The SAGE Handbook

of
Counselling and Psychotherapy

Second Edition

The SAGE Handbook

of

Counselling and Psychotherapy

Second Edition

Edited by

Colin Feltham and
Ian E. Horton

SAGE Publications
London • Thousand Oaks • New Delhi

First edition published 2000
Reprinted 2002, 2003, 2004, 2005
This second edition first published 2006

SAGE Publications Ltd
1 Oliver's Yard
55 City Road
London EC1Y 1SP

SAGE Publications Inc.
2455 Teller Road
Thousand Oaks, California 91320

SAGE Publications India Pvt Ltd
B-42, Panchsheel Enclave
Post Box 4109
New Delhi 110 017

British Library Cataloguing in Publication data
A catalogue record for this book is available from British Library

ISBN 1-4129-0274-6
ISBN 1-4129-0275-4 (pbk)

Library of Congress Control Number: 2005901771

Typeset by C&M Digitals (P) Ltd., Chennai, India
Printed on paper from sustainable resources
Printed in Great Britain by The Alden Press, Oxford

Contents

Contents

A list of resources (including useful websites for each chapter) appears at www.sagepub.co.uk/feltham&horton

List of Figures ○○○

List of Tables

○○○

Notes on Contributors and Editors ○○○

Geof Alred, PhD, is a BPS Chartered Psychologist, Honorary Fellow in the School of Education, University of Durham, a counsellor trainer and counsellor in Primary Care in the NHS and in private practice.

Kate Anthony, MSc, runs www.OnlineCounsellors.co.uk which provides online and offline consultancy services and training for practitioners using the internet. She is co-editor of *Technology in Counselling and Psychotherapy: A Practitioner's Guide* (Palgrave, 2003), is author of the *BACP Online Counselling and Psychotherapy Guidelines* (2nd edn, 2005) and is a regular contributor to journals, international conferences, media programmes and books. She is president of the International Society for Mental Health Online, and is completing her PhD within the field of online therapy.

Michael Barkham is Professor of Clinical and Counselling Psychology and Director of the Psychological Therapies Research Centre at the University of Leeds. He is also Visiting Professor at the Universities of Sheffield and Northumbria at Newcastle.

Nicola Barry is a Lecturer in the Department of Applied Psychology, National University of Ireland, Cork, where she is involved in counsellor and guidance counsellor training. In addition, she is a counselling psychologist in private practice.

Rowan Bayne, PhD, is a Professor of Psychology at the University of East London. He has been involved in counsellor training for over 25 years.

Debra Bekerian, PhD, a former Reader in Experimental Psychology at the University of East London, is now a supervisor, trainer and Gestalt practitioner working in private practice.

Elsa Bell is Head of Counselling at the University of Oxford and a Fellow of the BACP. Previously she worked as a counsellor in the Youth Service, and Further and Higher Education College and a Polytechnic. She is an executive member of the European Association for Counselling and former Chair of both the then Association for Student Counselling and the British Association for Counselling.

Jenny Bimrose, PhD, is a Principal Research Fellow with the Institute for Employment Research at the University of Warwick. She has over 30 years' experience of professional practice, project management, teaching at postgraduate level and research. Many of her research projects have focused on different aspects of gender and career counselling, both in the UK and Europe. She is a Fellow of the Institute of Career Guidance and Chair of its Ethics and Standards Committee.

Frances Blackwell, MA/Diploma in Psychoanalytic Psychotherapy, has retired from the NHS where she worked in the Disability Counselling Service (Tower Hamlets PCT) and she continues in private practice in North London.

Tim Bond, PhD, is Reader in Counselling and Professional Ethics at the University of Bristol, a Fellow, former Chair of the British Association for Counselling and member of the Executive Council of the International Association for Counselling.

Peter Bower is a psychologist and Senior Research Fellow at the National Primary Care Research and Development Centre (NPCRDC), a Department of Health funded unit at the University of Manchester. He currently conducts research on the effectiveness of psychological therapies in primary care and the relationship between mental health specialists and primary care professionals.

Joanna Brien is the counselling manager for Brook London, and, jointly with Dr Ida Fairbairn, wrote *Pregnancy and Abortion Counselling* (Routledge, 1996) and worked as a counsellor for the British Pregnancy Advisory Service (BPAS). She is also an antenatal teacher with the National Childbirth trust and baby massage tutor.

Adrian D. Coles is an independent trainer and consultant who is interested in management and leadership development. He is an accredited counsellor and recently published *Counselling in the Workplace* (Open University Press, 2003).

Jo Cooper has been involved with NLP since the mid-1980s and is certified by Richard Bandler as a master trainer. She is a founding partner of Centre NLP, a training and consultancy partnership, and has a private practice specializing in performance enhancement.

Nigel Copsey is Team Leader for Spiritual and Cultural Care in the East London and City Mental Health Trust where he has been responsible for establishing a new department based on research he had previously undertaken for the Sainsbury Centre for Mental Health. He has a passion to promote the integration of spirituality with mental health care and facilitates the Spirituality and Gestalt Interest Group for the Gestalt International Study Centre.

Dominic Davies is a BACP Senior Registered Practitioner who has been working with sexual minorities for 25 years. He is Director of Pink Therapy, the UK's largest private practice specializing in working with sexual minority clients (www.pinktherapy.com). He is co-editor (with Charles Neal) of the Pink Therapy trilogy of textbooks (Open University Press) and has taught and written extensively on the subject of sexual minority therapy in the UK and internationally.

Gill Donohoe is a BABCP accredited cognitive-behavioural psychotherapist working in Doncaster for the NHS. She is involved in training and supervision and has a mental health nursing background. She has a particular interest in service delivery models, the use of groups and self-management approaches.

Christa Drennan is a BACP accredited counsellor and has an MA in Counselling and Psychotherapy. She was a counsellor at the Homerton Hospital Fertility Unit for four years, and currently works for the NHS as Primary Care Mental Health Development Manager for Waltham Forest Primary Care Trust in north east London.

Windy Dryden is Professor of Psychotherapeutic Studies, Goldsmiths College, University of London. He is a Fellow of the BPS and BACP. He began his training in REBT in 1977 and became the first Briton to be accredited as an REBT therapist by the Albert Ellis Institute.

John Eatock, MA, is a BACP accredited counsellor and a Fellow of the BACP. He is the BACP Lead Advisor for Healthcare Counselling and Psychotherapy and a founder of the Faculty of Healthcare Counsellors and Psychotherapists. He is also Senior Counsellor with Bolton, Salford and Trafford NHS Trust and an occasional lecturer at the University of Salford.

Michael Ellis, MA, is a UKCP registered psychotherapist. He is a director of the Gestalt Centre London and a tutor on the MA programme in psychotherapy. He has a private practice working with individuals and couples, is a supervisor and works with organizations as a trainer and organizational consultant.

Meg Errington, MA, is a UKCP registered analytic psychotherapist and member of FPC working in London. She divides her time between her private practice, working with adolescents in an inner London comprehensive school, and teaching and supervising at the Westminster Pastoral Foundation.

Rose Evison is a counselling and occupational psychologist, working as an independent practitioner with organizations and in private practice. She has used and taught co-counselling for 30 years. Its emotionally expressive techniques form the basis for her private practice in Cognitive Emotional counselling and for the Blockbreaking methods she uses in her work with organizations.

Colin Feltham, PhD, FBACP, FRSA is Reader in Counselling, Sheffield Hallam University and Course Leader for the MA Professional Development in Counselling and Psychotherapy. His publications include the *Dictionary of Counselling* (2nd edn, with Windy Dryden) (Whurr, 2004), *Problems Are Us* (Braiswick, 2004) and *What's Wrong with Us?: The Anthropathology Thesis* (Wiley, forthcoming).

Fay Fransella is Founder and Director of the Centre for Personal Construct Psychology at the University of Hertfordshire, a Fellow of the BPS and Visiting Professor in Personal Construct Psychology at the University of Hertfordshire.

Linda Gask is Professor in Primary Care Psychiatry at the University of Manchester. She is also an honorary consultant psychiatrist at Bolton, Salford and Trafford Mental Health Partnership Trust and divides her time between primary care mental health research and research, teaching and clinical work as a general psychiatrist.

Richard Gater is a Senior Lecturer in Psychiatry in the School of Psychiatry at the University of Manchester and Honorary Consultant Psychiatrist at Lancashire Care NHS Trust. His interests are in mental health among ethnic minority groups and psychiatry in developing countries.

David Geldard is a psychologist and Member of the College of Counselling Psychologists of the Australian Psychological Society. He works in private practice as a counsellor for children, adolescents and their families, and as a trainer and supervisor of counsellors who work with children. He and his wife are joint authors of several counselling textbooks.

Kathryn Geldard is a Clinical Member of the Queensland Association of Family Therapists and a registered Occupational Therapist in the USA and Australia. She works in private practice as a counselling supervisor and trainer, and as a counsellor of children, adolescents and their families. She is a visiting lecturer at the University of Queensland and the Queensland University of Technology. She and her husband are joint authors of several counselling textbooks.

Paul Gilbert is a Professor of Clinical Psychology at the University of Derby. He has published a number of books in the area of mood disorders and shame and is currently researching compassion and compassion-based therapies. He is a fellow of BPS and ex-president of BACBP.

Ann Gledhill is a Consultant Clinical Psychologist for Somerset Partnership NHS and Social Care Trust and an Accredited cognitive-behavioural psychotherapist.

Susan Goodrich is a BPC Chartered Psychologist and BACP accredited Gestalt counsellor. She works as a trainer, supervisor and counsellor and is Director of Counselling Services for the Cambridgeshire Consultancy in Counselling.

Andrew Guppy is Professor of Applied Psychology at the University of Chester and is a Chartered Occupational Psychologist. He has been involved in the provision and evaluation of counselling and other interventions in the stress, alcohol and drug fields for the last 20 years.

Derek Hill retired as Relate's Head of Practitioner Training in 2000. He is a Fellow of BACP. Since his retirement he has devoted his time and energy to contributing to and editing several publications and to the role of Chair of the International Commission on Couple and Family Relations (www.iccfr.org).

Peter E. Hodgkinson, BA, MPhil, is a Chartered Clinical Psychologist. He has been involved in disaster- and trauma-related work for 17 years and is Senior Partner of the Centre for Crisis Psychology.

Richard Horobin is Honorary Senior Research Fellow in the Division of Neuroscience and Biomedical Systems, Institute of Biomedical and Life Sciences, University of Glasgow. He has used and taught co-counselling for 30 years.

Ian Horton has retired as Principal Lecturer and Programme Leader for the Postgraduate Diploma/MA Counselling and Psychotherapy at the University of East London. He is a Fellow of the BACP and member of the BACP Professional Standards Committee and formerly a BACP Senior Registered Practitioner and UKRC Registered Independent Counsellor.

Peter Hughes is a person-centred counsellor and counselling supervisor in independent practice. Counselling since the mid-1980s, and supervising since the early 1990s, Peter is also a freelance counselling and groupwork trainer, principally in higher and further education.

Francesca Inskipp is a Fellow and Accredited Supervisor of the BACP. She works freelance as a trainer, supervisor and counsellor.

Paul Jackson is a nurse therapist and a BACP accredited counsellor working at the Mount Zeehan Alcohol Unit, Canterbury, Kent and in private practice.

Peter Jenkins is a Senior Lecturer in Counselling at the University of Salford, a BACP accredited counsellor trainer, and member of the Professional Conduct Committee of the BACP. He has written widely on legal aspects of counselling, and has run a large number of training workshops on this topic. He is the author of a number of books on this issue, including *Psychotherapy and the Law* (Whurr, 2004) with Vincent Keter and Julie Stone.

Gordon Jinks is a Principal Lecturer in the School of Psychology at the University of East London where he is Programme Leader for the MA/Postgraduate Diploma in Counselling and Psychotherapy.

Rosemary Kent is a qualified social worker and a chartered counselling psychologist and is a lecturer at the University of Kent, providing training for practitioners in alcohol and other drug services. She has worked with substance misusers in the NHS and in non-statutory settings, and provides supervision and consultancy as an independent practitioner.

Tracy King is currently training as a clinical psychologist with Surrey Oaklands NHS Trust. She previously ran a private therapy practice, favouring an integrative approach along with complementary methods such as hypnosis.

Graz Kowszun is a UKCP Registered Integrative Psychotherapist and a BACP senior accredited counsellor and trainer. She is currently in the process of moving her integrative relational practice of psychotherapy, supervision and training from London and Kent to Aotearoa (New Zealand) and changing her name to Graz Amber.

Phoebe Lambert has an enduring commitment to working with adult learners: as literature tutor, curriculum developer and counsellor. She has recently completed her doctoral thesis on client perceptions of counselling.

Karina Lovell is Professor of Mental Health at the University of Manchester. She is an accredited cognitive-behavioural therapist and her research interests lie in developing accessible and effective interventions for anxiety and depression in primary care.

James Low works as a Consultant Psychotherapist at Guy's Hospital and in private practice. He is trained in a range of psychotherapies and remains sceptical about all of them.

Barbara McKay is a UKCP Registered Systemic Psychotherapist with experience of working with individuals, couples and families in statutory, voluntary and private contexts. She also holds Masters qualifications in Social Work and Systemic Supervision and continues to hold both clinical and supervisory caseloads. Barbara has taught on various courses for the KCC Foundation and Relate up to Master's level and continues to offer practice and supervisory workshops. She is currently Head of Training for Relate.

John McLeod, PhD, is Professor of Counselling at the Univeristy of Abertay, Dundee.

Gladeana McMahon is a Fellow of the BACP. She is a BACP Senior Registered Practitioner, a British Association for Behavioural and Cognitive Psychotherapies accredited cognitive-behavioural psychotherapist who is UKCP and UKRC registered.

John Mellor-Clark is Director of CORE IMS which offers a range of support services to CORE System users. He is also a Visiting Senior Research Fellow at the Psychological Therapies Research Centre at the University of Leeds, and an external specialist consultant to the Health and Social Care Advisory Service in London.

Tony Merry was a Reader in Counselling at the University of East London. He was a person-centred practitioner, a co-founder of the British Association for the Person-Centred Approach, the author of six books about the approach, and editor of *Person-centred Practice* (1993–2004). He died in August 2004.

Carol Mohamed is a Psychoanalytic Psychotherapist, occupational psychologist and social worker. She works within the NHS in Sheffield, as the Head of Psychological Therapies and Consultation Services for NHS staff. She has considerable experience within the public and private sectors offering supervision, coaching and consultancy services to managers and senior executives.

Lesley Murdin, MA (Oxon), MA (Sydney), MFPC is a UKCP registered psychoanalytic psychotherapist and Director of WPF Counselling and Psychotherapy. She is also a supervisor, trainer and writer.

Jill Mytton is a Principal Lecturer, Department of Psychology, London Metropolitan University. She is the Course Leader for the Practioner Doctorate in Counselling Psychology and a chartered counselling psychologist in private practice. She is co-author with Windy Dryden of *Four Approaches to Counselling and Psychotherapy* (Routledge, 1999).

Bill O'Connell is currently the Director of Training with Focus on Solutions Limited, a company specializing in the delivery of training in the solution focused approach. Until 2003 he was a Senior Lecturer at the University of Birmingham where he headed the MA in Solution Focused Therapy programme. He is a Fellow of the BACP and an accredited counsellor. He has a background in social work and youth work. He is the author of *Solution Focused Therapy* (Sage, 1998), *Solution Focused Stress Counselling* (Continuum/ Sage, 2001) and co-editor with Dr Stephen Palmer of the *Handbook of Solution Focused Therapy* (Sage, 2003). Email: focusonsolutions@btconnect.com.

Professor Eleanor O'Leary is the Head of the Department of Applied Psychology and Director of the Counselling and Health Studies Unit, University College Cork. She is a Fellow of the Psychological Society of Ireland and a chartered health and counselling psychologist of the British Psychological Society. She was Visiting Professor at Stanford University where she taught a postgraduate course on older adults. She has received European funding under the Fifth Framework initiative and is joint Principal investigator of the Size research project on quality of life and mobility in old age. She obtained the award for Outstanding Contribution to Psychology of the Psychological Society of Ireland in 2000.

Professor Stephen Palmer, PhD FBACP CPsychol is Founder Director of the Centre for Stress Management and the Centre for Coaching. He is President of the Association of Coaching and Vice President of the Institute of Health Promotion and Education, and the International Stress Management Association (UK). In 2005 he was Chair of the new British Psychological Society Special Group in Coaching Psychology. He is an Honorary Professor of Psychology at City University and Visiting Professor of Work Based Learning and Stress Management at NCWBLP, Middlesex University. He is an Accredited CBT and REBT therapist, and an Albert Ellis Institute Certified REBT Supervisor. He has written or edited over 25 books on a range of topics, including coaching, management, stress, suicide, trauma, counselling and psychotherapy.

Simon Parritt is a Chartered Counselling Psychologist in private practice. He is Honorary Senior Lecturer at the Institute of Sexuality and Human Relations and until 2003 was Director of the Association to Aid the Sexual and Personal Relationships of People with a Disability (SPOD). He has a particular interest in offering training and supervision of counsellors and health professionals working with disabled people and those living with long-term conditions.

David Pilgrim is Clinical Dean for the Teaching Primary Care Trust for East Lancashire and an Honorary Professor at the Universities of Liverpool and Central Lancashire. He has a background in both clinical psychology and medical sociology and has researched and written extensively on the sociology of mental health.

Bernard Ratigan, PhD, is a psychoanalytic psychotherapist who, until recently, worked as an NHS adult psychotherapist and teacher in the University of Nottingham Medical School. He is now in private practice in Leicester but continues working in NHS Gender Identity Clinics.

Tom Ricketts, PhD, is a BABCP accredited cognitive-behavioural psychotherapist and nurse consultant working in the NHS. He has developed and taught both qualifying courses for cognitive-behavioural psychotherapists and introductory courses for non-specialists. He has a particular interest in widening access to cognitive-behavioural therapy through the use of self-management approaches and the training of health professionals.

Sheila Ritchie is a psychoanalytic psychotherapist and a group analyst registered with the UKCP. She works in a range of settings: in the National Health Service, voluntary and statutory organizations offering psychotherapy, supervision, consultancy and training.

Maxine Rosenfield has 15 years' experience as a counsellor and trainer. She pioneered telephone counselling in the UK, writing *Counselling by Telephone* (Sage, 1997) and has contributed to counselling and social work texts in the UK and the USA. Now based in Sydney, Australia, she continues counselling, training and writing.

Diana Sanders, PhD, is a Chartered Counselling Psychologist in the Oxfordshire Mental Healthcare NHS Trust and BABCP accredited cognitive psychotherapist. She works in the Department of Psychological Medicine and Oxford Cognitive Therapy Centre, specializing in psychological approaches to health problems and health anxiety.

Joy Schaverien, PhD, is a Professional Member of the Society for Analytical Psychology in London, a training therapist and supervisor for the BAP and Visiting Professor in Art Psychotherapy at the University of Sheffield. A member of the International Association of Analytical Psychology she teaches for the CG Jung Institute in Copenhagen and co-coordinates the IAAP supervision programme in Moscow. Her many books include *The Dying Patient in Psychotherapy: Desire Dreams and Individuation* (Palgrave, 2002). She is in private practice in the East Midlands as a Jungian analyst, psychotherapist and supervisor. She is UKCP and BPC registered.

Michael Scott is a Chartered Counselling Psychologist, with a private practice in Liverpool. He has authored or edited six text books, including the best-selling *Counselling for Post-traumatic Stress Disorder* (2nd edn, with Stephen Stradling) (Sage, 2001). Recently he became external examiner for the MSc Cognitive and Behavioural Psychotherapies programme at University College, Chester.

Peter Seal is certified by Richard Bandler as a master trainer of NLP and is a fouding partner of Centre NLP. He is the originator of a simple and effective approach to working directly with unconscious processes and author of programmes encouraging others to access that approach.

Julia Segal trained with Relate in 1979 and the same year wrote her first book (*Phantasy in Everyday Life*) which discussed relationships using the insights of Melanie Klein. Currently, her interests include working with people with multiple sclerosis or other neurological conditions, and training others in this field. She works for the NHS and privately.

Irene Bruna Seu is a Lecturer in Social Psychology at Birkbeck College, University of London and a UKCP registered psychoanalytic psychotherapist in private practice. She has edited *Who Am I? The Ego and the Self in Psychoanalysis* (Rebus Press, 2000) and *Feminism & Psychotherapy: Reflections on Contemporary Theories and Practices* (Sage, 1998) (with C.M. Heenan). She is currently working on moral apathy in response to human rights abuses and on women's shame.

Charlotte Sills is a UKCP registered psychotherapist and supervisor in private practice and Head of the Transactional Analysis Department at the Metanoia Institute, London, which offers a Masters course and a Diploma course in TA Psychotherapy and BA (Hons) in TA Counselling. She is Visiting Professor at Middlesex University and the author or co-author of many publications in the field of psychological therapies, including (with Phil Lapworth and Sue Fish) *Transactional Analysis Counselling* (Speechmark, 2001) and (with Helena Hargaden) *Transactional Analysis: A Relational Perspective* (Brunner-Routledge, 2002).

Jonathan P. Smith is a Lecturer in psychology and also a psychotherapist and trainer. He works at the Faculty of Continuing Education at Birkbeck College and has also been a regular contributor to courses at the Guildhall School of Music and Drama, the Psychosynthesis and Education Trust, and the University of East London. He has a private practice offering Gestalt psychotherapy and runs workshops in Gestalt for various counselling organizations.

William B. Stiles is a Professor of clinical psychology at Miami University in Oxford, Ohio. He received his PhD from UCLA in 1972. He is a past President of the Society for Psychotherapy Research, and the former North American editor of *Psychotherapy Research.* He is currently co-editor of *Person-centered and Experiential Psychotherapies* and Associate Editor of the *British Journal of Clinical Psychology.*

Eddy Street, PhD, is a Chartered Clinical and Counselling Psychologist and is an elected Fellow of the BPS. For nearly all of his professional career he has worked in NHS Child and Adolescent Mental Health Services (CAMHS). His interests have involved family interaction, the effect of stresses on children, the means by which families deal with a variety of chronic physical conditions and child development in abusive environments. He has published widely on themes related to his work and is a past editor of the *Journal of Family*

Therapy for the Association of Family Therapy. He is currently Consultant Clinical Psychologist and Head of Psychological Therapies in the South Wales CAMHS Managed Clinical Network.

Gabrielle Syme works in independent practice as a counsellor, supervisor and trainer. She is a Fellow of BACP, a BACP accredited Counsellor and Supervisor and also a UKCP registered psychotherapist. Gabrielle is a former Chair of both the Association for University and College Counselling and the British Association for Counselling and Psychotherapy. She is author or co-author of books and articles in the field of bereavement, dual relationships, independent practice and ethical issues. The books are *Gift of Tears* (2nd edn) (Brunner-Routledge, 2004), *Counselling in Independent Practice* (Open University Press, 1994), *Dual Relationships in Counselling and Psychotherapy* (Sage, 2003) and *Questions of Ethics in Counselling and Psychotherapy* (Open University Press, 2000).

Keith Tudor has worked for nearly 30 years in the helping professions in a number of settings. He is a qualified and registered psychotherapist, group psychotherapist and facilitator, and has a private/independent practice in Sheffield offering therapy, supervision and consultancy where he is a Director of Temenos and its postgraduate diploma/MSc course in Person-Centred Psychotherapy and Counselling. He is a teaching and supervising transactional analyst, and an Honorary Fellow in the School of Health, Liverpool John Moores University. He is a widely-published author in the field of psychotherapy and counselling, with over 60 papers and seven books to his name. He is on the editorial advisory board of three international journals and is the series editor of *Advancing Theory in Therapy* (published by Routledge).

Emmy van Deurzen is Professor of Psychotherapy with Schiller International University in London, where she directs the New School of Psychotherapy and Counselling. She is also a Director of the Centre for the Study of Conflict and Reconciliation at the University of Sheffield and of Dilemma Consultancy in Human Relations. She has published widely on existential psychotherapy and counselling, including the best-selling *Existential Counselling and Psychotherapy in Practice* (Sage, 2002), and she is the founder of the Society for Existential Analysis.

Moira Walker is a registered psychotherapist and Fellow of the BACP. She is currently a Reader in the Institute of Health and Community Studies at Bournemouth University. She has considerable experience as a trainer, supervisor, practitioner and writer and has worked in the field of abuse for many years. She has worked in universities, the voluntary sector and in health and social services settings. Her books include *Surviving Secrets: The Experience of Abuse for the Child, the Adult and the Helper* (Open University Press, 1992), *Hidden Selves: An Exploration of Multiple Personality* (Open University Press, 1999) and *Abuse: Questions and Answers for Counsellors and Therapists* (Whurr, 2003).

Jenny Warner was a Speech and Language Therapy Manager in the NHS and an Adlerian therapist, family counsellor, supervisor, author and international trainer. She is now retired.

Diana Whitmore is President of the Psychosynthesis and Education Trust. She is on the UKCP National Register of Psychotherapists, a BAC Accredited Supervisor and a founding member of the Association for Accredited Psychospiritual Psychotherapists. She is the author of two books, *Psychosynthesis in Education: A Guide to the Joy of Learning* (Turnstone, 1986) and *Psychosynthesis Counselling in Action* (3rd edn) (Sage, 2004).

Paul Wilkins, PhD, is a person-centred academic and therapist working for Manchester Metropolitan University. He is a qualified psychodrama psychotherapist and applies his knowledge of the theory and practice of therapy to research.

Emma Williams, BSc, MPhil, PhD, is a Consultant Clinical Psychologist with West London Mental Health NHS Trust, based at Broadmoor Hospital. She is also Consultant Clinical Psychologist with Berkshire Healthcare NHS Trust providing an in-reach service to HMP Reading. She has worked as a clinical psychologist in the National Health Service for over 15 years, primarily in medium and high-security psychiatric hospitals and community forensic services.

Llynwen Wilson is Senior Counsellor in General Practice and a psychosexual psychotherapist at the Porterbrook Clinic for Sexual and Relationship Difficulties in Sheffield. She is UKCP registered and a BASRT accredited member and supervisor.

Sally Woods is Joint Programme Co-ordinator for the MSc Drug Use and Addiction at Liverpool John Moores University. She also lectures on the undergraduate Applied Psychology degree and is a member of BPS.

Val Wosket, PhD, is Senior Lecturer in Counselling (part-time) at York St John College and a founding partner of Synergy Counselling and Psychotherapy. She is a BACP accredited trainer, counsellor and supervisor.

Preface ⟡ ○○○

COLIN FELTHAM AND IAN HORTON

This second edition of a relatively large book in an ever-expanding field, appearing among hundreds of other books, requires some explanation and justification of its conception, structure, aims and limitations. It is our hope that this text brings together comprehensively, in a helpfully updated form, the fundamentals of counselling and psychotherapy for both trainees and experienced practitioners seeking expansion of their knowledge base. Notwithstanding one or two welcome distinguished authors from the USA and Australia, this is a mainly British text, reflecting the experiences and needs of clients and therapists in a multicultural society, in the early stages of the twenty-first century, represented by leading practitioners and academics who are all active in their fields. It brings together both the practical and theoretical aspects of the psychological therapies, including information of an introductory and sometimes advanced nature. Finally, although it must be in the nature of a book of this kind to present a good deal of established, relatively uncontentious knowledge, we have continued to encourage the injection of a degree of critical thinking, in the hope that colleagues will join with us in taking responsibility for challenging any elements of counselling and psychotherapy calling for change. We have in mind those elements which have permeated our collective professional wisdom, which are repeated by each generation of practitioners, yet often remain without a clearly articulated rationale or evidence base.

Counselling and psychotherapy

In the first edition we acknowledged transparently the agonizing that went into the decision behind the title of the book. At different stages the central terms were to be 'counselling' or 'therapeutic counselling' or 'psychological therapy', or even 'integrative therapeutic counselling'. Finally we opted for 'counselling and psychotherapy' for the following reasons: among those involved in the debate on what the real, if any, differences between counselling and psychotherapy are, we both belong to that group who believe the differences to be minimal and the commonalities to be vast; we hope that *all* 'clinicians' – counsellors, psychotherapists, counselling psychologists, clinical psychologists and others – may find this book useful; much more contentiously and ambitiously, we hope that the blend of information, perspectives and challenges given here will activate in some small way the thrust towards not only theoretical collaboration in this field, but also towards, if not professional integration, then at least wider acknowledgement and greater respect for different contributions of all colleagues in the field. Fortuitously, in 2000, shortly after the publication of the first edition of this book, the British Association for Counselling (BAC) changed its name to the British Association for Counselling and Psychotherapy. This shift has helped to normalize use of the two terms in conjunction.

In spite of our challenge to the longstanding, uncritical Americanization of theory and practice in this field (see below), it is worth pointing out that American textbooks routinely include the terms counselling and psychotherapy conjointly and unproblematically in their titles. Nevertheless, we have to acknowledge that some of our British colleagues, particularly those trained under the title of psychotherapist, may still have reservations about and objections to our merging counselling with psychotherapy. Hopefully, some degree of persuasion of the usefulness of this decision will come about from reading the book itself. This debate does, however, create some potential difficulties of cumbersome language use. Rather than use the term 'counselling and psychotherapy' throughout the text, we have advised contributors to use their discretion, to alternate terms, and so on; and the abbreviation 'therapy' has also been liberally employed.

For the most part we have encouraged the convention of referring to the recipient of therapy as the client rather than patient. Writers have been asked to avoid, for the most part, use of 'I' for stylistic reasons, but occasionally its use has been appropriate. References, collected at the ends of each section, have usually been limited for space reasons but we trust that those appearing are useful.

Socio-cultural perspectives

When we declared that this was a mainly British text, our association was not with nationalism but with the recognition that there is a need to address 'local' experience with (as far as possible) local knowledge. In spite of central European origins, most models or schools of counselling and psychotherapy for the last 50 or so years have been American or Americanized, and many influential texts in this field have been American. British society and its particular multicultural profile is quite distinct. Moghaddam and Studer (1997) rightly challenge the kind of psychology that has become an American export, or what they refer to as 'US-manufactured psychological knowledge' which, even in its guise of cross-cultural psychology, subtly marginalizes the different experiences, indigenous theorizing and unique problem-solving capacities of other cultures, particularly in the developing world. Continuing tensions between western-driven globalization on the one hand and the reassertion of Islamic beliefs among others – tragically configured in the unforgettable events of '9/11' – remind us to question our ethnocentric assumptions. Ritzer (2004) presents us with the challenge of international social problems, including the worldwide growth of mental health problems like depression. It is hard to resist the wisdom of the call to 'think globally, act locally'.

Two of the very few truly 'home-grown' traditions in Britain are represented by the Independent Group (Fairbairn, Winnicott, Bowlby, Balint, Bollas, Khan and others), who pioneered object relations work and sought to avoid the extremes of other affiliations (Rayner, 1991), and cognitive analytic therapy, which welds object relations with personal construct, cognitive therapy and related theories into a short-term, NHS-adaptable therapy

(Ryle, 1990). It may still be hoped – in spite of the slowness of its realization – that such traditions of locally created theory and practice will continue to respond to the histories, needs, strengths and changing conditions of British and other European societies with a culturally sensitive and pragmatically attuned consciousness.

The priority given here to socio-cultural issues aims to recognize, however incipiently, the necessity for all therapists actively to widen their theoretical base and clinical and personal awareness from a traditionally, predominantly individualistic focus towards a socio-culturally informed and inclusive one. This focus embraces all those groups in society – women, alienated men, children, older people, the working class, gays and lesbians, disabled people, as well as ethnic minorities – that have been marginalized or silenced in various ways by traditional therapeutic discourse and practice. Gradually we are becoming more aware of changing demographics in British society, towards greater longevity, for example, with its attendant problems of adjustment to longer employment, insufficient pensions and inter-generational strain, as well as the growth in single house-holds, single parent and step-family households and the predicted need for increaing immigration to address a falling birthrate and ensuing economic problems. While mindful of these trends, we nevertheless suspect that along with colleagues and other texts, we have our own unrecognized assumptions, resistances and 'blind spots' and that what is presented here is still a modest movement in the direction of greater socio-cultural awareness.

Comprehensiveness

Most of the larger handbooks of counselling, psychotherapy and counselling psychology have tended towards representing mainly clinical skills and interventions and/or particular theoretical orientations, or specific client groups, or settings. Our aim in this book has been to draw together in one text as much consensual information, practice wisdom, main-stream theory, and pertinently challenging material, as possible. Our own original brief for ourselves and contributors was to address what practitioners 'need to know, do, think, feel, use, reflect upon, change and abandon to be of most use to clients'. Accordingly, while in a text of this kind it is necessary to include a fair amount of traditional theory, we hope there is also due bias towards practicality and creative rethinking where possible. To some extent this brief has led us to incorporate a greater number of clinical theories in this edition.

Limitations

Necessarily, the comprehensive intention behind this book means that some areas tradi-tionally accorded considerable space – notably, the mainstream theoretical approaches – have quite limited space. Where this is the case, we hope that such digests of information are useful and stimulating rather than frustrating, and that readers will follow up any sug-gestions for more comprehensive reading given by authors. At least one critic of the first edition complained about thinness of material in certain sections but our aim has been to provide a good general text that remains manageable in size, and there is of course an ever-expanding literature base available for those seeking more detail.

No single volume can hope to be exhaustive and therefore this, like any other book, has its limitations. The very selection of theoretical approaches to be represented in Part 5, for example, means that many have had to be excluded. While we have consciously attempted to include 'mainstream' approaches, not everyone will agree on our definition of mainstream. In Part 6, another necessary exercise in selection means that what we perceive as among the most commonly presented problems may well not match the daily clinical experiences and interpretations of all practitioner-readers. Where omissions are evident, we hope that these are due to conscious editorial decisions on space grounds, however difficult and sometimes arbitrary, rather than to negligent oversight. We are also aware that in a field that is shared by different clinical professions and different historical and institutional affiliations, our own positioning in a primarily *counselling* tradition may lead to some unintentional biases.

Structure

Part 1 opens with a scene-setting, succinct introduction to counselling and psychotherapy, to definitions, historical background, professional affiliations and philosophical assumptions. The varied, and not always clear, goals of therapy are briefly examined, as are the formats or arenas of therapy, the settings in which it takes place and the employment prospects it holds out. Part 2 lays the foundation for a socio-culturally informed account of the client populations served by therapists. Part 3 outlines the most significant therapeutic skills, techniques and practice issues, including many in-session and ancillary skills, the latter often being taken for granted by many clinical texts. Part 4 looks at professional issues relevant to all therapists, including professional development, supervision, ethics and law, insurance and advertising, private practice issues, research and evaluation, and includes clients' views and other neglected areas. Notably, a section on evidence-based practice is included in this edition, this topic have grown hugely in importance during just the last six years. Psychotherapeutic theory is the focus of Part 5, first by looking briefly at the need for and the place of theory and its different applications, and second via 23 distinctive, relatively mainstream theoretical models, approaches or schools of therapy. In Part 6 the focus is on the question of what clients need from therapy, first, by examining the topic of psychopharmacology, then different perspectives on psychopathology and problems of living, and second by outlining 21 of the most commonly presented problem areas, plus special issues. Part 7 gathers together a number of specialisms, modalities and setting-specific practice topics.

The construction of this book has represented another huge collaborative effort. In any edited book there is some undeniable risk of discordant styles and discrepancies. We hope that these are, however, minimal and that the insights and information provided by the contributors collectively make for a rich source of contemporary practice wisdom, accurate data and critical challenge to improve our services to clients by reflecting continuously on this fascinating subject.

Resources

Although we received favourable feedback about the Resources section of the first edition of the *Handbook*, we also became aware of how quickly information – particularly web addresses – can change. Accordingly, this information has been transferred to a website maintained by the publishers: www.sagepub.co.uk/feltham&horton

References

Moghaddam, F.M. and Studer, C. (1997) Cross-cultural psychology: the frustrated gadfly's promises, potentialities, and failures. In D. Fox and I. Prilleltensky (eds), *Critical Psychology: An Introduction*. London: Sage.

Rayner, E. (1991) *The Independent Tradition in British Psychoanalysis*. London: Aronson.

Ritzer, G. (ed.) (2004) *Handbook of Social Problems: A Comparative International Perspective*. Thousand Oaks, CA: Sage.

Ryle, A. (1990) *Cognitive-Analytic Therapy: Active Participation in Change*. Chichester: Wiley.

Acknowledgements

○○○

We are very grateful to all those contributors who have conscientiously updated and rewritten their sections in this book as well as to those who have written entirely new sections. We would also like to thank the Sage team, particularly Louise Wise for her constant cheerful help and greater than usual input with this demanding book, and also Alison Poyner, Rachel Burrows, Joyce Lynch and Harriet Baulcombe. A book of this magnitude really cannot be composed and collated without a supreme team effort.

PART I
Counselling and Psychotherapy in Context

1.1 What are Counselling and Psychotherapy? ○○○

COLIN FELTHAM

Definitions and aims

No single, consensually agreed definition of either counselling or psychotherapy exists in spite of many attempts across the decades in Britain, North America and elsewhere to arrive at one. For the purposes of this book, the following provisional, working definition is offered:

> Counselling and psychotherapy are mainly, though not exclusively, listening-and-talking-based methods of addressing psychological and psychosomatic problems and change, including deep and prolonged human suffering, situational dilemmas, crises and developmental needs, and aspirations towards the realization of human potential. In contrast to bio-medical approaches, the psychological therapies operate largely without medication or other physical interventions and may be concerned not only with mental health but with spiritual, philosophical, social and other aspects of living. Professional forms of counselling and psychotherapy are based on formal training which encompasses attention to pertinent theory, clinical and/or micro-skills development, the personal development/therapy of the trainee, and supervised practice.

A brief, tentative definition of this kind offers some parameters but omits mention of the many, often competing, schools of therapy, the arenas and the several professions (sometimes in conflict) in which they are practised. Discussions of all such conflicting claims can be found in Feltham (1995) and James and Palmer (1996). The contention advanced by this book's editors is that counselling and psychotherapy, in spite of partly different historical roots and affiliations, have much more in common than they have serious and demonstrable differences

and that practitioners and the public stand to gain much more from the assumption of commonality than from spurious or infinitesimal distinctions. Certainly practitioners in this field work with many different types of goal, each of which may call for the use of somewhat different skills, but arguably little is to be gained practically from further controversy about professional titles and distinctions.

Development of psychotherapy and counselling in the UK

Sigmund Freud was developing psychoanalysis – often considered the grandparent of most of the diverse schools in existence today – in Austria in the late nineteenth and early twentieth centuries. Before Freud there were certainly many kinds of psychologically oriented therapies and many had already used the concept of an unconscious. However, Freud has come to mark the historical moment when previous centuries of religious, philosophical and pseudo-scientific theories and methods (from religious propitiation to shamanism, sleeping cures, magnetism, hypnotism, etc.) were challenged by serious aspirations to establish psychotherapy as a scientific discipline. Psychoanalysis is perched curiously between being perceived as a challenge to previous faith in reason (the Enlightenment) and as itself, the new grand narrative capable of rationally explaining all the psychological ills of humanity. Freud is often (although not by all) ranked with Darwin and Marx as one of the most significant scientific thinkers at the dawn of the twentieth century.

Psychoanalysis moved through Europe and North America in the first few decades of the twentieth century, the International Psychoanalytical Association being established in 1910 and the British Psychoanalytic Society in 1924. The British Association of Psychotherapists (originally the Association of Psychotherapists) was founded in 1951. In spite of much public and medical resistance to psychoanalysis (which was originally radically counter-cultural), interest and support grew, partly in connection with the two world wars and the search for remedies for 'shell shock' (the predecessor of Post-Traumatic Stress Disorder (PTSD)) and other problems experienced by military personnel. Concern about scientology led in 1971 to the *Foster Report* which had implications for psychotherapy, and in 1978 to the publication of the *Sieghart Report* on the statutory regulation of psychotherapists. During the 1980s conferences regularly held at Rugby (organized by BAC) led eventually, in 1993, to the now United Kingdom Council for Psychotherapy (UKCP). The British Psychoanalytic Council (BPC), representing training institutions with a strictly psychoanalytic affiliation (the UKCP is a broad-based body containing member organizations from humanistic, cognitive-behavioural and other traditions), was established in 1991.

The development of counselling is harder to trace, there being no single dominant figure like Freud, or monolithic theory like psychoanalysis. Hans Hoxter may, however, be credited as one outstanding individual for his part in creating the counselling movement, including bringing American training ideas to Britain. It is usually agreed that early American vocational guidance projects and associations (for example Frank Parsons' Vocation Bureau in Boston in 1908) laid the foundations of counselling, and guidance for the young generally was a strong element. This certainly features in the early career of Carl Rogers, who is probably the closest to being the 'founder' of (non-directive) counselling in the 1940s. Another player is perhaps Rollo May, who, influenced by Alfred Adler, wrote what many consider to be the first counselling text in the 1920s (May, 1992). In the USA counselling was also originally closely linked with personnel management and the workplace. In general it is true to say that counselling has *historical* roots in practical guidance and problem-solving issues, and was often agency based rather than associated with private practice. However, it is now mainly characterized as distinctly other than advice giving and as having a primarily facilitative function.

Seminal events in the UK included the establishment of the National Marriage Guidance Council in 1938, the importation of counselling training methods from the USA to the Universities of Reading and Keele in 1966 (to serve the pastoral needs of students), and the establishment of the Westminster Pastoral Foundation in 1969. The Standing Conference for the Advancement of Counselling in 1970 led to the formation of the British Association for Counselling in 1977, renamed the British Association for Counselling and Psychotherapy in 2000. It should be said that a great deal of cross-fertilization between these developments and others in psychotherapy was taking place and the emergence of psychodynamic counselling, for example, demonstrates these close links.

Alongside these developments we should also note pertinent developments elsewhere. Originally the Association of Medical Officers of Asylums and Hospitals for the Insane (AMOAHI, 1841), the Royal College of Psychiatrists was so named in 1971. The British Psychological Society was established in 1901. Significant mutual aid and voluntary organizations such as Alcoholics Anonymous (1935), the Samaritans (1953) and Cruse (1959) should also be included in this brief portrait, as should the parallel existence of the personal social services and its casework tradition which closely mirrored developments in counselling and psychotherapy.

Theoretically, psychotherapy and counselling develop continuously, some might say all too prolifically, with significant departures from psychoanalytic theory and practice observable from its earliest days. Jung and Adler were among the earliest to break away from Freud, and similar schisms, factions and developments are in evidence throughout psychotherapeutic history. Hence, the growth of what is now thought to be the more than 400 schools (also known as theoretical orientations, approaches, brand names) of therapy we have today. The question of whether such proliferation is desirable, and in clients' interests, or not, must be faced by thoughtful practitioners, and indeed the integrationist movement stemming from the 1980s represents shared concern for convergence. A summary of some of the key points of this necessarily succinct history of events is provided in Table 1.1.1. Readers may also like to consult Dryden (1997), Ellenberger (1970) and Feltham (1995).

Allied professions

Most (but certainly not all) would agree that counselling and psychotherapy – in so far as they *are* professions or emerging professions – are part of the health professions. Although Freud battled to have psychoanalysis recognized as separate from medicine and Rogers similarly battled with psychiatric and psychological colleagues, the psychological therapies today concern themselves largely with mental health promotion and mental illness reduction even where these terms are not used and where additional or different aims are espoused, such as personal growth and development, psycho-education, etc. (see Brown and Mowbray, 2002). Counsellors are therefore found in health and social care settings along with psychotherapists, clinical and counselling psychologists, psychiatrists and psychiatric nurses. A second group of related professionals includes social workers, probation officers, welfare officers, personnel managers, career guidance workers, occupational therapists, speech and communication therapists, occupational and health psychologists, and so on. Teachers, nurses, priests and others in caring roles have closely related functions. Members of the above groups, sometimes known as 'core professions', have been considered good candidates for counselling and psychotherapy training, and typical intakes to courses include members of all these groups.

Each professional group has its own professional body, history, and traditions of training and supervision. Each has designated tasks that obviously differ from those of others, depending on context and client group. Counselling and psychotherapeutic skills are used to degrees in all these professions and where individual workers possess dual or multiple qualifications (for example a social worker may be trained in family therapy), they may formally provide therapeutic services. However, BACP and other clinically oriented bodies strive to emphasize a distinction between casual, informal, transient or untrained and uncontracted use of *counselling skills*, and disciplined, contracted, ethically protected, formal counselling or psychotherapy. Parry (1996), too, distinguishes between:

- Type A: psychological treatment as an integral component of mental health care
- Type B: eclectic psychological therapy and counselling
- Type C: formal psychotherapy

The above-mentioned groups are also related to those involved in practising the so-called complementary therapies (often regarding their work as holistic/mind–body integrated), including acupuncture, homeopathy, reflexology, aromatherapy, Alexander Technique, spiritual healing, osteopathy, naturopathy, Bach flower remedies, etc. Again, practitioners may sometimes have dual qualifications and practise both psychological therapy and somatic or sensual therapies alternately or simultaneously, having due regard for appropriate contracting (Sills, 1997). Debates about the rights of certain of these groups to aspire to professional status cannot be ignored. In relation to distinctions between the titles of those engaged in closely related therapeutic professions, and their putatively distinctive skills and effectiveness, see Cheshire and Pilgrim (2004); Gask (2004); James and Palmer (1996); and Milton et al. (2004). Offering resistance to the professionalizing trend, which is sometimes perceived as unnecessarily bureaucratizing therapy, is the Independent Practitioners' Network (IPN) (see House, 2003).

A brief overview of the values of counselling and psychotherapy

The overarching values, and the professional ethics that stem from these, of counselling and psychotherapy were summed up in the concepts of integrity, impartiality and respect (Bond, 2000). These were developed and related by BACP (2002) to tenets of moral philosophy: fidelity (honouring the trust

Table 1.1.1 Key historical developments

Year	Birth/growth of institutions/ professional organizations	Significant events	Appearance of schools (approx. dates)
1900		Freud's *Interpretation of Dreams*	
1907	British Psychological Society		
1907	Vienna Psychoanalytic Society		
1908		First (careers) counselling centre, Boston USA (Frank Parsons)	
1910	International Psychoanalytical Association		
1913	National Vocational Guidance Association (USA)		Analytical Psychology (Jung)
1919	London Psychoanalytic Society		
1920	Institute of Psycho-analysis		
1921	Tavistock Clinic		Behavioural Psychology
			Psychodrama
1924	British Psychoanalytic Society		
1926	London Clinic of Psychoanalysis		
	Medico-Psychological Association MPA (previously AMOAH I, originally 1841)		
1935	Alcoholics Anonymous		
1936	Society of Analytical Psychology		
1937		Death of Adler	
1938	National Marriage Guidance Council (now Relate)		
1939		Death of Freud	
1940		British National Health Service	Client/Person-centred Approach
1948		First student counselling service (University College Leicester)	T Groups
1950	International Association for Vocational and Educational Guidance (IAVEG)		Gestalt Therapy
1951	Group Analytical Society	Rogers' *Client-centered Therapy*	
1952	American Association for Counseling and Development (AACD)	*Diagnostic and Statistical Manual* (*DSM*) lst edn	
	American Counseling Association (ACA) (originally NVGA)		

(Continued)

Table 1.1.1 (Continued)

Year	Birth/growth of institutions/ professional organizations	Significant events	Appearance of schools (approx. dates)
1953	Samaritans		
1955			Rational Emotive Behaviour Therapy (orig. RT then RET)
1957			Personal Construct Therapy B
1958			Transactional Analysis
1959	Cruse		Behaviour Therapy
	Scottish Pastoral Association		
1960		First fee-charging counsellor in private practice in UK Death of Melanie Klein	
1961		Death of Jung J.D. Frank's *Persuasion and Healing*	
1962			Cognitive Therapy
1965		Halmos's *The Faith of the Counsellors*	
1966		Counselling training at Universities of Reading and Keele	
1969	Westminster Pastoral Foundation Association of Humanistic Psychology (USA 1962, UK 1969)		
1970	First Standing Conference for the Advancement of Counselling (Annual) MPA becomes the Royal College of Psychiatrists	Death of Perls and Berne	Primal Therapy
1971		The *Foster Report* on Scientology	
1975	National Association of Young People's Counselling and Advisory Services (later Youth Access)		Neuro-linguistic Programming
1977	British Association for Counselling		
1978		*Sieghart Report* on statutory regulation of psychotherapists	
1980	Association of Humanistic Psychology Practitioners (AHPP)	Smith et al.: *The Benefits of Psychotherapy*	

(Continued)

Table 1.1.1 (Continued)

Year	Birth/growth of institutions/ professional organizations	Significant events	Appearance of schools (approx. dates)
1982		Rugby Psychotherapy Conference (set up by BAC)	
1983	Society for the Exploration of Psychotherapy Integration (SEPI)	First BAC Accreditation scheme	Solution-focused therapy
1987		Death of Carl Rogers	
1989	United Kingdom Standing Conference on Psychotherapy (UKSCP)		
1990		Death of Bowlby	Cognitive Analytic Therapy
1991	British Confederation of Psychotherapists		
1992	European Association for Counselling	BPS Charter of Counselling Psychologists. First UK Chair of Counselling (Windy Dryden)	
1993	United Kingdom Council for Psychotherapy (UKCP, orig. UKSCP). Advice, Guidance, Counselling and Psychotherapy Lead Body		
1994	Independent Practitioners' Network UKCP Register of Psychotherapists 1994	BPS Division of Counselling Psychology	
1995		BCP Register launched NHS Psychotherapy Services in England Review	
1996	United Kingdom Register of Counsellors (UKRC) (individuals) World Council for Psychotherapy	NHS Psychotherapy Services in England (Department of Health (DOH) Strategic Policy Review)	
1998	Association of Counsellors and Psychotherapists in Primary Care (CPC) UKRC (organizations)	Data Protection Act CORE introduced	
2000	BAC renames itself the British Association for Counselling and Psychotherapy (BACP) Universities Psychotherapy Association (UPA) adds 'Counselling' to its title, becoming UPCA	BACP's *Ethical Framework for Good Practice in Counselling and Psychotherapy*	

(Continued)

Table 1.1.1 (Continued)

Year	Birth/growth of institutions/ professional organizations	Significant events	Appearance of schools (approx. dates)
2001		Lord Alderdice's Psychotherapy Bill *Treatment Choice in Psychological Therapies and Counselling: Evidence-based Clinical Practice Guidelines* (DoH publication) BACP's *Guidelines for Online Counselling and Psychotherapy*	
2002		Health Professions Council (HPC) is identified as the regulatory body for all health professions, including counselling and psychotherapy – 'talking therapies'	
2003		UKCP establishes its psychotherapeutic counselling section BACP Service Accreditation Scheme Telephone counselling (contractual) is accepted by BACP for accreditation hours	
2004	College of Psychoanalysts British Psychoanalytic Council	Graduate Mental Health Workers in Primary Care British Confederation of Psychotherapists (BCP) was renamed British Psychoanalytic Council (BPC)	

placed in the practitioner); autonomy (the client's right to be self-governing); beneficence (concern for the greatest good); non-maleficence (to cause least harm); justice (concern for fairness); and the practitioner's self-respect (self-knowledge and care of self). Such principles are not without problems, however, since in practice there sometimes are conflicts between, for example, the wishes of a client and possible damaging consequences. Also, it is sometimes the case that what may be professionally ethical and desirable will be challenged as socially undesirable or questionable by others. Hence, the goals of individual autonomy and self-actualization, which are held by many writers as central values in psychotherapy (e.g. Holmes and Lindley, 1989), have been criticized by some sociologists as leading to an 'autonomy obsession', an undermining of social responsibility and to cultural insensitivity. It is therefore important to bear in mind that what we often call *professional ethics* (as advocated in professional codes) are not necessarily coterminous with *social ethics*.

It follows from basic principles that counsellors and psychotherapists value non-judgementalism *vis-à-vis* clients, that they owe a duty of care to clients (while remaining necessarily detached to varying degrees), and that their aim is the ultimate good of

the client balanced by respect for the client's own choices. Due to the weight placed on respect for self-determination, most therapists are opposed to people being coerced into therapy, into remaining in therapy when they wish to leave, and actively support the principle of informed consent to therapeutic procedures.

All professional bodies in this field have their own codes of ethics and practice – BACP's *Ethical Framework for Good Practice in Counselling and Psychotherapy* being a mature example – usually addressing issues of safety, contracting, competence, confidentiality, boundaries, law, advertising, complaints, and so on. There are few specific prohibitions, although sexual contact with clients, exploitation of clients and breach of confidentiality are prohibitions shared by all professional bodies. Nevertheless, often genuine and valid differences in values do exist between members of different professional bodies (and networks, such as the IPN, which oppose professionalization), and different theoretical affiliations. Understanding, and elaboration of the foundational philosophical assumptions of therapists, is an area of theory and training that is taking a long time to mature (Bennett, 2005; Erwin, 1997; Howard, 2000).

1.2   Types of Goal

COLIN FELTHAM

Counselling and psychotherapy have developed organically and, some critics would say, have flowed almost promiscuously into many areas of our lives, so that exactly what they are *for*, what their goals are, is not always clear. It is possible to state that the overall goal of therapy is to facilitate clients' own

resourcefulness, insight, problem-solving capacities, happiness, and so on, but critics are entitled to question such global terms. As Sandler and Dreher (1996) convey well, it is far from clear to many psychoanalytic practitioners exactly what the legitimate scope and aims of their work are and should be. Freud himself expressed various aims for psychoanalysis at different times, such as symptom removal, making the unconscious conscious, restoring the capacity to love and work, helping clients to move from neurotic misery to ordinary unhappiness, and conducting research into the human psyche. Each of the contemporary 'schools' of therapy has its characteristic and sometimes conflicting aims – some being altogether wary of 'aim attachment' and some being explicitly goal-oriented and driven to reach and demonstrate successful outcomes. Here we look at the range of actual and possible goals.

Support

The term 'supportive therapy' suggests that some clients may primarily need and benefit from a form of therapy that upholds current ego-strength and/or coping skills and does not seek to challenge or uncover. Some may need long-term supportive therapy, while others require short-term support in crises. Support may be in the form of warm, non-judgemental listening and encouragement and, although most therapy does not become advocacy, on occasion supportive therapy or counselling may also lean in this direction. Such supportive work remains disciplined and professional and distinct from befriending or friendship. Its aim is to support the person through a difficult time and/or towards a position of independence or readiness for more challenging therapy.

Psycho-educational guidance

A wide range of psychologically informed practices are to be found under this umbrella term. Appropriate information giving, administering of questionnaires, coaching, mentoring, provision of social skills, life-skills training, assertiveness and relaxation training, marriage enrichment programmes, parent effectiveness training, relapse-prevention programmes, stress inoculation training, emotional intelligence and positive psychology training, are all examples. All aim to identify improvable behaviour and to teach personal

skills in various areas of life. The goal is not to uncover presumed psychopathology but to directly enhance cognitive, behavioural and interpersonal functioning, to assist clients in meeting developmental challenges and to equip them with concrete coping techniques and philosophies.

Adjustment and resource provision

The idea that people may be helped simply to adjust to their circumstances has usually been severely criticized by counsellors and therapists. However, it is probably a fact in at least some counselling settings (e.g. employee assistance programmes (EAPs)) that clients seek short-term adjustment-oriented help that may include elements of supportive therapy, problem-solving skills, assertiveness training, brain-storming solutions, *plus* the provision of contextual information (e.g. how an organization works, how to complain about your boss harassing you, etc.) and other welfare-oriented information, such as that relating to welfare benefits, housing, childcare, pensions, etc. In such contexts counsellors may act *both* as non-directive facilitators *and* as providers of relevant information and in some cases as brokers between individual client and organizations.

Crisis intervention and management

These terms are used broadly here to include the intervention and support of professionals in the aftermath of large-scale (e.g. plane crash), small-group (e.g. bank raid) or personal disasters (e.g. road traffic accidents). Survivors and witnesses of critical incidents or breakdowns of many kinds are often offered immediate help which includes debriefing, support, practical and active-directive help, referral to specialist resources, and gradual restoration of normal functioning. The aim is to provide sensitive, non-intrusive, psychologically strengthening help in the first instance, avoiding connotations of psychopathology. Crisis intervention is concerned primarily with restoration of the level of functioning that existed prior to the crisis.

Problem solving and decision making

For a certain proportion of clients, the purpose of entering counselling or therapy is to examine a life situation or dilemma and come to a (probably quite early) resolution or decision. How to cope with nuisance neighbours and difficult relationships, whether to have a termination of pregnancy, when to retire and whether to live in sheltered accommodation, whether or not to have optional surgery, are some examples. The aim is to facilitate exploration of issues, feelings and practicalities; addressing anxiety and loss may be part of the process. In some approaches, a philosophy and techniques of problem solving may be imparted as a proactive tool for living.

Symptom amelioration

A symptom is a usually distressing or troublesome change of condition which manifests in a crisis, inability to function as normal, apparently inexplicable somatic phenomena, etc. A majority of people who seek or are referred to counselling/therapy for the first time want their symptoms to go away; they wish to return to their normal mode of functioning and self-image. Sometimes their goals are hazy or implicit; a depressed client may, for example, obviously want to be simply less (or not) depressed. Probably one of the greatest mismatches between clients' and (many) therapists' goals is that while the former seek symptom amelioration or elimination, the latter often have more ambitious agendas based on belief in presenting problems as merely the tip of an iceberg, as 'defence mechanisms' masking underlying, unconscious conflicts. Exceptions to this tend to be behaviour therapists whose main aim is the identification of problematic behaviour and its reduction or elimination in the most efficient time span; and practitioners who strive to respond to consumers' stated needs and stages of change (e.g. Burton, 1998; Elton Wilson, 1996).

Insight and understanding

Some clients, and many therapists, have as their primary goals the investigation of causes of problematic feelings, thoughts and behaviour. Both client and therapist may wish to pursue the search for historical causes and the reasons for persistently counter-productive behaviour in current life circumstances ('Why did this happen to me? Why am I like this? *Aha! – now I see where this comes from.*') For some practitioners and clients, the goal of therapy may be the attainment of deeper and deeper insights or a state of continuous understanding of self, of how conflicts arise, of motivations, etc.

Cure

Almost all therapists and counsellors avoid use of the term 'cure' and any client expectations that therapy will result in final and dramatic removal of suffering. This may be due to (a) clinical experience – clients are very seldom dramatically, comprehensively or resolutely cured; (b) dislike of medical connotations – suffering, problems in living, are not regarded as biological disturbances to be treated with medical interventions; or (c) resistance to engendering hopes of unrealistic outcomes (and perhaps the disappointment and even litigation that might accompany such expectations). However, at least one approach, primal therapy, conceptualizes human problems in unitary terms as *neurosis* (a psychobiological state) for which it possesses *the cure*. Increasingly, too, the pressure from the evidence-based practice lobby leads practitioners to speak explicitly in terms of successful outcomes.

Self-actualization

Under this heading may be included all aims towards becoming a better person, having greater self-awareness or self-knowledge and attaining a state of fully functioning personhood. The range of goals subsumed here may include, for example, anything from 'I want to be more assertive/risk-taking/happy', to 'I want to try out everything life has to offer, I want to overcome all obstacles in my life and find the real me.' Concepts of individuation, maturation, finding the real self, being true to oneself and increasing self-awareness fit here. Most observers accept that the concept of an end-point – the fully functioning person – is somewhat mythical; self-actualization suggests a continuous process, a valuing of the journey more than a need to reach a goal.

Personality change

Eschewed by the more cognitive-behavioural and short-term approaches, hints at least of the possibility of quite far-reaching personality change are either found in or projected into certain forms of therapy. At an illusory level, the rather retiring, somewhat unattractive and untalented person may fantasize that therapy will compensatorily convert him or her into everything that he or she is not. However, a number of client claims and testimonies based on dramatic disappearance of distressing symptoms or limitations ('Therapy completely changed/saved my life') have suggested major life changes as a desired outcome for some clients. Many, particularly humanistic, psychotherapists regard their work as 'life-transforming therapy'. This goal raises questions about the nature of the concept of 'personality' and what actually constitutes personality change.

Discovery of meaning and transcendental experience

Particularly in the wake of the relative decline of formal religion and loss of spiritual and moral leaders and mentors, it seems that therapy has become for many an avenue for the exploration of existential, spiritual or metaphysical meaning and transcendental experience. The existential, humanistic and transpersonal approaches lend themselves most explicitly to such aspirations. This 'movement' has been gathering momentum in recent years and may well change the nature of at least some therapy practice (West, 2004).

Systemic, organizational or social change

In some forms of therapy, change within domestic partnerships, families, task groups and other groupings is clearly a goal. But counselling and psychotherapeutic skills as human relations skills (sometimes based on an understanding of unconscious conflicts, sometimes not) are also applied to conflict resolution within and between organizations. Experimentation with group counselling and therapy where more than a dozen or so participants are involved, and sometimes hundreds of members participate, has often had goals of conflict resolution and other aspects of social change.

Clients may change their goals over time, and the aims of therapy negotiated between therapist and client may change. It is not unusual for some clients to begin with modest goals and to find further, more ambitious or deeper aims to work on. It has been said that some therapists may be satisfied with the client *feeling better* as an aim, when a more enduring aim might be to *get better*. It has also to be remembered that the types of goal previously identified refer to avowed types of goal. We know that there are also 'shadow goals': some clients may wish to be in a 'sick role', to prove how incapable they are, to maintain a therapist's attention, etc.; some therapists may primarily wish to prove something to themselves, to hold power, to perpetuate a livelihood, to find vicarious intimacy. In spite of ethical codes or frameworks, requirements for training therapy, supervision and other safeguards, unhealthy covert goals cannot be eliminated altogether.

1.3   Arenas

COLIN FELTHAM

Arenas – also sometimes referred to as arrangements or modalities – may include the constellations of people receiving therapy (individuals, peers, couples, groups, families) and the media through which therapy is delivered (telephone or email counselling, art therapy, dance therapy, writing therapy, etc.). The former group is the one most commonly included under the rubric of arena. Strictly speaking, forms of self-help such as self-analysis, therapeutic writing and meditation might be included here. The interpersonal arenas are all, usually, face-to-face, verbally mediated therapies.

Peer counselling

This refers to any kind of counselling or therapy provided on an egalitarian basis, with each party agreeing temporarily to take the role of counsellor with the other as client, and then reversing roles. It started perhaps in its most disciplined format with the Re-evaluation Co-counselling of Harvey Jackins but has been modified by other groups (see Part 7). Its benefits include mutuality, egalitarianism, economy and avoidance of professional intrusion; its potential problems include boundary issues, compromised ability to 'hold', and transferential dynamics.

Individual therapy

Overwhelmingly the most popular form of therapy, one-to-one therapy (client and therapist) may be conducted in the following ways:

- Fifty-minute sessions for up to five times a week for many years using a couch or chairs (psychoanalysis)

- Fifty- or sixty-minute sessions (or sometimes shorter or longer) once, twice or three times weekly for months or years (psychotherapy and counselling)
- Single-session therapy, short-term/brief counselling/psychotherapy (e.g. 6, 10, 20 sessions), open-ended, serial, or intermittent patterns of attendance.

Individual therapy clearly replicates the original relationship of infant and caregiver and professional relationships such as the doctor–patient one. This arena offers optimal confidentiality, privacy, attention, containment, intimacy and safety. The assumption that it is necessarily the best arena for each client should, however, be balanced by considerations which include the therapist's expertise (or lack of it) in various areas; potential for dependency, manipulation, acting-out and abuse. The usefulness of other arenas should always be considered instead of or in conjunction with individual therapy.

Couple counselling/therapy

Originating in marriage guidance and marital psychotherapy, couple work is now provided for unmarried as well as married and for homosexual as well as heterosexual partners. Like individual and other arenas, it is informed theoretically by different schools of thought. However, unique to couple counselling is the focus on the relationship between the partners. Conflicts over domestic arrangements, interpersonal and sexual issues, children, money, affairs, values, at conscious and unconscious levels, take many couples, together or separately, to counsellors and therapists. This work entails triangular dynamics and a need for conflict management skills that individual therapists do not necessarily possess.

Individual therapists whose clients persist in discussing conflicts with their partners are well advised to consider referral to a couple counsellor. A caveat to this is when a client needs privacy for personal exploration or exceptionally confidential disclosures, or when co-operation between the partners is impossible. See further discussions in Parts 6 and 7.

Family therapy

Like couple counselling, where other parties (other members of a client's family) are clearly implicated, family therapy should be considered as an option for referral. A client's difficulties may be considered systemically when, for example, there are indications that the client is 'carrying' the family's secret sexual abuse or unexpressed grief and/or is being scapegoated by other family members. Counselling a client who has to remain in a disturbed or disturbing family may be counter-productive. Conversely, vulnerable clients may be unable or unwilling to participate in family therapy alongside those who are abusing or frightening them. This arena is the least likely to be offered in private practice, as it requires suitable accommodation, often with one-way mirror and/or video facilities, but is usually associated with social and family service units. Family therapy has a rich, diverse theoretical and clinical tradition. See Part 7 for further details.

Group therapy

Again, there is a rich tradition of forms of group therapy and counselling (see Part 7). In groups, clients may discover that others experience similar problems as they do; that they are accepted by group members (which can generalize into everyday life); that they can give as well as receive help and insights; and that they can draw on others' experiences and perceptions. Peer or mutual aid groups like Alcoholics Anonymous derive much of their effectiveness from common experience and committed support. Women may feel safer to explore certain issues in an all-women group. Groups can

act as a bridge from individual therapy to everyday living; they can also act as a booster for therapeutic progress either after or simultaneously with individual work. Like couple and family therapists, group therapists require particular skills and this work is sometimes conducted with co-leaders or facilitators.

Counselling/therapy via other media

As we have mentioned, although face-to-face, individual therapy based on talking is the most common format, increasingly therapy is offered using alternative media and arenas. Child psychotherapy is a specialism in its own right, requiring particular training (see Part 7). Sex therapy, too, is usually regarded as a specialism, and may depart from conversation to behavioural rehearsal. Sometimes brief psychotherapy is considered a specialism or arena, for which all practitioners should also consider appropriate referral routes.

The expressive or arts therapies, which include art therapy, drama therapy, psychodrama, dance and movement therapy, therapeutic writing and use of other media (e.g. photography) are increasing in their extent, availability and professionalism. For certain groups (e.g. children, older people, those who dislike primarily intense verbal communication), one or another form of expressive therapy may be the arena or modality of choice. Bodywork may or may not fit here, but obviously is an alternative means of providing therapy; where there are clearly problems expressed somatically, therapeutic massage, breathing or other techniques may be considered viable alternatives.

It is a common assumption that most therapy or counselling is a face-to-face activity. However, the extent to which telephone helplines are used is often played down or regarded unfairly as an inferior form of therapeutic help. This assumption is increasingly, and we believe rightly, challenged (see Part 7). Some people *prefer* the safety or convenience of telephone (or other forms of 'distant' counselling, including e-mail therapy and bibliotherapy, or recommended self-help books); and some have no other option, often by virtue of a disability, whether physical incapacity or agoraphobia, for example, or because of geographical remoteness. Advances in information and communication technology also increasingly challenge our acceptance of the best apparent help available.

Differences between counselling and psychotherapy and the use of counselling skills have already been discussed. Here it is important to point out that people often receive sufficient help from alternative professionals or para-professionals who may use counselling skills. Social workers, probation officers, guidance workers, welfare officers, nurses, teachers, mentors, coaches and others, often become involved in a helping or therapeutic role and many have specific training in therapeutic knowledge and skill. It is quite likely that many people are helped by such professionals (either incidentally and by brief contact or by formal arrangement) who might not otherwise approach, trust or have access to helpers designated 'counsellors' or 'psychotherapists'.

1.4 Settings and Opportunities for Employment

COLIN FELTHAM

A brief look at the prospects for trainees and those developing a career is included here because the subject of employment, although of obvious interest, is rarely touched upon in textbooks (see, however, Ross, 1997). It is perhaps an open secret that in spite of the huge growth of interest in counselling and therapy and the expansion of their training markets, it remains the case that relatively few (full-time) jobs exist. The reasons for this are not easy to specify but no doubt include: (a) the fact that much counselling stems from and remains attached to the voluntary and pastoral sectors and a great deal of counselling is still provided as an unpaid service; (b) the emergence of counselling and therapy as valid and evidence-based forms of professional service deserving of statutory funding; and (c) their relatively 'soft' image in competition with the work of, for example, psychiatrists (Gask, 2004) and clinical psychologists (Cheshire and Pilgrim, 2004). Although a great deal of therapeutic work is conducted in private practice, the extent of this (and its economic success for practitioners) is hard to measure. Alongside the number of relatively few full-time jobs, there are of course patterns of part-time and sessional (hourly paid) opportunities, private practice (usually part-time), counselling/therapy-related work (e.g. supervision, training/lecturing, consultancy, writing) and the use of counselling and therapeutic skills in other roles (e.g. social work, mentoring).

Voluntary agencies

These include those with national coverage such as Relate, Samaritans, Cruse, Victim Support, Mind, Turning Point, etc. Provision of local women's therapy centres, rape crisis centres, HIV/AIDS agencies, and family-oriented, drug- and alcohol-related services is widespread. Many of these rely on a mixture of statutory funding, voluntary fundraising and donations, most concentrate on a specific client group and some may offer paid positions. The work is not always purely or solely counselling or psychotherapy, but may include telephone helplines, befriending, advocacy, information and advice giving, awareness raising and so on.

Residential care

Residential care projects may be based within statutory or voluntary services and obviously focus on clients whose needs involve more than talking therapy. Client groups include children at risk, vulnerable young people, the homeless, those with often multiple problems of poverty, domestic violence, alcohol and drug abuse, criminal behaviour, mental health problems, disabilities and special needs, illness and frailty. Quite typically such work involves degrees of physical care, welfare issues and liaison with multiple agencies (e.g. Social Services, Probation and medical and legal services). Clients are often helped by 'keyworkers', part of whose work may be to provide counselling or to refer elsewhere for counselling. Some kinds of intensive residential care are highly specialized, for example with victims of torture, those emerging from hostage or damaging cult experiences. There are many projects offering residential rehabilitation programmes following drug addiction and alcoholism, and which look for experience and/or qualifications in general and psychiatric nursing, social work, counselling and groupwork. Often this kind of work offers in-house training and may be regarded as a route towards further professional training.

Education

Schools, further and higher education and special educational projects are some of the longest established settings in which forms of counselling and therapy take place. While some schools offer specific counselling services (and the need is still frequently alluded to), therapeutic work is probably still more commonly carried out by educational psychologists, behaviour support workers, mentors, and by teachers with a pastoral brief, with referrals being made where necessary (and possible) to child psychotherapists.

Colleges of further and higher education and universities, although not providing uniform national therapeutic services for students, are an example of a setting in which counselling has been offered successfully for decades. In the transitional and vulnerable period between adolescence and adulthood, issues of career uncertainty, susceptibility to emotional, interpersonal and sexual problems, drugs and alcohol, homesickness, and educational pressures, require sensitive help. Student counsellors may have relatively high caseloads of self-referred clients presenting a wide range of personal concerns. Turnover is often high since the work is often crisis-oriented and determined by the pressures of the academic calendar. Student counsellors (and those with psychotherapy training may be found as much as those from a counselling background) work in one of the few areas with a relatively good, clear structure of pay, conditions and progression prospects.

The workplace

Increasingly this has been the site of developments in counselling and opportunities for employment. Employee counselling, established in the USA for decades, has also grown considerably in Britain. Just as student retention is one of the motives behind provision of student counselling, so prevention of absenteeism is a motive behind employee counselling services. Employers' concerns include drug and alcohol abuse, stress at work, employee relations, management of change, redundancy, accidents in the workplace, etc. Many large companies provide their own in-house counselling provision, sometimes as part of occupational health; some refer out to individual counsellors or group practices; many contract the services of external employee assistance programme (EAP) providers.

Primary health care

This has been the area of greatest growth for counselling and psychotherapeutic services in recent years, especially in GP surgeries (see Part 7). This is perhaps an area where divergence of interest between counsellors and some psychotherapists is apparent, since this work is typically short-term. It has been estimated that over 50 per cent of counsellors are now employed by the NHS, although most counselling in primary care remains part-time. It is within the primary care sector that many new challenges face practitioners wishing to secure employment. Counsellors and psychotherapists are also sometimes to be found in specialized roles in hospitals (e.g. providing debriefing and counselling after road traffic accidents; counselling in obstetrics, infertility clinics, etc.) depending on local policies in NHS settings.

Private practice

Traditionally the location for most long-term psychotherapy, based typically in practitioners' own homes, and sometimes in purpose-rented offices, private practice is also fully discussed in Part 5 of this book. North American texts have been issuing warnings for some years that this is the practice sector most under threat from 'managed care' and from consumers' greater sophistication, awareness of outcome research and precarious personal finances. Small private practices probably compose an element of many counsellors' and psychotherapists' workloads, quite typically supplementing part-time incomes in other settings (Clark, 2002; Syme, 1994; Thistle, 1998).

In addition to the above settings, therapy may be offered in a wide variety of community services and voluntary agencies (e.g. Mind, Alcohol Concern, Victim Support, women's therapy centres, etc.), statutory services (e.g. psychology departments; social and probation services – although far less so now than in the past); police services and prisons); religious and pastoral organizations (e.g. Jewish Care's Shalvata (Holocaust Survivors' Centre); Catholic Marriage Advisory Centres, etc.).

As mentioned earlier, while relatively few full-time salaried posts exist, many of these offer good pay levels. Some statutory employers pay well, and EAP providers – where they offer more than occasional sessional (hourly) work – can offer relatively

high remuneration. Otherwise, pecuniary rewards run from nothing (particularly for trainees and those working as volunteers in community agencies) to modest hourly pay, to average wages for caring professionals. In private practice, some practitioners have been known to generate quite high incomes, but a trend towards a probable relative decline in clients being seen predictably from twice to five times a week (as in traditional psychoanalysis) for some years, and the growth in short-term therapies, is likely to undercut high incomes for all but a very few.

References

BACP (2002) *Ethical Framework for Good Practice in Counselling and Psychotherapy*. Rugby: BACP.

Bennett, M. (2005) *The Purpose of Counselling and Psychotherapy*. Basingstoke: Palgrave.

Bond, T. (2000) *Standards and Ethics for Counselling in Action* (2nd edn). London: Sage.

Brown, J. and Mowbray, R. (2002) Visionary deep personal growth. In C. Feltham (ed.), *What's the Good of Counselling and Psychotherapy? The Benefits Explained*. London: Sage.

Burton, M.V. (1998) *Psychotherapy, Counselling and Primary Health Care: Assessment for Brief or Longer-term Treatment*. Chichester: Wiley.

Cheshire, K. and Pilgrim, D. (2004) *A Short Introduction to Clinical Psychology*. London: Sage.

Clark, J. (ed.) (2002) *Freelance Counselling and Psychotherapy*. London: Brunner-Routledge.

Dryden, W. (ed.) (1997) *Developments in Psychotherapy: Historical Perspectives*. London: Sage.

Ellenberger, H.F. (1970) *The Discovery of the Unconscious*. New York: Basic Books.

Elton Wilson, J. (1996) *Time-conscious Psychological Therapy*. London: Routledge.

Erwin, E. (1997) *Philosophy and Psychotherapy*. London: Sage.

Feltham, C. (1995) *What Is Counselling?: The Promise and Problem of the Talking Therapies*. London: Sage.

Gask, L. (2004) *A Short Introduction to Psychiatry*. London: Sage.

Holmes, J. and Lindley, R. (1989) *The Values of Psychotherapy*. London: Routledge.

House, R. (2003) *Therapy Beyond Modernity: Deconstructing and Transcending Profession-centred Therapy*. London: Karnac.

Howard, A. (2000) *Philosophy for Counselling and Psychotherapy: Pythagoras to Postmodernism.* Basingstoke: Palgrave.

James, I. and Palmer, S. (eds) (1996) *Professional Therapeutic Titles: Myths and Realities.* Leicester: British Psychological Society.

May, R. (1992) *The Art of Counselling.* London: Souvenir.

Milton, J., Polmear, C. and Fabricius, J. (2004) *A Short Introduction to Psychoanalysis.* London: Sage.

Parry, G. (1996) *NHS Psychotherapy Services in England: Review and Strategic Policy.* Wetherby: Department of Health.

Ross, R. (1997) *Counselling as a Career.* Oxford: Baldrick Press.

Sandler, J. and Dreher, A.U. (1996) *What Do Psychoanalysts Want? The Problem of Aims in Psychoanalytic Therapy.* London: Routledge/Institute of Psycho-Analysis.

Sills, C. (ed.) (1997) *Contracts in Counselling.* London: Sage.

Syme, G. (1994) *Counselling in Independent Practice.* Buckingham: Open University Press.

Thistle, R. (1998) *Counselling and Psychotherapy in Private Practice.* London: Sage.

West, W. (2004) *Spiritual Issues in Therapy.* Basingstoke: Palgrave.

PART II
Socio-cultural
Perspectives

2.1 Introduction

COLIN FELTHAM AND IAN HORTON

Counselling and psychotherapy have often been criticized for focusing on the psychology of the individual and on the internal life of the client while ignoring the impact of the social, economic and cultural environment in which people live. Some practitioners and writers have expressed concern about what they see as a general lack of critical awareness of the social context of the psychological therapies (du Plock, 1997). Others have taken the argument much further and see the origin of a client's pain and distress as not only located within but maintained by the client's social environment (Pilgrim, 1997). Samuels (1993) suggests that such polarities are in fact usually subtly intertwined.

This part of the book starts by presenting an analysis of various theoretical perspectives on social context and then, in subsequent sections, examines a range of issues including gender, race, culture, class, religion, age, sexuality and disability. The assumption is that therapists will respond more effectively to the needs of their clients if they understand at least something of the socio-cultural factors that affect, not only their own lives and the lives of their clients, but the wider societal context in which counselling and psychotherapy takes place.

Implicit in this assumption are three levels at which socio-cultural factors may impact on therapy and which therapists may find useful to address in ways that are either consistent with or constructively challenge their theoretical orientation.

Human development

It is possible to identify two extreme theoretical positions on human development. From one point of view, human development and the origin and

perpetuation of psychological problems are seen as a function of the interaction between individuals and their environment. From this position the assessment or clinical formulation of client presenting problems and the subsequent therapeutic planning or approach to working with the client, would need to be aware of and to incorporate the impact of socio-cultural factors (Smail, 1993). Proponents of this view may also argue that therapists need to acquire a specific working knowledge of those socio-cultural factors germane to the client group they are working with. The opposing theoretical position is that the origin and/or resolution of psychological problems is located primarily within the individual. From this position it could be argued that socio-cultural factors are secondary or largely irrelevant to counselling and psychotherapy.

Therapist–counsellor relationship

This level of awareness is concerned with the socio-cultural similarities and differences between the therapist and client. What is important here is the impact of these factors on the development of rapport and therapeutic alliance (or misalliance) and on the ways in which the dynamics of the relationship may be used as a window on the client's presenting problems and as a mechanism of therapeutic change. Clearly there are wide differences between the broad theoretical orientations concerning the value and function of the qualities, characteristics and dynamics of the relationship between therapist and client.

Ponterotto et al. (1995) argue that essential elements of multicultural therapy competence are the therapist's awareness of his or her own cultural heritage, worldview and the related values, biases and assumptions about human behaviour, and an understanding of the worldview of the culturally different client (see also Palmer, 2002).

Counselling and psychotherapy generally

The psychological therapies remain largely a construction of the white, western, middle-class and majority culture. People generally have widely differing views about the value (or otherwise) of counselling or psychotherapy and its place in present-day society. Few therapists would argue that socio-cultural/economic factors do not impinge in some way on the work they do, although the importance they place on this issue varies enormously. Issues of power and social control seem relevant at this level as do the dynamics, constraints and demands of working in particular institutions or organizational settings, for example, primary health care and employment (see Part 7).

Bimrose (1993) is critical of the fact that so little attention seems to have been given to social context or multicultural issues in relation to counselling and psychotherapy theory, training and practice. This part of the book is concerned with what Bimrose describes as the hitherto invisible issues.

References

Bimrose, J. (1993) Counselling and social context. In R. Bayne and P. Nicolson (eds), *Counselling and Psychology for Health Professionals*. London: Chapman and Hall.

du Plock, S. (1997) Social responsibility. In I. Horton with V. Varma (eds), *The Needs of Counsellors and Psychotherapists*. London: Sage.

Palmer, S. (ed.) (2002) *Multicultural Counselling: A Reader*. London: Sage.

Pilgrim, D. (1997) *Psychotherapy and Society*. London: Sage.

Ponterotto, J.G., Casas, J.M., Suzuki, L.A. and Alexander, C.M. (eds) (1995) *Handbook of Multicultural Counseling*. Thousand Oaks, CA: Sage.

Samuels, A. (1993) *The Political Psyche*. London: Routledge.

Smail, D. (1993) *The Origins of Unhappiness: A New Understanding of Personal Distress*. London: HarperCollins.

2.2 Gender

JENNY BIMROSE

The gender of an individual refers to their membership of a particular category, masculine or feminine, which aligns more or less to the two sexes (and, according to the fifth edition of the *Concise Oxford Dictionary*, sexlessness). It is, however, different from sex, sexual orientation, sexual preference and other categories or descriptions which relate to various behaviours and identities associated with the sexes. Gender is defined by reference to those attributes associated with 'being female' and 'being male'. These attributes are not, however, fixed. They differ between cultures or societies during any one period in history, and change within the same culture or society over time. To illustrate this last point, it is quite easy for most people to identify ways in which some of the attributes associated with being female or being male in their own society have changed over, say, a 20-year period. Such changes are bound up with role changes and are also linked to subtle changes in social attitudes and values. Gender, then, is constructed and defined by societies. Perhaps most importantly, it highlights the ways in which 'being male' and 'being female' are valued differently – different and not equal. This section will examine the nature of some of these inequalities and discuss approaches developed to ensure counsellors respond more effectively to gender in counselling and psychotherapy.

Gender inequality

Gender focuses us on social inequality and its study raises questions about how and why such inequality occurs. In a poster campaign in 1980 which was designed to raise international awareness about the extent of these inequalities, the United Nations estimated that although women constituted approximately half of the world's population, they performed nearly two-thirds of its work hours, received one-tenth of the world's income and owned less than one-hundredth of the world's property. Fifteen years later, the United Nations held its fourth World Conference on Women in Beijing, China (1995). Progress in addressing gender inequality was evident (particularly in many western countries), and was reflected in significant lifestyle changes to the way that women live their lives. In the UK, women were having their first child later than ever before; divorces had increased sixfold; the number of first-time marriages had decreased; and young women accounted for more first-time mortages than men. However, in addition to such lifestyle changes, many examples of inequalities and injustices routinely confronted by women in a whole range of areas in their daily lives were reported. For example, statistics on violence against women exposed some shocking truths. Of violent incidents *revealed* by women, 46 per cent were classified as domestic, compared with 4 per cent of violence against men (crime surveys are known to underestimate the

extent of domestic violence). Over nine in ten domestic incidents against women were perpetrated by men. The higher risk of violence that women face was confirmed by the statistics on homicide. Of female homicide victims, 40 per cent were killed by present or former partners (Department for Education and Employment, 1995: 86).

Recent evidence of gender inequality in the UK presents something of a mixed picture. For example, girls are out-performing boys, educationally, at ages 16 and 18. In their last year of compulsory education, 58 per cent of girls, compared with 48 per cent of boys, gained five or more A*–C grades at GCSE or grades 1–3 at SCE Standard/NQ. At A level, 43 per cent of girls compared with 34 per cent of boys, were achieving two or more passes or three or more SCE/NQ Highers (EOC, 2005). However, patterns of women's employment in the UK have been much slower to change. While their participation rates in the labour market are increasing, women dominate in part-time work, which tends to be low paid, has few promotional prospects and has limited training opportunities. The gender pay gap is persistent and even widening. Gender segregation means women are persistently underrepresented in many occupational sectors. Finally, sexual harassment in the workplace is a strong and recurrent theme in women's employment, but often regarded as not being a significant problem (Bimrose et al., 2003).

The impact of child bearing has always had a dramatic effect on the economic status and income of women in the UK and the ages at which women have children are strongly related to qualification levels. In the age group 25–34, 84 per cent of women without qualifications had dependent children compared with only 29 per cent of those with degrees or equivalent (EOC, 2001). Within employing organizations, the 'glass ceiling' for women (the situation where women can see but not reach higher-level jobs and so are prevented from progressing in their careers) still exists. Women still comprise less than a quarter of company executives and only one in ten company directors. Even where women have broken through the glass ceiling into management positions, their pay is often lower than men's. These inequalities in pay and income inevitably extend into retirement (EOC, 2001).

Many other examples of gender inequality can be found in other areas of life, including health care, legal rights, housing, training and welfare. An important question for counselling is to ask to what extent and in what ways should these inequalities be taken into account in practice?

Gender and counselling/ psychotherapy

Even though the majority of psychotherapists are women[1] (AGCAS, 2004), trainers may, when working with trainee counsellors or therapists, often be confronted with resentment and sometimes resistance at the suggestion that gender represents a dimension in the therapeutic relationship which deserves special consideration. When such reactions are further explored, they usually reveal concern about stereotyping clients – that is, grouping clients within a grand category, such as gender, risks generalizations being made which may not valid. Of equal concern is the suggestion that women (and girls) are any more deserving of special attention or consideration in counselling than men (and boys). Such concerns cannot be ignored and they highlight just some of the difficulties associated with focusing on gender as a special issue in therapy. However, the study of gender inequality has the potential for enhancing overall counselling competence since each statistic about women also tells a story about men: where women are the victims of domestic violence, men are usually the perpetrators; the 'success' of girls in education highlights boys' 'failures'.

Over the past decade or so, gender has begun to attract the attention of researchers, writers and practitioners, who argue that counsellors and therapists need to adapt their approach when working with women. A useful framework for reviewing these contributions comes from multicultural counselling and therapy (MCT). Ivey et al. (1997: 6) claim that multicultural counselling helps clients 'see how their difficulties may be related to societal injustice issues concerning race or ethnicity, gender, or socioeconomic status'. As such, it has direct relevance for gender. Sue et al. (1995: 625) proposed specific multicultural standards and competencies which define the 'culturally competent counsellor'. They are presented in a three-by-three matrix which accommodates these competencies. The three basic dimensions of this matrix are defined as: therapist awareness, understanding and skills. It is within these dimensions that approaches to gender in therapy will now be considered.

Gender-aware therapy (GAT) is one approach that specifically encourages therapists to explore gender-related experiences with both women and men (Good et al., 1990). If adopted, the principles of GAT would enhance all three dimensions of multicultural competence in practice. Five are identified: (1) gender issues must be integrated into counselling and therapy equally with women and men (for example, problems related to childcare are discussed with men in the same way as they would with women); (2) problems which arise in counselling must, where relevant, be linked clearly to their social origins (for example, stress and anxiety which are created by a lack of availability of quality childcare provision should be related to systems failure in the provision of this service); (3) collusion with gender stereotypical solutions to problems must be avoided (for example, women experiencing stress and anxiety because of a lack of quality childcare provision should *not* be encouraged to give up work or to work part-time); (4) collaborative therapeutic relationships must be developed in preference to an expert therapist role; (5) and most important, clients' freedom to choose must be respected, rather than imposing a value position. Overall, an important goal of GAT is to help clients learn to act in new ways that will allow them to develop in a manner not constrained by stereotypical gender assumptions.

Applying Sue et al.'s (1995) multicultural competency framework, the second GAT principle implies increased knowledge and understanding about the precise nature and extent of gender inequalities within all aspects of society, together with their consequences. The third GAT principle implies the need for all therapists to increase their own self-awareness about gender issues as well as their awareness of gender stereotypes which operate generally. The first, fourth and fifth GAT principles imply particular skills and techniques which should be adopted by therapists in practice. For example, the first would require a conscious exploration of issues with men in therapy which relate to matters often associated only with women.

Feminist counselling approaches gender in a similar way to gender-aware therapy, highlighting the destructive potential of gender, since it limits role expectations and relegates half the population to second-class status. Chaplin (1999) describes feminist counselling as being a different approach that implicates attitudes, values and ways of thinking. She argues that it relates more to the development of a different 'feminine' value system through raising awareness and the rejection of the dominant male values and characteristics typical of the society in which we live. Feminist counselling is concerned with inequality generally, not just that associated with gender. It is eclectic in approach, so can be used with any other approaches to therapy which accept that external factors contribute to the problems of clients. Ivey et al. (1997: 173) summarize the main features of feminist therapy as being: the creation of an egalitarian relationship in counselling; valuing and respecting individual difference; emphasizing the influence of external influences; assisting with support for clients beyond the individual therapy session (for example, mobilizing support groups, community services); an active and participatory approach to therapy (for example, using techniques like assertiveness training for women); a strong information-giving component in counselling sessions to ensure that clients understand the origins and nature of gender oppression and inequality; and helping the client to gain a more positive self-image and personal validation.

Applying Sue et al.'s (1995) framework for multicultural competence to feminist counselling, the approach emphasizes increased counsellor self-awareness of gender inequality together with knowledge about and understanding of the dimensions of social inequality. Such knowledge would be used beyond individual counselling sessions to influence, even change, structures and systems which create and maintain gender inequalities.

Gender approaches to therapy are still being developed. They represent a serious and reflective attempt to address issues raised by gender in therapy.

Ivey et al. (1997: 175) discuss how feminist therapy can be combined with multicultural counselling and therapy, highlighting the value that can be derived when therapists work beyond the level of the individual to, for example, the community. Indeed, a conscious approach to gender can be particularly valuable when working cross-culturally, where cultures and value-systems define strongly marked gender roles.

Conclusion

Over three decades have passed since legislation was implemented in the UK which made discrimination on the grounds of gender illegal. Yet scratch the surface and it is easy to see the extent of the continuing gender discrimination, inequality and injustice. Often difficult to separate from other types of discrimination (such as ethnicity or social class), it can be subtle and hard to detect. Even so, it is no less destructive in its impact on the individual and society. Gender represents a challenge for counselling and psychotherapy: should counselling support, 'heal' and assist clients to return to the systems and contexts which damaged them? Or should it seek to influence these systems contexts, as well as reflecting upon and changing those values and practices inherently discriminatory in practice itself? Gender-aware therapy, feminist counselling and multicultural counselling and psychotherapy are distinctive approaches that attempt to address gender-related issues. They are still evolving, but represent a constructive attempt to ask legitimate questions about practice and incorporate new and different ways of responding to clients.

Note

1 Information relating to the proportion of women in counselling could not be located.

References

AGCAS (Association of Graduate Careers Advisory Services) (2004) *Psychotherapist: Occupational Profile.*

Available online: www.prospects.ac.uk/downloads/occprofiles/profile pdfs/

Bimrose, J., Green, A., Orton, M., Barnes , S.A., Scheibl, F., Galloway, S. and Baldauf, B. (2003) *Improving the Participation of Women in the Labour Market.* Coventry: Local Skills Council. Available online: www.lsc.gov.uk

Chaplin, J. (1999) *Feminist Counselling in Action* (2nd edn). London: Sage.

Department for Education and Employment (1995) *United Nations Fourth World Conference on Women – Beijing 1995.* Report of the United Kingdom of Great Britain and Northern Ireland. London: HMSO.

EOC (2001) *The Lifecycle of Inequality.* London: Equal Opportunities Commission. Available online: www.eoc.org.uk (accessed 25 April 2004).

EOC (2002) *Women and Men in Britain: Management.* London: Equal Opportunities Commission. Available online: www.eoc.org.uk (accessed 25 April 2004).

EOC (2005) *Facts about Men and Women in Great Britain, 2003.* London: Equal Opportunities Commission. Available online: www.eoc.org.uk (accessed 25 April 2004).

Good, G.E., Gilber, L.A. and Scher, M. (1990) Gender aware therapy: a synthesis of feminist therapy and knowledge about gender. *Journal of Counseling and Development,* 68: 376–80.

Ivey, A.E., Ivey, M.B. and Simek-Morgan, L. (1997) *Counseling and Psychotherapy: A Multicultural Perspective* (4th edn). Needham Heights, MA: Allyn and Bacon.

Sue, D.W., Arrendondon, P. and McDavis, R.J. (1995) Multicultural counseling competencies and standards: a call to the profession. In J.G. Ponterotto, J.M. Casas, L.A. Suzuki and C.M. Alexander (eds), *Handbook of Multicultural Counseling.* Thousand Oaks, CA: Sage.

2.3 Disability

SIMON PARRITT

It is estimated that some 600 million people in the world today experience disabilities of various types and degrees (WHO, 2003) and that 10–15 per cent of the total European population is disabled. A conservative estimate is that there are more than 6 million disabled people in the UK alone. The World Health Organization (WHO, 1980) has defined disability as the resultant deficits of performance of activities as a result of physical impairment. Physical impairment is the deficit in structure or functioning of some part of the body and social handicap is the deficit in social functioning (Johnston, 1996). However, there is continuing debate concerning the definition of disability which uses a model based

upon 'able bodied assumptions of disability …' (Oliver, 1993: 61). Oliver sees this as not just a question of semantics but a challenge to researchers to find new ways of operationalizing 'the concept of disability based upon the notion that disability is a social creation' (p. 66). For example, while a person may have an impairment, which means he or she uses a wheelchair, the disability is the difficulty experienced in accessing buildings or services as well as in personal relationships which is a result of the inaccessibility, or of the attitudes of a predominantly non-disabled societal structure. However disability is defined, and this continues to raise controversy, its prevalence increases with age. According to a recent

World Bank study, one person in four is over 75 years of age, and as we face an ageing population, the percentage of people who either define themselves or are classified by others as disabled will increase over the next few decades. An understanding of the issues and experiences of disabled people is essential for counsellors, psychotherapists and counselling psychologists if they are to meet the needs of this substantial group of people and of society as a whole.

As a minority group, disabled people differ from most others in that anyone can become a disabled person at any time in their life. Despite this, or perhaps because of this, there is often a tendency for therapists to collude with a process of denial or to distance themselves, seeing disability as something that happens to others. A substantial number of people, however, will experience disability in one form or another during their lifetime. One might in fact suggest that it is the exceptional person who will live his or her life without experiencing disability or being close to someone who is disabled. To see disability as 'other' and not reflect upon one's own relationship to disability and impairment is a fundamentally flawed strategy for anyone, but especially for those of us who are counsellors, psychotherapists or counselling psychologists.

Historically, disability has been seen as punishment or possession. Demons, spirits and divine retribution have all been evoked as ways of making sense of arbitrary and random events experienced by individuals and societies. This placed disability firmly within the domain of religion and therefore of faith healers, shamans and traditional healers. However, with the separation of the physical from the spiritual, illness and disability have become the domain of the physician and surgeon, who have sought to 'cure', treat or prevent. The impact of this upon disabled people, while overtly helping by interventions which have cured or improved disabled people's lives, has also brought difficulties. Unfortunately disability itself is often conceptualized as bad or deviant, and interventions are aimed at individuals to alter them physically or psychologically towards what a non-disabled world sees as the accepted norm, rather than what may be in their best interests.

Therapists may be faced with clients who are forever seeking a cure, but at what cost? If it takes many operations and almost half a lifetime to no longer be a wheelchair user, is this what the client wants the bulk of their life to be about? What has been lost in terms of living and what has been gained? Therapists will need to think deeply about these issues both from a philosophical standpoint and about each client. There are no right answers but the questions, options and choices should be aired and explored.

The impact of a predominantly biomedical model upon the development of services for disabled people has been to focus upon active physical treatment and to marginalize the psychological and socio-political experience of disabled people. For those who medicine fails to cure or repair, interventions are aimed at helping them 'come to terms' with their disability and accept their new reduced role and usually reduced status in society. They are in danger of becoming the passive recipients of care and sympathy from others. It is this image of disability that charity advertising has historically played upon, portraying disabled people as either helpless, sad, brave or courageous. While lip service may be paid to self-determination and empowerment, the reality of most support is that it marginalizes such issues as access to work, entertainment, transport, sex and relationships. Therapists may be in danger of falling into this narrow 'rehabilitation' framework. There are obviously access issues, but even accepting economic and physical access barriers, it is worth considering how the philosophy which underpins a counselling or psychotherapy service may compound the above view.

Leaving aside hospital-based services, what of counselling or therapy that is delivered from a social model perspective which proposes that people are disabled not so much by their impairments as by the environment? Much 'non-medically based' counselling for disabled people, where it exists, is delivered by charities or self-help groups with the emphasis on peer counselling. Disability charities are often struggling with the problem of being organizations run by the non-disabled for disabled people, rather than organizations run by disabled people for disabled people. Many large charities, established by the great and good in a different era, often promote the medical model. While there is a genuine effort by some to change and encompass the social model, progress is slow and often superficial. The quality and professionalism of such counselling is an important issue. While it may be important for counsellors to 'understand the issues', any service to disabled people should offer the same professional standards as would be expected by any other service user, disabled or not. Empathy is important, but it is surely not sufficient as the basis of a professional service. Equally important is access to high-quality training that addresses the fundamentals of disability for both disabled and non-disabled counsellors and therapists.

Counsellors and therapists should also be aware of the multiplicity of cultural value systems around disability both at the individual and family level. There are many ethnic and culturally differing attitudes towards disability. However, while counsellors must be aware of cultural values and practices, they should also view disability from a cross-cultural perspective. For example, family members may expect to be present during sessions, or a young disabled client may be expected to remain dependent and cared for at home with the family as a duty, and not to work or have sexual relationships. While these attitudes can be rationalized within a particular cultural perspective, they are also common themes of oppression and disempowerment that pervade disabled people's lives. Therapists must be sensitive to all aspects of a disabled client's experience.

There are other, more subtle barriers, which may explain why therapists see few disabled people. Attendance for counselling, so often a therapeutic and funding issue, has to be viewed differently as clients experience transport/access problems or may be ill. The result can be that non-attendance is higher and throughput lower than with other counselling services, increasing costs. Counsellors and therapists need to be aware of and explain these factors when compiling statistics and writing reports for the funding bodies. It is also important to question whether time-limited work which restricts the therapeutic contract to six or eight sessions is the most suitable for disabled clients, and to consider what the research and theoretical basis is for such contracts.

Having been referred a disabled client, there are practical issues that need to be addressed. But probably most counsellors or psychotherapists actually see very few disabled, or perceived as disabled, people. One counsellor, when asked how many disabled clients she had, was quite clear she had none. However, following a conversation about the subject, she realized that one of her long-term clients was in fact disabled with multiple sclerosis. Why had she not realized? Another experienced therapist felt unable to help in research because she also had 'no disabled clients'. Again, following discussion, she realized she had several clients with long-term impairments such as heart disease and rheumatoid arthritis.

The reason behind this 'denial' or 'invisibility' of disability is complex, but as therapists we need to become aware of all the issues in which clients themselves are immersed. The invisibility of many disabled people in society is itself a major source of oppression. Why do few therapists have disabled clients? It may be that clients are reluctant to label themselves disabled, preferring to be ill. This can either reflect a reluctance to be associated with a stigmatized group, or a preference for being ill – as illness is something that doctors treat rather than being something that defines who you are. Remember that most disabled people's experience of professionals is from a medical, not a social model perspective. Cure and treatment are aspects of the medical approach, with which disabled clients are familiar from day one of their diagnosis. Therapists need to be aware of where they are coming from and what their experiences of and reactions to impairment are, as well as how these influence their approach. They will also need to understand the client's belief system as well as their own in relation to disability, impairment and chronic illness, and their role as the counsellor or therapist.

As stated earlier, the social model outlined by Oliver (1993) and others proposes that disabled people are disabled by the environment, not by their impairments. This is clearly true at a sociological level, but for the individual client it only partly illuminates the experience of disability. Counsellors are looking to develop a therapeutic relationship with clients as unique individuals, but come to them with their own beliefs, experiences and models of working. Impairment may have little or nothing to do with what the client wants to address, or it may be central. However, therapists may at least initially be occupied by the impairment, especially if it is visible or declared prior to the first meeting or assessment.

Images of disabled people are often polarized between the 'dependent cripple' requiring sympathy, care and total support, to the strongly independent wheelchair user. The truth is rarely that clear-cut, and the majority of disabled people are not wheelchair users despite that being the accepted symbol for disability.

Disabled people have attempted to claim a cultural identity in a similar way to that of other oppressed people. They need to own their experience and see it for what it is – a unique culture of experience. This does not mean all disabled people are the same or share the same view of disability. Counsellors and therapists, whether they themselves are disabled or not, have a duty to see the experience of disability in a cultural context just as they would if they were seeing a client from a different culture. For many clients, having an impairment and being a disabled person means that they have experienced pain in various forms. It would be unrealistic to deny this. But how and to what degree this is the focus of therapy is both critical for the client and central to a wider political context in which therapy takes place. Being disabled is not necessarily a reason in itself for needing therapy.

Research has consistently shown that outcome depends more upon the quality of the therapeutic relationship than upon the theoretical model used by the therapist. It follows that the way therapists (be they non-disabled or disabled themselves) relate to their non-disabled or disabled clients is the critical factor. Here are just a few of the issues which might militate against the therapist making a successful therapeutic alliance with a disabled client:

- the association of tragedy with disability
- fear of contamination
- disgust at physical appearance
- helplessness
- pity

- a concentration on loss
- not accepting the reality of discrimination
- early life experiences and biases.

The writer has seen a few clients for whom becoming a disabled person was in retrospect an opportunity to start again, and such clients may embrace the social model as a core belief system. This reaction can cause tension, for the therapist may only see the 'loss' or 'tragedy' of becoming disabled. For such a therapist, the source of distress and therefore the focus of counselling is the individual, not the wider social political environment, and he or she therefore finds it almost impossible to empathize with a position which does not view disability *per se* as negative.

More common are clients who are distressed by their impairments not just because of the disabling environment but because they are in pain. They may have less energy and experience a deep ongoing sense of loss at not being able to do things that were once available to them. To adopt a position where all this is seen as secondary, the real issue which is located outside the individual in the social environment would be, of course, as harmful as the previous example. Finding the balance between these two extremes is perhaps the hardest task as it requires the therapist to listen intently to the internal experience of the client, to the therapeutic process as it unfolds and to their own inner process. Supervision is of paramount importance here.

For all this, the therapeutic space is perhaps one of the few opportunities that disabled people have to explore all aspects of their life and relationships. The sad thing is that few do so and fewer counsellors feel able to offer it. Those who do, often still come from a medical perspective and therefore can be in danger of not listening to how the client's experience of disability relates to his or her other life experiences and presenting problems.

References

Johnston, M. (1996) Models of disability: challenging the WHO model. *The Psychologist*, 9 (5): 205–210.

Oliver, M. (1993) Re-defining disability: a challenge to research. In J. Swain, V. Finklestein, S. French and

M. Oliver (eds), *Disabling Barriers: Enabling Environments*. Milton Keynes: Open University Press/ London: Sage.

WHO (World Health Organization) (1980) *International Classification of Impairments, Disabilities and Handicaps: A Manual of Classification Relating to the Consequences of Disease*. Geneva: WHO.

WHO (World Health Organization) (2003) Available online: www.who.int/mediacentre/notes/2003/np24/en/(accessed 6 July 2005).

Recommended reading

Hales, G. (ed.) (1996) *Beyond Disability: Towards an Enabling Society*. Milton Keynes: Open University Press.

Swain, J., Finklestein, V., French, S. and Oliver, M. (eds) (1993) *Disabling Barriers: Enabling Environments*. Milton Keynes: Open University Press/London: Sage.

Shakespeare, T., Gillespie-Sells, C. and Davies, D. (1996) *The Sexual Politics of Disability*. London: Cassell.

2.4 Age   ○○○

DAVID PILGRIM

This section will consider the relevance of age for counsellors and psychotherapists by addressing three phases in the life-span. A more elaborate account of the contents of the chapter can be found in Pilgrim (1997). The topic of mental health in relation to childhood, young adulthood and old age will be considered here.

Childhood

The emotions

As far as emotions are concerned, social science has drawn largely upon psychoanalysis. It provides an account of the emotional life of individuals, while at the same time offering an explanation of how mental ill health is determined by society.

For Freud, civilization puts limits on the free expression and experience of inherited emotions. These limits lead to the need of the child to repress anti-social feelings in exchange for family and societal acceptance. According to classical psychoanalytic reasoning, this battle between emotions and

social conformity leads to the development of neurosis. However, Freudianism is a limited social theory. Freud's emphasis is on civilization leading to repression and neurosis. According to Freud, we are all neurotic (to some extent) for more or less the same reasons to do with balancing our instinctual needs with the constraints of reality made clear to us by our parents. Consequently, differences between social groups were not addressed systematically by his theory, although later analytically oriented writers have explored women's issues.

Freud offered an explanation for neurotic behaviour arising from anxiety. Later psychoanalysts also explored the genesis of depression (Bowlby) and psychosis (Winnicott and Laing) by examining the impact of poor care and separation on the infant (from birth to two years). However, as an example of the divergent views within psychoanalysis, the influential work of Melanie Klein is distinctive because it focused on the pathogenic impact of the infant's inborn aggression (rather than poor care). By contrast, the work of Bowlby, Winnicott and Laing was heavily environmentally oriented – it emphasized deprivation of parents and deprivation as the source of later mental health problems.

Clinical psychoanalysis tends to play down or ignore variables other than the family, such as the particular stresses associated with class, race, gender, age and sexuality. It also ignores the potentially powerful role of extra-familial social institutions, such as the school, in shaping the child's identity and their emotional life. Those psychoanalysts who have strayed into these wider areas of theorizing have tended to leave or be expelled from their professional culture. Psychoanalysis also assumes family relationships which are 'triangulated', that is based on a set of tensions, which engender anxiety, created by children relating to a mother and a father.

While these competing etiological or developmental theories centring on the early years continue, there is ample empirical evidence that early childhood adversity predicts later mental health problems (see Rogers and Pilgrim, 2003).

Primary socialization

Childhood is a time when most of the rules and mores associated with the society and particular class and culture which the child inhabits are learned. It is also a time when gender-specific conduct is acquired. Children learn gradually to control their bodies and their emotions in order to perform competently and efficiently in the presence of others. They learn the importance of a shared view of reality with their fellows in gaining security and in meriting credibility. All these learnt capacities are also bound up with an increasingly elaborate and defined sense of identity.

Competence can fail if the person lacks the intellectual capacity to grasp what to do ('learning disability') or if they lack confidence in their performance as a social actor ('phobic-anxiety') or if they are too sad to participate in everyday activities ('depression'). The competence can also be judged to have failed by others if the person does not comply with everyday expectations of appropriate behaviour in context or they make idiosyncratic claims about reality ('schizophrenia').

A final aspect of socialization relevant to understanding mental health is that children learn to control their emotions. The strong emotional expressions tolerated in childhood become less and less acceptable as the person matures to adulthood. Consequently, if an adult becomes more exuberant or sad than is deemed appropriate for the context by others, they may acquire the label of 'manic-depressive'.

Childhood sexual abuse

While the connection between sexual abuse and distress can be viewed as a unifactorial relationship, this does not imply that there is a consistent outcome for all victims. Individuals do vary in their responses to similar abusive acts, and the severity of the abuse, its duration and the relation of the perpetrator to the victim have all been linked to variable outcomes (Finkelhor, 1984). Another caution is that sexual victimization may be part of a wider picture of family disturbance which could be pathogenic.

Notwithstanding this valid caution, reviews of the literature on the immediate and long-term effects of sexual abuse on child victims come to the conclusion that there is strong evidence that they are significantly more prone to mental distress than non-abused children. Not only is this evidence compelling, but it points to a wide range of effects which may account, in part at least, for the higher rate of reported mental health problems in women than men. Overall, girls are at greater risk than boys of sexual victimization. This is certainly true of intra-familial abuse, although there is some evidence that boys may be at greater risk from stranger-perpetrators. The large gap between male and female victims in terms of abuse and rates of distressing consequences may be accounted for in part by the greater readiness of females to disclose on both accounts (Finkelhor, 1979). In addition, the discourse on females has been more wide-reaching than on males, with the bulk of the research on prevalence of abuse and its effects being focused on women not men.

Sexual abuse makes child victims more likely than non-abused children to demonstrate:

- aggression
- sexually inappropriate behaviour
- sexual aggression.

This trio of symptoms characterizing child victims of sexual abuse does not mean that they have only these problems. Other forms of distress reported include those suffered by non-abused psychiatric referrals (anxiety, depression, night terrors, language delay, hyperactivity, stealing, peer relationship difficulties, eating disorders, etc.). However, the trio does seem to mark sexual abuse victims off from non-abused children with emotional problems.

A number of epidemiological studies now indicate that these immediate externalizing effects in childhood translate into adult problems both of 'acting out' and of experienced distress. Studies of long-term effects on both clinical and community populations all show raised levels of mental health problems in survivors of childhood sexual abuse.

The stigma of the abused victim and the shame and criminality of the perpetrator make accurate estimates of child sexual abuse difficult. Baker and Duncan (1985) suggest child sexual abuse rates of 0.25 per cent for relative and 10 per cent (12 per cent female and 8 per cent male) for non-relative abuse in Britain. If these are accurate estimates, around 4.5 million British adults are victims of earlier sexual abuse. In the USA, Russell (1983) reports much higher rates in her community survey of women – 38 per cent reporting one experience of sexual abuse before 18 with 4.5 per cent of the sample reporting abuse by their biological or step-fathers.

Young adulthood

One of the most controversial questions in current debates about mental health is the nature of schizophrenia. The diagnosis is the most common one given to those deemed to be suffering from a 'major mental illness'. It is also the one which is given most commonly in young adulthood. Orthodox psychiatric descriptions depict the schizophrenic as a person who is socially withdrawn and who suffers from disturbances of cognition (thought disorder and delusions), perceptions (hallucinations) and emotions ('flat' or 'inappropriate' affect). Schizophrenia rests on value judgements about the person's unintelligible behaviour but has no equivalent of a blood test. This does not imply that diagnosis of physical illness cannot be deconstructed, nor that value judgements are absent in physical diagnoses. However, it does point to the particular construct validity problems of a diagnosis of schizophrenia and other 'functional' disorders.

The questions begged about schizophrenia are thus mainly about how it is negotiated or ascribed. This tack has been taken most systematically by Coulter (1973). He argues that focusing on debates about aetiology obscures the ways in which madness emerges, first through social negotiation in the lay area and then in the professional confirmation (a diagnosis). Coulter focuses on everyday expectations of normality and competence. For instance, in relation to hallucinations he argues that to maintain our credibility in a social group there has to be a consensus about what our senses detect around us. In most contexts if a person sees or hears something others do not, then their credibility, and therefore their social group membership, is jeopardized. However, it is possible in certain contexts that such idiosyncratic capacities might strengthen rather than weaken their credibility and group status. The Christian mystic and some African medicine men are expected to have extraordinary visions. Indeed, their social credibility may rest on having these abnormal experiences.

In some cultures where hallucinations are valued positively, the bodily circumstances which increase the probability of their occurrence (fasting, fatigue, drug taking, etc.) are often contrived deliberately. Al-Issa (1977) notes that in western society hallucinations offend rationality. Most of us suppress idiosyncratic perceptions because we learn that they are valued negatively. 'Schizophrenics', in contrast, act upon their idiosyncratic experiences. Community surveys indeed point to estimates of between 10 per cent and 50 per cent of the normal population who hallucinate.

Thus atypical idiosyncratic perceptions are not intrinsically pathological. Whether hallucinations are deemed to indicate a gift or defect depends on the roles people occupy in particular cultures. Likewise, weird speech patterns are highly valued in those Christian sects which respect the ability to 'speak in tongues' (or 'glossolalia'). Outside these sects, in everyday western life, they may be taken to be an offence to rational discourse and so encourage attributions of mad talk from their fellows. Later these may be reframed as evidence of schizophrenic thought disorder by a psychiatrist.

While most cultures have some notion of oddity or madness, because norms of sanity vary this notion is not constant. Nor is there a transcultural or trans-historical consensus on what causes oddity or how to respond to it when it emerges. Each culture may have a notion of what it means to lose one's reason but these notions vary across time and place and so undermine the claims of modern western psychiatry that 'schizophrenia' and its symptoms are a stable set of factors to be studied.

Old age

While dementia may have become a dominant modern culture image of becoming elderly, depression is actually more prevalent. Whereas the prevalence of dementia is about 5 per cent in the over-65s, rising to just under 20 per cent for those over 80, depression is much commoner in the younger age band of older people. Prevalence studies typically quote rates of 11 to 15 per cent (Copeland et al., 1987). The factors which contribute to depression in old age include:

- Multiple and chronic physical illness. The link between depression and physical illness in old age is highlighted by a recent review of several studies of medical (i.e. not psychiatric) inpatients, which concludes that only one in five recover from lowered mood state before death (Cole and Bellavance, 1997).
- The environment of residential homes for older people is often under-stimulating, and being moved to a residential facility is disruptive, entails a loss of previous surroundings and may mark a loss of personal control or autonomy.
- Relationships that have accumulated during the life-span are lost. Spouses, friends and siblings die off around a surviving older person, making the person prone to the aggregating effect of grief.
- Another social vulnerability factor is that of material adversity. In a community study of life events preceding depression in old age, Murphy (1982) found that poorer people who had experienced housing and financial difficulties were more prone to depression (both mild and severe proportions) than better-off older people. Blaxter (1990) found that psychological well-being of older people varied significantly with social class. Social classes 1 and 2 improved with age overall but those in social classes 4 and 5 deteriorated.
- Another consideration is the role of supportive and confiding relationships. Lowenthal (1965) found that the presence of a stable confiding relationship was a protective factor against depression in old age. She also found that those most vulnerable are old people who try to form relationships and fail, rather than people who have coped throughout life alone. Murphy (1982) found in her community survey that 30 per cent of those reporting the lack of a confiding relationship were depressed.
- A final factor which needs to be considered is that of abuse in old age. As with the abuse of children, prevalence and incidence are difficult to investigate accurately, given that abusers will typically deny the act. When the abuse occurs at the hands of paid carers, their job is at stake, as well as their reputation. Estimates of elder abuse rates in Scandinavia vary from 8 to 17 per cent of older victims across Denmark, Sweden and Finland (Hydle, 1993).

Discussion

Therapists have a differential interest in the topics raised above. The material on childhood and emotions has a central relevance to many of the models of counselling which are the bread and butter of schools and training courses. The latter rehearse assumptions about childhood development and its personal implications for adult clients. Childhood sexual abuse is clearly important. Even the conservative estimates of the prevalence of its survivors in mental health services suggests that the topic deserves serious consideration, both in training and in routine casework.

The brief discussion about psychosis raises a different question which is whether the traditional exclusion of this client group from many types of psychological treatment is any longer tenable. It poses particular challenges for therapists in their training and daily practice. As far as private practice is concerned, mad people are usually poor and thus permanently excluded from its ambit. Many trainers have had little or no contact with people with psychotic problems. The structured problem solving required in this type of work is also at odds with the neutrality of a psychodynamic approach and the non-directiveness of person-centred therapy. Freud and his followers typically argued that psychotic patients could not develop a transference relationship and were thus unanalysable.

Finally, older people have been overlooked by therapists in comparison to younger adults. Two factors influence this under-provision. The first is ideological – older people are considered by professionals to be fixed in their functioning and thus lack the capacity for change. The second is economic – older people tend to be poorer than those of a working age. Consequently private practitioners will see fewer older clients.

References

Al-Issa, I. (1977) Social and cultural aspects of hallucinations. *Psychological Bulletin*, 84: 570–587.

Baker, A.W. and Duncan, S.P. (1985) Child sexual abuse: a study of prevalence in Great Britain. *Child Abuse and Neglect*, 9: 457–467.

Blaxter, M. (1990) *Health and Lifestyles*. London: Routledge.

Cole, M.G. and Bellavance, F. (1997) Depression in elderly patients: meta-analysis of outcomes. *Canadian Medical Association Journal*, 157 (15 October): 1055–1060.

Copeland, J., Dewey, M., Wood, N. et al. (1987) Range of mental illness among the elderly in the community. *British Journal of Psychiatry*, 150: 815–823.

Coulter, J. (1973) *Approaches to Insanity*. New York: Wiley.

Finkelhor, D. (1979) *Sexually Victimized Children*. New York: Free Press.

Finkelhor, D. (1984) *Child Sexual Abuse: New Theory and Research*. New York: Free Press.

Hydle, I. (1993) Abuse and neglect of the elderly: a Nordic perspective. *Scandinavian Journal of Social Medicine*, 2 (2): 126–128.

Lowenthal, M. (1965) Antecedents of isolation and mental illness in old age. *Archives of General Psychiatry*, 12: 245–254.

Murphy, E. (1982) Social origins of depression in old age. *British Journal of Psychiatry*, 141: 134–142.

Pilgrim, D. (1997) *Psychotherapy and Society*. London: Sage.

Rogers, A. and Pilgrim, D. (2003) *Mental Health and Inequality*. Basingstoke: Palgrave.

Russell, D. (1983) The incidence and prevalence of intrafamilial sexual abuse of female children. *Child Abuse and Neglect*, 7: 133–145.

2.5   Social Class

DAVID PILGRIM

This section will discuss the relevance of social class for counsellors and psychotherapists and will cover the following topics:

- social class and mental health problems
- the historical root of class discrimination in therapy

- the social class of therapists and patients
- the social gap and its implications
- who is responsible for the class bias in psychotherapy.

There is a wealth of information now about the relationship between social class (or what is sometimes called socio-economic status) and mental health.

The following main points can be summarized at the outset:

- Mental health problems can be found in all social classes.
- Within the overall picture, class gradient exists – richer people are generally more mentally healthy.
- This class gradient amplifies with age – the mental health status of richer people improves with age, whereas that of poorer people deteriorates.
- This epidemiological summary is based upon correlational investigations – the question of the direction of causality remains contested about some aspects of the overall picture.

The final point is the most contentious in that while the class gradient in mental health statistics is unequivocal (as is the unequal pattern of mental health service delivery) the direction of causality is open to debate. Those retaining a strong bio-determinist approach to mental illness argue that patients become poor because of their social incompetence (the downward drift hypothesis). The opposing view is that of social causation: poverty makes people mentally ill. A third position is that genetically vulnerable individuals are differentially exposed to social stressors. The controversy essentially applies to the *causality* of psychosis. It does not apply either to relapse in psychosis nor to stress reactions nor to psychosomatic reactions. Here the evidence is unambiguous. For example, employment opportunities improve the prognosis of those with a diagnosis of schizophrenia. Low-paid and unemployed people are disproportionately likely to suffer a range of anxiety and depressive symptoms and are more likely to commit suicide and abuse drugs and alcohol. When psychosomatic symptoms are taken as a proxy for mental health (e.g. cardiovascular disease) then lower pay and lower task control in work are factors in the development of hypertension, strokes and heart attacks. This picture of unemployment and low pay adversely affecting mental health parallels the picture of physical health. Poorer people are sicker and die younger than richer people. For a fuller review of the relationship between labour market disadvantage and mental health see Rogers and Pilgrim (2003: Chapter 5).

One point which is indisputable is that poorer people are over-represented with mental health problems in specialist mental health services (and in primary care samples). Moreover, the class position of a patient is a predictor of their likely style of treatment.

The historical roots of class discrimination in therapy

It has been pointed out elsewhere (Pilgrim, 1997) that a central question under this heading is not whether but *why* psychotherapy is elitist. All of our research on mental health service utilization demonstrates that poorer people receive more physical treatments than richer people and vice versa in relation to talking treatments. The class gradient in access to talking treatments can be accounted for by the following factors:

- A dominant model of psychotherapy is based upon the psychoanalytic tradition. The latter originated in the middle-class outpatient work in which the fee not only became fetishized as an important symbol for interpretive work in therapy but was a practical necessity for the *therapist* to live. Freud made the point that 'we do analysis for two reasons – to understand the unconscious and to make a living'. Fee paying *ipso facto* debars poor clients from access to therapy – it is a discriminatory practice. However private practitioners rationalize their form of employment, its consequences are discriminatory.
- The origins of contemporary styles of psychotherapy can be traced to the growth of the 'psy complex' and the medical dominance in the state asylum system. In the early days of this in the mid-nineteenth century, a brief tension existed between lay managers of asylums, who wished to encourage 'moral treatment' (a precursor of the therapeutic community), and medical superintendents who argued that mental abnormality was a genetically determined defect requiring physical restraint and treatment. By the end of the nineteenth century, the medical view prevailed and set the pattern for the next 100 years – inpatients were to be mainly treated by physical means. As there was (and is) a preponderance of poorer people in inpatient settings, poverty and biological treatment become inextricably linked. In Britain by the

1990s over 90 per cent of psychiatric patients had received drugs but only 60 per cent had received any form of psychological intervention, which included access to the private and voluntary sector for counselling and therapy (Rogers et al., 1993).

- Although the above picture shows a class gradient in type of service access, it is a gradient and not a dichotomy. Psychological treatments are provided within the public sector. However, within this, a further class process has operated over time. In Britain this can be traced to the First World War and the problem of 'shell-shock', which created a crisis for the bio-determinism of Victorian psychiatry. Those who were breaking down in the trenches were either working-class volunteers or officers and gentlemen – they were 'England's finest blood' (Stone, 1985). A eugenic (genetic) account of mental abnormality was logically incompatible with this picture and was tantamount to treason. As a result, the asylum doctors lost legitimacy for a while during war conditions, as did their professional rhetoric about bio-determinism. Their authority was replaced by that of the shell-shock doctors who imported a *psychological* (eclectic or Freudian) model into state-provided mental health work. After the First World War outpatient treatment centres were set up, thus changing the configuration of mental health work. After that point the ambit of psychiatry began to include an interest in the neuroses. Prior to the war, medical interest had only been in madness. However, the expanded interest of psychiatry still made important distinctions in practice: soldier patient versus the civilian; the neurotic versus the psychotic; the outpatient versus the inpatient. Against the organizational backdrop we can see how poor mad patients continued to be treated in the way they always had been – via physical not psychological means.
- Apart from these historically rooted organizational biases which produced institutional discrimination against poorer clients, another factor to consider is the class background of therapists. This is influential in a number of ways to be considered next.

The social class of therapists and patients

A general sociological point made by Horwitz (1983) is that the class position of mental health professionals inevitably biases the way in which they make their assessments and conduct their treatments. This is not to say that all the fine-grain assessment and treatment is class determined but it does make the point that the class relationship between patients and their therapists is important. For example, the closer that therapists and clients are in their class position, the greater the probability of mutual agreement and understanding. Questions of empathy and intelligibility come into the frame here. Not surprisingly, the smaller the gap between therapists and clients, the greater the probability that the former will be empathic to the latter and the more they will be confident about intelligibility of presenting problems. By contrast the poorer client will be understood less readily. This then spills over into labelling – poorer clients are more readily given more serious or stigmatizing labels than their richer equivalents. Middle-class clients more readily accrue diagnoses of neurosis, whereas working-class patients more readily accrue diagnoses of psychosis. During the nineteenth century, for example, poorer depressed patients were described as 'melancholic', whereas richer ones were described as 'mopish'.

The social gap and its consequences have been used as an explanation for why lower-class patients do less well in psychotherapy. However, what remains ambiguous is both the evidence for this specific claim and the responsibility for its rectification, when and if it is proved to be the case.

The social gap and its implications

The whole question of social class and psychotherapy can be unpacked sequentially, starting with this selection. In his review of the topic, Bromley (1994) found that:

- The evidence on *client expectations* explaining referral bias was unequivocal. Some studies showed that working-class clients express a need for exploratory psychotherapy. Other studies show no class differences.
- The evidence on *professional expectations* was less equivocal. There is a consistent pattern in the studies of professionals in their referral and assessment decisions which shows that professionals have lower

expectations of lower-class clients in terms of their general suitability to form a therapeutic alliance and in terms of client capacity to utilize talk in a consistent way in a process of change.

- The great majority of studies of selection demonstrate that the higher the social class of the patient, the greater the probability they will be assigned to talking treatments rather than being treated physically.
- The evidence about early drop-out of working-class patients is equivocal. Some show early drop-out but others show no class difference. In those which suggested a pattern of early drop-out, it was not clear whether this was a function of client expectations, professional expectations or an interaction between the two.
- This selection bias is accounted for in part by the fee (which is prohibitive for poorer patients) and partly by the biases of professional referrers and assessors.
- Most of the studies' bias is from the USA but the fewer studies conducted in Britain and Scandinavia confirm a similar picture.

When I reflect on the above from personal experience of working for over 20 years in a variety of British mental health settings, in which I have only seen non-fee-paying clients, then a number of the findings make sense. I am aware of GP bias in the type of client they refer to the NHS (Pilgrim et al., 1997). I am also aware of the criteria which general psychiatrists working in acute mental health units operate about the suitability of patients for referral to some form of psychological treatment. Bias by diagnosis and class is evident. My own experience has also been that a problem-solving approach, rather than one which is either rigidly non-directive (attending *only* to the purported necessary and sufficient conditions of the central therapeutic triad) or psychodynamic (attending only to transference) is one that engages and profits NHS clients, whatever their class background, but especially those from a poor background. This question of personal experience is important not because it necessarily is telling evidence (Bromley's review needs to be accepted or critiqued in its own right as a balance-sheet of evidence) but because it shapes the message I choose to deliver, here. This question of a reflexive

turn on evidence is what I want to turn to next to round off this chapter.

Who is responsible for the class bias in psychotherapy?

In the light of the discussion above about the social history of class discrimination in psychotherapy and the evidence about professional biases in referral, who is responsible for reversing the current elitism? The first point to make here is that the question may be vital, irrelevant or discomfiting depending on the professional background of the therapist. Those working in private practice will either treat the question in an inconsequential way or they might offer justifications for their practice. By contrast, those practitioners committed to providing health care free at the time of need will argue that therapists must take some political responsibility for class discrimination. This was my very conclusion elsewhere (Pilgrim, 1997: 54). Those coming from a strong private practice background will deny the need for political responsibility. Strong tendencies exist among private practitioners to avoid or defuse political argument by, for example, using the euphemism 'independent practice', intimating that their critics may be 'envious', and in general resorting to psychological reductionism. Interested readers may wish to compare Pilgrim (1992) with Syme (1994: 108) on such points.

I mentioned above that I considered therapists to be partially responsible for class discrimination. This is not a straightforward matter of moralizing about private practices but it is a question about putting into context the relationship between therapists and their own cultural and organizational legacies. Three examples may illustrate this point. First, we cannot be responsible for inhabiting structural arrangements we inherit from the past, although we can be responsible for critical appraisal of their contemporary relevance. An example of this is the interpretive focus of the fee in psychodynamic work. This had a particular social history but therapists may wish to query its current necessity. Second, bias occurs in the referral process not just in the assessments of therapists. That is, referral routes precede the activity of individual therapists. Even here the latter can still be responsible for changing cultural expectations about these biases with their referrers. Third, psychological treatments in the NHS are restricted in part by lack of appropriately trained personnel. Some of this is about lack of volume in professions such as clinical psychology and part is to do with professional protectionism of mental health workers. If the availability of psychological treatment in the NHS is to increase then questions of numbers trained and restrictive practices need to be addressed by politicians, service managers and the leadership of the mental health professions.

References

Bromley, E. (1994) Social class and psychotherapy revisited. Paper presented at the Annual Conference of the British Psychological Society, Brighton.

Horwitz, A. (1983) *The Social Control of Mental Illness*. New York: Academic Press.

Pilgrim, D. (1992) Psychotherapy and political evasions. In W. Dryden and C. Feltham (eds), *Psychotherapy and Its Discontents*. Milton Keynes: Open University Press.

Pilgrim, D. (1997) *Psychotherapy and Society*. London: Sage.

Pilgrim, D., Rogers, A., Clarke, S. and Clarke, W. (1997) Entering psychological treatment: decision-making factors for GPs and service users. *Journal of Interprofessional Care*, 11 (3): 313–323.

Rogers, A. and Pilgrim, D. (2003) *Mental Health and Inequality*. Basingstoke: Palgrave.

Rogers, A., Pilgrim, D. and Lacey, R. (1993) *Experiencing Psychiatry: Users' Views of Services*. London: Macmillan.

Stone, M. (1985) Shellshock and the psychologists. In W.F. Bynum, R. Porter and M. Shepherd (eds), *The Anatomy of Madness*, vol. 2. London: Tavistock.

Syme, G. (1994) *Counselling in Independent Practice*. Buckingham: Open University Press.

2.6 Sexual Orientation

DOMINIC DAVIES

History of homosexuality

Representations of homosexuality have been found by anthropologists and historians around the world and from the earliest times. In some cultures homosexuality is seen as a natural and normal variation of human sexuality, in other cultures same-sex relationships are encouraged or given high status, and in some others still homosexuality is reviled and persecuted. What is clear, though, for anyone who has spent time exploring the issue, is that homosexuality is a naturally occurring phenomenon. Some people see their homosexuality as an *essential* part of their nature. Such people may say, 'I was born this way.' They may be able to give examples of childhood same-sex attractions and desires to support their experience. Others may say they have chosen their sexuality or maybe even that they have tried sexual relationships with the opposite sex, and prefer for a variety of reasons to have relationships with the same sex. Generally speaking gay men tend to use essentialist ideas (that they were born gay) to explain their homosexuality and lesbians tend to use arguments of 'choice'. Some people, following childhood sexual abuse, experience distress or confusion about their sexual orientation, although there appears to be no clear evidence that sexual abuse has any impact on the sexual object choice.

Sociologically, views of homosexuality are divided into two camps. There are those who see homosexual identity as a social construction particular to this place and time. In this view, homosexuality in, say, Thailand, Ancient Greece, or Pakistan has little in common with the modern gay man living in, let us say, London or New York. There are others who would argue that because there is evidence of people who have always been gay, in every culture and through time, there is something essential or natural about homosexual identity. These arguments continue to be discussed and evidence accrues in support of both views. Is it nature (essentialism) or nurture (social constructionism)? There is plenty of evidence to support both nature and nurture arguments for the individual seeking to understand why they are lesbian, gay or bisexual, and also plenty of evidence to support theories of homosexuality as *essentialist* and *socially constructed*. Most lesbian, gay and bisexual people, however, have little interest in why they are interested in same-sex relationships – it is just a given.

One common feature, highlighted by Grahn (1990), is that in many cultures lesbians and gay men are holding up a mirror to the way the society in which they live views sex, gender and sexuality. They are showing a different way of being a man or woman. In some societies this is supported by the culture, in others a separate culture exists to support the lesbian, gay or bisexual person. Lesbian, gay and bisexual people have been among the European witches and their rites – over a 400-year period, seven million witches were burned on piles of faggots (not simply bundles of wood, but piles of human bodies – there is evidence that many of these people would have been strangled gay men). They have been among the shamans and medicine men and women of the Native Americans (where many tribes, including the Sioux, Cherokee and Navajo, sanctioned same-sex love and held it in high regard). Lesbian, gay and bisexual people have been despised, tortured and murdered by, among others, Nazis in Germany, and in modern-day Iran and China and elsewhere. To varying degrees individual men and women participate in both the heterosexual and lesbian, gay and bisexual communities and cultures.

There is an invisible thread linking all sexual minorities. This thread is the way lesbian, gay and bisexual people have manifested and worked within societies throughout the world to facilitate a crossover in the way the genders operate with each other. When a lesbian cuts her hair short and wears 'male' clothing she is not trying to look like a man. She is showing another way of being a woman, in which she, as a woman, defines how she looks, rather than allowing men to define how she should look. A gay man wearing a 'camp', perhaps effeminate outfit of a loose-fitting shirt in pastel shades is not trying to look like a woman but to show a different way to be a man. There is a strength that comes from being able to reinvent oneself, and in creating different ways to be who one is.

It was only as recently as 1992 that the World Health Organization (WHO) removed homosexuality from their *International Classification of Diseases* (ICD9). This was two decades after the American Psychiatric Association declassified homosexuality from the *Diagnostic and Statistical Manual III*. There are still a great many practitioners, particularly those working in the mental health sector, who erroneously believe that to be lesbian, gay or bisexual is an illness or perversion. Few people learn much to the contrary on their training courses even today, although the national mental health charity MIND has been raising the issue within the mental health professions. Gay affirmative practitioners believe that it is *homophobia* which is the cause of mental distress and difficulties. Homophobia means a fear, dread or hatred of homosexuals or homosexuality (Weinberg, 1972; see also Davies, 1996a for more on homophobia and heterosexism).

For the last 100 years homosexuality has been seen by most 'helping' professionals as an illness. Some of the worst atrocities have been committed by people supposedly dedicated to helping and supporting people, in the name of trying to cure people of this 'disease'. Lesbians and gay men have been subjected to electric shock treatment, aversion therapy and crude attempts at psychosurgery. Others were subjected to long-term, intensive psychotherapy where they wrestled with their natural desire to love someone of the same gender, and society's (and often their therapist's) view that this was sick or perverted. The declassification of homosexuality as a mental illness has more or less brought an end to this persecution. However, equally of concern is the way so-called 'Christian Counselling' groups have sought to 'cure' lesbian, gay and bisexual people. The preying on confused and vulnerable people by those who have religious or moral objections to homosexuality continues to bring the notion of 'helping others' into disrepute and cause untold damage to their 'clients'.

This century of torture and abuse in the name of treatment and help has left a legacy. Most lesbian, gay and bisexual people seeking help from mental health professionals are likely to be guarded and self-protecting. They may be hypervigilant to any sign of homophobia in the therapist. This emotional and psychological guarding can result in a lack of spontaneity and a need for clear and open communication between client and therapist.

Homophobia as pathology

The last three decades, however, have slowly seen a growth in what have come to be known as *gay affirmative* models of therapy. Most work undertaken by lesbian, gay and bisexual therapists in the USA and Europe has sought to show non-pathological ways of viewing homosexuality and working with lesbian, gay and bisexual people. Maylon describes gay affirmative therapy thus:

> Gay affirmative psychotherapy is not an independent system of psychotherapy. Rather it represents a special range of psychological knowledge, which challenges the traditional view, that homosexual desire and fixed homosexual orientations are pathological. Gay affirmative therapy uses traditional psychotherapeutic methods but proceeds from a non-traditional perspective. This approach regards homophobia, as opposed to homosexuality, as a major pathological variable in the development of certain symptomatic conditions among gay men. (1982: 69)

The term 'gay affirmative' is not without its dissenters among lesbian and gay therapists. Du Plock (1997) and Ratigan (1998), among others, have rightly questioned who or what is being affirmed in gay affirmative therapy. The term can imply that the therapist is giving permission and is encouraging the client to be gay. This can make it difficult for the client to explore his or her own negative, internalized, self-oppressive structures and feel that these won't be accepted or affirmed by their gay-affirming therapist. 'Gay affirmative' can also be said to be quite gender biased, perhaps excluding other sexual minorities and gender-variant people. A more natural term, which is growing in usage, is simply *sexual minority therapy*.

Such non-pathologizing therapeutic approaches are now slowly being integrated into the syllabus of European therapy training programmes. In lamentably few courses is it placed within the core curriculum of the training institutes. More often it is at the request of individual students (usually lesbians and gay men), and sometimes it is only addressed through self-directed study (Davies, 1996b). This marginalization of sexual minority therapy issues only serves to perpetuate and reinforce the pathological models. Cayleff (1986), in discussing the ethical issues involved in counselling the culturally different (in which she includes lesbians, gay men and bisexuals), questions how therapists graduating from training programmes that do not require courses in working with the culturally different may ethically work with these populations. Since formal education is a socialization process that transmits the values of the dominant culture, the majority of counselling and therapy training programmes, through both course work and practice, continue to explore individual development, sex, gender, coupling, family and relationship issues solely within a heterosexual context (Iasenza, 1989).

Effects of homophobia and heterosexism on lesbian, gay and bisexual people

The stress of living with a stigmatized identity where one is seen as 'mad, bad and dangerous to know' has been demonstrated to contribute to poor mental health (Coyle, 1993; Rivers, 1997). Lesbian, gay and bisexual people may at some level feel shame about their sexuality, and this *internalized homophobia* can result in low self-esteem, self-medication through drug and alcohol misuse, over-work through trying to prove oneself, and avoidance of drawing attention to oneself. Lesbian, gay and bisexual people are also prone to discrimination and violence. In a survey, *Queer Bashing*, Stonewall (1996) found that 34 per cent of gay and bisexual men and 24 per cent of women had experienced physical violence because of their sexuality. In another study, the same organization (Stonewall, 1993) found that 37 per cent experienced workplace discrimination and almost half the respondents (48 per cent) had been harassed because of their sexuality. One does not need to have experienced the discrimination to *fear* that it will happen. This leaves almost all lesbians, gay and bisexual people vulnerable to anxiety and disorganization.

There are not only negative effects to living with a stigmatized identity. Lesbians, gay men and bisexuals who are open about, and comfortable with, their sexuality often experience a strong sense of identity as 'different but equal' to heterosexuals. These differences sometimes result in a freedom to reinvent themselves anew with values and attitudes that support their individual and collective identities. Lesbian, gay and bisexual people may, for example, have critiqued much about a heterosexual lifestyle and identity and decided this is inappropriate. Their culture, like those of other oppressed groups (Jews, African-Caribbean people, etc.) celebrates this diversity and different perspective in art, music, literature and other expressions.

Client–therapist matching

This hypervigilance to heterosexist thinking and homophobia in the therapist often leads lesbian, gay and bisexual clients to prefer to see someone who shares their sexuality. Where this is possible it should be acceded to, although it may be helpful, of course, to explore the assumptions that lay behind this request.

Clients may also be interested in the sexual identity of the therapist. Some therapists feel this is an unwarranted intrusion into their private lives or that it must only be addressed transferentially, although they may not give a second thought to the wearing of a gold ring on the third finger of their left hand. Often clients are attempting to check out the experience of and attitudes to lesbian, gay and bisexual people through such questioning. The British Association for Counselling and Psychotherapy *Ethical Framework for Good Practice* (BACP, 2002) makes it clear that therapists should be open about their qualifications and experience in working with clients. There is a strong case for arguing that questions about the therapist's own sexual orientation deserve to be answered honestly and directly.

Summary and key points

- Don't assume the client's sexual orientation is the cause of his or her difficulties. Lesbian, gay and bisexual people may present for counselling or therapy with a range of life issues (relationship breakdown, bereavement, anxiety, depression, work stress, etc.). Most of these issues bear little direct relevance to their sexuality, although they are often coloured by the experience of being a sexual minority in an oppressive and discriminatory society.
- Don't make assumptions about a person's sexuality. Many married, apparently heterosexual men have sexual relationships with members of their own sex. Significant numbers of gay men have sex with women. The corollary is also true for women.
- Don't make assumptions about the client's lifestyle. Clients may have different notions of what it means to be in a relationship ('monogamy' may not be the norm), or to be a family (many lesbian, gay and bisexual people will consider their friends as their family).

Lesbian, gay and bisexual clients may want to be a parent or may already be involved in childcare.

- Be aware of the client's hypervigilance and that you will be tested out for signs of homophobia and heterosexist thinking. Work with this and do all you can to learn more about lesbian, gay and bisexual culture and lifestyles. Be honest about your experience and work to create an open and non-defensive relationship.
- Reflect on your own attitudes to and experience of your sexuality and to homosexuality in particular. To be able to work effectively with sexual minority clients you need to be comfortable with who you are as a sexual being and to have examined your beliefs and prejudices about lesbian, gay and bisexual people. Everyone has them. The therapist who says they are not prejudiced is a therapist to be avoided, as they are probably extremely low on self-awareness. Therapists might like to consider what impact on the therapeutic relationship there might be for a sexual minority client working with them, if they have not examined their attitudes before working with clients.

Working towards good practice

There are perhaps three main ways in which we can prepare ourselves for working with lesbian, gay and bisexual people:

- Training workshops, which include both didactic presentations about lesbian, gay and bisexual psychology, including the various models of coming out (see Davies, 1996c), dealing with internalized homophobia and the social and political context of lesbian, gay and bisexual people. Most importantly, perhaps, experiential exercises aimed at addressing our attitudes to and experiences of lesbian, gay and bisexual people, as well as increasing understanding of our own sexuality. A leading training provider in this field is *Pink Therapy* (www.pinktherapy.com). They regularly run workshops and courses for therapists wishing to improve their knowledge and skill in this area.
- Personal therapy and self-awareness work to explore some of our sexual histories in some depth, with therapists who have themselves done the required work, which itself raises a complication: where does one find such people? Alongside this, specific supervision/consultation is advisable (see Pett, 1999) from experienced lesbian, gay and bisexual therapists on client work.
- Spending time with lesbian, gay and bisexual people at work and in recreation. Personal contacts through genuine friendships have been demonstrated to be powerful ways of changing opinions and behaviours. Become involved socially and politically with the lesbian, gay and bisexual communities. Manthei says, 'there is no short cut to being involved in and accepted by local communities so that you are known to be supportive and trustworthy' (1997: 31).

References

BACP (2002) *Ethical Framework for Good Practice in Counselling and Psychotherapy*. Rugby: British Association for Counselling and Psychotherapy.

Cayleff, S. (1986) Ethical issues in counselling gender, race and culturally distinct groups. *Journal of Counseling Development*, 64 (5): 345–347.

Coyle, A. (1993) A study of psychological well-being among gay men using the GHQ-30. *British Journal of Clinical Psychology*, 32: 218–220.

Davies, D. (1996a) Homophobia and heterosexism. In D. Davies and C. Neal (eds), *Pink Therapy: A Guide for Counsellors and Therapists Working with Lesbian, Gay and Bisexual Clients*. Buckingham: Open University Press.

Davies, D. (1996b) Towards a model of gay affirmative therapy. In D. Davies and C. Neal (eds), *Pink Therapy: A Guide for Counsellors and Therapists Working with Lesbian, Gay and Bisexual Clients*. Buckingham: Open University Press.

Davies, D. (1996c) Working with people coming out. In D. Davies and C. Neal (eds), *Pink Therapy: A Guide for Counsellors and Therapists Working with Lesbian, Gay and Bisexual Clients*. Buckingham: Open University Press.

du Plock, S. (1997) Sexual misconceptions: a critique of gay affirmative therapy and some thoughts on an existential-phenomenological theory of sexual orientation. *Journal of the Society for Existential Analysis*, 8 (2): 56–71.

Grahn, J. (1990) *Another Mother Tongue: Gay Words, Gay Worlds*. Boston, MA: Beacon Press.

Iasenza, S. (1989) Some challenges of integrating sexual orientations into counselor training and research. *Journal of Counseling and Development*, 68: 73–76.

Manthei, R. (1997) *Counselling: The Skills of Finding Solutions to Problems*. London: Routledge.

Maylon, A. (1982) Psychotherapeutic implications of internalized homophobia in gay men. In J. Gonsiorek (ed.), *Homosexuality and Psychotherapy*. New York: Haworth Press.

Pett, J. (1999) Gay affirmative supervision. In D. Davies and C. Neal (eds), *Theoretical Approaches to Pink Therapy*. Buckingham: Open University Press.

Ratigan, B. (1998) Psychoanalysis and male homosexuality: queer bedfellows? In C. Shelley (ed.), *Contemporary Perspectives on Psychotherapy and Homosexualities*. London: Free Association Books.

Rivers, I. (1997) The long-term impact of peer victimisation in adolescence upon the well-being of lesbian, gay and bisexual adults. Paper presented at the 5th European Congress of Psychology, University College Dublin, Eire, 9 July.

Stonewall (1993) *Less Equal than Others: A Survey of Lesbians and Gay Men at Work*. London: Stonewall.

Stonewall (1996) *Queer Bashing: A National Survey of Hate Crimes against Lesbians and Gay Men*. London: Stonewall.

Weinberg, G. (1972) *Society and the Healthy Homosexual*. New York: St Martin's Press.

Recommended reading

Davies, D. and Neal, C. (eds) (1996) *Pink Therapy: A Guide for Counsellors and Therapists Working with Lesbian, Gay and Bisexual Clients*. Buckingham: Open University Press.

Coyle, A. and Kitzinger, C. (eds) (2002) *Lesbian and Gay Psychology: New Perspectives*. Oxford: Blackwell.

Cabaj, R.J. and Stein, T.S. (eds) (1996) *Textbook of Homosexuality and Mental Health*. Washington, DC: American Psychiatric Press.

2.7 Religion within a Multi-faith Context

NIGEL COPSEY

The word 'religion' awakens in us a variety of responses, many of which are very negative. Ever since the world was shaken by the horror of the 'Twin Towers' massacre on 11 September 2001, a new awareness, fear and curiosity about religion has emerged. Our society seems unable to understand how, in the 'global village', fundamentalist disciples of an Islamic group were willing to sacrifice their own lives and those of so many others. As I write, the situation in Iraq is as volatile and dangerous as ever: different factions led by a number of clerics demand the attention of the media. The ongoing conflict in the Middle East also continues to highlight the major differences between two very strongly held belief systems. For the first time in many decades the Eurocentric belief systems on which counselling and psychotherapy are based are being challenged by a wider world founded on strongly held religious beliefs. This complicated picture has been highlighted in the early years of the twenty-first century by a US President and a UK Prime Minister who both hold Christian beliefs.

What follows is an attempt to illustrate such themes by reference to a Gestalt-informed mental health and multi-faith project. I live and work in an area of London that holds together all the polarities mentioned here. In the most recent Census (2001), the area of London was highlighted as having the highest proportion of people from minority ethnic groups. The London boroughs of Tower Hamlets, Hackney and Newham, which form the area covered by the East London and City Mental Health NHS Trust, are among the most diverse. The Census figures show that in Hackney Black Caribbeans form over 10 per cent of the population and in Newham Black Africans form over 10 per cent. The figures also show that Tower Hamlets and Newham have the largest Muslim populations in the country (33.45 per cent and 24 per cent respectively). Furthermore, the Census shows that Newham now has the smallest white minority population of 39.4 per cent, with Tower Hamlets and Hackney ranked closely behind. I have highlighted these figures because they help to provide the context for my findings. In earlier research I was able to show that such changes in the ethnic mix of the population can be understood only by linking the cultural changes with spiritual traditions (Copsey, 1997). It is not possible to understand the Bangladeshi community of Tower Hamlets without also appreciating the importance of Islam. Similarly, it is not possible to fully understand the Black African and Black Caribbean communities of Newham and Hackney without appreciating the importance of Pentecostal Christianity. The community of East London is made up of all the world faith communities. In addition to those already mentioned, there are also large Hindu, Sikh and Jewish populations.

Over the last decade there has been an awareness that psychological therapies and mental health services have failed to meet the needs of the new communities: this fact has been highlighted recently in a number of important health policy documents relating to minority ethnic groups, such as *The National Service Framework for Mental Health* (Department of Health, 1999) and *The NHS Plan* (Department of Health, 2000). Both documents highlight the fact that existing services are insensitive to the cultural needs of the new communities. In addition, recent research has indicated that suicide rates are higher for Asian women and young black men (Cochrane and Sashidharan, 1996). One major reason for this failure has been the unwillingness of providers of psychological therapies to acknowledge the centrality of spiritual beliefs within these communities (Copsey, 1997). It is only possible to understand the cultural complexity of these communities by also understanding the spiritual values which are foundational to them.

For the last five years I have had the privilege of establishing a Department of Spiritual, Religious and Cultural Care within the mental health services of East London. Our task has been to join with groups that have a history of polarization. At one end of the polarity there are the faith groups which span the whole spectrum of the different world faith traditions. Many are very rigid in the way they relate to the world around them: they live by a belief system which interprets mental health services and mental distress purely in spiritual terms. At the other end of the spectrum are the mental health services and psychological therapies which live by a Eurocentric belief system which excludes the spiritual dimension.

The challenge for our department has been to find a middle ground between these two polarities. The task was made even more complicated by the fact that each major faith community has a wide spectrum of belief within it: many groups within each tradition are often unwilling to be in contact with each other. Establishing this new department has provided us with a unique opportunity to revisit many of the assumptions associated with psychological therapies. The lessons we are learning will, I hope, provide some guidelines for counselling within a religious context. While these are clearly findings arising from the East End of London, this is the most richly diverse area in the UK, with lessons for all. It is worth noting here the established American Psychological Association's *Guidelines for Providers of Psychological Services to Ethnic, Linguisitic, and Culturally Diverse Populations*, which include the following statement:

Psychologists respect clients' religious and/or spiritual beliefs and values, including attributions and taboos, since they affect world view, psychosocial functioning and expressions of distress ... Effective psychological intervention may be aided by consultation with and/or inclusion of religious/spiritual leaders/practitioners relevant to the client's cultural and belief system. (Ponterotto et al., 1995: 612)

The complexity of the field

It was Lewin who first drew our attention to the importance of 'field theory'. The importance to Gestalt theory has been recently developed by Parlett (1997). It was from Lewin's theory that Perls was able to develop the concept of figure and ground. The significance of field theory is that it highlights our interdependence on each other. We are all interconnected. It is particularly the case in London that mental health services, psychological therapies and training institutes have failed to recognize the importance of the field. However, the cultural traditions, which have included the faith traditions, have also failed to have any major impact on our psychological services. In other areas of our lives these new traditions have enriched London and have contributed to it being the attractive capital that it has become. The spiritual traditions have been kept in a separate box, as if they do not properly exist. As these communities continue to grow, it is now no longer possible to ignore this central aspect of their identity. We are faced with the fact that in our midst is a highly complex collection of communities where the spiritual view of the world is considered normative. This is in stark contrast to secular western culture. It is at the point where mental health services and these cultures meet that we are now realizing that there is a polarizing of belief systems. Field theory provides the map for understanding the process. The aim of our department has been to heighten our awareness of the wider field in order to discover the richness of the new communities by allowing their beliefs and traditions to become more central to the raison d'être

of the department. It was at this point that we realized how little we understood!

Celebrating difference by joining with one another

Once we began to reach out and sought to be in relationship with those who were very different from ourselves, we realized how many differences existed: not only between different faith communities but also between those groups and the mental health services. As a process of dialogue was established, we came to realize that we all held very strong beliefs about the way we saw the world. It was these beliefs that kept us apart. Our aim was to be in relationship with each other, while at the same time reaching out and learning from one another. The core value was that we wanted to celebrate the differences among us and not to despise them. The process involved the hard work of being willing to reach out to those whom we would normally avoid! Our commitment was to create a 'safe place' where we could *join* with each other. We wanted to create an environment where we were curious about our differences: this meant asking questions of each other and seeking to fully understand the world from the other's point of view.

Such a process is risky as it involves becoming vulnerable and having to face and put aside the internalized messages which prevent contact. One such moment remains vividly in my memory. A Sikh priest was demonstrating to those of us in the group how important palm reading was to his spiritual tradition. This was the first time that those in the group from the Christian tradition had been exposed to such a way of understanding the world. I had never considered such a practice spiritual. I was to learn that celebrating our differences meant that I could understand why palm reading was important to this holy man while at the same time recognizing that it was something which I would not practise. This snapshot of religious believers being willing to learn from each other highlights a major tension. Traditional healing is regarded as normative by all the faith communities. The way in which such a view of the world informs a psychological framework is of crucial importance for true dialogue to take place.

A safe community

We quickly learnt that in order to take the risk to see one another with all our differences we needed to create a 'safe community'. This community needed to be a place where the members could take the risk to be themselves and know that the others in the group would really *see* them without being judged. Such a task was not easy! We have sought to create a number of such communities and a few have failed, the reason being that the majority of members have not been willing to *see* the others in the group. For the experience to be a success, *seeing* has to be a two-way process. There has to be a commitment to remain in relationship around difference. Group members need to have the courage to take risk in reaching out to others. Our experience has been that for such a venture to be successful there needs to be a community supporting that journey. We also learnt that in such a safe community, there needs to be an attitude on the part of all members of *genuine interest*. The person-centred tradition rightly emphasizes the need for genuineness and warmth in the therapeutic relationship. However, the heartfelt attitude of *genuine interest* takes the core conditions to a more intimate level: both parties discover the psychological courage to reach out to each other. When *genuine interest* is reciprocated, with both parties sharing the same level of interest, there is a joining which goes beyond that described by Rogers (Kirschenbaum and Henderson, 1990).

Implications for counselling and psychotherapy

Many practise a spiritual discipline which may include some form of prayer or meditation drawn from a spiritual tradition. Many others would express their spiritual life within the context of a faith community. There is now a great deal of evidence that shows that support for religious and spiritual needs has a positive impact on mental health (Koenig, 1998). In addition, the most recent user-led research undertaken by the Mental Health Foundation (1997, 1999, 2000) has clearly demonstrated that those coping with mental distress long for their spiritual needs to be recognized. This important fact has been recently adopted in the Care Programme Approach.

It is within this wider context of both the multi-faith society in which we now live and the growing recognition given by statutory services to matters of faith and culture that psychological therapies need to respond. I have sought to draw out a number of themes from the work undertaken in East London. These themes need to be applied to the counselling relationship. If they can be incorporated, then the counsellor or therapist can more fully understand the client's psychological conflicts. They can plan strategies which are compatible with the client's worldview and which utilize the spiritual resources that are available.

I believe that our task as counsellors and psychotherapists is to *join* fully with those who seek our help by reaching out to understand them from the context of their spiritual tradition. This means giving every aspect of their inner life a clear voice. It means being willing to learn from them and to discover how each aspect of their life intersects with their spirituality. We need to be able to suspend our own beliefs while at the same time showing a deep *genuine interest* in the world of our client, thus allowing us to understand their experience of the world through their own unique spiritual lens. I also believe that, when appropriate, we need to be able to share our own spiritual journey by connecting around a shared interest. This willingness to enter into a shared experience will strengthen the therapeutic relationship. It is my task to remain in relationship with my client while I celebrate the differences between us. If we can achieve this level of relationship, then I am certain that as counsellors we will be able to validate the healthy coping strategies drawn from spiritual traditions. From this strong foundation we will also be able to challenge those beliefs which are unhealthy. Clearly, this is a very complex area: it is only by being willing to *join* fully with the client that such a shared discovery can take place.

I am advocating a far greater awareness of the spiritual dimension of our lives within the counselling process, and an awareness that goes beyond even the assumption that western liberal spirituality applies to all clients (West, 2004). We need to be more proactive in reaching out to all our clients by asking questions which enable us to experience the whole field of the person's life. In this way clients will feel seen, and the bond of trust will provide a psychological safety which will give them the courage to move forward.

We have also learnt about the importance of the supportive community. Clearly, there are some communities that are neither supportive nor safe! I believe it is our role to help clients discover such safe communities. It is often the case that the work achieved in the counselling session cannot be 'lived out' because the group to which a client belongs does not feel sufficiently safe. Too often, religious communities cause a person to feel a deep sense of shame. It is very important to be aware of this and not to assume that a client can bear everything in relation to his or her community. It is often the case that it is only in the community of two that exists between the counsellor and the client that a person can be truly seen, as she or he seeks to integrate his or her own psychological journey with that of his or her own spiritual tradition.

This type of therapeutic journey involves a greater risk than we are often prepared to take. It is being prepared to *join* with someone at a level of shared intimacy with his or her deepest spiritual longings. At such a place, we as counsellors are vulnerable and realize our own limitations.

References

Copsey, N. (1997) *Keeping Faith: The Provision of Mental Health Services Within a Multi-Faith Context.* London: The Sainsbury Centre for Mental Health.

Cochrane, R. and Sashidharan, S.P. (1996) *Mental Health and Minorities.* CRD Report 5. York: University of York.

Department of Health (1999) *National Service Framework for Mental Health.* London: DoH.

Department of Health (2000) *The NHS Plan.* London: DoH.

Kirschenbaum, H. and Henderson, V.L. (eds) (1990) *The Carl Rogers Reader.* London: Constable.

Koenig, H.G. (ed.) (1998) *Handbook of Religion and Mental Health.* London: Academic Press.

Mental Health Foundation (1997) *Knowing Our Own Minds.* London: Mental Health Foundation Publishing.

Mental Health Foundation (1999) *The Courage to Bare Our Souls.* London: Mental Health Foundation Publishing.

Mental Health Foundation (2000) *Strategies for Living.* London: Mental Health Foundation Publishing.

Parlett, M. (1997) The unified field in practice. *Gestalt Review*, 1 (1): 16–33.

Ponterotto, J.G., Casas, J.M., Suzuki, L.A. and Alexander, C.M. (eds) (1995) *Handbook of Multicultural Counseling.* Thousand Oaks, CA: Sage.

West, W. (2004) *Spiritual Issues in Therapy: Relating Experience to Practice.* Basingstoke: Palgrave.

2.8 Race, Culture and Ethnicity

CAROL MOHAMED

This section considers race, culture and ethnicity as key concepts in the practice of counselling and psychotherapy. It also considers the profound impact that they have in defining different aspects of an individual's social and psychological experiences. The complexity and nature of the way that the concepts are used, that is, to classify individuals into various groupings as well as in a dysfunctional and socially pathological way, are explored. I will suggest that the psychological mechanisms employed in racism are universal and are liable to be engaged when the context is favourable. This could be when the political or historical circumstances provide a structure to support racism, such as the extreme reaction towards Muslims following the terrorist attack in the USA on 11 September 2001. Any full exploration of racism should include external dimensions such as social, political, historical, cultural and economic factors, as well as the psychological states of mind which enable an individual to engage with racist structures.

Psychological maturity is grappled with throughout life. Conflicts, which constantly arise, are an integral mechanism in the journey of psychological development. The defences employed by the psyche to ease and avoid these experiences are, I suggest, what are witnessed in racism. Racism can be seen as an arena within which many of the psychic conflicts that we all face are acted out. Ironically, while this structure is adopted as a defence against the experience of disintegration, the state of mind required to make use of the mechanisms involved is itself destructive and pathological.

Any therapeutic approach needs to consider these issues whether or not the therapist or client is from an 'other' racially categorized group. I will be using the term 'black' to refer to everyone who is not perceived as white skinned. The term black will not be limited to any specific cultural, ethnic or religious groups.

A transcultural therapy approach uses a western arrangement, in that the model is based in a dyadic relationship with a therapist in a commanding role and client in a deferential relationship to him or her. In addition, the approach interweaves, in a fundamental way, other factors such as a historical, political and cultural analysis, alongside a psychological approach. It advocates that therapists develop a self-awareness, knowledge and skills to ensure that the therapeutic situation takes account of the enduring history of oppression and racism in this society. Through this, a relationship and environment that does not replicate this experience can be offered.

Western psychoanalysis and counselling take little account of other cultural systems, and are therefore likely to offer a view which is liable to be ethnocentric and culturally specific. Fernando (1991) proposes that western concepts of mental health are influenced by racist ideology. The way that individuals develop a sense of themselves is through the dynamic interaction of internal (psychological) and external (social) circumstances. These include spiritual factors, instincts, emotions, and relationships. The attainment of a sense of well-being is dependent on the interplay between such factors and, in particular, the way that external experiences are internalized and made sense of. Erikson (1968) suggested that cultural factors have a direct impact on the development of personality, and may reinforce or suppress certain specific internal conflicts, such as the expression of anger.

The concept of mental health, in this society, is based on a western cultural paradigm, making it liable to cultural specificity. This is problematic because it excludes other perspectives, and is therefore somewhat biased against those whose behaviour does not fit what is expected within this culture. If the concept of mental health is culturally loaded, it has serious implications for those who do not belong to that culture. A transcultural approach argues for the inclusion of different perspectives.

Research by Mind (Hatloy, 2002), the mental health organization, found that black people had a rate of admission to medium-secure care that was seven times higher than their white counterparts. Research which focused on two psychiatric hospitals found that black people were over-represented among compulsorily detained patients compared with their number in the local population. Of the 224 patients admitted to one hospital, 51 per cent were black, 8 per cent Asian and 41 per cent white. Census data showed that 71 per cent of the local population were white, including 5.2 per cent Irish. The report states that:

> Black people are more likely to be given 'physical' treatments (drugs and ECT) than their white counterparts; this is well documented in the literature. African people are likely to be given higher doses of medication in comparison to other groups, and stand a greater chance of receiving this intramuscularly, which can be very painful. Black people are less likely to be offered counselling, other talking treatments or non-medical interventions than white people and are rarely offered counselling in a different language. (Hatloy, 2002: 5)

Fernando (1991) states that a transcultural view of mental health must address both racial and cultural issues. All therapeutic approaches should develop their theoretical and clinical aspects because they are about issues of great significance in understanding the interplay between the way that thinking and emotions develop in individuals.

Race and racism

The concept of race is itself questionable as a logical verifiable entity that actually exists. If this is the case, categorizing individuals on this basis is inappropriate.

It is the *use* that is made of these distinctions that is significant and relevant. Racism seems to encompass much more than just the hatred of a skin tone, cultural value or behaviour. It is as personal and meaningful to the racist as it is to the target. The possibility that the organizing category, race, might not itself even exist suggests that this phenomenon is both irrational and pathological.

The term 'race' is often used in everyday language to categorize individuals on the basis of skin colour. Race is usually characterized by physical appearance and as being determined by genetic characteristics. However, the idea of being able to categorize on the basis of belonging to a specific racial group is deceptive. Many writers (see Lane, 1998; Richards, 1997; Rustin, 1991; Young, 1994) argue that there is no scientific evidence to support the assertion that there are unique genetic features that distinguish one group of individuals from another. There are, however, economic, psychological and ideological roots that make this way of categorizing seem to be more about the expression of the destructive side of human nature than a scientific attempt to find distinguishing qualities between groups of individuals. Rustin (1991) describes race as both meaningless and as a powerful and destructive category, used in the pursuance of social control. He argues that the classic attributes of race are not able to explain any significant differences between groups of individuals. Lane (1998) also suggests that the concept of race is problematic from a scientific viewpoint because the visual features which commonly generate classifications of racial difference, such as skin colour, hair and facial features are, from an evolutionary standpoint, the most superficial. Variations on the basis of genetic traits do exist in a more significant way. Genetic patterns of variation cut across the traditionally perceived, visible categories, for example blood groupings.

Young (1994) describes racial differences as *naturalized* rather than natural and as an ideology firmly established within society. He argues that history has been manipulated in order to support racist notions and alter the truth. The cynical lack of regard for the truth occurs repeatedly, in order to advance the desired belief in the superiority of one group over another. It is also used to justify the social and economic gains that racism has provided at the expense of denigrated, dehumanized individuals. As Davids and Davison suggest: '*a feeling of superiority is a sublimation of a much more primitive feeling of hatred. Moreover, it is easier to rationalise a feeling of superiority than raw hatred*' (1988: 49, authors' italics).

With any classification or category, certain attributes and qualities are assigned to them and people within the groups become identified with these qualities. The problem with this is that they become more pervasive than individual characteristics and this leads to stereotyping. The categories are double-edged in that they are used to describe as well as to divide. This is especially the case if a classification does not take account of individual differences.

Richards describes *racism* as: 'attitudes and practices which are explicitly hostile and denigratory towards people defined as belonging to another "race". This implies some level of emotional psychological involvement on the racist's part' (1997: xi). The contemporary uses of the term 'race', and its concomitant generic terms 'black' and 'white', are used for 'political' purposes. One could therefore argue that the concept of race has emerged from racism itself rather than the reverse. If the aim of racism is the acquisition of power and control, grouping along racial lines defines who will be the oppressor and who will be the oppressed.

Rustin (1991) views racial differentiation as dependent on the distinguishing characteristics imposed by the 'Other'. The power of this definition, in spite of the negligible evidence of its existence in reality, suggests that it is not the actual factors but what they symbolize that is significant. He believes that this is conducive to psychotic thinking because the meaninglessness of the categories suggests that there is nothing, in reality, to think about, nor a real external object which can mediate against the projection of unwanted parts of the self. Here pseudo-thinking and lies are used as a defence against an acceptance of reality. What makes racism so powerful is the fact that this division is irrational and baseless. It is available to carry psychologically primitive or basic symbols, with little resistance from the conscious mind. Lane (1998) also argues that there are conscious and unconscious dimensions of racism. The strength of the irrational beliefs implies that psychic resistances are operating as a defence against an acceptance of reality. The extensive evidence refuting any notion of racial superiority appears to be ignored or resisted. Ward (1997) supports the notion of racism as irrational, making it difficult to understand if one attempts to apply a structure based on rationality. Wolfenstein makes an interesting distinction between race and racism when he suggests:

> … if we view race from an abstract, anthropological perspective, we recognize that a race is a natural or biological category which, as such, is devoid of political meaning. But racism is a relationship of domination and subordination based upon skin colour. (1981: 27)

This supports a view of racism as involving the projection and identification of hated parts of the self into other individuals and groups who are perceived and treated as possessing the attributes that have been evacuated. Rustin (1991) very strongly argues that racial prejudice is a product of social and cultural influences rather than innate behaviour. However, social and political aims cannot entirely explain its existence. I am, therefore, suggesting that the underlying phantasies of race need to be examined in order to truly understand what it is about. Ward (1997), Kovel (1970) and Fanon (1952) view racism and sexual aims as bound together. It is suggested that the underlying phantasies of racism are loaded with sexual impulses and anxieties, which are then translated into the commonly held beliefs and myths that are embedded within racist attitudes and behaviours. Agoro says: 'Black stud/black whore: relates to the sexualization of black people, typically being portrayed as sexually uninhibited, provocative and predatory' (2003: 19). In addition, Fanon suggests that: 'For the majority of white men, the Negro represents the sexual instinct (in its raw state). The Negro is the incarnation of genital potency beyond all moralities and prohibitions' (1952: 177).

The behaviour demonstrated by society provides the evidence to support such theories. For example, the 'sexual fetishizing' of blacks by whites is, for

Frosh (1989), an indication of the way that the 'Other' is constructed on the basis of the existence of a biological difference. Similarly, Moran (1999) describes the rational logic of racist ideology as concealing the deep-seated, powerful emotions which sustain it. Thus, racism is experienced deeply and as a passion that arouses intense feelings of anger and hatred. These feelings do not need outside stimulation to be aroused, as in provocation from a black person. They are irrational and are triggered by internal conditions. This passion is likened to psychotic states, a state which is universal and latent, liable to activation during times of stress and anxiety. Psychotic states are said to find racial categorizations ideal as containers. Through the splitting of objects into loved and hated, good and bad, they can then be projected on to an object that meets the need and expectations of the subject.

Kovel describes racism as:

> ... far from being the simple delusion of a bigoted and ignorant minority, is a set of beliefs whose structure arises from the deepest levels of our lives, from the fabric of assumptions we make about the world, ourselves and others and from the patterns of our fundamental social activities. (1970: 3)

It is a state of mind that requires a certain mental attitude to enable individuals to hold on to a set of beliefs and attitudes in spite of their irrationality. It also provides a context within which they are able to treat those, designated as belonging to a different race, in a dehumanizing, barbaric way. If this is the case, it supports the need for a psychological perspective, if racism is to be truly understood. Primitive aspects of the psyche find expression through the symbols and phantasies that underpin the structure of racism. The behaviours used to express these psychotic parts of the personality, such as oppression and dehumanization, demonstrate the way that individuals and groups are capable of using destructiveness in order to meet their own requirements. The human need to identify as an individual and as part of a group is central in the creation of an 'Other'. The most important feature of the Other, Kovel proposes, is that they are never as good as the self. This split between good and bad is essential in the maintenance of a sense of goodness. The justification for slavery stemmed from this notion of the Other and the perception of difference.

Culture

Richards (1997) describes *culture* as a social concept, referring to the features of an individual's environment. This encompasses all of the values, attitudes and behaviours common to a group, and is socially transmitted. As concepts, culture and race have historically been used in diverse ways, but have very significant concealed meanings. Cultures affect the way that we interact with the world, and conduct and define relationships. They determine the way that we react in certain situations and shape our ways of behaving and thinking.

Ethnicity

Ethnicity describes a way of life and can encompass both cultural and racial groups. It relates to the bonds that give an individual a sense of belonging to a group. This requires the ability to identify with the group, and for the group to be inclusive in its outlook.

These are interrelated concepts, often used interchangeably, sometimes in cynical ways. For example, ethnicity may be a less emotive way of describing racial difference. The classification of individuals into groups enables, in this society, the notion of the superiority of one group over another.

With any classification or category, certain attributes and qualities are assigned to them, and people within the groups become identified with these qualities. The problem with this is that they become much more pervasive than individual characteristics, and this leads to stereotyping. Agoro supports this notion:

> Perhaps most obviously there has been the phenomenon of associating people's skin colour to symbolic representations of white and black. White is portrayed as signifying spirituality, purity, goodness, divinity and beauty and generally associated

with positive characteristics, while black has been associated with evil, sin, dirtiness, death and mourning, sexual provocation, immorality, and a whole host of other negative connotations. (2003: 17)

This is especially the case as a classification does not take account of individual differences.

History and context

Racism is embedded in western culture, with a history that stretches back to the fourteenth century. It does not appear to be a stagnant ideology, but adapts to accommodate the socio-economic needs of the dominant society. Thus, during the slave trade, which flourished through the eighteenth century until the mid-nineteenth century, racism was justified under the guise of paternalism. The justification for slavery stemmed from the notion of the inferior Other and the perception of difference. The European reaction to Africans as heathen, naked and black, made them sufficiently different to enable a radical distinction between Self and Other to be made. The so-called savagery and aggression of the Other was sufficient to justify their enslavement. Africans were believed to be child-like and primitive, therefore needing the protection of their owners.

At times through history, Christianity has been used to justify barbaric European actions and the notion of the superiority of European culture. The conversion of uncivilized races to Christianity, which implied civilization, was considered unquestionably desirable. In South Africa, the system of apartheid has a strong connection with Christianity, through the Dutch Reform Church, and the use of the Bible to justify the structure. The idea that non-Europeans were barbarians and savages was described as emerging from their heathen or non-Christian beliefs. In the Bible, Ham was said to have been cursed, and his descendants destined to a life of inferiority. Ham's descendants are said to have been black. Indigenous or 'black' people were seen, at best, as uncivilized, primitive or savage, with a child-like view of the world, but also as subhuman – not human. The idea that Africans were savages and therefore incapable of experiencing mental ill health,

was used as an argument to support the continuation of slavery. Fernando describes the views of Babcock, a nineteenth-century American psychiatrist, who suggested that mental illness was achievable only by those who were civilized:

In a paper, *The Colored Insane*, Babcock juxtaposed the idea that mental disease was 'almost unknown among savage tribes of Africa' with the alleged observations in the United States on the 'increase of insanity [among African Americans] since emancipation'; he quoted such causes for this increase as the deleterious effect of freedom on 'sluggish and uncultivated brains', and 'the removal [during emancipation] of all healthy restraints', and forecast 'a constant accumulation of [black] lunatics in the years to come. (1991: 34)

This view is not dissimilar to that of early psychoanalysis. Jung, in reporting his East African trip, describes, with excitement and fear, his experience of the 'primitive' negro. While feeling drawn to Africa, he also describes a frightening dream, featuring a negro, which, he suggests, was 'as a warning that the primitive was a danger to me'. Jung's perception of non-Europeans was of having a primitive psyche that was a danger to Europeans. His perception of the emotional life of 'non-whites' was as naïve and un-integrated. He talks of the danger of 'racial infection' during a visit to America, and concluded that there was a psychological danger to white people if they continued to live in such close proximity to blacks. He states:

Now what is more contagious than to live side by side with a rather primitive people. Go to Africa and see what happens. When the effect is so very obvious that you stumble over it, then you call it 'going black'. The inferior man exercises a tremendous pull upon civilised beings who are forced to live with him because he fascinates the inferior layers of our psyche ... (Jung, 1967/1993)

Jung seems to have been moving towards a stereotypical concept of a racial psyche. He does not consider blacks as individuals who possess differences, nor does he contemplate the impact on an individual of the oppressive society in which they live. This is not to suggest that psychoanalysis and psychotherapy have no useful application in work with black clients, or in offering an understanding of racism. On the contrary, the psychoanalytic concepts of splitting, projection, and projective identification offer a very useful framework within which the phenomenon of racism can be analysed and understood.

Da Conceicao Dias and De Lyra Chebabi (1987) have written about psychoanalysis and black life in Brazil. The slave trade flourished in Brazil between the sixteenth and nineteenth centuries, due to the establishment of sugar plantations. The church did much to justify the trade, likening the plight of the slaves to Christ's suffering, unfortunate but necessary. The abolition of slavery was for cynical rather than humanitarian reasons. Africans are still, today, forced to integrate into white society and adopt this as their primary culture. The domination and oppression by whites, who are the minority in Brazil, still occurs as an integral part of Brazil's culture. Scientific theories supported the notion of blacks as retarded and in so doing gave strength to the theory of biological differences between the races.

A contrasting view to this is articulated by Richards (1997) when he describes the work of the black psychologist, Mosby. Mosby argues for the recognition of a unique black psychology. Richards states that Mosby's assertion takes account of the differences between black and white experiences. W.E. Cross Jnr proposed a developmental theory of black identity in white societies, which he termed 'nigrescence theory'. He suggested that an individual passes through five stages during the development of a black identity:

- pre-encounter – the individual possesses the negative white view of himself
- encounter – an event occurs leading to a change of view, and openness to considering other perceptions of his identity
- immersion – 'personal metamorphosis'
- internalization – conflicts are resolved, and a new viewpoint emerges
- internalization-commitment – 'lasting ideological change' (from Richards, 1997: 295).

This approach considers positively the different experiences of blacks and whites, and the impact of the experience of racism on the development of an identity. Whether or not one agrees with the developmental stages may not be as important as the idea that a black identity is defined within its own structure and with its own criteria rather than from within a white framework. This parallels the aim of a transcultural therapy approach. It does not, however, advocate that a black identity is a universal, undifferentiated entity, a view which racism promotes.

Racism and symbolism

I wonder about the symbolic meanings of the skin and of blackness which, in combination, have been moulded into such a powerful container for unbearable parts of the self. I believe that it is the phantasies underlying these symbols, combined with external social factors, which have created the phenomenon of racism. Kovel (1970) describes the structures upon which cultures are based as embedded with symbolism. They are liable to distortions and phantasies that have a powerful impact on beliefs and behaviours from within that culture. Racism is an example of such a distortion and phantasy. The symbolic meaning of whiteness and blackness are accepted and an ideology and belief system created.

Rustin (1991) suggests that the function of the skin in this matrix may relate to the importance of bodily sensation in early infancy. The initial relationship with the world is sensory, through touch, smell, sight and sound. If early relationships and communications are conducted in this way, it is likely that physical sensations will continue to be emotionally significant throughout life. The skin has an extremely important function during early infancy because at this time parts of the personality are not felt to have a binding ability. The skin takes on this function and becomes an important boundary between internal and external experiences. The skin acts as an early container and through this activity enables the introjection of an object capable of performing the function of containment.

Meltzer's (1975) view of a two-dimensional relationship, where the object is experienced in terms of its sensuous or surface qualities may expand an understanding of this phenomenon. It may offer an explanation for the significance of the skin as a dimension of racism where there is a surface relationship between the white subject and the black object of racism. It is as if the object is perceived as two-dimensional with no depth or space to possess a mind and as if the black person becomes a part-object whose surface colour is related to and controlled.

Some psychoanalytical theorists view the mechanism of racism as involving the splitting off of tabooed or feared aspects of the self, the violent projection of these aspects on to another and the scapegoating and stereotyping of this group identified as different and Other. This involves universal mechanisms which make it even more insidious because the processes involved are not pathological or rare. The mechanisms are accessible to everyone and are available to be employed as required. There might be some comfort in the belief that the dehumanizing of another, in order to preserve a sense of goodness and superiority, requires an unusual set of circumstances and the employment of extraordinary, pathological processes. However, I am arguing that this is not the case. It is about the everyday struggles that we all go through which somehow get transformed into raw hatred, aggression and destruction without the need for conscious thought. These initial anxieties and conflicts both in the self and in groups can be diminished through these projective processes. Young (1994) suggests that when the object takes on what has been projected and acts within the stereotype, a symbiotic dynamic is set up, with both sides partaking of a set of projections and reprojections. This may, however, be closer to a parasitic relationship because the subject uses the object for his or her own purposes. Agoro suggests that:

> The 'acting-out' of white stereotypes of blackness and other patterns of internalized racism are a reflection of the way black people survive the day-to-day realities of racism. For many black people, this acting out of white stereotypes of blackness has ensured their literal survival. (2003: 19)

Wolfenstein describes the dialectical relationship between the oppressor and the oppressed when he states that:

> Within this relationship, black people can think of themselves as fully human only by denying their true racial identity, while white people secure their humanity only at the price of black dehumanisation. … In this relationship the repressed sadistic tendencies of the dominating group become the self-hatred, the masochistic tendency, of the dominated group. Conversely, the alienated self-esteem of the dominated group becomes the narcissism of the dominating one. (1981: 145)

Taylor (1988) suggests that there is a connection between racism, psychotic states, and narcissism, because all three are rooted in primitive psychological states. Racism arouses intense emotions emanating from the life and death instincts. It is the experience of dependence which arouses intense feelings of hatred and envy and they relate to early infantile experiences. If anxiety and frustration are also experienced, there is a greater tendency towards paranoid and narcissistic reactions. Racism is an example of such a combination. Taylor suggests that superiority, the over-valuation of the self, is a defence against envy and hatred. When these are combined with other disturbing parts of the self and projected onto the object, it becomes hated and despised, and also feared. There is then a constant fear of retaliation by this dangerous object. I believe that racism operates by combining the internal mental organization of the individual with the cultural, political and economic factors of the external world, creating the phenomenon of racism. This becomes an effective way for individuals to be rid of unwanted feelings, in a way that does not employ reason or reality.

The explicit vilification of the Other is a crucial aspect of racism because it enables the dominant group and individual to be wholly good. If bad feelings are projected into the Other and they are identified as wholly bad, then the subject is freed to treat the object in this way and believe themselves to be good. The projection of negative aspects of the self is a dominant dynamic at work in racism. The problem is that this becomes a vicious circle in which persecutory anxiety, because of what has been projected, leads to further anxiety and the need to project even more. This process is not only damaging to the receiver but also to the projector. Thus the process of racism involves the projective identification of hated self attributes which are then phantasized to exist in members of a denigrated group.

The more common approach to a psychoanalytic exploration of racism is based primarily on the model of splitting and projection. Like Ward (1997), I have found this approach to be limiting, particularly because it excludes a crucial consideration of the concept of the 'Other' (see Tan, 1993; Timimi, 1997), and because it describes the mechanisms employed very effectively, but only goes part of the way towards explaining what racism is actually about. The phantasies underpinning the symbolic meaning of, for example, blackness, the function of the skin, and the powerful sexual component embedded in racism, are only partially addressed using this model alone. As Ward says:

> The process of altering reality in order to preserve a feature that seems to be essential to our psychical well-being, ... what are the anxieties that motivate such a manoeuvre? What we call racism involves all of these features and more. It is a composite structure which cannot be reduced to formulaic description, but rather should be taken apart, analysed, slowly, piece by piece. (1997: 91)

In his view, splitting and projection have been adopted as the model of racism because they can effectively describe the experience of feeling and being treated like a 'thing' for someone else, in a way which effectively obliterates who you are. He says:

> We can ask what it feels like to be regarded as an animal, monster, child, lump of shit, and so on. These are the ideas which seem to be the main templates on which the objects of racism are constructed. (1997: 91)

Like Ward, I think that the splitting and projection model is reductive, in isolation, because it does not explain what it is that is being so powerfully and overwhelmingly experienced, that it needs to be gotten rid of, and where these experiences originate. The model is of value, however, in explaining how these feelings are processed into bad experiences, and then dealt with through splitting and projective identification.

The main criticism of the dualistic model is that it fails to explain some of the elementary features of a racist ideology, and allows the structure of racism and racist thinking to be distanced from human beings. It can be disowned and denied as something out there, in this way, keeping it at a distance from ourselves. Ward also believes that the projective model, in isolation, neglects issues relating to envy, guilt, and reparation, and suggests that racism expresses issues about the symbolic role of the father. Ward's analysis of the creation of the 'Other' is a modification of Freud's concept of scapegoating. Here, ambivalence, that is, love and hatred, is experienced towards a person; this cannot be made conscious, so a second person is identified, and the ambivalent feelings, which cannot be expressed towards the original person, can be projected and satisfied through the relationship with the second. The triangular structure mirrors the oedipal situation. He describes the passion, controlling envy, and obsession that are embedded within racism, and the desire to possess and destroy. He also questions why, in the splitting and projection model, the subject might wish to destroy the container of the unwanted projections. This he considers to be a further weakness of the model. My understanding is that the container is hated and attacked because of what has been projected into it and what it is therefore felt to contain. I think that a sado-masochistic relationship is maintained with the container, involving experiences of envy and aggression. Also, a vicious circle, whereby anxiety arising from the fear of persecution by the object because of what has been violently evacuated into it, leads to the introjection of a persecuting object, and the need to further split and project.

Modes of thinking operating in racism

I want to return briefly to the mode of thinking which operates in racism because I have struggled to understand why black people are so strongly believed to be and to possess what has been projected. There must be a particular state of mind that can alter reality to such an extent that a lie can become a truth. If racism is irrational and illogical, how can otherwise thinking people alter reality to such an extent that the brutality involved can be justified and even sanctioned? Bion's (1970) model of thinking and lies can enable an understanding of the way that thinking can be altered or constructed to create the phenomenon of racism, and for it to be individually and socially sanctioned. If there is an agreement that the formulations and beliefs about black people, such as depravity, greed, stupidity, dirtiness, and the structure of racism, are all untrue, then it is important to understand the construction of the lie. Bion suggests that lies are formulations which are known by the thinker to be false, but are continued as a defence against knowledge that could lead to mental disintegration. The lie effectively acts as a buffer against this potentially damaging reality. The liar, he says, gains some pleasure from this false notion, and will not question the plausibility of the lie. In Bion's view, people do not necessarily believe that it is better to create than to destroy. If this is true, a conviction will be maintained regardless of the consequences both to the self and the object. If a lie conflicts with the perception of reality, there comes a point at which one has to know this, and the need to deny the truth becomes acute. This is, he argues, avoided at all costs.

Conclusion

I have attempted to explore the composite parts which combine to create the structure of racism. It has been argued that the psychological mechanisms which operate are universal and can come into play in particular ways for particular individuals when an individual feels the need to distance themselves from parts of themselves that are too anxiety provoking. I have highlighted examples of when this has been manifest in history and attempted to analyse why 'blackness' has been used as a readily available container in the pursuance of the relief achieved through the projections embedded in racism.

Racism is about the struggle in acknowledging and accepting the parts of the self that one finds detestable, and is therefore a psychological matter. This means that anti-racist practices can only go so far in legislating against this way of thinking and behaving. Differences are made into the Other and

are then projectively identified with what cannot be tolerated within the self. Psychological maturity and the ability to adopt reality mean that differences can be enjoyed rather than causing anxiety. As well as anti-racism legislation, the struggles need to be faced within oneself in order to move away from the need to just put on to someone else the things that cannot be tolerated within oneself.

One of the main aims of counselling and psychotherapy is to enable clients to develop ego strength, and a sense of positive mental health, through the medium of a therapeutic relationship. This is profoundly dependant on the qualities, skill, understanding and empathic abilities of the therapist. If the relationship is not able to manifest these very fundamental conditions, the therapeutic aim will not be achieved. It is the responsibility of therapists to ensure that they have sufficient knowledge and self-awareness of what they bring to every therapeutic encounter. This is particularly important in a transcultural situation. The concepts of race, culture and ethnicity, as well as ideas of individuality and a group identity have been explored. They are proposed as factors which have a profound influence in shaping us in deeply idiosyncratic ways, and as having major consequences for the way that we are perceived and treated by society.

Clients bring many ordeals that they have had to therapy but, for many black clients, racism is the most painful experience of their lives. It is therefore important to understand how this issue intensifies the struggles we all attempt to work through in our psychological development. Kovel makes the point very simply when he says: 'Everybody had to pay the penalty for the crime of Oedipus; and in the endless cycle of crime and retribution, the black man had to be continually re-created out of the body of the white culture' (1970: 75).

References

Agoro, O. (2003) Anti-racist counselling practice. In C. Lago and B. Smith (eds), *Anti-discriminatory Counselling Practice*. London: Sage.

Bion, W. (1970) *Attention and Interpretation*. London: Karnac.

Da Conceicao Dias, C.G. and De Lyra Chebabi, W. (1987) Psychoanalysis and the role of black life and culture in Brazil. *International Review of Psycho-analysis*, 14: 185–202.

Davids, F.M. and Davison, S. (1988) Two accounts of the management of racial difference in psychotherapy. *Journal of Social Work Practice*, November: 30–51.

Erikson, E.H. (1968) *Identity: Youth and Crisis*. London: Faber & Faber.

Fanon, F. (1952) *Black Skin, White Masks*. London: Pluto Press.

Fernando, S. (1991) *Mental Health, Race and Culture*. London: Mind Publications in association with Macmillan.

Frosh, S. (1989) Psychoanalysis and racism. In B. Richards (ed.), *Crisis of the Self: Further Essays on Psychoanalysis and Politics*. London: Free Association Books.

Hatloy, I. (2002) Race, culture and mental health. *Mind Factsheet*. London: Mind.

Jung, C.G. (1967/1993) *Memories, Dreams, Reflections*. London: Fontana.

Kovel, J. (1970) *White Racism: A Psychohistory*. London: Free Association Books.

Lane, C. (1998) The psychoanalysis of race. In C. Lane (ed.), *The Psychoanalysis of Race*. New York: Columbia University Press.

Meltzer, D. (1975) Dimentionality in mental functioning. In D. Meltzer et al., *Explorations in Autism: A Psychoanalytic Study*. Perthshire: Clunie Press.

Moran, A. (1999) The trauma of modernity or modernity's incorrigible impulse?: The psychoanalytic contribution to a theory of racism. *Psychoanalytic Studies*, 1 (1): 57–71.

Richards, G. (1997) *Race, Racism and Psychology: Towards a Reflexive History*. London: Routledge.

Rustin, M. (1991) Psychoanalysis, racism and anti-racism. In M. Rustin, *The Good Society and the Inner World: Psychoanalysis, Politics and Culture*. London: Verso.

Taylor, D. (1988) Commentary on Dr. Davison's and Mr Davids' Paper. *Journal of Social Work Practice*, November: 54–56.

Tan, R. (1993) Racism and similarity: paranoid-schizoid structures. *British Journal of Psychotherapy*, 10 (1): 33–43.

Timimi, S. (1997) Race and colour in external reality. *British Journal of Psychotherapy*, 13 (2): 183–192.

Ward, I. (1997) Race and racism: a reply to Sami Timimi. *British Journal of Psychotherapy*, 14 (1): 91–97.

Wolfenstein, E.V. (1981) *The Victims of Democracy: Malcolm X and the Black Revolution*. Los Angeles: University of California Press.

Young, R. (1994) *Mental Space*. London: Process Press.

PART III
Therapeutic Skills and Clinical Practice

3.1 Introduction

○○○

COLIN FELTHAM AND IAN HORTON

It has been said that, almost regardless of the many theoretical models, training issues, contexts and so on, in and against which therapy takes place, it is what therapists actually *do* in sessions that is significant (Hill, 1989). In this part of the book the concentration is on what therapists actually do when they are with clients and what they do in relation to clients. We refer to this area as clinical practice to distinguish it from other necessary but often indirect professional and theoretical issues, and we are mindful that certain practitioners dislike the epithet 'clinical' and its medical associations.

Various terms are used in this context: attitudes, skills, techniques, interventions, strategies, and so on. Here we make some attempt to clarify usage. *Skills* may be found at the most atomistic levels of practice, for example the micro-skills of responding to clients' utterances with apparently simple but carefully chosen supportive or reflective statements (or, as appropriate, judicious silences). A range of generic skills serves to aid the conversational flow and therapeutic communication between therapists and clients. As well as the micro-skills necessary for these therapeutically goal-directed interactions, there are the specific skills of assessment – calling for a certain cognitive acuity – and those of structuring the therapeutic process. Implied in all these skills, however intuitive they may sometimes appear to be, is an element of putting theory into practice. This, together with the exercise of putting experience and training into practice, is mediated by therapist decision making operating rapidly at perhaps different levels of consciousness (Dryden, 1991: 100–110).

Considerable debate continues as to whether clinicians are most effectively 'produced' by training which explicitly inculcates and reinforces all such skills, or by eliciting appropriate innate or pre-existing skills. Theorists and practitioners aligned with social learning and cognitive-behavioural traditions (e.g. Neenan and Dryden, 2004), particularly those promoting manualized therapeutic procedures, belong to the first group, while many psychoanalytic and humanistic therapists, including Lomas (1993) belong to the second. 'Use of the self' is a key concept here, with psychoanalytic and humanistic practitioners drawing heavily on the idea of *therapist attitudes* and *therapist self-awareness* as cultivated by personal (training) therapy and other forms of personal development work. The use of self is closely associated with therapeutic relationship issues, such as provision of a therapeutic climate. All the above groups agree, however, that counselling and psychotherapy are in fact skilled activities.

Dryden (1991: 103) has argued that *clinical strategies* lie between theory and technique, an example being the decision as to whether to provide a corrective emotional experience, which then leads on to technical implementation. The term *interventions* tends to be used differentially to refer to anything the therapist says or does or to conscious technical choices or directions, this last understanding being characterized for example by Heron (2001).

Techniques may be characterized as deliberately (strategically) employed, purposeful actions which are associated both theoretically and clinically with the therapeutic enterprise generally (e.g. empathy) and often with particular theoretical orientations (e.g. empty-chair work). While some traditions rely on a relatively small number of techniques (e.g. psychoanalysis) or may eschew the concept of techniques altogether or partially (Tolan, 2003), others spawn a large number (e.g. neuro-linguistic programming) and within eclectic practice is found an openness to the deployment of techniques from various sources (Lazarus, 1981; Thompson, 1996). Again, considerable debate exists as to the wisdom of techniques being anchored in their theoretical bases, versus techniques being freely applied, almost regardless of theory, to different clients with different needs. In addition, the contentious concepts of *treatment of choice* and *technique of choice* suggest that therapists need to think strategically both within a tradition (e.g. Barber and Crits-Christoph, 1995) and across traditions (Karasu and Bellak, 1980; Roth and Fonagy, 1996).

In this part of the book are included certain clinical practice issues and ancillary skills which are also widely necessary. Obviously each therapeutic tradition emphasizes the importance of certain skills, techniques and clinical protocols above others. We hope that readers interested in comparative therapeutic skills and potential rapprochement will cross-refer as desirable to other salient parts of the book, including the skills and strategies sections in Part 5.

References

Barber, J.P. and Crits-Christoph, P. (eds) (1995) *Dynamic Therapies for Psychiatric Disorders (Axis I)*. New York: Basic Books.

Dryden, W. (1991) *Dryden on Counselling*. Vol. 1: *Seminal Papers*. London: Whurr.

Heron, J. (2001) *Helping the Client* (5th edn). London: Sage.

Hill, C.E. (1989) *Therapist Techniques and Client Outcomes: Eight Cases of Brief Psychotherapy*. Newbury Park, CA: Sage.

Karasu, T.B. and Bellak, L. (eds) (1980) *Specialized Techniques for Specific Clinical Problems in Psychotherapy*. Northvale, NJ: Aronson.

Lazarus, A.A. (1981) *The Practice of Multimodal Therapy: Systematic, Comprehensive, and Effective Psychotherapy*. Baltimore, MA: Johns Hopkins University Press.

Lomas, P. (1993) *Cultivating Intuition: An Introduction to Psychotherapy*. Northvale, NJ: Aronson.

Neenan, M. and Dryden, W. (2004) *Cognitive Therapy: 100 Key Points and Techniques*. London: Brunner-Routledge.

Roth, A. and Fonagy, P. (1996) *What Works for Whom? A Critical Review of Psychotherapy Research*. New York: Guilford Press.

Thompson, R.A. (1996) *Counseling Techniques*. Washington, DC: Accelerated Learning.

Tolan, J. (2003) *Skills in Person-centred Counselling and Psychotherapy*. London: Sage.

3.2   The Client–Therapist Relationship   ○○○

WILLIAM B. STILES

There is a sprawling literature on the client–therapist relationship. What follows is a personal selection and understanding. I have practised, supervised and researched psychotherapy for some years (e.g. Stiles, 1999). My practice orientation is strongly person-centred, but my understanding of the research is that widely varying theoretical approaches are similarly

effective (Lambert and Ogles, 2003). This *equivalence paradox* – equivalent outcomes of diverse treatments despite manifestly non-equivalent intervention techniques, or 'Everybody has won and all must have prizes' (The Dodo, quoted in Carroll, 1865/1946) – has been the central puzzle driving psychotherapy research for generations (e.g. Beutler, 1991; Luborsky et al., 1975; Rosenzweig, 1936; Stiles et al., 1986; Wampold, 2001).

The concept of the therapist–client relationship offers to resolve the equivalence paradox. All therapy can be said to involve some sort of relationship, though the concept has to be stretched a little to encompass online therapy and bibliotherapy. Across very diverse treatments, including cognitive and psychopharmacological treatments (Krupnick et al., 1996), measures of the strength of the relationship, often styled as the *alliance*, have consistently been the strongest and most consistent process correlates of treatment outcome (Horvath and Bedi, 2002; Horvath and Symonds, 1991; Orlinsky et al., 2003). If the relationship is the main active ingredient, then it is understandable that any treatment approach can be effective – that is, providing the relationship is right (see Norcross, 2002).

But what *is* the client–therapist relationship? What do authors mean when they speak of the relationship, the alliance (helping alliance, working alliance, therapeutic alliance), or the therapeutic climate? This section considers three illustrative conceptual approaches: psychodynamic, person-centred, and psychometric. It concludes with some comments on recent research on the relationship.

Psychodynamic concepts of the relationship

Psychoanalytic and other psychodynamic theorists have focused on a distinction between the real relationship and the transference (Freud, 1958; Horvath and Luborsky, 1993; Zetzel, 1956). Some have further distinguished the working alliance (Gelso and Carter, 1985, 1994; Greenson, 1965). Theorists have made these distinctions in various ways. Gelso and Carter (1985, 1994) offered the following relatively succinct version:

> The real relationship is seen as having two defining features: genuineness and realistic perceptions. Genuineness is defined as the ability and willingness to be what one truly is in the relationship – to be authentic, open, and honest. Realistic perceptions

> refer to those perceptions that are uncontaminated by transference distortions and other defences. In other words, the therapy participants see each other in an accurate, realistic way. (1994: 297)

> The transference configuration ... consists of both client transference and therapist counter-transference. ... Transference is the repetition of past conflicts with significant others, such that feelings, attitudes, and behaviors belonging rightfully in those earlier relationships are displaced onto the therapist; and counter-transference is the therapist's transference to the client's material, both to the transference and the nontransference communications presented by the client. (1994: 297)

> [The working] alliance may be seen as the alignment or joining of the reasonable self or ego of the client and the therapist's analyzing or 'therapizing' self or ego for the purpose of the work. (1994: 297)

> The working alliance that exists between client and therapist both influences and is influenced by each of the other two components – the transference configuration and the real relationship. (1994: 298)

Thus, in Gelso and Carter's conception, the working alliance is only partially reality-based, and may additionally incorporate positive transferential elements, such as idealizing expectations about the therapist's ability to help.

Although all aspects of the relationship are arguably important, psychodynamic interest has focused on the transference. The transference concept is a way of understanding how past hurts, including early environments that interfered with or failed to support healthy development, can be manifested as problems in the present. Theoretically, the problematic relational patterns that brought the client into treatment tend to be re-experienced and acted out within the therapeutic relationship. This offers an experientially immediate opportunity for problematic patterns to be acknowledged, interpreted, understood and changed. By understanding and correcting distortions that arise in his or her feelings about the therapist, the client can resolve conflicts that have been interfering with daily life outside therapy.

Psychoanalytic theorists have elaborated the concept of transference in many ways. For example, Kohut (1971, 1977) distinguished between *mirroring transferences*, in which the therapist is experienced as an extension of the self, as a twin, or as an appendage whose function is mainly to support the client's (unrealistically) grandiose views of the self, and *idealizing transferences*, in which the client draws strength or reassurance from being associated with an idealized therapist's exaggerated virtues. In this view, progress may come when the therapist fails to fulfil these unrealistic expectations. The client's resulting frustration brings the expectations into awareness, making it possible to examine and change them within the treatment.

Manifestations of the transference in treatment can be dramatic and observations of transference phenomena have figured centrally in the psychoanalytic literature since Freud's case studies of Anna O. and Dora (Breuer and Freud, 1957; Freud, 1953). Reliable measurement has proved more difficult, however. Probably the most sustained and best-known effort has been the work on the *core conflictual relationship theme* (CCRT) (Luborsky, 1977; Luborsky and Crits-Cristoph, 1990; Luborsky et al., 2004). Theoretically, core conflicts are likely to appear repeatedly in many significant relationships, as well as in the therapeutic relationship. Consequently, then, a client's stories about relationships in or out of therapy are likely to manifest repeated patterns or themes that reveal the core conflicts. To assess them, accounts of relationships, called *relationship episodes*, are excerpted from the dialogue of therapy or of interviews with clients. Each episode is then analytically dissected into three components: (a) the *wish* (or needs, or intention) expressed by the client; (b) the *response from others*, actual or expected; and (c) the *response of self*, that is, the client's own thoughts, feelings and actions in the situation. A theme – a CCRT – is distinguished by a repetition of these components (i.e. similar wishes, responses of others and responses of self) across multiple episodes. The availability of reliable measurement of the CCRT has led to a productive line of research on psychodynamic concepts of the relationship (e.g. see reviews by Crits-Cristoph, 1998; Luborsky and Crits-Christoph, 1990).

Person-centred concepts of the relationship

Whereas psychodynamic theorists tend to view the transference as a distorted fragment impinging on a distinct real relationship, person-centred theorists have tended to take a holistic, here-and-now perspective (Rogers, 1957, 1980). Yes, people may transfer attitudes from past relationships to present ones, but to consider these as unreal is to deny or derogate the immediacy of the client's actual experience. Even if a client is acting on feelings derived from problematic primary relationships, those feelings are real in the present. Rather than seeking to judge and interpret client experiences, the therapist's job is to understand and accept them. Fully experiencing, acknowledging and stating ('symbolizing') experiences enables them to be considered and re-valued in light of current reality (see Greenberg's (1994) commentary on Gelso and Carter (1994)). The value placed on any particular experience is up to the client, not the therapist or the theory. This conceptualization directs attention not to the historical development of the client's problems but instead to the climate or conditions that the therapist provides within the therapy.

Rogers' (1957: 95) six therapist-provided 'necessary and sufficient conditions of therapeutic personality change' have been popularly reduced to three, which may be stated succinctly (my gloss, not Rogers') as: (1) *be yourself*; (2) *trust the client*; and (3) *listen*. Collectively, they prescribe a quality of openness to experience – the therapist's own experience and the client's. They demand at least tentative trust that the experience will not be overwhelmingly painful, and they underline the importance of creating a trustworthy environment. (The remaining three conditions were that client and therapist be in psychological contact, that the client is in 'a state of incongruence', and hence potentially motivated for therapy, and that the client perceives, to some degree, the presence of the other conditions (Rogers, 1957).)

Although the facilitative conditions, or *attitudes*, can be stated simply, they can be endlessly unpacked. Rogers did it this way:

The first element [*be yourself*] could be called genuineness, realness, or congruence. The more the therapist is himself or herself in the relationship, putting up no professional front or personal façade, the greater is the likelihood that the client will change and grow in a constructive manner. This means that the therapist is openly being the feelings and attitudes that are flowing within at the moment. The term 'transparent' catches the flavor of this condition: the therapist makes himself or herself transparent to the client; the client can see right through what the therapist is in the relationship; the client experiences no holding back on the part of the therapist. As for the therapist, what he or she is experiencing is available to awareness, can be lived in the relationship, and can be communicated, if appropriate. Thus, there is a close matching, or congruence, between what is being experienced at the gut level, what is present in awareness, and what is expressed to the client.

The second attitude of importance in creating a climate for change [*trust the client*] is acceptance, or caring, or prizing – what I have called 'unconditional positive regard.' When the therapist is experiencing a positive, acceptant attitude toward whatever the client is at that moment, therapeutic movement or change is more likely to occur. The therapist is willing for the client to be whatever immediate feeling is going on – confusion, resentment, fear, anger, courage, love, or pride. Such caring on the part of the therapist is nonpossessive. The therapist prizes the client in a total rather than a conditional way.

The third facilitative aspect of the relationship [*listen*] is empathic understanding. This means that the therapist senses accurately the feelings and personal meanings that the client is experiencing and communicates this understanding to the client. When functioning best, the therapist is so much inside the private world of the other that he or she can clarify not only the meanings of which the client is aware but even those just below the level of awareness. This kind of sensitive, active listening is exceedingly rare in our lives. We think we listen, but very rarely do we listen with real understanding, true empathy. Yet listening, of this very special kind, is one of the most potent forces for change that I know. (1980: 115–116)

Easy to say, hard to do. From a practitioner's perspective, being genuine (and distinguishing this from self-serving disclosure), accepting the client (who may hold beliefs or engage in practices contrary to your personal principles), and understanding empathically (when the client tells endless bland stories) can be difficult and taxing. Furthermore, under some circumstances, the conditions can be contradictory. If I disapprove (suicide, child molesters, etc.), do I disclose it? If I'm absorbed by my own problems, how do I empathize? Fortunately, the theory suggests that perfect adherence is not required. Approximations can be helpful, and beneficial effects can be expected to the degree that the conditions are fulfilled.

From the perspective of a therapist or a supervisor, the three conditions may seem distinct and even contradictory, but from the perspective of an observer, they can tend to merge. Although early attempts to measure therapist congruence, unconditional positive regard, and accurate empathy seemed promising, reviewers of the research found fault (Lambert et al., 1978; Mitchell et al., 1977). In my reading, the central difficulties lay in distinguishing the three conditions from each other and distinguishing any of them from global positive evaluation (e.g. Rappaport and Chinsky, 1972).

More recently, interest in the conditions has revived. In the report of a task force of the Psychotherapy Division of the American Psychological Association on the psychotherapy relationship (Norcross, 2002), the 'demonstrably effective elements' included empathy (Bohart et al., 2002) and the 'promising and probably effective elements' included positive regard (Farber and Lane, 2002) and congruence or genuineness (Klein et al., 2002). Nevertheless, the problem of empirically distinguishing the conditions from global positivity has not been fully resolved.

Psychometric concepts of the alliance

In a conceptualization that has proved seminal for psychotherapy process research, Bordin (1979, 1994) characterized the alliance as encompassing (a) the affective bond between client and therapist, (b) agreement on the goals of treatment, and (c) agreement on treatment tasks, or means of achieving those goals. Many subsequent alliance researchers have understood the alliance as multidimensional and have attempted to construct scales to assess the dimensions, for example, using ratings on items like 'I feel friendly towards my therapist' to measure bond or 'I am clear as to what my therapist wants me to do in these sessions' to measure agreement on tasks. Typically, investigators have administered a pool of such items to respondents – clients, therapists or external raters who have observed sessions or listened to recordings – and have then grouped the items into scales using factor analysis or related statistical techniques. The result is typically to confirm that items with similar meaning tend to be rated similarly (so that ratings are intercorrelated) and hence to load on the same factor. Results have offered some support for the multidimensional accounts (i.e. the factors often appear to correspond to conceptual dimensions). The factors tend to be substantially intercorrelated, however (for an example of such a factor analytic study, see Agnew-Davies et al., 1998).

Although researchers have concurred in conceiving the alliance as multidimensional, they have not concurred on the boundaries of the alliance construct or on the number or names of the dimensions. Some have used Bordin's (1979, 1994) concepts of bond, agreement on tasks, and agreement on goals (notably Horvath, 1994; Horvath and Greenberg, 1986, 1989). Some have combined or re-labelled these, for example, combining agreement on tasks and agreement on goals as *working strategy consensus* (Gaston, 1991) or *partnership* (Agnew-Davies et al., 1998). And others have added dimensions, such as *patient working capacity* and *therapist understanding and involvement* (Gaston, 1991; Marmar et al., 1989); *patient resistance* (hostile, defensive), *patient motivation* (acknowledged problems, wanted to overcome them), and *therapist intrusiveness* (fostered dependency, imposed own values) (Hartley and Strupp, 1983); or *openness, confidence,* and *client initiative* (Agnew-Davies et al., 1998). Each such additional dimension is defined and measured by a set of self-report items.

The alliance has sustained intense interest from researchers because of its replicated positive correlations with measures of psychotherapy outcome (Horvath and Bedi, 2002; Horvath and Luborsky,

1993; Horvath and Symonds, 1991; Martin et al., 2000; Orlinsky et al., 2003; Stiles et al., 1998). Clients who have strong alliances with their therapists also tend to have better outcomes. In the Norcross (2002) task force report on the psychotherapy relationship, the alliance was given pride of place among relationship aspects as the strongest and most consistent correlate of outcome (Horvath and Bedi, 2002). The research has not consistently supported the differentiation of the varied dimensions, however, and many researchers have ignored the dimensional scores, using total or aggregate scores meant to assess the overall strength of the alliance.

Thus, there is a disjunction between the multidimensional conceptual structure of the alliance instruments and the global implementation of the measures. That is, the clients and therapists who rate the alliance seem to respond more globally than was envisioned by the measures' creators. And investigators interpret their finding in terms of global alliance.

Evaluations and enactments

The lack of differentiation in applying the alliance dimensions points to a more general problem. Researchers had difficulty distinguishing any of the subtle concepts that theorists have developed to understand the client–therapist relationship. The weak differentiation of Bordin's dimensions or of Rogers' facilitative conditions is the tip of an iceberg. Theorists and clinicians use a far more differentiated repertoire of concepts than researchers measure.

A distinction between *evaluation* and *enactment* of the therapeutic relationship (Stiles and Agnew-Davies, 1999) can aid understanding of this research–practice gap. Whereas researchers tend to use terms such as '*alliance*' and '*relationship*' to refer to evaluations, clinicians consider the client's (changing) feelings towards the therapist as interwoven with a variety of interpersonal activities, and they use '*alliance*' and '*relationship*' as umbrella terms.

Evaluation involves the private experience of the participants – what they think and feel about each other, about the relationship, and about the process in which they are engaged. Thus, it is ironic that alliance evaluation has proved far more accessible empirically than has alliance enactment.

Enactments of problems and solutions within the therapeutic relationship are far more complex than can be represented adequately on a small number of evaluative (positive–negative) scales. Each alliance involves specific content, specific behaviours, specific people, and specific events, and understanding of the particularities requires longitudinal observation. For example, distinguishing between a mirroring transference and an idealizing transference is crucial for self-psychologists, following Kohut (1971, 1977), but doing this requires contextual knowledge of the case. The distinction is unlikely to be captured with the standardized items of alliance inventories.

It is always mathematically possible, of course, to project a multifaceted relationship on to a one-dimensional evaluative scale. That is, participants can always be said to have some degree of positive or negative feeling as part of the real relationship, the transference, the working alliance, or the degree of empathy, congruence, or trust. Moreover, the evaluation is often the most salient feature to participants, researchers and research consumers; the first thing people notice or want to know about a relationship (or anything else) is how good it was. But evaluations alone gloss over what makes relationships interesting and difficult. Differentiated clinical concepts like mirror transference are not so easily scaled. Studying relationships in their contextual complexity will probably require theoretically guided case studies, in which the distinctions made by clinical theories can be compared with observations in individual cases (Stiles, 2003).

Worryingly, many of the relationship measures considered as successful by researchers (because they correlate positively with outcomes) have the ring of evaluative rather than descriptive qualities – of valued achievements rather than volitional actions. As an illustration, in the Norcross (2002) task force report on the psychotherapy relationship, all of the *demonstrably effective* elements (therapeutic alliance, group cohesion, empathy, goal consensus and collaboration) and five of the seven *promising and probably effective* elements (positive regard, congruence or genuineness, repair of ruptures, management of counter-transference, quality of relational interpretations) were clearly achievements rather than volitional actions (Stiles and Wolfe, in press). Therapists work to achieve strong alliances, cohesive groups, empathic exchanges, high-quality interpretations, and so forth; they do not just decide that they will do these things. The behaviours that contribute to a strong alliance, accurate empathy, high-quality interventions, and so forth, differ across cases in response to the circumstances of each case. Close reading of the descriptions of the remaining two probably effective elements (therapist self-disclosure and feedback) suggests that they too were understood as achievements – as *appropriate* therapist self-disclosure and *appropriate* feedback, rather than *any* self-disclosure or *any* feedback. It is plausible that these achievements predict outcome, but it would be more informative to learn which actual activities predict outcome.

The dominance of one-dimensional evaluative scales may reflect asking people (clients particularly) to tell us things they do not know. It is too easy to assume that because people can report some things that are private and unavailable to others, they can report the thing we want to know, which is also private. They may not know whether they are having a mirroring transference, and they may not distinguish their therapist's genuineness from his or her positive regard, so they respond on rating scales with something they do know, which is their global evaluation of the relationship.

Developmental concepts: the rupture–repair hypothesis

To end this chapter on a more positive note, I want to briefly consider the emerging theory and research on how therapeutic relationships fluctuate and change over time. These developmental views address some of the potential oversimplifications of static conceptions of the relationship (Horvath, 2003). As one example, Gelso and Carter suggested that 'although the alliance is initially in the forefront of the relationship, it subsequently fades into the background, returning to the foreground only when needed' (1994: 301). For example, the alliance may fluctuate in connection with crises in therapy work, such as the therapist's failures to understand or the client's emerging resistances to understanding. The initially strong alliance may weaken towards the middle of therapy and rise again in a more realistic reaction to the therapist towards the ends of treatment. Some years ago, I proposed that therapeutic relationships develop in a pattern related to Erikson's (1963) 'epigenetic' (i.e. systematically emerging) sequence of stages of the life cycle. Psychotherapeutic relationships progress through issues of trust versus mistrust, autonomy versus shame and doubt, initiative versus guilt, industry versus inferiority, identity versus role confusion, intimacy versus isolation, generativity versus stagnation, and integrity versus despair, with each resolution containing the seeds of the next conflict (Stiles, 1979).

Perhaps even more promising is research on short-term fluctuations in the relationship, particularly rupture–repair sequences (Harper, 1994; Safran and Muran, 1996, 2000; Samstag et al., 2004). Ruptures in the therapeutic alliance may occur when previously hidden negative feelings emerge or when the therapist makes a mistake or fails to act as the client expects or wishes. Clients may then challenge the relationship by confronting the therapist or by withdrawing (Harper, 1994). If the therapist recognizes the challenge, it may prove to be an important opportunity for therapeutic interpersonal learning. Ruptures in the client's relationship with the therapist (one could say, in the transference) may recapitulate the client's relationship difficulties outside therapy. More generally, recognizing, acknowledging and overcoming relational difficulties can provide valuable experiential learning in the here-and-now of the session. Researchers are developing methods for identifying and isolating significant incidents using post-therapy interviews (Fitzpatrick and Chamodraka, 2004), detecting rupture–repair sequences in alliance ratings (Stiles et al., 2004) and in session tapes (Samstag et al., 2000), and describing steps in the task of repairing various types of rupture (Harper, 1994; Safran and Muran, 2000). By bringing research attention to processes occurring moment by moment within sessions, this work may succeed in building a bridge across the research–practice gap.

Conclusion

Clinical concepts of the relationship are complex, subtle and central to therapeutic practice. Depending on their theoretical orientation, therapists make extensive use of such concepts as the transference and the core facilitative conditions. Researchers using questionnaire and rating-scale methods have had difficulties coming to grips with the subtleties; measures of the relationship or the alliance tend to yield global evaluations rather than differentiated descriptions. There has been a great deal of research on the relationship in psychotherapy, but much of it repeats the broad finding that evaluations of the relationship predict evaluations of treatment outcome. This well-replicated result justifies the widespread conviction that the client–therapist relationship is central to the practice of counselling and psychotherapy but falls short of confirming or elaborating the clinical theories. Work on the development of the relationship, particularly rupture–repair sequences, holds promise of more differentiated and subtle scientific underpinnings.

References

Agnew-Davies, R., Stiles, W.B., Hardy, G.E., Barkham, M. and Shapiro, D.A. (1998) Alliance structure assessed by the Agnew Relationship Measure (ARM). *British Journal of Clinical Psychology*, 37: 155–172.

Beutler, L.E. (1991) Have all won and must all have prizes? Revisiting Luborsky et al.'s verdict. *Journal of Consulting and Clinical Psychology*, 59: 226–232.

Bohart, A.C., Elliott, R., Greenberg, L.S. and Watson, J.C. (2002) Empathy. In J.C. Norcross (ed.), *Psychotherapy Relationships That Work: Therapist Contributions and Responsiveness to Patient Needs* (pp. 89–108). New York: Oxford University Press.

Bordin, E.S. (1979) The generalizability of the psychoanalytic concept of working alliance. *Psychotherapy: Theory, Research, and Practice*, 16: 252–260.

Bordin, E.S. (1994) Theory and research on the therapeutic working alliance: new directions. In A.O. Horvath and L.S. Greenberg (eds), *The Working Alliance: Theory, Research and Practice* (pp. 13–37). New York: Wiley.

Breuer, J. and Freud, S. (1957) *Studies on Hysteria*. New York: Basic Books.

Carroll, L. (1865/1946) *Alice's Adventures in Wonderland*. New York: Random House.

Crits-Christoph, P. (1998) The psychological interior of psychotherapy. *Psychotherapy Research*, 8: 1–16.

Erikson, E.H. (1963) *Childhood and Society* (2nd edn). New York: Norton.

Farber, B.A. and Lane, J.S. (2002) Positive regard. In J.C. Norcross (ed.), *Psychotherapy Relationships That Work: Therapist Contributions and Responsiveness to Patient Needs* (pp. 175–194). New York: Oxford University Press.

Fitzpatrick, M. and Chamodraka, M. (2004) Participant critical events: a multi-perspective method for identifying and isolating significant therapeutic incidents. Manuscript submitted for publication.

Freud, S. (1953) Fragments of an analysis of a case of hysteria. In J. Strachey (ed. and trans.), *The Standard Edition of the Complete Psychological Works of Sigmund Freud* (Vol. 7, pp. 3–122). London: Hogarth Press. (Original work published 1905.)

Freud, S. (1958) The dynamics of transference. In J. Strachey (ed. and trans.), *The Standard Edition of the Complete Psychological Works of Sigmund Freud* (Vol. 12, pp. 99–108). London: Hogarth Press. (Original work published 1912.)

Gaston, L. (1991) Reliability and criterion-related validity of the California Psychotherapy Alliance Scales – patient version. *Psychological Assessment*, 3: 68–74.

Gelso, C.J. and Carter, J.A. (1985) The relationship in counseling and psychotherapy: components, consequences, and theoretical antecedents. *The Counseling Psychologist*, 2: 155–243.

Gelso, C.J. and Carter, J.A. (1994) Components of the psychotherapy relationship: their interaction and unfolding during treatment. *Journal of Counseling Psychology*, 41: 296–306.

Greenberg, L.S. (1994) What is 'real' in the relationship? Comment on Gelso and Carter. *Journal of Counseling Psychology*, 41: 307–309.

Greenson, R.R. (1965) The working alliance and the transference neuroses. *Psychoanalysis Quarterly*, 34: 155–181.

Harper, H. (1994) Developing the new paradigm in psychotherapy research: client confrontation challenges to the therapeutic relationship in a psychodynamic-interpersonal therapy. Unpublished PhD thesis: University of Sheffield, UK.

Hartley, D.E. and Strupp, H.H. (1983) The therapeutic alliance: its relationship to outcome in brief psychotherapy. In J. Masling (ed.), *Empirical Studies of Psychoanalytic Theories*, (Vol. 1, pp. 1–37). Hillsdale, NJ: Erlbaum.

Horvath, A.O. (1994) Empirical validation of Bordin's pantheoretical model of the alliance: the Working Alliance Inventory perspective. In A.O. Horvath and L.S. Greenberg (eds), *The Working Alliance: Theory, Research and Practice* (pp. 109–128). New York: Wiley.

Horvath, A.O. (2003) Alliance at the crossroad: an assessment of what has been achieved and the significant challenges that lie ahead. In T. Anderson (Chair), *Advances in Measuring the Therapeutic Alliance*. Panel presented at the North American Society for Psychotherapy Research meeting, Newport, Rhode Island.

Horvath, A.O. and Bedi, R.P. (2002) The alliance. In J.C. Norcross (ed.), *Psychotherapy Relationships That Work: Therapist Contributions and Responsiveness to Patient Needs* (pp. 37–69). New York: Oxford University Press.

Horvath, A.O. and Greenberg, L.S. (1986) The development of the Working Alliance Inventory. In L.S. Greenberg and W.M. Pinsof (eds), *The Psychotherapeutic Process: A Research Handbook* (pp. 529–556). New York: Guilford Press.

Horvath, A.O. and Greenberg, L.S. (1989) Development and validation of the Working Alliance Inventory. *Journal of Counseling Psychology*, 36: 223–233.

Horvath, A.O. and Luborsky, L. (1993) The role of the therapeutic alliance in psychotherapy. *Journal of Consulting and Clinical Psychology*, 61: 561–573.

Horvath, A.O. and Symonds, B.D. (1991) Relation between working alliance and outcome in psychotherapy: a meta-analysis. *Journal of Counseling Psychology*, 38: 139–149.

Klein, M.H., Kolden, G.G., Michels, J.L. and Chisholm-Stockard, S. (2002) Congruence/genuineness. In J.C. Norcross (ed.), *Psychotherapy Relationships That Work: Therapist Contributions and Responsiveness to Patient Needs* (pp. 195–215). New York: Oxford University Press.

Kohut, M. (1971) *The Analysis of the Self*. New York: International Universities Press.

Kohut, M. (1977) *The Restoration of the Self*. New York: International Universities Press.

Krupnick, J.L., Sotsky, S.M., Simmens, S., Moyer, J., Elkin, I., Watkins, J. and Pilkonis, P.A. (1996) The role of the therapeutic alliance in psychotherapy and pharmacotherapy outcome: findings in the National Institute of Mental Health Treatment of Depression Collaborative Research Program. *Journal of Consulting and Clinical Psychology*, 64: 532–539.

Lambert, M.J. and Ogles, B.M. (2003) The efficacy and effectiveness of psychotherapy. In M.J. Lambert (ed.), *Bergin and Garfield's Handbook of Psychotherapy and Behavior Change* (5th edn). New York: Wiley.

Lambert, M.J., DeJulio, S.S. and Stein, D.M. (1978) Therapist interpersonal skills: process, outcome, methodological considerations, and recommendations for future research. *Psychological Bulletin*, 85: 467–489.

Luborsky, L. (1977) Measuring a pervasive psychic structure in psychotherapy: the core conflictual relationship theme. In N. Freedman and S. Grand (eds), *Communicative*

Structures and Psychic Structures (pp. 367–395). New York: Plenum Press.

Luborsky, L. and Crits-Christoph, P. (1990) *Understanding Transference: The Core-conflictual Relationship Theme Method*. New York: Basic Books.

Luborsky, L., Singer, B. and Luborsky, E. (1975) Comparative studies of psychotherapies: is it true that 'everybody has won and all must have prizes'? *Archives of General Psychiatry*, 32: 995–1008.

Luborsky, L., Diguer, L., Andrusyna, T., Friedman, S., Tarca, C., Popp, C.A., Ermold, J. and Silberschatz, G. (2004) A method of choosing CCRT scores. *Psychotherapy Research*, 14: 127–134.

Marmar, C.R., Weiss, D.S. and Gaston, L. (1989) Towards the validation of the California Therapeutic Alliance Rating System. *Psychological Assessment*, 1: 46–52.

Martin, D.J., Garske, J.P. and Davis, K.M. (2000) Relation of the therapeutic alliance with outcome and other variables: a meta-analytic review. *Journal of Clinical and Consulting Psychology*, 68: 438–450.

Mitchell, K.M., Bozarth, J.D. and Krauft, C.C. (1977) A reappraisal of the therapeutic effectiveness of accurate empathy, non-possessive warmth and genuineness. In A.S. Gurman and A.M. Razin (eds), *Effective Psychotherapy: A Handbook of Research* (pp. 482–502). New York: Pergamon Press.

Norcross, J.C. (ed.) (2002) *Psychotherapy Relationships That Work: Therapist Contributions and Responsiveness to Patient Need*. New York: Oxford University Press.

Orlinsky, D.E., Rønnestad, M.H. and Willutzki, U. (2003) Fifty years of process-outcome research: continuity and change. In M.J. Lambert (ed.), *Bergin and Garfield's Handbook of Psychotherapy and Behavior Change* (5th edn, pp. 307–390). New York: Wiley.

Rappaport, J. and Chinsky, J. (1972) Accurate empathy: confusion of a construct. *Psychological Bulletin*, 77: 400–404.

Rogers, C.R. (1957) The necessary and sufficient conditions of therapeutic personality change. *Journal of Consulting Psychology*, 21: 95–103.

Rogers, C.R. (1980) *A Way of Being*. Boston: Houghton Mifflin.

Rosenzweig, S. (1936) Some implicit common factors in diverse methods of psychotherapy. *American Journal of Orthopsychiatry*, 6: 412–415.

Safran, J.D. and Muran, J.C. (1996) The resolution of ruptures in the therapeutic alliance. *Journal of Consulting and Clinical Psychology*, 64: 447–458.

Safran, J.D. and Muran, J.C. (2000) *Negotiating the Therapeutic Alliance: A Relational Treatment Guide*. New York: Guilford Press.

Samstag, L.W., Muran, J.C. and Safran, J.D. (2004) Defining and identifying alliance ruptures. In D.P. Charman (ed.), *Core Processes in Brief Psychodynamic Psychotherapy: Advancing Effective Practice* (pp. 187–214). Hillsdale, NJ: Lawrence Erlbaum Associates.

Samstag, L.W., Safran, J.D. and Muran, J.C. (2000) The rupture resolution scale and coding manual. Unpublished manuscript, Beth Israel Medical Center, New York.

Stiles, W.B. (1979) Psychotherapy recapitulates ontogeny: the epigenesis of intensive interpersonal relationships. *Psychotherapy: Theory, Research, and Practice*, 16: 391–404.

Stiles, W.B. (1999) Signs and voices in psychotherapy. *Psychotherapy Research*, 9: 1–21.

Stiles, W.B. (2003) Qualitative research: evaluating the process and the product. In S.P. Llewelyn and P. Kennedy (eds), *Handbook of Clinical Health Psychology* (pp. 477–499). London: Wiley.

Stiles, W.B. and Agnew-Davies, R. (1999) Brief alliances [Review of *The Therapeutic Alliance in Brief Psychotherapy* by J.D. Safran and J.C. Muran (eds)]. *Contemporary Psychology: APA Review of Books*, 44: 392–394.

Stiles, W.B. and Wolfe, B.E. (in press) Relationship factors in treating anxiety disorders. In L.G. Castonguay and L.E. Beutler (eds), *Principles of Therapeutic Change That Work*. New York: Oxford University Press.

Stiles, W.B., Agnew-Davies, R., Hardy, G.E., Barkham, M. and Shapiro, D.A. (1998) Relations of the alliance with psychotherapy outcome: findings in the Second Sheffield Psychotherapy Project. *Journal of Consulting and Clinical Psychology*, 66: 791–802.

Stiles, W.B., Glick, M.J., Osatuke, K., Hardy, G.E., Shapiro, D.A., Agnew-Davies, R., Rees, A. and Barkham, M. (2004) Patterns of alliance development and the rupture–repair hypothesis: are productive relationships U-shaped or V-shaped? *Journal of Counseling Psychology*, 51: 81–92.

Stiles, W.B., Shapiro, D.A. and Elliott, R. (1986) Are all psychotherapies equivalent? *American Psychologist*, 41: 165–180.

Wampold, B.E. (2001) *The Great Psychotherapy Debate: Models, Methods, and Findings*. Mahwah, NJ: Lawrence Erlbaum Associates.

Zetzel, E.R. (1956) Current concepts of transference. *International Journal of Psychoanalysis*, 37: 369–376.

3.3   Generic Skills

FRANCESCA INSKIPP

This section assumes that it is possible to identify a set of skills which are generally applicable to counselling and psychotherapy, irrespective of theoretical orientation. However, this is not a consensually agreed or proven assumption. Some of the skills, such as therapist self-disclosure, may be regarded as inconsistent with, for example, psychodynamic practice. In addition, micro-skills tend to be assumed to be present in psychotherapy training or to be imbibed in training therapy or analysis, but not necessarily trained in explicitly. Nevertheless, the assumption here is that although the concept of generic skills is contested at least by some therapists, it is just as relevant and useful for all to consider what remains a very influential area of training and practice.

Therapeutic skills imply a craft, but is therapy an art or a craft? At its best it is an art created by a unique individual in helping other unique individuals. However, a competent therapist needs to be skilled, especially in interpersonal communication, in building relationships and in self-awareness and self-management.

Counselling skills, like much of counselling theory, were an import from the USA, and initially met with considerable resistance; they were first taught on counsellor courses around 1970, and now are considered an essential part of counsellor education (BACP, 2002). Carl Rogers was the first person to move the training of counsellors and therapists from the realm of the mysterious into the realm of the observable and trainable by making audiotape recordings of sessions. He says in *A Way of Being*:

Then came my transition to a full-time position at Ohio State University, where, with the help of students, I was at last able to scrounge equipment for recording my and my students' interviews. I cannot exaggerate the excitement of our learnings as we clustered about the machine that enabled us to listen to ourselves, playing over and over some puzzling point at which the interview clearly went wrong, or those moments in which the client moved significantly forward. (1980: 138)

Research by Truax and Carkhuff (1967) confirmed the three core qualities, previously identified by Rogers (1957) – empathic understanding, unconditional positive regard and congruence – and their accurate communication, as essential elements manifested by counsellors who helped their clients change, whatever their theoretical base; this began the development of basic counselling skills to communicate these qualities. Carkhuff (1969) later added four other essential skills – concreteness, self-disclosure, confrontation and immediacy. Ivey (1971) developed the idea of micro-skills, identifying clearly delineated discrete behaviours such as attending, paraphrasing, reflection of feeling and summarizing, teaching them systematically and then integrating them in therapy practice.

Kagan (1975) is the third influence with his Interpersonal Process Recall (IPR) system of training. This is not focused on teaching specific communication skills but helps in the development and monitoring of the skills of internal awareness; the core of IPR is a unique recall process in which an 'inquirer' guides trainees as they review their video or audio-recorded sessions with clients. The overall purpose is to encourage practitioners to become more aware of the interaction process, to study aspects of their own interpersonal behaviour and become more attuned to their own sensations and thoughts in a safe recall situation. In developing this awareness by recall outside the session, they become more aware in the actual session, and can learn to communicate this awareness to develop the therapeutic

Table 3.3.1   Some typical inquirer leads

As you recall specific interactions or situations:
What thoughts were going on in your mind?
What emotions were going on for you – any others below the surface?
What did you sense in your body? Where specifically?
How were you breathing?
What did you imagine the client was thinking/feeling about you?
What did you want the client to think/feel about you?
Does the client remind you of anyone?
Did you have any images passing through your mind?
Did you have any fantasies about the outcomes? Or about the client?

relationship. It is based on the theory that even beginning practitioners perceive and intuitively understand much more of their communication with the client than might be expected, but often have no way of using this information. See Table 3.3.1.

IPR has not had such an impact on training in Britain, partly because it is time-consuming and not easy to incorporate into basic skills courses. However, it has great potential for developing the skills which depend on internal and interpersonal awareness, for example self-disclosure and immediacy. IPR can usefully be incorporated into supervision. Further details of this training are found in Inskipp (1996).

Connor (1994) gives detailed references to the main research on skills training in both the UK and USA. Most of the work and research on counselling and therapy skills has been with a white middle-class population, and has been undertaken by men; there is some work being done on how this relates to other cultures and, following research on brain differences in the sexes, how women may learn in different ways from men.

The competencies originally developed by the National Council for Vocational Qualifications in Advice, Guidance, Counselling and Psychotherapy (now abandoned) are used as a structure for generic in this section.

Key generic skills

- Establish contact with clients;
- Ensure a structured therapeutic setting;
- Develop the therapeutic relationship;
- Develop and maintain interaction with clients;
- Evaluate and develop work on self;
- Monitor self within the therapeutic process.

Generic skills include basic communication skills, but also more complex skills which a therapist needs. Skills can be learnt and practised and used as 'techniques', but the therapeutic use of them with the client depends not only on the communication skill but on the attitude and intention of the therapist – the inside 'energy' which comes from a commitment to understanding the person from his or her frame of reference.

Competent therapy depends not only on the skills therapists use to communicate with their clients, but on how well they are able to be aware and reflect upon what is going on inside themselves and between themselves and their clients – and what they imagine is going on inside their clients. This in turn depends on awareness of the therapist's own attitudes, beliefs, values, intentions and knowledge. Casement (1985: i) describes this internal supervision as 'a process of self-review in the session'. These skills of inside awareness are referred to here as 'inside or process skills' and those skills which can be seen and evaluated by an observer are referred to as 'outside skills'.

The 'inside skills' have not normally been taught as skills, but therapists in training have used personal development groups, experiential exercises and individual therapy to develop awareness of themselves and of themselves in interaction. Arguably counsellors and psychotherapists gain from making awareness of inner processes more specific and from finding ways to learn and practise these skills; IPR is especially useful for this.

Table 3.3.2   Inner and outer skills

Inner	Outer
Observing	Attending
Listening	Greeting
Body scanning for	Active listening
awareness of body sensations	paraphrasing
emotions	reflecting feelings
thoughts	summarizing
images	Asking questions
Impartial witnessing	Contracting
Discriminating	purpose stating
Reflecting	preference stating
	Clarifying counselling/psychotherapy and therapeutic role
	Technical skills of audio recording and introducing this to clients

Macro- and micro-skills

To learn and practise skills it is important to be able to break down a competency such as 'contracting' into smaller units, e.g. negotiating, and further into micro-skills such as listening, paraphrasing, reflecting feelings, etc. It is these specific micro-skills that can be identified, practised, internalized and developed into the practitioner's way of working – therapy is an art but it needs a good craft background for development into a creative artist.

Rogers warns against the mechanical 'reflection of the client's feelings', a caricature of 'false empathy'. By learning and practising micro-skills therapists can become good at 'portraying' empathy and congruence without necessarily developing the inner understanding and acceptance of the client. In a similar way therapists may become facile in analysing and give ill-judged interpretations. This emphasizes the importance of inner work running alongside outer practice.

Establish contact with clients and ensure a structured therapeutic situation

- Making psychological contact;
- Intake and assessment;

- Introducing tape recording;
- Contracting and clarifying therapy;
- Beginning to build a relationship.

The first meeting with a client requires a wide range of skills, both inner and outer, to accomplish the tasks and monitor the process. Table 3.3.2 lists the necessary skills.

Making psychological contact

Rogers' conditions for constructive personality change to occur have been immensely important in the development of counselling and therapy; however, one of the conditions, that 'Two persons are in psychological contact' has often been neglected, though revived in relation to work on 'pre-therapy' (Mearns, 1994). Psychological contact is hard to define; it is different from rapport, being in a relationship, or being empathic, but precedes and underlies them all. It may be seen as the intangible interpersonal process which changes from moment to moment, the 'dance' and exchange of energy between human beings.

Psychological contact between therapist and client depends on the skills, experience, attitudes, emotions, each bring to the situation. Clients present, on a continuum from those who appear to make no contact, to those who may seem overwhelming, invading the therapist's space. Therapists also vary in their ability to make contact, especially with a new person or possibly with clients who are different from themselves in culture, class, race, gender, age or sexual orientation.

The following skills are relevant to making psychological contact.

Inside skills

- **Awareness of your experience of initial interpersonal contact can be developed by self-reflection:**

    What feelings, thoughts, bodily sensations are engendered at first interaction?
    How do these vary when meeting with different individuals?
    Have I any particular 'allergies' to people?
    How different am I in the role of therapist from my everyday self?

- **Impartial witnessing** is concerned with the ability to observe inner processes without judging – to be an interested and curious observer of inner self is one of the greatest skills that can be developed. It can enable practitioners to use their thoughts, sensations, images, and emotions both to build the therapeutic relationship and to promote purposeful interaction with the client.
- **Awareness of how others experience you** in initial psychological contact can be developed by asking colleagues in training or supervision whether they experience you as, for example:

    warm or cool
    immediate or slow in contact
    anxious or relaxed
    engaged or distant
    congruent or incongruent
    strong or vulnerable
    fearful or open
    intrusive or distant.

    They can also be asked to describe your interpersonal style and whether they see you differently in the role of therapist.

Very useful skills for exploring psychological contact, especially emotional and subtle contact, are given in Tolan (2003). Major theory and practice are discussed in Wyatt and Sanders (2002). Other example of exploring 'inside processes', both in dyads and

in groups, are given in Crouch (1997). IPR can be used to increase self-awareness of the range and level of feelings experienced in initial contacts with clients.

Outside skills

- **Skills of greeting appropriately and starting the interaction** are concerned with the following kinds of issues:

    How do I encourage psychological contact?
    Does the therapist have any physical contact, e.g. shake hands?
    Does the therapist put the client 'at ease'? If so, how?
    What impression, if any, does the therapist want the client to have about him or her?
    How is the scene set which is not a social visit but is sufficiently welcoming?

How are adjustments made to a different culture or age? Some older people prefer to be addressed by their title of Mr or Mrs and dislike calling therapists by their first name. People from some cultures always shake hands at every meeting, some do not touch, or do not touch the opposite gender.

What does the therapist do if clients arrive early on their first visit? How should therapists indicate time is important without diminishing the welcome? How do therapists decide whether to see clients early if they are free and later discuss punctual starting, or whether to ask them to wait outside until the time of the appointment?

These nuances of first contact are opportunities for skill development. Therapists need to be aware of their own thoughts, emotions and physical reactions. These are the skills of self-management and enable therapists to make choices in handling beginnings – clearly mediated by the therapist's theoretical orientation.

Where a client's ability to make psychological contact seems impaired, pre-therapy is well suited as a source of inspiration and a departure point for highly concrete client–therapist interaction. The method is basically a way of making contact with the client by reflecting back concrete client behaviour and/or relevant elements from the surrounding reality, for example, 'You've come into my room and you're wondering which chair to sit in'. Although based on working with disturbed clients, these ideas can be adapted to work with clients who seem to make little or no psychological contact.

Example:

> *Client:* (Comes in, sits down, looks out of the window and says in a very quiet voice) Dr Evans sent me. (Therapist feels cut off, not seen.)
> *Therapist:* You've come to see me for counselling … You're not sure what to say … I notice you're looking out of the window and I wonder what you are seeing.

Responses like this can help clients be in touch with where they are, psychologically and literally, and can help to draw them into contact. Exploring the skills for making psychological contact is a fruitful field for further work. The concept can be particularly useful in supervision to help the therapist focus on the interaction.

Intake and assessment

In an intake interview or a formal assessment, specific skills are needed.

- **Asking for information.** Assessment sessions may involve asking set questions and it is important for the client to know the purpose of these questions. If the answers are written down it is necessary to explain what will happen to the records. However, many therapists never make any form of written record *during* a session.

Example:

> I'll need to ask you some personal questions to find out if my approach would be helpful and how we might work together – is this OK?
> I will be writing down your answers on a form. This will have a coded number, not your name, and will be kept in a confidential file.

- **Purpose stating – what the therapist wants to happen and what must happen.** This is an important skill in setting a scene of openness to clients so that they know the therapist's intentions or the purpose in asking questions. It helps the client to experience the therapist as congruent.

Example:

> Dr James suggested you came to see me, and it would be useful to spend time now talking, to decide whether therapy would be useful for you.
>
> or
>
> You know I am a student on a counselling course and after this session I need to check with my tutor whether I will be the most suitable counsellor for you – have you any questions about that?

- **Preference stating – what the therapist would like to happen.** Here the therapist says what needs to happen but is giving the client some choice.

Example:

> I would like to start by you telling me what brings you here today, but you might like to ask some questions first about psychotherapy or about me.

- **Saying 'No' to a client.** There may be clients for whom the therapist, or the therapist's supervisor, decide they cannot offer therapy. These clients may, or may not, need to be referred to somebody else. The issue here is how to communicate this and at the same time remain empathic, respectful and congruent.

Example:

> *Therapist:* When we talked last week I said I would have to consult with my supervisor before setting up counselling with you. I'm sorry but it seems that I may not have the relevant experience to be able to offer you the service you need, and I would like to refer you to a more experienced therapist if you are willing.
> *Client:* That makes me feel my problems are too difficult and I'm hopeless.
> *Therapist:* You're feeling worse because I'm suggesting you could be helped better by a more experienced counsellor?
> *Client:* Well you seemed a very understanding person last week when I told you all my troubles, and now I feel you're shutting me out …

The therapist gives the client time to explore feelings using paraphrasing, reflection of feelings, summarizing and restating that the referral is about his or her own inexperience.

Introducing tape recording

Many counsellors and psychotherapists find this very hard to do but it is now often a requirement for trainees, and many experienced therapists find this a great asset in developing their work and using recordings in supervision.

Technical skills are needed to set up equipment in order to obtain a good recording. Gaining the client's consent needs practice and confidence and an inner conviction that it is acceptable and useful for the therapist and the client. It needs to be part of the initial contract.

Contracting and clarifying therapy

Contracting is dealt with in more detail elsewhere in this section so the related skills will only be listed. Negotiating a contract with a client requires particularly the multiple skills of 'active listening' – paraphrasing, reflecting feelings, summarizing – and also 'asking questions', purpose and preference stating, the ability to be assertive enough and flexible enough. It is an ethical requirement of BACP, for example, that clients understand what they are committing themselves to, that expectations and intentions are clarified. Complaints by clients to BACP are often the result of poorly contracted arrangements.

If therapists are working in an agency or organization they also need these skills to clarify their work contract with the agency. They need skills to be able to communicate effectively with people who refer clients or manage their work, and sometimes skills to educate the agency about counselling or psychotherapy, and about what constitutes suitable referrals.

Further useful skills for intake interviews, assessment and diagnosis are given in Joyce and Sills (2001).

Beginning to build a relationship

The ability to communicate empathic understanding of the client, unconditional respect, and to be perceived as congruent, requires both inner and outer, receptive and responding skills. The client needs to hear that the therapist understands him from his point of view, accepting and not judging him, and is openly present for him, genuine in the role. The 'openness' conveyed by the therapist may vary with the orientation – for example, a psychodynamic role may require more reticence.

The skills which communicate this are:

Inside and outside skills

- **Attention giving** – shown non-verbally by alert and relaxed posture, body lean, eye contact and gaze (not staring), facial expressions and head movements.

Accessibility is expressed by being open to being influenced and affected by the client. This is an inner attitude, dependent upon the therapist's degree of awareness of sensitivity and vulnerability. There is a degree of anxiety and threat in all interpersonal relating. Therapists tend (as human beings) to like approval and fear rejection and this can interfere with their non-verbal messages of receptiveness to the client if they are not aware of, or have not worked on, their interpersonal anxieties.

Being completely present for the client is sometimes called 'presence' and signifies that all the energy is in the moment focused on being with the client. It takes considerable energy. Some barriers which deplete energy are:

- tiredness or being in poor physical condition;
- anxieties about self, performance, role, or present life;
- overlap of therapist's issues with the client's;
- not liking the client – unconditional positive regard does not necessarily mean liking him, but having respect and acceptance for him as a human being as he is at this moment.

Both verbal and non-verbal behaviour can indicate an open willingness to work with the client, a commitment to helping him.

Rogers (1980: 143) suggests:

> To be with another in this way means that for the time being, you lay aside your own views and values in order to enter another's world without prejudice. In some sense it means that you lay aside yourself;

this can only be done by persons who are secure enough in themselves that they know they will not get lost in what may turn out to be the strange and bizarre world of the other, and that they can comfortably return to their own world when they wish.

Some therapists find that relaxation or meditation before a session helps them to gather energy and stack their own issues on one side to be with the client. Ethically, therapists need to know when their energy is so depleted that they cannot give this attention, and refrain from therapy until they are re-energized or emotionally reasonably stable.

Feedback from others can help develop skills of good attention giving and opportunities to view self on video can enable therapists to check how skilled they are, or what might be improved.

- **Observing** – what do you look for? and why are you looking?

What? Physical appearance, posture, facial expressions, dress, grooming, tension, fidgeting, perspiration, blushing, breathing, smell.
Tone and volume of voice, pace, expressiveness, speech difficulties, articulation.
Awareness of and responsiveness to emotions.
Thinking: slow, fast, disjointed, rational.
Congruence between words and body language.
Why? To pick up clues to begin to understand the client from his internal reference point – his view of himself. Looking, listening and resonating give the clues to developing empathy.

'Scanning' your own body during observation can provide clues. People are much more sensitive than they think; they know they may pick up yawning from others, but they also pick up tummy rumbling, emotions and sometimes bodily pains, so by tuning into our own body we can begin to tune in to others. Mostly we need to protect ourselves from too much contact in a crowded world; however, we need to learn to shed this protection when necessary as counsellors or therapists.

- **Listening and hearing** – hearing is picking up the sounds; listening is an inner activity which is aligned with attention giving. Listening to *how* the words are said, the tone, intensity, emotional inflexion, pace, volume, and taking all this in, helps the therapist to catch the precise meaning of the speaker, and what this says about him as a person.

The barriers to good listening are the same as for attention giving. Listening takes a lot of energy. As therapists listen they are remembering, choosing and discriminating what to respond to, monitoring their own thoughts, feelings, images and bodily sensations – listening with their bodies as well as their ears.

Other barriers include the ability to block out or neutralize, dampen down, painful messages or other emotions such as anger, hurt and even joy or elation. Human beings survive in a crowded, often painful world by filtering what is allowed in, not hearing the starving or the abused because of the helpless feelings it engenders. Therapists need to be aware of their defences, their vulnerability to being hurt and sad, or their tendency to dampen down joy or excitement, and stay with what the client may bring, hearing his pain or joy, feeling it but not confusing it with their own.

When clients feel really listened to they are encouraged to talk and reveal themselves. Therapists will often get a lot of information in a first session without asking specific questions, allowing clients to tell their story in their own way, rather than through a formal assessment. On the other hand in brief counselling or therapy, it may be important to get relevant information quickly, then focused questions may be the most practical way.

Accurate listening can help clients to become more aware of their 'inner flow of experiencing'. Some clients may need to be encouraged to acknowledge, experience and express their thoughts and feelings. Good listening may reduce defensiveness and this may enable clients to focus on their own behaviour rather than on what others do to them. Good listening provides psychological space and support for clients' self-exploration.

- **Responding/facilitating skills – outside skills**
On the whole the skills discussed above are receptive ones, communicated through body language. Therapists also need good responding or facilitating

skills, sometimes called the 'active listening skills'. These demonstrate and communicate empathy and acceptance and facilitate exploration.

These skills are sometimes named 'first-level empathy' to distinguish them from 'deeper empathy'. This latter is generally used later in the relationship when the therapist has a deeper understanding of the client's inner world and can sense 'the music behind his words' or what he is not quite expressing, or perhaps emotions or thoughts with which he is not quite in touch. To use advanced empathy at an early stage is risking being inaccurate and may be too challenging for the client.

So, first-level empathy is communicating to the client how he is perceived at this moment. It needs to be as accurate as possible, without adding or subtracting and also identifying the *level* of feeling being expressed. This is sometimes called 'the interchangeable response', meaning it mirrors exactly what the client is expressing. It can be looked at as two skills, 'paraphrasing', picking up the meaning, and 'reflecting feelings'. This combined response is a checking, tentative one and needs to be in the form of a question – with an inflection at the end – not as a definitive statement:

Paraphrasing – picking up the meaning of the client's words and putting it back to him accurately, using your own words and/or his, using a tentative, almost questioning tone, checking you are understanding what he is conveying.
Reflecting feelings – identifying what the client is feeling, often mainly from the non-verbals – tone of voice, bodily expression, your own bodily resonance.

Example:

Client: My manager suggested I came to see you but I'm not sure you can help me, I don't think anybody can.
Therapist: You're not sure about being here, whether it's possible I or anybody can help you?

Done well it enables clients to really hear and understand themselves afresh. There is a saying 'I don't know what I mean until I hear what I say.' Often, hearing themselves will enable clients to explore further and clarify deeper meaning for themselves.

Example:

Client: I feel upset when I hear you say that, I desperately want help, but I am in such a mess I don't know what anybody could do and I think talking about it might make it worse.
Therapist: You sound as if you really want to get some help, but you're afraid that perhaps talking to me might make you feel worse?

Paraphrasing is not parroting – it means having an extensive vocabulary to reflect accurately the feeling and the meaning, and being able to use words that match the client's vocabulary, not using jargon. Notice how the therapist starts the response with 'you' and a 'feeling' followed by a 'thought'. This focuses on the client and his feelings and thoughts – his internal frame. If the counsellor had replied, 'People are often afraid talking will make things worse', that is an outside frame and does not encourage the client to be in touch with himself.

The level of feeling is important. In our culture we often decrease the level, especially of negative feelings, saying perhaps 'You are annoyed' when the client is angry. Therapists need to develop an emotional thesaurus of 'feeling' words, especially being able to distinguish levels. For example: raging, furious, angry, irritable, annoyed, fed up.

One student kept a notebook always with her and wrote down any feeling word she came across, so developing a very good range and ability to reflect accurately. Sometimes getting a reflection wrong enables the client to correct, showing he can express his experience accurately – what Gendlin (1981) calls a 'felt sense'.

Inaccurate reflections can also result from the use of generalized words such as worried, concerned, upset. These are safe in early stages of interaction but may neutralize the intensity of the feelings, avoiding painful feelings and keeping things safe, when it could be useful for the client to risk connecting with stronger feelings, deepening the process of therapy. However, therapists obviously need to be sensitive to different (e.g. class and cultural) subtleties in vocabulary (Kearney, 1996)

Example:

> *Client:* I can't go back to school, I might break
>   down in front of the class.
> not
> *Therapist:* You're too upset to go back to school?
> but
> *Therapist:* Breaking down in front of the class
>   would be very frightening?

Some feeling words are about the situation rather than the client's feelings. For example, to respond 'You feel rejected' describes the situation or something being done to the client, whereas the actual feeling may be sad, angry, frightened; a more accurate response would be 'You feel hurt when you are rejected.' Again this depends on the therapist being able to discriminate, or help the client discriminate, the finer feelings. This is often done by noticing the non-verbal communication from the client.

Sometimes, if the therapist does not express the feelings as exactly as the client experiences them, the client is able to restate them and both can then get an enhanced understanding. However, if the therapist is inaccurate too frequently, the client can begin to feel misunderstood and lose trust in the therapist.

There are further useful exercises in developing the capacity for empathic attunement in Lister-Ford (2002).

• **Summarizing** – is using a combination of the above skills to focus the therapist and client at appropriate points in the interaction. Summarizing can be used:

> as a check that you are together in your understanding;
> to pull out the main thoughts and feelings if a client has talked for several minutes or longer;
> as a bridge for the client to move on;
> to return to something significant;
> to structure the interaction if the therapist or the client is getting lost.

• **Asking questions** – and the kind of questions used, depends on intentions. A danger about asking questions is that it may move clients inappropriately from their internal framework to that of the therapist.

Questions which stay in the 'active listening role' are listed here with examples:

Open questions – questions which encourage the client to expand and say more on the subject:
'I'm not sure I quite understand you – could you say a bit more about your feelings about your brother?' (open and checking)
'Would you like to say how you think therapy could help you?' (open)

Closed questions – questions in which the answer is 'yes' or 'no', do not encourage the client to go on talking but may be the best way of collecting facts:
'Is this your first experience of therapy?' (closed)
'Was your last therapy useful?' (closed) as opposed to –
'In what way was your last therapy useful or not helpful?' (open)

It is often helpful to follow a question with a paraphrase or reflection. This often helps the client to expand further and does not set the interaction into a question/answer form where it may condition the client to wait for the therapist to ask questions.

• **Asking non-threatening questions** – some questions are experienced as threatening by clients because they do not know the therapist's purpose, e.g. 'What is your relationship with your father?' The therapist here is using an insight or theory without taking the client with them in their thinking. To encourage the client to work co-operatively it is ideal to state the clear purpose of questions so that he knows where the questions are coming from – the therapist's agenda is explicit to him. To do this therapists need to be clear of their intentions. 'You're saying you have difficulty with male managers and men in authority and I'm wondering what your relationship was like with your father'. In this last example the therapist has turned the question into a statement. Making statements instead of asking questions can be a very useful way to remove the possible threat from a question and to encourage trust in a client.

• **Questions beginning with 'Why …?'** – 'Why' questions are seldom useful and are sometimes threatening or confusing for the client. Questions using 'in what way', 'what' or 'how' are more encouraging for the client to explore himself: for example, *not* 'Why do you think you are depressed?' *but* 'Can you describe the sort of things that seem to bring on your depression?'

All these skills are the beginning blocks for building a relationship and for helping clients start to explore what they want from the therapist and therapy. In the main they are 'supportive' skills. Skills which continue to build the relationship and develop the interaction will be considered next. These skills are challenging, both for the client and the therapist.

Develop and maintain interaction with clients
Develop the therapeutic relationship: moving the client forward

The skilful weaving together of these two areas provides the on-going work with the client. The following skills are needed for developing both the relationship and the interaction:

Inner	Outer
All the previous skills plus	All the previous skills plus
self-awareness of attitudes to challenge	focusing
scanning inner maps or theories	summarizing
reflecting and recording	concrete examples: deeper empathy challenging appropriate self-disclosure immediacy

Support and challenge

The skills discussed so far can be considered as supportive – helping clients feel safe enough to begin to explore themselves and their situation. To move on in the relationship and the interaction requires skills which will challenge the client to explore further, to

gain new perspectives, new frameworks and see the world in a different way. How the client will receive the challenge will depend on the relationship which has been built and how it is maintained and developed; all the supportive skills will still be needed, appropriately interspersed with the challenging ones.

Inner skills

To challenge well requires inner skills of examining your own feelings about challenge. Do you dislike challenging others, are you afraid of getting angry and letting out negative feelings? Or afraid the client might get angry, leave, or shut down? You may be afraid to go deeper with the client in case you get out of your depth. Alternatively you may enjoy challenge and not be sensitive enough to a client who fears challenge. Timing and tentative challenge are important. It is probably better on the whole to be somewhat reluctant to challenge rather than to be too eager.

Most of these skills require good inner awareness of the therapist's 'process' and this needs practice and attention to personal development.

Clarity is needed on what theories of counselling are being used to develop the interaction. What implicit or explicit theories are guiding the chosen responses? Replaying audiotapes and reflecting on the sessions, especially in supervision, can help identify what values, beliefs, thoughts, feelings, sensations and images are guiding the choices.

Outer skills

Responsible challenging needs well-practised communication skills:

- **Focusing skills** – If clients are to move forward the therapist may need to help them focus. *Summarizing*, as already mentioned, provides bridges, drawing themes together, keeping track, and can be used in three specific ways:

1 Summarize and ask the client to make a *choice*:

   Example:

   Therapist: You're not sure Robert – you're saying your girlfriend is pregnant and is thinking about an abortion which you feel is wrong –

whether you should influence her as you don't really want a permanent relationship with her. It seems as if you're confused about what you want to do, what you ought to do and what others expect of you. You'll perhaps need to explore all those, but which of those might it be useful to start with?

2   Summarize and ask the client for a *contrast*:

Example:

Therapist: Robert, you're worried about Gill deciding on an abortion for your child and that, although you're in love with her, you don't think you want a permanent relationship with her. Would it be useful to look at how you would feel if she left you now and disappeared out of your life?

3   Summarize and bring out the *main focus* as you see it:

Example:

Therapist: Robert, you say Gill is considering an abortion. You feel strongly against it but are not sure how much you should influence her when you don't really want to make a commit- ment to her. You're also aware of your parents' feelings, but it seems as if your main confusion is about how responsible you feel for Gill, for the baby and for yourself. Would it be useful to talk a bit more about that?

Summarizing is a useful skill, requiring: (i) accu- rate listening; (ii) the ability to sort out relevant thoughts and feelings; and (iii) the ability to com- municate them clearly. It is also useful at times to ask the client to summarize, perhaps at the begin- ning or ending of a session, or before a review of the work together.

• **Focusing – asking for concrete examples –** Sometimes it can be useful to ask clients to be more specific about their experiences or their thoughts or feelings.

Examples:

Therapist: You say you feel really angry because you're always being drawn into rows with your mother. Perhaps it would help us both to see how this happens if you could describe in detail the last time this occurred for you.

Therapist: You say you are very frightened of this teacher. Perhaps it would help us both if you could tell me what it is your teacher says to you that frightens you so much.

Both summarizing and focusing provide challenge to clients, as they ask them to look more closely at themselves or at what is happening.

• **Communicating deeper empathy** – This skill is to pick up 'the music behind the words', thoughts and feelings of the client which are perhaps buried, out of reach, implied and which may come to the therapist as an intuition or hunch. The skill is to put it into appropriate words when the timing is right.

Example: identifying a pattern of behaviour and emotion:

Therapist: It seems Jo, from several things you have said, that you don't like to look ahead and plan; you'd rather let things happen. It's almost as if you want surprises and feel life would be dull if you knew what was coming? Perhaps like wanting a surprise birthday present, even if it's not what you really want. Does that make sense to you?

Client: Yeh, I suppose that's true. I've never thought about it that way, and I suppose I often don't get what I really want because I don't want to think ahead. Surprises can be horrid sometimes.

Example: expressing what is only implied:

Client: I could wait to hear from her, but I suppose there's nothing wrong in phoning her to see how she's getting on.

Therapist: You seem to be talking about getting in touch with her, but somehow I feel there doesn't seem to be much enthusiasm in your voice.

Client: You're right, I really don't want to see her – I feel so guilty – and if I get in touch with her, I'll be dragged in again.

The response moves the client on to expressing his real feelings.

• **Challenging** – entails gently confronting clients to change their perspective, see a bigger picture, recognize strengths they are not using, discrepancies between verbal and non-verbal behaviour, or behaviour which is destructive to them or others. Challenging is *an invitation to see* things differently.

Examples:

> *Therapist:* Sue, what I'm hearing from you is that at work you are a very good organizer, you consult and delegate with staff, but don't seem to use those skills to run the home, and I'm wondering if it could be useful for you to look at that? What do you think?
>
> *Therapist:* You're saying, Robert, that you can't choose which of these women you want to live with. Could you change this to 'won't choose' and see how that feels?
>
> *Therapist:* You're telling me how frightened you are of your father, but you're smiling as you say it, and I'm wondering what's going on in your mind, what you're feeling inside?
>
> *Therapist:* You say you want to explore your difficult relationship with your mother, but I notice you move off on to other members of the family. I imagine it's painful for you and I wonder what would help us to stay with you and your mother?

In summary, these skills require risking moving in closer to clients, being sensitive to intentions and to timing, and being able to choose appropriate words and tone of voice. If clients get defensive, be flexible. Supportive skills can be used to explore hurt or anger; to encourage self-challenge; to earn the right to challenge by being open to challenge; to be tentative, build on successes, be specific, challenge strengths rather than weakness and respect the client's values.

• **Self-disclosure** – In some sense therapists cannot help but disclose themselves by all the ways they respond, or even by not responding to the client. By verbal and non-verbal clues the client is construing the meanings, the personality of the therapist, evaluating who and what they are. There are two sorts of therapist self-disclosure – disclosing some experience from the therapist's own life and disclosing some thoughts or feelings the therapist has about the client or his or her experiences.

• **Helpful and unhelpful disclosure** – When is it helpful, purposefully, to disclose some of your experience? It is usually not helpful in the beginning stages when you are concentrating on staying with the client's experience and it needs discrimination what to disclose and when.

Advantages

- It can act as a model for the client to talk more openly about him or herself.
- It can build the relationship.
- It can shorten the psychological distance between the client and counsellor, produce more intimacy, more trust.
- If the therapist discloses difficulties he or she has overcome – e.g. bereavement, addiction – it can encourage and challenge the client; many self-help groups work on this principle.

Disadvantages

- The client may feel unsafe to see the therapist as less well adjusted.
- It can be too challenging, and increased intimacy may threaten the client.
- Clients may see themselves or their difficulties as very different from their therapists and therefore are not encouraged to help themselves.
- Self-help groups may work because it is 'peer' experience, but the therapist is not a peer.
- Intentional self-disclosure is considered by some therapists to be always poor practice.

As with all challenge it needs a secure enough relationship. It needs to be used selectively and focused flexibly – an art, not a science.

Example:

> *Client:* Since my partner died I can't face the day, there doesn't seem any point to anything. I just feel lost all the time and my daughter worries I'm not looking after myself.
>
> *Appropriate response:* You sound as if it's hard for you to get through the day. I remember when my partner died I felt as if all the structure to my life had disappeared and it was very hard to make myself do anything.
>
> *Inappropriate response:* I know how you feel; when my partner died I was like that, but I got over it and recovery happened in time.

Example:

> *Client:* I don't know what it is really. I just feel very low and know I could do better but I can't make the effort. I worked hard at school to get here and I've wanted to be a lawyer for as long as I can remember, but now I'm here I should be feeling happy but I just feel fed up and depressed.
>
> *Appropriate response:* I think when I was at university I was often critical and bored but I think I knew it was what I wanted. It seems, perhaps, it is different for you. Although you say you always wanted to be a lawyer, perhaps now you know more about it you're not sure it's what you want to do?
>
> *Inappropriate response:* I can remember my second year and I felt just like that, so I know how badly you must feel. But I managed to stick at it and get my degree and that's got me where I wanted to be.

Inappropriate responses are often just relating the therapist's experience and sometimes sounding rather smug. However similar the situation, each individual will experience it differently and may not want to be classified as similar to you, especially if they perceive you as very different in class, race, age, etc.

• **Sharing the therapist's own thoughts or feelings** – can be useful in sharing some transferential patterns:

Example:

> *Therapist:* I noticed I was feeling very sad when you talked about your mother and your easy relationship with her. I wondered, is there, perhaps, some sadness there for you?

Or sharing thoughts or feelings:

> *Therapist:* As I think about your life, both at home and at work, I'm wondering, perhaps trying to do two full-time jobs would make *me* want to give up one of them.
>
> *Therapist:* Nasreen I'm finding it quite hard to imagine not sharing such an important decision with your husband.

Responses such as these can be a challenge to the client, maybe to enable them to see alternative frames of reference.

Things to remember about self-disclosure:

• Don't use it too soon in a session.
• Keep the focus on the client.
• Be brief.
• Don't overburden the client with your concerns, and be flexible.
• 'If I were you' usually means 'if you were me'.
• Use only if it is for the good of the client, not for your need to share.
• Recognize your power to influence the client.

• **Immediacy** – is one of the most useful skills of counselling and psychotherapy, and probably the most difficult to do well. It is sometimes called 'you–me talk' or 'I messages'. It is about discussing directly and openly with the client what is happening between the therapist and the client, at the moment, or about something that has happened in the recent past. It involves awareness of what is going on inside the therapist and imagining or guessing what is happening in the client and between the therapist and the client.

Example:

> *Therapist:* Jim, when you said you were afraid to tell me because I would disapprove of you, I admit I felt hurt that you couldn't share it with me. Would it be useful to explore how far you feel you can trust me?

It is quite a difficult thing to say, but does help clients open up what may be a difficult area for them. It also provides a model of speaking about thoughts and feelings not usually expressed.

Immediacy can also help clients understand how their behaviour may be affecting other people:

Example:

> *Therapist:* When you say 'that's not the way it ought to be', I feel a bit battered by you, as if you're forcing me to see your point of view and I wonder if that's how your wife feels, and if that makes it difficult for her to discuss things with you. Do you think that might be so?

Immediacy can sometimes help when the therapeutic relationship seems otherwise to be foundering.

Example:

> *Therapist:* I felt last week that you went home angry with me, but you didn't express it, and I wondered if I had upset you. Would it be useful to talk about it?

Immediacy is a complex skill involving competence in attending, listening, empathy, self-disclosure, and making self-involving statements. It requires the therapist to be assertive, have courage to take risks and also, most importantly, an awareness of 'process', or of what is happening from moment to moment internally, inside the client and in the 'dance' between therapist and client. Using IPR can be very helpful in developing this skill. Using audio or video recall to explore these processes, and to put into words what *might* have been said, enables the therapist to become more aware and to become competent at using the skill. It is important to develop an 'impartial witness' of feelings and thoughts, not to judge but to acknowledge them and be able to use them in the way the therapist works with the client. Practice with IPR also helps in identifying transference and counter-transference.

Part of the skill of immediacy is knowing when to use it – it can be useful when:

- a session seems bogged down;
- there is tension in the relationship;
- trust is an issue;
- there are differences in class, race, sexuality, etc., which need to be explored;
- dependency or attraction seems to be blocking;
- the therapist is confused by the client.

Used well it can build or repair a therapeutic relationship, promote a shared working situation, develop congruence, and deepen the interaction. It is also a very useful skill in all human relationships.

All the skills in this section require a lot of practice with feedback, both for developing the inner and outer skills. This leads on to the last section.

Monitor self within the therapeutic process
Evaluate and develop own work

These competencies need all the previous skills plus the additional skills listed here.

SELF-MANAGEMENT SKILLS

- developing a caring acceptance of yourself and an impartial witness of your internal processes;
- identifying and using resources to meet learning, emotional, physical and spiritual needs;
- on-going identification and checking of values, beliefs and theories;
- planning on-going training and personal development;
- reflecting, recording, presenting and using supervision;
- reviewing with clients;
- asking for feedback from clients.

The above skills are necessary to develop as a foundation for the supporting and challenging skills. It is the learning and practising of these skills that enables the therapist to translate theory into competent practice with clients. Skills do not make a counsellor or psychotherapist but an unskilled therapist may harm rather than help clients.

References

BACP (2002) *Accreditation of Training Courses* (4th edn). Rugby: BACP.

Carkhuff, R.R. (1969) *Helping and Human Relations I: Selection and Training.* New York: Holt, Rinehart and Winston.

Casement, P. (1985) *On Learning from the Patient.* London: Routledge.

Connor, M. (1994) *Training the Counsellor: An Integrative Model.* London and New York: Routledge.

Crouch, A. (1997) *Inside Counselling.* London: Sage.

Gendlin, E. (1981) *Focusing.* New York: Bantam Books.

Inskipp, F. (1996) *Skills Training for Counselling.* London: Cassell.

Ivey, A.E. (1971) *Microcounseling: Innovations in Interviewing Training.* Springfield: Charles C. Thomas.

Joyce, P. and Sills, C. (2001) *Skills in Gestalt Counselling and Psychotherapy.* London: Sage.

Kagan, N. (1975) *Influencing Human Interaction.* Washington, DC: American Personnel and Guidance Association.

Kearney, A. (1996) *Counselling, Class and Politics: Undeclared Influences in Therapy.* Manchester: PCCS Books.

Lister-Ford, C. (2002) *Skills in Transactional Analysis Counselling and Psychotherapy.* London: Sage.

Mearns, D. (1994) *Developing Person-centred Counselling.* London: Sage.

Rogers, C.R. (1957) The necessary and sufficient conditions of therapeutic personality change. *Journal of Consulting Psychology*, 21: 95–103.

Rogers, C.R. (1980) *A Way of Being.* Boston: Houghton Mifflin.

Tolan, J. (2003) *Skills in Person-centred Counselling and Psychotherapy.* London: Sage.

Truax, C.B. and Carkhuff, R.R. (1967) *Toward Effective Counseling and Psychotherapy: Training and Practice.* Chicago: Aldine.

Wyatt, G. and Sanders, P. (eds) (2002) *Rogers' Therapeutic Conditions: Evolution, Theory and Practice.* Ross-on-Wye: PCCS Books.

3.4   Specific Strategies and Techniques   ○○○

GORDON JINKS

This section is intended to give the reader an awareness of the range of intervention strategies available to a counsellor or therapist operating in an integrative or eclectic way. The relative merits of this as against operating from a single theoretical framework will not be discussed here except to make the pragmatic point that the use of a range of techniques from different theoretical traditions appears from the research to be very common. This is not intended to be a comprehensive manual for the use of the strategies outlined, and therapists must ensure that they have the necessary underpinning to use whatever techniques they employ and work safely with material that might be raised for the client. Counselling and therapy are contracted activities which involve a working alliance between therapist and client. The values underpinning the alliance – described as client empowerment, respect, and genuineness by Egan (2001) – imply that the client has a right to take part in decisions about how they are to be helped: to set their own goals, to understand the techniques which might be used to help them, and to exercise choice about what techniques are used. It is therefore important that therapists become skilled at discussing possible helping strategies with clients, and empower them to take an active part in therapeutic planning. We must also be aware of the need to use techniques genuinely at the service of the client, not in order to be seen to be doing something as a substitute for the hard work of sustained listening and empathy, or because we have preference for a particular technique. The section is subdivided to cover techniques which primarily address behaviours, feelings, imagery, cognitions, and interpersonal factors.

Behaviours

A wide range of techniques have been developed in behaviour therapy (see, for example, Wolpe, 1990), which can be adapted for eclectic or integrative therapy.

Modelling, rehearsal, reinforcement

The sequence of modelling, rehearsal and reinforcement is a powerful one for helping clients to develop desired new behaviours, and is frequently used in developing assertiveness, social skills, or confronting feared situations. Modelling is based on the principles of social learning theory (Bandura, 1977): that much learning is derived from observing role models; that individuals tend to select models whom they respect, trust, and perceive as competent; and that the most useful models are those whose level of performance is seen as achievable and not so skilled as to seem out of reach. Rehearsal and reinforcement are based on operant conditioning – that behaviour is most likely to be repeated if it is positively reinforced.

The process begins by the client and therapist discussing the behaviour the client would like to achieve, and trying to develop a clear picture of what it might look like. Examples of behaviours which could be addressed in this way are dealing more assertively with colleagues at work, sharing feelings more openly, public speaking, and managing conflict or aggression. The more specific the client can be about what they want to be able to do, and to what standard, the better. (An important check here is to explore any possible negative consequences of a change that the client is considering, and this may need to be returned to when the client is ready to begin putting changes into practice.) The client then observes a model of the desired behaviour. They may have identified an external role model, who behaves as they would like to in a given situation, and can be observed. Alternatively, the modelling may fall to the therapist, who can role-play a situation demonstrating the behaviour the client wishes to be able to achieve. The client should be asked to give feedback on the extent to which the therapist's performance reflects what they see as desirable and achievable, and the role-play modified until the client is satisfied with what they are seeing. The client may also develop some useful insight during this process by taking the other role in the role-play.

The client then rehearses in role-play with the therapist (or some other situation if appropriate),

until they are able to achieve a performance that they are happy with and feel they can reproduce in the real situation. After each rehearsal the client should be encouraged to recognize what they were happy with about their performance, rather than focusing on shortcomings, and receive congruent praise from the therapist. In the next rehearsal the client will try to repeat what has gone well, but also develop the behaviour in other aspects – a technique known as *shaping* in the terminology of behaviour therapy. For example, in rehearsing assertive behaviour the client may be able to act assertively up to a certain point, at which something said by the other causes them to 'crumple'. It will be most useful if the client can see this as a success *up to* that point, rather than a failure *at* that point. They can subsequently try to repeat the success, but add something new to deal with the response that caused the crumple. The success of this process is influenced by the atmosphere in which it is undertaken, so the therapist's sensitivity to the needs and responses of individual clients is likely to be crucial. While it can be presented as a series of steps in a technical manner, the therapeutic benefit will be greater if the client is really engaged in the process, and maybe even has a bit of fun, but also sees it as sufficiently realistic to be a meaningful rehearsal for the real situation. This requires the therapist to continue to relate to the client with empathy during the process, rather than adopting a detached didactic position. As ever, achieving a balance between supporting the client and challenging them to stretch themselves is an important part of what the therapist should be aiming for.

Helping the client to implement the new behaviour in the real situation benefits from careful planning. Important considerations will be the sequencing of where and when this is to be attempted, how it can be positively reinforced, and contingency planning for what might go wrong. Some will benefit from fairly elaborate timetables with target dates and reward schemes, while others may prefer a looser, more evolutionary approach, with a mechanism for monitoring of progress. The therapist will often be a useful part of the monitoring process, particularly in the early stages, but it is important that the client develops self-monitoring strategies, perhaps involving significant others, if changes are to be sustained. Ongoing reinforcement for the new behaviour can be explored with the client, and *social reinforcers* identified – ways in which the new behaviour will be rewarded by the client's social circumstances and environment. If the client is more consciously able to recognize the benefits of the changes they are making, the new behaviours are more likely to be sustained.

Desensitization

Desensitization is a structured technique designed to help individuals come to terms with anxiety-provoking stimuli in a gradual and step-wise way, using relaxation techniques as a counter-measure against the anxiety. The client must first become practised in a relaxation technique that is effective for them (see p. 92), then uses this prior to exposure to their feared stimulus, initially in a very mild form, then gradually increasing in strength as they become desensitized to its effect. The client can determine a suitable pace for him or herself and advance in steps of a manageable size. The intention is that at each step of the process the strength of the anxiety-provoking stimulus will be sufficient to generate a noticeable anxious response, but not sufficient to disrupt the relaxation previously induced. The client can then experience feeling the anxiety, but being able to control it, and feeling it subside with time. The therapist's role is to explain the technique, structure the process, provide support and encouragement during sessions, and help to monitor and evaluate progress. Pacing of this process is important – the client needs to see each step as manageable and experience success, but each step also needs to be challenging enough so that meaningful progress is seen to be made. Ongoing evaluation may lead to some steps being condensed together, or other steps being inserted as a programme unfolds. If a given step does turn out to be too much, a return to the previous level and the insertion of one or two intermediate steps is called for. The client usually benefits from feeling actively involved in designing and maintaining the programme. So, for example, a client with a powerful anxiety reaction to rats was helped to draw up a programme of increasingly powerful stimuli beginning with simple line drawings, progressing to black and white pictures, colour pictures, and then video. The client took control of the process, uncovering pictures when she felt ready, and using a remote control with video images. Each step was repeated by the client between sessions to reinforce success. The sessions culminated with some visits to come into contact with and handle live rats, and the client was very surprised with what she was ultimately able to achieve by taking gradual steps. A useful principle in desensitization programmes is to try to help clients reach a level which is a little beyond what they will normally have to cope with to allow room for some 'slippage' after the programme is finished. The process of dealing with difficulties in a step-wise fashion underlies a number of the techniques which follow.

Exposure

Exposure techniques rely on the fact that if one is exposed to a feared stimulus, and is able to stay with it rather than retreating, then in time the level of anxiety will inevitably decline. On a physical level this occurs because the body will not sustain the same level of stimulation in the face of an ongoing threat as is generated when the threat first appears; while on a psychological level, time spent in the presence of a feared stimulus which does not result in harm leads the individual to re-assess the threat posed by the stimulus. The reduction in anxiety serves as a positive reinforcement for facing the fear. A rather extreme way of using these in-built processes is known as *flooding* and involves immersing oneself in the worst feared situation until the anxiety declines to a manageable level. While this has considerable risks as a therapeutic procedure, some clients have been known to apply this technique to themselves – 'I'm just going to get in there and face it, and if it doesn't kill me then I'll have beaten it'. However a more cautious approach or *graded exposure* is usually preferable. The client can be asked to list feared or difficult situations, covering a range from the relatively mild to the most severe. These would be rated for difficulty, and ordered with the least difficult first. The client would be helped to develop strategies for confronting and coping with each situation in turn, including ways of managing negative emotions, such as relaxation or scripted messages to repeat to themselves. The technique of step-wise exposure to difficult situations can be applied to the level of exposure as well as to the difficulty level of the situation. Thus a given situation can be confronted in fantasy (the client imagines themselves in the situation, perhaps as an observer first, then a participant); in rehearsal or role-play; and then *in vivo* (real life). This might be used, for example, with a client who has to attend a difficult meeting or interview.

Exposure *in vivo* is often a crucial step in any programme of assisting a client to change their behaviour, as it represents the move from talking about or imagining change to actually doing it. A programme of exposure *in vivo* may be developed as homework for a client, but it is also worth considering 'therapist-assisted exposure' – being present with the client while they confront a situation – where this is practical within the established contract/boundaries. The counsellor/therapist's skills are useful in supporting and challenging the client while they take a step forward, they can assist the client in monitoring anxiety (perhaps using rating scales) and can prompt the client to employ prepared coping mechanisms. Understanding of the client is likely to be deepened and the working alliance strengthened by such activity.

Response prevention

Response prevention is a technique which has been developed primarily for use with sufferers from obsessive-compulsive states and is used in combination with various types of exposure. The technique relates to the situation where an individual feels compelled to act in a certain way in response to a given stimulus – a typical example might be someone who feels compelled to wash their hands after touching a door handle. Response prevention involves delaying that response for increasing periods to help the client gain control of the behaviour. So initially the client might wait for a minute before going to wash their hands, then two minutes, then five minutes, ten, and so on – using relaxation techniques to learn to control the anxiety in the intervening

period of time. The key here is that the client is not initially denying themselves the compulsive response, but is learning to control it rather than be controlled by it. At some point it becomes unnecessary to carry out the compulsive behaviour at all. Some clients are able to adapt this technique for use with a variety of apparently compulsive behaviours such as smoking, spending, eating, self-harm, seeking reassurance or making self-deprecating remarks. Many clients also report that the period of delay tends to lessen the severity of the compulsive behaviour when it is carried out.

Homework

Various ways in which homework can be incorporated into the therapeutic process have been alluded to above. The norm for counselling and psychotherapy in the UK in many contexts seems to be moving in the direction of a relatively small number of sessions at weekly intervals, and if real change is to be achieved and sustained under such a contract it seems sensible to think carefully about the part that homework might play. At the most open-ended this might involve asking the client 'What could you be doing between now and the next time we meet which would consolidate or develop what we've been doing today?'. Many approaches would allow or even encourage the therapist to be more directive in the setting of homework tasks, but developing homework tasks in collaboration with the client will give them more ownership of the process and is desirable. Homework can have a number of different aims. Often it will be about facing a difficult situation, trying a new behaviour, or putting into practice something which has been rehearsed or prepared in a session – in a sense tasks which are part of the outcome of the therapeutic journey. However, homework might also be part of the process, and could involve reflecting on a particular aspect of one's situation, continuing to work on a list of ideas or the detail of a plan, getting feedback from others, or gathering resources. It also provides the opportunity for significant others in the client's life to be involved in the helping process by being engaged for support, reinforcement or feedback.

- Making or expanding lists: for example, anxiety-provoking situations, desired achievements, strategies

- Practising steps of desensitization or graded exposure programmes

- Relaxation techniques

- Diary keeping

- Bibliotherapy

- Classes – for example, assertiveness

- Dream recall – maintaining a dream diary

- Practising specific behaviours in specific situations

- Writing – creative or autobiographical

Figure 3.4.1   Examples of homework

The therapist needs to be sensitive to the client's motivation. If a client seems reluctant to undertake a particular activity it may be useful to revisit the goal for that activity. If the client feels that this goal is worth achieving then other ways can be examined for achieving it, and hopefully a different homework activity agreed on. For example, a client was working on dissatisfaction with her social life, and had become aware of how she tended to discourage new people she met in social situations, closing down opportunities to get involved in conversation. Discussing homework, she somewhat reluctantly said that she thought she was 'going to have to try' to have a conversation with someone new in the next week. Previous experience of this client suggested a tendency to set herself up for failure, so it seemed appropriate to reflect the reluctance before asking what having this conversation would achieve. It became clear that the client wanted to take a risk of being rejected, and stay with it, so other ways of achieving this which she might be more willing to try, and more likely to succeed with, were explored. The homework task settled on was visiting an acquaintance unexpectedly, and a successful conversation with someone new happened a few weeks later without formal planning. See Figure 3.4.1 for a summary of examples of homework tasks.

Diary keeping

From a behavioural standpoint keeping a diary can be useful in exploring relationships between stimuli, behaviours and reinforcerment. Sometimes patterns become apparent which might not otherwise have been so clear – for example, periods of drinking tend to follow disagreements at work, or angry outbursts are being reinforced by the allowances made by others afterwards. If a particular behaviour is to be focused on, an A–B–C (antecedent–behaviour–consequence) format can be used in the diary, whereby each incidence of the behaviour is recorded in the form of a description of what happened before it occurred, the details of the behaviour itself, and the events that followed. The client and therapist can then discuss this record and perhaps clarify patterns. Links between behaviour and other aspects of experience such as thoughts, feelings and perceptions may also become clearer as a result of diary keeping. Figure 3.4.2 shows an example of a structured format for diary keeping which can be varied to suit the individual needs of the client. Once the client is engaged on a change programme, a diary can be a useful tool for monitoring progress, and can serve as both stimulus and reinforcement in itself by highlighting target dates, and being a place where success is recorded. Some clients find it useful

Day/Date	Time	Significant event (What happened?)	Antecedents (What had been happening before?)	Thoughts (What were you aware of thinking?)	Consequences (Including feelings and behaviour)

Figure 3.4.2   Example of a diary format

to develop ground rules about how they will use the diary, perhaps to ensure that it does not solely become a place for complaining about others or criticizing oneself.

A diary can also be valuable as a tool for reflection, and clients may wish to do this in a structured way. A simple structure for reflecting on key events is: *what?* (description and exploration of the event); *so what?* (implications, new understanding: what have I learnt?); *now what?* (goals and actions: what am I going to do as a result?). Clients may also be able to recognize and own their feelings more effectively when they have the activity of writing about them to focus on, and those who have difficulty expressing their feelings in conversation may be able to do so on paper. Some may also enjoy using diaries not just for writing, but to include drawings, pictures, cuttings, and poetry, if given permission to do so. The currently expanding field of 'therapeutic writing' (see, for example, Bolton et al., 2004) is worth exploring for the benefits it can offer clients.

Relaxation

There is now a wide range of resources available to help an individual learn the skills of relaxation, including self-help books, tapes, videos, alternative therapies, and classes, so regular relaxation may not be the most cost-effective way a therapist and client can use their valuable time together. The therapist's role may rather be to help clients clarify their needs, and choose from the available resources. However, a counsellor or psychotherapist may still need a repertoire of relaxation techniques to deal with anxiety 'on the spot' if it becomes acute within a session, or to teach clients to use for themselves. A repertoire of techniques is important because clients vary greatly in their responses to the techniques available, and each individual may need to try several before finding one which suits them. Relaxation techniques are most useful when developed as a habit carried out every day. The habit tends to diminish one's general level of stress or anxiety, and one also becomes skilled at inducing relaxation, which can then be done in time of need.

Relaxation involves the interplay of physical and psychological factors and the feedback loops which exist between the human body and psyche. It is difficult for the mind to remain tense when the body is relaxed, and vice versa, so relaxation techniques can focus on either physical or psychological relaxation. Physical techniques most commonly employ muscle or breathing control. The tensing and relaxing of various muscle groups in turn, working through the whole body, or just face and neck, helps the client to bring into clear awareness the differences in sensation between muscle tension and relaxation, and learn to control this for themselves. The control of breathing makes use of the powerful links that exist between breathing and state of arousal. A state of relaxation is related to a slower and deeper pattern of breathing and to the use of the abdominal and diaphragm muscles to draw in breath, rather than the chest muscles. If one can learn to adopt such a breathing pattern by conscious control it becomes very difficult to sustain a state of psychological tension.

Psychological techniques usually involve giving the mind a task to perform which is absorbing yet relaxing. Guided imagery is a common example – the client is asked to adopt a relaxed posture and close their eyes if it is comfortable to do so, before being guided in imagining a relaxing scenario or series of experiences. Care needs to be taken in constructing these experiences, first to avoid any imagery which might be distressing to a particular individual, but also in the use of language and what is specified as against what is left to the client's imagination. A general principle is to avoid specifying anything which will jar with what the client has already imagined for themselves, and to use different channels of experience as a means of elaborating an experience rather than specific detail. So, for example, if a client is instructed 'Imagine yourself lying on a warm sandy beach', a fairly detailed image is likely to occur quite quickly for most clients. If the person guiding the relaxation then starts to specify details such as the texture of the sand, the colour of the sky, or how crowded the beach is, which are not what the client had imagined, this is unlikely to be experienced as relaxing. More useful would be instructions such as 'Notice the texture of the sand … and the colour of the sky … Focus on the sounds you can hear …'. Some clients like to have tapes of guided imagery in a voice they are familiar with to assist them in practising at home.

Other psychological relaxation techniques which can be suggested to clients include immersing themselves in favourite pieces of music, and the technique of 'noticing'. Here, one focuses one's attention on a specific object, and spends a period of time attending to the object in great detail, trying to take in as much as possible about its shape, colour, texture and detail. It can be a pleasant surprise how much there is to be seen even in apparently simple objects. This technique can also be practised on a walk, where trying to notice as much detail as possible about one's environment is often experienced, paradoxically, as relaxing.

Once an individual client has learned to achieve a state of relaxation, classical conditioning can be used to help them to access that state in times of stress, by establishing a link with a key word, image, or physical sensation they can bring about unobtrusively. The key word, image or sensation might be part of the relaxation technique which the client finds effective, or can be introduced into it when the client has become practised. So, for example, the word 'warm' repeated inwardly, an image of a soft blanket, or gentle pressure on the back of one's hand might be used to help a client trigger relaxation more quickly than by going through the full process they have learned.

Affects/feelings

Levels of empathy

In terms of the activity required of the therapist, empathy can be described as having four dimensions: *perception* (what the therapist hears or sees from the client), *affect* (what the therapist feels when listening to the client), *cognition* (what the therapist understands and imagines about the client's experience), and *communication*. The therapist communicates empathy both verbally and non-verbally, and this communication can selectively include each of the other three dimensions – feeding back what the therapist has heard or seen, checking the validity of understanding or imagining, and sharing the therapist's emotional response.

Levels of empathy can be defined in terms of the depth of understanding achieved and communicated (Carkhuff, 1969; Egan, 2001). Basic or primary empathy involves understanding and communicating what has been expressed by the client directly, and is generally communicated by relatively simple empathic responses such as paraphrasing, summarizing, and reflecting feeling. Advanced empathy involves awareness of the client at a deeper level – that which has only partly been expressed or alluded to. This involves a much closer attention not just to what is said, but to how it is said, and to the therapist's own affective responses. There is more scope for inaccuracy here – the therapist may have a hunch about what is going on for the client, but should also have some awareness of the origins of the hunch, and should share it with the client only when basic empathy has been established. Advanced empathy may be expressed by interventions such as: 'I notice some tension in your face when you say … and I wonder if that might mean …', or: 'As I was listening to you I noticed that I began to feel … and I was wondering if any of that was around for you'. Some practitioners focus particularly on the client's idiosyncratic metaphors and imagery, trying to develop understanding of the complexity that is conveyed, while others (e.g. Mahrer, 1996) attempt to work wholly within the client's affective experience by closing their eyes and speaking 'with' the client: 'I'm feeling heavy, sad …'. Advanced empathy may communicate understanding of aspects of the client's experience that the client was not fully aware of, so should be used tentatively, and seen as opening up an area for exploration if the client wishes.

The consideration of a level of empathy relating to cultural understanding seems a useful addition to the concept. Cultural empathy is about striving for understanding of the interactions between the client, the client's culture (including experiences, values, and beliefs), the therapist, and the therapist's culture, and recognizing that communication between therapist and client can be influenced by any of these factors. Expressing and checking one's understanding of these interactions, and inviting the client to do the same will be useful interventions in building a strong empathic bond.

Cathartic work

Cathartic work can be very challenging for the therapist, because it involves the client making contact with and expressing their feelings, often feelings which are painful to face or difficult to contain. All of us at times will experience reluctance towards opening the 'can of worms' which we fear we may struggle to deal with. It is equally possible, having got over this reluctance, to fall into a way of thinking that sees counselling and psychotherapy as being all about catharsis, and develop the habit of making cathartic interventions when this is not what the client has come for or wants, but rather what the therapist feels they need. Therapists need to walk a fine line here: neither discouraging clients from making contact with difficult feelings (possibly colluding in efforts to deny them); nor pulling down clients' carefully constructed defences without their permission. Clients tend to know when they are ready and able to get in touch with deeper emotions, and signal this to the therapist in some way (sometimes non-verbally, perhaps through moist eyes or clenched fists). There needs to be agreement to undertake cathartic work and clients should have a clear idea of what they are hoping to achieve. However, release of powerful emotion can occur unexpectedly, and it may sometimes be appropriate to check quickly whether the client wishes to go on, rather than lose the moment through contracting and goal-setting procedures.

In the least structured way of approaching cathartic work, the therapist concentrates carefully on accurate empathic responses, both basic and advanced, and this will almost inevitably lead a willing client into a deeper contact with their emotions. Empathic responses in cathartic work are most effective when the work is done in the present tense and the focus is on what the client is experiencing in the here and now (e.g. 'You are looking very sad as you talk about your brother'). Although this may involve re-living or re-experiencing past traumas or painful memories, the therapist will communicate empathy more effectively by responding to what the client is feeling as they re-experience, rather than focusing on what they were feeling in the past. Careful pacing, appropriate use of silence, and attention to non-verbal communication will help the client to actually feel and experience, rather than talk *about* their feelings. The therapist should not be afraid of silence while the client cries or experiences their anger. Staying in touch with the client and one's own responses, being open about sharing these, and providing a safe holding environment where the client can feel able to discharge emotion are the essential skills in managing this process, rather than needing to be completely in control of the course of the session. Some thought needs to be given to how the boundaries of the therapeutic hour will be managed in relation to cathartic work, and whether any flexibility is to be allowed. In planned cathartic work it may be advisable to allow for a specific session to be longer (e.g. 90 minutes). Near the end of a cathartic session it is useful to ask the client what they would like to do in order to prepare themselves to leave. It will often be helpful to shift into a more cognitive processing of what has happened, asking the client what they have discovered or learned during the session. Some clients also find brief visualization exercises helpful, for example visualizing themselves closing a book and putting it away, or symbolically packing up the contents of the session into a suitable container until they decide to look at them again.

More structured approaches to cathartic work (for example Heron, 1990; Mahrer, 1996) tend to be tailored to the type of material being worked with. Single traumatic events can be approached by re-telling at different levels. The client begins with a literal description of the event, so that both parties can be clear about what happened. This is followed by a first-person, present-tense account – as though it were happening now, with greater attention to the emotional content, in particular the feelings which arise for the client during the re-telling. The therapist should attend carefully to the client's non-verbal communication, and listen for slips of the tongue, brief asides and throwaway comments, blocks and pauses, and elements which the client appears to skate over. Sharing what has been noticed with the client and inviting them to respond will often lead to a deeper examination of a more difficult aspect of the client's feelings.

If an event cannot be clearly recalled, the client can be invited to describe what they imagine might have happened, and work with this in a similar way. A number of cautions are important here. The client is being helped to process their present feelings about what might have happened in the past, not to uncover what actually did happen. If the client's goal is to determine what actually did happen, then asking them to imagine what might have happened is probably inappropriate, and certainly unreliable. Such cathartic work on past events will at times lead to the recovery of memory, sometimes in the form of dramatic and sudden flashbacks which can be very distressing for clients. Clients should enter this sort of work from a position of informed consent, aware of the possible consequences, and it is important to consider strategies for dealing with flashback experiences if they occur – in particular being clear about who the client can turn to for support between sessions. Clients and therapists need to be aware that the validity of such recovered memories is a matter of dispute within the legal system, but the prime concern of the therapist remains the welfare of the client. This may necessitate processing such recovered memories, whether or not they can be considered legally valid, though clearly there is a need to be very cautious in avoiding implanting suggestions.

In working with sequences of events, or recurring patterns in the client's life, catharsis can be facilitated by encouraging the client to move from generalizations towards specific and detailed descriptions of examples. They can be asked to pick an event that seems particularly significant, a typical example, the oldest, most recent, or first example that comes to mind, and explore it in more depth as described above. On the other hand, some clients find themselves getting lost in detail of specific events and cartharsis may only occur when the therapist helps them to become aware of themes and recurring patterns. When issues of loss are involved, objects or photographs which help the client to connect with the loss can be a useful focus for cathartic work. Physical acting out of difficult emotions may also help clients who have problems experiencing them fully, for example using cushions as a focus for anger, or to hold on to. Clients can also be invited to repeat emotive phrases, address an absent person directly as 'you', use the therapist as a 'stand in', or complete emotive sentences.

Empty chair work

Empty chair work (Houston, 1990; Zinker, 1977) can be very helpful for raising awareness in clients and bringing feelings, relationships, or conflicts to life in the therapy room, rather than being a subject for speculation or discussion. Used judiciously, it can benefit clients who struggle to express difficult emotions such as grief or anger. The client is encouraged to act out both sides of a dialogue, perhaps between themselves and some significant other person, between different parts of themselves (for example 'confident me' and 'insecure me'), between their present self and some past or future self, or between themselves and some more abstract entity (such as the organization they work for or the place they live). The client should change position when adopting different roles, so two (or more) chairs will be used. This is a potentially powerful technique, and is probably best presented to a client as an experiment they might like to try, with no pre-set outcome. The therapist should suggest that clients take their time and try to feel free to go with whatever occurs to them during the exercise. Clients should be given permission to stop the process at any point if they wish to, and any resistance or reluctance should be responded to empathically and explored. As is often the case, there may be more therapeutic benefit in exploring the resistance than in forging ahead with whatever is being resisted.

The dialogue is best conducted in the first person present tense from each position to make it more present and real. Some clients will find this a bit awkward at first and may begin with statements like, 'Well, I would say that he shouldn't be so critical of me', while looking at the therapist. A gentle suggestion to 'Say it to him', while indicating the empty chair, will often get the dialogue going. When the client seems to have expressed what they want to from one position they can be encouraged to try out the other chair and respond to what has been said, and move backwards and forwards as much as they wish, to play out the dialogue. At times the therapist may wish to share an observation or ask a question of one of the roles, but should be careful not to interrupt the flow of the dialogue too much for the client, as spontaneity will often lead to useful insights. A so-called 'top dog–under dog' dialogue may emerge, where one party appears to be in a position of power over the other or be communicating from a 'critical parent' position. The therapist

can then support the under dog in expressing its point of view, and dealing assertively with the top dog. When the client has taken the dialogue as far as they wish, they can be invited to reflect on what has happened, and what seemed significant. Useful feedback to the client during this process will generally be observations, rather than interpretations. Discussion may suggest some further dialogue work, or lead into an evaluation of what has been learned or is different as a result. Clients report a variety of benefits from such work, including new insights into their feelings and conflicts, or what might be going on for others; new ideas about how to move forward or resolve conflicts; a sense of satisfaction at having got something off their chest, even if only to an empty chair; decisions made; or a raised awareness of deeper feelings. They are often surprised about how much such an exercise seems to have changed their perspective, and may need time to talk this over to make sense of it.

Imagery

Use of metaphors

Metaphors can be useful either when therapists respond to the metaphorical communication of clients, encouraging them to elaborate and explore their imagery; or when therapists use metaphorical communication themselves to communicate their understanding, share a new perspective, or convey a message to clients. In either case metaphors offer an opportunity for communication that is less concrete, more creative and flexible, and can sometimes bypass normal inhibitions or limitations (see, for example, Riikonen and Smith, 1997).

Metaphorical communication is often ignored. When a client talks about experiencing a knot in their stomach, it would be quite normal for the therapist to assume a shared understanding of what that feels like, and proceed as though the client had described tightness or tension. The metaphor of the knot is an opportunity to work in a different way to transform the experience. The client can be asked to describe the knot in more detail as a metaphor, exploring its texture, shape, and colour to engage more fully in the experience it represents, and may even wish to draw it. The client can then visualize its disentangling. In learning to take control of the image they may be able to take control of the reality, using the image of the knot being disentangled as an aid to relaxation. So in listening to clients a therapist should try to notice the images and metaphors which clients use to express themselves. The bridges, crossroads, gulfs, mountains, lights, tunnels, fogs and swamps which clients mention can all be picked up, elaborated, and used to deepen empathic understanding, and possibly to transform meaning and experience – either through visualizing changes, or linking back to objective description by exploring what would be involved in clearing a path through the swamp, or how the bridge could be made more secure. Metaphorical communication can help clients to conceptualize their difficulties more clearly or differently, and to look for solutions from a new perspective.

Emotive imagery

Emotive imagery techniques involve working with images or imagined scenarios to help clients change or control their emotional responses to particular stimuli. Clients will usually be encouraged to relax, using whatever means they are familiar with, before immersing themselves in a particular image, designed to provoke a predetermined emotional response. This image may have been discussed beforehand, may be described by the therapist, or may be developed by dialogue with the client (for example, 'Imagine yourself in a place where you would feel very peaceful – describe it to me as the image becomes clear'). A stimulus, which would normally generate a different emotional response, is then introduced, but at a level which will not totally disrupt the response to the initial image. In this way the emotional response induced by the initial image can be used as a means of controlling (though not replacing) the response to the introduced stimulus. For example, if a particular individual generates a very angry response in a client, which the client would like to learn to control, they may first imagine themselves relaxing in a warm, comfortable room, listening to some favourite music. When they

are suitably comfortable in that image, they can introduce a small black-and-white photograph of the problem individual into the room, and take as long as they need to become comfortable and relaxed with that. This process can be repeated with increasingly powerful stimuli being introduced (larger pictures, colour, and ultimately perhaps the person themselves, silent, then talking) until the client has learned to control their angry response to the individual.

Conversely, clients can imagine themselves in a situation where they normally have an undesired emotional response, and introduce suitable stimuli to modify that response. The technique has been adapted for use in rational emotive behaviour therapy (Ellis and Dryden, 1987), where the modifying stimuli would be the therapist or client disputing the irrational beliefs which lead to the undesired response. As with all imagery techniques it is important that clients are given permission to take control if they need to and change the image for themselves or stop the activity. Positive double binds such as 'Take as long as you need to relax' and 'Do whatever you need to do in order to feel safe' can be useful in helping clients to control imagery for themselves and feel empowered in using such techniques.

Lazarus (1989) suggests using visualization techniques to help clients not only in dealing with their presenting or immediate issues, but also as 'anti-future shock imagery', preparing themselves for changes which they are likely to have to deal with in the future. Clients are asked to identify life events (e.g. children leaving home, retirement) which are likely to lie ahead for them, and visualize themselves coping effectively with the changes. As well as preparing for potentially difficult events, such visualizations of coping positively in the future may also help clients to get in touch with what they really want from life, and identify developmental goals.

Some clients may prefer to work with imagery in a more externalized way than has been described so far, and might benefit from using objects to represent significant people, feelings or experiences. A variety of objects can be put together in a *sculpt*, where their arrangement and proximity says something about the interrelationships of the factors they represent. Clients can be invited to represent and explore the current situation in this way, and then move the objects into a more desirable arrangement, often with surprisingly powerful results. Such sculpts can be undertaken with any objects that are to hand (coins, contents of pockets, handbags), but many therapists choose to keep a box of varied stones, buttons and so on available for this purpose.

Dream work

Clients often wish to share their dreams in therapy because they seem significant, or are a source of concern. Dreams can be seen as a means of accessing unconscious material such as repressed wishes, fears or memories, and their content seems frequently to be symbolic or metaphorical. Dreams can also be seen as a normal creative expression, part of the psyche's mechanism for maintaining healthy equilibrium, and include symbolic projections of current concerns and rehearsals for events anticipated in waking life.

Work with dreams can follow a number of different approaches (see, for example, Cushway and Sewell, 1992), and three techniques are outlined below. It is good practice to enable the client to work with their dreams in a way that makes sense to them, so some discussion of what the client hopes to gain from dream work and the opportunity to choose from a range of approaches is indicated. Dream work techniques can bring clients into contact with material which was previously out of their awareness, so they should enter into any work knowing this, and be able to stop or withdraw if they choose. It is often helpful to examine relationships between the themes and symbols in dreams and the client's waking life, and explore what messages or learning might be drawn from these.

Clients who wish to recall their dreams but have difficulty doing so might be encouraged to keep a dream diary. This is kept by the bed, and the client should be told to expect to wake briefly during the night to write some notes. They should make these notes immediately on waking as recall tends to fade quickly. The notes need only be reminders but in enough detail to stimulate memory later. Many find it helpful to give each dream a name that has some significance.

Dreams can be worked with in a cognitive way, discussing and trying to understand what the dream might mean and how it relates to other aspects of the client's experience. To do this, the client is first asked to recount the dream in the first person present tense as a way of getting into contact with it again. They can then describe their *actions* during the dream in the third person as a way of adopting a more objective perspective. After this, the therapist helps the client to reflect and explore: they may ask what the client sees as central in the dream; what contrasts or similarities they perceive between characters, events or feelings; what may be symbolic; what is resolved, what is not (and how it might be); what relationships might exist between anything in this dream and other dreams or waking life. The therapist should always be clear that the dream belongs to the client, and focus on facilitating the client in making sense of the dream for themselves, not interpreting it for them. After exploring the dream content in this way it is helpful to ask the client to summarize how they see the dream now, what they have learned from it so far, and any action they may wish to consider as a result. If working with nightmares or recurring dreams, it can help to repeat this process a number of times so that the client becomes used to confronting the dream content, and thus less afraid of it. Where disturbing events take place in dreams with characters known in waking life, it is useful to share with the client the idea that all characters in dreams can be thought of as representations of aspects of the self. For example, this enabled a client who had dreamed of killing a close family member to examine what aspect of herself that person might represent, and thus make sense of the dream.

A more active technique for working with dreams is used by Gestalt therapists to explore the richness of a dream and integrate its elements into the client's awareness. Once again the client begins by recounting the dream in the first person, present tense. The client then identifies the main elements (characters or objects) in the dream, and picks out those which generate curiosity, uncertainty, or powerful feelings. (This technique also assumes that the elements in the dream represent aspects of the dreamer, and this is useful in diminishing the fear associated with some nightmare figures.) The client is invited to take on the role of some of these elements in turn, beginning with 'I am …', and either tell the story of the dream from that perspective, or explore their feelings towards other characters or objects. The type of empty chair dialogue described above can be developed between key dream elements where it seems there are potential conflicts or blockages. After the client has explored whatever dialogues seem appropriate they might be asked to reflect on what messages this dream may have about how they are living their life, but the purpose of the technique is less to explain or interpret the dream than to raise the client's awareness of its elements and how they relate to each other.

A third approach to dream work involves using imagery to help the client re-enter their dream world, and take control of the dream. A number of techniques exist for doing this, and the approach outlined here has been described as an adaptation of the cultural practice of the Senoi tribe in Malaysia (Johnston, 1975). The client is encouraged to settle comfortably, relax in any way that works for them, and begin talking about an aspect of the dream which seems like a 'way in' or key. This might be the start, a snippet that is recalled clearly, or a particularly strong image or feeling. The client is then helped to go through a period of embellishment by continuing to explore the world of the dream and describing the experience in the first person present tense. This may result in re-telling the dream as it first happened, but the therapist should encourage the client to follow whatever images come to mind, rather than trying to stay close to the original dream. Often a main figure (most significant character, or object) will become apparent as the embellishment develops, and if it does not the client can be asked to identify what seems to be the most important element in the dream and imagine engaging it in dialogue. It is useful to discuss this process with clients in advance so that they can anticipate what will be asked of them, and feel empowered to take control of their imagery. It is also helpful to agree suitable language for engaging in dialogue with inanimate objects or abstract entities. (For example, can we refer to the 'spirit' or 'essence' of an object such as a tree and communicate with it?) The client

might begin dialogue with the main figure by asking 'How can I help you?', and wait for their imagination to provide a response. The objective is to make an ally of the main figure even if it is initially hostile, and positive double binds such as 'Summon whatever help you need …', 'Do whatever you need to do to make things safe for yourself …' can help the client to create a situation where they can safely communicate with the main figure. For example, a client who had recurring nightmares about swarms of insects found she was able to imagine a swarm of wasps contained in a large plastic bubble, and then allow one of the wasps to come outside to engage in dialogue. Following the dialogue, the client is encouraged to ask the main figure for a gift to symbolize their new alliance. If something abstract such as 'peace' is offered it seems to be useful to suggest the client ask for a more concrete gift (to symbolize the peace). At this point the client can say goodbye to the main figure and the dream world, and return their full awareness to the present when ready to do so. After processing the experience, many clients find it helpful to represent the gift for themselves, perhaps by drawing, or finding an object which resembles what they imagined. This technique seems to be particularly useful for exploring confusing dreams, or for working with nightmares and recurring dreams. Clients can be encouraged to visualize ways to safely subdue threatening figures, which can sometimes be used if they have further nightmares, though they rarely continue to be terrorized in their dreams by a main figure after confronting it in this way.

Cognitions

Cognitive restructuring

The techniques of cognitive restructuring are designed to help clients take control of what they think and believe in certain situations, and, by doing so, enable them to change their emotional or behavioural responses. Cognitive restructuring interventions rely on clients being able to report and examine their cognitive processes, learn how these are connected to other aspects of their experience, and be amenable to challenging and changing these cognitive processes.

At the most informal level, any counsellor or psychotherapist can listen for things the client might say which indicate a tendency towards self-defeating beliefs or cognitive responses. These can be evident in a tendency to over-generalize ('Nothing I do ever works out'), to use 'musts' ('I must be more confident'), or catastrophize ('This is terrible, I can't cope'). The therapist can challenge and begin to change such patterns of expression and thought by gently inviting the client to try expressing what they have said in a more realistic form and reflect on how it feels. (For example, 'Try saying "A lot of things I do aren't wholly successful/I'd like to be more confident/This is hard, and it will be difficult to cope" and tell me how that feels'.)

Rational emotive behaviour therapy (REBT) (see Part 5 of this book) makes the assumption that events in themselves do not necessarily lead to negative emotional consequences, but that negative emotions are the result of what one believes about an event. If a more 'rational' belief can be substituted, then the individual will be better able to respond to events. The intervention sequence for doing this begins by helping the client to learn the A–B–C model, where A represents an Activating event; B the Belief one holds about oneself, other people, or the world, which is called into play by the event; and C the emotional and behavioural Consequences of that belief. For example, if a client fails at a job interview (A), and believes that this is another example of *always* getting knocked back when it really matters (B), then they may be unlikely to apply for any further posts (C). If that belief can be changed to something more pragmatic, practical, and reality-based, such as 'although there was a candidate judged to be better on this occasion, that need not always be the case', then the outcome is likely to be different. Specific target beliefs are identified with the client, goals for change negotiated, and then the therapist engages with the client in disputing their irrational beliefs, and helping them to learn to do this for themselves. Techniques for disputing include challenging the logic of the belief; challenging the evidence for the belief and finding exceptions; drawing attention to the ultimate consequences of

holding such a belief; using humour or exaggeration; using self-disclosure; or adopting a didactic style to explain why the belief is irrational. Generally speaking, asking questions which encourage the client to challenge their own beliefs will be preferable to therapist self-disclosure and the didactic style as they encourage the client to focus on their own experience and see the flaws in their interpretations for themselves. Having done this, the client can be encouraged to state specifically a more rational belief, explore the effects of this and the new feeling generated, and develop a programme to practise disputing the old belief, reinforce the new belief, and put the resultant changes into operation.

Other approaches to cognitive restructuring (Beck, 1989; Meichenbaum, 1977) focus more on automatic thoughts and 'self-talk'. These can be tackled in a similar fashion, asking clients to identify problematic events and talk about the thoughts that they engender or the things they might say to themselves in such situations, and the way these are linked to their emotional and behavioural responses. It can be useful to encourage clients to explore these connections on paper, setting out events, cognitive, emotional and behavioural responses in the form of a chart. They can rate the strength of automatic thoughts and emotions as an aid to prioritizing. The therapist then helps the client to develop a more 'adaptive' healthy response which they would like to substitute, i.e. a new thought, its emotional and behavioural consequences. The therapist can help the client to practise substituting the adaptive response by rehearsal in fantasy. The client imagines and describes the situation in order to generate the automatic thought. When this has happened the therapist says 'Stop', or uses some other stimulus to interrupt the automatic thought pattern, and asks the client to repeat the adaptive cognitive response or positive self-talk to themselves before imagining the new desired behavioural response. This process is repeated until the client is able to stop the automatic response for themselves and substitute the adaptive response, before undertaking an action plan designed to practise and reinforce this process in real life. It is important to note that cognitive restructuring is not merely 'positive thinking', but is more personalized and subtle, and can be used as the basis for extensive personal development, not just for superficial situational help.

Developing new perspectives

New perspectives might be available to the client around ownership of problems. If they have always conceptualized themselves as being powerless in a given situation (e.g. 'My boss makes unreasonable demands of me', 'He makes me feel …') it may be very useful to encourage them to look at the situation in terms of what is within their control (e.g. 'How do you respond to these unreasonable requests?', 'What does he do, and how does that lead to your emotional response?'). Positive challenging involves helping clients to experiment with viewing things differently – problem situations as opportunities for change, difficulties as challenges, mistakes as learning opportunities – and become more aware of the strengths and resources they are able to employ rather than focusing on weaknesses and shortcomings. Dexter and Russell (1998) provide a useful exploration of this area. The point is not that the client will feel better if only they can change their perspective on a situation, but that by experimenting they may find a perspective which gives them more autonomy. They may see a chance to act differently. This is an example of the technique of *reframing* – helping the client to find a new way of viewing the problem in which they are able to see choices, opportunities, or possibilities for solution where previously they did not.

The concept of the 'empathy sandwich' for challenging interventions is useful. The intervention is preceded by an empathic response to check that the therapist has understood the client's current perspective (first layer of sandwich). The intervention to facilitate a new perspective is then offered (filling), and the therapist attends carefully to the client's reaction, which is responded to with empathy (second layer of sandwich). Hence:

Therapist:	So the current situation is very difficult and you're feeling a lot of pressure, but I get the sense that you're also feeling more aware of the need to change things.

Client:	(thoughtfully) Actually that's true, and I probably could have gone on being dissatisfied for years if things hadn't got this bad.
Therapist:	So it sounds like you're thinking that this crisis might not be all bad.

The empathy sandwich can help to reinforce the new perspective if successful, but can also be a means of re-establishing an empathic relationship if the client responds with irritation or defensiveness. In this case the second layer of the sandwich may be more like 'You seem a bit unhappy with what I've just said, maybe because it seems I don't appreciate how bad it really feels at the moment. Have I got that right?'

Making connections, past and present

A useful technique for uncovering connections begins by identifying common patterns of feeling and belief. The client talks about their present situation, and the therapist listens carefully to the feelings expressed, reflects these back to ensure they are properly understood, and tries to help the client be aware of the subtleties of their emotional experience. It may seem that the client's emotional responses are not entirely explicable in terms of their current situation, so the therapist can ask the client if these feelings are familiar to them from previous experiences. If so, they can be asked to talk about these if they are prepared to. The relevance of these past situations will often be illuminated by helping the client to look at them from two different perspectives. First, the client explores how they made sense of the experience and coped with it at the developmental stage when it occurred; and, second, they consider what insights are possible from their current developmental stage that were not possible when the past experiences took place. Having explored past situations in this way, the client can be encouraged to look again at their present experience, and consider what new insights are available. They will often be able to understand present feelings, behaviours, irrational beliefs, or automatic thoughts in terms of learning from past events, ways of coping at an earlier stage of development which are no longer appropriate, or responses which were developed in specific circumstances which have been generalized beyond their useful limits. For example, while it may be a valuable survival strategy for a child to be submissive in the face of a bullying teacher, it will be useful to have a range of ways of responding to bullying in adult life rather than be limited by the emotional response which is triggered due to connections with the past experience. If the client discovers these connections, they begin to be empowered to change their responses.

The process of connecting past and present might at times be deepened either by developing an empty chair dialogue between the past and present selves to help one share some insight with the other, or highlight differences in ways of understanding and coping with situations; or by encouraging the client to compose letters in which past and present selves exchange messages. If one of these selves is the individual in childhood, it may help the client to access that part of themselves by writing with their non-dominant hand. It should be noted that such techniques can bring about powerful cathartic experiences for clients, helping them access deep feelings associated with past events, or feelings of loss associated with different developmental stages, and thus need to be engaged in with caution. The client needs to be clear about what is being done, what they are hoping to achieve, what the possible consequences are, and give their informed consent.

If clients seem to value talking about their past and do not explicitly make connections with the present, it is likely to be useful for the therapist to invite them to do so. This can be achieved by asking the client if the feelings they have been describing in relation to past events are familiar to them in any aspects of their present, or simply if they can identify any parallels with their present experience, or interactions with others. Perhaps more obliquely, it can also be useful for the therapist to help the client become aware of the similarities and differences which are apparent between the emotions they are describing in relation to past events, and the emotions that they seem to be experiencing as they describe them. These similarities and differences can then be used as a means of bringing the client

into the present and exploring the relevance of past material.

Malan's 'triangle of insight' (Malan, 1979), which has *the past ('back then'), the present ('out there'),* and *the therapy relationship ('in here')* at its corners, offers a guide to ways connections and parallels may be identified and worked with in therapy between any two or all three of these sets of experience. It is likely that patterns learned by the client in the past and played out in the present will also be played out in the therapy relationship. The relationship will thus provide opportunities for learning, and for experimentation with new patterns, which the client can then take 'out there'.

Identifying personal beliefs and ways of construing

The A–B–C technique from REBT outlined earlier is one way of helping clients to get in touch with their beliefs initially in relation to specific events and situations. It will often be the case that after looking at a number of situations some core beliefs about self, others and the world in general emerge. Different formulations of REBT list different sets of common irrational beliefs about how things must be in order for self, others, or life in general to be acceptable – such as 'I must always succeed', 'Others must always treat me reasonably', 'The world must always be just and fair'. Encouraging the client to test their own beliefs against these can be challenging, and can help to develop a more pragmatic and reality-based outlook.

Personal construct theory (Kelly, 1991) offers some useful techniques for helping clients to be more specific about how they view themselves and others and what they believe, although the approach itself would describe this as understanding how clients construe, rather than what they believe. A 'self-characterization sketch' is a short written piece by a client describing what they see as their own most important features. The client is asked to write about themselves from the point of view of someone who knows them well and looks upon them favourably. They are asked to write about themselves fairly briefly, but in enough detail to help an actor who was preparing to take their role in a film prepare for the part. What the client has chosen to include or leave out, and how easy it was to write from the perspective asked, can then be useful topics for further exploration.

The examination of 'bipolar constructs' can also be illuminating in helping the therapist to understand the client's worldview. Bipolar constructs are not exactly opposites in the linguistic sense, but represent concepts which an individual sees as being mutually opposed. The individual nature of such constructs is important, so that for example where one person may have the opposite pole of 'tidy' as 'messy', another may have it as 'relaxed', and these clearly represent quite different ways of looking at things. An interesting technique for eliciting such constructs from an individual is to ask them to consider three people whom they know fairly well, and develop a list of ways in which any two of them are the same as each other and different from the third, giving a name to what the two have in common and the way the third is different. (As an example: 'A and B are open while C is careful', 'B and C are optimistic while A is realistic' are statements which begin to give some insight into the construing of the individual and open up interesting avenues for discussion.) It may then be appropriate to explore how rigid or flexible the individual's constructs are and work on new perspectives by exploring the pros and cons of opposite poles (e.g. 'What might be good/bad about being optimistic/realistic?').

The *scripts* of transactional analysis and the *schemas* of cognitive therapy represent protracted, sometimes lifelong, patterns of personal belief, which can be dysfunctional. These are analysed over a period of time in therapy, often by a process of induction from exploration of critical incidents. Client and therapist attempt to uncover patterns in relating, thinking, and feeling, and the beliefs and predictions about self, others and the world, which underlie them.

Positive asset search

The positive asset search helps the client to re-evaluate their experience in order to find new meaning in something previously seen as negative, or new resources in themselves (Ivey et al., 1987).

The technique involves the use of listening skills and selective attention to positive assets, but is not about the denial of negative aspects of a situation, rather the drawing of the client's attention towards positive perspectives previously overlooked. The therapist listens carefully to the client as they describe a situation or experience, paraphrasing and reflecting the feelings in what they hear in order to develop a clear empathic understanding of how the client sees the situation, but in particular draws the client's attention to things they have said which include a neglected positive element. So, for example, when a client is describing a stressful situation in the past, the therapist should not ignore what the client is saying about how difficult they found it, but should also be listening for what is said about how they survived the situation – what internal and external resources they were able to draw on, who helped them get through, and what they learned from the situation. Achieving an appropriate balance is crucial here – clients are likely to become frustrated if the therapist seems to be ignoring their pain in order to search for positives, but the therapist can demonstrate genuine empathic understanding of a client's difficulties while at the same time helping them to find new meanings and resources in their lives.

Goal setting

Goals can be set with the client both in relation to the therapy itself and achievements outside of the therapeutic situation. Clients will often have goals for both of these areas at some level of awareness, but may have difficulty in expressing them clearly, or in thinking explicitly in terms of wants and outcomes as opposed to problems and difficulties. Clear goals encourage a sense of self-determination and empowerment; give a focus for activity both during and between sessions; a sense of hope for a better future; and are something to keep in view even if specific strategies do not prove successful (Egan, 2001). Keeping goals in focus does not necessarily mean that the client will not have the opportunity to explore negative feelings, or traumatic experiences, but that they will be clear about what they are hoping to achieve in doing so, and will be 'signed up' to that as a desirable goal. This is not to deny the possibility of unintended or surprise outcomes, or to encourage practitioners to tie down every aspect of the therapeutic encounter into a dry and logical process, but to encourage both therapist and client to keep an eye on the agenda.

Clients might initially be encouraged to talk about their aims or wants in a fairly general way, by asking 'How would you like things to be?' The therapist might also try offering the client the imaginary chance to use a magic wand, or ask a 'miracle question' (De Shazer, 1985) – 'If you woke up tomorrow and a miracle had happened giving you what you want, how would you become aware that it had happened?' – as ways of helping clients free their imagination when thinking about goals. The use of other media such as drawing and sculpting can also be considered as a way of engaging the imagination. Clients can be asked to create an image to represent themselves at some point in an imagined future, when things are going well. They could also be asked to sculpt their present situation using suitable buttons, stones or other objects to represent themselves, significant others and their interrelationships; and then to move the objects to represent a more desirable configuration and talk about the changes they have made. Even if clients' initial responses to some of these interventions are not achievable, useful material can be gleaned by exploring what the client would like to be feeling, and incorporating this into a realistic goal. Asking clients who are beginning to be able to express a rather vague goal (e.g. 'a better relationship with X') how they will know when they have achieved it, might well help them to state the goal in more measurable terms ('We'd only fall out once a week instead of every day'). The acronym SMART is often used as a guide to help clients shape up a goal from an initial statement of intent. Therapists can ask questions or prompt clients to consider how the goal can be stated specifically (S), in a measurable form (M), to consider its appropriateness (A) and realism (R) in relation to their individual situation, and to give some thought to the time (T) by which they would like to achieve it.

It can be useful to encourage the client to look at what they want to achieve in terms of short-, medium-, and long-term goals, or perhaps to break down a major project into a series of goal steps. The technique of *scaling* (De Shazer, 1985) might be incorporated here. The client is asked to rate where they currently are on a scale for which 0 represents the worst things could be, and 10 represents the achievement of their long-term goal, or the best things could be. They can then be asked to specify what would be involved in moving up by one scale point, two points, and so on. Once again clients are likely to benefit from recording some of this on paper as a way of productively fixing ideas, and holding on to specifics. Some clients (and indeed therapists) will find it difficult to talk about goals without quickly moving into thinking about strategies for achieving those goals, and may find the two becoming blurred – for example, is discussing one's feelings with a partner a goal or a strategy? If this seems to be occurring, the therapist might usefully try an intervention such as 'That sounds like something that you might do, but perhaps it would be useful first to try to be clear about what you would be hoping to achieve by doing it.'

Force field analysis

Force field analysis (Lewin, 1969) is a technique which can be used to help clients explore the ways various factors in their situation might be operating to help or hinder them in achieving their goals or putting action plans into practice. This is a process which involves a number of steps, and it is often advisable to record the process on paper. The therapist begins by asking the client to list all the factors they can think of which might help or hinder them in achieving their goal or implementing an action plan. This can be further structured by inviting the client to consider factors about themselves, significant others, and the broader environment if appropriate. If there are a lot of factors identified, it may then be useful to ask the client to rate each on a scale from 1 to 10 in terms of its power to influence their success or otherwise, as an aid to prioritizing. The client should then be able to visualize their goal or action plan located within a 'force field' of helping and hindering factors pulling them towards success or failure, and this can be useful in assessing the realism of a given goal or plan. If the force field analogy does not appeal or make sense, clients can

Facilitating forces	Strength (out of 10)	Restraining forces	Strength (out of 10)
• motivation to improve the relationship	8	• guilt about not being with the children	6
• shared interests	5	• difficulty finding babysitters	3
• the enjoyment we know we can have together	7	• tendency to let other priorities dominate (particularly work)	6
• the chance of breaks from domestic routine	3	• inertia	4
• chance to revisit some old haunts	4	• feeling tired or stressed after work	8
• encouragement from two particular friends	6	• problems sustaining the strategy as the novelty wears off	4
		• a lot of things we'd like to do cost money	5

Strategies for strengthening facilitating forces	Strategies for weakening restraining forces
• list benefits of improved relationship • remember current dissatisfaction • careful planning and selection of things to do together that we'll both enjoy • share feedback on 'quality time' spent together • spend time individually with the two friends etc. …	• plan 'quality time' around predictable work stresses • plan 'quality time' well in advance • be more assertive at work about leaving on time • do things together as a family at weekends • don't automatically take responsibility when a crisis occurs at work etc. …

Figure 3.4.3 Example of force field analysis

instead visualize a tug-of-war, with the helping and hindering factors pulling against each other. The therapist then encourages the client to examine the most powerful factors on each side and think about ways of strengthening the effects of the helping factors, and weakening the effects of the hindering factors. Specific strategies for doing this can be developed and built into the client's action plans. Figure 3.4.3 shows an example of the use of this technique.

Decision making

Strategies for helping clients with decision making can be used when a choice has to be made between competing goals, or between mutually exclusive strategies for achieving goals (e.g. career choice, college course, relationships, divorce, early retirement). Encouraging clients to adopt some form of balance-sheet method (Egan, 2001), and put their ideas down on paper, can often move them forward or get them unstuck. A balance sheet can be as simple as a list of pros and cons for each of the competing choices, but it is also possible to structure the technique to tailor it more effectively to individual needs. So, for example, a balance sheet may be composed which has two columns for each choice in which to list advantages and disadvantages, but under a series of subheadings to suit the individual, for example career, social life, home life, significant others, organization, environment and so on. The client can be asked to rate each factor listed for importance. It may also be helpful to ask clients to specify and list what is appealing to them about particular choices and what is not. Interestingly, not all clients act on the basis of the numerical result or apparent balance of such exercises – some decide that they want to follow a particular course in spite of what the balance sheet shows them, but if they take enough time over the process, most report being clearer about what they really want as a result.

A simple but often effective technique in decision making can be used in response to the client asking the therapist what they would do. If the client is asked what response they would like or are hoping for from the therapist, the processes underlying the client's inability or resistance to making that decision for themselves can be explored.

Interpersonal factors

Interpreting transferential patterns

If a known client's way of being seems surprising in a particular session, charged with emotions which seem out of context, or if they seem to want the therapist to adopt a particular role with them, then it may be worth exploring the possibility of transference as an explanation. Knowledge of the client may already suggest how earlier relationships might be influencing the therapist–client interaction, but often it will not. Interpretation should not take the form of an explicit statement telling the client about the transference they are supposedly experiencing, but should be tentative and offered to the client as an area for exploration – interpreting transference

can be seen as a joint activity. An initial intervention may draw attention to a behaviour or emotion that the therapist has become aware of, for example, 'I notice you've seemed quite angry with me today', or a sense of what the client wants – 'It feels as though you'd like me to sort this out for you'. The client can then respond with their perspective on the situation, and the origins of the feelings may begin to become apparent. If this does not happen, the client can be asked if the feelings they are experiencing are familiar to them, and encouraged to talk about other instances, which will often clarify the transference. One of the relatively unusual aspects of the therapist–client relationship is that it can be discussed and examined between the parties in a way that would be difficult in many other relationships. Exploring and interpreting transference in the relationship may allow the client to understand themselves better in other relationships. It can enable them to work through issues in the relationship with the therapist which resolve past negative experiences and help them to behave differently in other present relationships. For example, if the client is able to become aware of their fear of rejection, explore its origins in past experiences, and learn to manage that fear appropriately in the relationship with their therapist, then hopefully they can also learn to manage it more effectively in other significant relationships. On the other hand, opening up exploration of transference may bring therapist– client relationship issues to the fore inappropriately, and impede the client's ability to focus on their real goals. (See Kahn (1996) for a useful discussion.)

Clearly a therapist needs to be aware of their own patterns of relating and responses to clients if they are to respond appropriately. If they are not, the danger exists of being flattered inappropriately by the client's positive transference, feeling inadequate in response to negative transference, or being drawn into an inappropriate co-dependent relationship. The therapist's counter-transference will often be material for supervision or personal therapy, and consideration needs to be given to the extent to which it is shared with the client. There will be times when the therapist owning their own feelings towards the client will be helpful in enabling the client to see the therapist as genuine, modelling openness in the relationship, giving feedback on how they are being received, and developing insight into the dynamics of the relationship; and other times when it would be experienced as distracting or indulgent. Once again, it is useful to be guided by the client's goals, and the extent to which these will be furthered by working with the transference relationship, and it may be helpful to involve the client in such decisions. Increasingly, forms of transference interpretation are used in even ostensibly non-psychodynamic approaches such as cognitive therapy, in order to work on cognitive distortions within the 'laboratory' of the therapeutic relationship.

Here-and-now awareness

Therapists need to develop the habit of continually monitoring their own awareness, and learning to share this appropriately with the client. This involves attending to one's own feelings during the encounter, and processing these. The therapist can consider: how their feelings relate to the developing relationship with the client; the nature and quality of the work currently being done; any resistance in themselves or perceived in the client; and can evaluate any hunches or intuitions they may experience in the light of what they are seeing, hearing and feeling. The therapist can choose to disclose something of their own awareness, and invite the client to reflect and share their own perspective. The skill of immediacy is used in this context. So, for example, the therapist might say, 'I'm feeling a bit confused by what you've just said, but I normally feel we understand each other quite well. How does it seem to you at the moment?'; or 'I notice I'm feeling quite enthusiastic about the work we've done today. How is it for you?'; or 'I'm aware that I'm feeling some anger towards X and I'm wondering what feelings are around for you?' These kinds of intervention, used intentionally and appropriately, have the potential to encourage the client to stop and think about what is happening, experience the therapist as congruent, take permission to share their own feelings or perceptions openly, and be involved in monitoring and shaping the helping process for themselves. The therapist's awareness is used as a stimulus for a joint exploration, and becomes a model for developing the client's own awareness.

If used inappropriately or excessively, such interventions also have the potential to leave the client feeling confused as to their purpose, and lacking confidence in the therapist. The therapist is again required to exercise judgement, and to have a clear intention for what might be achieved by sharing their awareness, or sufficient experience to trust their sensitivity to the situation and know when immediacy is likely to be beneficial. A thoughtful pause is often useful to check in with oneself before using such an intervention.

Corrective emotional experience

An example of how the therapist–client relationship can be used as a medium for correcting previous experience is given above when considering use of the transference relationship. Using the relationship intentionally to correct the client's previous learning is often a feature of work with a client who has been subject to some form of abuse in an earlier phase of their life. If, for example, the client has been the victim of a relationship where their dependence or trust has been exploited, they may have developed a range of difficulties around trust, guilt, self-esteem and responsibility, which now cause them problems in engaging in trusting relationships or a vulnerability to exploitative relationships. The counselling or psychotherapy relationship offers the opportunity to experience something different, and can be used as a model of a healthy relationship, to enable the client to have a positive experience of trust, intimacy, non-exploitative co-operation, and the maintenance of appropriate boundaries. The client can experience sharing their emotions, and understanding from another, without having their vulnerability exploited or needing to defend themselves, and they can experience being valued and trusted rather than being discounted. If this is to be effective, it requires some care from the therapist, who will ideally model congruence, acceptance, and both clarity and flexibility about boundaries. Therapists who are too rigid in their application of boundaries, for example refusing to engage in conversation with clients outside session times, can be experienced as not genuinely caring.

Those who are too lax and allow the boundaries between the therapeutic relationship and friendship to become blurred can be experienced as exploitative or vulnerable to exploitation. The therapist needs to monitor the developing relationship carefully and keep in touch with their own responses, as well as learning about the client's previous experience, exploring the deficits in terms of learning about relationships, and considering how the therapeutic relationship might be used to correct these deficits. At times this might involve modelling appropriate parental behaviour – nurturing, setting limits within the relationship, or responding non-defensively but assertively to challenges and threats. Modelling such as this can enable the client to develop a more adaptive 'internal parent' and enable them to be more nurturing towards themselves, or to maintain more appropriate boundaries and limits. At other times the therapist might be involved in modelling a trusting and co-operative adult relationship, wherein both parties can share their feelings openly, accept and understand each other, and respect each other's limitations. These processes are unlikely to proceed smoothly, as clients who have been involved in exploitative relationships may well have evolved coping strategies which are experienced as hostile and rejecting; and will probably need to test this new relationship before they are able to accept it as safe. This may involve giving the therapist the opportunity or even encouragement to exploit their position, or to reject the client, and can leave the therapist feeling angry, exposed or threatened. The therapist's ability to stay in touch with their own responses and share these with the client while maintaining the core conditions of congruence, acceptance and empathy will be vital in helping the client to gain insight into the evolving relationship, genuinely experience it as different, and learn from it.

What has been presented here is an outline of a range of techniques and strategies drawn from a wide spectrum of counselling and psychotherapeutic approaches, which individual therapists may find they can use or adapt to their own style or context. It is likely that many therapists will at least occasionally work in an eclectic fashion, even if they are unable to go along with Lazarus' assertion that it is techniques, not theories, which help clients (Lazarus, 1989). It seems certain at this stage in the development of knowledge about therapy that no one approach has a monopoly on the truth, and many of the techniques described above seem to have a utility which can be separated out from their theoretical rationale. The way a given technique works can be explained from a number of perspectives, so the possibilities for integration are many. Such use of techniques needs to be thoughtful, sensitive to the client's needs, pay due regard to contra-indications, and should give the client a voice in the way they are helped. Many therapists will feel the need for additional specialized training in relation to some of the techniques they would like to adopt, if their previous training does not provide them with an adequate framework for their use, and the skills to use them safely and deal with the possible consequences.

References

Bandura, A. (1977) *Social Learning Theory*. Englewood Cliffs, NJ: Prentice-Hall.

Beck, A.T. (1989) *Cognitive Therapy and the Emotional Disorders*. Harmondsworth: Penguin.

Bolton, G., Howlet, S., Lago, C. and Wright, J. (eds) (2004) *Writing Cures: An Introductory Handbook of Writing in Counselling and Psychotherapy*. Hove: Brunner-Routledge.

Carkhuff, R. (1969) *Helping and Human Relations*, Vols. I and II. New York: Holt, Rinehart and Winston.

Cushway, D. and Sewell, R. (1992) *Counselling with Dreams and Nightmares*. London: Sage.

De Shazer, S. (1985) *Keys to Solution in Brief Therapy*. New York: Norton.

Dexter, G. and Russell, J. (1998) *Challenging Blank Minds and Sticky Moments in Counselling*. Preston: Winckley.

Egan, G. (2001) *The Skilled Helper* (7th edn). Pacific Grove, CA: Brooks/Cole.

Ellis, A. and Dryden, W. (1987) *The Practice of Rational Emotive Therapy*. New York: Springer.

Heron, J. (1990) *Helping the Client: A Creative Practical Guide*. London: Sage.

Houston, G. (1990) *The Red Book of Gestalt* (5th edn). London: Rochester Foundation.

Ivey, A.E., Ivey, M.B. and Simek-Downing, L. (1987) *Counseling and Psychotherapy: Integrating Skills, Theory, and Practice*. Boston: Allyn and Bacon.

Johnston, J. (1975) *Elements of Senoi Dreamwork Applied to Western Culture* (monograph). San Francisco, CA: California School for Professional Psychology.

Kahn, M. (1996) *Between Therapist and Client: The New Relationship* (revised edn). New York: Freeman and Co.

Kelly, G.A. (1991) *The Psychology of Personal Constructs*. London: Routledge.

Lazarus, A.A. (1989) *The Practice of Multimodal Therapy*. Baltimore, MD: Johns Hopkins University Press.

Lewin, K. (1969) Quasi-stationary social equilibria and the problem of permanent change. In W.G. Bennis,

K.D. Benne and R. Chinn (eds), *The Planning of Change*. New York: Holt, Rinehart and Winston.

Mahrer, A.R. (1996) *The Complete Guide to Experiential Therapy*. New York: Wiley.

Malan, D.H. (1979) *Individual Psychotherapy and the Science of Psychodynamics*. New York: Butterworth.

Meichenbaum, D. (1977) *Cognitive Behavior Modification: An Integrative Approach*. New York: Plenum.

Riikonen, E. and Smith, G.M. (1997) *Re-imagining Therapy*. London: Sage.

Wolpe, J. (1990) *The Practice of Behavior Therapy* (4th edn). New York: Pergamon.

Zinker, J. (1977) *Creative in Gestalt Therapy*. New York: Vintage.

3.5 Assessment and Case Formulation

GLADEANA MCMAHON

Assessment

An earlier section dealt with the importance of the therapeutic relationship, without which positive outcomes are unlikely to be achieved. When a therapist undertakes an explicit assessment of a client and his or her problem(s), it is necessary to balance the need to maintain the quality and continuity of this relationship against the therapist's possible need to develop a full and appropriate picture of the client as an aid to case conceptualization and therapeutic planning (Milner and O'Bryne, 2004).

Assessment is normally undertaken during the first session or so, and if assessment forms part of the therapist's approach, then it is helpful for the client to know this in advance so that he or she is suitably prepared (Palmer and McMahon, 1997). Nonetheless, there are exceptions. Rules and normal practice are 'made to be broken' if the situation or the needs of the client demand it, and it is not unethical

to do so. The physical, mental or emotional state of the client, or difficulties in establishing communication or rapport, can sometimes rule out or postpone an assessment process.

The therapeutic orientation of the therapist will influence the type of assessment and the type of information sought. For example, psychodynamic psychotherapists will seek to identify aspects such as the client's defence structure, core conflicts and ego strength, with greater attention being given to early life experiences and influences. Person-centred therapists will see their main task as 'being' with the client and establishing the most helpful therapeutic climate to enable the client to facilitate change rather than seeking information about the client's history or problems. Cognitive-behavioural therapists, however, are more likely to focus on 'here-and-now' problems, underlying schemas and self-defeating behavioural patterns. In addition, systems-based family therapists will assess the way the family interacts and the roles each person enacts to enable the system to operate.

Even when a psychotherapist's therapeutic approach does not include assessment in a formal sense, it is difficult to avoid some form of subjective evaluation or internal assessment of clients and their needs. The evaluation of situations and people is a process learned from an early age as a necessary survival technique. Training may reduce the negative effects of such judgements, but whether it is ever possible to be totally judgement-free and 'with' the client in a completely accepting spiritual meld is more debatable.

In any event, basic information needs to be gathered, if only as a bare minimum for contact purposes. Arguably, unless you are a 'super-therapist' trained in every possible technique, including medical and psychiatric assessment, and are able to deal with psychotic and/or violent clients, you will be obliged to make a judgement, evaluation or assessment as to whether you and the client can work successfully together. Thus, some form of assessment seems unavoidable. The question is one of extent, formality, the 'when' and 'how'.

Therapists employed by an agency may have little choice in the matter, being constrained by the agency's procedures, which may include the completion of standard forms or questionnaires. In private practice, therapists still have accountabilities – under the law, to their codes of ethics and practice, to whichever professional body they belong. Such accountability may include their clinical supervisor, who has responsibility for monitoring clinical and ethical standards, and may extend to colleagues, perhaps, and certainly to clients and, not least, to themselves. A failure to assess presenting problems and keep appropriate records can be construed as unprofessional and a robust defence would be needed to refute such a charge (McMahon, 1994). The remainder of this section is based on the assumption that some form of assessment is both necessary and desirable.

When does assessment take place?

Assessment starts with the receipt of any information concerning the client, be this through self-referral,

referral letters, case records or an initial telephone contact, but develops more completely, and perhaps more reliably, with the first therapy session. It is hard to overestimate the importance of this first session and the mutual impressions gained by the therapist and client. Mistrust and suspicion can jeopardize any future relationship. As mentioned above, it is helpful for the client to know in advance something about the therapist and the fact that the first session is likely to be devoted to assessment. To reduce uncertainty on behalf of the client as to where she is going, how she will get there, who she will see and what she might expect, a brief information pack, together with a very basic client details form (see Figure 3.5.1), which can be completed before or at the end of the first session, may prove helpful.

It is also possible to provide the client with a list of topics or questions she may wish to consider or ask before or during the first session as an aid to understanding what might reasonably be expected from therapist and from therapy. Such a list has been compiled by Palmer and Szymanska (1994) (see Figure 3.5.2). Thus assessment can be a two-way process and not just something a counsellor or psychotherapist 'does' to a client. Whether we like it or not, clients will assess the quality of the therapeutic relationship and the effectiveness of any therapeutic plans, though some may be more able and objective than others in doing this.

History taking

While the client is telling her story, the therapist will be an active listener. In her preparation for the assessment, the therapist should have examined whatever background information was available. This information, together with the client's story, provides a partial picture. A more complete picture at this stage can be obtained with questions of who, what, when, where and how, but it may not be helpful to use questions involving motivation which may be premature.

How will you remember all the client tells you?

This is a matter of what works best for you and your clients and whether you are obliged to follow any

---

CLIENT RECORD SHEET   Client Identifying Code:

Last name: _____

First name: _____

Home address: _____

_____

Post Code: _____

Telephone numbers: Home: _____ Work: _____

Mobile: _____

Email: _____

Doctor's Details

Doctor's name: _____

Address: _____

_____

Post Code: _____

Telephone number: _____

Statement
I have read and understood all the information supplied to me about the therapy I am being offered. I give my permission for my therapist to contact the appropriate external agencies if my therapist believes I am either a danger to myself or to others.

Signed: _____   **Date:** _____

Figure 3.5.1   Client details form (adapted from McMahon, 1994)

externally imposed procedures. It can also depend on the client and how she is likely to react to a record being made at the time. At one extreme, a video camera can be used to record not only every word spoken, but also every physical movement, expression, appearance, gesture, etc., but this is rarely, if ever, done. It is also common practice for some therapists to tape-record sessions, whereas others believe this

Here is a list of topics and questions you may wish to raise when attending your first therapy (assessment) session:

(a)   Check that your therapist has relevant qualifications and experience in the field of therapy/psychotherapy.

(b)   Ask about the type of approach the therapist uses and how it relates to your problem.

(c)   Ask if the therapist is in supervision (most professional bodies consider supervision to be mandatory; see note).

(d)   Ask whether the therapist or the therapy agency is a member of a professional body and abides by a code of ethics. If possible, obtain a copy of the code.

(e)   Discuss your goals/expectations of counselling or psychotherapy.

(f)   Ask about the fees, if any (if your income is low, check if the therapist operates a sliding scale) and discuss the frequency and estimated duration of therapy.

(g)   Arrange regular review sessions with your therapist to evaluate your progress.

(h)   Do not enter into a long-term therapy contract unless you are satisfied that this is necessary and beneficial to you.

If you do not have a chance to discuss the above points during your first session, discuss them at the next possible opportunity.

General issues

1.   Therapist self-disclosure can sometimes be therapeutically useful. However, if the sessions are dominated by the therapist discussing his/her problems at length, raise this issue in the therapy session.

2.   If at any time you feel discounted, undermined or manipulated within the session, discuss this with the therapist. It is easier to resolve issues as and when they arise.

3.   Do not accept significant gifts from your therapist. This does not apply to relevant therapeutic material.

4.   Do not accept social invitations from your therapist, for example, dining in a restaurant or going for a drink. However, this does not apply to legitimate therapeutic assignments such as being accompanied by your therapist into a situation to help you overcome a phobia.

5.   If your therapist proposes a change in venue for the therapy sessions (for example, from a centre to the therapist's own home) without good reason, do not agree.

6.   Research has shown that it is not beneficial for clients to have sexual contact with their therapist. Professional bodies in the field of therapy and psychotherapy consider that it is unethical for therapists to engage in sexual activity with current clients.

7.   If you have any doubts about the therapy you are receiving then discuss them with your therapist. If you are still uncertain, seek advice, perhaps from a friend, your doctor, your local Citizens Advice Bureau, the professional body your therapist belongs to or the therapy agency that may employ your therapist.

8.   You have the right to terminate therapy whenever you choose.

Note: Therapy supervision is a formal arrangement where therapists discuss their therapy in a confidential setting on a regular basis with one or more professional colleagues.

Figure 3.5.2   Issues for the client to consider in counselling or psychotherapy (adapted from Palmer and Syzmanska, 1994)

to be intrusive. At the other extreme, no notes or recording of any sort may be undertaken. If records are made during or after the assessment, the client needs to be aware of the purpose of keeping such notes, as well as access and storage issues and the boundaries relating to client confidentiality.

During the assessment session it is likely that a wealth of information will have been gleaned and there are a number of ways in which this information can be written up: unstructured or structured, brief and focused or wide-ranging and detailed. Unstructured records will look very different for each client and will probably reflect the emphasis and priority given by the therapist to the information given or elicited. Brief and focused records will tend to concentrate on the presenting problem(s), with a minimum of relevant background information. Structured records will tend to follow a number of standard headings or supply answers or observations to a list of standard questions. In turn, the list of headings or questions can be fairly short or very long and wide-ranging. Examples of structured record headings might include:

- occupational and educational background
- family and personal relationships, past and present
- medical and psychiatric history
- previous therapy outcomes
- ethnicity, sexuality and disability
- client goals
- related problems
- recurring themes (for further detail see Palmer and McMahon, 1997)

A Mental State Exam can be used, based directly on the therapist's observations. The Mental State Exam focuses on the client's appearance, speech, emotions, thought processes and content, sensory perception, mental capacities and attitude towards the therapist. A detailed set of questions under each heading aims to help the assessor form impressions of the client's possible state of mind (see Figure 3.5.3; and Lukas, 1993). Some may object to possible prejudices and cultural stereotypes implicit in Lukas's list. However, most items can be intuitively and judiciously adapted.

The Multimodal Life History Inventory (MLHI) (Lazarus and Lazarus, 1991) is another example of an assessment tool. This is a highly detailed and comprehensive questionnaire extending over 15 pages and is completed by the client, usually after the first session. The MLHI is based on seven modalities of personality: Behaviour, Affect, Sensation, Imagery, Cognition, Interpersonal and Drugs/biology (BASIC ID).

Of course it may not be possible for a full assessment to be carried out after just one session. Time and judgement may not allow for a number of questions to be asked and answered. The advantage of any structured form of assessment is that any outstanding gaps are visible to the therapist and are not just overlooked.

The therapist's preferred theoretical perspective will tend to influence the content of the assessment session (or whether, in the case of person-centred therapy, an assessment is undertaken at all) and the emphasis given to the different aspects of the client's personality, situation and presenting problem.

The Mental State Exam contains a number of general areas of observation and has also been seen as a useful tool for assessing children, provided it is adapted to their developmental level.

For a therapist using an integrative approach, choosing an appropriate perspective to fit the client and the client's situation, a more extensive coverage of relevant client information is likely to be required before such a choice is made. Upon completion of an adequate client history, probably in written format, the therapist is obliged to consider the next steps. Again, this can vary from a confident analysis by an experienced and knowledgeable therapist to a situation of near panic by a trainee wishing that his or her clinical supervisor was sitting in the room too. Whatever the case, the next step is case conceptualization and therapeutic planning.

Case conceptualization

When a therapist has a preferred theoretical approach, he or she is likely to conceptualize the client's problems in terms of that orientation and it could be said that the client is 'fitted' to this orientation.

When a cognitive-behavioural therapist is referred a client who is experiencing a range of difficulties, the therapist uses the assessment session to undertake a 'collaborative case conceptualization' (Padesky and Greenberger, 1995), using this to assist both parties understand what has happened (see Figure 3.5.4).

An alternative approach, utilizing the information already generated about the client and the client's presenting problems, would be to select a particular

APPEARANCE
1. How healthy does the client look?
2. Is the client disabled?
3. How is the client dressed (clothing, cleanliness, etc.)?
4. What do you notice about the client's body language (e.g. eye contact, facial expression, etc.)?

SPEECH
1. Pacing, pitch, etc.?
2. Speech impairment?

EMOTIONS
1. Client's predominant mood?
2. Client's predominant emotion?
3. Does the client's emotion vary?

THOUGHT PROCESSES AND CONTENT
1. Does the client demonstrate loose associations or flight of ideas?
2. Does the client exhibit delusions, persecution, thought broadcasting, etc.?
3. Are there any obsessive thoughts, compulsive behaviour or is the client phobic?
4. Indications of suicidal ideation?

SENSORY PERCEPTION
1. Does the client have significant hearing or sight problems?
2. Does the client suffer from illusions or hallucinations?

MENTAL CAPACITIES
1. Is the client oriented to time, place and person, memory or judgement problems?
2. Does the client appear to be of average intelligence, have a capacity for concentration?
3. Client's sense of self-worth?
4. Does the client appear to have a capacity for insight?

ATTITUDE TOWARDS THE INTERVIEWER
1. Client's attitude towards the therapist, including changes?
2. Client's ability to emphathize?

Figure 3.5.3　Mental State Exam (adapted from Lukas, 1993)

focus bearing in mind the capabilities of the client to respond to the approach, the immediacy of the problems and the time available for therapy. This approach takes the view that no single perspective can provide a total 'truth' about the client, although each may still provide a valuable insight into the client's problems. This approach could be said to 'fit' the orientation to the needs of the client.

This second approach can only realistically be adapted by practitioners who have been trained in more than one orientation or in cases where they are able to refer clients to a colleague who does possess knowledge and experience in the selected orientation. For example, in the case of a client with a history of violence, a behavioural approach is likely to focus on an analysis of symptoms and immediate life circumstances. Recent violent episodes would be relatively easy for the client to recall, together with the antecedents and consequences. Therapy would tend to focus on developing anger control and learning new patterns of behaviour. A psychodynamic approach is likely to focus on the unconscious psychological

```
┌────────────────────────────────────────────┐
│              Early experiences               │
└────────────────────────────────────────────┘

┌────────────────────────────────────────────────────────┐
│  • Father left when client was 6 years old              │
│  • Mother found it difficult to cope and was treated     │
│    for depression                                        │
│  • Mother relied on client for support and was very      │
│    critical                                              │
└────────────────────────────────────────────────────────┘

┌────────────────────────────────────────────┐
│          Formulation of core beliefs         │
└────────────────────────────────────────────┘

┌────────────────────────────────────────────┐
│  • I am a failure                            │
│  • I am a bad person                         │
└────────────────────────────────────────────┘

┌────────────────────────────────────────────┐
│    Formulation of conditional assumptions    │
└────────────────────────────────────────────┘

┌────────────────────────────────────────────┐
│  • If people like me, then I am okay         │
│  • If I work hard, I will succeed            │
└────────────────────────────────────────────┘

┌────────────────────────────────────────────┐
│               Critical incident              │
└────────────────────────────────────────────┘

┌────────────────────────────────────────────┐
│  • Not getting a promotion                   │
└────────────────────────────────────────────┘

┌────────────────────────────────────────────┐
│         Beliefs/assumptions activated        │
└────────────────────────────────────────────┘

┌────────────────────────────────────────────────────────┐
│  • I should have worked harder and I am a failure       │
│  • I did not try hard enough to make an impression       │
│  • I am a failure                                        │
└────────────────────────────────────────────────────────┘

┌────────────────────────────────────────────┐
│          Negative automatic thoughts         │
└────────────────────────────────────────────┘
```

(Continued)

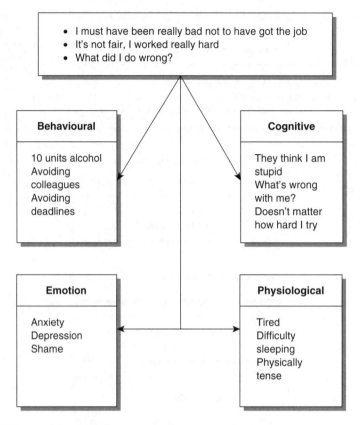

Figure 3.5.4   CBT case formulation

conflicts which give rise to such violence. An exploration of the distant past may be necessary to provide an understanding of how an aggressive lifestyle has developed as a means of coping with everyday problems. Adaptive behaviour can then follow the client's insight into unmet and unrecognized needs.

In case conceptualization, consideration should be given to the ease and understanding with which it can be read at a future date, possibly by a third party. Again, a standard structure may be helpful in this as well as imposing discipline on the therapist.

Two components are required: an overview of the client written from the chosen theoretical perspective and the supporting material which backs up the overview. The overview can come either at the beginning of the written case conceptualization, which makes for quick and easy reading, or at the end, where it will tend to be seen as the logical conclusion drawn from the supporting material. The overview of the client should be concise, provide an analysis of the client's core strengths and weaknesses, and tied to the assumptions of a stated theoretical perspective.

The supporting material is likely to be more extensive and to provide all the evidence on which the overview is based. The supporting material will also include an in-depth analysis of the client's strengths and weaknesses (again from the same theoretical perspective). Relevant information will be included from the client's past and present histories, observations made during the assessment and from other sources.

Therapeutic planning

Therapeutic planning is usually regarded as a collaborative effort between therapist and client and is a theory-driven action plan to produce constructive client change. The implementation of such a plan frequently calls for considerable effort and determination on the part of both therapist and client. As a result, it is usual to list both long-term goals, which represent the longer-term aims of the client, and a series of more manageable, short-term steps or goals from which the longer-term aims can be achieved.

In evaluating the relevance and efficacy of therapeutic plans, Egan (2001) has provided a set of criteria which include the following questions:

- Is the strategy clear?
- Is it relevant to the problem or goal?
- Does it appeal to the client?
- Is it consistent with the client's values?
- Is it effective enough?

Further useful reference can be made to Egan (2001).

The choice of long and short-term goals is clearly tied to the client but will tend to differ with the theoretical orientation used (Berman, 1997). For example, in the case of a recently bereaved widow with young children, who experiences depression, anxiety and low self-esteem, a cognitive approach may suggest long-term goals of:

1. Replacing maladaptive beliefs in perfectionism and absolutist standards with realistic perceptions and adaptive coping.
2. Becoming aware of gender-role stereotypes and how they distort and restrict her ability to grieve and parent effectively.

Short-term goals might be:

1. Learning to monitor, interrupt, analyse and challenge maladaptive self-talk.
2. Reducing contact with those who are reinforcing problematic thoughts and behaviour and increase positive social support to maintain any changes she makes in therapy.

In the case of a male, black teenager perceiving white people as condescending, showing no respect, and as a result behaving in a way that can elicit the very negative behaviour and stereotyping he most hates and fears, a time-limited psychodynamic approach (after the therapist has established to what extent his views of discrimination are reality-based) may have a long-term goal to:

1. Use his experience within the therapeutic relationship to increase the flexibility of his internal model of the interpersonal world with non-blacks.

Short-term goals might be:

1. To become aware of his emotions, fantasies, wishes and perceptions involving non-blacks and how these have resulted in his good/bad categorization.
2. To become aware of how negative community stereotypes of black people have affected him.
3. To become more aware of his eliciting manoeuvres, their impact on his non-black relationships and their potential for increasing negative stereotyping.
4. To experience more fully his emotions associated with any discrimination he faces.

Berman (1997) clearly states that case conceptualization and treatment planning aims to integrate theory with clinical practice; that the aim is to provide quality care; and that material can be reworked in the light of new information or a change of direction in the therapy. Treatment planning is an attempt to meet client needs as accurately as possible, yet effective therapy seeks to help clients help themselves. The therapist's main task is to bring together the respect for the therapeutic relationship with the discipline of treatment planning.

See also section 6.3, 'Conceptualizing clients' problems' (p. 356).

References

Berman, P.S. (1997) *Case Conceptualization and Treatment Planning*. London: Sage.

Egan, G. (2001) *The Skilled Helper* (7th edn). Pacific Grove, CA: Brooks/Cole.

Lazarus, A.A. and Lazarus, C.N. (1991) *Multimodal Life History Inventory*. Champaign, IL: Research Press.

Lukas, S. (1993) *Where to Start and What to Ask*. New York: Norton.

McMahon, G. (1994) *Starting Your Own Private Practice*. Cambridge: National Extension College.

Milner, J. and O'Bryne, P. (2004) *Assessment in Counselling: Theory, Process and Decision-Making*. Basingstoke: Palgrave.

Padesky, C. and Greenberger, D. (1995) *Clinician's Guide to Mind Over Mood*. New York: Guilford Press.

Palmer, S. and McMahon, G. (eds) (1997) *Client Assessment*. London: Sage.

Palmer, S. and Szymanska, K. (1994) Referral guidance for participants attending stress management training courses. *Stress News*, 5 (4): 11.

3.6 Structuring Work with Clients   ○○○

IAN HORTON

This section will examine the structure and process of counselling and psychotherapy. It is based on the assumption that, irrespective of theoretical orientation, it is possible to conceptualize the therapeutic process in terms of a framework of broadly defined phases or stages. Each phase is characterized by particular process goals or tasks that need to be achieved as a prerequisite of moving forward to the next phase (Beitman, 1990; Egan, 2001; McLeod, 2003). As a structural overview of the developmental process, the framework provides therapists with a sense of grounding and direction. But it is only a cognitive map and as such cannot reflect the actual experience or dynamics of a process that seldom, if ever, follows a straightforward linear progression through discrete and clearly defined phases. As the relationship between therapist and client develops, new issues may emerge, goals are evaluated and often redefined and earlier phase-related tasks may be revisited and worked on more deeply. It is a fluid, multidimensional and complex process.

A simple generic model of the Preparatory, Beginning, Middle and Ending phases of therapy is used here as a heuristic framework for examining the typical structure, process and procedures of counselling and psychotherapy. The therapist's own theoretical orientation will largely determine the relative emphasis and importance placed on the various aspects of the four-phase model. Some psychotherapists regard initial and on-going frame management as the main, if not the only kind of legitimate structuring (e.g. Smith, 1991) and many psychoanalytic therapists are unconcerned with temporal and outcome issues.

Preparatory phase

Many practitioners believe that the therapeutic relationship actually begins before any face-to-face contact with clients. Several factors may influence both the client's and the therapist's expectations of each other and therefore the beginning of their relationship and the subsequent development of the therapeutic process. For some counsellors or psychotherapists, the normal procedure may be for a senior therapist to conduct an intake assessment, followed by allocation to a suitable therapist – a process which in itself may structure expectations and norms.

Prior knowledge

The therapist may have a referral letter or report containing detailed information about the client and her or his presenting problem and history. Casual comments made by the receptionist or other people working in the agency or service setting may unwittingly influence the therapist's expectations of the client.

Clients themselves will often come to therapy with preconceptions about counselling or psychotherapy and project them on to the particular therapist. Previous experience of some form of psychological or psychiatric help, or accounts of the experiences of others may similarly influence the client's expectations. The client may have heard something about the reputation of the particular therapist or agency.

Introductory leaflet

Many agencies or therapists produce information leaflets to give to potential clients. The purpose is to inform the client about the conditions and procedures to follow and what to expect when coming for counselling or psychotherapy. The leaflet, read carefully by some potential clients and probably ignored by others, is nevertheless an opportunity to help establish positive and accurate expectations of what therapy is about. An information leaflet for clients will normally contain the following information:

- some explanation of what counselling and/or psychotherapy is about;
- examples of the kinds of problems people might come with and how therapy can help;
- background information about the particular agency or service offered;
- qualifications, experience and professional affiliation of the therapists providing the service;
- how to make an appointment;
- fees and how these are paid;
- cancellation procedures, fee implications and period of notice required;
- typical duration and frequency of sessions and length of contract;

- theoretical orientation and approach to counselling or psychotherapy;
- where the counselling or therapy will take place, postal address, name and telephone number of therapist or contact person.

First telephone call

Often the first direct contact between client and therapist is through a telephone call. Many people do not find it easy to be a client and have to admit to others (and to themselves) that they have problems they cannot cope with. Some people agonize for some time before picking up enough courage to make the initial telephone call. The client may be upset, diffident about making the call or sceptical about counselling or psychotherapy. The reception he or she receives, what the therapist says and how it is said, may influence the caller's feelings and attitudes. The therapist may be very busy or tired, but if he or she is able to offer a place for an initial appointment, this is the first opportunity to start building rapport by communicating some degree of warmth and concern and perhaps by responding to callers by mirroring the way they speak. In one sense the therapeutic relationship starts at this point. The client needs to feel accepted, welcomed and understood. What happens next and what is being offered needs to be explained simply and clearly.

If the person taking the call is not a counsellor or psychotherapist the same considerations still apply. Receptionists may need training in how to take calls from potential clients. Beginning therapists may find it useful to rehearse the kind of things they want to say.

Letter of appointment

In some situations the letter offering a first appointment may be the first contact with the client, who, even from this limited source of information, may begin to develop some impression of the therapist and the service offered. Therapists may want to convey a balance of warmth and professional formality in what and how they write to clients. Letters, usually typed or neatly handwritten on headed A4-size notepaper, would normally include information about the location, date, time and duration of the first session, as well as the contact telephone number and, if appropriate, how and by when the client should confirm acceptance of the appointment. Somes examples of letters to clients can be found in the next section on ancillary skills.

Physical setting

The room in which the therapy takes place contributes to the client's initial impression of the therapist. Generally therapists believe that while it may inevitably reflect the therapist's personality and preference of what seems comfortable and welcoming, it should be relatively neutral with no distracting objects or very personal things such as family photographs on show.

Unless the therapist always works on floor cushions or with the client on a couch, two comfortable chairs of the same height and style are used by most practitioners. The chairs are usually positioned slightly at an angle to each other to avoid direct eye contact, which some clients may find overly confronting. Lighting may be an issue too. Care should be taken to avoid having the source of light or the window directly behind the therapist and with the light directly into the face of the client. The client may then see the therapist as a partial silhouette and feel vulnerable and threatened. Soft or dim lighting is usually thought preferable to a bright light, especially the kind of strip light found in many offices.

What is essential is to ensure the optimum level of privacy. Every effort should be made to avoid being disturbed by any extraneous noises such as people talking in the corridor outside or in adjacent rooms or by telephones ringing. The client should not be visible to anyone passing outside and looking in through the window. Many therapists use a 'Please don't disturb' notice on the door and insist that everyone else in the building knows that they are 'not to be disturbed'. Many of these contextual issues are discussed in Lago and Kitchin (1998) and are important in that they help the client to relax and feel safe.

Preparation before the client arrives

Few if any therapists would disagree that it is absolutely essential to arrive on time and before the client arrives. Beginning practitioners often like to arrive early to check the room, read through the referral report or their case notes and maximize their level of 'free attention'.

Practitioners vary in their attitude towards referrers' reports. Some like to study the reports carefully, noting issues to explore with the client or at least hold as 'silent hypotheses'. Some agencies adopt a policy of asking clients to complete a pre-interview questionnaire on background history and personal details. Other practitioners want to meet the client without being influenced by the apparent facts and opinions provided by the referrer. They deliberately do not read the referral letter until after their first meeting with the client. The risk with this procedure is that the referrer might mention some critical issue which the therapist really does need to be aware of *before* meeting the client – for example, a record of frequent violent or aggressive behaviour or recent suicide attempts. The key issue is for the therapist to be aware of her or his assumptions or inferences drawn from what can sometimes be highly subjective and often dated information about the client.

Immediately prior to the expected arrival of the client, some therapists follow deliberate procedures to enable them to relax and focus attention on what they are about to do. Simple physical relaxation or breathing exercises or just sitting in silence for a few minutes can help the therapist to prepare mentally.

Beginning phase

The first face-to-face meeting with the client sows the seeds of attraction, uncertainty or dislike and the beginning of the therapist's assessment of the client. People are often unaware of the source of their feelings or immediate reactions to others, although counsellors and therapists are trained to be aware of the way in which they may prematurely interpret what they notice about the dress and demeanour of others or project feelings or attitudes derived from previous relationships or situations on to their clients. But of course this is a two-way process: clients will have feelings too and make assumptions about the therapist on their first meeting. Both parties will be tentatively sizing the other up.

Initial greeting and seating

Practitioners vary in the degree of formality with which they greet their clients. Many do so warmly, but wait for the client to indicate tentatively whether they expect to shake hands. It is important to get the client's name correct and it is useful to become familiar with the naming conventions of different cultures. If in doubt, it is an idea to ask clients how they wish to be addressed or at least initially to adopt a more formal manner of address, leaving the choice to become more familiar, later. Some culturally different names may be difficult for the therapist to pronounce. Again it may be appropriate for the therapist to ask the client how to pronounce her or his name. This at least communicates that it matters to the therapist to get the client's name right. Especially in some cultures, counsellors and psychotherapists are seen as powerful people and clients initially feeling overwhelmed are unlikely to correct the therapist's pronunciation of their name or the mode of address and may feel put down or feel that the therapist does not really care about them as individuals.

Another concern for some therapists is whether to leave it to clients to decide or, more conventionally, whether to indicate where the client should sit. To leave it to the client may, albeit in a small way, help the client to feel more equal in an inevitably unequal relationship, but it can mean that the client has yet another unfamiliar decision to make at a time when they are already feeling anxious about what is going to happen.

Introduction

'How can I help you?', 'What brings you here?', 'We have 50 minutes together; how would you like to use the time?' are some of the ways in which therapists encourage the client to start talking as soon as possible. Some psychoanalytic therapists think it important to say *nothing* from the outset. However, other practitioners prefer to start by setting the scene, being aware that once some clients launch into telling their story it is hard to stop them, while other more reticent clients appreciate some time to relax into their new surroundings with a stranger and have little or no idea how the therapist might be able to help them or how to use the time. There is some 'collective wisdom', if not clear research evidence, that indicates a strong correlation or association between successful outcome and a shared understanding between therapist and client of the purpose of what they are doing together and how they are going to try to achieve it. This shared understanding is the basis of an effective working or therapeutic alliance, so some therapists prefer to start by saying something like: 'The purpose of our first meeting today is for us to get to know each other and for me to begin to understand something of the problems or issues that bring you here. At the end of the hour we may be in a position to decide whether we want to continue to work together and we will discuss the necessary arrangements'. Some clients may have been sent by their GP or persuaded by a friend to come and may be sceptical about the value of counselling or psychotherapy. In this situation the task is to try to establish whether or not there is a basis for working together and the therapist may suggest to the client that they leave it to a subsequent session before formally contracting to work with the client. This would give the therapist an opportunity to consult her or his clinical supervisor before seeing the client again.

Therapist's agenda

Theoretical orientation, personal preference and style, and agency setting and organizational constraints or procedures are some of the factors that may determine the way in which the first session is structured and managed. While most therapists tend to adopt a similar way of working with all their clients, some vary what they do according to perceived client needs and expectations. The style and approach differs enormously between therapists – even those of the same orientation – and varies along a continuum from formal and highly structured to open, flexible and very much client-led.

Nevertheless, whether it is explicit or not, most practitioners will have a similar agenda for the first few sessions or for the beginning phase of their work with clients. This agenda may typically include the following process goals or tasks, irrespective of whether they are achieved through listening to the client's story, intervening as appropriate as the story gradually unfolds, or asking questions in a more structured interview.

Some therapists listen for or deliberately ask about the client's expectations and previous experiences of counselling or psychotherapy. This information will help the therapist to assess the client's needs and level of readiness and to know how best to begin to facilitate a strong therapeutic alliance.

For clients for whom counselling or psychotherapy is a truly new and unfamiliar experience the therapist may need to explain what therapy is about, the roles of therapist and client and what is going to happen. Beginning therapists may find it a very useful exercise to prepare and rehearse the actual words they might use to define or explain counselling or psychotherapy to clients.

The whole idea of therapy as an approach to problem solving or self-development is culture bound. Seeking help with psychological problems from someone outside the family is alien to some cultures and clients may need time to discuss and assimilate the implications and consequences of doing so. Similarly, counselling and psychotherapy goals are culture bound. For example, such concepts as self-awareness or self-actualization and the emphasis on individualism may be inappropriate as explicitly stated goals when working with some clients in cross-cultural settings.

At some point in the first (few) session(s) it may be helpful for the therapist to say something about the ground rules or boundaries of counselling or psychotherapy. Issues about privacy, confidentiality and its limits, the length of sessions and time boundaries may need to be explained and discussed. If the therapist is culturally close to the client, some clients may feel an instant rapport and trust, but others may fear a loss of confidentiality and feel as if they risk what they say being known by everyone in his or her cultural community. The therapist may need to reassure the client that he or she respects confidence and that therapy is in no way compatible with socializing. Some clients may disclose something critical near the end of the session, in what feels like the safety of the session ending; other clients may be unfamiliar with the strict time-keeping of middle-class western practice and be left feeling resentful when invited by the therapist to raise the issue again in their next session.

Facilitating client self-disclosure is the primary task of the beginning phase of therapy. Talking about themselves and their problem is after all exactly what the client has come for. The therapist will listen to the client's story and explore the client's social and cultural background, history and experiences, the onset of the problem, current stresses and issues, coping behaviours and motivations. This will enable both the therapist and the client to begin building a picture of the problem and to consider if and how therapy might help.

Some therapists start to develop a formal assessment or clinical formulation of the client's presenting problem and, from this, an initial therapeutic plan or possible therapeutic goals and approach to working with the particular client.

At this point, usually at the end of the first session, therapists need to make a decision. Basically there are four options:

- to offer counselling or psychotherapy;
- to offer to refer the client to another therapist or agency;
- not to offer counselling or psychotherapy if the therapist thinks it would be inappropriate or not useful to the particular client at this time;
- to defer the decision to contract until a later session.

Therapists approach contracting with clients with varying degrees of formality, clarity and explicitness. It is possible to identify two types of contracting: therapeutic and business contracts. The first is concerned with negotiating and identifying with the client the sort of desired outcomes the therapy might achieve, and the initial focus or aspect of the problem the therapist and client intend to work on together and how they might approach this. The nature of the therapeutic contract and whether it is stated explicitly and even written down will depend very much on the therapist's theoretical orientation and personal preference. Some therapists assume that the therapeutic contract is part of the client's induction into therapy and a largely unspoken yet integral part of the gradually evolving therapeutic process.

The business contract is important and few therapists disagree that it needs to be concrete and explicit. The business contract concerns such things as the duration, frequency, number, day and starting time of sessions, fees and how they are to be paid, procedures for the cancellation of sessions, and fees for missed sessions. Some therapists like to give this information in written form and include the date and time of the next appointment.

Comprehensive details of contracting from the perspectives of different theoretical orientations are given in Sills (1997).

Ending the first session is an opportunity to clarify administrative details and handle any questions the client may still have about the therapy, before confirming the next appointment and parting.

Summary: beginning phase process goals

The beginning phase may last for one, twenty, or more sessions depending on the nature of the contract, theoretical orientation and progress made. The process goals or tasks that need to be accomplished are summarized here:

- Build the relationship, establish rapport and an effective working alliance, clarify boundaries, conditions, and the client's role and work towards developing mutual aims about the work of therapy.
- Facilitate client self-disclosure, identify the client's presenting problem through understanding the client's worldview and experiences, exploring antecedents, precipitating events, social/cultural context and assessment of client strengths and resources. The therapist may begin to develop a tentative assessment of the nature, origins and ramifications of the client's problem(s) in a way that suggests a possible target for change. In some psychodynamic work the early fostering of a positive transference might be a key task.
- Negotiate therapeutic and business contracts, and monitor and review progress.

Middle phase

This is typically the longest phase in counselling or psychotherapy. It is the work phase in which conflicts and problems are more clearly defined and worked through. It is within this phase that the biggest variation in practice exists. What therapists are trying to achieve and how they approach the work are largely determined by their theoretical orientation and how they explain the origin and maintenance of psychological problems and the principles and process of change. Nevertheless, at least in broad terms, it is possible to identify the kinds of process goals or tasks generally associated with this phase.

Summary: middle phase process goals

- The aspect of the counselling or psychotherapy process most strongly associated with successful outcome is the quality of the therapeutic relationship and the strength of the working alliance. In the middle phase work continues to maintain and develop further the relationship between therapist and client. Where appropriate and consistent with the therapist's theoretical orientation, the dynamics of the relationship, or what is going on within both therapist and client and between them, may be used as a basis for learning and motivation. The dynamics of the relationship between therapist and client can often provide a 'window' on the client's presenting problem and any hidden conflicts or issues.
- In the middle phase the therapist is concerned with facilitating learning and change, congruent with the identified therapeutic goals and theoretical assumptions about change. It is also the phase in which sometimes unexpected memories, discoveries, obstacles, crises and ambivalence or defences may arise. The process goals of this phase may involve searching for patterns and key themes in the client's experiences and behaviours, affirming and, where possible and appropriate, using the client's strengths and ways of coping, working towards new perspectives, deeper self-awareness or understanding and learning different ways of thinking, feeling and/or behaving.
- Therapists vary in how and whether they explicitly monitor progress. Some formally contract to hold regular review sessions with their clients, others rely solely on clinical supervision, personal reflection and writing case notes to review progress, while some believe in suspending the notion of anxiety about progress altogether.

Reviewing

Some practitioners strongly advocate the need to include regular review sessions in their contract with clients, so that every five weeks or so the client will know that at least part of the session will be spent reviewing progress. Other therapists will review only informally, whenever it seems appropriate or when something comes up, or alternatively only when the work has reached an impasse, when things feel stuck and little, if any, progress is being made. However, clients are entitled to a competently delivered service that is periodically reviewed (BACP, 2002).

The arguments for explicitly monitoring progress with the client include:

- To check out the therapist's assumption about how things are going and if necessary use the opportunity to make changes or improve ways of working.
- To reinforce learning and change or the conditions for change.
- To share power with the client by involving the client in evaluating progress and to help re-establish that the therapist is working *with* the client rather than for, or doing something to, the client.

Arguments against any formal review sessions might be that they interrupt the whole therapeutic process and that any impasse, stuckness or resistance is better worked through as a natural part of the therapy. Review sessions could be seen as a way of avoiding or even perpetuating resistance to change and potentially damaging the transference relationship and may be misinterpreted by some clients as a review of *them*.

Review session structure

Review sessions will be conducted with varying degrees of structure and formality. In standard long-term psychoanalytic psychotherapy, any form of review may be discouraged, while some therapists adopt the practice of asking at *each* session 'what the client wants' and 'how it went' etc. However, a full review agenda would usually involve discussing the following aspects:

- Client and therapist expectations and understanding of what it is they are trying to achieve together.
- Therapeutic goals: What has been achieved? What changes have occurred? What evidence is there of any change?
- Client's experience of the therapeutic process and relationship. What has the client found helpful, unhelpful or difficult? What problems, if any, do the therapist and client have in working together?
- Negotiate ways forward. Review and confirm, or, if necessary, revise the therapeutic goals or focus of the work, and discuss possible alternative ways of working.
- Review the business contract and re-contract for a further period before the next review session.

Ending phase

The ending phase of therapy may represent a real or symbolic loss for many clients. It can provide a potent force in changing a client's frame of mind. In thinking about how best to orchestrate endings or the termination of counselling or psychotherapy, therapists will need to have views, although not necessarily clearly articulated views, on several issues (Leigh, 1998).

- How explicit is the issue of ending therapy with clients? How important is it to prepare for the ending? Some therapists discuss the ending at the beginning of their work with clients, others use a 'countdown' system to remind clients about how many sessions they have had and how many remain. Who decides when therapy should end? Is it decided by the client, therapist or by mutual agreement?
- How rigid is the decision about ending? Will the therapist adhere strictly to the agreed ending date? This decision is usually linked to the nature of the therapeutic goals, type of contract and sometimes negotiated or otherwise implicit completion criteria. Clearly, therapists need to be aware of what, if any, are the circumstances that justify an extension and how flexible they can be and what the ramifications are.
- What may be the special existential or developmental needs of the particular client around loss and ending?

For some clients separation and loss may have been a key theme or conflict in their work with the therapist. Ending therapy may mean a reworking of earlier loss or a celebration of a new beginning. Ending may be more critical in some types of time-limited contracts and therapists need to pay attention to managing effectively client resources and deficits.

Summary: ending phase process goals

Most therapists will pay attention to some or all of the following tasks in working towards a satisfactory ending with their clients:

- Seeking resolution of the client's issues around ending.
- Exploring ways of consolidating learning and change through helping clients to apply and assimilate change into new ways of being or living and through identifying obstacles and ways of sustaining and expanding change.
- Evaluating the outcomes of therapy and the effectiveness (or otherwise) of the therapeutic process and relationship.

A high percentage of counselling and psychotherapy contracts end by default rather than by design. That is, clients may just stop coming for therapy, sometimes not even letting the therapist know and not replying to the therapist's letter. Incomplete ending by default can haunt therapists for some time. It is all too easy to slip into imagining all sorts of circumstances or reasons, including the therapist's own mistakes or incompetence, for clients failing to attend to the end of a negotiated contract or agreed period of therapy. These things are best worked through in clinical supervision. However, most therapists will have the opportunity to formally complete their ending work with a client.

Ending session structure

Ending can be viewed as a process in itself. The aim is to help clients integrate their views of what has happened and reinforce the positive aspects of the experience. The intention is to enable clients to sustain any change.

There are five areas that can be usefully explored with clients at the end of counselling or psychotherapy:

- What has been achieved?
  What changes have occurred or are anticipated by both client and therapist?
  Were the goals met?
- What still needs to be achieved?
  Is it possible to anticipate any return of symptoms in particular circumstances? Will the client be able to cope with old problems using the new 'solutions' or ways of coping learned in therapy?
- Why has change happened?
  How does the client attribute cause or responsibility for change?
  The client's story about therapy is the best predictor of whether useful changes will last. Clients need to know the ways that they contributed to or are responsible for any change, attempts to change and the quality of the relationship.
- What may happen in the future?
  Is it possible to anticipate any stresses or 'rough spots'? What resources are available for support? Sometimes it is helpful to try to identify signs or indicators of the need to start therapy again.
  Will the therapist offer a one-off follow-up in say six to eight weeks or invite the client to contact him or her again if necessary? What possible messages might that give to the client? What seems important is that a 'good ending' will help to ensure that clients will have positive feelings about the prospect of returning to therapy – and not see it as a failure, but as a normal occurrence in developmental change.
- What has been the nature of the therapy relationship?
  This can be threatening to the therapist and some see it as irrelevant to identifying what qualities were helpful and/or difficult in the relationship. The client may be encouraged to identify what has been learned from the therapy relationship that may help the client in other relationships.

Many of the skills and procedures mentioned in this section are developed in the following section on ancillary skills.

References

BACP (2002) *Ethical Framework for Good Practice in Counselling and Psychotherapy*. Rugby: British Association for Counselling and Psychotherapy.

Beitman, B.D. (1990) Why I am an integrationist (not an eclectic). In W. Dryden and J.C. Norcross (eds), *Eclecticism and Integration in Counselling and Psychotherapy*. Loughton: Gale Centre.

Egan, G. (2001) *The Skilled Helper* (7th edn). Pacific Grove, CA: Brooks/Cole.

Lago, C. and Kitchin, D. (1998) *The Management of Counselling and Psychotherapy Agencies*. London: Sage.

Leigh, A. (1998) *Referral and Termination Issues for Counsellors*. London: Sage.

McLeod, J. (2003) *An Introduction to Counselling* (3rd edn). Buckingham: Open University Press.

Sills, C. (ed.) (1997) *Contracts in Counselling*. London: Sage.

Smith, D.L. (1991) *Hidden Conversations: An Introduction to Communicative Psychoanalysis*. London: Routledge.

3.7 Ancillary Skills

COLIN FELTHAM

As well as the many overt, in-session, interpersonal, therapeutic or clinical skills, there are many ancillary skills necessary for good practice. These are largely 'before and after' skills, and relate to mediated communication with clients, the setting for therapy, safety, recording and reflecting on practice; a set of skills falling somewhere between clinical and professional/business skills. While 'ancillary' may not be the best word for those internal skills of reflecting on the moment-to-moment encounter with clients, reference to these as a form of self-monitoring is nevertheless included here. To some extent how extra-therapeutic communications are managed depends on ordinary social skills, yet there are often subtle psychological and ethical considerations involved, which render them quite complex. Practitioners need to find an appropriate balance between the routine and practical, and ethically challenging issues that can arise at any time (BACP, 2002).

Receiving referrals

The manner in which clients make contact with therapists – directly or via intermediaries or certain media (letter, telephone, etc.) – depends a great deal on the nature of the practice setting. Inward referral issues are discussed here. The word 'clients' is used throughout here, even though some contacts will be inquirers only.

Contact variations

- 'Cold' contact via telephone, where the client's call is the first communication about them. This is common in private practice.
- Expected telephone contact, where an intermediary has already alerted both parties to the possibility of a referral.
- Message taken or appointment made by a receptionist, colleague or senior.

- A (usually senior) colleague allocates the client to a particular therapist following assessment.
- The client attends a 'drop-in' service and, depending on availability, may be seen almost immediately.
- Some clients initiate contact by written correspondence if they are wary, tentative or have mobility problems.
- Formal written referral and (psychiatric/mental state/history) report from GP or psychiatrist.

Two quite different scenarios are involved in all this: (i) In single-handed private practice, first contacts are typically by telephone, and frequently the caller will be completely unknown; this is especially likely when therapists advertise. This scenario immediately raises considerations of *preparation* (a practice diary, a rehearsed or spontaneous response to requests for counselling or therapy, etc.) and of *safety* (protection of client and practitioner safety). Preparation and safety issues are discussed later in this section. (ii) In counselling or psychotherapy agencies or private practice collectives, it is quite typical for new clients to pass through a process entailing elements of telephone inquiry, waiting lists, assessment, allocation and first appointment. Many agency-oriented issues are dealt with in Lago and Kitchin (1998) and the focus here is mainly on private practice and/or lone practitioner issues (Clark, 2002).

Telephone issues

Certain telephone skills are discussed in Part 7 of this book. Clearly, it is necessary to consider who will answer the telephone (particularly in a multi-occupancy house or busy office) and what unintended first impressions clients may formulate. Background noises of children, music, television, office staff laughing, etc., are likely to detract from a professional image and could inadvertently convey the impression that the therapist or agency is too busy with other matters to give full attention to the client.

A separate practice line most usefully deals with some of the potential problems since an answerphone message can be tailored to meet the calls of clients telephoning when no one is available to answer in person. ('This is the counselling/psychotherapy practice of Mary Jones. I'm sorry I'm unavailable at the moment. Please leave your telephone number and I will call back as soon as possible, or try calling again between 10 a.m. and 1 p.m. on Wednesdays and Fridays.') Different practitioners may disagree on the levels of warmth and informality, as opposed to neutrality and professionalism, they wish to convey by tone of voice and selection of phrases. However, therapeutic relationships begin both consciously and unconsciously at these earliest stages, and even a slightly unfriendly tone of voice or hint of impatience or incompetence may take on personalized negative proportions in some clients' minds. It is important to remember too that many people dislike telephone answering machines and there is some risk of frustrating callers and losing business or take-up of the service when no personal response is available. As in all extra-sessional (outside the session) communication with clients, sensitivity and alertness have to be exercised at all times with regard to the possibility of third parties (on your own or the clients' side) compromising confidentiality.

'I wonder if you can help me. I've been given your name by X organization. I've had a lot of problems and I've been signed off sick with stress.' This is a not unusual opening, although inquiries may of course be anywhere on a range from brief, curt and anxious to lengthy, complex and demanding. Sometimes potential clients may wish to 'interview' the therapist on the telephone, or ask for immediate opinions on their condition, or for recommendations of other therapists. Some will want to know full details of fees, available times, and so on, while others may be too embarrassed or distressed to go into such details. In some instances the client's friend, partner or parent will telephone on their behalf, and the therapist needs to anticipate appropriate responses (i.e. to accept or not to accept anything other than a self-referral).

Probably only experience can teach each practitioner what suits her or his situational needs and preferences, but everyone will need to prepare to discuss early on their availability, the range of presenting concerns they feel competent to take on, and preferred referral and assessment procedures. In determining availability, therapists should allocate themselves very specific hours if possible, and anticipate all breaks, holidays and possible clashes of commitments as far in advance as they can. Some prefer to keep telephone contact minimal, for example by offering to meet at no cost for an initial assessment or 'exploratory meeting'. Others, however, offer a specific, sometimes longer initial session for which payment is due. Some have printed leaflets containing details of services, fees, availability and location, which may be sent out prior to a first meeting.

Safety

For ethical, legal and obvious personal reasons, all practitioners must anticipate certain issues concerning their clients' and their own physical safety and security.

Attending to client safety

Clients' physical safety may be inadvertently compromised by any of the following:

- The potentially hazardous nature of the neighbourhood in which the therapist lives or works; street lighting; transport; parking; anonymity; privacy; etc.
- Hazardous features in access to residence, office and room, including slippery pathways; loose roofing slates/tiles; steep steps; loose carpets; problematic stairways; faulty wiring; fire hazards; etc.
- Potential health emergencies, such as asthma attack; fainting; epilepsy; cardiac arrest; psychotic episode; etc.
- Possible intrusion and assault by third parties, for example in busy agencies with a mixed clientele.

In most cases the remedy is obvious – property maintenance, adequate insurance, training in first aid, etc. – but it is recommended that self-initiated systematic surveys of potential hazards are carried out and remedies considered. Attention to outward aspects of safety is also, in an important sense, an integral reflection of the provision of psychological containment for and protection of the client.

Practitioner safety

Therapists owe it to themselves, and to any colleagues or family members who may be affected, to consider necessary self-protection and security measures. Again, thinking over issues of particular relevance to private practitioners (but also to others), these items are significant:

- Working alone: if possible, this should be avoided, simply by having other people present in other parts of the house or building, especially if the client is a different sex from the therapist.
- In case of risk of being physically attacked, steps should be taken to install alarm buttons or other means of summoning help, if possible. Where possible, *downstairs* rooms near to exits should be used as consulting rooms.
- Careful consideration should be given to what could ensue from accepting referrals involving clients with histories of crime, addiction and related activities. Easily removed valuables and potentially dangerous objects should certainly be removed before seeing clients.
- Unwanted intrusions by 'out of hours' telephone calls, unexpected visits, etc. should be addressed as far as possible by clear contracting at the outset.
- While many practitioners and some clients object to tape recording of sessions, this is one way of faithfully recording what happens in sessions in case of unjustified accusations of malpractice.
- Since some therapists have unfortunately been harassed or stalked by clients or ex-clients, thought should probably be given to prevention (e.g. rigorous assessment), and to how such eventualities will be dealt with should they occur.
- Possible aggression from clients or third parties (e.g. angry partners) should be anticipated, and appropriate methods of defusion employed when necessary. Practitioners, especially those working regularly in or with the criminal justice system, also need to consider and use supervision to reflect on issues pertaining to 'difficult clients' (Norton and McGauley, 1998) and aggressive behaviour (Sills, 1997).

A list of this kind may appear overly and unattractively defensive at first sight. However, the North American experience of litigation has alerted UK practitioners to these areas of concern. Professional indemnity insurance protects practitioners from unnecessary and distracting worry, thus leaving them more able to be fully present for their clients. Another valid objection to such issues is that there may simply be no way of anticipating the many anomalous challenges posed by clients. Perhaps the most that can be suggested is that careful thought be given to *preparation, assessment, contracting, alertness to real threat, and robust and sensitive interpersonal skills for managing unexpected challenges.*

General risk assessment

It could be argued that a therapist has an ethical and professional responsibility to take all reasonable steps to ensure not only their own safety, but also that of their clients and, as a result of their client's behaviour, the safety of others. If called to account, therapists should be able to demonstrate that they have taken 'all reasonable steps' and this might include evidence of having conducted a general assessment of risk, either before the therapy starts, as a result of what is already known about the client or situation, or subsequently, as a result of emerging indicators of a potential risk. Evidence of the nature and severity of the hazard or risk should be identified and the likelihood that it will actually happen should be assessed. A simple model for general risk assessment has three elements and can be applied to potential risks to self, client and/or others:

1. **Hazard severity**

   - Low (slight or very minor and easily managed)
   - Medium (potentially serious)
   - High (major risk with possible risk of injury or to life)

2. **Likelihood**

   - Low (seldom present)
   - Medium (frequently present)
   - High (certain or near certain that it could happen at any time)

3. **Overall risk rating**

   - Low (no action or low priority)
   - Medium
   - High (urgent action and high priority)

Clearly, a written record should be kept of the evidence for each decision and the therapist would be advised to discuss the overall rating with her or his clinical supervisor and, if necessary and appropriate, with the agency manager.

Preparing the physical environment

Therapy has been referred to by some as a labour-intensive cottage industry requiring no equipment or props besides a room and two chairs. This is not quite true, however. Jung used the Greek term *temenos* (referring to a sacred precinct, as in 'temple') for the 'out of the ordinary' atmosphere of therapy, and some therapists have extended this metaphor to refer to the psychological significance of the physical environment of the consulting room. Considerable thought and expenditure can go into preparation of the room, including, in some cases, structural alterations to buildings – creating a separate, private entrance and/or waiting area, installing soundproofing, etc. Practicalities and limited finances may often govern such matters but privacy, safety and adequate comfort must be provided, and sometimes this may necessitate specific building, conversion and decorating work.

It is important to consider what ambience will be conducive to privacy, psychological safety and reflection; and (a neglected area) what emotional impact thoughtful aesthetics may have on clients. Those working within the humanistic tradition may wish to incorporate evocative imagery into their décor, as well as using floor cushions or other therapeutic aids. Many therapists weigh up the advantages and disadvantages of using a couch instead of a chair, and in some cases may offer the client a choice. Preferably lighting should be adjustable. It has been suggested that warm and dimly lit interiors encourage (possibly long-term) introspection, while well-lit, businesslike interiors may be suited to the outward-looking briskness of shorter-term therapy (Molnos, 1995). Heating too must be efficient and adjustable enough to provide comfort without inducing drowsiness. Décor will obviously reflect the occupant's taste, but thought should be given to creating optimal conditions by perhaps *not* keeping personal possessions in the consulting room; striking a balance between sparseness (obliging the client to look inward) and usefully evocative features (pictures, artefacts, plants, etc.) which can often become therapeutically useful metaphors.

Some writers go as far as arguing that the therapeutic environment should be both minimalist and constant. In other words, furniture and other items should be no more than necessary – two chairs of the same height and style, perhaps a couch, a small table on which to place a diary, invoice, tissues, but very little else. There should be no telephone, no filing cabinet, computer or other office equipment. In no circumstances should any windows be overlooked or walls be thin enough to hear through. All such precautions provide psychological safety. Other writers and practitioners are more pragmatic, perhaps believing that clients learn as much (or more) from the normal challenges of compromised environments as from special, arguably infantilizing conditions. In many cases therapists have little choice but to practise in far from ideal agency settings. However, anticipation, thoughtfulness and planning in relation to the setting are all significant skills that can add to or detract from the therapeutic experience the client has. Guidance on many of these issues is given in Lago and Kitchin (1998) and Thistle (1998). Rowan (1988) also points out that the therapy environment can unwittingly transmit important political messages to clients.

Record keeping

Care should be paid to all records involving clients. These often commence with a note of the first appointment in a diary. A completely separate practice diary ensures that your personal diary does not accidentally reveal details of clients' names and telephone numbers. Earlier in this part of the book, suggestions are made as to useful written intake formats. It isn't always obvious that sufficient time has to be allocated within anyone's practice for administrative matters, and in some services a ratio of about 2:1 is used as an indication of practice to administration hours needed (that is, 24 one-hour practice sessions +1 hour supervision: 12.5 hours administration (including meetings) = a 37.5 hour week). Record keeping includes appointments, case notes, financial records, reports, copies of correspondence, etc.

Case notes

It is good practice to keep regular case notes, although it is not, as is sometimes claimed, necessarily unethical *not* to keep detailed notes. Case notes may also help to demonstrate evidence of professional and ethical responsibility in cases of threatened or potential litigation. However, some means of monitoring one's competency and progress *is* always essential. The precise character of case notes will be determined by individual style, theoretical orientation and other considerations. While some therapists use pro formas, including headings such as referral source, pre-interview data, first impressions, content/process of sessions, therapeutic plan, supervision issues, etc., others prefer a 'free-writing' format. Sometimes referred to as personal case notes to distinguish them from purely factual client data, these may be records of the following:

- The therapist's first impressions, observations, inferences, associations. This may be a mixture of facts, feelings and guesses – e.g. *The client is a tall, elegant man who seemed to bow as he entered the room. His very first words were 'This is cosy', and I was unsure whether this was meaningless small-talk, part of his charm, or a subtle form of defensive sarcasm.* In this example, simple visual observation and a record of actual words spoken is mixed with the therapist's speculations, possibly including implicit elements of counter-transference. Such notes do not claim to be objective and do not aim to be judgemental or diagnostic. Their purpose is (a) immediate reflection and speculation (when made very soon after a session); (b) as an *aide-mémoire*; and (c) as part of an on-going record of progress to be reviewed from time to time.
- Significant and outstanding phrases, images, dreams, new material (e.g. first disclosure of feelings about father), declared aims, hopes, fears. Often, in a busy practice, very brief notes made immediately or soon after a session are all the therapist may have time for. *Said she'd felt better after last week's session. It had helped to get it all out in the open. She felt ready to look in more depth at the effect of her mother's death when she was 10. Mentioned her two brothers, how they seemed to protect her. She looked directly and appealingly at me several times.*
- The therapist's intentions, on-going notes on strategies, their usefulness or otherwise, etc. *I had asked her*

to bring any dreams/try keeping a diary/consider using the relaxation exercise we discussed, etc. ... Today's session seemed to become stuck, arid; next time perhaps I need to challenge, to disclose how that made me feel and prompt the client to express how she feels about it. ... We looked at the extent to which the client has been able to tolerate being in the supermarket; there was marked progress – 20 minutes – and it may be time to increase frequency. It may be apparent that records of this kind are *personal* (i.e. for the therapist's use) and are *notes* (they do not have to be written in polished English, and do not have to make sense to others (unless an agency specifies this). Training in certain approaches (e.g. cognitive-behavioural therapy) may require a detailed record of the implementation of interventions and their impact. In the case of manualized therapies in particular, pro forma checklists of staged interventions may be part of regular record-keeping procedures.

- Reflections on counter-transferential patterns, congruence or transpersonal material. *Felt peculiarly drowsy today when seeing X, which seems odd, since he was talking about being beaten up. ... I realize that although my grandfather used to terrify me by the look he gave me, this client really has a similar look; there is perhaps something in him that wants to terrify others. ... Don 't know why, but I had recurring images of a calm lake when Paul was talking today, and as if we were both floating on it.* Notes of this kind may not even make immediate sense to the writer, but can be returned to and/or taken to supervision later.
- Use of supervision. Notes may be especially useful for marking queries, doubts, concerns, counter-transferential material and ethical matters to be brought up in supervision. Indeed it is customary in some supervision traditions for the therapist to refer directly to their notes. Additionally, therapeutic intentions arising from supervision sessions may be included in the notes, and the impact of supervision-inspired interventions can be further noted. *It had never occurred to me that I might be trying too hard to help this client. ... In the next session, I consciously relaxed, allowed the silences to develop, and X suddenly burst into tears. ... My supervisor suggested that I seem cynical and resistant to everything she says when I discuss Angela, and wondered whether this was the effect Angela has on me; she does!*

Case notes should be kept in a secure place, separate from any identifying details of the client concerned, and should not themselves identify clients.

Coding systems and pseudonyms should be used. Notes should not be trivializing of or demeaning towards clients. Clients should be informed that records are kept and secured, and that you have plans for their safe disposal. Notes should be dated, with some indication of their 'shelf life' and who may have access to them. It is not normal practice to routinely show clients the notes made about them but they have the right to see them. Advance thought should be given to the eventuality of the police requesting to see case notes, or making them the subject of a subpoena, in court cases (Jenkins, 1997). Personal case notes (even when these are kept separately from 'official' notes) are not necessarily regarded as private under the law. Jenkins and Palmer (2000) stress the need for counsellors and psychotherapists to review all their record-keeping and data-processing practices to ensure compliance with the Data Protection Act (1998) which came into force in March 2000. The Act gives clients an increasing right to know what is recorded and written about them. It gives clients the right of access to all computerized data processing. However, 'manual' or handwritten records which are kept in some form of structured system like a card index file are also covered by the Act, although the clients' right to see handwritten notes remains to be clarified by the courts and the Data Protection Commissioner. Some of the key principles of the Act governing our client record systems include the following:

- data must be kept only for specific purposes;
- data must be relevant, accurate and up-to-date;
- data must be kept no longer than is necessary for the purpose;
- data must be protected against misuse;
- data must respect the client's rights, especially 'sensitive personal data' such as the client's race, religious beliefs, union membership, mental and physical health and sexual history. A counsellor's or psychotherapist's records are now classed as 'sensitive personal data'.

Counsellors and therapists, and agencies providing a service, are now required to notify the Data Protection Registry where computerized data processing is being carried out. If the only records are manual records kept as part of a 'relevant filing system', notification is not required.

Table 3.7.1   Record of clients seen – week beginning 14/2/04

Date	Client code	Session number	Presenting/major issue/outcome	Comments
14/2/04	BX5	3	Continuing conflict with partner: Anger. Client needs to talk at length	
14/2/04	BX2	16	Bereavement. Reasonable progress in making new sociable contacts	Review session due in two weeks
14/2/04	CA01	1	G appears severely depressed; agreed to contact GP	GP agrees to make contact. Raised in supervision
15/2/04	BX4	6	Stress at work. Client reports feeling much better	Client wishes to end at agreed session
15/2/04	CY3	5	DNA	Wrote to extend invitation to make another appointment
15/2/04	AX9	37	On-going working through sexual abuse memories	
15/2/04	BY5	1	Disfigurement	Check any support groups available
16/2/04	BY4	9	DNA	Client phoned in ill
16/2/04	CY5	5	Low self-esteem. Social skill problems	Assertiveness programme well under way
16/2/04	AY3	24	Renewed motivation to overcome anxiety	Client returned after two-month interval
16/2/04	BY7	2	Complex problems of debt, loneliness, shyness, bereavement	Need for focus/ prioritization
16/2/04	BX1	11	Anxiety, remorse *re*: rejection by ex-partner	Counter-transference issues

On-going cases summary

It may be a requirement in training situations, in certain agencies or for accreditation purposes, to keep a running record of clients seen, with brief details. A simple format is given in Table 3.7.1. Obviously this can be modified as necessary. Some therapists prefer to keep a *separate* sheet for each client. A benefit to therapists themselves is that this offers an 'at a glance' picture of caseload, workload, length of cases, typical issues, etc. This is a quite separate exercise from data gathering specifying items such as gender, age, ethnic identity, etc., used mainly by agencies.

Case study

A case study is a relatively formal exercise used for training, accreditation, research or publication purposes. One of its main advantages is that it obliges the therapist to think analytically, in depth, and in a detailed manner about a particular client, applying and reflecting on theory, and making links with in-session and across-session phenomena, assessment and case conceptualization skills, use of self, supervision, outcomes, and so on. Case studies in this field have been used for many decades. Freud himself was perhaps one of the most gifted writers in this genre; he certainly wrestled with the difficulties of accurate recall but stressed the significance of detail for understanding the deeper meaning of his patients' own lapses in memory (Freud, 1977 [1925]). A case study may be written as a well-crafted narrative, but the aim is not usually to produce polished literature but to stimulate and demonstrate therapeutically significant learning.

Below are common useful ingredients of a case study. In this instance, the case is retrospective, but case studies may also relate to on-going work.

Elements of a case study

Depending on the specific purpose of the case study, it may include all or some of the following elements:

Initial information

- Description of the client in terms of age, appearance, demeanour, etc.
- Outline of the referral/intake process, other parties involved, etc.
- Setting in which therapy took place, including any conditions or constraints.
- First or early impressions of the client, including the therapist's own feelings, tentative hypotheses, etc.
- Initial assessment, including the client's reported problems, goals, etc.
- Contract/agreement on times, fees, etc., plus initial shared goals.
- Further personal history and relevant background material.

Assessment or clinical formulation

- Identification of patterns revealed in the client's story.
- Any classical diagnostic 'hooks' provided (whether or not these are worked with).
- Emerging themes accounting for the nature of the client's difficulties and for indications of a possible therapeutic plan.

- Observations on defence mechanisms, games, obstacles, or threats to the therapeutic alliance.
- Any subtle or tangential factors that may have some bearing on the outcome.

Therapeutic process

- A record of interventions deployed, with some indication of degree of success.
- Theoretical reflections – i.e. reference to one's training orientation and/or main theoretical allegiance and its ability to explain and predict in this case.
- Key issues and themes, as well as critical moments or turning points in the therapy.
- Specific use of supervision and a note of the usefulness of supervisory inputs.
- Reference to research evidence consulted to clarify or support the work with this client (e.g. consulting literature on outcomes in therapy with eating distress).
- An indication of the structure of sessions and pattern of change (or otherwise) across time (e.g. beginning, middle and ending phase characteristics), linked with client material and therapist interventions.
- Reflections on use of (therapist's) self, counter-transference, congruence, significant components of the therapeutic relationship.

Evaluation

- Indications of success, goal attainment or client satisfaction, including any formal or informal evaluation mechanisms used.
- A statement of what the therapist has learned from this case for their own future development, including identification of any training needs, and any impact the case may have on the therapist's emerging 'personal philosophy' of therapy.

Some psychotherapy training demands extensive case study, fully documented with detailed references to clinical literature. It is quite typical for trainees in counselling to be required to write succinct case studies of anything from 1,000 words upwards. A key feature is often to demonstrate coherence between theory and practice. Case studies are valuable vehicles for learning but care has to be taken that they do not become empty exercises in simply fitting the client to the theory. *Protection of the client's confidentiality by (where appropriate) seeking explicit permission from them, and attending to anonymity, disguising identifying details, physically securing the written article, and limiting the readership, is essential (especially if the case study is to be published).*

Written and other communication with or for clients

Apart from initial telephone contact and on-going face-to-face contact with clients (except where telephone counselling/therapy *is* the medium of therapy), the other main forms of communication are probably periodic telephone and written correspondence. The need for such communication usually arises from cancelled or missed sessions but can also include agreed tasks such as the goodbye letters characteristic of cognitive analytic therapy, letters of support or reports required by solicitors, notification of progress with a waiting list, and occasional correspondence of a social support or therapeutic nature.

Communication relating to missed appointments

Consternation at unexpectedly missed appointments (DNAs – 'did not arrive/attend') is often expressed by trainees in supervision. What is the most appropriate way of discovering why a client did not turn up, reassuring them that they may return, and knowing where you stand with them? Such eventualities may be anticipated by comprehensive verbal contracting ('If you do not arrive for your next session, I will assume you will be here the following week at the same time, and you have agreed to pay for all missed sessions.' Or 'If you do not give at least 24 hours notice of cancellation, I will make contact with you by phone or letter.') Where leaflets are used, they may spell out exactly what happens following a non-arrival. There are numerous possible permutations here, and differing preferences and traditions. Quite typically, therapists may assume that unexpected telephone contacts may be unwelcome, and that therefore letters may be preferable. Below are two examples:

Dear Nasreen

I'm aware that you were unable to attend your last appointment with me at 3p.m. on Tuesday 22 September. As agreed, I intend to keep the same time (3p.m.) available for you next week on Tuesday 29 September, unless I hear from you by telephone or letter to the contrary.

I look forward to seeing you.

Yours sincerely

Margaret Smith

Practice counsellor

Dear Anthony

I'm sorry you could not attend yesterday's appointment with me. In the light of recent events in your life and your own expressed uncertainty about therapy, I assume that you don't want to continue. However, I would like you to know that you are very welcome to get in touch again at any time, either to make another appointment or simply to let me know how you're getting on.

All best wishes

Yours sincerely

Ved Patel

The first example is businesslike and reiterates a previously agreed contract. The second, written to a client after some months of therapy, is more personal, warm and tailored. *There is no one correct form of correspondence in these circumstances.* In spite of the norms inculcated by different training traditions, it is advisable to adapt appropriately to the unique set of demands constituted by knowledge of the client, the client's circumstances, organization or agency procedures/requirements, ethical, professional and business considerations, as well as preconceived theoretical traditions about breaks and endings.

Other kinds of correspondence may be appropriate at times. For example, 'Here is the address of the occupational psychologist I mentioned to you', or 'I am writing to say that my hospital treatment is now completed and I would welcome the opportunity to resume therapy with you, if you would like to get in touch', or 'Thank you very much for your letter telling me why you have decided not to continue with therapy', etc. Otherwise, unsolicited communication is not advised, unless it serves specific and justifiable purposes, for example a greetings card for a special occasion. Of course, in some traditions, almost all such exceptions (including the giving or receiving of gifts) may be regarded as compromising the therapeutic frame, but in others flexible, responsible, ordinary human responses may be regarded as helpful and particularly important with clients from some minority cultures (Ridley, 1995).

Report writing

Counsellors and psychotherapists would not normally be required to write official reports on or for their clients unless employed by an agency with a specific brief to do so. For example, those involved in adoption counselling, or forensic psychotherapy, may have certain statutory responsibilities. Psychiatrists and clinical psychologists are the professionals more likely to be called upon for reports on clients' mental state, assessments, and professional opinions. Sometimes counsellors and psychotherapists may be approached by solicitors, clients' advocates or clients themselves with requests for written reports in connection with stress at work, post-traumatic stress or marital disputes. The motivation for such requests may be straightforward but there are potential dangers – the therapist may not be a suitable 'expert', may become involved in complex disputes and could be called to support any written statement in court. Before agreeing to any such request, a supervisor should be consulted and possible legal ramifications explored (Jenkins, 1997). However, an example is given below of a possible brief report.

Director of Human Resources

Zephyr-Kopf Laboratories plc

Dear Sir/Madam

re. Mrs Anita Clarke (dob: 13.4.58)

I write at the request of Mrs Clarke, who I have been seeing for counselling since December last year.

Mrs Clarke initiated contact following a distressing incident at her workplace last November. As I believe you know, she witnessed a near fatal accident in the laboratory where she works. She tells me that since that time she has been unable to sleep normally, has had to take several weeks off from work, and her GP has prescribed medication. I understand that she has tried returning to work but still feels too shaky to resume her full duties.

Mrs Clarke appears to have become somewhat more relaxed than when she first saw me. However, since she is still very troubled by sleeping difficulties and occasional nightmares, which in turn seem to affect her ability to concentrate at work, my recommendation is that she sees a clinical psychologist, Dr R. Brown, specializing in treating her symptoms. With her agreement I am very willing to pass contact details on to you, and I understand that you may be willing to meet any costs she may incur if seen by this psychologist.

It is my view that Mrs Clarke is suffering from a degree of post-traumatic stress but I do not claim to possess specialist assessment qualifications, and I recommend that she and you communicate with Dr Brown on this matter.

Yours sincerely

Moira McDonald, MA, Dip. Couns.

Counsellor in Private Practice

It is important in all such communications that therapists do not claim to know more than they really do, do not make unjustified categorical statements, and use appropriately simple and tentative phrases. Obviously the client's permission is needed, and the therapist should be convinced that there is a strong case for their written intervention (for example, the client has no other professional advocate). All practitioners should be warned that even ostensibly innocent, compellingly humanitarian responses of this kind *can* backfire, and should be undertaken only with extreme care. Always consider how many parties are involved, what their respective interests are, what ulterior motives *may* be at work, and what potential minefields lie hidden beneath simple requests. *Always secure the client's full permission and collaboration, perhaps by asking the client to sign a copy of the letter, and keep copies of all correspondence.* Having said this, there may well be occasional requests for reports that are completely justified and appropriate. A rule of thumb is to write as factually as possible (avoiding unwarranted speculations), and concisely, although sometimes lengthier reports are necessary. Questions of related fees and any other implications should be discussed with supervisors, colleagues or employers as appropriate.

Reflecting on and monitoring one's work

This section examines briefly the issues involved in continuing professional self- monitoring. The relevant activities include in-session self-reflection, reviewing, using supervision, and deploying suitable means of evaluating the limits of one's skills and effectiveness.

Self-reflection in the session

Beginning therapists sometimes become caught in self-conscious 'spectatoring' as they try mentally to juggle what the client is expressing, what their trainers and supervisors have said, what they have read, and their own aspirations and self-doubts. In time this tends to be converted into a skilled form of self-observation, whereby the therapeutic process can be appropriately, undistractedly scanned and evaluated from time to time within each session. Highly experienced or gifted therapists may be able to cultivate an exquisite sensitivity to the ever-shifting nuances of their clients' moods and disclosures, while almost simultaneously tracking and testing out their own internal responses. This is what Casement (1985) has referred to as 'internal supervision'. The therapist integrates in his moment-to-moment practice a disciplined, reflexive alertness to the interaction between his statements and the client's unconsciously coded communications. This kind of awareness and *in vivo* self-supervision is increasingly incorporated into non-psychodynamic therapies, even into cognitive therapy.

Reviewing

Reviewing refers to consciously planned sessions or parts of sessions in which therapist and client agree to review their work together in terms of progress, satisfaction, problems, the relationship itself, any new material or goals. Broadly speaking, there are probably two ends of a spectrum of opinion about reviewing. It can be argued that reviewing is a constant, vital, implicit part of the therapeutic process and needs no additional formal structure. Others, however, suggest that it is good practice to hold mini-reviews at the end of each session (quite common in cognitive therapy), reviews at every four or six sessions; or, in longer-term therapy, three-monthly or six-monthly reviews.

For a review to be meaningful and not merely a compliant ritual, it may be helpful to adhere to a checklist of relevant items. For example:

- General impressions of both client and therapist.
- The client's view of progress in relation to explicit goals as agreed at assessment/first meeting, including sense of how well time has been used.
- The therapist's view of progress.
- The client's reservations about any aspect of therapy, disappointments, misunderstandings, need for clarification, etc.
- Any impasses that are evident and how they might be addressed (Leiper and Kent, 2001).
- Both parties' views on the relationship between them, its therapeutic value, any obstacles evident.
- The therapist's hypotheses about obstacles, defences, gaps in the client's story.
- Possible alternatives to current therapy (e.g. referral elsewhere).
- Any newly emerging issues or goals.
- Anything relating to structure, arrangements, fees, possible termination.

The nature and precise choice of the items discussed must relate to the client's needs, to the therapist's theoretical orientation, level of competency, and ethical and professional considerations. It can be useful to give clients a checklist of this kind to think over before the agreed review session. In some therapies regular reviews are integral to the therapeutic process, rather than an optional add-on, and in some cases written records are made of them, with duplicate copies for the client. It is *always* crucial to introduce and explain the meaning and purpose of reviews clearly and sensitively, and not to use them mechanically, or in an ill-timed manner. It is also realistic to expect at least some degree of consciously or unconsciously withheld feelings and views.

Using supervision

Counselling and psychotherapy traditions differ in regard to clinical supervision. Accredited BACP members *must* receive regular supervision (a minimum of 1.5 hours monthly) throughout their career, however experienced they are. In some professions and countries regular supervision is primarily associated mainly or exclusively with training. In certain clinical professions or specialisms 'high dose' supervision is either recommended or mandated. Without entering into these debates (see Section 4.3 on clinical supervision, pp. 165–173), the focus here is on a summary of *preparation for and optimal use of supervision.*

Preparation

Presentation of clinical issues in supervision is touched on elsewhere. Here, a brief outline is given of the kinds of areas that are typically focused upon in supervision, that often require a certain amount of forethought (adapted from Horton, 1993):

- *Identification* – How will the client be 'named' or disguised? How will you describe them to the supervisor?
- *Antecedents* – How the client came to see you; the context of counselling; pre-counselling knowledge of the client; any previous contacts.
- *Presenting concerns and contract* – Summary of the main concern or concerns and their duration; precipitating factors; initial assessment; current conflicts or issues.
- *Questions for supervision* – What, exactly, do you wish to address in supervision (given that time in supervision may need to be used very efficiently)?
- *Ethical and professional issues* – It is always important to consider whether there are any significant ethical or legal issues to be aired (BACP, 2002). More generally, therapists may wish to reflect on any continuing professional development needs that are thrown up for them by clients. 'What does the research have to

say about this particular presenting problem?' is a highly relevant question here.

- *Focus on content* – How does the client see their situation? What are pertinent work and relationship factors? How does the client see him or herself (i.e. identity)? What other elements are pertinent (e.g. early history, strengths and resources, beliefs and values, fears and fantasies, socio-cultural factors)?

  Part of the content focus is also (a) problem definition (how the client construes current and desired scenarios); (b) assessment and reformulation (how the therapist understands the presenting concern, related patterns, themes for exploration, useful theoretical constructs, helpful hunches, etc.; (c) unmentioned material, silent hypotheses, blind spots and underlying contributory factors.

  A therapeutic plan may or may not feature (depending on theoretical orientation). What might be the direction of future work? What goals are emerging? What criteria for change and its measurement exist? Reviewing progress and new possibilities also comes in here.

- *Focus on process* – What strategies and interventions have been used? Consider therapeutic intentions, the impact of interventions and possible alternative interventions. A large part of the process is of course about the relationship: what happened between you and the client? What transferential or other interpersonal patterns are you aware of? What variety of relational factors may be at work (Feltham, 1999)? In what ways are such issues played out in the parallel process between therapist and supervisor? Finally, how is the process being evaluated? What alternatives exist?

- *Critical incident analysis* – Supervision is extremely useful for disclosing and analysing key moments in the therapeutic process: what did the client say or do, how did you respond (and feel internally), what might this signify and what clues could it yield to further work?

- *Covert communication* – Supervision also offers space for considering what might be happening between therapist and client that is unspoken, subtle, taboo, and so on. Supervisees can beneficially ask themselves how the client 'makes them feel', what subtle sensations, images and thoughts are associated with particular clients, aside from the overt content of sessions. Recalled changes in voice quality, idiosyncratic choices of words or phrases, encoded statements – any of these may yield significant insights into non-verbal and para-verbal communication and its meaning for therapy.

Self-monitoring

It may be helpful to think of self-monitoring in the following ways:

- Moment-to-moment awareness of all that may transpire consciously and unconsciously within the session.
- Insights, hunches; anomalous, intermittent or persistent internal (counter-transferential) reactions; hypotheses and conjectures: voiced to the client or otherwise.
- Consciously withheld thoughts, feelings, responses (relating to the client), to be noted, further developed, and/or taken to supervision.
- Observations about one's own occasional lapses, errors, skill deficits, or recurrent 'own material' to be taken to supervision or own (occasional, intermittent or on-going) therapy.
- Awareness of times when fatigue, illness, emotional difficulties, etc. may amount to an impairment affecting competency to practise and the need to make contingency plans and take appropriate action.
- Tape recordings or written notes to be studied, analysed and learned from. This is a potentially large subject in its own right and many of the practical and ethical issues involved are discussed in Bor and Watts (1999).
- Alternative, formal means of self-evaluation, such as a personal audit of skills, knowledge, issues of congruence or counter-transference, etc.

Conclusion

Reference may be made to those parts of this book addressing the wide range of generic micro-skills, clinical practice skills, strategies and techniques, professional issues and common presenting problems. By checking one's therapeutic practice challenges – that is, the ways in which diverse clients present with widely different issues at different levels of difficulty – against the potential range of skills and interventions, one may measure and monitor one's development in competency terms.

References

BACP (2002) *Ethical Framework for Good Practice in Counselling and Psychotherapy.* Rugby: British Association for Counselling and Psychotherapy.

Bor, R. and Watts, M. (eds) (1999) *The Trainee Handbook: A Guide for Counselling and Psychotherapy Trainees.* London: Sage.

Casement, P. (1985) *On Learning from the Patient.* London: Tavistock.

Clark, J. (ed.) (2002) *Freelance Counselling and Psychotherapy: Competition and Collaboration.* London: Brunner-Routledge.

Feltham, C. (ed.) (1999) *Understanding the Counselling Relationship.* London: Sage.

Freud, S. (1977 [1925]) *Case Histories I: 'Dora' and 'Little Hans'.* Vol. 8, Pelican Freud Library. Harmondsworth: Pelican.

Horton, I. (1993) Supervision. In R. Bayne and P. Nicolson (eds), *Counselling and Psychology for Health Professionals.* London: Chapman and Hall.

Jenkins, P. (1997) *Counselling, Psychotherapy and the Law.* London: Sage.

Jenkins, P. and Palmer, I. (2000) *Record Keeping and the Data Protection Act 1998.* Rugby: BACP.

Lago, C. and Kitchin, D. (1998) *The Management of Counselling and Psychotherapy Agencies.* London: Sage.

Leiper, R. and Kent, R. (2001) *Working Through Setbacks in Psychotherapy: Crisis, Impasse and Relapse.* London: Sage.

Molnos, A. (1995) *A Question of Time: Essentials of Brief Dynamic Psychotherapy.* London: Karnac.

Norton, K. and McGauley, G. (1998) *Counselling Difficult Clients.* London: Sage.

Ridley, C.R. (1995) *Overcoming Unintentional Racism in Counseling and Therapy.* Thousand Oaks, CA: Sage.

Rowan, J. (1988) Counselling and the psychology of furniture. *Counselling*, 64: 21–24.

Sills, C. (ed.) (1997) *Contracts in Counselling.* London: Sage.

Thistle, R. (1998) *Counselling and Psychotherapy in Private Practice.* London: Sage.

3.8   Clinical Practice Issues   ○○○

TIM BOND, GEOF ALRED AND PETER HUGHES

Length, frequency and duration of sessions

When referring to length and duration of counselling and psychotherapy, there is an ambiguity about whether it is one session being discussed or a sequence of sessions. In what follows, we have referred to length of a session and duration of a sequence.

The 'therapeutic hour' is a term synonymous with 'the 50-minute hour'. Drawn from psychoanalytic psychotherapy, the '50-minute hour' 'has been adopted by many psychodynamic counsellors' (Jacobs, 1999: 65), and by many others as: 'long enough to get depth in interviewing but not long enough to get too tired!' (Trower et al., 1988: 37). On the other hand, person-centred therapists may be more relaxed about the length of a session, in which 'clients have wanted and benefited from sessions lasting two or three hours or even longer' (Mearns and Thorne, 1999: 123). McLeod (2003: 436) reports on research undertaken by Turner et al. (1996) in which a student counselling service 'reduced the length of each session to thirty minutes. They found that clients seemed to gain as much from these shorter sessions'. In this case, the number of sessions was retained. McLeod (2003: 436) also reports on work by Rosenbaum (1994), in which the focus was on limiting the number of sessions, preferably to one, and the length of the session 'was allowed to extend to 90–120 minutes'. A distinction between the different approaches is the extent to which significance is given to boundaries: 'Acknowledgement of the boundaries between people, demonstrated in the counselling itself, is important in the making of [more reliable inter-dependent] relationships' (Jacobs, 1999: 83). Egan (2001: 36), on the other hand, with his action-orientated approach, is much more concerned with efficient use of time: 'helping can be lean and mean and still be fully human' with sessions lasting as little as five minutes.

The literature is less varied about frequency of sessions, typically opting for 'once a week, or more frequently in the case of crises' (Trower et al., 1988: 37). A person-centred approach tends to be keen to find out what the client wants, recognizing that there are people 'who may welcome a longer period between sessions' (Mearns and Thorne, 1999: 123). Perhaps it is because the lives of many people are chunked into week-long units that 'less frequent contact strains continuity and decreases the likelihood of keeping the client to the "contract"' (Trower et al., 1988: 37). However, Richard Nelson-Jones suggests that a possible way of drawing a counselling relationship towards a conclusion 'is to *fade* the relationship by seeing the client less frequently' (1982: 295). Psychodynamic therapists, on the other hand, are likely to make use of the impact on the client of impending separation as important material.

A variety of factors impinges on the duration of a therapy sequence. Some therapy relationships are open-ended, whereas others are limited to a specified maximum. The psychoanalytic tradition pulls the psychodynamic therapy process towards several years of work. Jacobs writes of 12 weeks seeming a 'fairly short period' (1999: 84). Emmy van Deurzen-Smith (1996: 182), writing about existential therapy, considers that 'therapy ends … probably within a span of three months to a year'. Person-centred therapy is concerned to put the client in charge of the duration of the therapy, and for this reason 'person-centred therapists will find it difficult to work in agencies where policy dictates that clients can have a certain number of sessions and no more' (Mearns and Thorne, 1999: 123). However, their approximate expectation is for 'a few weeks, a month or two, or, where the difficulties seem particularly severe, a few months perhaps' (1999: 123). Diana Whitmore (2000: 69), writing about psychosynthesis therapy thinks 'it is advisable to set boundaries rather than leave it open-ended. Often a psychosynthesis therapist will propose an initial contract of six sessions, to be reviewed and assessed before continuing.' From a cognitive-behavioural perspective, the number of sessions suggested is 'six to ten initially, with a review at the end of the period' (Trower et al., 1988: 36).

Most counselling and psychotherapy approaches have addressed the issue of brief therapy, although what is understood by the term varies enormously: 'Malan (1976) … argues that one of the key factors in the efficacy of brief therapy (of about 30 [weekly] sessions) is the ability of the therapist to interpret the significance to the patient of the ending. Time-limited work makes a virtue out of necessity …' (Jacobs, 1999: 156–157). The person-centred approach simultaneously recognizes that good work can be done even in one session alone, but that therapist or agency determination of the number of sessions is an obstacle to effective therapy (Mearns and Thorne, 1999: 124). McLeod (2003: 436) has considered research which demonstrates that a significant proportion of clients can achieve long-term improvement in their problems as a result of one (extended) therapy session.

Time management

At its simplest, the management of time in therapy concerns the start and end times of sessions. Should these times repeatedly differ from shared expectations, most therapy approaches would view such divergence as significant in terms of resistance, reluctance or stuckness. Each approach would then address the issue in its own way. Arguably, the person-centred therapist is faced with the greatest difficulty: the therapeutic imperative to enter the client's frame of reference challenges the importance of issues such as punctuality.

At a deeper level, however, time management also involves holding the therapeutic process within a

session, and over a period of sessions. A significant issue is the extent to which the therapist takes responsibility for the process and its pacing, as distinct from sharing these with the client. Egan expresses a bias towards action, and the terminology of his helping skills model points towards a process in almost perpetual forward motion, the therapist probing, challenging and looking for points of leverage. Person-centred therapists, however, are considered less effective when imposing their own values on the process (see the case study example given by Mearns and Thorne, 1999: 133–143).

Contracting

Clear contracting in advance of counselling and psychotherapy is generally considered to demonstrate respect for client autonomy. Conversely, retrospective attempts to impose conditions and terms are frequently considered unethical and are unenforceable legally. Although these views are generally supported, they can be problematic to implement. In the experience of many therapists, clients may be least interested in contractual terms at the outset of therapy. Many are so concerned to unload the emotional distress or the urgency of their situation that it may be some sessions later that they are willing to consider contractual issues. One widely used way of resolving this dilemma is to provide the basic contractual terms and conditions with a pre-therapy information sheet and to review the client's understanding of these and their appropriateness. For some clients, the review will take place at the beginning of the first session. For others, the first session will involve little more than agreeing to work according to the terms of the information sheet, with more detailed discussion deferred until later.

Counselling and psychotherapy contracts tend to be complex and involve several different aspects. The first aspect concerns *administrative* matters. These include details of any fees to be charged, method(s) of payment, notice required for cancellations by clients, therapist holidays, cancellations by therapist due to illness, unavoidable delay, bad weather, etc. Level of confidentiality and limitations are also important administrative matters. In

English law, limitations of confidentiality in order to protect adult clients from suicide or self-harm are legally unenforceable and would not protect a therapist from possible legal claims for breach of confidence. The law prioritizes the adult client's right to informed consent including the right to refuse life-saving treatment (St George's Trust v S. [1998] 3 All ER at 692). In the absence of a legal requirement to disclose, therapists have professional discretion over whether to disclose to protect people other than the client from harm or to assist in the prevention and detection of child abuse. This contrasts with jurisdictions elsewhere in Europe and in the US, where there may be legal obligation to restrict confidentiality or to disclose in order to prevent suicide, harm to others and child abuse (Bond, 2000; Corey et al., 2002).

The *professional* aspects of the contract concern the nature, aims and valid considerations of therapy. Legally and ethically, it is considered unwise to promise positive outcomes, but it is appropriate to indicate methods of working and the possible benefits of therapy based on the therapist's experience or research. Some of these might be included within pre-therapy information.

The *psychological* aspects of the contract are more difficult to capture in advance as they concern the focus of the therapist's struggle. They will often involve the clarification of boundaries of responsibility and undertaking to work in specific ways by client, or therapist, or both.

Therapists vary considerably in their approach to contracts (Sills, 1997). Some treat them as rules that are unilaterally created by the therapist and non-negotiable. Others view them as bilaterally negotiable between therapist and client (Tudor, 1998). Another way of classifying contracts would be to distinguish between non-negotiable rules or negotiable terms: open-ended or fixed-term (usually short) contracts; and those that exclude or include periodic review. As with different approaches to fees, the challenge is finding the appropriate form of contract rather than assuming one type of contract is universally superior to all other types of contract.

Oral contracts are as ethically and legally binding as written contracts. However, the lack of evidence and potential for misunderstanding is considerable.

Therefore it is considered best practice to record important contractual terms in writing. The methods for doing so can be quite varied. Written pre-therapy information, letters sent to clients confirming the contractual agreement, signed and dated agreements, and contemporaneous notes of agreements in the therapy records are valid forms of evidence. Perhaps the most important reason for carefully considering the contractual basis of therapy is the sense of security and clarity that a well-drawn contract can give both therapist and client.

Negotiating fees

Attitudes to charging fees vary considerably between therapists. Some attach little significance to fees, and take the view that it is simply a pragmatic transaction. For others, the exchange of services for money is full of symbolic meaning and the way the client responds may be therapeutically informative. In one of the most informative articles on the issue of fees, Tudor (1998) reflects on the significance of various omissions and errors made by clients when paying by cheque. He speculates that missing out the therapist's name may be a way of discounting the therapist; not dating the cheque may indicate withdrawal from the immediate present; leaving out the amount may indicate resentment about the amount charged; and not signing the cheque may indicate a passive-aggressive response to the therapist. Interpretations of this kind are made from the therapist's perspective. Just as therapists vary in their views about the significance of money, clients are similarly varied in their opinions. In these circumstances, it is therapeutically desirable to be systematic and clear about issues concerning fees so that areas of difficulty are minimized and their significance can be discerned as they occur.

Ethics and law reinforce the therapeutic desirability of clarity about fees. Ethical requirements from BACP state that, 'Good practice involves clarifying and agreeing the rights and the responsibilities of both the practitioner and the client at appropriate points in their working relationship' (2002: section 3) and '[c]lients should be adequately informed about the nature of services being offered.

Practitioners should obtain adequately informed consent from their clients and respect a client's right to choose whether to continue or withdraw' (2002: section 12). These requirements are both ethical and legal. No legal obligation to pay can be incurred without having agreed the terms of payment in advance.

The combination of therapeutic ethical and legal considerations all reinforce the importance of the therapist having decided on a policy over fees prior to offering therapy. There are several options including setting a fixed fee, setting a variable fee usually related to the client's financial circumstances, waiving a fee by providing free therapy, bartering and accepting fees from sources other than the client, often referred to as third-party payment. The main advantages and disadvantages of each are considered below.

Fixed fees have the advantage of being the easiest to calculate (i.e. overheads plus payment for the length of the session) and create a high degree of certainty about income and cost to therapist and client respectively. However, fixed fees may exclude people from receiving therapy who have limited income or a high number of dependents relative to their income. Many practitioners do vary their fees according to their clients' capacity to pay or offer some of their clients reduced fees. This approach extends the availability of therapy but can sometimes create unhealthy dynamics within the therapeutic relationship, if the client feels second class or the therapist resents the reduced fee. Free therapy is one way of significantly widening the accessibility of therapy to everyone. The desirability of free therapy may be counterbalanced by the potential for the therapeutic relationship being inhibited by the client's gratitude or the potential for widening the power imbalance between helper and helped by the dependence of the client on the therapist's charity! The bartering of therapy for goods or other services provides an alternative way of making therapy more accessible, but raises potential areas of difficulty over determining the value of what is being bartered. Establishing the value may require the involvement of someone outside the therapeutic relationship. Another complication is the potential disruption of the therapeutic relationship if the goods or services turn out to be deficient. Third-party payments,

usually by an employer or relative, may make possible the provision of adequately resourced therapy, but have the potential disadvantages of introducing additional people into the therapeutic relationship who may be more favourably motivated towards therapy than the client – for example a parent paying for a teenager. This very condensed survey of the different approaches to fees demonstrates that each has advantages and disadvantages and the challenge is maximizing the former while minimizing the latter.

Another factor to be considered in advance is whether to require a single method of payment – for example cash, cheque, or standing order – or whether the method of payment is negotiable. It is generally considered sound advice to avoid the accumulation of large sums of money owed to the therapist, both because of the way this can influence the therapist–client relationship and because of the increased risk of not being paid. Equally, any payment in advance should, in our view, be exceptional and limited to a few sessions. The usual practice is payment 'as you go' supported by clear agreements about other administrative aspects of therapy.

Evaluation of process and outcomes

Evaluation of process and outcomes is an integral part of therapy. It builds the initial contract (Bordin, 1994), makes significant contributions to client progress (Wills, 1997) and enhances the quality of the therapeutic alliance (Egan, 2001). Different approaches to evaluation emphasize and focus upon different dimensions of the alliance, namely the working relationship between client and therapist; mutually agreed goals; and therapeutic tasks carried out to achieve the goals (Bordin, 1979).

In cognitive-behavioural and problem-oriented approaches progress is evaluated primarily in terms of goals. These are set in the initial phase of therapy, and also as the therapy proceeds, and include the overall goals of the therapy, an agenda of therapeutic tasks, and homework. A straightforward example of this kind of evaluation is the Goal-attainment

Model (Sutton, 1989) in which clients rate progress towards individual goals on a numerical scale. In cognitive analytic therapy (CAT) (Ryle, 1990; Ryle and Kerr, 2002), rating scales are also used for evaluation of progress, and in the spirit of using written as well as spoken communications in CAT (Ryle, 2004), therapist and client exchange goodbye letters, making explicit outcomes and prospects for progress continuing once therapy is over. There is also evaluation of the client's progress in performing therapeutic tasks, such as disputing irrational beliefs in REBT. Towards the end of therapy, evaluation covers learning from the therapy and how this can be sustained and built upon (Wills, 1997). Evaluation of process focuses on tasks and the working relationship as, for instance, in Egan's challenge for helpers to ask in what way a technique or method contributes to the 'bottom line', that is, to outcomes that serve clients (Egan, 2001: 38). Evaluation is an important and on-going aspect of collaboration between client and therapist, and it also takes place formally in review sessions at regular negotiated intervals.

Sutton (1989) maintains that the Goal-attainment Model can be applied to any approach. This view is unlikely to be accepted by humanistic counsellors, who recognize that the achievements by the client in therapy cannot always be clearly specified, and do not always need to be. Saying specifically what has changed does not add anything to the client's conviction that she has changed, in that, for instance, she feels less anxious, or more resolved, or more in touch with people who matter to her. What helps is to appreciate the process by which change has occurred and to reflect on this, as a way to chart progress and link what goes on in therapy to what brought this client to therapy and to changes she wants to make in her life in general. Hence, evaluation takes place within the general flow of the therapeutic process and relationship, as well as in formal review sessions. Evaluation may draw upon the practitioner's own experience of the therapy process. For example, if the practitioner considers that the process is stuck, she may share this with the client and check how the client is perceiving the process at this time. Or, if the practitioner believes that the client is becoming more self-accepting, she

may reflect this back to enable the client to evaluate herself. The timing of reviews is important, and there needs to be flexibility in any arrangements to review. There are times when the client is vulnerable and needy and a review would be counter-productive.

In psychodynamic therapy, as with person-centred therapy, evaluation is interwoven into the therapeutic process and relationship, and takes place at specific times. The central aim of finding meaning through interpretation and the triangle of insight provides for the client the basis for assessing progress and change. Evaluation may draw on non-specific aspects, such as the emotional atmosphere in the therapy room, as well as specific changes the client notices. A particular area of attention in psychodynamic therapy is the ending of the therapeutic relationship. This is often planned and may extend over a period of several sessions. Reviewing the therapy as a whole is part of breaking the relationship and enabling the client to experience the loss as fully and constructively as possible.

Purpose, selection and definition of outcome goals

Clients come to therapy with an intention to change their lives for the better, and to live in a more satisfactory and resourceful way. The intention may not be clearly known or articulated. The therapist responds by helping the client to establish aims in relation to areas of a client's life he or she wishes to change, and may help the client set goals, which translate aims into statements of specific desired changes. A major source of difference among counselling and psychotherapy approaches concerns those which advocate 'goal-directedness' (e.g. Dryden and Feltham, 1994; Egan, 2001) and those which pursue intentions and aims without specific goals (e.g. Jacobs, 1999; Mearns and Thorne, 1999; Worrall, 1997).

In person-centred therapy, the underlying aim is 'freeing the natural healing process in the client' (Mearns and Thorne, 1999: 146). This is not necessarily achieved by identifying specific outcomes. In relation to contracting in person-centred therapy, Worrall states that: 'Not only does such a contract not need to deal with outcomes, it is philosophically and therapeutically essential that it be independent of outcomes' (1997: 66), arguing that client distress often stems from 'contractual living' in which the individual, through seeking the approval of others, loses autonomy, sense of purpose and effectiveness.

In contrast, many practitioners employ goals to build with their clients a shared sense of therapeutic purpose. When clients are confused or distressed, they may not know what goals they have, they may feel directionless, lost or stuck. Setting goals helps to give the client a sense of direction, and a basis for charting progress and clarifying further work to be done. As the client begins to focus on what he or she wants to change, and as issues are explored, goals that are implicit in what brought the client to therapy begin to emerge. These will include goals associated with the presenting issue, of which the client has some awareness at the outset of therapy, and may also include new kinds of goals discovered in therapy. For example, through addressing a particular source of stress, a client may come to realize the value of looking at his reaction to stress in general.

There are general guidelines for goal setting, such as making them specific and achievable, which provide a useful rule of thumb, and which are given prominence in some approaches (e.g. Egan, 2001; Sutton, 1989). A more fundamental concern is ensuring that goals are negotiated and truly reflect the client's needs and desires, as 'ethically it is the client's right to determine the goals and the limits of his or her interest in counselling' (Dryden and Feltham, 1994: 31). There needs to be openness about the therapist's goals as well as those of the client, to avoid the therapist having a different, possibly more ambitious, therapeutic agenda than the client.

For therapists using an integrative or eclectic approach, a central issue is to avoid an unhelpful polarization between outcome goals and relationship, and to balance working towards specific outcome goals with attending to the relationship and its therapeutic potential. For example, Ryle states that the central task at the outset of therapy is 'to establish a working relationship, to maximize the powerful and non-specific effects of therapy on morale and to convert passive suffering to active engagement in problem-solving' (1990: 11). Attending to this balance is particularly important in brief and time-limited therapy (Bor et al., 2004; Houston, 2003; Hudson-Allez, 1997), which is essentially outcome orientated.

Conceptualization of client problems: levels of problem

A potential client may or may not have a clear idea of *what* is 'out of joint', or of what is required to *put right* what is out of joint, but is more than likely to feel, think or believe that something *is* out of joint. The person will probably present for therapy because they seek remedy for their uncertainty, unease or distress. The orientation of the therapist will not, in the first instance, restrict the therapist's awareness of the client's agenda about, say, coping with the death of a parent; or a desire to unlock the shackles of past abuse; or a yearning to leave a current partner. Remaining more central to the client's overt frame of reference is made all the easier when the client chooses a therapist who prefers to work with particular issues (e.g. bereavement), and not others (e.g. sexual abuse).

Different therapy models, however, hold divergent views about what therapy is intended to achieve (outcome), and how best to achieve it (process). Each approach conceptualizes a client's problems differently, and demands that the client accepts, or at least suspends disbelief about, some theoretical tenets central to that approach. In making this demand, the model is not only attempting to conceptualize about the client, her problematic situation, and an appropriate therapeutic course of action, but also that the client becomes willing to view matters in the same way.

Therefore, whose conceptualization of a client's problems prevails? This apparent polarization partly involves the extent to which the therapy addresses the client's issues from the client's phenomenological point of view, and how she talks to herself about her situation, as distinct from a more theory-laden point of view (e.g. projection and transference, stages of grieving and tasks of mourning, self-concept and organismic self).

For instance, person-centred therapy is concerned with personal growth mediated through a therapeutic relationship. The person-centred practitioner respects insight (deeper and fuller understanding), and, through the medium of the therapeutic relationship, encourages the client to value insight. The client's agenda is completely respected, and yet the process of person-centred therapy in effect transforms the client's material into footsteps towards greater self-knowledge. 'The therapist will … focus not on problems and solutions but on communion' (Thorne, 1996: 129). Rogers (1951) describes many indicators of therapeutic movement: 'They tend to move away from façades … from oughts … from meeting the expectation of others …'. He describes seven stages of psychological development, which for most people will be quite independent of any therapeutic endeavour, but for a client may be enhanced through the therapeutic process. A client in the earliest stages is unlikely to present for therapy, whereas a client in the latest stages is likely to be able to draw on a wide range of resources, of which therapy will be only one. A client in the middle stages of development, however, is likely to be able to make best use of person-centred therapy. For the person-centred practitioner, therefore, the client's issues are not significantly conceptualized as problems, but as opportunities for the client to get to know, understand and accept herself more fully. There is little sense of level of problem, more a recognition that some clients require or desire the help, short-term or long-term, of a therapist in order to take them further along their journey.

Cognitive-behavioural therapy promotes the view that the client learns to think and act in different, more effective, ways. The therapist challenges what is dysfunctional and directs towards greater functionality. While a client might express the view that her shyness is problematic to her because she would like to meet new people, the therapist will consider the client's shyness to result from faulty beliefs or faulty thinking: 'emotional distress and problematic behaviour, C, are the consequences not of the events themselves, A, but of negative inferences and evaluations of these events, B' (Trower et al., 1988: 21). From the therapist's point of view, therefore, the 'problem' is how the client thinks about herself and the world she inhabits. From this perspective, the therapist's focus is not on the inconvenience or intractableness of the presenting problem, but on the range and persistence of faulty beliefs and thoughts. A client who clings tightly to a wide range of faulty thoughts and beliefs may well require longer therapy than a client who is eager to learn to challenge her own dysfunctionality.

Of all counselling models, a problem-management model, such as the *Skilled Helper* model of Egan (2001), places presenting, and subsequently revealed, problems at centre stage. 'Many clients become clients because, either in their own eyes or in the eyes of others, they are involved in problem situations they are not handling well' (2001: 4). These clients need ways of dealing with, solving or transcending their problem situations. By focusing on a clear articulation of a specific problem, and on step-by-step approaches to its solution, the problem-management model gives paramount importance to the client's stated problems and their solution. The counsellor is unlikely to restate the problem in different theoretical terms, but is likely to challenge the client to view the problem from some other perspectives to discover where is leverage and opportunity, and to let go of inadequate solutions. It is unlikely that a problem cannot be articulated. However, a problem may be intricately entwined with other problems, in which case it is the counsellor's role to help the client tease out the different strands. A client with many intertwined problems may require more counselling than a client with only one. A client familiar with, and fluent at, personal reflection and self-challenge may require only a few sessions.

In their own unique ways, then, different counselling and psychotherapy approaches conceptualize the person of the client and her problems, the purpose of therapy and its methods, in radically different ways. Necessarily their perspectives are tied to the theoretical and philosophical foundations on which they are based.

Approaches to diagnosis

Diagnosis is controversial in counselling and psychotherapy. Some practitioners are highly critical of the possibility of therapist-determined diagnosis.

Practitioners working in person-centred and many other humanistic traditions are most likely to take this view. Their approach emphasizes the client's ability for self-diagnosis and capacity for self-healing, sometimes referred to as the 'wisdom of the client'. The therapist's role is to provide the conditions, particularly the quality of relationship, in which the client's wisdom can flourish. These approaches are frequently founded on a critique of the medicalization of human relationships, and a concern to avoid replicating the inherent power imbalance between patient and medical practitioner.

An alternative way of resolving some of the disempowering aspects of diagnosis is to teach clients to diagnose for themselves. Transactional analysis operates primarily in this way by teaching accessible models of the way people view themselves and interact with others and by encouraging the client to develop new insights and self-assessment (Midgley, 1998). Another very popular approach has been developed out of the Jungian psychoanalytic tradition that helps people to distinguish different personality types and understand where they stand in the Myers–Briggs classification (Bayne, 1993).

Problem management, as advocated by Egan (2001) and others, provides a variation on 'insight' models of diagnosis by combining humanistic insights into the counselling relationship with a more active counsellor facilitation of the client's problem. For example the process of engaging the client in focusing on one of several potential issues to be considered in counselling distinguishes between different kinds of problem, e.g. contained and urgent or chronic and pervasive, and a joint counsellor–client evaluation of which should be the subject of counselling.

Some approaches to counselling and psychotherapy are much more accepting of the desirability of diagnosis, for example family therapists are concerned to distinguish functional and dysfunctional interactions within families based on their impact on the family which is understood as a closed or semi-closed system of relationships. The process of diagnosis and therapy is taken so seriously that it is classically undertaken by at least two therapists working together (Waldron-Skinner and Watson, 1987). Similarly, the interventions in rational emotive

behaviour therapy developed by Albert Ellis (Ellis and Dryden, 1998) also depend on diagnosing dysfunctional patterns in order to challenge these and substitute ways which are considered more functional.

Psychodynamic therapists have generally been stereotyped as being most accepting of diagnostic techniques within their therapeutic techniques. In reality some are extremely reluctant to move swiftly to diagnosis. Nonetheless the notion of 'unconscious' implies something that is invisible to the client, and which may be visible to the therapist. In this context diagnoses of 'resistance', 'transference' and 'defence mechanisms' as ways of understanding the therapeutic relationship may be meaningful to the therapist and eventually to the client. Some diagnoses may be problematic because they encode evaluations about suitability for therapy or imply a pessimistic prognosis, for example 'borderline' or 'sociopathic'. Some therapeutic approaches resist the implied moral judgements and the immutability of these kinds of diagnoses, and question their place in therapy.

Generally, diagnostic systems are more widely accepted in psychiatric services and clinical psychology and form an important part of the therapist's regime. The best known of the diagnostic systems has been developed by the American Psychiatric Association (2000), which is widely used as an international classification. In some countries psychologists, counsellors and psychotherapists are expected to know this system although that is not a general expectation in Britain. However, therapists working closely in association with psychiatric and drug rehabilitation services may find it helpful to familiarize themselves with this system in order to enhance communication between services, whether or not such diagnoses are incorporated within therapy.

Reluctance, resistance and stuckness

Counselling and psychotherapy approaches diverge widely, and may be distinguished from each other by their conceptualizations of the terms 'reluctance', 'resistance' and 'stuckness'. Different writers consider quite differently the sources of these features, perceive quite differently their manifestations within the therapeutic relationship, and hold quite different views about the ways in which these issues can most appropriately be addressed. For instance, to a person-centred practitioner, the term 'resistance' has judgemental and unempathic connotations, and is unlikely to be used, whereas a client who shows 'reluctance' is dubious or suspicious of the therapist or of therapy as a form of help for themselves, presenting the therapist with an opportunity to build trust and rapport (Mearns and Thorne, 1999). The term 'stuckness', in terms of lack of movement in the therapeutic process, points to the opportunity for the client to assimiliate and integrate fresh insights into their frame of reference, and for the therapist to stay with and track that process (Mearns and Thorne, 1999).

In contrast, for an integrative/eclectic 'skilled helper', reluctance and resistance are similar, although recognition of the fine distinction between them may be crucial. 'Reluctance ... refers to the ambiguity clients feel when they know that managing their lives better is going to exact a price. Clients are not sure that they want to pay that price. The incentives for not changing drive out the incentives for changing'. On the other hand, 'Resistance refers to the reaction of clients who in some way feel coerced. It is their way of fighting back' (Egan, 2001: 163). While Egan concedes that some resistance may be normative, he sees reluctance and resistance as features to be overcome. 'Stuckness' arises out of a failure of some part of the therapeutic process, and probably demands that the therapist takes responsibility for backtracking to the stage which was left incomplete. For Dexter and Russell, a client's resistance to the counselling process is a response to what a counsellor is doing, or not doing, and therefore the counsellor should do something differently (Dexter and Russell, 1997: 11–22).

'Analysis of resistance is a major part of the psychodynamic technique, freeing the client ... to understand more of himself, and releasing him to make the changes which he wishes' (Jacobs, 1999: 98). Psychodynamic therapy considers that clients' failure to function fully is due to the defences they use to avoid acknowledging something:

> Resistances are the expression (or tactics) of the defences, particularly as employed in the therapeutic relationship. Both defences and resistances serve a definite ... purpose, defending people either against feelings which are too strong and threaten to overwhelm them or others, or against the self-criticism of a punitive and persecutory super-ego (or conscience). (1999: 98)

In consequence, the psychodynamic therapist may go in search of resistance as a major part of the therapeutic process.

Cognitive, gestalt, psychosynthesis therapists and so on, each conceptualize these terms as differently as the approaches addressed above, arising out of how each views the path and purpose of the therapy process.

Clinical issues: tape recording

Some (few) clients desire their therapy sessions to be recorded on audiotape. They may bring a cassette tape with them to the therapy room. It would be unusual for a client to bring audio recording equipment. The recording quality of pocket-portable equipment, such as dictaphones and personal stereos, tends to be unsuitable for conversations between two or more people. An ordinary tape recorder and a multidirectional microphone are sufficient, and can be part of therapy room equipment. In this case, operation of the equipment may well fall on the therapist.

In the initial contracting process, a therapist may be able to offer the client use of audio recording facilities. This demonstrates not only a transparency about the therapy process, but also a desire for the client to listen to the content, pattern and movement in their disclosures, and to reflect on the insights, challenges and modelling of the therapist. There may be occasions when the content or manner of disclosure is traumatic in some way. Tape recordings of such material can valuably form the basis of further therapy. Parkinson (1995: 168) gives a fine example of a couple who listen in detail to each other for the first time, and gain valuable insight into their manner of communication, as a result of an audiotape recording.

Some therapists feel uncomfortable about the tape recording of sessions, and in certain psychoanalytic approaches, recording is viewed as abusive. It is seen as an unwarranted inhibition of the client's opportunity to explore sensitive and/or unconscious material. Some therapists, regardless of therapeutic orientation, are wary about requests from clients to record their sessions. They might sense that the client's request has a potentially malicious or defensive ulterior motive. Alternatively, a therapist might fear exposure of their own perceived incompetence. It is worth exploring any request by a client to audio record the session, and what value taping sessions has for the client. Equally, the therapist's own internal and articulated responses may hold valuable learning to be explored in counselling or psychotherapy supervision.

When it is the therapist who wishes to audio record the session, the situation is different. Parkinson (1995) is sceptical about the value to the client of a therapist analysing what a client talks about. In so far as therapy is about developing a relationship, not curing a patient's illness, his point is valid. However, the situation is different when the focus of the recording is to analyse the therapist's role in the relationship. A therapist in training may ask a client for permission to record some specific piece(s) of work. It is not unusual for therapists on training courses to be asked to analyse and present some recorded work with a client. The client may have little notion about how the therapist will subsequently listen to the disclosed material, and even if it is contractually agreed that the tape will subsequently be wiped, there is a risk that the client may feel exploited regardless of any assurances and safeguards. In an early paper, Rogers (1942) considered training/supervision to be 'probably the most significant use of [audio] recordings ...'. He reported that, by means of careful analysis and discussion, supported by full transcripts, trainees were able to critique their own practice in detail:

The recorded interviews show ... clearly those techniques which lead towards insight and reorientation .... Such close analysis of these interviews gives to the inexperienced and experienced counselor alike a new understanding of the therapeutic process. This new understanding vitalises and improves their treatment interviewing.

A more recent example of this kind of use of interview recording is Interpersonal Process Recall (IPR), formulated in the early 1960s by Norman Kagan. It is appropriate for a therapist to request permission to audio record for the purposes of therapy supervision or training and to ensure that any consent is both informed about the use of the tape and that the consent is freely given. As a significant purpose of supervision and training is to enhance the quality of therapy for clients, it is likely that the costs of intrusion will be considered to be worth the benefits.

A final circumstance in which audio taping may be used concerns research into counselling and psychotherapy. While some clients may feel uneasy about having their sessions recorded for research and refuse consent, others are willing participants. Therapists are similarly divided in their views about the validity of requesting permission to record sessions for research. Traditionally, psychodynamic therapists have the strongest reservations in contrast to others. Rogers (1942) was enthusiastic for 'electronic recording' to aid counselling research.

Testing, psychometric and other questionnaires

For many therapists, the idea of 'testing a client' runs counter to their core values and beliefs about what makes their work therapeutic. There are fears of labelling, de-humanizing and pathologizing people who come for therapy. However, the use of tests is common and is an integral part of the history of counselling and psychotherapy, especially in the US, both in research (e.g. Rogers and Dymond, 1954) and in practice (Watkins and Campbell, 1990). Dryden and Feltham (1994) have argued that when used flexibly and pragmatically, tests of various sorts can be of value to all practitioners. The main purposes for using questionnaires, inventories and other exercises are assessment and clarification of the client's needs; making catalytic interventions as part of the therapy process; and evaluating client progress and the effectiveness of therapy.

A wide spectrum of tests is available, ranging from standardized psychometric tests to informal information-gathering exercises. Standardized tests can be used to assess such psychological variables as anxiety, depression, social support and interpersonal functioning (Anastasi, 1992). There are inventories associated with particular therapies, such as the Beck Depression Inventory (Beck, 1978) and cognitive therapy, and Lazarus' (1981) Multimodal Life History Questionnaire and multimodal therapy. There are also questionnaires designed to gather information about specific issues, such as post-traumatic stress disorder (Scott and Stradling, 2000) and risk of suicide (Curwen, 1997).

A variety of exercises and questionnaires can be used catalytically, to initiate dialogue or to help a client get unstuck. These are not formal tests, but exercises that give sufficient structure and stimulus to reveal useful information. An example is completing sentence stems such as 'I get sad when …'. Another, from transactional analysis, uses written or diagrammatic descriptions of key aspects of a client's situation. In reality therapy, Glasser (1989) challenges clients with questionnaires that expose problematic attitudes and behaviour.

Some tests help in deciding what therapeutic approach is most suitable for a client. This helps the therapist to adapt his approach or to consider referral. An example is the Opinions About Psychological Problems Questionnaires (Barker et al., 1983, reproduced in Dryden and Feltham, 1992) which reveal what theoretical orientation may best help a client. A more general test, the Myers–Briggs Type Indicator, assesses preferred ways in which people relate to the world and others, using Jungian concepts of psychological type. This can be also be used to provide useful insights about how best to intervene with a client (Bayne, 1993).

Questionnaires can be used to assess client change and to gauge progress. This is particularly helpful with depressed or sceptical clients, who can gain concrete feedback of changes they have made. This is a feature of reality therapy and cognitive analytic therapy, and of cognitive-behavioural therapies in general. Questionnaires can also be used to evaluate a therapy service. An example is given in Carroll (1996: 222–224).

The decision to use tests, of whatever kind, depends upon a number of factors, such as the therapy setting, the therapist's theoretical orientation, and referral procedures where these are involved. The guiding principle is that the quality of the therapy is enhanced, for the individual client, and over time for the therapist, and the therapeutic service. This is most likely to be achieved when the rationale of a test is clearly understood and its use is closely linked to other aspects of working with the client within the therapeutic alliance.

Crisis management

Managing crises is an inevitable part of counselling and psychotherapy. Clients may seek therapy because they are already in crisis or anticipating crisis. Often, the circumstances that have created the crisis originate outside the therapy from some other aspects of the client's life, for example the ending of a close relationship or difficulties at work. Where the source of crisis is external to therapy, one of the functions of therapy is to act as a refuge, a place of relative calm and safety for the client. For the therapist this means creating an appropriately peaceful physical environment, free of interruptions, and, being in a state of personal calm and order. Predictably, routine and a sense of the therapist's calm will usually be beneficial to the client.

However, the boundary between an externally generated crisis and the therapy is seldom so clearly delineated. External crises can contribute to crises within the therapeutic relationship that may be imported by the client, therapist, or someone else. Some examples of each may help to establish a range of circumstances in which crisis management is required.

The major challenge in managing any crisis is avoiding the sense of crisis taking over. This requires a combination of the therapist's personal/professional resourcefulness, attitude and technique. Useful techniques that have been tried and tested in practice include:

Table 3.8.1 Sources of crisis in therapy

Source	Example
Client	Extreme distress due to trauma, difficulties in relationship, physical or mental illness of sufficient severity to raise doubts about client's capacity to cope at end of session.
Counsellor	Personal difficulties due to illness, unforeseen disruptions, own emotional issues. Practical disruptions like loss of therapy room due to fire, flood or burglary.
Other	Unexpected events like client's angry partner bursting in and threatening therapist/client.

- Mentally counting to ten to allow space for initial reflection and reduce the sense of overwhelming urgency.
- Controlling own breathing, by breathing deeply, slowly and concentrating on exhaling.
- Focusing personal and professional resources on managing the crisis.
- Breaking the source of the crisis into its component parts or more manageable 'chunks'.
- Maintaining a sense of hope, purpose, and knowledge that the person most affected by the crisis is not alone in experiencing this kind of crisis.

The therapist's capacity to manage any crisis is considerably enhanced by preparation for such eventualities. Clinical supervision provides an excellent opportunity to review periodically the management of past crises and to anticipate other reasonably foreseeable ones. Discussion with experienced colleagues may also provide important insights.

Many therapists work alone with their clients. This is often unavoidable, especially in independent practice. However, this aspect of the work makes crisis management particularly demanding. Although therapy tends to be a professionally solitary activity, it need not be isolated. Therapists can learn from the way emergency services, such as the ambulance and fire services, manage the recurrent crises that characterize their work. Belonging to a network of therapists working in similar circumstances provides an opportunity to replicate the opportunities for informal debriefing and joint problem solving. Issues of confidentiality may prevent disclosure of the personal identity of clients but nonetheless many of the ways of providing positive support used

in emergency teams can be adopted. As in their case, formal debriefing may be required if managing the crisis has proved to be personally traumatic. The knowledge that adequate personal and professional support is available enhances the therapist's confidence to concentrate on managing the crisis without becoming unduly distracted by the personal consequences of exposure to crisis. A well-managed crisis can often prove to be both a critical and beneficial turning point in the therapeutic process (Roberts, 2000).

Referral

There are many reasons why therapists consider making referrals to other services. Sometimes it is at the client's request. A client who is emotionally depressed by financial worries may want specialized financial advice in addition to therapy about depression. There are times when a client presents problems of such severity that they are inappropriate for therapy or may be beyond the competence of a specific therapist. For example, a client might benefit from being prescribed anti-depressants by a doctor (Thistle, 1998). Ethical boundaries may also indicate the desirability of referral, for example to avoid therapy with friends and colleagues.

Most practitioners find responding to requests for referral made by clients more straightforward than raising the possibility of referral in response to their own assessment. There is the possibility of a client feeling personally rejected, or receiving implicit negative messages when the therapist raises the possibility of referral. That is, someone who is being referred because of the therapist's concerns about their own competence may misinterpret the process as a comment on the severity of the client's problems rather than the limitations of the therapist. Considerable tact, transparency and reinforcement of key statements may be required to ensure that both therapist and client are communicating their feelings and intentions accurately.

Making a referral is likely to be an infrequent procedure in most counselling and psychotherapy services. This means that there are usually no fixed procedures nor expectations of the potential agency to whom the client is being referred. This can complicate any exploration of the desirability of referral and the client's active involvement in the process. It is increasingly common practice for the therapist to have discussions with the potential provider of new services about:

- the eligibility of the client to receive the service
- service availability, e.g. waiting lists
- type of service(s) available
- any requirements of the client
- confidentiality
- referral arrangements.

These discussions will usually take place with the client's consent but may also be made in ways which protect the client's identity, for example anonymously. The purpose of these discussions is to gain information, which enhances the quality of the decision to make a referral.

It is most consistent with the ethical basis of therapy to work in ways that enable clients to refer themselves to further services, especially where they are open to self-referral. However, there may be times when the client is too troubled to make a self-referral, or explicitly requests the assistance of the therapist. Some agencies will accept only professional referrals. In these circumstances, best practice is to negotiate the basis of referral with the client so that the client is clear about what is being communicated or withheld. Anecdotal evidence suggests that there is considerable variation in the amount of information passed to the receiving service. In terms of efficiency and respect for client privacy, it is usually best to restrict information to that which is relevant to the delivery of the service and which has been explicitly agreed with the client. Most receiving services would expect to be informed if the person being referred poses a threat to other service recipients or staff.

It is common practice to make referrals in writing, usually by letter or brief report. This has the potential advantage of the therapist being able to discuss the contents with a client prior to sending if it is considered personally sensitive, or of sending a copy to the client so that the process is transparent. This maximizes the client's participation. Practice varies in whether the person making the referral expects a brief report of the outcome. It is therefore best to request a report if this is considered desirable.

The major challenge in making referrals is making them in ways consistent both with the quality of relationship and with ways of working required for therapy (Leigh, 1998).

References

American Psychiatric Association (2000) *Diagnostic and Statistical Manual of Mental Disorders: DSM–IV–TR* (4th edn). Washington, DC: American Psychiatric Press.

Anastasi, A. (1992) What counselors should know about the use and interpretation of psychological tests. *Journal of Counseling and Development*, 70: 610–615.

BACP (2002) Guidance on good practice in counselling and psychotherapy. In BACP, *Ethical Framework for Good Practice in Counselling and Psychotherapy*. Rugby: British Association for Counselling and Psychotherapy. pp. 5–10.

Barker, C., Pistrang, N. and Shapiro, D.A. (1983) Opinions about psychological problems. Unpublished manuscript. Sub-department of Clinical Psychology, University College London.

Bayne, R. (1993) Psychological type, conversations and counselling. In R. Bayne and P. Nicholson (eds), *Counselling and Psychology for Health Professionals*. London: Chapman and Hall.

Beck, A.T. (1978) *Depression Inventory*. Philadelphia, PA: Center for Cognitive Therapy.

Bond, T. (2000) *Standards and Ethics for Counselling in Action*. London: Sage.

Bor, R., Gill, S., Miller, R. and Parrot, C. (2004) *Doing Therapy Briefly*. Basingstoke: Palgrave Macmillan.

Bordin, E.S. (1979) The generalizability of the psychoanalytic concept of the working alliance. *Psychotherapy: Theory, Research and Practice*, 16: 252–260.

Bordin, E.S. (1994) Theory and research on the therapeutic working alliance. In O. Horvath and S. Greenberg (eds), *The Working Alliance: Theory, Research and Practice*. New York: Wiley.

Carroll, M. (1996) *Workplace Counselling: A Systematic Approach to Employee Care*. London: Sage.

Corey, G., Corey, M.S. and Callanan, P. (2002) *Issues and Ethics in the Caring Professions*. Pacific Grove, CA: Brooks/Cole.

Curwen, B. (1997) Medical and psychiatric assessment. In S. Palmer and G. McMahon (eds), *Client Assessment*. London: Sage.

Dexter, G. and Russell, J. (1997) *Challenging Blank Minds and Sticky Moments in Counselling*. Preston: Winckley Press.

Dryden, W. and Feltham, C. (1992) *Brief Counselling: A Practical Guide for Beginning Practitioners*. Buckingham: Open University Press.

Dryden, W. and Feltham, C. (1994) *Developing the Practice of Counselling*. London: Sage.

Egan, G. (2001) *The Skilled Helper: A Problem-management and Opportunity-development Approach to Helping* (7th edn). New York: Brooks/Cole.

Ellis, A. and Dryden, W. (1998) *The Practice of Rational Emotive Behaviour Therapy*. London: Free Association Books.

Glasser, N. (ed.) (1989) *Control Theory in the Practice of Reality Therapy*. London: Harper and Row.

Houston, G. (2003) *Brief Gestalt Therapy*. London: Sage.

Hudson-Allez, G. (1997) *Time-limited Therapy in a General Practice Setting*. London: Sage.

Jacobs, M. (1999) *Psychodynamic Counselling in Action*. London: Sage.

Lazarus, A.A. (1981) *The Practice of Multimodal Therapy*. New York: McGraw-Hill.

Leigh, A. (1998) *Referral and Termination Issues for Counsellors*. London: Sage.

McLeod, J. (2003) *An Introduction to Counselling* (2nd edn). Buckingham: Open University Press.

Malan, D.H. (1976) *The Frontiers of Brief Psychotherapy*. New York: Plenum.

Mearns, D. and Thorne, B. (1999) *Person-centred Counselling in Action* (2nd edn). London: Sage.

Midgley, D. (1998) *New Directions in Transactional Analysis Counselling: An Explorer's Handbook*. London: Free Association Books.

Nelson-Jones, R. (1982) *The Theory and Practice of Counselling Psychology*. London: Holt, Rinehart and Winston.

Parkinson, F. (1995) *Listening and Helping in the Workplace: A Guide for Managers, Supervisors and Colleagues who Need to Use Counselling Skills*. London: Souvenir Press.

Roberts, A.R. (ed.) (2000) *Crisis Intervention Handbook: Assessment, Treatment and Research*. New York: Oxford University Press.

Rogers, C.R. (1942) The use of electronically recorded interviews in improving psychotherapeutic techniques. In H. Kirschenbaum and V.L. Henderson (eds) (1990), *The Carl Rogers Reader*. London: Constable. pp. 211–219.

Rogers, C.R. (1951) *Client-centered Therapy: Its Current Practice, Implications and Theory*. Boston: Houghton Mifflin.

Rogers, C.R. and Dymond, R. (eds) (1954) *Psychotherapy and Personality Change*. Chicago: Chicago University Press.

Rosenbaum, R. (1994) Single-session therapies: intrinsic integration. *Journal of Psychotherapy Integration*, 4: 229–252.

Ryle, A. (1990) *Cognitive-analytic Therapy: Active Participation in Change: A New Integration in Brief Psychotherpy*. Chichester: Wiley.

Ryle, A. (2004) Writing by patients and therapists in cognitive analytic therapy. In G. Bolton, S. Howlett, C. Lago and J.K. Wright (eds), *Writing Cures: An Introductory Handbook of Writing in Counselling and Therapy*. Hove: Brunner-Routledge.

Ryle, A. and Kerr, I.B. (2002) *Introducing Cognitive Analytic Therapy: Principles and Practice*. Chichester: Wiley

Scott, M.J. and Stradling, S.G. (2000) *Counselling for Post-traumatic Stress Disorder*. London: Sage.

Sills, C. (ed.) (1997) *Contracts in Counselling*. London: Sage.

Sutton, C. (1989) 'The evaluation of counselling: a goal-attainment approach. In W. Dryden (ed.), *Key Issues for Counselling in Action*. London: Sage.

Thistle, R. (1998) *Counselling and Psychotherapy in Private Practice*. London: Sage.

Thorne, B. (1996) Person-centred therapy. In W. Dryden (ed.), *Handbook of Individual Therapy*. London: Sage. pp. 121–146.

Trower, P., Casey, A. and Dryden, W. (1988) *Cognitive Behavioural Counselling in Action*. London: Sage.

Tudor, K. (1998) Value for money? Issues of fees in counselling and psychotherapy. *British Journal of Guidance and Counselling*, 26 (4): 477–493.

Turner, P.R., Valtierra, M., Talken, T.R., Miller, V.I. and DeAnda, J.R. (1996) Effect of session length on treatment outcome for college students in brief therapy. *Journal of Counseling Psychology*, 43: 228–232.

van Deurzen-Smith, E. (1996) Existential therapy. In Windy Dryden (ed.), *Handbook of Individual Therapy in Britain* (3rd edn). London: Sage. pp. 166–193.

Waldron-Skinner, S. and Watson, D. (1987) *Ethical Issues in Family Therapy*. London: Routledge and Kegan Paul.

Watkins, C. and Campbell, V. (eds) (1990) *Testing in Counseling Practice*. Mahawa: Lawrence Erlbaum Associates.

Whitmore, D. (2000) *Psychosynthesis Counselling in Action* (2nd edn). London: Sage.

Wills, F. (1997) Cognitive counselling: a down-to-earth and accessible therapy. In C. Sills (ed.), *Contracts in Counselling*. London: Sage.

Worrall, M. (1997) Contracting within the person-centred approach. In C. Sills (ed.), *Contracts in Counselling*. London: Sage.

PART IV
Professional Issues

4.1 Introduction

COLIN FELTHAM AND IAN HORTON

Apart from the descriptive factors in therapy – what therapy attempts to do, in what settings – and its clinical or therapeutic ingredients, and the wider social context in which it takes place, there is a set of issues perhaps best described as *professional* issues. While use of this term may be usefully read against critiques of the *professionalizing* trend in therapy (see House, 2003), we believe that all practitioners, from whatever tradition, are obliged to at least consider their own version of the issues presented in this part of the book.

First, there is a cluster of matters – professional and personal development, supervision, ethical and legal considerations – that all must address in one way or another. Training institutions and professional bodies differ in their requirements for professional and personal development, but all expect that counsellors and therapists will take initial and further training seriously, and all have their own perspectives on and requirements for clinical supervision. Given that the therapist's *use of self* is such a central part of the work, and that it sometimes entails difficult judgements as to boundaries between subjectivity and professionalism, it behoves all therapists to weigh up carefully such issues. Equally, all must address the questions posed by ethical frameworks and the kinds of dilemma that can arise in the ethical and legal domain.

Most, if not all, practitioners will at some time need to consider the question of insurance. However, not everyone has to examine issues arising from private practice settings, including the matter of advertising; nevertheless, this is a very large area of provision and is necessarily included here. While, likewise, not everyone has to consider the relevance of research, a challenge is issued here to all practitioners to weigh up their own position and the advantages that research has to offer. Quality assurance is something that many practitioners may not need urgently to confront, but increasingly many must do so and all are advised to anticipate the likelihood of future demands from employers and others for evidence-based practice informed by research and regular and systematic monitoring of clinical effectiveness Evidence-based practice has in fact risen to far greater prominence since the first edition of this book.

We have also included in this part of the book a brief section on clients' experiences of the therapeutic enterprise since clients both deserve and are gradually and rightfully getting a larger voice in the development and monitoring of therapy.

Reference

House, R. (2003) *Therapy Beyond Modernity: Deconstructing and Transcending Profession-centred Therapy*. London: Karnac.

4.2   Professional and Personal Development

PAUL WILKINS

Professional development and personal development are widely acknowledged as essential components of the training of counsellors and psychotherapists and as an ongoing obligation of practitioners. The major professional groupings to which counsellors and psychotherapists may belong (for example, the BACP, UKCP and the Counselling Psychology Division of the BPS) all make reference to continuing professional development (CPD) in their codes of ethics and practice and/or in their schemes for registration, and usually to a responsibility to ensure personal development too. For example, the BACP *Ethical Framework* refers both to the need for practitioners to care for themselves, which 'includes seeking counselling or therapy and other opportunities for personal growth' (2002: 3) and a commitment to maintaining competent practice which 'requires practitioners to keep up to date with the latest knowledge and respond to changing circumstances. They should consider carefully their own need for continuing professional development and engage in appropriate educational activities' (2002: 6).

Although professional associations require a commitment to professional and personal development on the part of their members, what is not immediately apparent is just what each of these comprises, nor how much is 'enough'. Also, there is confusion as to the boundary between the two and whether one can in some sense contain the other (Wilkins, 1997: 4–6). Perhaps professional development includes all those things a counsellor must do to continue to be 'fit to practise'. Broadly speaking, this includes the updating and increasing of knowledge, the continual honing of skills, the purposeful expansion of awareness and the maintenance of a healthy psyche. The relevance of the two latter arises

from the importance attached to the therapist's use of self, which is emphasized in psychodynamic and humanistic approaches but which is (arguably) of less importance in, for example, cognitive-behavioural therapy and other skills-based approaches. Of necessity, personal development (including personal growth) must be contained in professional development. The reverse is equally true. Personal therapy which would seem to be unequivocally part of personal development may also be an opportunity to learn about how it is to be a client and to assimilate the techniques and strategies of another therapist. This is clearly professional development.

The exact nature of appropriate continuing development will depend upon the stage of professional life, theoretical orientation and (not least) the interests and preferences of the practitioner. What constitutes 'enough' will also vary with the individual and the requirements of a professional body. Most professional bodies expect practitioners (especially candidates for registration) to provide evidence of serious efforts towards continuing development but are more likely to be impressed by effective and appropriate measures than sheer quantity. It is not possible to be prescriptive about what a suitable programme might be for any individual; this must be a reflection of the career ambitions of the practitioner, needs made apparent in current practice and through supervision, and the resources at the practitioner's disposal. What matters is 'to be able to explain convincingly why you did what you did, how you did it and how as a result of it your practice is different or you are different' (Wilkins, 1997: 18). In other words, it is necessary to have a coherent strategy for development, a way of monitoring and evaluating progress, and to be able to give a reasoned account of that progress. Places to decide upon developmental needs include discussion with peers, by reflection upon current work (what client needs are you unable to meet?) and, perhaps most of all, in supervision. Whatever the needs, there are a number of components to consider when deciding upon an appropriate programme of professional and personal development and, for the purpose of clarification and exploration, it is convenient to consider these separately.

Professional development

Professional development embraces the extension of skills in, and the expansion of knowledge with respect to, the theory and practice of therapy. This goes beyond a concentration on technique and orientation and includes, for example, ethics, the needs of clients and use of supervision. For many, the fundamental step on the ladder of professional development is to join a professional organization. This amounts to an intent to grow and develop as a practitioner and a commitment to safe, ethical practice. Further training or advanced study may constitute professional development and, as a scan of the world wide web will reveal, many institutions offer programmes to contribute to CPD. Research, too, can be a valid form, whether this is of a traditional and formal nature or follows one or more of the newer approaches concentrating on learning from human experience. The former approach is usually considered the most appropriate when the quest is for 'evidence-based practice'. That is as a way of providing empirical evidence that is reliable and valid and which supports, for example, a particular 'treatment'. Attending conferences, workshops and short courses, and the reading of books and journals also constitutes professional development, as does working towards registration or extending skills into a related area (e.g. supervision or training). Lastly, doing something for others is a way to develop professionally. This may be, for example, by presenting your knowledge in writing or via a workshop or through contributing in a practical way to a professional body, for example by serving on a committee.

Joining a professional body

Although some psychotherapists and counsellors elect not to do so, joining one or more of the appropriate professional bodies is for many a first step on the ladder of professional development. The BACP seeks to represent the interests of counsellors and psychotherapists of any orientation, the UKCP has constituent organizations drawing on a variety of therapeutic orientations (and it is usually these that set requirements for and monitor professional development), and the BPS has a division of Counselling Psychology. Other organizations include the British Psychoanalytic Council (BPC) and the Independent Practitioners' Network (IPN). With the Scottish organizations (e.g. the Confederation of Scottish Counselling Agencies or COSCA), these are the major national bodies to which individual practitioners may affiliate. There are a number of smaller organizations which represent special interests, such as a particular orientation or client group. In addition, practitioners increasingly have the option of joining supranational bodies operating on a European or world stage. Membership of a professional body indicates that the practitioner subscribes to a particular code of ethics and practice. This in turn means that aggrieved clients have recourse to a properly managed complaints procedure.

All professional bodies have criteria which must be met for a practitioner to be eligible for membership. These criteria are specified in the literature produced by the organization and, if they have one, on the relevant website. Most professional organizations produce a journal, newsletter or both, organize training conferences and represent the interests of their members in the wider professional and political arenas.

Accreditation, registration and chartering

Accreditation (BACP), registration (UKCP) or chartering (Counselling Psychology Division, BPS) are increasingly seen as qualifications in their own right. It is rare now to see an advertisement for a counseling or psychotherapy post which does not ask that the prospective post holder is professionally recognized or is eligible for or working towards such recognition. This alone may make it desirable, but achieving the goals necessary for professional recognition is also professional development.

Membership of a professional organization is a prerequisite for 'registration'. As indicated above, the major organizations all have schemes that offer members a recognition of their professional status and a guarantee to clients that the practitioner is trained at least to a specified minimum standard. To satisfy the relevant criteria, practitioners must be members of the organization in good standing and demonstrate that they meet the specified requirements for training, practice, supervision and CPD. These requirements tend to be modified and updated fairly frequently and prospective candidates for these schemes are advised to check that they have the most up-to-date information. This is most easily obtainable from the organization's website.

There are now a number of registers of practitioners of counselling and/or psychotherapy, that is of those members who meet and maintain the standards demanded by the relevant body. The UKCP publishes a register of psychotherapists in which the names, addresses and professional affiliations of its members appear. The BPS has a register of chartered counselling psychologists and practitioners, who are accredited by BACP, COSCA or UKAHPP (United Kingdom Association of Humanistic Psychology Practitioners) and are eligible for inclusion in the United Kingdom Register of Counsellors (UKRC). There are also registers produced by a number of smaller, specialist organizations.

The government seems to remain committed to the establishment of some form of statutory regulation of the 'talking therapies'. The current proposal is that the various regulatory bodies should be accountable to the new Council for the Regulation of Healthcare Professionals (HPC, 2003) and through that Council to Parliament. However, as yet, no clear decisions have been made on how the standards of education and training and the approval process (HPC, 2004) will impact on counsellors and psychotherapists. Currently, only Art therapists are regulated through the HPC (Health Professions Council).

Further training

Because it offers intellectual and professional satisfaction and increased prestige, a tempting avenue for professional development is further training. This is also of value because, however good primary training was, it is bound to have gaps and it does become dated. There is a professional obligation to address these gaps and to become familiar with advances in theory and practice and with current debates. The counselling and psychotherapy press and innovative series of books (e.g. the Sage series *Professional Skills for Counsellors*) are valuable indicators of current issues practitioners may wish to address by further training.

Further training may involve the extension of current expertise, acquiring knowledge of the skills and practices of another orientation or becoming proficient in a therapy-related area such as supervision or training. It takes a variety of forms, ranging from a prolonged course of study leading to a higher degree to attendance at a short course or training conference. For some purposes, 'self-teaching' may suffice. For example, it may be possible to learn a lot about another orientation by reading, but any attempt to incorporate such learning into practice should be approached with caution and be under the guidance of an experienced supervisor. Each form of training has its advantages and is appropriate to different professional needs. A taught higher degree (e.g. MA but also increasingly at doctoral level) provides an opportunity to reflect upon and develop practice within the rigour of an academic framework. It will also usually require the student to engage in a research project, the scale of which will vary with the level and nature of the course. A higher degree by research usually involves a deeper and lengthier research study. University websites are good places to discover opportunities for these forms of further training.

Short courses and workshops, which can be taught in a traditional didactic way, experientially or some fusion of the two, provide a contained way of, for example, updating knowledge or becoming more familiar with a particular technique, client group or issue. Attending a training conference provides an opportunity to dip into a variety of such events and to meet and debate with colleagues.

Purposeful reading, too, can contribute to further training. There is an ever-increasing number of books on counselling and psychotherapy and there are specialist journals as well as broad spectrum journals such as *British Journal of Guidance and Counselling*, *British Journal of Psychotherapy* and *Counselling and Psychotherapy Research*. Collectively, these represent a rich source of information and ideas. Reading fiction too can increase knowledge of human nature and the conditions in which people live. Knights (1995) has written about the relevance of imaginative literature to the practice of counselling and argues that some texts are particularly relevant. A great advantage of reading as development is that books and journals are accessible through the local and academic library systems and need not involve purchase.

Research

As with any other form of contributing to the increase of knowledge, research is seen as a valid form of professional development and McLeod (1994: 2–3) lists five reasons for doing counselling research. Although, as McLeod (2003) points out, counselling and psychotherapy professionals as a whole may still be reluctant to read research articles and consider research as not particularly relevant to their work, there has been a shift in recent years. For example, this is reflected in the fact that the BACP now regularly publishes a research journal (*Counselling and Psychotherapy Research*) and holds an annual research conference.

Although it remains important (especially given the perceived need for 'evidenced-based' evaluations), positivistic outcome research (i.e. research which is about the formulation and testing of an hypothesis, an attempt to link cause and effect, usually involving some kind of 'objective' measurement) is not the only kind relevant to psychotherapy or counselling. Qualitative research, both of a traditional kind and that deriving from a variety of schools of thought such as feminism, postmodernism and action research (all of which include reflection on the nature of 'power'), is equally valid and may indeed be seen as particularly sympathetic with the philosophy and aims of therapy.

In the course of practice, many practitioners encounter a 'burning question'. Research is the systematic and rigorous attempt to answer this question by one or more methods. The question may be simply framed and easily answered or it might involve a complex study over time, requiring a collaborative effort with others. It might be an individual and private endeavour or take place in the context of higher education and lead to a higher degree (e.g. MA/MSc, MPhil or PhD, depending upon the nature and depth of the research). Whatever the nature of the research, the basic process is the same (see Wilkins, 1997: 117). Practitioners considering a research project of any size are advised to become familiar with the literature on research methods, survey the publications relevant to the particular issue and, where possible, consult with an experienced researcher. It is possible that researchers based in institutions of higher education will be prepared to offer supervision or collaboration, even if a higher degree is not an objective. This would open the door to a richer library, online and computing resources than is otherwise the norm.

Writing for publication

Normally, an objective of research is to place the results of that research in the public domain. Most commonly, this is through publishing in an appropriate journal, many of which are now available in both traditional 'hard copy' forms and as electronic versions on the world wide web. Indeed, there is an increasing number of journals existing only in electronic form. It is not only the dissemination of research which constitutes professional development through publication. Written contributions can take many forms. At one end of a spectrum is the presentation of a large body of knowledge in the form of a book. This is probably only appropriate for experienced writers and only then when a publisher has seen and approved a plan or draft. At the other end of the spectrum, writing a letter to a journal or contributing to a newsletter may be a way of beginning the process of committing ideas and views to print and entering public debates. Writing for journals would seem to fall somewhere between. Actually producing a journal article can be an arduous business. There are limitations of length and there is the process of peer review which, although a constructive and helpful process, may involve considerable additional effort as suggested revisions are incorporated. Rarely is a paper accepted in its initial form.

When considering writing for a journal, there are a number of issues to be addressed. The first is to consider which journal is most appropriate. This will depend on the subject matter (specialist papers may be best placed in specialist journals), whether it is theory- or research-based (an academic journal might be a suitable home) or dealing with practical issues (perhaps a professional journal), and so on. Once a suitable journal has been decided on, it is really important to write in the format indicated in the 'notes for contributors'. These are usually to be found in copies of the journal and on the relevant website. Guidelines specify the acceptable length of a paper and other aspects of house style. It makes sense to incorporate these from the outset.

Personal development

'Personal development' and 'personal growth' are both discussed in the area of counselling training. Irving and Williams (1999: 517–526) take the view that these are two different concepts which tend to be conflated. They state that 'development is something that can be planned; growth cannot. Growth is what may happen as a result of personal efforts to develop' (1999: 518). Certainly, it is useful to consider

personal development as structured towards definite professional aims whereas personal growth may be about ways of being. For counsellors and psychotherapists, personal development is

> the process of attending to our own needs in such a way as to increase our ability to be with our clients in a way that is not only safe for both parties but which incrementally improves our effectiveness. It is about dealing with our blind spots and resistance so that we may better accompany our clients on their painful or challenging journeys rather than risk blocking them because they seek to enter areas which are frightening or painful for us. It is also about resourcing ourselves so that we have the energy and enthusiasm that effective work demands. (Wilkins, 1997: 9–10)

Personal development and therapy training

Personal development has long played a part in counsellor and therapist training although, as Johns (1996: 9) points out, 'the balance and extent has varied from course to course'. This depends on the model and philosophy in which training is grounded. For example, training rooted in the person-centred tradition often includes an obligation to participate in 'personal development' and/or community groups, and the emphasis on personal therapy in the psychoanalytic/psychodynamic tradition is well known. Courses drawing more on cognitive-behavioural models tend to pay less attention to this element.

In this context of training, personal development is most often understood in terms of personal growth or personal therapy. For some courses, a specified period in the client role is a prerequisite, others demand that the student be in therapy for some part of the course and others make no such demands – sometimes because it is not necessary in terms of the espoused model, sometimes out of a belief that coercion of any kind is anti-therapeutic. Broadly speaking, training courses focus either on the acquisition of skills and techniques (e.g. cognitive-behavioural programmes) or on meaning and growth (most humanistic and psychodynamic courses). Personal therapy is seen as having more relevance to the latter, but forms of personal development which emphasize the thinking process may legitimately be part of the former.

With respect to counsellor training, Johns (1996: 27) recognizes four models in which personal development work can operate. These are:

- Discrete and specific within the course, labelled as personal development through focused activities, undertaken at some depth in groups, structured exercises and in individual tasks.
- Through reflection on, implications for and application to the individual of all other elements of the course, such as skills work, feedback opportunities, theoretical and conceptual study, and assessment experience.
- Through the learning from, and application of supervision of, direct work with clients.
- Through the individual student's experience as a client in personal counselling/therapy.

Johns (1996: 83–99) sees personal development through individual exploration as facilitated by:

- personal counselling
- supervision
- tutorials
- journal keeping
- other writing and recording
- reading (including the 'imaginative engagement with literature of all kinds').

These, in some philosophically consistent combination, together with structured activities (e.g. the use of videotapes or creative and expressive work) and groupwork of some kind (large groups, task-oriented groups, personal development groups) would be ways of addressing personal development as an element of training.

On-going personal development

Whatever personal development is appropriate to training, what is pertinent, on-going personal development (like professional development) will vary between individuals and with time. However, the principal issues and the means of addressing them are much the same. Addressing any limitation of self-awareness and awareness of others is likely to be useful and this may be through personal therapy, although reading, writing, dreamwork and contemplative reflection might also serve. On-going personal development also includes a number of other strategies for maintaining 'fitness to practise'. These can include strategies to manage or reduce not only stress resulting from practice, but also stress in other areas of life, and deliberate efforts to refresh body, mind and spirit.

For those for whom it has relevance, personal therapy provides:

- an opportunity to address personal material (which may be understood in terms of unresolved trauma, irrational beliefs, life scripts, conditions of worth, defence mechanisms or whatever else is personally meaningful);
- experience in the client role which aids the therapist's understanding of how *their* clients may be experiencing therapy;
- a learning opportunity. However subtly, as clients we are aware of how our therapist responds, what techniques are used. This awareness may very well inform our own practice and so is at least to some extent professional development;
- a way of stimulating natural creativity and spontaneity and the imagination and exploring a variety of issues;
- a means of identifying personal conflicts (unresolved issues or ingrained attitudes and prejudices) which practitioners need to manage in their own practice (Wilkins, 1997: 10).

Choosing a therapist

Deciding that therapy may be an effective contribution to personal development immediately involves a number of considerations. There is an abundance of approaches to therapy from which to choose. This abundance reflects not only the plethora of orientations but also modes of delivery. As well as individual therapy, there are group approaches and various forms of peer counselling – each of these may be offered on a regular basis (perhaps most usually weekly) or in blocks. Each of these has its advantages and perhaps the choice depends upon individual need and resources.

Except where the nature of the training course requires the trainee to be in a particular kind of therapy, the first choice is whether to be in therapy with a therapist of the same or similar orientation or with somebody who practises another. Choosing someone of the same orientation can be affirming and instructive but, because the commitment to an orientation is often a matter of deeply held belief, somebody operating from quite different principles may prove to be of very limited help in the growth process. Conversely, an experienced therapist may learn much from someone who practises differently *if* their values and model of the person are not experienced as alien. An alternative which may offer considerable personal learning is to work with a therapist who operates from the same philosophical and theoretical framework but uses a different medium. This may be as simple as someone whose practice is one-to-one opting for group therapy, but there are also a large number of therapists who use creative or expressive techniques in their work (e.g. they may be dramatherapists or art therapists but informed by psychodynamic principles) and some whose approach is physical, offering dance movement therapy from, for example, a Jungian perspective, or primal integration therapy with a person-centred bias. Sometimes, these different, unfamiliar channels offer a radical slant on old material and a way of bypassing or overcoming ingrained defences.

A second choice is between individual therapy, a group approach, or some reciprocal arrangement with a colleague ('co-counselling'). Individual therapy offers the undivided attention of the therapist and privacy and confidentiality of a high degree. This may afford an atmosphere of acceptance and intimacy in which deep, revealing self-exploration and self-disclosure can take place. Group therapy does not offer this same protected environment but it does have other advantages. In groups, the way the individual acts and reacts becomes part of the agenda. This is awareness raising in a way that individual therapy is not. Group approaches to therapy 'all offer the opportunity for participants to learn about themselves, themselves in relation to others, and human communication and interactions in general' (Wilkins, 1997: 78).

The third option, peer counselling, is to be approached with caution. While there are advantages to a pair or small group of practitioners coming to some arrangement whereby they offer each other therapy, there are also risks of collusion which are more easily avoided in other forms. This said, a properly constructed and supervised arrangement may prove suitable for experienced therapists.

Alternatives to therapy

> The objectives of personal therapy include the maintenance of psychological, emotional and spiritual health, increasing understanding of human nature and personal growth, and there might be other ways of achieving each or all of these. (Wilkins, 1997: 79)

Alternatives to personal therapy, which may have the same result or at least contribute to the same process, are numerous. These include a variety of spiritual or meditative practices which, by tradition and experience, lead to increased awareness, systematic reflection on personal experience, perhaps in the form of dreamwork or journal keeping, the reading of imaginative and creative literature, creative approaches to relaxation and so on. What is important is choosing activities which expand awareness and/or reduce stress and replenish psychological, emotional and physical resources. Good practice depends upon the fitness of the practitioner. Each of us has an ethical and professional obligation to take care of ourselves. 'Rest, work and play' – each is necessary to on-going development.

References

BACP (2002) *Ethical Framework for Good Practice in Counselling and Psychotherapy.* Rugby: British Association for Counselling and Psychotherapy.

HPC (2003) *Guidance for Occupations Considering Applying for Regulation by the Health Professions Council*. London: Health Professions Council.

HPC (2004) *Standards of Education and Training and the Approval Process – Consultation Paper*. London: Health Professions Council.

Johns, H. (1996) *Personal Development in Counsellor Training*. London: Cassell.

Irving, J.A. and Williams, D.I. (1999) Personal growth and personal development: concepts clarified. *British Journal of Guidance and Councelling*, 27 (4): 517–526.

Knights, B. (1995) *The Listening Reader: Fiction and Poetry for Counsellors and Psychotherapists*. London: Jessica Kingsley.

McLeod, J. (2003) *Doing Counselling Research* (2nd edn). London: Sage.

Wilkins, P. (1997) *Personal and Professional Development for Counsellors*. London: Sage.

4.3 Clinical Supervision   ○○○

VAL WOSKET

What is supervision?

Supervision is a structured and formal collaborative arrangement whereby a counsellor or psychotherapist reflects regularly on their clinical work with someone who is an experienced therapist and supervisor. The aim of supervision is to promote the efficacy of the therapist–client relationship and the therapeutic work. It therefore has a primarily development function. Clinical supervision is *not* training, personal therapy, or line management, although it may contain elements of these. BACP (undated) describes supervision as 'a process to maintain adequate standards of counselling and a method of consultancy to widen the horizons of an experienced practitioner'.

Supervision at its best is a restorative process that nourishes the supervisee and helps to replenish emotional energy. As such it has a preventive mental health function and counteracts the effects of stress. Clinical supervision does not have a disciplinary function and within supervision the therapist should feel free to discuss their difficulties in working with clients without fear of disapproval or judgement. Supervision is different from line management in that the focus of the work is the interaction between the practitioner and the client, rather than the management of casework. Ideally practitioners are not supervised by their line managers. Where this occurs by necessity, it is important that the therapist also has access to external, objective consultative support to complement their line management supervision. In essence, then, effective supervision:

- promotes therapeutic competence, knowledge and skills development;
- enhances the quality of the therapeutic work;
- safeguards the welfare of clients by monitoring ethical, professional and anti-discriminatory practice;
- encourages the growth of insight and self-awareness through reflective practice;
- provides the therapist with a protective mechanism against stress and burnout.

Clinical supervision has three key functions which are to support, develop and monitor the supervisee and the work that she or he is undertaking with clients. The supervisor's role is to encourage the autonomy of the practitioner within safe boundaries and limits and to provide a relationship and process that will enable the practitioner to develop their own way of working effectively with clients. The ultimate success of supervision depends to a large extent upon the quality of the relationship between the supervisor and the therapist. Research is now emerging to show that the relationship in supervision is a key determinant of its effectiveness (see Page and Wosket, 2001, for a full discussion and references). Some key findings from this research indicate that:

- supervisees rate the quality of the supervisory relationship as the most pivotal and crucial component of good supervision. Positive relationships with their supervisors contribute significantly to supervisees' overall satisfaction with the supervision they receive. Conversely, where supervision relationships are deemed unsatisfactory by supervisees they tend to rate these as the most significant aspect of negative supervision.
- there is a positive correlation between supervisees' perceived levels of rapport with their supervisors and their ability to disclose difficult and sensitive issues in supervision. Therefore the quality assurance function of supervision may be importantly mediated by the quality of the supervisory relationship.
- where supervisees experience good relationships with their supervisors, they identify the positive elements of these relationships as empathy, a non-judgemental stance, a sense of affirmation or validation, and a tendency to encourage exploration and experimentation.
- supervisees who experience relationship difficulties with their supervisors learn to protect vulnerable aspects of the self by hiding certain problems and conflicts in their work from fear of an unsympathetic reaction if they revealed them to their supervisor. This experience then tends to be paralleled in supervisees' client work as they learn to use avoidance tactics when dealing with difficult interpersonal relationships with clients.

One particular aspect of supervisory relationships that has been shown to be significant is the supervisor's use of self, particularly through the use of self disclosure. Research in this area (see Page and Wosket, 2001) indicates that:

- self-disclosure by the supervisor, as a way of using the self within supervisory relationships, serves two important purposes:
  (i) building and enhancing the supervisory relationship and
  (ii) repairing the relationship when it becomes problematic.
- the use of legitimate self-disclosure by the supervisor is particularly important in providing modelling to supervisees about how to address conflicts and tensions in their relationships with clients.
- the degree of supervisor self-disclosure appears to predict the strength of the supervisory working alliance.
- excessive or inappropriate self-disclosure by the supervisor tends to significantly undermine the supervisory process and relationship.
- the willingness of a supervisor to share their vulnerability through disclosing their own struggles with therapeutic dilemmas is particularly appreciated by supervisees and helps to correct the power imbalance in the relationship.
- the more frequently a supervisor (legitimately) self-discloses, the greater is the agreement between the supervisor and the supervisee on the goals and tasks of supervision and the stronger is the emotional bond between the two.

An analysis of data gathered in research studies suggests the following key indicators about the significance of the supervisory relationship:

- The relationship is not an end in itself, but importantly expedites the task and process in effective supervision.
- In particular, supervisor self-disclosure and genuineness appear to move the process of supervision forward and encourage open exploration whenever the supervisee feels vulnerable, resistant or inhibited.
- In unsatisfactory supervision, supervisees become very focused on the negative characteristics of the supervisory relationship.
- In particular, inflexibility on the part of the supervisor seems to seriously inhibit supervisees' productive exploration and can lead to irreconcilable impasses.

Requirements for supervision

Clinical supervision as a formal, ongoing requirement for all counsellors is stipulated in BACP's *Ethical Framework for Good Practice in Counselling and Psychotherapy* (2002). Current recommendations made by BACP (2000) advise that counsellors (including those in training) should receive a *minimum* of one and a half hours of supervision per month in order to be eligible for Individual Counsellor Accreditation. This is considered to be an absolute minimum and BACP recommends that careful assessments based on variables such as case loads, complexity of client issues, work setting and experience of the counsellor are made to determine how much supervision individual practitioners need for ethical and safe practice. Where supervision is undertaken in a group, counsellors may count a proportion of presentation time (rather than the total time that the group meets) towards their supervision hours. Proportions are based on the size of the group and BACP can advise on current ratios.

UKCP and other professional bodies governing psychotherapists, psychoanalysts, clinical psychologists and counselling psychologists expect clinical practitioners to be engaged in on-going personal and professional development, including supervision, but stop short of stipulating mandatory specified amounts of career-long supervision. Increasingly, on-going supervision for trainees and qualified practitioners is becoming embedded in the broader spectrum of mental health professions (Scaife, 2001), perhaps most noticeably in nursing (Butterworth et al., 1997).

Types of supervision

Supervision can be undertaken in a one-to-one relationship with an individual supervisor, within a group, or between two therapists as co-supervision. Normally, in individual supervision, the supervisor will be a more experienced practitioner than the supervisee. Group supervision can either be peer-facilitated or have a leader. Where it is led by a supervisor, group members may be supervised in turn by the leader or they may engage in peer supervision

that is structured and facilitated by the leader. The latter model allows for greater use to be made of the resources and responses of all members of the group in the process of understanding and exploring the client work presented.

Peer group supervision is not recommended as the only, or main, form of supervision for trainee counsellors, who are considered to require the discipline and individual attention provided by regular one-to-one access to an experienced supervisor. Co-supervision occurs where two counsellors take turns in supervising one another. This form of supervision is only suitable for very experienced therapists and may not be appropriate for all practitioners.

Finding a suitable supervisor

Counsellors and psychotherapists in training will often have their supervisor appointed or recommended by their tutor from an approved register of supervisors maintained by their training institution. Where trainees are required to make their own supervision arrangements, it is important that they check on the suitability of their supervisor to meet the requirements for the type and standard of supervision laid down by the training course. A trainee therapist should have a supervisor who is trained or well versed in (and supportive of) the core theory or model of training that the supervisee is learning on their course. Continuity is also important for trainees. Once settled with a supervisor who suits them, it is helpful for the student to stay with the same supervisor throughout their training. The supervisor can then provide feedback and encouragement that arise from in-depth knowledge of the student's work as it develops over time and with a variety of clients.

Qualified practitioners may benefit from supervision provided by someone who can offer a range of perspectives that extend beyond their own original training model. Therapists who work in organizations do well to choose supervisors who are willing and able to work with organizational issues and dynamics as well as interpersonal ones. Those who work in primary health care and other specialized settings, or who offer time-limited contracts or work with specific client populations, are similarly advised to seek out a supervisor who is familiar with and able to take account of the context-specific nature of their work. Therapists need to feel both supported and stretched in their learning and development. Supervision that is experienced merely as a cosy exchange of interesting observations is likely to diminish a therapist's work with clients rather than enhance it. Vigorous and active challenge, coupled with support and encouragement, are the important components of a healthy and creative supervision relationship and without an optimum balance of these elements supervisees and their clients are unlikely to thrive.

It is important for therapists to choose supervisors who are experienced clinical practitioners, have sound supervisory knowledge and experience, and can offer the kind of relationship in which the supervisee feels able to reveal their concerns and dilemmas freely and honestly. BACP publishes an annual *Counselling and Psychotherapy Resources Directory* that provides details of supervisors under geographical listings and indicates those who are accredited practitioners. Prospective supervisees should not fight shy of asking for detailed information about a supervisor's background, training, experience and style of supervision, and own supervision arrangements before deciding whether to work with that person. They should expect that time will be given in an initial meeting to contracting, which includes looking at the supervisee's needs and preferences as well as what the supervisor has to offer. Supervisees can expect to have regular reviews in which mutual feedback is given and received on the supervision task and relationship, and should ask for these if they are not offered.

Negotiating a supervision contract

Once supervisor and supervisee have agreed on the possibility of working together, they need to form a contract to establish ground rules for the process and relationship that are designed to ensure that the work is safely structured and proceeds in a constructive manner. Contracts can be written or verbal and should be regarded as consisting of a process as well as having content, in that they can be added to and re-negotiated as the supervision work develops. Examples of supervision contracts are provided by Page and Wosket (2001) and Scaife (2001). The supervision contract will encompass a range of factors dependent on the nature and context of the supervision and whether it is with a trainee or experienced therapist. Common to all supervision contracts are likely to be discussion and agreement on the following elements:

- *Time, place, duration and frequency* – of supervision meetings and arrangements for between-session contact, emergency supervision and cancellations.
- *Fees* – amount, when and how fees are to be paid and whether payment is required for sessions that are cancelled.
- *Boundaries* – in which the differences and similarities between supervision, training, therapy and line management are explored and clarified and boundaries between any (potential or existing) overlapping roles and relationships are established.
- *Confidentiality* – where common understanding and agreement about the parameters of confidentiality governing the supervision relationship are agreed.
- *Codes of ethics and practice* – agreement on which professional codes of practice will govern the supervision and counselling work. If supervisor and supervisee adhere to different ethical frameworks, they will need to familiarize themselves with one another's. Negotiation should take place on how ethical concerns will be managed if they arise.
- *Accountability* – any lines of accountability need to be made explicit. In particular the supervisor should be clear with the supervisee about any responsibility they have to report back to an organization, training institution or line manager and how this will be done. It is good practice for the supervisee to have some input into any evaluation of their work through, for example, the compilation of a joint learning statement or report that includes sections written by both supervisor and the supervisee.
- *Expectations and preferences* – of both the supervisor and supervisee need to be discussed. Clarification of responsibilities towards one another and the supervisee's clients should cover considerations of anti-discriminatory practice, for instance through displaying sensitivity to issues of race, disability and sexual orientation as they may arise in relation to clients and supervisees.

Using supervision effectively

Arguably, supervision is primarily about enabling therapists to use themselves more effectively in the service of their clients' therapeutic needs (Wosket, 1999). It is important for supervisees to prepare well in order to make good and economical use of the creative learning space that supervision affords. Supervision that is largely taken up with recounting background details and blow-by-blow accounts of therapy sessions leaves scant room for immediate and constructive exploration of the supervisee's issues in a way that will enhance the therapeutic work. It can be helpful for the supervisee to attempt a focused presentation of their issue, for instance by starting with a phrase such as: 'My dilemma with my client is …'. (Note that this is different from saying: 'The problem with my client is …' which may only serve to objectify the client and take the focus of the supervision away from the interaction between client and therapist.)

Presenting issues for supervision

The issues that supervisees bring to supervision can be wide-ranging and extend well beyond an exploration of the content and process of counselling sessions. However, it is important that issues brought are in some way clearly related to the client work to preserve the integrity of the supervision task and process and prevent it lapsing into something else, such as teaching or counselling. Some examples of issues which supervisees might present for supervision are: a boundary problem; a difficulty with a beginning or ending; a sense of stuckness; a power issue; strong feelings – for instance of frustration, dread, shame, hostility or sexual attraction; a concern about working in a culturally sensitive manner; an organizational issue; feelings of stress or anxiety; a loss of motivation or commitment; a personal issue, such as pregnancy, illness or a bereavement, that is impacting on the work with clients; a concern about client dependency, or a sense of achievement or success.

Supervision issues can be presented in a number of ways, including the bringing of audio or video tapes, case notes or transcripts of sessions. The bringing of tapes to supervision is especially useful in the supervision of trainees as tapes provide immediate and concrete examples of work that is actually taking place with clients and can enable the supervisor to give specific feedback based on behavioural observations. It is, of course, crucial that tapes of client work are presented only with the informed consent of clients. Using written consent forms is best practice (a sample consent form can be found in Page and Wosket, 2001). Where tapes are used it is important for the supervisee to select a significant portion of a session to present to their supervisor, for example, where they feel they made an excellent or a very poor intervention; where the session stalled or became confusing; or where there seemed to be a sudden, unexplained surge or drop in energy. Supervisor and supervisee can then explore what might have been occurring within the counselling process and relationship and consider together possible alternative interventions or responses to the client.

Creative and intuitive approaches to the presentation of client work can also be employed, such as the use of imagery and metaphor; creative drawing; sculpting with coins, stones or shells. Within group supervision dramatic and active forms of supervision, such as inviting group members to represent and speak as aspects of the client's world, can be utilized in order to make use of the dynamics of the group to throw light on the relationship between therapist and client.

Working within the supervision space

Whatever methods of presentation are employed, their purpose is to lead the supervisor and supervisee into a collaborative exploration of issues within the supervision space. Within this space supervisor and therapist work together to explore possibilities, issues and dilemmas arising from the supervisee's work with clients. The focus of the work will shift according to which aspects of the supervisee's issue are most pressing. Where the focus is squarely on a particular therapy session, it can be helpful for supervisor and supervisee to differentiate between:

- *focus on the content of the session* – how is the client seeing their problem; how does the counsellor see it – are their views similar or different? What patterns and themes are emerging and what are the underlying issues, if any? What else might usefully be explored?
- *focus on the process* – what therapeutic strategies are being used and why? How is the client responding? Would it be helpful to consider other perspectives and ways of working? How is the overall process of the work being managed and paced? Are any adjustments needed?
- *focus on the relationship* – what is the relationship like between client and therapist? How sound is the working alliance? What impact is the therapist having on the client and the client on the therapist? What needs attention in the relationship? What might be going on in the relationship that isn't being talked about? Is anything happening in the supervisory relationship that may parallel or reveal something that is happening in the therapist–client relationship? Can any of this be named and discussed with the client?

Within the supervision space the supervisee is enabled to find their own best way of working with clients with the support and guidance of the supervisor. If effective work is taking place, the therapist will feel both challenged and affirmed by the supervisor as they are helped to reflect on their work in ways that lead to the development of fresh insight and awareness. Information and suggestions about how to work more effectively with clients may be given by the supervisor if they would be welcomed by the supervisee. Trainee and novice therapists are likely to seek more guidance and advice from their supervisors than are experienced practitioners. The supervisor's role is to provide sufficient guidance for the therapist to feel securely 'held' and increasingly competent in their work, but without disenfranchising the supervisee by taking over and standing in as a surrogate counsellor of his or her clients.

Culturally sensitive supervision

Responding to the many aspects of difference and diversity that arise in supervison requires a readiness on the part of the supervisor and supervisee to acquire a broad range of culture-specific knowledge, competence and sensitivity. Bradley and Ladany (2001)

have usefully identified five domains of competency within multicultural supervison that supervisors and supervisees might use to identify their strengths and areas for development as they work towards more culturally sensitive practice. Briefly, these domains include the following competencies:

1. *Personal development* (for both supervisor and supervisee). This would include exploring and challenging attitudes and biases and increasing knowledge of diverse populations and alternative approaches to helping other than those based in North American and Northern European contexts.
2. *Conceptualization*. This includes supervisors enabling their supervisees to understand the impact of racism, oppression and discrimination on clients' lives and their presenting issues and helping them to avoid pathologizing clients on the basis of cultural differences.
3. *Skills/interventions*. This involves supervisors encouraging supervisees to offer flexible interventions that do not rely solely on strategies that take the pursuit and accomplishment of individual goals as the norm and, in so doing, take proper account of group and community action and responsibility.
4. *Process*. Attending to process involves addressing power dynamics within supervision and therapy relationships. Supervisor modelling here should show the willingness to adopt a collaborative way or working with supervisees to establish jointly agreed goals, ways of working and feedback mechanisms. Supervisees are then encouraged, through such modelling, to offer respect for diversity and equality in working with their clients.
5. *Outcome/evaluation*. This involves supervisors taking responsibility for engaging in on-going collaborative evaluation of their own and their supervisees' strengths and weaknesses in transcultural practice. Supervisors who are competent in this area recognize their duty as gate-keepers to the professions of counselling and psychotherapy and are willing to act to ensure that their supervisees are working in culturally accountable ways and to take steps to address evident deficiencies in transcultural competency when these are apparent in their supervisees (or in themselves).

The reader is referred to Bradley and Ladany's text (2001) for a full and thorough account of a broad range of transcultural issues and recommended responses to these within supervision training and practice.

In assisting themselves and their supervisees to develop as culturally sensitive practitioners it has been suggested (Campbell, 2000) that the supervisor should attend to two crucial questions. The first of these is to ask how transcultural differences might be affecting the supervisory relationship and how the supervisor should respond to these differences. The second is to ask how transcultural issues may be affecting the client work and what response may be needed here.

In relation to the first question, supervisors have a responsibility to understand how the supervisory relationship will be mediated by cultural differences. This becomes particularly important where the supervisor has a role in evaluating the supervisee's competence. As Campbell (2000: 175) observes, 'variables such as assertiveness, expression of feelings, sense of time, respect, and ability to function independently all have a cultural component'. Awareness of cultural norms should closely inform the supervisor's understanding of their supervisee and he or she should be especially careful about fixing supervisees with labels such as resistant, dependent, lacking in confidence, or reluctant to work with feelings, when these may be more indicative of cultural differences between the supervisory couple than incompetency by the supervisee.

In relation to the second question, supervisors have a duty to challenge, through supportive exploration and confrontation, supervisees' unexamined attitudes and beliefs towards clients who do not share their own cultural identifications and life experience. They need to be constantly alert to inviting supervisees to consider the impact that their own cultural identifications have on their understanding of clients' problems and the therapeutic strategies they choose to employ.

Ethical issues in supervision

It is good practice for supervisors to allow their supervisees to determine what they wish to explore in supervision. Therapists should be encouraged to bring their flaws, errors, omissions and misjudgements to supervision safe in the knowledge that their vulnerability and fallibility will be accepted and respected. Yet at the same time the role of supervisor brings with it certain ethical responsibilities involved in monitoring the work of supervisees to ensure that the welfare of clients is safeguarded. On occasion the supervisor may have to step in and clearly indicate to the counsellor that an ethical issue needs attention. The task for both supervisor and supervisee will be more easily accomplished here if the ground has been prepared in advance, preferably at the contracting stage.

A useful question for the supervisor to ask when contracting with a supervisee is: 'If I have concerns about your practice with clients, how would you like me to address these with you?' An open invitation such as this clearly lets the supervisee know that their supervisor is comfortable with the quality assurance aspects of supervision and also allows them to have some say in how their work will be monitored. As part of the discussion the supervisor should at some point clearly declare what action they may take in the event that the counsellor appears to be engaged in practice that constitutes a breach of ethics and may lead to clients being harmed.

Where the supervisor has ethical or professional concerns about a therapist's practice this should first be raised with the supervisee, preferably invoking relevant ethical frameworks and principles so that the supervisee is clear about the rationale for the supervisor's concerns and interventions. Where discussion fails to resolve the issue, possible courses of action open to the supervisor are: to inform the organization and/or training institution to which the supervisee is accountable; to invoke the complaints procedure of the supervisee's professional association; and to refuse to continue to supervise the therapist. Unilateral courses of action should normally only be taken after the supervisor has consulted with their own supervisor or consultant and with the supervisee's knowledge. In all cases the clear mandate that the supervisor holds to ensure that clients are not harmed needs to be balanced against the supervisee's right to work as an autonomous practitioner.

Recent developments and perspectives

While the importance of supervision for therapists in training remains largely undisputed, debates about the desirability and necessity of mandatory, career-long supervision for qualified practitioners have recently been aired in the professional literature (Feltham, 1999; Lawton and Feltham, 2000). Some of the arguments voiced against career-long supervision include the following:

- The perceived lack of research evidence to show that supervision makes therapists more effective in their work with clients.
- To other professions, the requirement for obligatory, career-long supervision arguably gives out the message that counselling is a profession that needs constant surveillance and that therapists cannot be trusted to work independently.
- The requirement for mandatory supervision infantilizes the more senior and experienced members of the counselling profession.
- Practitioners may find supervision more effective if they seek it voluntarily and only when they feel the need, rather than being obliged to have a set amount at regular intervals, where the danger then exists that the activity will degenerate into an empty ritual.
- Supervision is supposed to safeguard the welfare of clients, yet it relies largely on second-hand reporting of issues by counsellors. It is therefore possible that unscrupulous and unethical practitioners may simply censor what they bring to supervision and use supervison as a smokescreen to endorse bad practice.

The credibility of supervisors and the professional bodies to whom they are accountable rests, to a large degree, on their openness to interrogation by those within and outside their ranks. These are sensible criticisms and ones which the professions of counselling, psychotherapy and supervision must continue to engage with through ongoing debate and research. One forum in which such issues have, and continue, to be vigorously debated is the annual conference of the British Association for Supervision Practice and Research (BASPR). Over the last decade, the themed BASPR conferences have provided a stimulating mix of keynote addresses and interactive workshops on a variety of key aspects of supervision theory and practice, including: power, authority and accountability in supervision; integrative models of supervision; men, masculinity and supervision; and women, femininity, intimacy and supervision.

A recent significant contribution to the professional literature, and one that attempts to address concerns regarding the perceived lack of supervision research in the British context, is Wheeler's landmark systematic scoping search entitled *Research on Supervision of Counsellors and Psychotherapists* (2003). This publication reveals that while most of the published research in this area stems from America, there are significant studies beginning to emerge from the United Kingdom. It is to be hoped that this comprehensive and accessible resource document will act as a stimulus to researchers and students of supervision in the British context to produce further studies designed to challenge and develop current thinking and practice in this growing field.

It may well be that a number of the criticisms noted above have more to say about incompetent and ineffective supervisors than about deficiencies in the practice and function of supervison, *per se*. Wherever supervisors take measures to effectively enhance their supervision relationships, to attend to aspects of difference and diversity in their work and to adopt flexibile approaches that take account of their supervisees' differing needs and expectations as they gain experience, they may do much to avert such criticisms. Herein, perhaps, lies the best hope that supervision has of occupying a continuing and valid place in the on-going development of counsellors and psychotherapists as they are engaged in moving towards greater personal and professional authenticity as self-determined, autonomous practitioners.

References

BACP (undated) Information Sheet S2. *What Is Supervision?* Rugby: British Association for Counselling and Psychotherapy.

BACP (2000) Information Sheet S1: *How Much Supervision Should You Have?* Rugby: British Association for Counselling and Psychotherapy.

BACP (2002) *Ethical Framework for Good Practice in Counselling and Psychotherapy.* Rugby: British Association for Counselling and Psychotherapy.

Bradley, L.J. and Ladany, N. (eds) (2001) *Counselor Supervision: Principles, Process and Practice* (3rd edn). Philadelphia, PA: Brunner-Routledge.

Butterworth, T., Faugier, J. and Burnard, P. (eds) (1997) *Clinical Supervision and Mentorship in Nursing* (2nd edn). Cheltenham: Stanley Thornes.

Campbell, J.M. (2000) *Becoming an Effective Supervisor: A Workbook for Counselors and Psychotherapists.* Philadelphia, PA: Accelerated Development.

Feltham, C. (ed.) (1999) *Controversies in Psychotherapy and Counselling.* London: Sage.

Lawton, B. and Feltham, C. (eds) (2000) *Taking Supervision Forward: Enquiries and Trends in Counselling and Psychotherapy.* London: Sage.

Page, S. and Wosket, V. (2001) *Supervising the Counsellor* (2nd edn). London: Brunner-Routledge.

Scaife, J. (2001) *Supervision in the Mental Health Professions.* London: Brunner-Routledge.

Wheeler, S. (2003) *Research on Supervision of Counsellors and Psychotherapists: A Systematic Scoping Search.* Rugby: British Association for Counselling and Psychotherapy.

Wosket, V. (1999) *The Therapeutic Use of Self: Counselling Practice, Research and Supervision.* London: Routledge.

4.4 Private Practice, Insurance, Advertising

GABRIELLE SYME

Psychoanalysis and psychotherapy are considerably older professions than counselling. Freud first used the word psychoanalysis to describe his way of working in 1896. From the very beginning he and his successors worked only in private practice. Many people hoped that the advent of the NHS in Britain in 1948 would make both psychoanalysis and psychotherapy readily available to the general public but for a number of reasons this did not occur. Even now the provision of psychoanalysis and psychotherapy within the NHS is minimal compared with clinical psychology.

In contrast to psychoanalysis and psychotherapy, counselling started in the voluntary sector and was therefore free at the point of delivery. The first counselling was offered by volunteer lay counsellors with the National Marriage Guidance Council in the late 1940s. Shortly afterwards the first courses in counselling were set up in universities to offer teachers

in-service training in counselling. Again counselling was to be offered free. In my private enquiries I found a counsellor who set up in private practice in 1960; possibly he was the first person to do so in the UK. From then on there was a slow but steady growth in private practitioners, with 127 entries in BAC's first referral directory published in 1979. From 1987 onwards there has been an accelerated growth in private practitioners. A survey by BACP in 2001 suggests that 67 per cent of its members (about 14,600 people) do some paid private practice (BACP Membership Survey, 2002). Of course the actual number will be considerably larger since many private practitioners will not be members of BACP.

In many respects private practice is more difficult than working in a voluntary agency or for an organization such as a school or university. The main reason for this is the lack of both institutional and peer support. Therapists in private practice have to organize their own support and supervision, manage their own caseloads, organize their own timetables, collect their own fees and pay their bills, keep accounts, and so on. Similarly, if they are ill they have to ring their clients to cancel appointments. All these difficulties have led the UKRC to demand higher qualifications and more experience of people registered as independent practitioners. Unfortunately not everyone working in private practice recognizes the need for this rigour.

Some issues that follow, such as insurance and advertising, are common to all counselling and psychotherapy regardless of context, but with specific detail for the private practitioner, whereas bookkeeping, accounts and invoicing are more commonly issues solely for the private practitioner. Evidence of the importance of insurance cover and accurate advertising can be seen from their mention in the *Ethical Framework for Good Practice in Counselling and Psycotherapy* published by BACP (2002), in the *Code of Conduct* published by BPS (2000) and in *Ethical Requirements for Member Organisations* published by UKCP (2003) and in Article 6 of the Constitution of BPC. In addition, evidence of insurance cover is one of the essential requirements demanded by UKRC of anyone registering or re-registering as an independent counsellor.

Insurance

Insurance is addressed in BACP's *Ethical Framework*. Under a heading of 'If things go wrong with own clients', the advice is as follows: 'Practitioners are strongly encouraged to ensure that their work is adequately covered by insurance for professional indemnity and liability' (2002: Clause 36). UKRC asks the counsellor to send evidence of insurance cover when registering or re-registering. BPS also requires its members to have professional indemnity insurance and UKCP and BPC require that their member organizations ensure that their Codes of Ethics and Practice insist that their members are 'adequately covered by appropriate indemnity insurance' (UKCP, 2003: 2.9). This cover is necessary for the safety and protection of both the client and the counsellor.

Even when all resonable steps are taken to prevent physical injury by either removing obvious sources of danger, such as wobbly chairs or sharp edges, or drawing attention to hazards such as uneven steps, accidents can still happen. Should an accident happen, the client has the right to seek compensation and to receive adequate payment for any injury. It is therefore prudent to have adequate insurance cover at a sufficient level to cover the worst possible accident with the highest likely level of damages (Bond, 2000: 74). In fact the accidents that would happen in a therapist's premises are unlikely to draw huge compensation claims and so the premiums are relatively low.

If a therapist works from home, the ordinary household insurance will not cover injury while the counsellor is using their home for business unless this has been specifically disclosed and covered. Failure to disclose the business use may invalidate the whole policy. It is essential that this is checked out with a competent insurance broker, who will also recommend the necessary level of public liability cover. Therapists renting rooms should check with the lessors whether they hold public liability insurance. If not, the therapist is responsible for arranging this cover.

Ensuring that a client does not suffer psychological harm is considerably more burdensome than preventing physical harm. If it is proven that one has caused psychological harm through error, malpractice or omission, then the claims are frequently substantial, as are the legal costs. In addition, records show that false charges have been made by malicious clients and simply defending oneself can cost a considerable amount in legal fees. It is therefore essential to have professional indemnity insurance. However, it is important that practitioners decide for themselves, on the basis of evidence, the likely risk of being sued and therefore the appropriate cover. It should be remembered that insurance companies make money from insurance cover. The Psychologists Protection Society (2003) gives some advice on how to assess the risk of being sued and therefore the relevant level of indemnity. The actuarial evidence is that the risk of being sued is small and therefore PPS's economy scheme, which is a mutual scheme, offers £30,000 indemnity and

£1 million public liability cover. This is probably adequate at the present time (2004) for a careful practitioner who minimizes the risks of being sued by following good standards of practice. However, if a higher level of insurance would reduce worry or one's employer insists on it, then £500,000 cover is probably adequate. If the work is in an area of higher risk, such as reporting to courts, providing sexual or marital therapy or reporting on individuals to companies, then at least £1 million or even more cover may be necessary. A number of Employee Assistance Programmes insist on £1 million. Some of these providers may be influenced by the UK having become a considerably more litigious country in recent years and by their parent company being in the USA. Another trend in the UK is that more practitioners are being investigated and disciplined by their professional associations. This can cost a considerable amount in legal expenses and therefore additional legal expenses cover for such an eventuality is also available from some insurers.

It is common for policies to include Libel and Slander and Product Insurance, though the interpretation of this, as far as counselling is concerned, is currently unclear.

A private practitioner has to consider loss of income owing to sickness or even inability to earn because of total and permanent disability following a serious illness or injury. Insurance is available to cover such eventualities but the premiums are vastly more if cover for sudden illness is wanted, than if the cover is only to commence after three or even six months of illness. Cover for permanent illness or chronic disability which prevent any earnings is less expensive than insurance against sudden illness. As with all insurance issues it is essential to consult with an insurance broker, who will possibly need to have specific experience of this market.

Advertising

It is always difficult, particularly when starting out in private practice, to know whether to advertise and if so where and how. In addition, the profession has regulations to prevent the public being misled. The BACP's *Ethical Framework* states, first, that 'all information about services should be honest, accurate, avoid unjustifiable claims, and be consistent with maintaining the good standing of the profession', and, second, that 'particular care should be taken over the integrity of presenting qualifications, accreditation and professional standing' (2002: Clauses 52 and 53). In the case of BPS, their response to the frequent requests for guidance on advertising from members and complaints from the general public was the publication of 'Guidelines on Advertising the Services Offered by Psychologists' by the Professional Affairs Board (BPS, 1998). These directives are very similar to those of BACP and of UKCP, but there is considerably more detail.

Advertising can be very important when first starting out. Once established, most referrals come by word of mouth from satisfied clients and their networks of friends and from colleagues. Some people find it useful to place an entry in the *Yellow Pages*, although others have not found this so because few people coming by that route kept their initial appointment. Obviously advertisements can be placed in local newspapers and on notice boards in doctors' surgeries, in post offices and shops. Perhaps the most effective place is an entry in a popular directory. In some cities directories of alternative therapists are published. These lists will include the name of practitioners offering a wide range of therapies, such as acupuncturists, reflexologists, aromatherapists, and including counselling and psychotherapy. In most of these directories there are no standards to be met, simply payment of a registration fee. A directory which does set standards for entry and is an effective source of referrals is the *Counselling and Psychotherapy Resources Directory*, published annually by BACP. To have one's name included, an applicant must be one or more of the following:

1 a BACP registered counsellor
2 a UKCP registered independent counsellor
3 an individual member of BACP who has completed their initial training as a counsellor, or Registered Associate
4 a member of the UKCP National Register of Psychotherapists
5 a Chartered Counselling Psychologist or Chartered Psychologist with counselling training

6   a member of the BPC Register of Psychotherapists
7   a COSCA Accredited Counsellor
8   an IACP Accredited Counsellor.

The applicant's status with the relevant organization(s) is checked. This procedure offers some safety to clients in that all entrants belong to associations with codes of ethics and complaints procedures, and for the counsellor some security in being on a list with others, all of whom have been vetted and reached an agreed standard. There is an additional safeguard for clients if the counsellor is from category 3, because these people have their work supervised, which is a form of quality assurance. Similar directories or registers are published by UKCP, BPS and BPC and can be found from their respective websites.

In some areas it is becoming much harder to set up in private practice. This may be because in recent years there has been a huge output of trained therapists, though the standard of courses available is very variable. Some clinical supervisors will pass a supervisee's name on to people seeking therapy if they themselves have no vacancies, but it should not be presumed that this will be the case. It is becoming more common for new counsellors and psychotherapists to inform colleagues in their locality that they have just started working and have vacancies. Many therapists are reluctant to recommend someone or even mention their name when the person and their work is unknown to them. It may be preferable to mention that there are directories to which they can refer rather than name a stranger, albeit one who is qualified as a counsellor or psychotherapist. It is clear, then, that the therapist has no responsibility for the recommendation, particularly if the recommended practitioner's work is subsequently found to be incompetent or unethical. It also has to be recognized that therapists in the private sector are in competition with each other, which can lead to rivalry. It would be naïve to think otherwise.

Book-keeping, accounts, invoicing

It is a legal requirement of all UK residents to pay tax on their earnings above a set threshold and therefore an important part of professional accountability and credibility is to keep financial records so that the tax can be assessed. Laws change from time to time so it is essential to obtain the most up-to-date versions of leaflets produced by the Inland Revenue. The current ones are 'Thinking of Working for Yourself?' and 'Self-assessment: A General Guide to Keeping Records'. The Inland Revenue also produces free of charge to anyone starting up in business a comprehensive guide called *The Right Way to Start Your Business: Cutting through the Red Tape.*

The self-employed are responsible for paying their own tax and even if an accountant is employed, they remain responsible for the accuracy of the accounts. To be able to guarantee accuracy it is essential that all business transactions are separated from personal finances and are recorded, backed up by evidence of payment by clients (see later), invoices and receipts, bank statements and cheque stubs. In addition, it is important to note down immediately all postage and telephone costs and the mileage of all journeys associated with the business (the mileage driven to and from supervision is a legitimate charge). It is important to be very disciplined about this as the Inland Revenue will only allow for a small number of unsubstantiated items. Should there be no receipt for small items of cash expenditure, and this should be the exception, then make a note of what this was for, the date and the amount spent as soon as possible. I would recommend buying an account book or a computer accounts package from a commercial supplier for the book-keeping so that business income and expenses are recorded clearly and effectively. From this either you or an accountant can derive the necessary information for the annual return to the Inland Revenue. The amount of detail needed depends on the business turnover before expenses. Currently, a simple three-line summary of turnover, purchases and expenses and net profits is all that the Inland Revenue require provided the business turnover before expenses is below £15,000 for a full year.

The Inland Revenue do not insist that clients are given invoices, although some clients like to receive them. Nonetheless it is essential to keep a record of exactly what a client has paid. In doing so, it is important to have a system so that the client's anonymity is maintained. One way of doing this is to assign each client a unique code number, which is always stored separately from their name and address. This code number is all that is seen in the records.

The self-employed are also responsible for paying their own National Insurance Contributions. Information on this can be found in 'Thinking of Working for Yourself?' and *The Right Way to Start Your Business: Cutting through the Red Tape*, mentioned earlier and in 'National Insurance Contributions for Self-employed People, Class 2 and Class 4', all published by the Inland Revenue.

When winding up a practice, the local Tax Office must be informed of the date on which business will cease or has ended and whether the termination is due to cessation of work or changed employment. As soon after the ending as possible, accounts must be submitted for the period of work from the last date on which prepared accounts were submitted to the Inland Revenue.

More details on all aspects of insurance, advertising, accounting and tax issues can be found in books by Syme (1994) McMahon (1994) and Thistle (1998).

References

BACP (2002) *Ethical Framework for Good Practice in Counselling and Psychotherapy*. Rugby: British Association for Counselling and Psychotherapy.

BACP Membership Survey (2002) Released as insert in *Counselling and Psychotherapy Journal*, 14.

Bond, T. (2000) *Standards and Ethics for Counselling in Action* (2nd edn). London: Sage.

BPS (2000) 'Guidelines on advertising the services offered by psychologists', in *Code of Conduct, Ethical Priniciples and Guidelines*. Leicester: British Psychological Society.

McMahon, G. (1994) *Setting Up Your Own Private Practice in Counselling and Psychotherapy*. Cambridge: National Extension College.

Psychologists Protection Society (2003) *The Assessment of Risk*. Alloa: Psychologists Protection Society.

Syme, G. (1994) *Counselling in Independent Practice*. Buckingham: Open University Press.

Thistle, R. (1998) *Counselling and Psychotherapy in Private Practice*. London: Sage.

UKCP (2003) *Ethical Requirements for Member Organisations*. London: United Kingdom Council for Psychotherapy.

4.5 Ethical Codes and Guidance

TIM BOND

No one reads codes of ethics because of their entertainment value or their aesthetic qualities. Codes and guidelines about professional ethics are functional documents designed to fulfil many purposes. First and foremost they are written to offer guidance about the parameters of ethical behaviours that are considered acceptable conduct by the membership of a specific professional body. As someone who has been involved in the production of codes for counsellors and who has taken a wider interest in the codes of the caring professions, I have been frequently consulted about how to resolve ethical challenges within the terms of specific codes or to interpret the potential meanings of a specific ethical statement. This section builds on this experience by setting out a series of observations about how to get the best out of codes and guidelines by using them to inform your own capacity for ethical analysis and personal judgement. I have deliberately phrased the preceding sentence to emphasize the primacy of your owner-ship and control of the ethical decision making. I am also writing in the first and second person to reinforce this point.

The personal responsibility for making profes-sional decisions is frequently understated because of the way codes are written – in particular their 'voice' tends to be one which seems to encourage compli-ance rather than the exercise of personal judgement. As an individual person reading a code it is easy to be intimidated by the sense that the code states the collective voice of your professional organization. The language is often explicitly or implicitly laden with 'shoulds' or 'oughts'. Failure to observe these injunctions carries the potential for being caught up in a professional complaints or disciplinary proce-dure which adds to the potentially intimidatory effect. As if to reinforce the authoritative effect, codes are usually written as though there is only one view of ethical issues, that is, the view taken by that code. Faced with the semblance of such monolithic authority, it is tempting to say 'I submit. Just tell me what to do.'

Other factors may compound this sense of dependency on the code. In the midst of an urgent ethical crisis or dilemma, most of us do not feel at our most rational or personally robust. A pressing crisis with a client, conflict with an agency, or an impending court case can make the possibility of an authoritative answer seem very attractive. In any of these circumstances, many counsellors turn to their code as a lifeline to rescue them from the turbulent waters that sometimes surround our work. This is an understandable response. However, these are not the circumstances in which to be considering a code for the first time. The sense of personal crisis not only enhances the potential dependency but may also undermine a capacity for understanding what are in reality quite complex documents. It is said that drowning people will clutch at straws. In my experi-ence, counsellors in acute ethical difficulty will clutch at clauses that seem to offer a degree of protection.

These clauses are often taken out of context. It is a strategy that is seldom successful, because codes need to be read as a whole document. Taken out of context, an individual clause can be deceptive and the interpretation favoured by the counsellor or psychotherapist is unlikely to stand close scrutiny. If you find yourself clutching at clauses, it is better to recognize this as a sign of personal pressure and to seek supportive facilitation in considering the ethical issue that confronts you. However, it is much better to reduce the risk of finding yourself consult-ing a code for the first time in a crisis by reviewing the relevant ethical guidelines in advance of any crisis and periodically revisiting them to assess how they relate to your practice. In this way, you will acquire a sense of the totality of the contents and how different provisions are interrelated, as well as some of the strengths and weaknesses of a code for your particular area of work. This considered approach to codes will put you in the best possible position to use them constructively as a support to your practice. You will also be better placed to see through some of the authoritarian tendencies of some codes.

In the next section I will examine the authorita-tive voice of codes and suggest that understanding the context within which codes are produced makes them less intimidating and maximizes their capacity to be informative. This is followed by a comparison between the codes produced by three major national professional organizations for counsellors and therapists. I will conclude with suggestions for ethical problem solving.

Decoding the ethical instruction

Codes and guidelines should be taken seriously. They usually represent an important version of the collective experience of the organization that pro-duced them. They will also have been subject to scrutiny and debate before gaining the support of a majority at an adoption meeting, usually an annual general meeting. However, they are not definitive statements. All organizations find it necessary to publish supplementary guidance and periodically to revise their codes. Some of these changes are due to changes within the profession and are in response to the challenges of new areas of work.

Other changes are determined by broader trends within society. As a result, codes and guidelines are never comprehensive. The codes currently available from the major national professional organizations all tend to share the same omissions. Ethical issues concerning work with young people, counsellors or psychotherapists working within multidisciplinary teams like primary health care, and within organizational settings such as places of education and employee assistance programmes, receive relatively scant attention in comparison to the therapist working independently with an adult client. These are issues that will doubtless receive fuller attention in the future as experience accumulates. The omission or partial treatment of a particular issue may simply indicate that practice is still evolving and no consensus has emerged about a particular issue.

There have been occasions when the publication of a code has provoked controversy about some of its provisions. Some insight into how codes are constructed will explain how these controversies emerge. The creation of codes is always a combination of ethical analysis and political process working towards creating a statement that will at least achieve majority support at its formal adoption. Within BACP and many other professional organizations, the process of developing a code is usually informed by a consultative process. This process will inevitably evoke a wide range of views on any issue. Those writing the code have to exercise judgement about any minority views that are incompatible with the majority view. The outcome of that judgement is likely to be that a minority view will be:

- ignored with/without debate and due consideration;
- rejected with clearly articulated reasons to elicit further discussion or to encourage negotiation within the consultative process;
- accommodated by 'finessing', that is artfully accommodating the minority view by creating a more inclusive and consequently more ambiguous and generalized phraseology;

- treated as an exception for which special provision is made;
- validated as being of sufficient importance to justify reconsidering the majority position and possibly initiating an educational programme.

As codes are designed to cover people working in a wide range of therapeutic orientations with their respective values, ethos and ethical predispositions and in a wide variety of settings with a variety of established practices and practical constraints, there are always minority issues to be taken into consideration. Depending on their composition, committees may move between actively supporting the ascendancy of a particular section of membership or taking a wider view of being as inclusive as possible of the full range of ethical practice. These are difficult judgements and like all human endeavours are fallible. It is always possible that a specific provision is unduly restrictive and may as a consequence not only be oppressive to an individual or group of counsellors or psychotherapists, but also constrain the future development of psychological therapies. On the other hand, a provision might be over-cautious in seeking to prevent unethical behaviour.

A comparison of ethical guidelines

A comparison of published professional guidance by three major national organizations in Britain reveals a considerable similarity in the range of issues considered to be particularly relevant to counselling. These are identified as themes in Table 4.5.1. However, there are also significant differences in tone of voice and concerning supervision and confidentiality.

When making comparisons between the specific provisions, it is important to distinguish between those ethical guidelines that set out the obligations of members directly (BACP and BPS) and those which state the minimum requirements for the production of codes by organizational members (UKCP). In each case, the level of obligation would only apply to members of that organization but the provisions are of interest and often useful to others working in the same or closely related fields.

Table 4.5.1 Comparison of published professional guidance

Requirements	British Association for Counselling and Psychotherapy	British Psychological Society (Counselling Psychology Division)	United Kingdom Council for Psychotherapy
Accuracy in statements about professional qualifications	✓	✓	✓
Therapist competence	✓	✓	✓
Fitness to practise	✓	✓	
Indemnity insurance	*	✓	✓
Respect for client self-determination			
• working with client's consent	✓	✓	✓
• non-exploitative	✓	✓	✓
• management of dual relationships	✓	✓	✓
• non-discriminatory	✓	✓	✓
Contracting			
• clarity about terms	✓	✓	
• communicated			
– in advance of any liability	✓	✓	
– at client's request			✓
Arrangements for illness or death	implied	✓	
Confidentiality			
• importance emphasized	✓	✓	✓
• any limitations to be communicated			
– in advance	✓	✓	
– at client's request			✓
• communications with other professions require			
– client consent	✓		
– assessment of client's best interests			✓
– endeavour to inform client		✓	
• disclosure permitted to save life or prevent serious harm	✓	✓	implied
Knowledge of relevant law	✓	✓	
Supervision			
• regular	✓	✓	
Research			
• integrity in treatment of data	✓	✓	
• clarity of agreement with participants	✓	✓	✓
• participant identity to be protected	✓	✓	✓
Detrimental behaviour of other members to be reported	✓	✓	✓

Key: ✓ – obligatory
      * – recommended

Sources: BACP, 2002, 2004; BPS, 2000, 2001; UKCP 1998

Each of these guidelines is written in a distinctive style and tone of voice. The BACP *Ethical Framework for Good Practice in Counselling and Psychotherapy* (2002) and *Ethical Guidelines for Researching Counselling and Psychotherapy* (2004) combine statements about professional obligations directed towards public safety with more educational passages to support practitioners in engaging with the ethical intricacies and complexities of their practice. The aim is to enhance ethical mindfulness throughout practice and to support practitioners in taking appropriate ethical responsibility and exercising accountability. These documents represent a move away from a more rule-based system of ethical governance into one designed to encourage members to ask, 'What is right?' rather than the less ethically challenging question, 'What is allowed?' These developments in the BACP (2002, 2004) contrast with those in the BPS. The latest version of *Professional Practice Guidelines: Division of Counselling Psychology* (BPS, 2001) has become more focused on stating practitioner obligations and has removed the more educational passages from the earlier version. These latest *Guidelines* also appear to have a much closer structural resemblance to the generic *Code of Conduct, Ethical Principles & Guidelines* (BPS, 2000), which is applicable to all members of the BPS. It is tempting to conclude that this simplification and focusing of the ethical infrastructure was part of the preparatory work for taking applied psychology within the regulatory framework of the Health Professions Council. It is highly probable that psychology will be admitted several years ahead of counselling and psychotherapy and, therfore, is at a different point in the cycle of meeting the challenges of regulation. The UKCP's *Ethical Requirements for Member Organisations* (1998) have remained relatively unchanged over several years but are believed to be under review as the organization considers the best structure from which to face the transition to statutory regulation.

It is difficult to anticipate what the full implications will be for the development of ethical infrastructures for any professional body concerned with the provision of talking therapy ahead of statutory regulation.

The process of enforcement and disciplining practitioners who act below acceptable standards will rest with the regulatory council. However, this activity affects only relatively small numbers of practitioners, often those working in fairly untypical circumstances. Most routine practice will be above the purview of the regulatory standards in the sense that it will never be reviewed as part of a disciplinary process as it is undertaken by ethically well-intentioned and reasonably competent practitioners. However, this is not a reason for neglecting the ethical needs of typical routine practice. It is in the interests of clients and practitioners to ensure that the ethical basis of all routine practice is adequately supported and, whenever possible, enhanced. This is likely to remain an important activity for all the professional bodies. The alternative is ethical complacency.

The analysis of current ethical guidelines in Table 4.5.1 reveals some differences in approach to confidentiality and the requirement for supervision. Although there is consensus around the importance of confidentiality to clients, there are subtle differences in how any limitations to confidentiality are communicated to clients. The BACP (2002: 7, s.16) and the BPS (2001: s.4) require that the client be informed of any limitations in advance of the provision of services. The UKCP (1998: 2.3) merely requires the communication of any limitations when the client requests this information. There are also differences in the communication of confidential information to other professionals. The BACP (2002: 9, ss.47 and 49) stresses a client's knowledge of the terms on which a service is being provided and the significance of a client's consent in routine disclosures. The BPS (2000: 42) requires psychologists to 'endeavour to make clear ... the extent to which personally identifiable information may be shared between colleagues'. The UKCP (1998: 2.4) requires that the decision to inform relevant professionals be based on 'the client's best interest'. Both the BACP (2002: 6, s.7) and the BPS (2001: 2.1.2) require regular supervision. The UKCP has no comparable general requirement.

When these comparisons are taken into account alongside the earlier discussion about how codes are produced, it becomes possible to identify a number of basic tips on how to consult codes and guidelines from professional organizations (see below). Following these tips should enable you to identify any requirements of your professional organization(s) for your specific therapy context. These requirements form an important component in ethical problem solving but are only part of the picture, albeit an important one.

Tips on consulting codes and guidelines

- Use the most recent version. Out-of-date versions may be seriously misleading.
- Avoid taking sections out of context, by considering the document as a whole.
- Distinguish between statements on obligatory practice and those on recommended practice.
- Interpret supplementary guidance and recommendations by reference to core codes and guidelines.
- Consider the implications for your specific therapy context.

Ethical problem solving

A useful strategy for problem management is breaking the problem down into its component parts. This helps a problem which is already overwhelming, or has that potential, to become more manageable. Effective ethical problem solving follows this approach. A six-step approach is recommended, which I know has proved to be extremely helpful to many practitioners (Bond, 2000: 223–236). Each of the steps builds progressively on the previous step(s) but does not exclude the possibility of creating new insights which might involve some reworking of an earlier step and proceeding again from that point. The steps are:

1 *Produce a brief description of the problem or dilemma*

   The aim is to produce a clearer statement of the main elements in the problem. It is very difficult to make progress until the problem can be expressed clearly.

2 *Consider who holds responsibility for resolving the problem*

   Another way of approaching this step is to ask 'Whose problem is it anyway?' This is particularly significant in therapy where a great deal of responsibility for the outcome of the therapy rests with the client, e.g. whether to confront someone, etc. There are occasions when the responsibility rests with the therapist, for example a client has started talking about someone who is already known to you in another context. Sometimes the problem is a shared responsibility and can only be resolved by discussion between therapist and client – for example, the client has selected you as therapist because of her sense of you as a person from knowing you in another context. The therapeutic orientation might determine whether the responsibility would rest with the therapist (more likely in a psychodynamic orientation) or could be resolved by joint exploration of the implications (more likely in humanistic and cognitive-behavioural approaches).

3 *Consider all the relevant ethical and legal guidance*

   It is unusual if a significant problem is resolved at this step. For all the reasons given earlier in this section, it is probably better to view professional guidance as establishing accepted parameters within which to exercise your ethical judgement. Sometimes you may consider that the specific circumstances of your problem challenge these parameters and that you may have to consider how to proceed against the usual guidance. This would be a major step and should be taken with professional and legal advice. Nonetheless the aim of this step is not to be prescriptive but to inform the ethical and legal decision making. At the end of this step, it ought to be possible to identify an ethical goal.

4 *Identify all possible courses of action*

   It is unusual to find that there is only one possible course of action. Often there is a choice between doing nothing or doing something, which may include saying different things to your client, to someone else, or challenging accepted practice within the profession. Listing all possible courses of action avoids the frequent misconception that because one approach appears to be right, there are no other solutions. Many solutions may be possible from which a selection can be made.

5   *Select the best course of action*

A good test of your level of conviction that you have found an appropriate solution is to test it against three standards first proposed by Holly A. Stadler, a former chairperson of the American Association for Counseling and Development (now ACA):

- Universality

    - Could my chosen course of action be recommended to others?
    - Would I condone my proposed course of action if it was done by someone else?

- Publicity

    - Could I explain my chosen course of actions to other counsellors?
    - Would I be willing to have my actions and rationale exposed to scrutiny in a public forum, e.g. at a workshop, in a professional journal, newspaper or on radio/TV?

- Justice

    - Would I do the same for other clients in a similar situation?
    - Would I do the same if the client was well known or influential?

If you find yourself answering 'no' to any of these questions, you may need to reconsider your chosen outcome. A final step in identifying the best course of action may be checking whether the resources are available to implement what is proposed.

6   *Evaluate the outcome*

After you have implemented your course of action, it is useful to evaluate it in order to learn from the experience and to prepare yourself for any similar situations in the future.

- Was the outcome as you hoped?
- Had you considered all relevant factors with the result that no new factors emerged after you implemented your chosen course of action?
- Would you do the same again in similar circumstances?

Conclusion

My aim in writing this section is to challenge any expectation that codes of ethics and guidance should be regarded as authoritative commandments to be followed in blind obedience. The BACP Professional Conduct Committee has adopted a short saying to inform their work: 'Rules are for the obedience of fools and for the guidance of the wise.' This saying is a reminder that any code is a social construction and, as such, has value as a pooling of shared experience and reflection. However, no code can be universal or infallible and therefore must be applied with discernment. Surrendering a personal and professional responsibility to any external authority would have the paradoxical effect of undermining the ethical basis of even the most appropriate action. Sometimes, it may be ethically appropriate to inform your professional organization about a limitation or weakness in current guidance, particularly if you find it ethically desirable to override an explicit requirement. The nature of counselling or psychotherapy is such that the ethical integrity of the practitioner is paramount. All the codes of ethics and practice for therapy, known to me, share a common aim in seeking to support the development of ethical awareness and practice. Being ethical is a continual challenge.

References

BACP (2002) *Ethical Framework for Good Practice in Counselling and Psychotherapy.* Rugby: British Association for Counselling and Psychotherapy.

BACP (2004) *Ethical Guidelines for Researching Counselling and Psychotherapy.* Rugby: British Association for Counselling and Psychotherapy.

Bond, T. (2000) *Standards and Ethics for Counselling in Action* (2nd edn). London: Sage.

BPS (2000) *Code of Conduct, Ethical Principles & Guidelines.* Leicester: British Psychological Society.

BPS (2001) *Professional Practice Guidelines: Division of Counselling Psychology.* Leicester: British Psychological Society.

UKCP (1998) *Ethical Requirements for Member Organisations.* London: United Kingdom Council for Psychotherapy.

4.6 Client Experiences

COLIN FELTHAM AND PHOEBE LAMBERT

Despite constant reminders given by trainers and therapists themselves – to put each unique client first, to enter the client's inner world, to learn from clients, and to respect the self-determination of the client – therapy is now a highly organized enterprise. When therapists meet their clients they are 'armed' with experience, training, theories and a professional infrastructure. The client, however, is more often than not someone in some degree of distress who knows little if anything of the theory of therapy, and their agenda may be quite different from the therapist's. In spite of requirements for therapists to have their own therapy, it is quite likely that such experiences only partially resemble those of distressed clients. For all these reasons – plus an increasing emphasis on accountability generally – this section looks at the client's perspective and commends an attitude of raised awareness among therapists about implications for their own practices.

What clients have said about their experiences of therapy

Presented here is a collated summary of views published unprompted by consumers, formally researched, or gleaned from clinical experience.

Help-seeking patterns

It is important to put in perspective the fact that the vast majority of people with problems resolve them themselves or with peer support, and that although up to about 20–25 per cent of the population at any one time may suffer from a diagnosable psychological problem, probably only about 5 per cent receive formal help. (A recent, uncorroborated figure of 25 per cent has been reported.) A disproportionate number of clients are women, it being speculated that men are less ready to acknowledge personal problems. Many people will have tried other things before turning to professionals almost as a last resort, often waiting months or years before seeking therapy. Of course many, even after presenting, must wait months for a first appointment, and while waiting up to about 14 per cent resolve their problems to their own satisfaction. Typically, many seek word-of-mouth recommendations to private practitioners, while those eligible for services free at the point of delivery may have quite different experiences of choicelessness, waiting lists, etc. Leong et al. (1995) summarize these and many additional obstacles to effective help for ethnic minority groups. Although clients are sometimes advised to 'shop around' for a service or practitioner with whom they feel comfortable or in whom they have confidence, obviously many feel too distressed to endure such an exercise or are not sufficiently assertive to do so.

Service anxiety

It has been noted that on top of the 'problem anxiety' that brings clients to therapists, it is common and understandable for them to feel anxious and uncertain about telephoning for an appointment, attending first appointments, knowing what to say and how to behave, and deciding whether what they are receiving is indeed helpful for them. They may have only a hazy notion of whether or not counselling can be helpful to them. In addition, it is quite typical for a power imbalance to exist, especially in counselling or psychotherapy agencies, with the therapist being styled and naturally perceived as the one who is qualified, who knows, who embodies sanity (whose powers may apparently border on telepathy), and who may hold the key to an exit from misery. Where discrepancies exist between the status, age, class, race, gender and sexual orientation of therapist and client, an imbalance of power may become all the more problematic and anxiety-engendering. Usually the client must visit the therapist's premises (which could be experienced as frighteningly clinical, for example) and agree to the therapist's conditions, rules and ethos of therapy. Counselling and psychotherapy – we can easily forget – are for many people very strange, counter-cultural experiences: sitting sometimes silently in a room with a stranger, being (or feeling) stared at, and expected to make intimate disclosures. According to some psychoanalytic thinkers, clients are acutely aware of the necessity of consistent physical and business arrangements and will communicate unconsciously to therapists their anxieties about any inconsistencies and subtle abuses. *Service anxiety* is discussed by Howe (1989). Additionally, Pipes et al. (1985) detailed some common client fears, which are summarized below.

Client fears

- Is therapy what I need?
- Will I

  - be treated as a case?
  - be taken seriously?
  - be made to do things I do not want to do?
  - find out things I don't want to?
  - lose control of myself?
  - be thought of by my friends as crazy?

- Will the therapist

  - share my values?
  - think I'm a bad person?
  - think I'm more disturbed than I am?
  - discover things I don't want him or her to discover?
  - be competent?

Recent research (e.g. Le Surf and Lynch, 1999; Setiawan, 2004) shows that although clients know they need help, they do not know enough or are not given enough opportunity to know about what happens in counselling. Additionally, there may be ambivalence about wanting advice and yet not wanting to be controlled.

Common factors

Initially surprising to many in the field, but now accepted as highly significant, a majority of clients have expressed the view (or it has been inferred from their accounts) that attention from a socially sanctioned healer in a sanctioned setting plays a large part in setting positive expectations. People are often reassured by appropriate settings, by a professional manner, qualifications, and an explicit rationale for therapy. For some, simply being told or reassured by a mental health professional that they are not mad is in itself 'therapeutic' (and for some it is all that is required). A large proportion of clients report the importance of being taken seriously; being listened to respectfully and non-judgementally; being understood; experiencing warmth and genuine concern; feeling contained; being helped to make sense of their otherwise ostensibly chaotic life stories (Howe, 1993). Finding a therapist with whom one can make an optimally therapeutic match is increasingly regarded as significant: this *may* include theoretical orientation but is more likely to involve perceptions of warmth, attractiveness, expertness, personality and so on (Feltham, 1999). Most clients appear uninterested in clinical theories or the nomenclature attaching to them, except where this is a vital part of the on-going therapy (as, for example, in transactional analysis or cognitive therapy); many clients report that counsellors' and psychotherapists' publicity material is sometimes too jargon-oriented and is not sympathetic to the client's perspective. If this is surprising to readers, it may be because many of us are surrounded by colleagues and friends who are therapeutically involved, whereas a statistical majority of clients, especially first-time clients, seek solutions to distress or confusion, and are very rarely fascinated by or steeped in therapeutic theory.

Scope, depth and length of therapy

It has been a sobering realization for many therapists that clients not only seek crisis resolution, symptom amelioration or removal but are often satisfied to terminate therapy when these goals have been reached. A discrepancy between the pragmatic, short-term goals of many consumers and the often more ideologically driven goals of in-depth, long-term, psychic exploration and personality overhaul of therapists, is something that has to be reckoned with. Also, while many clients have appreciated the space for reflection and empathic understanding offered by therapists, they have sometimes been mystified by long unexplained silences and lack of normal social conversation, for which therapists themselves have rationales (e.g. non-directiveness and therapeutic neutrality). Rather, for some clients, a naturalistic style of therapy is preferred which may include more self-disclosure and simple practical advice than practitioners are willing to give. Related to this is the finding that many clients expect their counselling or therapy to be relatively short-term (one estimate has it that therapists typically think therapy will take at least three times longer than clients think it will take) and many clients may prefer an intermittent pattern of attendance as indicated by felt need, rather than a 'once and for all time' model of therapy.

Therapist abuse, exploitation and ineffectiveness

Unfortunately, for a significant number of clients therapy has turned out to be – in spite of therapists' duty of care – a negative and damaging experience (Sands, 2000). Even allowing for media exaggeration, client bias and resistance, and a small proportion of unjustifiably litigation-orientated clients, it is clear that abuse (sexual, emotional, physical) occurs, along with other forms of exploitation and ineffectiveness of therapy. Sex between clients and therapists is perhaps the most publicized. While it is easy to *understand* how the intimacy of one-to-one therapy can slip into inappropriate sexual contact, accounts of how damaging it usually is for clients has led to its prohibition by all professional bodies. Formalized complaints procedures now offer those wronged the opportunity to seek redress, even though this may be rather too late. Emotional abuse (for example, using demeaning language, inappropriate confrontation, engaging in reciprocal emotional entanglements,

'dropping' clients who are regarded as difficult) is reported by some clients. Examples of clients being (or feeling) financially exploited are not so well publicized, but no doubt exist. The question of whether most clients prefer to pay something for their therapy and are likely to show more commitment when paying than if they do not, has not been resolved, although increasing clinical experience might suggest that direct payment is not the critical variable in commitment and motivation that it was once assumed to be. The ineffectiveness of some counsellors, psychotherapists and their services gives cause for concern, some clients having reported spending a great deal of time and money in therapy with no discernible results and sometimes experiencing deterioration (Striano, 1988). The extent of this is contradicted by Seligman (1995), but its sting has helped to lead to concern for evidence-based practice (Roth and Fonagy, 1996; Rowland and Goss, 2002).

Client–therapist differences

Although no figures are available, it is evident that a majority of counsellors and psychotherapists in Britain are white, middle-class liberals. Therapeutic theory reflects this bias as well as certain assumptions of secular individualism and, as is pointed out elsewhere in this book, (psychology-saturated) training often marginalizes or neglects the experiences of non-dominant social groups (Palmer, 2002; Shoaib and Peel, 2003). Hence, historically, gay clients have often been assumed to need treatment to reverse their homosexuality; the needs of clients with disabilities have been played down or ignored; women have been assumed to be 'hysterical' (and more recently to all want a career outside the home); older people have been considered too old to benefit from therapy; and different cultural norms pertaining to expressiveness, dress, religion, etc. have either been misinterpreted or ignored. There is now enough evidence from clients' reports to know that therapists can be ignorant, patronizing, and in some cases dangerous in relation to these factors. The question of *client–therapist matching* is not clear, there being mixed views on whether black people, for example, generally prefer to be seen by black therapists, or not. There is concern about low awareness of counselling in Asian communities, and more information is needed about the existence and nature of counselling services (Netto et al., 2001; Setiawan, 2004). Client–therapist age difference is a similarly uncharted or disputed area. Where some trend exists, it is that many women prefer to see a woman therapist when they have a choice, and when they sense that their concerns might be better understood and more sensitively handled by another woman. Similar preferences have been shown to exist among gay and lesbian clients (Liddle, 1996). Often, clients do not want to have to explain matters of daily oppression that are obvious to them. The converse of this picture is that in some cultures it may be the norm to expect mental health professionals to be authorities to be looked up to, and who will duly dispense expert advice. *All such cultural differences are mediated by individual differences between the parties, adding another layer of complexity.* Additionally, factors of emotional distress, transference and countertransference mean that therapists must be aware of complex interrelationships involving socio-cultural factors (including peer, family and media influences) and individual psychology.

Appreciation

The above views need to be balanced by a reminder that many consumers have expressed great satisfaction with their therapy. Client reports and formal research both affirm the overall effectiveness and/or satisfaction levels achieved by therapists (Seligman, 1995). Clients have often said that therapy 'changed my life' or that 'I couldn't have got by without counselling'. Surveys of users of mental health services have confirmed that they overwhelmingly value the talking therapies in preference to medication. Appreciating the common factors mentioned above, clients are often surprisingly unconcerned or forgiving about therapists' occasional mistakes (e.g. clumsy interpretations, forgetting factual details, etc.). Modest changes are often appreciated by clients when therapists are hoping for more radical or dramatic changes. Clients have sometimes reported having 'internalized' the therapist, that is, having a helpful inner (imaginary) dialogue with them between sessions and after therapy has ended. As might be expected, to some extent client evaluations will always represent *some* mixture of the appreciative and the negative (Bates, 2006; Dinnage, 1989; Feltham, 2002).

Conclusions

It is noteworthy that (a) discrepancies may well exist between the views and goals of therapists and clients; (b) the inherent imbalance of power in the therapeutic relationship can easily lead to forms of abuse, infantilization or insensitive treatment, and their concealment; (c) training analysis or personal therapy/counselling for the trainee is not sufficiently similar to the experience of clients to address the need for understanding; and (d) the complexity and privacy of therapeutic relationships means that clients' views have implications not only for initial training, but for on-going development, in-session awareness and reflection, and accountability and evaluation. The objection of some therapists that an overly consumerist view of the therapeutic process is unwise must certainly also be factored into our consideration: clients do not *always* know what is best for them, and may *sometimes* unconsciously introduce confusion and revenge seeking into the enterprise (Sutherland, 1987). Nonetheless there is increasing interest in the UK in the involvement of consumers in the audit and evaluation of mental health services. Procedures for, and satisfactory outcomes of, monitoring and assuring quality are (increasingly) linked to continued funding.

Taking consumers' views seriously has already led to increased concern for *informed consent* (verbal and written explanations and contracts) which extends to publications advising consumers (e.g. Dryden and Feltham, 1995) and better publicized complaints procedures. Mental health agencies such as MIND have long championed users' rights to be heard, for example by taking part in management committees. New evaluation procedures seek consumers' views in order to improve services. Knowledge about the differential effectiveness of therapies in relation to different client issues calls for greater awareness of referral issues. Clearly, the overall trend is necessarily towards greater transparency, knowledge-sharing, fairness, and constant updating of therapists' knowledge in view of clinical research results and the changing nature of society.

References

Bates, Y. (ed.) (2006) *Shouldn't I Be Feeling Better by Now? Client Views of Therapy.* Basingstoke: Palgrave.

Dinnage, R. (1989) *One to One: Experiences of Psychotherapy.* London: Penguin.

Dryden, W. and Feltham, C. (1995) *Counselling and Psychotherapy: A Consumers' Guide.* London: Sheldon.

Feltham, C. (ed.) (1999) *Understanding the Counselling Relationship.* London: Sage.

Feltham, C. (2002) Consumers' views of the benefits of counselling and psychotherapy. In C. Feltham (ed.), *What's the Good of Counselling and Psychotherapy? The Benefits Explained.* London: Sage.

Howe, D. (1989) *The Consumer's View of Family Therapy.* Aldershot: Gower.

Howe, D. (1993) *On Being a Client: Understanding the Process of Counselling and Psychotherapy.* London: Sage.

Leong, F.T.L., Wagner, N. and Tata, S.P. (1995) Racial and ethnic variations in help-seeking attitudes. In J.G. Ponterotto, J.M. Casas, L.A. Suzuki and C.M. Alexander (eds), *Handbook of Multicultural Counseling.* Thousand Oaks, CA: Sage.

Le Surf, A. and Lynch, G. (1999) Exploring young people's perceptions relevant to counselling: a qualitative study. *British Journal of Guidance & Counselling,* 27 (2): 231–243.

Liddle, B. (1996) Therapist sexual orientation, gender, and counseling practices as they relate to ratings of helpfulness by gay and lesbian clients. *Journal of Counseling Psychology,* 43: 394–401.

Netto, G.S., Thanki, M., Bondi, E. and Munro, M. (2001) Perceptions and experiences of counselling services among Asian people. In G.S. Netto et al., *A Suitable Space: Improving Counselling Services for Asian People.* Bristol: The Policy Press and Joseph Rowntree Foundation.

Palmer, S. (ed.) (2002) *Multicultural Counselling: A Reader.* London: Sage.

Pipes, R.B., Schartz, R. and Crouch, P. (1985) Measuring client fears. *Journal of Consulting and Clinical Psychology,* 53 (6): 933–934.

Roth, A. and Fonagy, P. (1996) *What Works for Whom? A Critical Review of Psychotherapy Research.* New York: Guilford Press.

Rowland, N. and Goss, S. (eds) (2002) *Evidence-based Counselling and Psychological Therapies: Research and Applications.* London: Routledge.

Sands, A. (2000) *Falling for Therapy: Psychotherapy from a Client's Point of View.* Basingstoke: Palgrave Macmillan.

Seligman, M. (1995) The effectiveness of psychotherapy. The Consumer Reports Study. *American Psychologist,* 50: 96–104.

Setiawan, J.L. (2004) Indonesian undergraduates' attitudes to counselling: a study of areas of concern, perceptions relevant to counselling, willingness to seek help and sources of help. PhD thesis (unpublished). University of Nottingham.

Shoaib, K. and Peel, J. (2003) Kashmiri women's perceptions of their emotional and psychological needs, and access to counselling. *Counselling and Psychotherapy Research,* 3 (2): 87–94.

Striano, J. (1988) *Can Psychotherapists Harm You?* Santa Barbara, CA: Professional Press.

Sutherland, G. (1987) *Breakdown: A Personal Crisis and a Medical Dilemma* (revised edn). London: Weidenfeld and Nicolson.

4.7 Therapy and the Law ○○○

PETER JENKINS

Therapists are discovering that they increasingly need to have at least a basic working knowledge of the law, whatever their reservations about the legal system or the law itself. Whether in terms of keeping client records, responding to requests for information by external agents, such as the courts, or in deciding whether to break confidentiality in order to protect a child or client at risk, therapists are finding that from time to time they urgently need access to well-informed legal advice. All too often, their basic understanding of how the law impacts on psychotherapeutic practice has been left relatively untouched by their professional training, or subjected to conflicting and sometimes even inaccurate messages about their duties and options under the law.

This section sets out some of the main parameters of the interface of counselling and psychotherapy and the law in the UK. The main points of reference relate to the civil law in England and Wales, with the law in Scotland and Northern Ireland operating in distinct, but still broadly parallel ways. The emphasis will be on describing the key trends and professional issues to be considered by practitioners, rather than setting out the precise detail, which can be followed up in the references and resources supplied. The section briefly sets out:

- how legal principles applying to counselling and psychotherapy are mediated by the practitioner's context for practice, employment status and client group
- legal aspects of managing professional relationships with clients
- legal obligations and options in handling risk
- legal principles applying to the management of sensitive information.

Making links between psychotherapeutic practice and the law

Therapists often look for general principles, and even for absolute certainty, when encountering the law. While, as practitioners, we try to encourage our clients and colleagues to contain, stay with and *work through* ambiguity and uncertainty, our own strong preference is very often to have clear and very definite answers to the professional dilemmas which we face. The following example might illustrate this process at work:

> Paul did some unpaid weekly counselling sessions for a small voluntary agency. He became concerned about his client, Sarah,

who seemed to be increasingly depressed and self-absorbed, to the extent that her pre-teenage sons, who were involved in illicit drugs and joy-riding, seemed to be 'running wild' and almost beyond her control as a single parent. The senior counsellor at the agency was unable to provide any clear guidance on how he should respond to the risks he perceived for the sons, given that there was no specific evidence of child abuse. Any attempt to explore her problematic relationship with her sons, or to express his own anxiety about this situation as a counsellor, seemed to produce little response from her, possibly due to her somewhat depressed emotional state. However, Paul's supervisor was increasingly concerned about the client and the risk to the sons' welfare. His supervisor felt strongly that Paul should make contact with social services, given the apparent reluctance or inability of the client to take any action herself.

From a professional and ethical point of view, a therapist's first point of reference should be with regard to their code of ethics, such as the BACP's *Ethical Framework for Good Practice in Counselling and Psychotherapy* (2002). This kind of dilemma contains classic issues, namely of promoting client autonomy versus protecting the welfare of the client and also of third parties. From a legal point of view, the practitioner's responses will be framed by a number of key factors, which are highly specific and will vary according to:

- the *context* in which the therapist practises
- the therapist's *employment* status
- the nature of the *client group*.

The interaction of these key factors provides a clue to the complexity of the law as it relates to counselling and psychotherapy. Exploring the possible options and responses to particular legal dilemmas is often highly specific, as general principles have to be applied carefully to this particular counsellor, working in this *setting*, on this *employment* basis, with the *client* group. Thus there may well be significant differences between the child protection reporting requirements faced by therapists working in a statutory setting and for a counsellor, such as

Paul, who is counselling in a voluntary agency. Alternatively, a counsellor such as Paul, who is either directly employed or who is seen by the law to approximate to 'employed' status, may have little real discretion in deciding how to respond to issues of client or third-party risk, due to agency policy. A therapist in private practice, on the other hand, generally has substantially greater freedom of action in deciding how best to work with these issues. Therapists working with children, or with adults experiencing mental health problems, may similarly face certain pressures to act, which are *not* obligatory when working with other client groups, who are deemed to be less vulnerable.

The resulting combination of legal pressures means that therapists often encounter a wider and more varied range of legal issues than do other comparable professionals, such as social workers or psychiatric nurses. Therapists need, therefore, to consider carefully how well they are prepared for recognizing and responding to such professional dilemmas, which necessarily carry a *legal* element as well as an ethical or professional set of choices.

Legal aspects of managing professional relationships with clients

Having emphasized the *variability* of the law as applied to different psychotherapeutic situations, the following sections now provide a brief outline of more general legal principles, which will need to be adapted to a range of specific situations. The core of counselling and psychotherapy work consists of the therapeutic relationship and its essential boundaries. These mark it as being distinct from other professional stances, such as teaching or social work, or other helping relationships, such as friendship or mentoring. From a legal perspective, the key factors relating to the therapist's therapeutic relationship with clients are framed by the concepts of:

- contract
- duty of care
- liability.

Defining a contract

Counsellors and therapists often use the term 'contract' in a rather loose way, referring to a set of arrangements guiding contact with the client, the purpose of the counselling and psychotherapy, and arrangements for supervision and recording. While the use of formal written agreements with clients may be considered a hallmark of good practice, these documents may not be considered to constitute a contract in a proper legal sense. A legal contract requires the fulfilment of a precise set of conditions (Jenkins, 1997: 48):

- *capacity* for the parties involved, i.e. not mentally disordered or under 18 years of age
- a firm *offer* and unequivocal *acceptance*
- a clear *intention* of both parties to create a legally binding agreement
- a contract that is supported by *consideration*, i.e. an exchange of goods or services for payment.

Many therapeutic contracts would *not* meet all these conditions, particularly regarding payment, as much counselling or therapy is provided *without* charge to the client, for example in schools, in the NHS, or by voluntary agencies. In private therapy or supervision practice, however, the agreement would, in all likelihood, constitute a legal contract. As a result, a therapist, supervisor, supervisee or client could take legal action for breach of a contract in the Small Claims section of the County Court, should there be an alleged breach of the contract (Jenkins, 2002).

Rather than constituting a legal contract as such, therapists may be using a document which is actually better termed a consent form or a working agreement. This can be useful and necessary for setting out the limits to confidentiality, for example. In this way, a client may give their advance consent to their General Practitioner being contacted in the case of becoming suicidal. The counsellor then has substantial protection in law against any later charge of breach of confidence from an aggrieved client. Consent forms, or working agreements, are also important in documenting the client's *informed consent* to therapy. While this is still a developing area of law, it is emerging as a significant shift within the NHS, where obtaining the patient's full, informed and *continuing* consent to physiological and psychological treatments has become part of a major policy drive on this issue.

Duty of care

Not all counsellors or psychotherapists will be covered by the law of contract. However, therapists will be subject to a duty of care towards their client, and supervisors will be similarly bound to their supervisees. The following vignette illustrates some features of this crucial part of the law relating to psychotherapeutic practice.

> Niki was a newly qualified psychotherapist, working in the NHS with clients who had been subjected to extensive domestic violence, and who often had previous histories of experiencing serious childhood sexual abuse. Interested in trauma work, Niki began experimenting by using some radical hypnotic techniques with her client, after attending a week-long workshop in the USA. Unfortunately, the client's mental condition began to deteriorate rapidly soon afterwards, and she was admitted for psychiatric treatment. Following this, she then brought a civil case against Niki as her former psychotherapist for breach of duty of care, alleging that the psychotherapeutic techniques had caused her lasting psychological damage and resultant substantial loss of earnings.

Action of this kind is brought under tort law, for the infliction of non-intentional harm, and requires the fulfilment of the following conditions:

- the existence of a duty of care between practitioner and client
- breach of that duty
- resultant foreseeable harm to the client as a direct result of the breach.

For counselling and psychotherapy clients, the alleged harm will normally be *psychological* rather than physical in nature. However, the law sets a very

high threshold for such damage. It requires that the alleged harm meets the diagnostic criteria for a psychiatric illness, such as clinical depression, generalized anxiety disorder or post-traumatic stress disorder, rather than simply taking the form of the more everyday human emotions of anger, distress or disappointment.

Case law concerning therapists

Many therapists are somewhat apprehensive of being sued by their clients, particularly when the latter are very aggrieved about some aspect of the therapy provided. However, the relative lack of reported cases in the UK suggests that the law actually presents very formidable barriers to clients successfully winning this type of case. Derived from medical case law, therapists subject to this type of action will be judged according to the *Bolam* test, namely whether their actions were consistent with the 'practice of competent respected professional option'. Relying on the evidence of expert witnesses, the judge needs to decide whether the therapist was working *within* the parameters of their chosen approach, such as psychodynamic, person-centred or other method. In practice, it is very difficult for clients to prove that the therapist's actions directly *caused* their psychological damage. In the case of Niki above, the client's *prior* history of abuse and possible evidence of psychiatric treatment *in the past* may well be used in court to invalidate her claim or, at the very least, reduce any damages eventually awarded to her.

Liability

Therapists are often keen to assume a professional duty of care towards their clients, as this is consistent with their overall professional stance and their obligations under a code of ethics. From a legal point of view, liability is defined in rather narrower terms and takes specific forms, which are determined by the therapist's *employment* status, rather than simply by the existence of a therapeutic relationship with the client. Liability can take the form of:

- *personal* liability, where a therapist doing paid private work holds *direct* responsibility for any non-intentional harm caused to the client
- *vicarious* liability, where an *employer* holds liability for the work of employees and volunteers.

Returning to the points made earlier, Niki's liability would be primarily determined by her status as an employee of the NHS Trust. The client would need to sue her *and* the NHS Trust together. To that extent, a psychotherapist in Niki's position would be 'protected' by their employer, which may have its own legal department and extensive experience in responding to claims and litigation. There remains a strong case, nevertheless, for therapists to keep their own professional indemnity insurance, rather than rely totally on the goodwill of their employer. Holding such insurance gives the therapist access to independent legal advice and, if necessary, separate legal representaion in court, should this be necessary (Jenkins et al., 2004).

The barriers against clients succeeding in this case remain substantial. It needs to be remembered that clients also have access to a non-legal route of redress, namely by bringing a *complaint* against the therapist, either to the therapist's employer or to their professional association. Given the shift towards establishing accessible and user-friendly complaints procedures by both sets of organizations, it is probably much more likely that counsellors and psychotherapists will face at least one serious professional or organizational complaint during their working career, rather than undergo actual litigation in court.

Legal obligations in handling risk

Therapists often express real concern about the ethical tension and conflict existing between their obligations towards the client and towards other members of society, who may be put at risk by the client's actions. In fact, the concept of risk can take a number of forms:

- risk to *client*, via deliberate self-harm, actual or attempted suicide

- risk to a *third party*, such as child abuse, domestic violence, serious crime or terrorism
- risk to *therapist*, via assault or stalking.

Therapists subscribe to an ethical commitment to promote the client's autonomy and to protect their well-being. This may come into conflict with real or imagined *legal* obligations, particularly when counter-balanced against an expectation that therapists should avoid harm to the client or others, by breaking client confidentiality if necessary. This might be in order to take preventative action by alerting the authorities concerned, for example, in the case of suspected child abuse.

As discussed below, therapists have a duty of trust and confidence towards clients. There are few overriding, absolute legal requirements to break confidentiality, and these concern instances of terrorism and drug money laundering. Therapists may be required by their contract of employment or agency policy to report suspected child abuse or threatened client self-harm or suicide when working for statutory agencies such as health, education and social services. However, even these requirements need to be balanced against the therapist's fiduciary duty of trust and confidentiality towards the client. This broad fiduciary duty to clients has been recognized by independent legal opinion, despite it conflicting on occasion with forceful employer demands for blanket policies on the reporting of risk (Bond, 2000: 156).

In fact, in situations involving non-terrorist crime, therapists (outside Northern Ireland) have the *right*, but not necessarily a *duty*, to break confidentiality in the wider public interest. A therapist *could*, therefore, contact the police to report criminal activity by a client, such as an undetected murder, or a credible threat of revenge towards a former partner, or to report a client who was stalking the therapist herself. From an ethical, professional and therapeutic point of view, any such decision to report clearly needs to be prefaced wherever possible by discussion with the client, and consultation with a supervisor and experienced colleagues. However, the law will generally support such action if taken in a measured, responsible and accountable manner, as evidenced by the introduction of statutory provision for 'whistleblowing' facilities into the workplace.

Legal principles applying to the management of sensitive information

Therapists learn a great deal of highly sensitive information about clients during the course of their work. In terms of the law, therapists owe a duty of confidence to clients by virtue of the nature of the special, indeed *trusting*, relationship which underpins therapeutic work. This duty can also be assumed to apply in the case of a contract for the psychotherapeutic work (see earlier section). The legal protection for client confidentiality has been further strengthened by recent statutes, such as the client's right to *respect* for privacy under human rights legislation, and, more emphatically, by the provisions of data protection law. This requires therapists to adopt transparent forms of record keeping which are consistent with the fundamental rights of citizens to know and, wherever appropriate, to have substantial access to such records. In contrast with past legislation, current data protection law covers manual records kept in systematic form, as well as computerized records, together with audio- and video-tapes. The continuing impact of data protection law has spelled the end of the former practice by many therapists of keeping 'private' sets of notes on an open-ended basis for untold purposes, which were unknown to the client or agency concerned.

Access by third parties to client records

Part of the therapist's role in managing sensitive client data has been to limit unauthorized access by other interested parties, such as the partner of a client undergoing therapy. What now appears to be developing is a rising interest by external agencies in requiring access to client records for use in legal proceedings. These agencies include:

- *solicitors* representing clients in legal proceedings, such as litigation for workplace stress
- *police officers* seeking evidence for a prosecution in the case of alleged child abuse
- *courts* requiring the surrender of counselling and psychotherapy records, including personal and supervision notes, to assist the court in its deliberations.

Counsellors and psychotherapists do not possess legal privilege, unlike solicitors, and cannot simply refuse to comply with court-ordered demands for notes, except at the risk of being held in contempt of court. Practitioners faced with court-authorized demands for release of client records need to take legal advice, but are faced with the reality that client confidentiality is outweighed by the wider public interest on this issue. Therapists, trainers and professional associations need to take fuller account of this issue, where client and therapist confidentiality is ultimately provided with limited protection by the law, that is when the law itself declares an interest in accessing client secrets confided within the therapy session.

Summary

Therapists need to be familiar with the broad outline of the civil law and the specific ways in which it impacts on their practice. In reality, the relationship of law to counselling and psychotherapy is mediated by a number of factors, such as the therapist's context for practice, employment status and client group. In terms of managing professional relationships with clients, therapists need to be aware of the principles underlying contracts, if in private practice, and to work within the parameters of accepted professional norms in discharging their duty of care to clients. The process of managing risk presents a number of challenges to therapists, where there are relatively few absolute requirements to break client confidentiality. Data protection law has eroded previous therapist latitude regarding record keeping, and subjected it to wider principles of public transparency, access and accountability. Finally, while the law is generally supportive of client confidentiality, therapists do not possess the legal protection of privilege, and must normally comply with court-authorized demands for access to client records in the public interest.

References

BACP (2002) *Ethical Framework for Good Practice in Counselling and Psychotherapy.* Rugby: British Association for Counselling and Psychotherapy.

Bond, T. (2000) *Standards and Ethics for Counselling in Action* (2nd edn). London: Sage.

Jenkins, P. (1997) *Counselling, Psychotherapy and the Law.* London: Sage.

Jenkins, P. (ed.) (2002) *Legal Issues in Counselling and Psychotherapy.* London: Sage.

Jenkins, P., Keter, V. and Stone, J. (2004) *Psychotherapy and the Law: Questions and Answers for Counsellors and Therapists.* London: Whurr.

4.8   Responding to Complaints

TIM BOND

Developing satisfactory ways of responding to complaints has been considered fundamental to good practice for several reasons. Pragmatically, there is only one thing more damaging to the reputation of a service than being a cause for complaint. This is allowing a complaint to go unexamined and ignored, as this compounds the sense of grievance and may eventually poison the reputation of the service. Responding to complaints is a clear indication that the service takes its responsibilities seriously. Ethically, responding to complaints is a major way of addressing possible inequalities of power between therapist and client. In some cases, the complaints procedure may be the client's only way of redressing serious abuses of power. However, complaints procedures should not be thought of solely in terms of benefiting the aggrieved client. They have often been presented as an important source of learning for the profession or organization. A good complaints procedure may be viewed as an important aspect of enhancing the quality of the entire service by drawing attention to areas of difficulty.

Types of complaint

The subject matter of complaints varies in its origins and in its seriousness. Based on her experience of several years of co-ordinating complaints heard by the BACP and the UKCP, Palmer Barnes (1998) suggests that the causes of justifiable complaint fall into four categories. Illustrative examples from my experience as the Chair of the BACP Professional Conduct Committee have been added:

- Error or mistake that is the result of a slip in good practice. This might include missing an appointment due to making an entry on the wrong page of a diary, confusing the identity of two people without serious consequences, or forgetting the details of less significant parts of an oral agreement reached with the client.

- Poor practice is a failure to deliver good practice, whether intentional or not. Examples include a therapist working inconsistently within the therapeutic model that he has described to a client as his way of working; a therapist missing the significance of something communicated by the client relating to a therapeutically important issue; or, a therapist giving out-of-date information. Poor practice and negligence are frequently indistinguishable.
- Negligence arises from lack of proper care or attention in circumstances where someone owes a duty of care, like a therapist to client or supervisor to supervisee. An example would be a therapist setting behavioural tasks for a client as homework between sessions, which expose the client to serious harm or prosecution, where the harm or illegality ought to have been known by the therapist.
- Malpractice is intentional misconduct. All malpractice associated with counselling and psychotherapy is serious because it undermines trust that is so essential. However, contrary to some views, it is arguable that the level of seriousness varies. Less serious forms of misconduct might include inappropriately blurring boundaries with clients between therapy and social contacts without significant harm to clients, or failing to honour significant but not critically important terms of an agreement made with clients. Gross misconduct includes serious exploitation of clients for the therapist's sexual, financial or other benefits; or serious misrepresentation of experience or qualifications in order to obtain clients or employment as a therapist.

Awareness of the different categories of conduct that might lead to a justifiable complaint is important because they imply different levels of culpability and seriousness, which arguably should be reflected in the kind of response that the complaint evokes. A relatively trivial mistake would not justify a full investigation by an independent investigator and an extensive adjudication leading to serious sanctions. Similarly, consideration of the seriousness of any misconduct might lead to different kinds of outcome, with the less serious first-time acts of misconduct justifying greater leniency than gross misconduct, especially if the gross misconduct has been repeated several times. Sometimes the gravity of the alleged source of grievance is not readily apparent at the outset of any procedure. However, there are times when the seriousness is readily apparent and this could inform decisions by the complainant, the complained against, and the managers of the complaints process.

Initiating a complaints procedure

There are two main initiators of complaints. Most complaints tend to be started by someone who is feeling aggrieved about the conduct of their service provider. A more recent and growing source of new complaints are members of the same profession who are concerned to protect the standards and conduct of their profession. Over the last ten years most professions have been moving from merely encouraging members of a profession to report serious concerns about the conduct of others in the same profession to making this an explicit ethical requirement. All the major professional organizations in counselling and psychotherapy include this requirement. Whether or not the complaint is initiated by a client or another professional, it is usual practice to insist that there is an attempt to resolve the complaint informally where this would be appropriate. These informal attempts at resolving complaints are largely invisible to the profession, especially if they are successful. As a consequence, it is impossible to be confident about the level of matters that were of sufficient seriousness that someone considered making a complaint. Known levels of grievance concern those complaints that could not be resolved informally or were considered to be of sufficient seriousness to make informal resolution inappropriate. Other reasons will be considered later in this chapter for suspecting that the numbers of complaints that enter any kind of formal procedure are only a fraction of potentially valid complaints. However, if the complainant decides to initiate a complaint, she will usually have two ways of proceeding.

The main choice will usually be between seeking a remedy from the courts or using some form of professional complaints procedure. Using the County

Court, especially the small claims court, is an option that deserves serious consideration by fee-paying clients, especially if the grievance concerns breach of a contractual term. The procedures are user-friendly and the legal costs are relatively small with little risk of unforeseen costs. Most other types of claim are likely to fall outside the courts because of the difficulty in bringing claims for negligence against counsellors or the high cost of taking cases to more senior courts (Bond, 2000). In these circumstances, the only realistic alternative is to use a complaints procedure run by the agency providing the counselling or an appropriate professional organization. This will be the organization(s) to which the therapist belongs, as these organizations will only hear complaints against their own members.

Most agencies and organizations will only hear complaints that are made in writing against a named person who is member of their organization and that specify the nature of the complaint. The British Psychological Society provides examples of potential complaints. These include acting beyond one's competence, breach of confidentiality, exploiting a client's trust, damaging the interests of clients or failing to obtain adequate consent (BPS, 2001). BACP (2002) currently requires that the complaint be presented as a succinct statement of the concern and the events giving rise to this concern. All these procedures may be changed as psychology and the other talking therapies are brought within the Health Professions Council or other forms of statutory regulation.

The complaints procedure

Most organizations that hear complaints have found that, with experience, they have wanted to refine their procedures. It can be a complex and demanding process to manage which is complicated by the inevitable stress that is experienced by most of the people involved, but especially the complainant and the complained against. It is possible to discern a common pattern emerging in the most recently revised procedures within the talking therapies. Typically the stages include:

- An initial screening of the complaint, which must have been submitted in writing, in order to ensure that there are sufficient grounds for proceeding. Obviously ill-founded and vexatious complaints may be stopped at this or the next stage.
- An investigatory process in which usually two or more people are given the task of gathering pertinent information and recommending whether the process should move to a formal hearing for adjudication. In most procedures the investigators also have the possibility of facilitating conciliation between the complainant and the person complained against when this is appropriate. Generally conciliation is considered more appropriate to resolving issues that have arisen by error and is inappropriate to malpractice.
- The adjudication process involves hearing both sides of the complaint and usually a panel of adjudicators deciding whether or not to uphold the complaint. The way that this process is conducted varies between organizations. Some adjudication procedures may parallel the criminal law in which both parties have relatively unlimited time in which to present their case and may be legally represented. This is the process adopted by the Disciplinary Committee of BPS and the General Medical Council. Typically the case for upholding the complaint is taken over and presented by the professional body rather than the complainant. An alternative model is to give both the complainant and complained against equal time to present the main elements of their case, which will have already been submitted more fully in writing prior to the hearing. This creates an opportunity for both parties to question each other and for the adjudicators to ask questions. In this system legal representation is not usually permitted and the power to call witnesses is restricted to the panel. This procedure is generally less costly in time and money for the people directly involved and therefore may be more accessible to a greater number of complainants. There is the possibility of the professional body taking over a complaint after a complaint has been withdrawn by the complainant, if the matter is considered sufficiently serious. However, the complainant retains the possibility of remaining more actively involved in the complaints process, if that is desired. In many ways this process parallels the more accessible forms of civil hearings. This is the procedure that is currently preferred by BACP.
- The announcement of a decision and any sanctions that have been imposed typically takes place a few days after the adjudication and is given in writing.

- There is usually a set period within which any appeal against the adjudication must be lodged. Any appeal process must be completed before the next stage.
- Publication of the results of any complaint that has been upheld usually includes the name of the person concerned, the nature of the complaint or malpractice, and the sanctions that have been imposed. The complainant's name is not disclosed.

Perhaps one of the more disturbing but frequently reported findings of those most directly involved in hearing complaints against therapists is that a significant number could have been resolved at a very early stage. It is a frequent observation that the official complaints procedures would be unnecessary if the counsellor or therapist had simply apologized. This is particularly appropriate when the cause of complaint was due to error rather than malpractice. One of the motivations of complainants in pursuing a complaint is to have their sense of loss or hurt acknowledged when they believe that this is justifiable. Withholding an appropriate apology is probably not only anti-therapeutic because it invalidates the client's personal experience but is also inflammatory.

Basic principles of hearing complaints

Once a complaints procedure is under way there is an ethical and often a legal obligation to ensure a fair investigation and hearing within the rules of natural justice. These consist of (a) the *right to a fair hearing*; and, (b) the *rule against bias*. The exact implications of these rules are frequently considered in the courts. In general terms, the right to a fair hearing requires prior notice, an opportunity to be heard, a fairly conducted hearing and a decision made supported by the reasons for it. The rule against bias has two main elements. The adjudicator undertaking these tasks should be independent and without any direct personal interests in the outcome. Any potential conflicts of interest that might prejudice or merely seem to prejudice the procedure sought to be declared and probably that person should withdraw. Another element requires that

someone should not be judged by his accuser. Similarly it would be inappropriate for someone who has been involved in investigating a case to act as adjudicator. Unless these rules are observed, any decision will lose moral authority. Some hearings may also be subject to judicial review, which means that the courts may overturn them. Hearings by national professional bodies in counselling and psychotherapy are subject to judicial review in the High Court.

Tensions between adjudication and therapy

It is not unusual to find that counsellors and psychotherapists are often uneasy about taking on a role that involves judging the behaviour of other therapists. The personal qualities and values that motivate most therapists are usually closely related to a commitment to trying to understand someone's experience, as perceived by that person. This usually involves suspending any attempt at moralizing. Some therapeutic approaches require more of the practitioner than mere abstinence from moralizing, for example the person-centred counsellor regards non-judgemental positive regard as an essential core condition of the therapeutic relationship. In other words, the client's subjective experience is positively valued independently of any moral considerations. Almost all approaches to therapy require that understanding the client's subjective experience takes priority over making an objective assessment of behaviour against what is considered to be competent or moral. This means that the ethos and ethic that pertain to being an effective therapist are usually very different from those which pertain to being an effective adjudicator. The role of adjudicator is much less concerned with subjective experience than determining by objective observation and rational deduction what has occurred and then considering whether the person complained against is culpable. The adjudicator is concerned to match the imposition of any sanctions with the gravity of any malpractice. In effect the adjudicator's role could not be much further removed from that of the therapist, as each requires constructing a relationship which is almost the antithesis of the other. This may lead to therapists who take on the role of adjudicator either being too punitive or too lenient as they step outside their usual way of working. This is one of the reasons why it is highly desirable to include non-therapists in the adjudication panel. There are other reasons why this is desirable, which are considered later.

The case that has brought therapeutic and psychological complaints procedures into national controversy concerned the sanctions imposed on a senior member of BPS (Lunt, 1999). Despite being found responsible for repeated inappropriate sexual relationships with clients after having been previously disciplined for similar misconduct, he neither lost his fellowship nor was he expelled from membership of the Society. Instead the Disciplinary Board chose to accept an undertaking that he would stop seeing clients. This case has evoked an intense debate about when it is appropriate to take a constructive and formative view about helping someone back into practice and when it is more appropriate to view a professional's behaviour as culpable and therefore subject to sanctions including expulsion.

I will confine my next observations to general principles rather than any specific case. The difference in attitude to wrongdoing between the courts and professional bodies over sexually inappropriate behaviour could not be more marked. When people are convicted of paedophilia the latest practice is not simply to punish them by incarceration but also to offer treatment. On discharge they are usually dissuaded from resuming unsupervised contact with children in order to maximize the safety of potential victims. When a professional body decides to accept an undertaking that the abusing therapist will seek treatment or will temporarily cease seeing clients until 'cured', that professional body is prioritizing the welfare of its member over the protection of the public by working towards the very situation where temptation is greatest. This may be a plausible response for a first example of malpractice where no significant harm has been caused, but it seems both implausible and irresponsible where there is sound evidence of serial abuse and a formative approach has already been tried and failed. Such responses seem to discredit the claim that the primary function of the way that a profession regulates itself is to protect the public.

There is need of a major study to discover whether professional bodies tend towards leniency in matters of serious malpractice or whether it is exceptional. In either case it would be informative to know the basis for decisions to impose sanctions and, perhaps more importantly, why they are not imposed. There may be many motivations. Seniority and prominence in the field may create an understandable reluctance to discredit a key member because to do so could seem like discrediting the entire profession. The offending therapists often offer explanations about having an alcohol problem and acting under the influence, being untypically disinhibited by treatment for depression, or some other reason which suggests diminished responsibility which would respond to treatment. However, one of the characteristics of sexual offenders is plausibility, which deceives others, and effective rationalizing, which distances them from the pain that they are causing their victims and increases self-deception. It may be that a combination of some or all these factors in a profession that values empathy creates an irresistible tendency towards mitigation. Anyone who has been involved in any of these cases knows that they are extremely hard to adjudicate. Nonetheless it is important to the credibility of any profession's claim to be able to regulate itself that it strikes an appropriate balance between protecting the public and the welfare of an individual member. A failure to appreciate the difference between the values and expertise required for adjudication and providing therapy increases the risk that inappropriate decisions will be made by adjudicators of misconduct by therapists.

Sanctions

Most adjudications appear to be fairly uncontroversial and appear to be accepted by the professional members and others as a fair outcome. Many of the less serious examples of malpractice can be appropriately dealt with by an admonition, a requirement for some retraining or a period of additional supervision of practice. Temporary suspension from practice or membership can also be used in many professional hearings to mark the seriousness of what has occurred and to provide some limited protection of the public. Expulsion from membership carries different consequences according to whether the procedure forms part of a voluntary or statutory system of professional regulation. In a voluntary system such as that operated by BACP there is no way of stopping someone from continuing to practise as a counsellor after being expelled from membership. For as long as counselling and therapy are unregulated anyone may set up as a counsellor even if they have just been discharged from prison for serious fraud or assault. Statutory regulation provides some protection by restricting the people who can make use of a particular professional title but it is important not to exaggerate the level of protection that is offered. Even after expulsion it is possible to continue to practise in closely related roles or in organizations that are unconcerned about conforming to a system of regulation. This means that in sectors like therapy and counselling where many people are self-employed, statutory regulation will have only limited impact.

People who have had complaints upheld against them often say that their concern about the sanction that had been imposed was eclipsed by their feelings when the outcome of the hearing was published in the appropriate professional journal. The primary justification for publishing the results of adjudications is educative, in order to alert the profession to potential malpractice so it is as well as to identify the individual concerned. The person concerned frequently experiences a sense of loss of face and shame that is sometimes considerably greater than the seriousness of the malpractice or error appears to justify. It is one of the paradoxes of professional complaints procedures that the dissemination of the finding against someone, which is not usually viewed as a sanction, is the outcome that is most dreaded by the person concerned.

Challenges to the importance of complaints procedures

The view that having an effective complaints procedure is an indication of a commitment to quality is widespread within the world of therapy and beyond. However, this widely accepted opinion can be challenged from a number of points of view.

Most complaints procedures managed within agencies and professional organizations are vulnerable to the suspicion that they may be no more than a mechanism for a professional group protecting its own. It is important that strategies are sought to minimize this suspicion because of the deterrent effect on well-founded complaints being presented for consideration. To be credible a complaints procedure must involve people from outside the field of activity under consideration. A complaints procedure is only as good as its protection of its own integrity. The mere perception that a complaints procedure lacks integrity has consequences that extend beyond this area of work to damaging the reputation for integrity of the profession as a whole. Accounts of the work of the Prevention of Professional Abuse Network (POPAN) make salutary reading for anyone concerned to enhance integrity in this area of work. Most of the complaints procedures within the caring professions are found to be problematic for bona fide complainants, especially if they are third parties concerned that a relative or friend may be being abused by a practitioner (POPAN, 2003).

Complaints procedures are expensive to run in terms of time and resources. They are extremely difficult to run effectively within small organizations. They require a critical size in membership in order to ensure that the people representing the profession in the procedure are truly independent. They require sufficient financial resource in order to obtain adequate legal advice that can be expensive. Small organizations can overcome some of these difficulties by collaborating in the development of joint schemes. However, adequacy of resources in terms of time and funds is an important factor in being able to conduct an effective procedure.

Complaints procedures are still seen as an important method of redress for people who have well-founded grievances. However, the standing of complaints procedures as a mechanism for quality control has diminished relative to other strategies. A well-managed complaints procedure can only address those instances where there is the possibility that the quality of service has fallen below acceptable standards. Usually this will only concern a minority of the cases seen by therapists. The challenge of quality management is to enhance the standards of service of all the therapy that is provided. In particular, quality management aims to ensure that therapy which is 'rattling along the bottom but just above unacceptable standards' becomes 'good enough'. Complaints procedures make limited contributions to addressing concerns about the adequacy of quality and its consistency which are better addressed by strategies that cover the full range of service provision. It may be that the involvement of professional bodies in the development of better quality control mechanisms for use by their membership will do more to enhance the standing of the profession than has been achieved so far by the use of complaints procedures. Complaints procedures are important, especially for those who are directly involved in them, but it is equally important to be realistic about what they can achieve.

References

BACP (2002) *Ethical Framework for Good Practice: Counselling and Psychotherapy.* Rugby: British Association for Counselling and Psychotherapy.

Bond, T. (2000) *Standards and Ethics for Counselling in Action* (2nd edn). London: Sage.

BPS (2001) *Complaints about Psychologists.* Leicester: British Psychological Society.

Lunt, I. (1999) Disciplining psychologists. *Psychologist,* 12 (2): 59.

Palmer Barnes, F. (1998) *Complaints and Grievances in Psychotherapy: A Handbook of Ethical Practice.* London: Routledge.

POPAN (2003) New service for concerned others: POPAN encourages third party reporting. *POPAN Newsletter,* 13: 2 [No volume number].

4.9   The Relevance of Research   ○○○

JOHN MCLEOD

Background

Skills and awareness in research have become increasingly important for counsellors and psychotherapists in recent years. The professionalization of counselling and psychotherapy, and the emphasis placed within healthcare on evidence-based practice, has contributed to an expectation that therapists will be informed about research findings relevant to their work. There is a growing trend for institutions and agencies which fund therapy services, and also for consumer groups, to demand research evidence about effectiveness. The development of new therapy settings, client groups and interventions has also required research support.

It is widely acknowledged that there exists a 'gap' between research and practice in the field of counselling and psychotherapy. Few therapists read research articles or regard them as being useful sources of information in relation to practice. Practitioners complain that research depends too much on statistical generalizations and does not ask the appropriate questions.

At the present time there exist opposing pressures around research in therapy. On the one hand, there are demands that therapists become more tuned in to research. On the other hand, many therapists are resistant to becoming more involved in an activity that does not appear to produce advantages in respect of work with clients. The remainder of this section describes some of the ways in which these conflicting demands might creatively be reconciled.

Using the research literature

The research literature represents an immense resource for therapists. It includes articles on many different kinds of therapy applied to the problems of a diversity of client groups. In the past this information was only available in university libraries. It is now possible to scan or review much of this literature using personal computer access to the Internet or to online databases such as psyc-LIT. Information and instruction in how to use these resources is available at most local libraries. *Bergin and Garfield's Handbook of Psychotherapy and Behavior Change*, edited by Lambert (2003) and now in its fifth edition, is an authoritative review of contemporary research and a good place to start when looking for research studies. Therapy research articles are published in a wide range of places; among the most important journals are *Counselling and Psychotherapy Research, Psychology and Psychotherapy, Journal of Consulting and Clinical Psychology, Journal of Counselling Psychology* and *Psychotherapy Research*.

All research papers begin with an Abstract which summarizes the main features and conclusions of this study. Readers can use the Abstract to decide whether or not to look at the article in more detail. Although an increasing number of research studies employ qualitative methods, it is still the case that the majority rely on statistical forms of data analysis. To make sense of these papers, it is therefore necessary to have some familiarity with statistical concepts (see Barker et al., 1994; McLeod, 2003). When reading research papers it is important to adopt a critical, questioning perspective, particularly in relation to the implications of the study for practice. In research studies, the definition and measurement of key variables, the selection of participants, or the therapeutic interventions that are used may not mirror what happens in everyday therapeutic practice.

The therapist as researcher

There are several reasons why the participation of therapists in research is essential. If therapists do not actually engage in research, then the research base of the profession will continue to be dominated by the interests of government departments or academic psychologists and psychiatrists. However, it can also be argued that doing research can make a contribution to therapist personal and professional development (McLeod, 1997). Research is a way of reflecting on practice and on assumptions about the therapeutic process. Doing research forces therapists to think clearly, conceptualize and find ways of communicating personal experience to others. Reading the research literature exposes therapists to alternative ideas about therapy.

Therapists who appreciate the potential relevance of research are often deterred by the compromises they assume they need to make in order to collect data. For example, practitioners may be worried about compromising the confidentiality of client material, using standardized questionnaires that do not match the client's experience, or by a perceived requirement to collect data on large numbers of cases. It is crucial in practitioner research that ethical considerations and the well-being of the client should take first priority. Nevertheless, there are many ways in which practitioners can engage in meaningful research, for example through systematic case study methods, qualitative analysis of therapy transcripts, or participation in practitioner inquiry groups. Various approaches to practitioner research are introduced in McLeod (2003).

Problems and issues

It is easy to see that, at the moment, therapy research does not always effectively relate to practice. However, it is no easy matter to remedy this situation. Therapy research at present is dominated by psychological assumptions and methods. Although there is an increasing acceptance of the idea of methodological *pluralism* (the use of many different research methods), it will only be when research techniques and ideas from fields such as sociology, anthropology and philosophy begin to make an impact on therapy research that an appreciable difference will be felt. Other critical issues relate to the use of theory in therapy research. The emergence of eclectic and integrative approaches has been accompanied by a turning away from formal theories of the type espoused by Freud, Jung, Rogers, Kelly and other founding figures. The absence of theoretical awareness acts as a limiting factor in research because it has the result that research is restricted to recording and observing, rather than testing interesting and provocative hypotheses. A final issue arises in relation to the nature of the knowledge base of therapy. While disciplines like medicine, nursing and even social work are able to make use of well-defined clinical rules or procedures, therapy depends much more on the quality of the relationship between therapist and client, and the capacity of the therapist to improvise interventions rather than following guidelines that are specified in advance. (Some branches of cognitive-behavioural therapy may differ from the psychodynamic and humanistic therapies in this respect.) It is therefore difficult for therapy research to generate new clinical rules or interventions that can be 'slotted in' to practice. Perhaps the best that therapy research can achieve is to enrich the awareness and understanding of practitioners.

In conclusion, it is important that both researchers and practitioners strive to find ways of making research more relevant for practice. It is also important to recognize that the complexity and ethical sensitivity of therapy research presents distinctive problems.

References

Barker, C., Pistrang, N. and Elliott, R. (1994) *Research Methods in Clinical and Counselling Psychology*. Chichester: Wiley.

Lambert, M. (ed.) (2003) *Bergin and Garfield's Handbook of Psychotherapy and Behavior Change* (5th edn). Chichester: Wiley.

McLeod, J. (1997) Reading, writing and research. In I. Horton and V. Varma (eds), *The Needs of Counsellors and Psychotherapists*. London: Sage.

McLeod, J. (2003) *Doing Counselling Research* (2nd edn). London: Sage.

4.10 Evidence-based Practice in Counselling and Psychotherapy: Definition, Philosophy and Critique

PETER BOWER AND MICHAEL BARKHAM

The term 'evidence-based practice' (EBP) is ubiquitous within the health professions. Just as there can be little doubt that the concept of EBP has had significant impact on the delivery of care, there is also some residual unease concerning the relevance of the concept in the area of counselling and psychotherapy. This section seeks to consider the definition of EBP, to consider its main strengths and limitations, and review ways in which the concept of EBP may be usefully applied in the context of counselling and psychological therapy.

Evidence-based practice: definition and methods

EBP developed within the context of medicine. The originators of 'evidence-based medicine' (EBM) defined it as 'the conscientious, explicit, and judicious use of current best evidence in making decisions about the care of individual patients' (Sackett et al., 1996: 71). Like any complex construct, EBM defies simple description, but is fundamentally concerned with shifting the basis of decision making about the treatment of patients from ill-defined 'clinical expertise' or appeals to tradition or authority towards the use of objective evidence from rigorous research designs. These 'rigorous research designs' include technologies such as the randomized controlled trial (Bower, 2003), the systematic review (Gilbody and Petticrew, 1999), and meta-analysis (Smith et al., 1980).

Randomized controlled trials treat the provision of counselling and psychotherapy like any other treatment, and seek to provide a valid measure of their effectiveness by randomly allocating some patients to receive a particular treatment and the others to a control group, which might be no treatment, a placebo, a waiting list or another brand of psychotherapy. Implemented correctly (and there are a large number of criteria relating to the 'quality' of trials), such studies can effectively rule out all other possible causes of changes in client outcome (such as the passage of time) to determine whether the observed effects on outcome are genuinely related to the treatment provided (Bower, 2003).

Systematic reviews are designed to provide a comprehensive accounting of all randomized controlled trials relating to a particular therapy or problem area. Trials are located through methods such as electronic database searching, and the review follows a pre-planned protocol to determine which studies have the appropriate level of quality and are thus eligible for inclusion in the overall summary of the available literature (Gilbody and Petticrew, 1999).

Meta-analysis goes one step beyond systematic review and uses statistical techniques to quantify the summary of the literature. Thus Smith et al. (1980) summarized 475 studies of counselling and psychotherapy and reported that, based on this massive database, the average psychological therapy client was better off than approximately 80 per cent of patients who did not receive psychotherapy.

EBM and its technologies are best exemplified by the Cochrane Library, which is advertised as 'the best single source of reliable evidence about the effects of health care', and is a repository of 446,156 trials and 2356 systematic reviews (as of early 2005) of various treatments.

Evidence-based practice as applied to counselling and psychological therapies

Although EBP had its roots in medicine, the emerging technology has a familiar history in counselling and psychological therapy, as debates about the importance of research evidence had been in existence since Eysenck's critique of the evidence concerning the effectiveness of psychoanalytic psychotherapy (Eysenck, 1952). Indeed, the meta-analysis of Smith et al. (1980) on the effectiveness of psychotherapy can be seen as one of the first applications of the systematic review technique and meta-analysis conducted specifically in response to Eysenck's challenge. Certainly, many of the objections to meta-analysis discussed in response to the Smith et al. review have been recycled within the medical journals. Thus it may be argued that EBP was not a new development in the context of counselling and psychological therapy.

However, even if the technologies and the arguments were not new, the impetus was significantly greater. In part, this related to the status and power of medicine as a profession compared to other health-care disciplines. Equally important was the development of the debate in the context of health systems such as the UK National Health Service and managed care organizations in the USA, which were increasingly influenced by resource constraints or a desire to limit spiralling costs. Finally, there were changes in the wider political landscape that led to an increasing focus on the issues of accountability and performance measurement among the professions, which were in turn facilitated by developments in information technology. Now counselling and psychotherapy practitioners are required to prove their worth, not only in terms of differences between therapies, but also in terms of their worth in comparison to all the treatments currently provided in the wider context of health care.

Summary of the evidence base in counselling and psychological therapies

There is a very large literature concerning randomized controlled trials of counselling and psychological therapy, and a developing literature integrating this evidence base into systematic reviews and meta-analyses concerning particular therapies and problem areas. Again, this literature defies simple summary, but the main findings are as follows:

- Counselling and the psychological therapies (i.e. active interventions) are more effective than placebos which, in turn, are more effective than no treatment. This was the outcome of the original meta-analysis of Smith et al. (1980) and has been confirmed by most major reviews since (Churchill et al., 2002; Elliott, 2002; Roth and Fonagy, 1996). However, the importance and value of those changes are still debated, and there is an increasing focus on the value of these benefits in relation to their costs (Tolley and Rowland, 1995).
- When different therapies are directly compared with each other, there are generally few differences between them in terms of outcomes despite their technical diversity – the so-called Dodo Bird verdict (Luborsky and Singer, 1975).
- However, there may be differential treatment effects for certain types of problem. For example, the available evidence suggests that anxiety problems are more effectively treated by exposure-based treatments and other cognitive-behavioural therapies than by other treatments such as psychodynamic or humanistic therapies (Department of Health, 2001).

Critique of evidence-based practice in the context of counselling and psychotherapy

The rise of EBP has resulted in a significant number of critiques of the concept within medicine (Graham-Smith, 1995), and its application in the context of counselling and psychological therapy is in some ways particularly controversial (Bolsover, 2002). Some doubt the relevance of experiments (such as randomized controlled trials) or quantitative methods in the context of counselling and psychological therapy. Such debates reflect fundamental tensions about the nature of knowledge and thus tend to be unaffected by empirical findings and remain somewhat static in nature. A more fruitful challenge is ensuring that evidence drawn from differing research paradigms is equally valued.

Other critiques are concerned with the particular application of EBP within counselling and psychological therapy. EBP generally focuses on distinct treatments (often described in a written manual) and patient groups (usually defined by diagnosis). This is sometimes called the *specific factors model*. However, as suggested earlier, there is evidence that the differences in effectiveness between counselling and psychotherapy treatments are relatively small, which leads to the argument that their effectiveness is based on *common factors* across therapies, such as aspects of the *therapeutic alliance* between patients and therapists (Horvath et al., 1993). Critics suggest that trying to make sense of such complex interpersonal processes within the context of randomized controlled trials is a somewhat Procrustean solution. However, there is increasing interest in ensuring that common factors are viewed with the same rigour as specific factors (Norcross and Goldried, 2003).

Another related concern is that certain therapies and techniques are far more amenable to test within the context of randomized controlled trials. This applies particularly to brief treatments and those which are structured (such as cognitive-behavioural therapy). Because of this, the research literature is particularly skewed towards certain treatments. Generally, cognitive-behavioural treatments have significantly greater amounts of evidence of effectiveness than other treatments (Churchill et al., 2002; Department of Health, 2001). However, 'absence of evidence' should not be taken as synonymous with 'not effective'. Rather, it should imply the need to commission research to provide the necessary data. Nevertheless, there is a tendency for treatments with the most evidence to be seen as the only legitimate contenders, which runs counter to accepted scientific principles which are concerned to disprove existing hypotheses rather than only seeking evidence that supports them.

In addition, there is concern that the findings from trials undertaken in research settings often relate to highly selected patient populations and standardized treatments that do not reflect the way in which treatments are provided in routine contexts, such that the relevance of the data is unclear (Morrison et al., 2003). There are also undoubtedly complex psychological and social reasons why EBP is resisted in the context of counselling and psychological therapy. Although a somewhat crude generalization, there may be some conflict between the personality that is drawn to the profession of counselling and psychological therapy and that which is drawn towards quantitative research.

In addition, counselling and psychological therapy practitioners are not alone among the professions in resenting philosophies which restrict their professional freedom. However, this may be heightened in counselling and psychological therapy, for the following reasons. Treatments within EBM are not themselves closely tied to the profession of medicine, and thus the results of trials of particular interventions do not challenge the legitimacy of the profession of medicine *per se*. The situation is different in counselling and psychological therapy because most practitioners are more firmly wedded to particular theoretical orientations. A medical clinician can easily replace one medication with another, but a psychoanalytic practitioner who is faced with findings suggesting that their approach is ineffective cannot so easily modify their work so as to make their therapeutic practice evidence-based, given the time required to retrain in more evidence-based approaches and the number of different approaches potentially required. The resistance of counselling and psychological therapy practitioners may (in part

at least) reflect this perceived threat to their legitimacy.

In summary, the question is not '*Can* counselling and psychological therapy be understood and evaluated in the context of the randomized controlled trial and EBP?' – the existence of several thousand trials examining therapy indicates that it can. Rather, the question is whether it *should* be understood and evaluated in such a way. Given that there is increasing agreement that evaluation and accountability are required to protect patients and ensure the efficient use of resources, the question becomes, what form should an appropriately 'evidence-based' counselling and psychotherapy take?

Alternative models of EBP in the context of counselling and psychological therapy

One approach is to move away from a focus on the model of evidence-based practice applied to medicine, which concerns decision making about the provision of particular interventions within an individual consultation, towards a more general 'evidence-based philosophy', which is more concerned with the application of an appropriately critical perspective to counselling and psychological therapy. Again, this argument is not new, as the requirements for an 'evidence-based philosophy' may look very similar to the *scientist-practitioner* model (Stricker, 2002). However, despite the popularity of this model in theory, it is clear that the promise of the scientist-practitioner has not been entirely fulfilled, with much of clinical practice within counselling and psychological therapy unaffected by current research findings. One problem, discussed briefly above, is that a closer fit needs to be found between the particular decision-making contexts in which counselling and psychological therapy operate and the particular approaches and technologies available to assist in those decisions.

The last part of this section will consider how a broad 'evidence-based philosophy' may be applied in three key decision-making contexts: health policy, organizational setting of services, and individual practitioners.

- *EBP at the level of health policy.* This concerns the role of trials and systematic reviews in the overall planning of services (e.g. determining the range of treatments that should be available in a particular geographical locality). At this level, the application of traditional EBP is most relevant. However, it should be noted that, even in this setting, the simplistic application of the results of randomized trials is always qualified by lack of relevant data, restrictions on what can be evaluated, and other key issues, such as patient preferences. The recent psychological therapy guidelines in the UK are a good example of the way in which research evidence is interpreted and translated into feasible recommendations that reflect the research evidence and a host of other factors. Another context for the application of traditional EBP might be the training and development of therapists, where the long-term aim would be to ensure that the mechanisms for producing professionals are appropriately informed by the evidence so as to create an appropriately skilled workforce.
- *EBP at the level of the organization.* Within statutory services, counselling and psychological therapy are increasingly delivered within organizations. It may be beyond the remit of such organizations to deliver rigorous randomized controlled research, but the critical perspective required of evidence-based philosophy may lead to a focus on some aspects of EBP, such as rigorous outcomes measurement. Such measurement can be used in *benchmarking* services, to ensure that the treatments recommended at the policy level are being delivered in a local context in a way that is effective, efficient and acceptable, and that there is not excessive variation in the outcomes obtained by services working in similar contexts (Barkham et al., 2001). This may involve *provider profiling*, which attempts to examine the strengths and weaknesses of particular practitioners with particular types of patient (Lutz et al., 2002). An alternative may be the application of rigorous measurement methods, not just to outcomes, but also in the evaluation of common factors (such as the therapeutic alliance) which may be equally important determinants of outcome.
- *EBP at the level of the individual clinician.* If one rejects the relevance of the medical model of the individual practitioner selecting treatments on the basis of the evidence base, the issue remains one of ensuring an appropriately critical perspective is applied to individual clinical decision making within counselling and psychological therapy. This has traditionally been the preserve of supervision and the 'reflective practitioner', but such processes may not meet current standards for accountability and transparency.

An alternative model is 'practice-based evidence', and there are several developments that may be of relevance there. An example relates to work on *patient profiling*, which seeks to estimate a patient's expected outcome during treatment based on baseline variables, and then compare this estimate with the actual outcome observed, in order to determine the success or otherwise of the particular treatment. This is in contrast to the traditional application of EBP, where the focus is on providing the correct 'evidence-based' treatment, which it is assumed will produce the best outcome for an individual patient. The key advantage of the patient-profiling approach is that it does not seek to impose the logic and technology of EBP on the decision making of counselling and psychological therapy practitioners, where it may feel highly inappropriate. Rather, it seeks to use the source of evidence that is most salient to practitioners (i.e. *practice-based clinical experience*), but to systematize and codify it in a way that is transparent and demonstrably influential on routine practice.

Summary

Although EBP may be a relatively new term, many of its philosophical roots and assumptions have a long history in the context of counselling and psychological therapy. Significant developments have occurred in understanding the tensions raised by EBP and the limits of its application in this context. Future developments need to focus on methods that allow these tensions to be dealt with constructively. In this way, the philosophy of evidence-based practice can be applied to counselling and psychological therapy in a way that is sensitive to their particular history and context, and to the values of practitioners while still serving the needs of policy makers, insurers, managers and patients.

References

Barkham, M., Leach, C., Lucock, M., Evans, C., Margison, F., Mellor-Clark, J., Benson, L., Connell, J. and Audin, K. (2001) Service profiling and outcomes benchmarking using the CORE-OM: toward practice-based evidence in psychological therapies. *Journal of Consulting and Clinical Psychology*, 69 (2): 184–196.

Bolsover, N. (2002) Commentary: the 'evidence' is weaker than claimed. *British Medical Journal*, 324: 294.

Bower, P. (2003) Efficacy in evidence-based practice. *Clinical Psychology and Psychotherapy*, 10: 328–336.

Churchill, R., Hunot, V., Corney, R., Knapp, M., McGuire, H., Tylee A. and Wessely, S. (2002) A systematic review of controlled trials of the effectiveness and cost-effectiveness of brief psychological treatments for depression. *Health Technology Assessment*, 5 (35).

Department of Health (2001) *Treatment Choice in Psychological Therapies and Counselling: Evidence-based Clinical Practice Guidelines*. London: Department of Health.

Elliott, R. (2002) The effectiveness of humanistic psychotherapies: a meta-analysis. In D. Cain and J. Seeman (eds), *Humanistic Psychotherapies*. Washington, DC: American Psychological Association, pp. 57–81.

Eysenck, H. (1952) The effects of psychotherapy: an evaluation. *Journal of Consulting and Clinical Psychology*, 16: 319–324.

Gilbody, S. and Petticrew, M. (1999) Rational decision-making in mental health: the role of systematic reviews. *Journal of Mental Health Policy and Economics*, 2: 99–106.

Graham-Smith, D. (1995) Evidence-based medicine: Socratic dissent. *British Medical Journal*, 310: 1126–1127.

Horvath, A., Gaston, L. and Luborsky, L. (1993) The therapeutic alliance and its measures. In N. Miller et al. (eds), *Psychodynamic Treatment Research: A Handbook for Clinical Practice*. New York: Basic Books, pp. 247–273.

Luborsky, L. and Singer, B. (1975) Comparative studies of psychotherapies: is it true that everyone has won and all must have prizes? *Archives of General Psychiatry*, 32: 995–1008.

Lutz, W., Martinovich, Z., Howard, K. and Leon, S. (2002) Outcomes management, expected treatment response, and severity adjusted provider profiling in outpatient psychotherapy. *Journal of Clinical Psychology*, 58 (10): 1291–1304.

Morrison, K., Bradley, R. and Westen, D. (2003) The external validity of controlled clinical trials of psychotherapy for depression and anxiety: a naturalistic study. *Psychology and Psychotherapy: Therapy, Research and Practice*, 76: 109–132.

Norcross, J.C. (ed.) (2002) *Psychotherapy Relationships That Work: Therapist Contributions and Responsiveness to Patients*. Oxford: Oxford University Press.

Norcross, J. and Goldried, M. (2003) *Handbook of Psychotherapy Integration*. New York: Oxford University Press.

Roth, A. and Fonagy, P. (1996) *What Works for Whom? A Critical Review of Psychotherapy Research*. London and New York: Guilford Press.

Sackett, D., Rosenberg, W., Gray, J., Haynes, B. and Richardson, W. (1996) Evidence-based medicine: what it is and what it is not. *British Medical Journal*, 312: 71–72.

Smith, M., Glass, G. and Miller, T. (1980) *The Benefits of Psychotherapy*. Baltimore, MD: Johns Hopkins University Press.

Stricker, G. (2002) What is the scientist-practitioner anyway? *Journal of Clinical Psychology*, 58 (10): 1277–1283.

Tolley, K. and Rowland, N. (1995) *Evaluating the Cost-effectiveness of Counselling in Health Care*. London: Routledge.

4.11 The CORE System: Developing and Delivering Practice-based Evidence Through Quality Evaluation

JOHN MELLOR-CLARK AND MICHAEL BARKHAM

In the first edition of this handbook we introduced CORE as a quality evaluation system designed to offer a cost-free, practical and theoretical enhancement to the limitations of traditional approaches to service evaluation (Mellor-Clark and Barkham, 2000). In this update, we place the philosophy of quality evaluation as one of the key components in the paradigm of practice-based evidence, re-profile the structure and content of CORE as being a robust system for delivering practice-based evidence, and describe new innovations that have emerged from this research–practice collaboration. These include the development of bespoke evaluation software to offer empirical support to reflective practice, and the growth of practice-based evidence to help develop CORE Performance Indicators (i.e. benchmarks) to support services which wish to assess the relative quality of their local service delivery. We begin by reviewing the aims and objectives of quality evaluation.

The aims of evaluation

It is out belief that the *raison d'être* of evaluation should be to enhance the quality of service provision, and hence client care. Moreover, the activity of evaluation carried out by practitioners in routine settings is the means by which we can build an evidence base for counselling and psychotherapy which is grounded in practice and owned by practitioners. We have referred to this as *practice-based evidence* (Barkham and Mellor-Clark, 2000, 2003), which complements the research-driven paradigm of *evidence-based practice* (see Bower and Barkham, this volume). Practice-based evidence provides the foundations for generating questions which are grounded in the practice context and, for this reason, are seen to be relevant to practitioners and the delivery of routine services. Such questions may be pragmatic or theory-driven but have in common a fundamental relevance to practice and provide evaluation activity which can operate at local, national or international levels via the development of practice research networks (for details, see Audin, Mellor-Clark et al., 2001).

Unfortunately, in reality, all too often counselling and psychological therapy service evaluation is undertaken for evaluation's sake. Typically, the most common method of evaluation is to rely on clients to provide most, if not all, information, and to choose measures on the basis of their accessibility, rather than their clinical and management utility. In short, it is all too common for evaluation to be about being seen to be doing the 'right' thing. However,

irrespective of whether practitioners believe that evaluation *is* the right thing, it is critical to do it for the *right* reason. This should be the primary aim of evaluation – to employ appropriate methods and measures capable of informing on the quality of service provision, identify inadequacies and thereby give information that assists the development of service delivery. This we term *quality evaluation*, and suggest that its pursuit should be the cornerstone of accountable service delivery and continuing professional development. In the earlier edition of this section (Mellor-Clark and Barkham, 2000) we proposed the ideal and pragmatic aims of quality evaluation should be to:

- demonstrate the *appropriateness* of service structures
- enhance the *accessibility* to service provision
- monitor the *acceptability* of service procedures
- ensure *equity* for all potential service recipients
- demonstrate the *effectiveness* of service practices
- improve the *efficiency* of service delivery.

If evaluation could begin to address such aims, we suggested that this would be a vast improvement on simply letting the need to evaluate predominate as the reason for involvement. But, what methods are best employed to collect these quality evaluation data, and from what sources are they most appropriately secured?

Methods for quality evaluation

It appears that one of the most common confusions for practitioners interested in, or challenged with, evaluating their service provision, relates to understanding the relationship between research, evaluation and audit. We've previously stated that the tradition of evaluation methodology had a heavy (if not exclusive) reliance on the client as therapy consumer to provide evaluation data (Mellor-Clark and Barkham, 2000). In light of the aims of quality evaluation summarized above, it is unfortunate that the central focus of evaluation tends to be on measuring effectiveness, with little regard for the necessary contextual information profiling structure (provider and setting) and process (therapy) determinants.

These interrelations are the hallmark of formal therapy research and, we argued, needed urgently to be included in both evaluation methods and practice. Explicitly, we suggested that quality evaluation should borrow from the best traditions of research, evaluation and audit, collecting data from both provider and consumer to link service *context* and *process* to *outcome* – to ultimately inform the development and enhancement of practice. Practical ways in which the methods (and aims) of research, evaluation and audit may be combined to provide quality evaluation are now explored in more detail.

There is increasing recognition that the major strength of formal therapy *research* (i.e. randomized controlled trials) has been the pursuit of a secure base of supportive evidence (e.g. Bower, 2003; Bower and King, 2000) to identify 'best' evidence of good practice (e.g. Cape and Parry, 2000; Parry et al., 2003). As scientific rigour is the hallmark of such formal therapy research, there has been a traditional emphasis on methods being *replicable* (using treatment manuals), *controlled* to strengthen causal inference (using randomization), and *measured* via valid and reliable instruments completed by both providers and research subjects. Such research is then comprehensively analysed and documented in a highly structured and traditional format for academic journals. The yield from such rigorous research has provided not only 'more, and better quality, scientific evidence to support psychotherapy than for many other interventions in health care today' (Roth and Fonagy, 1996: viii), but in addition:

- a growing body of valid and reliable research measures having multiple foci (see Froyd et al., 1996);
- an increasing sophistication of psychotherapy research methodology evolving through generations of inquiry (see Lambert, 2004);
- an established knowledge base of potentially efficacious therapies with supporting initiatives to collate and disseminate research evidence acting as guidelines for 'best' therapy practice (see Department of Health, 2001; Parry et al., 2003);
- consistent recognition of the need for methodological pluralism to help evolve investigative rigour to have wider relevance and utility (see Barkham and Mellor-Clark, 2003; Goss and Rowland, 2000; Lambert, 2004; McLeod, 1999).

In sum, rigorous research methodologies, using standardized measures assessing multiple domains, collected from the dual sources of both practitioners and clients have achieved much, but what are the relative 'products' of therapy evaluation?

In contrast to research inquiry, *evaluation* has traditionally been far less concerned with enhancing theory and adding to the established knowledge base. Instead, the emphasis of evaluation, while aspiring to the utilization of scientific rigour, has all too often used a 'ragbag of measuring tools' (Parry, 1996: 424) to aid decision making and solve operational problems, the 'ragbag' ultimately disseminated for purely local consumption. As a consequence, evaluation has existed as a limited public information source relative to formal therapy research, as even most large-scale studies have remained unpublished, and hence have been unable to inform the national development of therapy (and evaluation) theory and practice (Hemmings, 2000). This is something that urgently needed to change. There is a critical requirement to enhance the credibility and utility of evaluation methods and measures to both inform national service development and guide others interested in evaluating their practice. This is irrespective of whether evaluation is undertaken for personal interest, professional development, or to meet contingent funding demands.

As suggested earlier, the principal problem of traditional approaches to evaluation is their reliance on therapy consumers to provide information, and the consequent paucity of *context data* (i.e. presenting problems/issues, therapy interventions, therapy durations, social environment factors, etc.) to ultimately clarify what determines effectiveness and ineffectiveness. In an attempt to illustrate some of the real costs of this reliance on the therapy consumer, in the earlier edition of this section we reviewed data-collection figures from four large-scale evaluation studies involving over 6,000 clients (Audin and Mellor-Clark, 1998; Goss, 1997; McCarthy et al., 1998; Shapiro and Barkham, 1993). Collectively, these studies helped demonstrate that it was not unusual for high-volume client evaluation studies to report on less than 50 per cent of client throughput, severely limiting confidence in the reliability of any interpretation. This finding has been subsequently supported by findings from other large-scale studies (e.g. Audin, Margison et al., 2001; Barkham et al., 2001; Evans et al., 2003; Lucock et al., 2003; Mellor-Clark, Connell et al., 2001).

In light of these data, personal evaluation experience, and appraisals by other researchers reviewing evaluation studies (e.g. McLeod, 2001), there can only be one conclusion. In short, the traditional sole reliance on therapy consumers to supply evaluation data, while having considerable strengths for offering objectivity, also carries weaknesses that at best limit the representativeness of outcome measurement, and at worst undermine the time and energy devoted to data collection in relation to its ultimate informativeness. Explanations for such large levels of data loss can be found in the original studies and is addressed later in this section. Here, the simple summary profiles of data attrition help to reinforce our suggestions that quality evaluation requires information collection to be more appropriately shared between both practitioner and client. This not only has the advantage of being able to provide more representative (albeit subjective) data than traditional approaches but, as stated previously, makes it possible to record crucial information detailing the contexts and processes which ultimately determine outcome. We now move on to consider the relative contribution of audit.

Traditionally, *audit* has been considered and conceptualized by many as simple counting: counting the number of patients seen; the number of DNAs; inappropriate referral rates; waiting times; and session durations, to name but a few examples. However, this is a severe dilution of clinical (or medical) audit philosophy. The more realistic and pragmatic focus of audit is about measuring elements of service delivery against agreed standards. For example, a service may well audit its appropriate referral rates by simple counting – content to report that, like many others, 15–25 per cent of its referrals are inappropriate. Clinical audit, however, goes several steps further. Having identified an inappropriate referral rate, the service then sets a realistic reduction target, maybe suggesting that an improvement in service appropriateness (and hence efficiency) would be to reduce the inappropriate referral rate by 10 per cent, thereby reducing both the waiting list and waiting times. Consequently, the service evaluates the main

sources of inappropriate referrals from its evaluation data, implements some educative strategy for inappropriate referral sources (e.g. sends out guidelines for appropriate service referrals), and continues to monitor appropriate referral rates (and their impact on waiting lists/times) in the hope that their educative intervention strategy improves service quality. If it doesn't, further change strategies are tested and the cycle repeated. This is quality evaluation in action.

Another example emphasizing the philosophical contribution of clinical audit to the evaluation process focuses attention on the use of data derived from research questionnaires used to evaluate the effectiveness of service delivery – the preoccupation of traditional evaluation research methodologies. Here, while the aims of evaluation may be to demonstrate the proportion of clients who can be empirically shown to have 'changed', the philosophy of clinical audit, with its emphasis on the enhancement of service delivery, suggests that it may be more appropriate to focus on client groups who are identified as showing no change, or worse – deterioration. Once again, building these sorts of foci into our evaluation endeavours demonstrates quality evaluation in action.

In summary, if the central aim of *research* is to improve the knowledge base for practice by demonstrating what can be achievable, and the central aim of the traditional *evaluation* approach is to assess the effectiveness of what is achieved in practice, then *audit is* the natural complement to close the gap between the two. This is accomplished by assessing whether actual practice lives up both to research-evidence potential and to internal standards of quality service delivery. If we recall that the explicit aim of quality evaluation is to give us information to assist the development of service delivery, then audit, with its emphasis on measuring process and context data relative to internal standards, is the ideal vehicle for helping us use our collected data to ensure that the *raison d'être* of evaluation is achieved.

Measures for quality evaluation

In the first part of this section, we hope to have communicated that evaluation measurement is not simply about choosing a measure (or even a 'rag-bag' of measures) which focuses solely on the changes in clients' personal functioning. Rather, we would hope to have delivered a case to support our view that measuring such change is but one component of a multiplicity of measurement requirements necessitating a plurality of methods and tools to achieve the principal aim of quality evaluation – enhancing service provision. Now, we concentrate on two related practice-based areas. First, we briefly review the availability and utilization of outcome measures in both research and practice. Second, we focus on summary descriptions for the use and utility of the CORE System (Mellor-Clark et al., 1999) and innovative supporting resources developed to jointly act as a potential resource or guide.

As service quality evaluation has increasingly become a funding and/or policy requirement over the past decade or more, it should be no surprise that the subject of therapy outcome measures and measurement practice has been the focus of attention in several reviews. These include three investigations collectively addressing the availability of therapy effectiveness measures and UK measurement practice:

- Froyd et al. (1996) published a review of 'efficacy' measures used in therapy outcome studies reported in 20 international journals over a five-year period. In total they identified 1,430 measures, of which 851 (60 per cent) had only appeared in the literature once.
- Mellor-Clark et al. (1999) reported on a survey of NHS purchasers and providers of psychological therapies in the UK, assessing both practice and preference for outcome measurement. Here, a sample of 220 services was found to be using 77 different outcome measures, 51 (66 per cent) used by single sites only, with only 16 per cent of services using the same measures pre- and post-therapy.
- Mellor-Clark, Simms-Ellis et al. (2001) reported the results of a national survey of over 1,000 counsellors working in general practice. One of the findings suggested that although 62 per cent of practitioners were undertaking some form of effectiveness evaluation, a third used their own outcome measures, and only 15 per cent evaluated their counselling effectiveness via published measures.

The picture that emerged from these surveys suggests a vast array of outcome measures being used to assess the effectiveness of therapy service delivery. While this is laudable for illustrating practitioners' dedication to outcome evaluation, the collective picture unfortunately reinforces the early conclusions of Froyd and his colleagues, who stated that 'without some direct action, psychological therapy outcome measurement will remain in a state of disarray, if not chaos, with individual practitioners or separate mental health entities selecting outcome measures without thought for communication across practitioners, treatment sites or problem domains' (1996: 14). Equally, such findings reinforced our own beliefs in the benefits of developing a standardized approach to outcome measurement for enhancing communication not only between practitioners, treatment sites and problem domains but also between research, management and national policy development (see Barkham and Mellor-Clark, 2000, 2003; Barkham et al., 1998; Margison et al., 2000). In short, we believed that if a standardized system were nationally implemented, the benefit could be substantial. We thus conclude with a summary introduction to the CORE system, and a brief profile of complementary innovations that have evolved from the unique national research–practice collaboration that developed through the growth of a broad user base.

The CORE (Information Management) System

The CORE System was developed by a multidisciplinary group of practitioners and researchers having a common interest in producing appropriate methods and tools to realize the benefits of quality evaluation (see Barkham et al., 1998, 2001; Barkham, Gilbert et al., 2005; Evans et al., 2000, 2002; Mellor-Clark et al., 1999 for a full developmental account). The content of the system was informed by extensive collaboration with practitioners, managers and service commissioners (Mellor-Clark et al., 1999). The system comprises three tools, sharing the onus of evaluation data provision equally between clients completing a CORE Outcome Measure (CORE-OM) pre- and post-therapy, and practitioners completing CORE Assessment and End of Therapy Forms. This paired data-collection strategy facilitates the collection of a comprehensive set of process and outcome data informed by the relative strengths of research, evaluation and audit. Descriptions follow.

The CORE-OM (see Figure 4.11.1) is a double-sided, 34-item, client-completed questionnaire which addresses the clinical domains of *subjective well-being* (4 items), *symptoms* (12 items which include anxiety, depression, trauma and physical symptoms), and *functioning* (12 items which include close relations, social relations and life functioning). In addition, the measure contains six items which address components of *risk or harm* which can be used as indicators of clients being at risk to themselves or to others. The measure has been extensively validated (Evans et al., 2000, 2002) and a series of publications demonstrate that it has considerable utility for both clinical assessment and service evaluation (Barkham et al., 2001; Evans et al., 2003; Mellor-Clark, 2003, 2004; Mellor-Clark, Connell et al., 2001).

Operationally, the measure is used by the client responding to each of the 34 statements (e.g. 'I have felt terribly alone and isolated'), indicating, on a five-point scale, how often they have felt that way over the last week. In practice, the client completes the questionnaire at both the beginning and end of their contact with the service. More frequent administration of the measure within therapy would also support 'outcomes management' (Okiishi et al., 2003) and the production of 'report cards' (Dickey, 1996) to review and (if necessary) revise therapeutic intervention.

Irrespective of the frequency of administration, once the client has completed the questionnaire the practitioner can then score the items on the questionnaire (literally, in the right-hand 'office use only' column) and calculate mean scores for each of the four clinical domains. At intake, responses to individual items allow the practitioner to identify the frequency of specific issues over the previous week and the aggregate scores will inform the practitioner of the overall severity level as well as the severity level for each of the domains. In-therapy administrations will naturally help track 'progress', and administering the measure at discharge will inform the practitioner of the remaining severity levels for each of the domains as well as the overall remaining

severity. Individual item responses highlight any specific issues remaining or occurring over the last week. In sum, for individual clients the CORE-OM is easy to score and use for communicating the extent of change to clients, referrers, supervisors and service managers. But what do the scores mean and what of aggregate scores for a series of clients?

In designing and piloting the CORE-OM, there has been an emphasis on developing a user-friendly, pragmatic measure having a high level of utility for use in routine practice (Barkham et al., 1998; Evans et al., 2000; Mellor-Clark et al., 1999). Consequently, the CORE System Group collected clinical data from a variety of service settings and client groups, including 'clients' and 'non-clients' from the general population (Barkham, Culverwell et al., 2005; Evans et al., 2002). These latter data are critical to the ultimate utility of the measure. In short, the publicly available aggregate data from these two client groups allow the practitioner to calculate easily the proportion of their caseload who scored within a client-group at intake, and the proportion who moved to a 'non-client' or 'general population' group at discharge. The process by which this is done requires the simple calculation of the mean CORE-OM score for each individual client, a comparison with the 'cut-off' scores, and a final determination as to the population the client score now most closely matches. Subsequently, the philosophy of quality evaluation places an emphasis on reviewing those cases where there was no identified change, or where there was deterioration. *The CORE System User Manual* (CORE System Group, 1998) gives more detail on these methods and can be downloaded from the CORE Support website (see end of the section).

To complement the CORE-OM and provide client contextual detail, the double-sided CORE Therapy Assessment Form (see Figure 4.11.2) captures a 'core' set of contextual information that aids the quality of both client/patient assessment and overall service development (Mellor-Clark et al., 1999). To enhance patient assessment, the form collects important contextual information, including patient/client support; previous/concurrent attendance for psychological therapy; medication; and a categorization system to record presenting difficulties,

CLINICAL OUTCOMES in ROUTINE EVALUATION

OUTCOME MEASURE

Site ID ☐☐☐☐☐
letters only   numbers only
☐☐   ☐☐☐☐☐☐

Client ID

Therapist ID   numbers only (1)   numbers only (2)
☐☐☐   ☐☐☐   ☐☐☐

Sub codes

D D   M M   Y Y Y Y
☐☐ / ☐☐ / ☐☐☐☐
Date form given

☐☐   **Age**

Male ☐
Female ☐

Stage Completed
S Screening   **Stage**
R Referral   ☐
A Assessment
F First Therapy Session
P Pre-therapy (unspecified)
D During Therapy
L Last Therapy Session   **Episode**
X Follow up 1   ☐
Y Follow up 2

IMPORTANT – PLEASE READ THIS FIRST

This form has 34 statements about how you have been OVER THE LAST WEEK.
Please read each statement and think how often you felt that way last week.
Then tick the box which is closest to this.
Please use a dark pen (not pencil) and tick clearly within the boxes.

Over the last week	Not at all	Only occasionally	Sometimes	Often	Most or all the time	OFFICE USE ONLY
1 I have felt terribly alone and isolated	0	1	2	3	4	F
2 I have felt tense, anxious or nervous	0	1	2	3	4	P
3 I have felt I have someone to turn to for support when needed	4	3	2	1	0	F
4 I have felt O.K. about myself	4	3	2	1	0	W
5 I have felt totally lacking in energy and enthusiasm	0	1	2	3	4	P
6 I have been physically violent to others	0	1	2	3	4	R
7 I have felt able to cope when things go wrong	4	3	2	1	0	F
8 I have been troubled by aches, pains or other physical problems	0	1	2	3	4	P
9 I have thought of hurting myself	0	1	2	3	4	R
10 Talking to people has felt too much for me	0	1	2	3	4	F
11 Tension and anxiety have prevented me doing important things	0	1	2	3	4	P
12 I have been happy with the things I have done	4	3	2	1	0	F
13 I have been disturbed by unwanted thoughts and feelings	0	1	2	3	4	P
14 I have felt like crying	0	1	2	3	4	W

Please turn over

(Continued)

Over the last week	Not at all	Only occasionally	Sometimes	Often	Most or all the time	OFFICE USE ONLY
15 I have felt panic or terror	0	1	2	3	4	P
16 I made plans to end my life	0	1	2	3	4	R
17 I have felt overwhelmed by my problems	0	1	2	3	4	W
18 I have had difficulty getting to sleep or staying asleep	0	1	2	3	4	P
19 I have felt warmth or affection for someone	4	3	2	1	0	F
20 My problems have been impossible to put to one side	0	1	2	3	4	P
21 I have been able to do most things I needed to	4	3	2	1	0	F
22 I have threatened or intimidated another person	0	1	2	3	4	R
23 I have felt despairing or hopeless	0	1	2	3	4	P
24 I have thought it would be better if I were dead	0	1	2	3	4	R
25 I have felt criticized by other people	0	1	2	3	4	F
26 I have thought I have no friends	0	1	2	3	4	F
27 I have felt unhappy	0	1	2	3	4	P
28 Unwanted images or memories have been distressing me	0	1	2	3	4	P
29 I have been irritable when with other people	0	1	2	3	4	F
30 I have thought I am to blame for my problems and difficulties	0	1	2	3	4	P
31 I have felt optimistic about my future	4	3	2	1	0	W
32 I have achieved the things I wanted to	4	3	2	1	0	F
33 I have felt humiliated or shamed by other people	0	1	2	3	4	F
34 I have hurt myself physically or taken dangerous risks with my health	0	1	2	3	4	R

THANK YOU FOR YOUR TIME IN COMPLETING THIS QUESTIONNAIRE

Total Scores

Mean Scores

(Total score for each dimension divided by number of items completed in that dimension)

(W)   (P)   (F)   (R)   All items   All minus R

Figure 4.11.1   CORE Outcome Measure

Source: CORE System Group

The CORE Outcome Measure © MHF & CORE System Group

CLINICAL
OUTCOMES in
ROUTINE
EVALUATION

THERAPY ASSESSMENT FORM v.2

Site ID [ ][ ][ ][ ]   **Age** [ ][ ]

letters   numbers
Client ID [ ][ ] [ ][ ][ ][ ][ ][ ]   **Male** [ ] **Female** [ ]

TH ID number   SC2 numbers   SC3 numbers
Sub Codes [ ][ ]   [ ][ ][ ]   [ ][ ][ ]   **Employment** [ ] [ ]

Referrer(s) [ ][ ]   [ ][ ]   [ ][ ]   **Ethnic Origin** [ ] [ ]

Referral date   D D / M M / Y Y Y Y   [ ][ ] / [ ][ ] / [ ][ ][ ][ ]

Total number of assessments [ ]   Episode

First assessment date attended   D D / M M / Y Y Y Y   [ ][ ] / [ ][ ] / [ ][ ][ ][ ]

Previously seen for therapy in this service?   Yes [ ]   No [ ]

Last assessment date   D D / M M / Y Y Y Y   [ ][ ] / [ ][ ] / [ ][ ][ ][ ]

Months since last episode [ ][ ][ ]

Is this a follow-up/review appointment?   Yes [ ]   No [ ]

Relationships/support   *Please tick as many boxes as appropriate*

Living alone (not including dependents) [ ]   Full time carer (of disabled/elderly etc) [ ]

Living with partner [ ]   Living in shared accommodation (e.g. lodgings) [ ]

Caring for children under 5 years [ ]   Living in temporary accommodation (e.g. hostel) [ ]

Caring for children over 5 years [ ]   Living in institution/hospital [ ]

Living wiht parents/guardian [ ]   Other [ ]   [   ]

Living with other relatives/friends [ ]

Current/previous use of services for psychological problems?
Please tick as many boxes as appropriate

		Concurrent	<12 mths	<12 mths
Primary	GP or other member of primary care team (eg practice nurse, counsellor)...	[ ]	[ ]	[ ]
Secondary	In primary care setting	[ ]	[ ]	[ ]
	In community setting	[ ]	[ ]	[ ]
	In hospital setting on sessional basis	[ ]	[ ]	[ ]
	Day care services (e.g. day hospital)	[ ]	[ ]	[ ]
	Hospital admission <=10 days	[ ]	[ ]	[ ]
	Hospital admission >=11 days	[ ]	[ ]	[ ]
Specialist	Psychotherapy/psychological treatments from specialist team (sessional)	[ ]	[ ]	[ ]
	Attendance at day therapeutic programme	[ ]	[ ]	[ ]
	Inpatient treatment	[ ]	[ ]	[ ]
Other	Counsellor in e.g. voluntary, religious, work, educational setting	[ ]	[ ]	[ ]

(Continued)

Is the client currently prescribed medication to help with their psychological problem(s)? Yes ☐ No ☐

If yes, please indicate type of medication:

Anti-psychotics ☐ Anti-depressants ☐ Anxiolytics/Hypnotics ☐ Other ☐
(neuroleptics/major tranquillizers) (minor tranquillizers)

Brief description of reason for referral

Identified Problems/Concerns

severity	<6 months	6-12 months	>12 months	Recurring/continuous	severity	<6 months	6-12 months	>12 months	Recurring contin.
Depression	☐	☐	☐	☐	Trauma/Abuse	☐	☐	☐	☐
Anxiety/Stress	☐	☐	☐	☐	Bereavement/Loss	☐	☐	☐	☐
Psychosis	☐	☐	☐	☐	Self-esteem	☐	☐	☐	☐
Personality Problems	☐	☐	☐	☐	Interpersonal/Relationship	☐	☐	☐	☐
Cognitive/Learning	☐	☐	☐	☐	Living/Welfare	☐	☐	☐	☐
Eating Disorder	☐	☐	☐	☐	Work/Academic	☐	☐	☐	☐
Physical Problems	☐	☐	☐	☐	Other (specify below)	☐	☐	☐	☐
Addictions	☐	☐	☐	☐					

Risk

	None	Mild	Mod	Sev
Suicide	☐	☐	☐	☐
Self-harm	☐	☐	☐	☐
Harm to Others	☐	☐	☐	☐
Legal/Forensic	☐	☐	☐	☐

ICD-10 CODES

1 F/Z ☐ Main Code ☐☐ . Sub-code ☐   3 F/Z ☐ Main Code ☐☐ . Sub-code ☐

2 F/Z ☐ Main Code ☐☐ . Sub-code ☐   4 F/Z ☐ Main Code ☐☐ . Sub-code ☐

What has the client done to cope with/aviod their problems? *Please tick, and then specify actions*

Positive actions ☐   Negative actions ☐

Assessment outcome *(tick one box only)* | *If the client is not entering therapy give brief reason*

Assessment/one session only ☐

Accepted for therapy ☐

Accepted for trial period of therapy ☐

Figure 4.11.2 CORE Therapy Assessment Form

Source: CORE System Group
CORE Therapy Assessment Form © The CORE System Group

their impact on day-to-day functioning and any associated risk. To enhance the development of service quality, the form collects data on critical assessment audit items that profile the accessibility and appropriateness of service provision. These include patient/client demographics, waiting times, and the suitability of referral.

Finally, for client discharge, the CORE End of Therapy Form (see Figure 4.11.3) complements the other components and captures a 'core' set of treatment descriptors that aid the interpretation of CORE-OM scores to (again) help contextualize therapy outcomes and inform service development. To contextualize the outcomes of therapy, the form collects profile information that includes therapy length, type of intervention, modality, and frequency. To enhance the development of service quality, the form collects data on critical discharge audit items that profile the effectiveness and efficiency of service provision. These include problem and risk review, therapy benefits, session attendance rates, and therapy ending (i.e. planned or unplanned). Ways in which users of the CORE System data are supported to help maximize the data yield for service management and development is the focus of the final part of this section.

CORE System Data Utilization Support

Historically, following the national launch of the CORE System in 1998, the central research and development team offered support by providing services with data entry, analysis, and standardized reporting. In short, using a traditional retrospective model, services usually collected 12 months worth of CORE data and then sent them to the support team for batch-processing. Initially, this worked well as services valued and appreciated the research support that enabled them to pass on the onerous tasks of data mounting, statistical analysis and report production. However, despite such initial attractive advantages, there were a number of limitations with a hands-off/data export approach. The limitations included: the lack of engagement with the aggregated results (which may be up to 12 months old);

critical data quality problems only being recognized retrospectively; the relative high cost of providing finer-grained analysis such as individual–practitioner feedback; and an inability for services to interact with their data by exploring clients in specific data categories. Examples of this latter limitation included a desire to explore filtered data for those clients showing deterioration, or those having excessive waiting times, or else terminating therapy suddenly through a loss of contact with the service.

For these and other reasons, and in consultation with system users, we explored the potential usefulness of developing software which would support the use of CORE running on a personal computer (PC) – hence, the development of CORE-PC – to support in-house analysis and reporting. Through such innovation we also hoped to meet the more top-down (but equally demanding) challenges offered by the National Health Service policy requirements for evidence-based practice, clinical governance, and performance assessment of *National Service Framework* standards (for fuller accounts see Mellor-Clark, 2000, 2001; Rowland and Goss, 2000).

CORE-PC was designed to promote quality evaluation as a dynamic activity that recommended weekly data-quality checking and input, and quarterly data synthesis, reporting, and in-house review. In short, CORE-PC provided services with a support resource to take control of their own evaluation on an on-going basis to promote a 'research–practitioner' model, rather than export data to external expertise. In this initial early pilot phase the four key strengths of having on-site support were reported to include:

(a) the ability to provide information to service stakeholders as and when it was requested;

(b) the ability for service practitioners to analyse their own data for personal feedback (that generated a sense of shared ownership);

(c) the ability to be able to categorize easily client outcomes according to whether their CORE outcome profile categorized them as 'improved', 'deteriorated', or 'the same'; and

(d) the ability to explore meaningful sub-sets of clients for insight into potential problems with service organization and delivery (Mellor-Clark, 2004).

CLINICAL OUTCOMES in ROUTINE EVALUATION

END OF THERAPY FORM v.2

Site ID ☐☐☐☐

Client ID letters ☐☐ numbers ☐☐☐☐☐☐☐

Sub Codes Therapist ID ☐☐☐ SC4 numbers ☐☐☐ SC5 numbers ☐☐☐

Date therapy commenced D D ☐☐ / M M ☐☐ / Y Y Y Y ☐☐☐☐

Date therapy completed D D ☐☐ / M M ☐☐ / Y Y Y Y ☐☐☐☐

Number of sessions planned ☐☐☐

Number of sessions attended ☐☐☐

Number of sessions unattended ☐☐☐

What type of therapy was undertaken with the client? *Please tick as many boxes as appropriate*

Psychodynamic	☐	Person-centred	☐
Psychoanalytic	☐	Integrative	☐
Cognitive	☐	Systemic	☐
Behavioural	☐	Supportive	☐
Cognitive/Behavioural	☐	Art	☐
Structured/Brief	☐	Other *(specify below)*	☐

What modality of therapy was undertaken with the client? *Please tick as many boxes as appropriate*

Individual	☐	Family	☐
Group	☐	Marital/Couple	☐

What was the frequency of therapy with the client?

More than once weekly	☐	Less than once weekly	☐
Weekly	☐	Not at a fixed frequency	☐

Which of the following best describes the ending of therapy?

Unplanned ☐		**Planned** ☐	
Due to crisis	☐	Planned from outset	☐
Due to loss of contact	☐	Agreed during therapy	☐
Client did not wish to continue	☐	Agreed at end of therapy	☐
Other unplanned ending *(specify below)*	☐	Other planned ending *(specify below)*	☐

(Continued)

Review of Identified Problems/Concerns

Severity		Therapy Issue	Severity		Therapy Issue
☐	Depression	☐	☐ Trauma/Abuse		☐
☐	Anxiety/Stress	☐	☐ Bereavement/Loss		☐
☐	Psychosis	☐	☐ Self-esteem		☐
☐	Personality Problems	☐	☐ Interpersonal/Relationship		☐
☐	Cognitive/Learning	☐	☐ Living/Welfare		☐
☐	Physical Problems	☐	☐ Work/Academic		☐
☐	Eating Disorder	☐	☐ Other *(specify below)*		☐
☐	Addictions	☐			

Risk

	None	Mild	Mod	Sev
Suicide	☐	☐	☐	☐
Self-harm	☐	☐	☐	☐
Harm to Others	☐	☐	☐	☐
Legal/Forensic	☐	☐	☐	☐

Contextual Factors

	Poor	Moderate	Good
Motivation	☐	☐	☐
Working Alliance	☐	☐	☐
Psychological Mindedness	☐	☐	☐

Benefits of Therapy

	Improved Yes	No	Not addressed		Improved Yes	No	Not addressed
Personal insight/understanding	☐	☐	☐	Control/planning/decision making	☐	☐	☐
Expression of feelings/problems	☐	☐	☐	Subjective well-being	☐	☐	☐
Exploration of feelings/problems	☐	☐	☐	Symptoms	☐	☐	☐
Coping strategies/techniques	☐	☐	☐	Day-to-day functioning	☐	☐	☐
Access to practical help	☐	☐	☐	Personal relationships	☐	☐	☐
Other benefits	☐						

Tick box and then specify below

Has contact with this service resulted in a change of medication? Yes ☐　No ☐　Not applicable ☐

If yes, is this change likely to be of benefit to the client?　Yes ☐　No ☐

Details of change:　Started ☐　Discontinued ☐　Increased ☐　Decreased ☐　Modified ☐

Has the client been given a follow-up appointment?　　**Number of months until appointment**

Yes ☐　　　　No ☐　　　　☐☐

Figure 4.11.3　CORE End of Therapy Form

Source: CORE System Group
CORE End of Therapy Form © The CORE System Group

Table 4.11.1   A five-stage model representing the generic client journey into and through counselling and psychological therapy related to CORE performance quality indicators

Stage	Description	Service quality indicators
Referral	The point of potential entry when either the client and/or referrer decide that therapy may be potentially helpful.	• % equity of referral (by gender, ethnicity, age, and employment) • Distribution of referrals • % clients above CORE-OM cut-off
Waiting	The clients wait for an available first contact appointment usually measured in weeks or months.	• Average waiting time to first contact • Distribution of waiting time • % first session contact DNA
First contact outcome	The clients' first contact experience where they describe their current concerns and difficulties to the practitioner/assessor and they co-explore the potential for the service to help alleviate them (note the two-way process of 'assessment').	• % accepted into therapy • % single session • % onward referral • % inappropriate referral
Therapy	The period of attending a series of regular counselling or psychological therapy appointments.	• % unattended appointments • Distribution of attended sessions
Therapy ending	The termination of therapy which can be characterized by either co-planned ending, or planned by either the client or therapist deciding to end	• % planned/unplanned endings • % clinical and/or reliable change • CORE data quality profiles

Source: CORE IMS, 2002

Constructive feedback has suggested ways we could improve the structure and utility of the automated reports to enhance the use of the system for service management and development.

First, it was very apparent that the vast majority of services using the CORE System struggled to obtain a high percentage of client-completed CORE-OM both before and after therapy. In routinely administered evaluation, published figures suggested that the volume of post-therapy completed CORE-OM may actually address little more than one in seven of those clients completing forms at referral (Lucock et al., 2003). Naturally, at a local level such findings severely limit a service's confidence in the representativeness of their measures outcomes. At a national level they raise questions about clients' journeys into and through therapy services. We therefore felt that it would be a pragmatic improvement to support our philosophy of quality evaluation if we promoted an analysis model within the CORE-PC software that pragmatically focused on tracking clients through a set of discreet stages in their journey into and through services.

We believed that a useful starting point in aligning the philosophy of quality evaluation with national NHS performance assessment requirements (Department of Health, 1996, 1999, 2004) and local service quality self-assessment (Commission for Health Improvement, 2003) was to harness service quality performance indicators to a generically applicable client pathway of five discreet (contact) stages summarized in Table 4.11.1.

Building such a stage-wise approach to data analysis encouraged services to consider the progressive attrition of their clients over the 'journey' and helped them focus on specific aspects of their CORE data that could help them understand and ultimately reduce attrition. But how would a service know if their service profile on a given indicator was good or less good? For example, at referral, if a service only had 50 per cent of their clients scoring above clinical threshold on the CORE-OM, would this be something they should be concerned about? Or, for waiting-stage indicators, if the average waiting time between referral and first contact was eight weeks, is that a long or a relatively short wait? And finally, if 40 per cent of clients drop out of therapy with 'a loss of contact', is this 'normal'? These and other similar questions led to the development of a set of CORE National Comparative Performance Indicators and Service Descriptors (CORE IMS, 2002) to act as a benchmarking guide.

In developing a set of CORE performance indicators we wanted to help services understand the relativity of their own service profiles, while respecting and protecting the traditional culture of anonymity and confidentiality central to counselling and psychological therapy philosophy and activity. Consequently, we developed a graphical indicator which took the form of a 'thermometer' approach, as illustrated in Figure 4.11.4. The thermometer format summarizes the range of percentages for a specific indicator (from 51–88 per cent in this example). In its usual coloured representation the band at the top of the thermometer is green and shows the range of percentages profiled for the top 25 per cent (i.e. quartile) of services, the second quartile band (in yellow) and the third band (in amber) show the mid-quartile ranges, and the lower band (in red) shows the range of percentages for the lowest quarter of all services (in this case 51–73 per cent). A percentile to the right of the thermometer is usually displayed to indicate the national average profile (in this case 70 per cent). In use, a service compares their own service profile on a specific indicator to those of the performance thermometer to get an indication of their relative performance. As stated, roughly speaking, if a

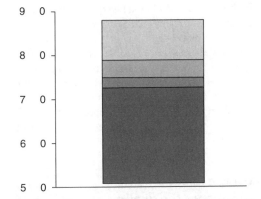

Figure 4.11.4 CORE System Comparative Performance Indicator for the quartile percentages of clients having clinical and/or reliable change on the CORE outcome measure

Source: CORE National Comparative Performance Indicators and Service Descriptors (CORE IMS, 2002)

service's profile is in the green, it is assumed to be 'good' or 'desirable', while red equates to 'bad' or 'not so desirable'. So what happens if a service finds aspects of their service profile in the 'not so desirable' band? How can they explore potential contributory factors without time-consuming, complex statistical analysis requiring expert resources in input?

The third and final innovation in the ongoing development of the utility of CORE and CORE-PC for service management and development is the ability to 'data-drill' (i.e. transforming quantitative empirical data cells containing percentiles into listings of the individual ID numbers of clients that meet that criteria and thus populate the cell). Practical examples commonly of interest to services include the client ID numbers for all clients waiting over a specified time for their first contact session; the client IDs for all those scoring below clinical cut-off on the CORE-OM; and the client IDs for all clients leaving the service with a total loss of contact. Additionally, other forms of data-drilling consider the contribution of individual practitioners to help explore, explain and potentially improve certain service (performance) characteristics. Collectively, we believe that these procedures help practitioners *quantify* their service profile and *qualitatively* explore individual cases to better understand important local service phenomena. In this way, this approach fulfils the recent calls for methodological pluralism (Barkham and Mellor-Clark, 2003; Goss and Rowland, 2000; Lambert, 2004; McLeod, 1999).

Using evaluation data to enhance the quality of service provision

The aim of this section has been to introduce the concept, utility and operationalization of quality evaluation as a practical enhancement to traditional methods and practice of evaluation in order to deliver practice-based evidence on counselling and the psychological therapies. This has been attempted by reviewing some of the limitations of current approaches, and advocating the utilization of the best methods of research, evaluation and audit to collect data on context, process and outcome to ultimately inform and enhance service provision. As guiding materials and potential resources, the CORE-OM, CORE System, CORE-PC, and CORE benchmarking have been introduced and summarized as products of a multidisciplinary group of researchers and practitioners who have striven to design, implement and have a standardized system adopted as a resource for the national enhancement of therapy provision. As we did with our earlier version of this section, we close with a series of questions to help you self-assess your local evaluation systems and/or data analysis methods and rate their potential to enhance therapy service provision and improve client care. Only this time we cite a selection of self-assessment questions drawn from *A Framework for Markers of Best Practice*, based on Department of Health guidance on organizing and delivering psychological therapies (Department of Health, 2004), and service self-assessment material provided by the Commission for Health

Improvement (2003) to help clinical teams prepare for formal service inspection:

- Do you target your service resources on accepting client *referrals* that have a demonstrable potential to benefit from counselling or other psychological therapies?[1]
- Do you know what the *waiting times* and access issues are for your service and do you have actionable plans to improve them?[1,2]
- In *first session contacts,* can the service give accurate advice across a wide range of possible modalities and act as 'broker' to ensure that clients end up with the most appropriate help?[1]
- Do you work in partnership with service users and carers so they contribute to the *planning, monitoring and evaluation of your therapy* services?[1,2]
- Do you use a range of up-to-date clinical indicators (i.e. benchmarks) to monitor and improve *clinical outcomes* for service users and carers?[2]
- Do you receive and *act upon information* about the quality of all aspects of the service you provide?[2]

(*Sources:* 1. Department of Health, 2004. 2. Commission for Health Improvement, 2003)

Recommended reading

For a comprehensive overview of the evolving political and policy contexts of evaluation and service audit we suggest the suite of Department of Health publications *NHS Psychotherapy Services in England: Review of Strategic Policy* (1996), *National Service Framework for Mental Health* (1999), and *Organising and Delivering Psychological Therapies* (2004). For background reading on the philosophical underpinnings of the concept of quality evaluation we suggest R. Pawson and N. Tilley's (1997) text on *Realistic Evaluation.* For a comprehensive overview on the challenge of evidence-based practice for the psychological therapies we suggest *Evidence-based Counselling and Psychological Therapies,* edited by N. Rowland and S. Goss (2001). Finally, for more information on the CORE System, relevant publications and the range of resources to support users, visit www.coreims.co.uk.

References

Audin, K. and Mellor-Clark, J. (1998) *Composite Evaluation Report 1997: Leeds CMHT Clinical Psychology, Psychotherapy and Counselling Unit.* Leeds: Psychological Therapies Research Centre.

Audin, K., Margison, F., Mellor-Clark, J. and Barkham, M. (2001) Value of HoNOS in assessing patient change in NHS psychotherapy and psychological treatment services. *British Journal of Psychiatry*, 178: 561–566.

Audin, K., Mellor-Clark, J., Barkham, M., Margison, F., McGrath, G., Lewis, S., Cann, L., Duffy, J. and Parry, G. (2001) Practice research networks for effective psychological therapies. *Journal of Mental Health*, 10: 241–251.

Barkham, M. and Mellor-Clark, J. (2000) Rigour and relevance: the role of practice-based evidence in the psychological therapies. In N. Rowland and S. Goss (eds), *Evidence-based Mental Health*. London: Routledge. pp. 127–144.

Barkham, M. and Mellor-Clark, J. (2003) Bridging evidence-based practice and practice-based evidence: developing a rigorous and relevant knowledge for the psychological therapies. *Clinical Psychology & Psychotherapy*, 10 (6): 319–327.

Barkham, M., Culverwell, A., Spindler, K., Twigg, E. and Connell, J. (2005) The CORE-OM in an older adult population: psychometric status, acceptability, and feasibility. *Aging and Mental Health*, 9: 235–245.

Barkham, M., Evans, C., Margison, F., McGrath, G., Mellor-Clark, J., Milne, D. and Connell, J. (1998) The rationale for developing and implementing core outcome batteries for routine use in service settings and psychotherapy outcome research. *Journal of Mental Health*, 7: 35–47.

Barkham, M., Gilbert, N., Connell, J., Marshall, C. and Twigg, E. (2005) Suitability and utility of the CORE-OM and CORE-A for assessing severity of presenting problems in psychological therapy services based in primary and secondary care settings. *British Journal of Psychiatry*, 186: 239–246.

Barkham, M., Margison, F., Leach, C., Lucock, M., Mellor-Clark, J., Evans, C., Benson, L., Connell, J., Audin, K. and McGrath, G. (2001) Service profiling and outcomes benchmarking using the CORE-OM: towards practice-based evidence in the psychological therapies. *Journal of Consulting and Clinical Psychology*, 69: 184–196.

Bower, P. (2003) Efficacy in evidence-based practice. *Clinical Psychology & Psychotherapy*, 10 (6): 328–336.

Bower, P. and King, M. (2000) Randomised controlled trials and the evaluation of psychological therapy. In N. Rowland and S. Goss (eds), *Evidence-based Counselling and Psychological Therapies: Research and Application*. London: Routledge. pp. 79–110.

Cape, J. and Parry, G. (2000) Clinical practice guidelines development in evidence-based psychotherapy. In N. Rowland and S. Goss (eds), *Evidence-based Counselling and Psychological Therapies: Research and Application*. London: Routledge. pp. 171–190.

Commission for Health Improvement (2003) *Mental Health Trusts Clinical/Care Team Self Assessment.* London: CHI.

CORE IMS (2002) *CORE National Comparative Performance Indicators and Service Descriptors* (1st edn). Rugby: CORE IMS.

CORE System Group (1998) *The CORE System User Manual.* Leeds: Psychological Therapies Research Centre.

Department of Health (1996) *NHS Psychotherapy Services in England: Review of Strategic Policy.* London: HMSO.

Department of Health (1999) *National Service Framework for Mental Health.* London: HMSO.

Department of Health (2001) *Treatment Choice in Psychological Therapies and Counselling.* London: HMSO.

Department of Health (2004) *Organising and Delivering Psychological Therapies.* London: HMSO.

Dickey, B. (1996) The development of report cards for mental health care. In L.I. Sederer and B. Dickey (eds), *Outcomes Assessment in Clinical Practice*. Baltimore, MD: Williams & Wilkins. pp. 186–160.

Evans, C., Connell, J., Barkham, M., Marshall, C. and Mellor-Clark, J. (2003) Practice-based evidence: benchmarking NHS primary care counselling services at national and local levels. *Clinical Psychology & Psychotherapy*, 10: 374–388.

Evans, C., Connell, J., Barkham, M., Margison, F., Mellor-Clark, J., McGrath, G. and Audin, K. (2002) Towards a standardised brief outcome measure: psychometric properties and utility of the CORE-OM. *British Journal of Psychiatry*, 180: 51–60.

Evans, C., Mellor-Clark, J., Margison, F., Barkham, M., McGrath, G., Connell, J. and Audin, K. (2000) Clinical Outcomes in Routine Evaluation: the CORE-OM. *Journal of Mental Health*, 9: 247–255.

Froyd, J.E., Lambert, M.J. and Froyd, J.D. (1996) A review of practices of psychotherapy outcome measurement. *Journal of Mental Health*, 5: 11–15.

Goss, S. (1997) *Patient Outcomes Following the Introduction of a Counselling Services into Primary Care in Lanarkshire: Follow-on Evaluation Report.* Glasgow: Lanarkshire Health Board.

Goss, S. and Rowland, N. (2000) Getting evidence into practice. In N. Rowland and S. Goss (eds), *Evidence-based Counselling and Psychological Therapies: Research and Application*. London: Routledge. pp. 191–205.

Hemmings, A. (2000) Counselling in primary care: a review of the practice evidence. *British Journal of Guidance and Counselling*, 28: 233–252.

Lambert, M.J. (ed.) (2004) *Bergin and Garfield's Handbook of Psychotherapy and Behavior Change* (5th edn). New York: Wiley.

Lucock, M., Leach, C., Iveson, S., Lynch, K., Horsefiled, C. and Hall, P. (2003) A systematic approach to practice-based evidence in a psychological therapy service. *Clinical Psychology & Psychotherapy*, 10: 389–399.

McCarthy, P., Walker, J. and Kain, J. (1998) *Telling It as It Is: The Client Experience of Relate Counselling*. Newcastle upon Tyne: Relate Centre for Family Studies.

McLeod, J. (1999) *Practitioner Research in Counselling*. London: Sage.

McLeod, J. (2001) *Counselling in the Workplace: The facts. A Systematic Study of the Research Evidence*. Rugby: British Association for Counselling and Psychotherapy.

Margison, F., Barkham, M., Evans, C., McGrath, G., Mellor-Clark, J., Audin, K. and Connell, J. (2000) Measurement and psychotherapy: evidence-based practice and practice-based evidence. *British Journal of Psychiatry*, 177: 123–130.

Mellor-Clark, J. (2000) *Counselling in Primary Care in the Context of the NHS Quality Agenda: The Facts*. Rugby: British Association for Counselling.

Mellor-Clark, J. (2001) How can quality be enhanced in counselling services? In P. Bower, J. Foster and J. Mellor-Clark (eds), *Quality in Counselling in Primary Care: A Guide to Effective Commissioning and Clinical Governance*. Manchester: National Primary Care Research and Development Centre.

Mellor-Clark, J. (2003) National innovations in the evaluation of psychological therapy service provision. *The Journal of Primary Care Mental Health*, 7 (3): 82–85.

Mellor-Clark, J. (2004) A review of the evolution of research evidence and activity for NHS primary care counselling. *Psychodynamic Practice*, 10 (3): 373–393.

Mellor-Clark, J. and Barkham, M. (2000) Quality evaluation: methods, measures and meaning. In C. Feltham and I. Horton (eds), *The Handbook of Counselling and Psychotherapy* (1st edn). London: Sage.

Mellor-Clark, J., Barkham, M., Connell, J. and Evans, C. (1999) Practice-based evidence and need for a standardised evaluation system: informing the design of the CORE System. *European Journal of Psychotherapy, Counselling and Health*, 2: 357–374.

Mellor-Clark, J., Connell, J., Barkham, M. and Cummins, P. (2001) Counselling outcomes in primary health care: a CORE System data profile. *European Journal of Psychotherapy, Counselling and Health*, 4: 65–86.

Mellor-Clark, J., Simms-Ellis, R. and Burton, M. (2001) National survey of counsellors working in general practice: evidence of professionalisation? *Occasional Paper 79*. London: Royal College of General Practitioners.

Okiishi, J., Lambert, M.J., Nielsen, S.L. and Ogles, B.M. (2003) Waiting for supershrink: an empirical analysis of therapist effects. *Clinical Psychology & Psychotherapy*, 10 (6): 361–373.

Parry, G. (1996) Service evaluation and audit methods. In G. Parry and F.N. Watts (eds), *Behavioural and Mental Health Research: A Handbook of Skills and Methods* (2nd edn). London: Erlbaum. pp. 423–449.

Parry, G., Cape, J. and Pilling, S. (2003) Clinical practice guidelines in clinical psychology and psychotherapy. *Clinical Psychology & Psychotherapy*, 10 (6): 337–351.

Pawson, R. and Tilley, K. (1997) *Realistic Evaluation*. London: Sage.

Roth, A. and Fonagy, P. (1996) *What Works for Whom? A Critical Review of Psychotherapy Research*. New York: Guilford Press.

Rowland, N. and Goss, S. (2000) *Evidence-based Counselling and Psychological Therapies: Research and Application*. London: Routledge.

Shapiro, D.A. and Barkham, M. (1993) *Relate – Information Needs Research*. Final Report to the Department of Social Security. Rugby: Relate.

PART V
Theory and Approaches

5.1 Introduction

COLIN FELTHAM AND IAN HORTON

Counselling and psychotherapy are activities shaped, supported and guided by theory. In other words, an undeniable characteristic of the therapeutic enterprise is its theoretical underpinning. This is not to say that theory is without problems – critics have long attacked the theoretical rationale of psychoanalysis, for example, and some commentators argue that as therapists we need to be clearer about the exact place that any theory has in relation to clinical practice (Feltham, 1999; Horton, 1996) – but it is to assert that therapy in its current form seems inseparable from various theories. Therapy or healing *may* occur without or apart from theoretical preparation or influence, but is commonly driven or justified by theory.

This part of the book addresses some of the theoretical ground of therapy. First, we look at some aspects of contextual psychology, specifically developmental, social, evolutionary and positive psychology, and their relevance for practice. Psychological type theory deriving ultimately from Jung is examined as a valuable trans-theoretical tool. Possible reasons for, and the structures of, the myriad models of therapy and attempts at their theoretical integration, are then outlined. The largest component is then given over to a selection of distinct approaches to therapy (or core theoretical models, or approach-specific theories) as described below. Hopefully the space and positioning accorded to such theories here reflect their historical importance and continuing influence, but we acknowledge our own contention that theories are not perhaps quite the crowning feature of therapy or accurate explanations of therapeutic change that they have often been considered. Readers may of course discern implicit theoretical assumptions in most other parts of the book.

References

Feltham, C. (ed.) (1999) *Controversies in Psychotherapy and Counselling*. London: Sage.

Horton, I. (1996) Towards the construction of a model: some issues. In R. Bayne, I. Horton and J. Bimrose (eds), *New Directions in Counselling*. London: Routledge.

5.2 Contextual Psychology

COLIN FELTHAM

Counselling and psychotherapy constitute a field of knowledge and practice in their own right. Although psychoanalysis was associated with nineteenth-century neuropsychiatry and speculative psychology, it evolved similarly to theology, almost as a subject *sui generis*. Counsellors and psychotherapists draw upon their own emerging tradition of knowledge which includes but is arguably not reliant upon psychology (Thorne and Dryden, 1993). Counselling and clinical psychologists are, of course, exceptions to this rule.

There are, however, some areas of psychology of real significance in the training of therapists: developmental and life-span psychology, social psychology and evolutionary psychology. Wilkinson and Campbell (1997) include the first two of these topics in their consideration of personality, emotion, memory, thinking, states of consciousness, stress, coping, health and illness, and psychological disorders. We focus briefly here on some aspects of these as well as on the fertile fields of evolutionary psychology and psychotherapy, and positive psychology.

Developmental and life-span psychology

An understanding of how human beings typically develop or grow is considered essential by some practitioners (e.g. the psychodynamic) but of far less relevance by others (e.g. those practising REBT). Psychodynamic practitioners have their own developmental theories (e.g. Freudian, Kleinian, Eriksonian, Bowlby-inspired, etc.) which are often not shared – indeed may be disputed – by classical (academic) psychologists. The concepts of early childhood memory, repression, and maternal deprivation, form the basis of three such disputes, for example. Nevertheless, there are certain good reasons for all therapists to familiarize themselves with the fundamentals of human development:

- Clients may present from a wide age-range, from childhood to old age, and a knowledge of common age-specific characteristics can assist in assessment and therapeutic planning and referral.
- Therapists themselves will usually have analysed and grappled with their own significant developmental issues – past, present and future – and may benefit in terms of self-understanding from consulting relevant texts (Sugarman, 2004).
- All therapeutic schools inherit and generate implicit or explicit developmental theories, which are associated with different theories and practices of assessment, intervention and prognosis.

- Many therapeutic traditions rest on notions of a 'presenting past', in other words the belief that all present crises and problems in some sense represent or repeat earlier developmental stages and unresolved traumas.

While developmental psychology has traditionally focused on the years from infancy to adolescence, and perhaps to early adulthood, it is now quite usual to think in life-span terms from birth to death. Humanistic psychology has forced on to the agenda the significance, for example, of birth (e.g. birth trauma) or even earlier formative events; and transpersonal psychology commends consideration of 'past lives', near-death and 'posthumous' experiences, as well as challenging the traditional, pessimistic assumptions of old age as decline. Increasing longevity too takes psychology into advances in psycho-gerontology, the study of old age. The emergence of evolutionary psychology commends the usefulness of examining ways in which humans as evolved beings carry forward certain archetypal behaviours, both healthy and unhealthy; and advances in transgenerational psychotherapy (Schutzenberger, 1998) also widen the potential for expansion in our understanding of human development.

In addition to simple *chronology*, life-span psychology embraces different frameworks for understanding development, including the metaphors of journey and narrative, transitions and life events, models of the life-course, and developmental tasks. Typically, texts focus on early developmental milestones (especially cognitive achievements, following Piaget's work), attachment, moral development, family influences, etc., and thereafter on themes of physical and sexual development, identity, career-seeking, forming partnerships, establishing families, and so on, into the crises, transitions and losses of midlife, retirement and old age.

Feminist and social theorists have criticized typical white, western, individual-centred, linear models of human development propagated by psychology, particularly those focusing uncritically on the central role of the mother, and those implying direct links between statistically 'normal' development and psychological health (Burman, 1993). D'Augelli and Patterson (1995) argue for specific recognition of lesbian, gay and bisexual life-span issues. Existential and phenomenological therapists too question orthodox deterministic models. Some Jungians interpret the life-course less as a constant recovery from past hurts and general recapitulation of the past, and more in teleological terms as a forward movement to fulfil purpose and destiny.

Social psychology

Traditionally social psychology has been concerned with the topics of intimate, group and wider social relationships, focusing on interpersonal perceptions, attributions, attraction, aggression, influence, power, roles and social skills. More recently, attention has been given to aspects of the self, including self-concept, schemas, subpersonalities and the body, and also to bisexual, lesbian, gay, ethnic/cultural and other psychologies of difference.

In relation to therapy, one of the most significant social psychological contributions has been that of social influence. While many therapists have concentrated on the nuances of unconscious communication in therapy, more obvious issues of power, influence, coercion, authority and attractiveness, in the therapeutic context have often been neglected. Social learning theory suggests that much dysfunctional behaviour is learned in childhood by imitation, conditioning, avoidance, punishment, habit, and so on. Many psychologists in the 1960s and 1970s (e.g. Claiborn, Dorn, Strong) exploited these insights via empirical work which led to the conclusion that therapists' *trustworthiness*, *attractiveness* and *expertness* were key indicators of successful therapy. In other words, clients' *perceptions* of their therapists' ability to help them were highly significant.

These developments, mirrored in the work of Carkhuff, Cormier, Egan, Ivey, Nelson-Jones, Truax and others, suggested that improvement by concerted practice of skills associated with certain therapist in-session behaviours would enhance working alliances and hence outcomes. Important work has been carried out too on the effects of judicious therapist self-disclosure, on client reactance or preference for certain relational styles, and on relevant non-verbal behaviours. Social psychological theories of

close relationship development (i.e. friendships, romantic bonds, partnerships), studies of compliance with therapy, different communication styles according to gender, and psychological type, have informed some therapeutic practice developments. It is now widely accepted that early consolidation of the therapeutic alliance, consciously forged by therapists, is a key to successful outcomes. Such findings have now influenced cognitive-behavioural therapists, for example, towards paying greater conscious attention to *specifically relational factors in therapy*.

These developments appear to endorse Jerome Frank's durable observations and suggestions about persuasion effected by social psychological factors in therapy, now much discussed as common factors in therapy (Feltham, 1999).

Evolutionary psychology and psychotherapy

One of the missing (or inadequately developed) pieces of the counselling and psychotherapy jigsaw is a compelling account of the origins of human behaviour patterns, why they are so often entrenched, that is, why psychological dysfunctions can remain so difficult to change and what may be done to change them. While much psychoanalytic theory has focused on the deep-seated nature of psychopathology and defence mechanisms, humanistic and cognitive-behavioural approaches have shown far greater interest in understanding and implementing change processes; broadly, in understanding the nature of present behaviour and how it can be improved. Evolutionary psychology (Barrett et al., 2002), and in its clinically applied form of evolutionary psychotherapy (EP), offers explanations, for example, for proclivities towards and common experiences of depression, anxiety, obsessions, eating disorders, schizoid behaviour, schizophrenia and homosexuality, among others (Stevens and Price, 2000).

Where genetic explanations for behaviour start and end at the genetic level of the neurologically hard-wired, evolutionary accounts seek to speculate about the prevalence and obduracy of certain contemporary behaviours and their beginnings in the conditions in which early human beings lived. Not everyone can be a leader, and subservience has a necessary function. But too much subservience can lead to chronic low-ranking and low self-esteem. On the other hand, ancient communities of humans needed their inspired, visionary and aggressive leaders. But too much of such behaviour can lead to distorted perceptions (e.g. some aspects of schizophrenia) and in-group violence (as in domestic violence, psychopathy and murder). Horrobin (2001) has suggested that schizophrenia may have roots in the distant past, being linked with changes in diet towards fatty acids, increasing brain size and a need for gifted visionary members of the group. But what was once necessary in certain circumstances backfired later in others.

It is of course unsurprising that many therapists remain either indifferent or opposed to the tenets of evolutionary psychology. Evolutionary psychotherapy may not seek to suggest that behaviour is wholly determined but, along with sociobiological accounts, does lean in this direction. If you can establish good reasons why some human beings had to act extra-vigilantly for long evolutionary periods, for example, you undermine to some extent the arguments that heightened anxiety is learned in our early years from parents or that it follows personal traumatic experiences. Notions of individual self-determination are undermined.

Evolutionary accounts do not in themselves suggest particular, if any, therapeutic remedies. However, in a manner typical of this field, an array of authors from Jungian, psychoanalytic, primal, cognitive-behavioural and psychopharmacological therapies have drawn selectively on evolutionary explanations for behaviour to underpin their rationales for diagnosis and treatment. Evolutionary psychology and psychotherapy offer promises for an integrative aetiology of psychological disturbances: we act in these dysfunctional ways because we have inherited certain behaviours that were once – and probably for a very long time – necessary but no longer are. Most therapists agree that *awareness* of such behavioural roots in ourselves should help us to understand how and why they function, and that they are anachronistic. But EP in itself is agnostic about how we can, or whether we can, reliably change such behaviour.

Positive psychology

Positive psychology, pioneered by Seligman (2002), Carr (2004) and others, is a relative newcomer to the discipline of psychology. Unlike the tendency of clinical and abnormal psychology to look for deficits, positive psychology looks for the causes, perpetuating factors and learned ingredients of human psychological strengths. Instead of learned helplessness, learned optimism is its focus. Although not the diametrical opposite of evolutionary psychology, positive psychology has an emphasis on functional not dysfunctional behaviours, on the study of happiness not misery, on learnable not inherited behaviours. It is unashamedly about strengths, hope, emotional intelligence, the values of relational attachment, giftedness, creativity, self-esteem and even 'positive illusions'. Denial and repression, for example, are valued as sometimes necessary and helpful defence mechanisms. Optimism in the face of objective adversity is promoted.

Clearly positive psychology, which its proponents regard as not identical with positive thinking since it has a fairly sophisticated research base in academic psychology, resonates well with many aspects of humanistic psychology and psychotherapy but also with cognitive-behaviour therapy and solution-focused therapy. It is forward-looking, reinforcing the significance of learning coping skills and preventing future problems. Carr (2004) advocates deep relationships, absorbing work or activity, and an optimistic outlook, all held in balance with each other, as crucial to good mental health.

Critics of positive psychology suggest that it is *not* so far from positive thinking and Pollyannaish behaviour, that it ignores the social distribution of psychological dysfunction and its myriad social causes, and that its over-reliance on positive illusions or benign self-deception is highly questionable. Carr's recipe – 'to value the future more than the present' (2004: 348) – is also open to serious criticism. Nevertheless, it chimes well with government policies for well-being and mental health enhancement and with an educational rather than psychopathological orientation. It represents a challenge to those therapies dwelling on uncovering past hurts.

References

Barrett, L., Dunbar, R. and Lycett, J. (2002) *Human Evolutionary Psychology*. Basingstoke: Palgrave.

Burman, E. (1993) *Deconstructing Developmental Psychology*. London: Routledge.

Carr, A. (2004) *Positive Psychology: The Science of Happiness and Human Strengths*. London: Brunner-Routledge.

D'Augelli, A.R. and Patterson, C.J. (eds) (1995) *Lesbian, Gay and Bisexual Identities over the Lifespan: Psychological Perspectives*. New York: Oxford University Press.

Feltham, C. (ed.) (1999) *Understanding the Counselling Relationship*. London: Sage.

Horrobin, D. (2001) *The Madness of Adam and Eve: How Schizophrenia Shaped Humanity*. London: Corgi.

Schutzenberger, A.A. (1998) *The Ancestor Syndrome: Transgenerational Psychotherapy and the Hidden Links in the Family Tree*. London: Routledge.

Seligman, M. (2002) *Authentic Happiness: Using the New Positive Psychology to Realize Your Potential for Lasting Fulfilment*. New York: Free Press.

Stevens, A. and Price, J. (2000) *Evolutionary Psychiatry: A New Beginning* (2nd edn). London: Routledge.

Sugarman, L. (2004) *Counselling and the Lifecourse*. London: Sage.

Thorne, B. and Dryden, W. (eds) (1993) *Counselling: Interdisciplinary Perspectives*. Buckingham: Open University Press.

Wilkinson, J.D. and Campbell, E.A. (1997) *Psychology in Counselling and Therapeutic Practice*. Chichester: Wiley.

5.3 Psychological Type Theory

ROWAN BAYNE

Psychological type theory is Isabel Myers' clarification and development of some of Jung's ideas about personality. It has two distinctive features and several applications to counselling and psychotherapy. The distinctive features are that it takes the individuality of therapists and clients unusually seriously, and its positive and constructive tone. In particular, it is intended to be a step towards understanding and valuing each person's individuality, rather than a set of restrictive and stultifying 'boxes'.

The applications that follow from these features include:

- an increased chance of quicker and deeper empathy, acceptance and self-acceptance

- ideas about matching clients and practitioners in style and expectations of therapy
- ideas about matching clients and techniques (and perhaps especially how therapists present techniques)
- a perspective on how much clients can change.

Each of these applications is discussed briefly in this section.

Myers' theory (e.g. Allen and Brock, 2000; Bayne, 2004) is widely applied in organizations and with individuals. More than 2 million copies of the associated questionnaire, the Myers–Briggs Type Indicator (MBTI), are completed each year and there is now a substantial research base, though so far, like this section, it is focused on the basic level of the theory

Table 5.3.1 The four pairs of preferences

Extraversion (E) or Introversion (I)
Sensing (S) or Intuition (N)
Thinking (T) or Feeling (F)
Judging (J) or Perceiving (P)

Table 5.3.2 Some general characteristics associated with the preferences

E	More outgoing and active	
		More reflective and reserved I
S	More practical and interested in facts and details	
		More interested in possibilities and an overview N
T	More logical and reasoned	
		More agreeable and appreciative F
J	More planning and coming to conclusions	
		More easy-going and flexible P

Table 5.3.3 The preferences and aspects of learning style

E	Action, talk, trial and error.
I	Reflection, work privately.
S	Close observation of what actually happens. Start with the concrete and specific, with ideas and theory later.
N	Theory first. Links and possibilities. Surges of interest.
T	Analysis and logic. Critiques.
F	Harmonious atmosphere. Care about the topic.
J	More formal. Organized. Clear expectations and criteria.
P	Flexible. Not routine. Bursts of energy. Work as play.

much more than on the deeper levels of type dynamics and type development.

The key concepts are 'preference' and 'psychological type'. Tables 5.3.1 and 5.3.2 summarize the preferences and Table 5.3.3 expands a little on their meaning in relation to aspects of 'learning style'. Preference can be defined as 'feeling most natural and comfortable with'. For example, the theory assumes that everyone behaves in both Extraverted and Introverted ways but that we each prefer one of them, and therefore tend to behave in that way more often and with less or no sense of effort.

Each psychological type includes one from each of the four pairs of preferences, e.g. ENTP or ESTJ,

and there are 16 possible combinations and therefore 16 types.

A few therapists will only work with clients who have completed the MBTI questionnaire, discussed their results, and made a provisional decision about which psychological type they are. However, most therapists who use the approach have it in the background like any other framework or concept (e.g. loss or assertiveness) to consider applying when relevant. Sometimes the application will, if the therapist has passed the appropriate training, include the MBTI questionnaire.

More often, the theory is used informally, to say for example, 'Some people like and *need* to plan ahead more than others, and that seems to be true of you', or 'You seem most comfortable making decisions through analysing the arguments for and against, and this usually works well for you. *This* decision, though, is different and you're stuck and baffled. Would you like to try adding another element to your analysis: how right or not each possibility *feels*?' In the spirit of type theory, both examples could equally well have been phrased in terms of the opposite preferences – 'Perceiving' in the first example, and 'Feeling' in the second.

Several more specific applications of psychological type theory were suggested at the beginning of this chapter. Taking empathy first, the theory illustrates in a very concrete way how difficult empathy can be. According to the theory it is impossible to *really* understand what it is like to have the opposite preferences(s) to your own, even though each of us uses all of them. But at the same time, knowing this limitation and knowing how profoundly people differ, may make genuine empathy more likely. It may – probably should – mean that empathy, or sufficient empathy, occurs more quickly too. The obstacle of 'people are like me' or assumed similarity is less prominent, or more consciously present and therefore more readily countered.

Similarly, type theory should encourage quicker and deeper acceptance. Its major theme is that most people most of the time are behaving differently from ourselves because they are different and equally valid 'types', *not* because they are being awkward, weird or incompetent. Moreover, the different ways of being can be equally effective. For example, someone with a preference for Perceiving (which is developed sufficiently) will tend to produce their best work at the last minute, energized by the deadline which someone else, with a preference for Judging, has tried to avoid by starting early. A major problem can occur of course when the two people are collaborating or when one is the manager of the other. Type offers a refreshing perspective on such problems and on various combinations of people, including people of the same type. Similarity is not seen as ideal. On the contrary, any combination can work well but the best work is more likely to result from partnership between people of different types who value each other's (complementary) strengths.

A helpful matching of clients and counsellors on type is similarly subtle, not just or even primarily a question of INTPs being the best counsellors for other INTPs, etc. (Bayne, 1999). Indeed, type development is probably the most important factor: how versatile therapists can comfortably and authentically be in their use of all the preferences when they are most appropriate. This is not to say that all therapists should aim to be versatile. Rather, people of some psychological types (in theory ENTP and ENFP) are more naturally versatile and versatility tends to develop with practice (and therefore age). The logic of the theory's model of development is to develop true preferences first and one's 'other side' later, often in middle age or older.

According to type theory the different psychological types tend to have different expectations of counselling and therapy. For example, as Table 5.3.3 suggests, clients who prefer Extraversion will usually want a more active approach. Similarly, some techniques will be more palatable, though not necessarily more effective, with clients of some types, for example guided fantasy with clients who prefer Intuition. The principle here is not a rigid, mechanistic one. Rather, it is to use the theory as a guide to being sensitive about how, when and whether to suggest a particular technique, to reviewing the outcome, and to deciding whether to continue with it or not (Bayne, 2004; Provost, 1993). Type theory can also make referral more acceptable.

Finally, psychological type theory offers a distinctive view of change. We know that some behaviour can generally change quite easily – for example panic attacks, problems with being assertive, sexual problems. Type theory suggests that people can (and do) develop all the preferences but that their true preferences do not change. A 'laid-back' person (clue for a genuine preference for Perceiving) does not – at least not without a punitive amount of effort which continues to be punitive – change into a highly organized person. However, we *can* usefully add a little of the opposite preference. The stability of type may be regarded as positive: it is part of having a sense of identity and it can lead to realistic expectations of counselling and psychotherapy and change. Moreover, there is a special case. When someone has lived as a psychological type other than their own (usually because of an extreme upbringing), they tend not to feel 'right' and can sometimes change rapidly and dramatically to express their true preferences.

References

Allen, J. and Brock, S.A. (2000) *Health Care Communication and Personality Type*. London: Routledge.

Bayne, R. (1999) The counselling relationship and psychological type. In C. Feltham (ed.), *Understanding the Counselling Relationship*. London: Sage.

Bayne, R. (2004) *Psychological Types at Work: An MBTI perspective*. London: Thomson.

Provost, J.A. (1993) *Applications of the Myers–Briggs Type Indicator in Counseling: A Casebook* (2nd edn). Gainesville, FL: Center for Application of Psychological Type.

5.4 Models of Counselling and Psychotherapy

○○○

IAN HORTON

Norcross and Grencavage (1990) reviewed various surveys which indicated that between 1959 and 1986 the number of arguably different or distinct models or approaches to counselling and psychotherapy rose from 36 to over 400. The proliferation of new approaches or attempts to combine elements or aspects of existing approaches in reconstituted or integrated models seems to have continued unabated to the present day. Theoretical and clinical innovation remains something of an enduring preoccupation that exercises the imagination and creativity of some practitioners and researchers.

Historically, models or approaches to counselling and psychotherapy have tended to be seen as synonymous with psychological theories of personality with only tenuously related indicators of methods of treatment or change. However, the last decade or so has seen a shift towards the view that models or approaches to counselling and psychotherapy may,

but will not necessarily, subsume aspects of personality theories, and are quite distinct from them in the emphasis they place on 'therapeutic operations' (Orlinsky et al., 1994) and change processes.

The concept of model or theoretical orientation is complex. It is hard to measure. Poznanski and McLennon (1997) report that few of the multi-item self-report instruments designed to measure theoretical orientation show evidence of reliability, and even fewer of validity. They suggest that this may be explained by the evidence indicating theories or models of counselling and psychotherapy as multiple concepts made up of four positions:

1 Personal therapeutic belief systems which are not always clearly articulated or accessible.
2 Theoretical school affiliation or the practitioner's self-reported adherence to one (or more) theoretical schools.

3   Espoused theory or the theoretical concepts and techniques that practitioners say they use.
4   Theory-in-action or what observers believe the practitioner is actually doing.

There seems to be a relatively strong link between theoretical school affiliation and espoused theory, but often a contradictory or at least a much weaker association between espoused theory and theory-in-action. Practitioners do not always seem to be doing what they say or think they do. This compounds the problems and issues faced by researchers trying to evaluate and compare the outcomes of different approaches and may be taken as evidence to support Clarkson's (1995) doubts about the usefulness of theory and Feltham's (1997) doubts about the emphasis professional bodies place on the need for a coherent core theoretical model.

What is a model or theory of counselling and psychotherapy? Relatively little has been written on this subject and there is no consensus on what actually constitutes the parts or elements of a comprehensive model or theory. However, four common elements are either explicit in the literature or can be inferred from most descriptions of particular models of counselling and psychotherapy (Horton, 2000): (a) basic assumptions or philosophy; (b) formal theory of human personality and development; (c) clinical theory which defines the goals, principles and processes of change and provides a cognitive map which gives a sense of direction and purpose; and (d) the related therapeutic operations, or skills and techniques. The basic assumptions or philosophical elements of a model or approach will typically be concerned with two aspects. First, worldview or how people construct reality and attribute meaning to their life experiences. In some models or approaches this may include reference to socio-cultural factors as well as psychological influences and personal values and beliefs. The second aspect is the therapeutic process and basic assumptions about the characteristics of the therapeutic relationship and the values, purpose and goals of therapy. While the basic assumptions or philosophy might be seen as setting the stage for the selection and adoption of the formal and clinical theory elements, it is not always clearly articulated or understood.

The formal theory element[...] human development and may [...] of those characteristics of a per[...] consistent patterns of behaviou[...] or healthy development, as wel[...] aetiology of psychological prob[...] are perpetuated or maintaine[...] or otherwise of these aspects of theory may be explicit in the formal theory description or be inferred from how it is described. Not all models or approaches emphasize the importance of the genesis of psychological problems and are more concerned with how problems can be modified or changed.

In a clearly articulated and internally consistent model or approach the clinical theory element will interpret the largely abstract concepts contained in the formal theory in ways which are amenable to the delivery of therapeutic services.

Clinical theory may imply or make explicit general principles of change and account for the psychological processes which enable change to take place. Different models or approaches seem to be based on different assumptions about the mechanisms or process of change and may not necessarily be made explicit in the theory of the model. The common mechanisms or processes of change include such variables as the quality of the relationship between therapist and client, the expression of emotions or catharsis, the provision of new perspectives through some explanation or interpretation of the problem and/or of the interaction between the therapist and client, reinforcement of client strengths and resources, increasing levels of 'exposure' to the problem thus enabling clients to face and confront what was previously being avoided, and a working towards deeper understanding or awareness of unconscious processes. Some models or approaches involve psycho-educational interventions – skills training and information giving – as an integral part of the change process. Much research still needs to be done to establish exactly what therapists do that actually contributes to helping clients change.

The most concrete and visible element of a model or approach is the therapeutic operations or the skills and strategies a therapist uses to implement the clinical theory.

This analysis of the elements of a model or approach to counselling or psychotherapy assumes a coherent and internally consistent relationship between them, with each element developing from the previous one. However, other than in very broad terms the actual relationship between the elements and how each informs the other is not always explicit. It is not always apparent how what a therapist does actually interprets his or her philosophy or theory of human development in a consistent and coherent way. More experienced therapists seem to make decreasing use of abstract concepts (Skovholt and Ronnestad, 1995), placing greater emphasis on what is referred to here as clinical theory. Bond's (2000: 319) pictorial metaphor of a 'pond' illustrates the relationship between the four elements. He describes the basic assumptions or philosophy as the 'dark, murky and stagnant water at the bottom of the pond, containing rich and fertile soil, living creatures, flora and fauna and the unregenerate sludge and detritus of our own culture'. Above that in the still relatively dark and murky water is the level of formal theory. The translucent level just below the surface represents the clinical theory with the clearly visible water on the surface of the pond representing the therapeutic operations and what the therapist can actually be observed doing.

These four elements of a model or theory of counselling and psychotherapy are used as the basic structure for the description of the different models included later in this part of the book.

References

Bond, T. (2000) Bond's pond. In S. Palmer and R. Woolfe (eds), *Integrative and Eclectic Counselling and Psychotherapy*. London: Sage.

Clarkson, P. (1995) *After Schoolism*. London: PHYSIS.

Feltham, C. (1997) Challenging the core theoretical model. *Counselling*, 8 (2): 121–125.

Horton, I. (2000) Principles and practice of a personal integration. In S. Palmer and R. Woolfe (eds), *Integrative and Eclectic Counselling and Psychotherapy*. London: Sage.

Norcross, J.C. and Grencavage, L.M. (1990) Eclecticism and integration in counselling and psychotherapy: major themes and obstacles. In W. Dryden and J.C. Norcross (eds), *Eclecticism and Integration in Counselling and Psychotherapy*. Loughton: Gale Centre.

Orlinsky, D.E., Grawe, K. and Parks, B.K. (1994) Process and outcome in pyschotherapy – noch einmal. In A.E. Bergin and S.L. Garfield (eds), *Handbook of Psychotherapy and Behavior Change* (4th edn). New York: Wiley.

Poznanski, J.J. and McLennon, J. (1997) Theoretical orientation of Australian counselling psychologists. Unpublished paper. Victoria, Australia: School of Social and Behavioural Sciences, Swinburne University of Technology.

Skovholt, T.M. and Ronnestad, M.H. (1995) *The Evolving Professional Self*. Chichester: Wiley.

5.5 Integration   ○○○

IAN HORTON

Most counsellors and psychotherapists, including those who espouse pure form models, tend gradually to develop their own personalized conceptual systems and individual styles of working (Skovholt and Ronnestad, 1995). Although they may not necessarily describe themselves as integrative, many practitioners appear to assimilate explanatory concepts and techniques that can be attributed to more than one theoretical perspective (Poznanski and McLennon, 1997). Skovholt and Ronnestad's (1995) model of the evolving professional self demonstrates the widespread and often significant changes in beliefs about psychological change and the ingredients of optimal therapeutic practice that occur as practitioners develop through the 'exploration', 'integration', 'individuation' and 'integrity' post-training stages of their professional practice. In this sense it could be argued that integration is a personal process undertaken or instinctively evolved by individual therapists and that all therapists become to some degree, integrative practitioners. It is the view of some academics and researchers that 'pure form' approaches to practice exist only as a myth – a view that may be hotly contested by others. In this section the term 'integrative' is taken to subsume ideas of technical and systematic eclecticism. Any haphazard and arbitrary pick-and-mix approach to counselling and psychotherapy ideas and methods is not considered here. For a useful discussion of the different traditions within psychotherapy integration, see Feixas and Botella (2004). They distinguish among pragmatic, theoretically guided and systematically technical eclecticisms and differentiate between hybrid and extended models of theoretical integration and discuss the common factors perspective.

What is clear is that there is no one approach to integrative counselling or psychotherapy. Broadly speaking it is possible to identify two types of integration – fixed (or relatively stable) and open integrative – systems which seek to combine aspects developed originally within separate schools and approaches. For example, CAT (Cognitive Analytic Therapy) could be described as a fixed system in that it combines identifiable and specific aspects of cognitive and analytic models in a predetermined and explicit way. Relatively fixed systems such as CAT are perhaps destined to become the single or pure form approaches of tomorrow. Arguably models or approaches such as gestalt therapy and psychosynthesis could be described as fully integrative hybrids of ideas and techniques previously developed or which, at least partially, existed elsewhere, yet which have been combined and have been subsequently developed in such a way that in the resulting synthesis the components or influences have

virtually lost their original identity and a new and distinct model of counselling or psychotherapy has emerged.

The other type of integration is within a relatively open system, utilizing some kind of overarching framework or higher-order or trans-theoretical concept that provides internal consistency while at the same time allowing for the assimilation of explanatory concepts and/or methods from other schools or approaches. The core integrative framework or concept is fixed but allows the individual practitioner to develop gradually his or her own synthesis of ideas and practice. Examples of such open system approaches might include Egan's 'skilled helper' model and other generic skills models, Andrews' 'self-confirmation' model and Garfield's 'eclectic-integrative' approach.

Integration can occur at different levels, with varying degrees of overlap between and within the different elements of a model in what can be broadly categorized as theoretical and technical integration. Theoretical integration takes place between the more abstract levels of formal theory and basic or meta-theoretical assumptions whereas technical integration takes place primarily at the surface and more concrete levels of clinical theory and therapeutic operations. Arguably, high-level synthesis of any two or more models or part models of counselling or psychotherapy is only feasible to the extent that they share theoretical and meta-theoretical or basic assumptions. High-level integration can only take place between epistemologically compatible systems. However, the term high-level refers to the extent of structural integration possible between the deeper and more abstract elements of a model, rather than to the more limited degree of integration at a clinical procedural level. It should be clear that there is no evidence that high-level integration correlates with or can even be associated with the efficacy of clinical practice.

While there are some research findings supporting the effectiveness of some fixed type integrative models, such as CAT, there is little if any objective and empirical research to support the effectiveness of more open integrative systems. This is largely because of the methodological problems of measuring personal and individualized combinations of ideas and methods and the existence of factors that may account for psychological change and which are common to all or most approaches.

A comprehsive account of the historical development of counselling and psychotherapy integration (Hollanders, 2000), a detailed description of some current and diverse paradigms and a useful discussion of issues and debates can be found in Palmer and Woolfe (2000).

References

Feixas, G. and Botella, L. (2004) Psychotherapy integration: reflections and contributions from a constructivist epistemology. *Journal of Psychotherapy Integration,* 14 (2): 192–221.

Hollanders, H. (2000) Eclecticism/integrative historical developments. In S. Palmer and R. Woolfe (eds), *Integrative and Eclectic Counselling and Psychotherapy.* London: Sage.

Palmer, S. and Woolfe, R. (eds) (2000) *Integrative and Eclectic Counselling and Psychotherapy.* London: Sage.

Poznanski, J.J. and McLennon, J. (1997) Theoretical Orientation of Australian Counselling Psychologists. Unpublished paper. Victoria, Australia: School of Social and Behavioural Sciences, Swinburne University of Technology.

Skovholt, T.M. and Ronnestad, M.H. (1995) *The Evolving Professional Self.* Chichester: Wiley.

5.6 Approaches to Counselling and Psychotherapy: Introduction

COLIN FELTHAM AND IAN HORTON

Not only are there disagreements about the exact number of therapeutic approaches in existence, but also there are disputes about how these are best grouped. In this part of the book 23 different schools of therapy are presented in summary form. The intention has been to include a representative selection of the currently more mainstream or influential approaches. Obviously the allegedly 400 and more approaches in existence today cannot all be included. However, it has been customary to organize approaches (also often known as theoretical orientations, models, schools or brand names) according to their affiliation with the three main traditions of psychoanalytic, humanistic, and cognitive-behavioural therapy. This convention has been utilized and extended here by adding an eclectic-integrative

heading, honouring the recency and trans-theoretical identity of certain approaches. Under each approach heading, alphabetical rather than chronological order has been adopted.

Even so, we are aware that some adherents may dispute the location of their approach in the present schema and, in addition, some may feel strongly about the absence of what has sometimes been called the 'fourth force', multicultural counselling and therapy (MCT). This is understood here not as a separate or distinct category, or group, but as a theme that should permeate and enrich the psychodynamic, cognitive-behavioural, existential-humanistic and eclectic-integrative approaches by focusing on issues of culture, ethnicity/race, gender, sexuality, disability, class and other factors.

Writers for each approach have been asked to give a brief history, followed by a succinct account of the basic assumptions, explanation of origins and maintenance of problems (mechanisms of), change, skills and strategies, and any research indications, pertinent to the approach. While even this schema, with these headings, is not found conducive by all, we hope this is a useful way of organizing and condensing a considerable amount of material in a way that facilitates comparison.

It may be useful to have a sense of the historical context of each school of therapy in order to weigh up the influences upon it and perhaps to understand how well it has endured and in what socio-cultural milieu it best operates. Every approach has some, often implicit, basic assumptions which should be understood. Possibly of more theoretical interest to many therapists is how exponents of an approach explain causes or origins of individual humans' psychological problems in living, and how these problems (or concerns, issues, or disorders) persist in time. Of most clinical interest are explanations about personal change and how therapists' approach-specific skills and strategies help to effect desired changes in clients' lives. Here it should be noted that these very brief introductions to each approach are just that: there is no claim or pretence that these provide therapeutic instructions or clinical skills in a nutshell, and recommended texts should be studied by any reader wishing to gain further in-depth knowledge. Finally, any specific research relating to each approach has been highlighted, although again there are obviously major differences between approaches about valid research methodologies.

The brevity of these descriptions is acknowledged, and this is very much an overview intended to demonstrate the distinctiveness of different approaches, their key characteristics, and to show collectively the diversity of the field. Counselling and psychotherapy literature found elsewhere already abundantly represents the different schools of therapy. Obviously readers may adopt a 'magpie' strategy of surveying the particular attractions of these approaches. Alternatively, we might commend a reasonably systematic reading of follow-up texts towards becoming an informed student of comparative counselling and psychotherapy. To this end, the following kinds of questions may usefully be asked of these approaches, probably in conjunction with further detailed readings:

- Exactly how was each one discovered and/or constructed?
- On what kinds of knowledge, experience and methodology does it draw?
- Why do creators, developers and affiliates of therapeutic traditions have different assumptions, interpretations of distress, change and effectiveness?
- In what ways can these approaches be judged as significantly similar to or different from each other?
- What indications are there that they are philosophically defensible, empirically testable, and effective for clients in general, and/or for specific kinds of presenting problems or goals?
- To what extent is this theoretical and institutional diversity helpful or unhelpful, and will such differences persist, or reduce as therapies become more integrated?

PART V
Theory and Approaches

PSYCHODYNAMIC APPROACHES

5.7 Adlerian Therapy
(Alfred Adler, 1870–1937)

○○○

JENNY WARNER

Brief history

Adlerian therapy has grown from the ideas and practice of Alfred Adler, a Viennese psychiatrist and contemporary of Freud. In 1911 Adler left the Viennese Psychoanalytical Society, after a disagreement with Freud, formed his own school of psychology called Individual Psychology, and fellow doctors used his approach; they were particularly interested in people with hysterical disorders who had physical symptoms which were caused by psychological difficulties. After the First World War Adler returned to Vienna and changed his focus of attention to prevention of mental ill health and to education. He worked with teachers and pupils in open sessions to enable as many people as possible to learn his approach. He gave lectures at the People's Institute, the equivalent of evening classes in our time. He wanted people to understand themselves and each other better so that society could be more harmonious and each person could reach his or her potential and make the fullest contribution possible. Adler was Jewish and had to emigrate to New York in 1934. After his death another Adlerian psychiatrist, Rudolf Dreikurs, went to America and eventually started Adlerian therapy training, teacher training and parent education. There are Adlerian Institutes throughout the world with mainstream university training in many countries. The Adlerian approach of establishing democratic relationships is used in all forms of counselling and psychotherapy and in management training as well as teacher and parent education.

Basic assumptions

- *Holistic* – Adler was one of the first to recognize holism in people. The *individual* of Individual Psychology is a poor translation and means 'indivisible'. The client's consistent overriding pattern of behaviour, goals, thoughts and emotions must be viewed as a whole. Adlerians refer to this as the lifestyle.
- *Social* – people develop their personalities in social groups, in the first four or five years of life, and their behaviour can be viewed in relation to the group. All human beings are social in order for the human race to survive and the focus in therapy is to understand the nature of their belonging.
- *Goal-directed* – all behaviour has a purpose and a goal. Clients' goals are identified and the purposes of their behaviour revealed. Clients are not usually aware of what their goals are, nor of the ideas and beliefs that underpin their movement through life.
- *Belonging* – most people feel inferior and strive to be superior in order to belong. Adler considered that everyone is born with the potential to belong as a social equal and he used the term *gemeinschaftsgefuhl* to describe this; he preferred the translation of social interest although the concept also includes a feeling of belonging or community. Dreikurs showed how parenting and education can nurture social interest. Therapy identifies the discouraging beliefs that clients have that prevent them from realizing their full potentials as equal human beings.
- *Creative and responsible* – we create our own personalities or lifestyles by the time we are 5 years old through trial and error and are very much influenced by our siblings. Our behaviour is the result of our own subjective perceptions. Our beliefs which underpin our unconscious goals are called our private logic;

the ideas make sense to us but are not necessarily common sense. We are responsible for our goals, behaviour, beliefs and feelings and therefore it is in our power to change if we should wish to do so.

- *Unique* – in order to understand people we must look at their own unique subjective view of life and themselves and the decisions they have made about their movement through life.

Origin and maintenance of problems

Although people are born with the potential to feel they belong as equal human beings, frequently this potential is not nurtured by their early experiences. We live in a mistake-centred society where mistakes are commented upon, disruptive behaviour is responded to, competition is encouraged and personal self-esteem is considered more important than contribution to the task in hand. We all have different degrees of inferiority feelings. Young children are dependent for many years and parents can increase this dependency by doing things for them that they can do for themselves; this pampering is the most disabling form of parenting (Sonstegard, n.d.) and it is rife in modern society. Children feel incapable and fearful of making decisions and if the pampering continues into teenage years they will very likely make some bad decisions. They will develop feelings of inferiority and believe that they will always need others to help them through life. Some parents will spoil their children, giving them what they want, so that they develop a mistaken idea that they can always have what they want. School can be a rude awakening for such children – a spoiled child and a spoiled adult can be very unpopular. Many children refuse to accept their parents' authority. Parents can respond to this in different ways either by giving in to the child so he or she gains power over them, or by punishing the child into submission. A punished child may feel hurt and seek revenge. In order to hurt their parents they may also hurt themselves, so failure at school, anti-social or even criminal behaviour, drug taking, or teenage pregnancy may be revenge-seeking behaviours.

Inferiority feelings are uncomfortable and people compensate for these feelings by striving for superiority; their goals involve elevated self-esteem and feeling better than others. This would involve putting others down. This attitude towards one's siblings, schoolmates, work colleagues and intimate partners causes social and relationship problems. People are engaged in power plays and competition and their concern is their personal status in the group rather than co-operating and contributing to it. This will lead to distancing from other people and/or a lack of intimacy and spontaneity. Goals of superiority are often unattainable and that causes discomfort so the person will develop alibis to justify why the goal is not achieved. Adler recognized neurotic behaviour in people, such as developing illnesses or disabilities or making excuses for not achieving their over-ambitious goals.

Change

Therapists need to establish a relationship of equality with their clients and work with them to uncover their mistaken ideas or private logic, and their unrealistic goals. It is then the client's choice whether to make changes or not. The therapist will also show clients that they are responsible for their own behaviour and their decisions to change or not to change. If clients embark upon reorientation then the therapist encourages them by showing them how to focus on their strengths and what they appreciate about themselves. New behaviours may be successful and this could change the person's beliefs. Therapy enables people to develop a new flexibility so they have a variety of responses available to them.

Some clients will resist change and it is up to the therapist to show them that they are trusted with their own destiny. This democratic co-operative relationship may be the first such experience for some clients where they are afforded equal rights, equal respect and equal responsibility.

Clients gain insight and become aware of their beliefs and ideas and the goals of their behaviour and they are shown how their presenting problems have occurred due to their view of life and habitual pattern of responding. Once the goals are revealed clients can no longer pursue them with such energy.

The next stage of the process is reorientation. At this point the therapist and client need to agree on mutual therapy goals. This usually involves changes in behaviour. The therapist must ensure that clients want to change their personal goals and ideas, and, if they do, to what extent. It takes time for the client to consciously own ideas, beliefs and goals that have been unconscious for many years. Insight will occur first after the behaviour has taken place, then during the behaviour, and lastly before the behaviour. When the awareness occurs before the behaviour, clients have an opportunity to behave in a different way. Assignments can be set which challenge the old private logic, so clients agree to do something they do not usually do or have never done. Clients report back to the therapist or group. They may feel very pleased that they have achieved something new or they may feel the experience was not good and it merely confirms that they should never have done it in the first place. The therapist will now be looking towards the life tasks and the client's presenting problems. Full participation in the three life tasks of occupation, social life and an intimate relationship, as an equal who is able to contribute and co-operate, was considered by Adler to be the measure of a mentally healthy person. Non-participation in one of these tasks, or overtime spent in one at the expense of the others, was considered unhealthy and an avoidance of one's obligation to the human race.

Nowadays Adlerians take a more flexible attitude towards the life task of occupation as it is not possible or necessary from the point of view of the human race for everyone to have paid employment. It is no longer considered necessary for everyone to be engaged in heterosexual marriage and producing a family for the human race to survive, so single parents and homosexual and bisexual relationships are not considered mentally unhealthy. The social life task permeates all of life and the other life tasks and requires that people should get on with their fellow human beings and co-operate and contribute. The therapist and client explore the client's participation in the life tasks. Assignments might be set to enable clients to start to participate in work, friendships or more intimate relationships if they agree they would like to make changes in these parts of their lives.

The client is taught the art of encouragement. Most people are discouraged to some extent, feeling bad about mistakes and expecting more to come, and dwelling on their failings. Most people have unrealistic goals which are a constant source of discouragement because they are never attained. Clients are taught to focus on strengths and regard mistakes as an opportunity to learn rather than evidence of failings. Mistakes are seen as just part of normal human experience. Once clients become more encouraged they are able to encourage others, thus creating a more optimistic yet realistic environment, which will further enhance the encouragement process. This encouragement can be especially powerful in group sessions. Realistic, attainable goals and a more flexible attitude towards life will enable clients to feel good about their achievements and worth. As their feelings of inferiority diminish and their social interest increases, they feel equal to their fellows and willing to co-operate and make their contribution.

Skills and strategies

- *Equality* – The therapist establishes a relationship of mutual respect in which clients are accepted and not judged. Clients are listened to carefully in order to understand their unique point of view. The therapist will also want respect from the client and will not accept disrespectful behaviour; for instance, it will be expected that mutual agreements are kept.
- *Establishing a democratic relationship with the client* is a skill that develops through the therapist's own self-awareness. Adlerian therapists take an active role and it is easy to lapse into a power relationship with the client. Therapists may feel that they know what is best for the client but they must trust clients to make their own decisions. If a relationship of mutual respect cannot be established and continued throughout the sessions, then they must be terminated.
- *Lifestyle assessment* – in order to understand the client a lifestyle assessment can be carried out. Information is gathered about the client and his or her presenting concerns and how the client is participating in the three life tasks. Then the therapist will want to elicit the client's situation as a child; this is

where personality or lifestyle are formed. The therapist will want to establish how clients interpret their childhood position in the family and how they decided to become the sort of people they are. Interpretations of the client's early memories are then explored with the client. The therapist is looking for a consistent pattern or theme.

- *Analysing early memories* is a skill which also grows as therapists develop their own self-awareness. Therapists need to put their own interpretations and attitudes on hold so that they can truly empathize with clients and see with their eyes. Each hypothesized guess will have to be checked out with the client and this is where the therapist needs to be sensitive to the client's reactions to their guesses. Experienced therapists see clearly the moments of insight as the client reacts non-verbally or verbally to acknowledge a new insight. Dreams can also be analysed or interpreted with the client. Dreams and early memories contain symbolic messages about the client's basic view of self or the world or of other people or of how he or she should move through life. The client's own unique and creative symbolic thought must be understood. The client's unconscious belief system is explored and hypotheses are put to the client for verification.
- *Mutually agreed assignments* are set that challenge the client's private logic.

Also used are:

- *Mirror technique* – where the therapist points out the recurring patterns of behaviour as the client pursues the same goals.
- *Paradoxical intention* – which involves encouraging the client to intensify the mistaken behaviour or develop the symptom more. The client may then stop resisting change and see the sense in making a change.

Research evidence

Adler was a practical man rather than an academic and many of his books are translations of lectures he gave to large audiences. Adlerian therapists endorse their practical approaches, and academic evaluation is carried out in university departments in the USA and Europe where many aspects of Adler's theory of personality and his practical approaches are validated by small studies. Family constellation and the effects of psychological birth order, the technique of analysing early memories as a projective technique and measurement of lifestyle themes have been investigated and numerous studies on the effectiveness of encouragement by teachers and parents and the positive effects of co-operation in the classroom and the benefits of democratic parenting have been conducted (Dinkmeyer et al., 1987; Sweeney, 1989).

References

Dinkmeyer, D., Dinkmeyer, D.C. and Sperry, L. (1987) *Adlerian Counseling and Psychotherapy*. Columbus, OH: Merrill Publishing Company.

Sonstegard, M. (n.d.) *Creating Harmony in the Family*. Aylesbury: Adlerian Workshops and Publications.

Sweeney, T. (1989) *Adlerian Counseling*. Muncie, IN: Accelerated Development Inc.

Recommended reading

Adler, A. (1927) *Understanding Human Nature*. Trans. Colin Brett (1992). Oxford: Oneworld Publications.

Adler, A. (1931) *What Life Could Mean to You*. Trans. Colin Brett (1992). Oxford: Oneworld Publications.

5.8 Analytical Psychology
(Carl Gustav Jung, 1875–1961)

JOY SCHAVERIEN

Brief history

Analytical Psychology was the term given by C.G. Jung to the form of depth psychology which is now also known as Jungian analysis or psychotherapy. The term counselling is not usually used in this context. Jung was the son of a Swiss pastor. He studied natural science and medicine at the University of Basel and then became a psychiatrist. He worked for nine years from 1900 to 1909 at the Burgholzli psychiatric clinic in Zurich as assistant to the well-known psychiatrist Eugen Blueler. It was here in his work with patients suffering from psychotic illnesses (in those days called Dementia Praecox) that his lifelong interest in the psyche began. In 1900, he read Freud's *Interpretation of Dreams* and recognized in it an affinity with his own areas of interest. They met in 1906 and the interchange between them was very creative. At that time Freud's patients were mainly neurotic, while Jung worked with inpatients who were suffering from psychotic illnesses. Although this later changed, it may be that this contributed to his understanding of the more disturbed aspects of the personality. In 1914 irreconcilable differences emerged which led to the end of their close association.

This break was a personal blow to both of them and Jung's psychological crisis, which led to his self-analysis, occurred at this time. It is clear from *Memories, Dreams, Reflections* (Jung, 1963) that dreams and art had played a major part in his childhood. However, it was in this period that much of his conviction in the innate potential of the psyche to heal itself – given the right conditions – was established.

Jung travelled widely and was influenced by Eastern philosophies. He writes that it was only after he had developed his theory of individuation that he discovered that he had been 'unconsciously led along that secret way which has been the preoccupation of the best minds of the East for centuries' (Jung and Wilhelm, 1931: 86). This aspect of his work has sometimes led to the view that Jung is a mystic or that his psychology is semi-religious. There are those who are attracted to his work because of this and others who dismiss it for the same reason. However, to take too fixed a view of this one aspect of his work is to miss the complexity of his immense and original contribution to psychotherapy and particularly its applicability for clinical practice.

Jung founded the C.G. Jung Institute in Zurich and there is now an International Association for Analytical Psychologists with member organizations in many different parts of the world. In Britain there are four different societies affiliated to the IAAP. The Society of Analytical Psychology is the oldest of these; it was formed in 1946, by Michael Fordham and Gerhard Adler. Later Adler formed a breakaway group, the Association of Jungian Analysts. There are also the Independent Group of Analytical Psychologists, and the British Association of Psychotherapists Jungian Section. These societies reflect the history of some of the theoretical differences within analytical psychology in Britain. In part these differences are evident in the number of times a week clients are seen. Certain Jungian analysts work rather like psychoanalysts, seeing clients four or five times a week, considering that it is only then that the core self can be mediated. Others see their clients once or twice a week. This may reflect a personal preference, the needs of the client, or the training of the analyst.

In the USA a group of analytical psychologists called the 'archetypal psychologists' have developed Jung's ideas with particular attention to the healing potential of the imaginal world: dreams, myth, art and culture. James Hillman (1978) is their main exponent.

Basic assumptions

The central tenet of analytical psychology is *individuation*. This is the idea that the personality can realize its potential through the development of a symbolic attitude. In therapy, split off and disowned aspects of the personality may be differentiated and a conscious attitude to them attained. Jung made a distinction between the *personal* and the *collective unconscious*.

The *collective unconscious* is the source of consciousness. This is a layer of the psyche which underlies the personal unconscious. It is sometimes likened to geological strata where, as one layer is revealed, it is discovered to be founded on another. The collective unconscious is the deepest and least accessible of these layers. Jung considers that this collective unconscious can never be fully known and suggests that all we can hope for is to attain a conscious attitude in relation to it. The assumption is that all human beings are, at some fundamental level, linked to each other, not separated but related. This has been developed in relation to theories of the cultural unconscious and has an influence when working with groups as well as with individuals.

The collective unconscious is expressed through *archetypes*. These are recurring instinctual patterns which have no form in their own right: they are not tangible, or visible, but rather sense perceptions. They are the underlying patterns from which images take form in dreams, myth and art. Archetypes are often attributed with human form and characterized by figures, such as the 'hero' and the 'great mother'. They may manifest themselves in generational aspects of the personality, such as 'senex', where a young person may have an elderly outlook on life, or 'puer', the Peter Pan character who does not grow up.

Psychological types – The terms introvert and extrovert are commonly used but many people are unaware that Jung was the originator of them. The introvert is a person in whom inner-world reflection is a dominant mode of being, while the extrovert is more attuned to the outer world. There are different psychological types and, although aspects are present in some form in all of us, one or other may be dominant. Thus some people are predominantly feeling types, while others are sensation or thinking types.

The psyche is made up of *opposites*; that is to say, any conscious attitude is compensated by an unconscious one. This is a dynamic force in the psyche that Jung likens to the first law of thermodynamics. It is an energetic principle which is a precondition of all psychic life.

The shadow is the unconscious aspect of the psyche. It is the negative, unwanted or rejected aspect of the personality. It is based on the idea that any substantial object casts a shadow (Samuels et al., 1986) and may be understood as a metaphor for the psyche. Thus conscious elements cast an unconscious shadow and may result in unconscious acts or in attribution of the split-off element into an 'other', who may then be blamed.

Anima and animus attribute gendered status to the opposites. The psychological manifestation of these opposites may take embodied form. Very often in dreams or fantasies the desired other is seen in the guise of an idealized figure – a lover, for example. The anima is often regarded as the soul image.

The persona is the public face – the one that the person presents to the world. Sometimes this may be experienced as a mask.

The self – the centre of being – is the innermost core. It is a unifying principle within the human psyche. The self is understood as an integral aspect of being but its realization is also considered the goal of therapy.

Origin and maintenance of problems

Split-off or denied aspects of the personality remain unconscious. There may be unconscious compensation, which results in limitations in the personality. For example a person may be over-controlled, in unconscious denial of aggression. This may result in psychological distress. The aim in therapy is to bring the split-off elements to consciousness.

The main areas of theoretical disagreement between Jung and Freud were based on their views regarding the aetiology of sexuality and the unconscious. While Freud attributed much of the disturbance in adult life to infantile sexuality, Jung was inclined to see sexuality in a more positive light. He considered that the purpose of eros and regression in the transference, for example, was a need for a temporary return to a previous state, from which to grow forward. Thus the absence of eros might be considered to be the problem rather than its presence.

The personal unconscious is the product of an interaction between the collective unconscious and the environment. The personal unconscious is composed of complexes and, while Freud thought complexes involved only illness, Jung saw them as part of the healthy mind (Stevens, 1990: 31).

Psychotic areas of the personality are considered to be an integral part of normal development which may be contacted in the process of analysis.

Change

The individuation process comes about through the emergence of consciousness of the disparate elements in the psyche. This leads to a gradual separation, differentiation and autonomy.

Psychological transformation may be a result of acknowledgement and subsequent integration of previously unconscious material.

Transference and counter-transference are central elements and Jung elucidated this through an alchemical text which he discovered. Jung realized that *The Rosarium Philosophorum* (Jung, 1946) was applicable as a metaphor for the individuation process as experienced in the transference and counter-transference. He considered that the analytic journey was rather like the alchemist's quest. The alchemist mixes different chemicals in a vessel where they come together and are transformed by their union into something new – in this case – gold.

Jung applied this as a metaphor for the analyst and analysand engaged in the therapeutic relationship. Here it is psychological elements of both which meet and mix and a new aspect of the personality develops out of the union. Sometimes both are changed through the experience.

Skills and strategies

- *Active imagination* is achieved through dreams, art and associations which lead the client into contact with the depths of her or his unconscious. The aim is to become familiar with these, to observe the contents and so integrate them with consciousness.
- The *transcendent function* is understood to be one means of mediating between conscious and unconscious and between the 'opposites'. Often the recounting of dreams or the bringing of pictures may mediate in this way.
- Jung painted as part of his own individuation process and found that he was making circular forms similar to the mandalas which he had witnessed being made as a meditation in India. He realized that the psyche spontaneously finds such imagery when it needs to organize chaotic elements. He encouraged his clients to paint 'to escape the censor of the conscious mind' (Jung and Wilhelm, 1931), but he emphasized that this cannot be achieved by asking a client to make a mandala picture. Such imagery is only useful if arrived at spontaneously.

Research evidence

Jung regarded empirical data as integrally linked with the personality of the researcher. Thus his own life's work was indivisible from his life and research (Stevens, 1990).

Research in analytical psychology has led to major developments in understanding. Fordham (1976) became interested in infant observation. The studies, which he conducted in association with the Tavistock Institute in London led to a significant contribution to understanding of child development. He combined his observations with Jung's view of the self as a central organizing principle of the psyche. Fordham realized that the infant is not merely a mass of undifferentiated sensations, which are organized and contained by the mother. Rather, he noticed that the mother responds to the demands of her infant. This is a relationship that is present from the very beginning. The infant when awake de-integrates; that is, relates to the environment and generates responses from it. Then in sleep it integrates, that is, returns to its 'self'. This presumes that the self is the core of being which is present from the earliest moments of life.

The first chair in Analytical Psychology was founded in Dallas, USA, at the Texas A&M University. In Britain, the first chair in Analytical Psychology was created in 1995, jointly founded by the Society of Analytical Psychology and the University of Essex. This has led to the development of research programmes in Analytical Psychology at Masters and PhD levels.

References

Fordham, M. (1976) *The Self and Autism*. Library of Analytical Psychology, vol. 3. London: Heinemann Medical Books.

Hillman, J. (1978) *The Myth of Analysis: Three Essays in Archetypal Psychology*. New York: Harper Torch.

Jung, C.G. (1946) *The Psychology of the Transference*, *Collected Works* 16. London: Routledge and Kegan Paul.

Jung, C.G. (1963) *Memories, Dreams, Reflections*. London: Fontana.

Jung, C.G. and Wilhelm, R. (1931) *The Secret of the Golden Flower*. London: Routledge and Kegan Paul.

McGuire, W. (1979) *The Freud/Jung Letters*. London: Picador.

Samuels, A., Shorter, B. and Plaut, F. (1986) *A Critical Dictionary of Jungian Analysis*. London and New York: Routledge.

Schaverien, J. (1991) *The Revealing Image: Analytical Art Psychotherapy in Theory and Practice*. London and New York: Tavistock/Routledge.

Schaverien, J. (1995) *Desire and the Female Therapist: Engendered Gazes in Psychotherapy and Art Therapy*. London and New York: Routledge.

Stevens, A. (1990) *On Jung*. London and New York: Routledge.

Recommended reading

Fordham, M. (1978) *Jungian Psychotherapy: A Study in Analytical Psychology*. Chichester: John Wiley.

Samuels, A. (1985) *Jung and the Post Jungians*. London and New York: Routledge.

5.9 Psychoanalytic Therapy (Sigmund Freud, 1856–1939)

MEG ERRINGTON AND LESLEY MURDIN

Brief history

In the 1880s and 1890s Sigmund Freud, a Viennese neurologist, discovered that he could relieve many of his patients of debilitating hysterical symptoms, if they could be helped to recall and to talk about painful childhood experiences. Freud listened to their dreams and encouraged them to talk about whatever came into their minds, and from this he developed the principles of psychoanalysis – the talking cure. He was struck by the extent to which patients were preoccupied with thoughts and feelings of a sexual nature and concluded that their difficulties often derived from sexual frustration.

Freud's ideas outraged many of his contemporaries. Nonetheless, he continued to apply his methodology as scientifically as possible, developing and testing out hypotheses with his patients, leaving behind his research in the 20 volumes of his writings known as 'The Standard Edition'. He succeeded in attracting many influential followers as well as critics. Arguably most of the current models of counselling and psychotherapy have been inspired either by the work of Freud or by a reaction against his ideas. His observations have influenced the world, not only extending the range of psychoanalysis but proving influential in the related fields of education and social work and infiltrating into literary and cultural theory and the media. W.H. Auden, in a poem about Freud written in the 1940s, describes how he has become 'a whole climate of opinion'. Those most faithful to a strictly Freudian legacy include writers as diverse as Eric Berne and Jacques Lacan.

Basic assumptions

The unconscious mind – a part of our mind which is always a mystery to us. It can be revealed through dreams, slips of the tongue, and the gaps in speech that indicate some hidden force that determines our feelings and behaviour.

Developmental stages – connected to the erotogenic zones – the mouth, the anus, and the genitals. Bodily and emotional needs converge at these zones. If needs are not met in a satisfactory way or if the individual's conscience or superego cannot deal with impulses and drives to love and to hate, then complex character traits emerge connected to each stage – greed at the oral stage or hoarding and sadism from the anal stage, for example. The way the mind works influences development just as much as development influences the way the mind works.

Conflict – throughout life we struggle with our impulses and drives, pushed and pulled between love and hate. These concepts are rich in meaning, synonymous with growth and stagnation, eventually with life and death itself – the mighty Eros pitted against the equally mighty Thanatos.

Structure – the prevailing Freudian metaphor is that of the brain/mind as an electrical transmitter sending out units of energy round a circuit. From birth, experiences of pleasure and pain are charged with significance and have repercussions on our development. The unconscious mind has no concept of negation or limit. Overcharged experiences which threaten to overwhelm the psyche are not allowed into consciousness unless they are attached to something more tolerable and less anxiety provoking. The unconscious mind changes and represses intolerable ideas, although they return usually in the form of symptoms.

Libido – a sexual energy which undergoes vicissitudes throughout development. First it is invested in ourselves and our own bodies. We begin life as narcissistic and in love with ourselves. Our development as moral and healthily functioning individuals depends on our relinquishing this self-love and on our ability to move on and to relate to others.

The Oedipus Complex – the nucleus of every neurosis and the backbone of the orthodox Freudian approach. It derives from the genital stage and leads to the capacity to love and to enjoy healthy sexual relations. As in the Greek myth, Oedipus had to confront his desire to marry his mother and to kill his father, so as individuals we cannot avoid the awareness of our desire for sexual union with our opposite-sex parent or the dilemma of harbouring death wishes towards our same-sex parental rival. The little girl has to come to terms with her intense envy of the male penis and little boy with his fear that father will retaliate against him and castrate him. Health comes at great cost to the individual. Controversially, Freud came to believe that many patients phantasized that they had sexual relations with parents, like children telling fairy tales, but that this had rarely actually happened.

Origins and maintenance of problems

- *Conflict* – Freud saw the origin of neurosis as stemming from conflict – between the individual and the world and within the various strata of the individual mind. Freud's final model of the mind – the Structural Model – divides up the mind into an 'I', an 'Above I', and an 'It'. In the English translation of Freud's texts these terms become 'Ego', 'Superego' and 'Id' (terms frequently criticized for being depersonalized and soulless). The I or ego is charged with imposing the demands of the real world on the pleasure-seeking id. The id is amoral. The superego is supermoral. We struggle as divided selves to preserve our integrity in the face of overwhelming amoral and subversive forces within us. Conflict is the pervasive character of mental life since instinctual drives are incompatible with the moral, ethical and social side of the personality. Humans are instinctual beings, the achievement of pleasure through the expression of instincts being the aim of all life. This animal nature puts us at loggerheads with ourselves and the whole world.
- *Anxiety* – is a signal of impending danger. It is also a signal of conflict. The unconscious mind is a storehouse of wishful impulses in opposition to the world of order. Unacceptable impulses towards sexuality and aggression hold sway over what we usually perceive to be the central elements of our personality. These unacceptable impulses of love and hate are repressed by the mind and turned into anxiety. We strive to master this anxiety through the unconscious production of symptoms.
- *Trauma* – overwhelming anxiety is experienced as trauma, rendering the individual helpless. Throughout life we repeat unresolved trauma in the hope of resolving feelings of helplessness once and for all.
- *Developmental obstacles* – the strength of instinctual demands at any stage can lead to difficulty in moving on to the next stage.
- *Defences* – counter-productive defensive measures (e.g. denial, displacement, projection, repression) may be taken by the ego in order to protect the individual from experiencing the pain of self-knowledge.
- *Domination* – a part of the psyche such as the superego may be too powerful, leading to anxiety and attempts to escape. If the unconscious overwhelms the ego, the result may be what is known as a 'borderline' state or full-blown psychosis.

Change

- *Consciousness* – Freud's aim was always for the individual to gain greater self-knowledge, to make the unconscious conscious. Consciousness does not automatically bring about change but it helps to locate the areas of conflict and developmental arrest.
- *Transference* – in the therapy situation past trauma is unconsciously repeated or transferred into the present, often onto the therapist as a symbolic parent figure. This is a supremely creative and mutative moment when the past can be reconstructed or explored in depth. Above all, past trauma is re-experienced in the present, unearthing hidden feelings and liberating creative potential for new resolutions to difficulties and the prospect of taking greater responsibility for actions.
- *Interpretation* – change is brought about when repression is lifted. Timely interpretation that links the transferred elements from the infantile trauma with the present relationship with the therapist may enable the client to let go of some defences.
- *Reliability* – models that emphasize development will expect most improvement to come from the experience of a relationship with the therapist that is more austere and less retaliatory than the experience in the past.

Skills and strategies

- *Free association* – in sessions is encouraged. That is, the client is to say anything which comes to mind, and to talk about any dreams. The therapist maintains a state of reverie, making links between associations and waiting for signs of repression shown through hesitation or resistance to ideas or the person of the therapist. Such inhibitions or blockages indicate the existence of psychological conflict just as symptoms do or general unhappiness or the inability to relate well to people. The aim is to help clients gain knowledge of their unconscious.
- *Evenly hovering attention* – the therapist must pay attention to the conscious material and to what is not said. The therapist must use counter-transference, or his or her internal response to the client's repetition of the past in the present.
- *Depth and intensity* – work that seeks to identify unconscious processes through the relationship with a therapist needs usually to be of several years' duration

and benefits from the intensity of sessions that are at least once per week and frequently more often.

- *Basic facilitation skills* – linking, empathy.
- *Interpretation* – most therapists use a version of Malan's model of the triangle of defence and the triangle of transference (Malan, 1979). The three points of the triangle of defence are the pain, the anxiety that it causes and the defence against it. The triangle of transference has the three points of the past relationship, the present relationship outside the therapy and the relationship that develops with the therapist. Interpretations link two or more points of a triangle.
- *Boundaries* – of time, place, fees and the absence of gratification, for example in physical contact or direct answers to questions, are carefully maintained.
- *Blank screen* – it is no longer thought to be possible or desirable for therapists to be merely receptors but they will try to minimize their own interference in what happens in order to allow transference to appear as clearly as possible. Self-disclosure is minimal.

Research evidence

- *Outcome research* – this is notoriously difficult and studies have not shown a differential advantage for any one model (see Elton Wilson and Barkham, 1994). On the other hand, this model can claim results that are as good as any other.

- *Testability* – there is an inherent difficulty in testing outcomes and effectiveness for a model of therapy which is not known. The client and the therapist are both limited to what is conscious. For a discussion of this problem and its corresponding value for therapeutic work see Gellner's chapter and Frosh's rebuttal in Dryden and Feltham (1992).

References

Dryden, W. and Feltham, C. (eds) (1992) *Pyschotherapy and Its Discontents*. Buckingham: Open University Press.

Elton Wilson, J. and Barkham, M. (1994) A practitioner-scientist approach to psychotherapy process and outcome research. In P. Clarkson and M. Pokorny (eds), *The Handbook of Psychotherapy*. London: Routledge.

Malan, D. (1979) *Individual Psychotherapy and the Science of Psychodynamics*. London: Butterworth.

Recommended reading

Bettelheim, B. (1983) *Freud and Man's Soul*. London: Chatto and Windus.

Jacobs, M. (1988) *The Presenting Past* (revised edn). London: Butterworth.

5.10 Psychodynamic Therapy
(Melanie Klein, 1882–1960)

○○○

JULIA SEGAL

Brief history

Psychoanalysis provides the basic understanding underlying insight-based counselling and psychotherapy.

Melanie Klein was a psychoanalyst who came to England in 1926 from Vienna via Berlin. Her insights were deeply controversial at first but have gradually become more accepted, with Kleinian analysts receiving world recognition. Segal (1992) describes this in more detail.

Kleinian pychodynamic therapists and counsellors recognize and use the insights of Kleinian analysts while modifying their techniques to fit the different requirements of their particular settings.

Klein developed a new language with which to talk about ways we think, feel and behave; and about ideas, assumptions and beliefs people hold about themselves and others. Her discovery that babies and infants are active participants in relationships with their mothers and others around them, having both feelings and awareness, was contrary to opinion of the time. Kleinian ideas can seem strange to begin with, but bring new possibilities for understanding and new relief from anxieties.

Basic assumptions

Emotional understanding is a powerful tool. An understanding relationship can allow an individual to develop their capacities to feel, to think, to understand themselves and others better.

Facing feared reality, working through the associated feelings and fantasies and grieving for real losses brings long-term reduction in anxiety. Any kind of illusion or defence is maintained by and maintains anxiety.

People often hide their own emotions from themselves; for example, someone may light up a cigarette to prevent themselves feeling angry. Exploring emotions which are kept out of conscious awareness brings new understanding of the self in relation to others.

Difficulties in relationships with caregivers (involving accepting food and other necessities, taking in and learning, for example), underlie many problems both in the past and in the present. They manifest themselves not only in relationship difficulties, but also in disturbances in the individual's relationship with themselves. (The emphasis on relations with others makes Kleinian theory an Object Relations theory.)

The understanding of the counsellor or therapist includes the capacity to face unpleasant, destructive,

shameful feelings as well as deeply loving ones, in themselves as well as in the client. Their training should ensure that they have experienced the pains as well as the pleasures of a relationship with a therapist and that they have no sense of superiority towards their clients.

However, no relationship with a therapist or counsellor is truly one of equals. The therapist offers something which the client supposedly wants. This relationship therefore has the potential to arouse emotions such as hope, longing, desire, rivalry, envy, fear of loss, anger and aggressiveness; in therapy some of these can be understood and the associated behaviour, fears, attitudes and beliefs explored. The client's relationship with the therapist provides an opportunity to reassess the client's feelings and behaviour in connection with being cared for in the past. This can improve relations with others and with the self in the present.

The therapist's help in thinking directly about relationships with others and the self may also bring considerable relief.

The idea that we can envy and even hate those who give us what we want is particularly controversial, and distinguishes Kleinian theory from some others. These feelings manifest themselves in various forms of attack on those we love or need. We may denigrate them; or idealize them to make them useless to us; or dismiss what they say or offer, for example. Kleinian therapy involves paying close attention to such attacks by the client on the joint work of the client and therapist.

Kleinians also believe that we very much want to 'make reparation'; to repair damage which we feel we have caused by such attacks.

Origin and maintenance of problems

Our understanding of the world around us, and of ourselves in relation to it, grows with us. What Klein called 'phantasies' (Segal, 1981; Segal, 1995) are formed. To understand this concept, think of the way babies gradually begin to recognize people. Some kind of picture or model or 'phantasy' is formed. These phantasies are dynamic; they change and develop as the people around come and go and interact with each other. When the baby is happy, their phantasies of their world, including the people in it, are happy, loving ones; when the baby is feeling bad in some way, the phantasies may be frightening, disturbing ones.

Phantasies are unconscious constructions; we are not aware of our own contribution to our perceptions; we just see things that way. As a small child we may just *know* our father can do everything; as a teenager we may simply see him as the greatest fool in the world. One adult just knows the world is a friendly place; another lives in constant fear of attack.

As we grow up we generally begin to see those around more realistically. Phantasies we have of other people include characteristics derived from our knowledge and experience of ourselves; so a child who is missing a parent may believe that the absent parent is sad, for example; if the child is angry with the parent for being away, they may believe the parent is angry with them. A teenager afraid of embarrassing themselves may see a parent as embarrassing.

Problems can arise if very infantile phantasies do not get modified through play and through age-appropriate relationships with real people. Problems with our parents affect our phantasies about the world. We have phantasy relationships with our parents even when they are not there, so someone whose father disappeared when they were two may expect all men to disappear from their lives after about two years, and may behave in such a way as to make it happen. Their phantasies about sexual partners and fathers may remain on a level more appropriate to the knowledge and beliefs of a two-year old. Later experiences may lead to modifications to such beliefs, but phantasies created very early on under painful conditions (such as loss) are hard to change since recurrence of the pain is feared.

Problems arise too because of the ways we manipulate phantasies and emotions in response to conflicts. For example, bad feelings can seem so frightening that they have to be separated from good ones. In order not to feel jealous, envious,

angry and left out, for example, we may see ourselves as having and being everything desirable and our mothers as poor, weak, foolish creatures with no understanding. Unfortunately such phantasies may leave us not only vulnerable to collapse when we discover we do not live up to our own expectations but also unable to turn then to her for comfort.

Reality often brings emotional pain; 'splitting' is used to attempt to avoid such pain. However, the splitting itself is not only insecure but also deeply damaging. Denial, idealization and denigration (forms of splitting used in the Madonna and Whore images for example) may temporarily get rid of the jealous envy attached to knowing that women in general, and our mothers in particular, can have sex as well as have children; but reliance on such splitting would prevent us from combining the two.

Phantasies get rid of unbearable, uncontainable feelings into other people are common. Kleinians call this *projective identification*. This may be involved, for example, when a father of a small child finds a new lover. Instead of feeling left out of the relationship between his wife and the child, he feels that *they* are left out of his exciting new relationship. He may be trying to get rid of feelings of being cruelly left out when he was a child. He does not think to himself 'I will leave my child then he or she will feel the pain instead of me'; he simply feels an overwhelming urge to be cared for and loved exclusively; the excitement helps him to split off awareness of his own cruelty. The hope must be to find a new, better solution this time; the risk is that the 'solution' will be equally or more damaging – to the father himself as well as to his family.

Both external and internal conditions can cause problems in development. A baby or child subjected to ill-treatment may respond in many ways which distort his or her long-term development. However, some babies and children seem to respond badly to even normal good and loving care, and, contrariwise, some can make use of even the smallest opportunity for love in an otherwise problematic environment. Klein thought people had different capacities to use the good they were offered. Some babies seem to enjoy life more from the beginning; others to find it difficult and unpleasant, or even unbearable. Mothers who have to cope with difficult babies often blame themselves; people with a Kleinian orientation are more likely to sympathize than to blame.

Change

Change depends on modifying the underlying phantasies we have about the world and which we use to orient ourselves.

In therapy or counselling the client has the opportunity to experience a relationship in which her or his emotional state can be understood, tolerated, recognized and felt in a way which they have not been before.

The aim of psychodynamic counselling is to increase the client's capacity to use and accept more aspects of themselves; to free their processes of thought and feeling and to remove existing damaging restrictions on them. New, better possibilities for dealing with internal and external conflicts remain after counselling ends.

Other relationships also allow both good and bad phantasies to be modified. Teachers and other close adults in childhood, and lovers and friends later on can change us. So can giving birth or other forms of creativity. Work of all kinds provides an opportunity to test significant phantasies about whether we can make the world a better place or only damage and destroy. Successful parenting provides an opportunity to revisit phantasies created in childhood, and to bring them to a new, more satisfying conclusion. All of these experiences can evoke old, problematical phantasies and the accompanying feelings in a new situation, thus providing us with the opportunity to change them. However, significant changes generally involve experiencing pain, such as the pain of guilt or sorrow. Change probably occurs most when *not to change* itself involves considerable emotional pain.

The significance of the relationship affects the amount of change which can be brought about. In psychoanalysis five times a week an analyst may be almost constantly 'there' in the patient's mind and in reality reliably there and closely in touch with the client's emotional state on an almost daily basis. This relationship can contain and modify very deep anxieties. Psychodynamic psychotherapy two or three times a week can also have far-reaching effects. Counselling or therapy once a week or less, while bringing significant relief, cannot be expected to modify the deepest anxieties or change whole personality structures. The personal qualities and emotional capacities of the counsellor or other therapist matter hugely.

Grieving can initiate powerful processes of change. Grief handled alone often results in attacks on the self and other people as attempts are made to get rid of the pain; but grief worked through with someone who can tolerate painful thoughts and feelings may gradually bring new awareness and new strengths.

A significant point in development is reached when a baby recognizes that the mother he or she loves is the same as the mother he or she hates, and the self doing it is the same person too. Recognizing and taking responsibility for one's own attacks on the work with one's therapist can be a similarly important step in therapy. The consequent sense of guilt may be tolerated because it is accompanied by feelings of liberation, as the client gains control over processes recognized as destructive.

Skills and strategies

A Kleinian practitioner is expected to have an ability to recognize and tolerate their own true state of mind in the presence of a client.

Since offering anything to a client has important implications for the relationship, skill is involved in knowing when and how to share an idea or to suggest a thought for the client to consider, and in picking up the consequences.

Skill is involved in deciding when to discuss an issue raised by the client in terms of the overt meaning, and when to pick up a more covert meaning. For example, a client complaining about their sister may need help in thinking about her – but they may also need help in thinking about ways in which the sister at this moment is being used to talk about some aspect of themselves or the counsellor. Negative feelings towards the therapist or therapy are often raised in such ways, providing an opportunity to draw attention to, discuss and modify processes of splitting.

Skill is also needed to interpret what clients bring to the counsellor, both verbally and non-verbally. Since feelings, both negative and positive, can often be hidden by the client from their own awareness, the therapist has to be aware of signals conveying them. As they were hidden in the first place for very powerful reasons, bringing them to the attention of the client raises many issues about the relationship with the counsellor as well as about the client's state of mind and, when it is done, has to be done skilfully.

Research evidence

There seems to be no quantitive research explicitly looking at Kleinian psychodynamic therapy.

Malan (1975) reported a qualitative study in which a team of psychoanalytically trained analysts and psychotherapists offered brief psychotherapy to patients selected for insight therapy. He found that effective outcomes of therapy correlated with 'transference interpretations'; by this he meant *observations made by the therapist on the client's feelings towards the therapist.*

His conclusion was that prognosis is best when enthusiasm for treatment in both patient and therapist is high; when transference arises early and becomes a major feature of therapy; and grief and anger at termination are important issues (1975: 274).

Roth and Fonagy (1996), reporting research on therapy for people diagnosed with mental illnesses, comment on the dearth of research into outcomes for psychodynamic psychotherapy or counselling. However, they suggest that therapists should refer on people whose conditions can be classified as mental illnesses: 'The balance of evidence suggests that generic counselling is most appropriate to the least chronic and least severely impaired individuals within a patient population' (1996: 262). They list four factors they consider important: (a) a friendly and sympathetic attitude to the client; (b) the encouragement of a collaborative relationship; (c) therapist interventions aimed at addressing the client's negative feelings toward the therapist; (d) direct attention to the in-therapy relationship (1996: 253).

References

Malan, D.H. (1975) *A Study of Brief Psychotherapy.* London: Plenum Press.

Roth, A. and Fonagy, P. (1996) *What Works for Whom? A Critical Review of Psychotherapy Research.* New York and London: Guilford.

Segal, H. (1981) *The Work of Hanna Segal: A Kleinian Approach to Clinical Practice.* New York: Aronson. Republished as *Delusion and Creativity* (1986) London: Free Association Books.

Segal, J. (1992) *Melanie Klein.* London: Sage.

Segal, J.C. (1995) *Phantasy in Everyday Life.* London: Karnac.

5.11 The Attachment Theory of John Bowlby (1907–1990)

○○○

TRACY KING

Why is greater airtime not given, in all models of counselling training, to John Bowlby's (1969) theory of attachment and how it can be used to gain greater understanding of the client–therapist relationship in the 'here and now'?

Brief history

John Bowlby was born in 1907. He studied medicine at the University of Cambridge. Training in psychiatry and psychoanalysis provided Bowlby with an environment in which to develop his own ideas in what would later become known as developmental psychology. Bowlby felt that psychoanalysis put far too much emphasis on the child's fantasy world and far too little on actual events. He expressed this view in the paper, 'The influence of early environment in the development of neurosis and neurotic character' (1940), which contained many of the ideas that later became central to attachment theory. He emphasized the adverse effects of early separation, advising mothers to visit their young children in hospitals, and linked separation to neurosis.

In 1945, Bowlby became head of the Children's Department at the Tavistock Clinic. In 1948, he hired James Robertson to do observations of young children who were hospitalized, institutionalized or otherwise separated from their parents. In 1952 Robertson and Bowlby made the film, '*A two-year-old goes to hospital*'. This film played a crucial role in the development of attachment theory and also helped to improve conditions for children in hospitals in Britain and many other parts of the world. As a result of this research at the Tavistock Clinic, he received and accepted a request from the World

Health Organization to write a report, *Maternal Care and Mental Health* (1951) on the condition of homeless children in post-war Europe.

Bowlby's first formal statement of attachment theory was presented in London in three classic papers read to the British Psychoanalytic Society. The first, *The Nature of the Child's Tie to His Mother* (1957), reviewed the then current, psychoanalytic explanations for the child's attachment to the mother. In the next paper in the series, *Separation Anxiety* (1959), Bowlby suggested that excessive separation anxiety is usually caused by adverse family experiences, such as repeated threats of abandonment or rejections by parents, or to parents' or siblings' illnesses or death for which the child feels responsible. In the third major theoretical paper, *Grief and Mourning in Infancy and Early Childhood* (1960), he advanced the view that grief and mourning appear whenever attachment behaviours are activated but the mother continues to be unavailable either physically or emotionally.

Basic assumptions

There are three principal patterns of attachment that are reliably thought to extend to adulthood:

1. 'Secure'. Individuals are confident that their attachment figure will be available and responsive should they encounter adverse situations. They are bold in their interactions with the world.
2. 'Anxious-resistant/ambivalent'. Individuals are uncertain whether their attachment figure will be available and responsive when called upon. They are prone to separation anxiety.

3. 'Anxious-avoidant'. Individuals have no confidence that when they seek care they will be responded to. They try to become emotionally self-sufficient.

Origins and maintenance of problems

In later work, Bowlby (1988) suggested that 'attachment style' can change either through self-reflection or corrective relationships. One relationship that can achieve this is the therapeutic one. Relationships are important for understanding the origins and course of most conditions. Research has illustrated that many presenting issues are linked to attachment difficulties. Anxiety disorders are associated with histories of anxious-resistant/ambivalent attachment. Aggression and conduct disorders have been found to be related to anxious/avoidant attachment.

Despite these findings, little related research has been conducted on the client–therapist relationship with regard to attachment theory. This relationship acts as a 'secure base' and interaction between client and therapist parallels outside-world attachment patterns. This may suggest that working on the dynamics of the interaction between therapist and client may help to shift 'real-world' attachment patterns accordingly and help alleviate the presenting issue. This highlights the importance of self-awareness of the therapist's own attachment patterns, gained through personal therapy, training and life experience, to understand how their style interacts with that of their clients.

So how can theoretical knowledge about attachment inform thinking and interventions? The work of Main (1990) emphasizes the relative lack of importance of content in a client's story. It is not what kind of story the client tells but where, when and how this story breaks down. There are two important questions that the therapist can bear in mind for the client and also for examination of their own patterns:

1. How is the story told?
2. What can the client allow themselves to know, feel and remember in telling the story?

Generally, anxious-ambivalent individuals appear to be overly emotional and completely caught up in their feelings. Anxious-avoidant people appear to be caught up in thinking and speak in a way that is detached from the emotion of an event. Secure people have a healthy balance between these two polarities.

Essentially, it is the quality of the relationships a client has in his or her life that is informed by attachment theory. Areas to explore are: the history of their caregiver's responsiveness, whether there was any loss of a key caregiver and the attachment of the client can give clues to the way the therapy may go. There are a number of different pointers to what a therapist can do with different attachment presentations that Harris (2003) has formulated. These are based around a psychodynamic way of working but are informative for any school of therapy.

Harris (2003) suggests the following. If a caregiver is consistently rejecting or unresponsive to needs, then a client may go from not speaking much at first, to speaking a lot but not about their own needs. This pattern displays obedience in order to avoid rejection. The therapist needs to create a non-judgemental environment where expression of needs will not be seen to lead to rejection. If a caregiver was controlling and consistently unresponsive to needs, then the client may be able to speak freely but may experience some interventions as controlling or intrusive and be unwilling to listen. The action to take is to pace interpretations gradually until the client feels there is room to be him or herself. A client with a history of a caregiver who was consistently unresponsive and who has never been taught the value of relating may not have much to say. They may need encouragement to speak and may need to learn how to relate on the basis of examples provided by the therapist. An inconsistently responsive caregiver may 'produce' a person/client that gets stuck, as the therapy relationship reawakens ambivalence and they may try to manipulate some sort of unhelpful change in boundaries. Therefore, initial flexibility in boundaries may be important as it disconfirms the prior experience of inconsistent responsiveness. Too rigid boundaries may make the relationship feel unsafe.

So it seems a secure base can create a space for exploration whether this is in a child's immediate environment or through exploration in therapy in later life. If, as research indicates, lack of a secure base is present in many presenting conditions, then knowledge of the use of the attachment framework within the therapy room is not only desirable but essential. It must, however, be remembered that attachment is not the only concept that defines human experience, so rather than advocate 'attachment therapy', it should inform rather than define thinking and interventions.

Unfortunately, there are many schools of therapy that do not refer to this and there are varying levels of its application from therapist to therapist. Although this position has shifted over recent years, with more 'scientific' research being conducted, there is still relatively little research with regard to the implications of attachment theory within the paralleled secure base of the client–therapist relationship. Until this balance is redressed and researchers cease to be resistant or avoidant in approaching this area, then the strong benefits of the theory informing the therapy relationship also have no secure base beyond anecdotal case studies. However, as the therapeutic relationship is different with every client, perhaps anecdotal case studies are all that is required to encourage the application of Bowlby's theory within the therapy room.

References

Bowlby, J. (1940) The influence of early environment in the development of neurosis and neurotic character. *International Journal of Psychoanalysis*, 21: 154–178.

Bowlby, J. (1951) *Maternal Care and Mental Health*. Report prepared on behalf of the World Health Organization. Geneva: World Health Organization and Department for Children and Parents, Tavistock Clinic, London, England.

Bowlby, J. (1957) *The Nature of the Child's Tie to His Mother*. Report prepared on behalf of the World Health Organization. Geneva: World Health Organization and Department for Children and Parents, Tavistock Clinic, London, England.

Bowlby, J. (1959) *Separation Anxiety*. Report prepared on behalf of the World Health Organization. Geneva: World Health Organization and Department for Children and Parents, Tavistock Clinic, London, England.

Bowlby, J. (1960) *Grief and Mourning in Infancy and Early Childhood*. Report prepared on behalf of the World Health Organization. Geneva: World Health Organization and Department for Children and Parents, Tavistock Clinic, London, England.

Bowlby, J. (1969) *Attachment, Vol 1 of Attachment and Loss*. London: Hogarth Press.

Bowlby, J. (1988) *A Secure Base*. New York: Basic Books.

Harris, T. (2003) Implications of attachment theory for developing a therapeutic alliance and insight in psychoanalytic psychotherapy. In M. Cortina and M. Marrone (eds), *Attachment Theory and the Psychoanalytic Process*. London: Whurr.

Main, M. (1990) Cross-cultural attitudes of attachment organization: recent studies, changing methodologies and the concept of conditional strategies. *Human Development*, 33: 48–61.

PART V
Theory and Approaches

COGNITIVE-BEHAVIOURAL APPROACHES

5.12 Behavioural Psychotherapy

KARINA LOVELL

Brief history

The origins of behavioural psychotherapy can be traced back to early work on animal learning. Among the earliest is Ivan Pavlov's work on classical conditioning. In recognizing that dogs automatically salivated when presented with food (unconditioned response), he paired the ringing of a bell with food (conditioned stimulus). After a number of presentations the dogs would salivate when the bell was rung in the absence of food. This response is known as the conditioned response. Later studies found that when the bell was rung but no food followed the conditioned response (salivation) extinguished after a few trials.

Another important concept was that of operant conditioning (also referred to as instrumental conditioning and reinforcement). B.F. Skinner, following on from earlier work by researchers in the United States, demonstrated that the likelihood of the occurrence of given behaviours could be increased or decreased by that behaviour being followed by an event which 'reinforced' that behaviour. The event if positive (praise, money, food, etc.) would increase the likelihood of the targeted behaviour, and was thus termed as a positive reinforcer. The event might be the omission of an aversive response (as in criticism, additional work duties, etc.) which also acts as a reinforcer to the target behaviour. This is referred to as negative reinforcement. The development of classical and instrumental conditioning led to the important development of Mowrer's two-factor theory of learning fear and avoidance, to explain fear and anxiety. In essence this theory suggested that fear was acquired through classical conditioning and maintained through operant conditioning.

Although these and other theoretical models were the basis of much of early behavioural psychotherapy, the precise mechanisms for the acquisition and maintenance of fear and avoidance remain unanswered today. Further, there are also differing perspectives as to the relevance of theory in respect to the practical application of treatment, and since the development of the practice of behavioural psychotherapy there has been a greater emphasis on the pragmatic rather than the theoretical approach.

The actual practice of behavioural psychotherapy began in 1958 when Joseph Wolpe developed systematic desensitization. This treatment involved teaching phobic clients relaxation techniques while imagining the feared situation or object. Throughout the 1960s behavioural psychotherapy was developed further and treatment techniques refined by well-known researchers such as Jack Rachman, Vic Meyer, Aubery Yates and Isaac Marks. By the 1970s behavioural psychotherapy was well established and a number of large well-designed research studies demonstrated its efficacy with some of the anxiety disorders (Marks, 1987). During the latter half of the 1970s treatment failures were starting to be examined and some notable individuals began to emphasize the role of cognition and behaviour. The last 30 years have seen a rapid growth in cognitive therapy, and while cognitive therapy describes a number of approaches the most widely known and practised is that developed by Aaron Beck. Cognitive therapy and cognitive behaviour therapy incorporate many behavioural techniques but place greater emphasis on the patient's internal experiences such as thoughts, feelings, wishes, daydreams and attitudes.

Over time behavioural and cognitive interventions have been incorporated into a general inclusive discipline referred to as Cognitive-Behaviour Therapy

(CBT). While this chapter will deal with, in the main, behavioural principles as applied in clinical practice, few therapists use solely behavioural approaches in their clinical work (just as few clinicians use wholly cognitive interventions).

Basic assumptions

While behavioural and cognitive approaches to psychotherapy have been developed and refined in the last few decades, all interventions emphasize:

- the empirical validation of therapy
- a treatment focus on the here and now of the client's life
- the use of explicit, agreed and operationally defined treatment strategies
- the specification of treatment goals (chosen by the client) to bring about desired changes in their life
- the use of collaborative therapeutic strategies between client and therapist.

Behavioural psychotherapy is a short-term, collaborative, problem-orientated, active and directive treatment and has been applied to a wide range of problems. A number of interventions are utilized and treatment techniques include exposure therapy (both in vivo and imaginal), response prevention, behavioural activation, coping enhancement strategies, self-monitoring, social skills training, education, role rehearsal, modelling and contracting.

Behavioural psychotherapy is offered to clients if:

- the problem behaviour can be defined in terms of observable behaviour
- the problem is current and predictable
- the client and the therapist can agree on clearly defined outcomes (goals)
- the client understands and agrees to the treatment plan.

Cognitive-behavioural interventions have been applied to a range of clinical problems (Department of Health, 2001). The following list shows some areas where treatment efficacy has been demonstrated or at the very least shows much promise.

- phobias (including agoraphobia, social phobia and specific phobias)
- obsessive-compulsive disorder
- post-traumatic stress disorder
- habit disorders
- sexual difficulties
- mild to moderate depression
- generalized anxiety disorder
- chronic fatigue syndrome
- psychosis
- behavioural medicine (behavioural interventions have been applied to a whole range of physical disorders).

Origin and maintenance of problems

It is beyond the remit of this chapter to discuss the range of difficulties that behavioural psychotherapy is applicable to, hence only anxiety will be detailed. Lang (1979) provides the most useful model of anxiety in describing three inter-related response systems: behavioural, physiological and cognitive. For example, an individual suffering from agoraphobia will avoid certain situations or stimuli such as crowded places, queues or public transport (behavioural). In such situations they will experience physical symptoms of anxiety such as tachycardia, breathlessness and dry mouth (physiological). In addition they will describe fearful thoughts such as 'I am going to have a heart attack and die' (cognitive).

The maintenance of anxiety disorders can be explained by the three-systems approach described above. As described in Figure 5.12.1, a feared situation or object that causes anxiety will lead to the desire to avoid or escape that situation. Escape results in a reduction or relief from the distressing sensations associated with anxiety, but the next time the client confronts the object or situation they experience these feelings again, and thus a vicious circle develops. It is argued that for fear reduction to occur the feared stimulus must be confronted without avoidance or escape. Thus therapy focuses on breaking this vicious circle.

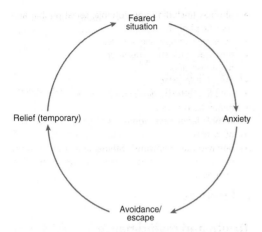

Figure 5.12.1 The vicious circle of fear and avoidance

Skills and strategies

Prior to the commencement of therapy it is important that a thorough assessment is conducted. As with all CBT interventions, a client-centred assessment should be undertaken. A detailed analysis of the current problem is gathered along with the antecedents and consequences (impact), onset, and course of the problem. A brief history, including social contacts, current substance use and risk, is taken. Following the assessment, the client and the therapist collaboratively write a formulation (i.e. a shared understanding) of the client's difficulty. Most therapists use a range of clinical measures, which include both process and outcome measures. The measures tend to be both client specific (e.g. a measure of the client's problems) and standardized measures. The purpose of measurement is important in that if repeated regularly it gives therapist and client valuable information regarding their progress. It also allows the therapist to change intervention if a specific intervention is not working. Clinical measures are also repeated after treatment, during the follow-up stage, to ensure that therapy gains are maintained.

Many techniques are used in behavioural psychotherapy and are detailed in the literature. One of the most frequent interventions for anxiety reduction is exposure. Exposure is the treatment of choice for many of the anxiety disorders including phobias and obsessive-compulsive disorder. This tried and tested intervention is based on the above theoretical view.

Confronting a feared stimulus as a means of reducing fear is reviewed by Marks (1987). Therapeutic interventions which include the exposure principle have been in use since the late 1950s. Exposure techniques persuade the client to confront feared situations or stimuli until fear subsides.

Exposure needs to be prolonged (one continuous hour or more) for reduction of anxiety (habituation) to take place.

Exposure can be used in imagination or live. Live is usually the preferred method but imaginal is used when the feared stimulus or situation is difficult or impractical (such as a fear of flying), or as a first step in therapy when a client is particularly fearful. In clinical practice a graded hierarchy of feared situations is defined with the client. For example, a client with agoraphobia would be encouraged to go to the local shops once daily, eventually building up to go to the local shopping centre alone by bus. The client is encouraged to confront the anxiety-provoking situation or object for at least one hour and to repeat this exercise on a daily basis as homework until anxiety reduction has occurred. Once the client has mastered the first step of the hierarchy they move on to the next step, and so forth, until all situations or objects are no longer avoided.

Research has demonstrated that it is unnecessary for the therapist to accompany the client with exposure tasks and that the main tasks for the therapist are to assist the client with setting exposure homework, and to help solve difficulties that may occur. At the end of treatment the therapist needs to spend time explaining the necessity of continuing exposure and discussing relapse-prevention strategies. After treatment it is important that clients are followed up for at least a year to ensure that treatment gains are maintained.

To summarize, the main principles of live exposure are that it should be

- graded
- prolonged
- repeated
- homework based.

Research evidence

Cognitive and behavioural psychotherapy is the most researched of all the 'talking' therapies (Department of Health, 2001). Research has travelled the scientific route from single-case studies, case series, uncontrolled studies, through to controlled studies comparing CBT to no treatment, and CBT with other psychotherapies and drug treatments. More recently, studies have compared the efficacy of cognitive treatments alone, behavioural treatments alone and combined with a range of disorders.

The research literature clearly demonstrates the efficacy of behavioural techniques with a range of anxiety disorders and CBT has been found to be the treatment of choice for obsessive-compulsive disorder, specific phobias, social phobia, blood/injury phobia and agoraphobia. Cognitive-behaviour therapy has strong support for many disorders including post-traumatic stress disorder, depression, chronic fatigue syndrome, habit disorders, relationship difficulties and, more recently, in the treatment of psychosis.

There is a wealth of literature to which the practising clinician can refer regarding the efficacy of cognitive and behavioural interventions.

References

Department of Health (2001) *Treatment Choice in Psychological Therapies and Counselling: Evidence-based and Practice-based Guideline*. London: Department of Health.

Lang, P.J. (1979) A bioinformational theory of emotional imagery. *Psychophysiology*, 61: 495–512.

Marks, I.M. (1987) *Fears, Phobias and Rituals: Panic Anxiety, and their Disorders*. Oxford: Oxford University Press.

5.13 Cognitive Therapy
(Aaron Beck, 1921–)

JILL MYTTON

Around the middle of the last century, two eminent American clinical psychologists, Albert Ellis and Aaron Beck, became separately dissatisfied with the psychoanalytic approach in which they were trained. Ellis went on to develop rational emotive behaviour therapy and Beck to develop what has become the most used cognitive approach to therapy today. Both these therapeutic approaches echo the ideas of the Greek, Roman and eastern philosophers who argued that the way we think about our world and ourselves plays an important role in our emotions and behaviours. Gautama Buddha once observed,

'We are what we think. All that we are arises with our thoughts, with our thoughts we make the world.'

Aaron Beck had noticed that the dreams and thoughts of his depressed clients were focused on unrealistic negative ideas, and in 1963 and 1964 published two seminal papers on the relationship between thinking and depression. He analysed the dreams and psychotherapeutic sessions with 50 of his patients and found evidence of negative bias in their thinking. He later called this bias the negative cognitive triad; depressed people typically have a negative view of themselves, the world and the future. Beck hypothesized that depression was a form of 'thought disorder' and concluded that psychoanalytic theory was inadequate to account for his findings.

Over the next decade, Beck extended his ideas to other psychological disorders, in particular anxiety. In 1976 he published *Cognitive Therapy and the Emotional Disorders* in which he described his model of cognitive processing and therapy which focused on teaching his clients to identify and change their thought patterns. Since then Beck's original model has been extended and adapted to the treatment of all forms of psychological problems including depression, anorexia, phobias, schizophrenia, chronic fatigue syndrome and tinnitus. In Britain researchers such as Blackburn, Teasdale and Clarke have developed and evaluated Beck's cognitive therapy and in the USA his daughter Judith has extended his ideas (Beck, 1995). Beck's therapy is the most evidence based, influential and popular of cognitive approaches in use today.

Therapeutic approaches constantly evolve. Over the last decade there have been a number of developments in cognitive behaviour therapy, including cognitive-analytic therapy (Ryle, 1989), dialectical behaviour therapy (Linehan, 1993) and more recently mindfulness-based cognitive therapy (MBCT) (Segal et al., 2002). MBCT brings together Eastern meditative practices with CBT perspectives. Developed mainly to prevent relapse in depression, MBCT teaches individuals to become more aware of their thoughts and see them not as facts or aspects of the self but as 'mental events'. Jon Kabat-Zinn describes this process as 'the simple act of recognizing that your thoughts as thoughts can free you from the distorted reality they often create and allow for more clear-sightedness and a greater sense of manageability in your life' (1990: 69–70).

Basic assumptions

Human beings have cognitions. We can think, we process information coming in through our five senses, and we make interpretations, inferences and evaluations about that information. In this way we interact with our environment.

These cognitions are believed to be linked to feelings, behaviour and physiology. Thus if a situation is perceived (cognition) as a threat by someone, adrenalin will be released into the body increasing the heart and breathing rates (physiology), the person will feel fear (affect or emotion) and will react ('flight or fight' behaviour).

Cognitions are available to our conscious minds – we can think about our thoughts and therefore we can change them. Beck described three types of cognition which strongly influence an individual's feelings and behaviour:

- *Information processing* – individuals are constantly receiving information from the internal (for example, their own bodily reactions) and external environments which their brains process and make sense of.
- *Automatic thoughts* – many of an individual's thoughts occur as if 'out of the blue'. Beck called these spontaneous cognitions 'automatic thoughts' and they are part of the person's internal dialogue, described as unplanned moment-to-moment thoughts that flow through our minds. Often on the edge of awareness, they can be difficult to recognize.
- *Schema* – this is a term given to hypothetical cognitive structures which act as templates to filter incoming information. They are the unspoken rules or underlying core beliefs learned through early experiences, which every individual holds about self, others and the world. When an event occurs schemas filter out unwanted information, enabling the person to attend to that which is considered important. In some areas we have well-developed schema – for example, when driving a car it is important for the driver to be able to filter out unimportant information to prevent

overload. In new situations the schema are less well developed and it is harder to filter out this unimportant information. Thus, people learning to drive can become confused by the variety of information in their environment.

Origin and maintenance of problems

Beck's cognitive model proposes that distorted or dysfunctional thinking underlies all psychological disturbance. It is not people's experiences or situations that make them angry, depressed or anxious but the way they process the information and think about those experiences.

Schemas can be adaptive and healthy or maladaptive and unhealthy. Maladaptive schemas tend to be negative, rigid and absolute. When unhealthy schemas are activated they affect all the stages of information processing. Thus a person with the schema 'I am worthless' will tend to distort incoming information to match this belief. Positive information that would discount this belief may be ignored or distorted: 'The teacher only gave me a good mark because she wants something from me.'

Faulty information processing – when people become disturbed they tend to make errors in this process. Beck has identified a number of these 'logical errors', including:

- *Arbitrary inference* – people sometimes draw conclusions about events without any supporting evidence.
- *Dichotomous thinking* – thinking in extreme terms, for example using the words 'never' and 'always' rather than 'sometimes', or placing experiences in one of two opposite categories such as beautiful and ugly.
- *Maximization and minimization* – events are evaluated as much more or much less important than they really are. A normally calm mother losing her temper one day with her child may exaggerate the event and conclude that she is a very bad mother.

When unhealthy schema are activated the individual tends to be prone to negative automatic thoughts. For example, an anxious person will automatically and repeatedly think 'I can't cope with this', and a depressed person may think 'I'm useless, I'll never be able to do this, I give up.' Although healthy people can also experience such automatic thoughts, they are more frequent and disruptive in people with emotional problems.

Beck proposes a multi-factorial theory to explain how these maladaptive cognitive schemas, automatic thoughts and cognitive distortions leading to emotional disturbance are acquired. His model suggests that people become vulnerable to psychological problems as a result of the following interacting factors:

- *Genetic predisposition* – individuals differ genetically in their vulnerability to different kinds of distress. For example, it has been shown that some forms of depression tend to run in families.
- *Childhood experiences* – specific traumas and negative treatment in childhood are thought to contribute to a vulnerability to psychological problems throughout life. Underlying dysfunctional schema are developed which can later be activated. In addition, child-rearing practices of the parents may not have provided the child with the experiences needed to learn coping skills.
- *Social learning* – children learn through observation of significant people in their lives. For example, they learn through imitating their parents' behaviour, and through rewards for behaviour. The child tends to learn from its parents and other significant people both helpful and unhelpful cognitive patterns and underlying assumptions.

Precipitating factors such as physical disease, severe and sudden external stress, and chronic external stress are thought to be responsible for activating the unhealthy cognitive processes.

Problems are thought to be maintained by the cognitive distortions. Once the unhealthy schema are activated the individual tends to continue to think and behave in ways that maintain this activation. Any information received is filtered through the person's schema to render it consistent with their belief systems. For example, a depressed person will minimize or negate achievements and positive experiences and will maximize failures and negative experiences. This biased information processing also affects the automatic thoughts. The result is a reinforcement of the unhealthy cognitions leading to a continuation of the emotional difficulties.

Change

Change in cognitive therapy usually means an alleviation of the emotional problems and a change in behaviour. It is a goal-orientated, problem-solving and structured approach. Cognitions are the primary target for change in therapy.

Cognitive therapy requires a sound therapeutic alliance and in recent years there has been an increased focus on how to use the relationship as an active ingredient in therapy. The role of collaboration between the client and the therapist and the active participation by the client in bringing about change are emphasized.

The process of change begins with the cognitive therapist educating the client about the cognitive model and the role of thoughts in emotions and behaviour. The emphasis is on conceptualizing the client's problems, teaching the cognitive model and providing some early symptom relief. The process continues with the therapist helping the client to set goals, identify and challenge cognitive errors, automatic thoughts and schema and plan behavioural change. Ultimately the client is helped to become their own therapist and relapse prevention is emphasized.

Long-lasting change results from the modification of the person's underlying distorted and dysfunctional beliefs.

Cognitive therapy is based on the cognitive model which we have seen relates the way we think to our emotions and behaviours. This model is used to conceptualize the client's problems. Cognitive therapists believe that the clearer this formulation is, the easier it becomes to find methods to solve these problems. A formulation is a tentative hypothesis about the origins and maintenance of the client's difficulties and is conceptualized in terms of:

- The client's current thinking patterns by assessment of their information processing, automatic thoughts and schema.
- Precipitating factors – a consideration of current stressors will help understanding of what has precipitated the present difficulties. These might be related to home, work, family or friends, and examples would include loss, illness, traumatic events or life changes.
- Predisposing factors can include past traumatic events, childhood experiences, genetic vulnerability, and personality factors.

As therapy progresses the therapeutic team of counsellor or psychotherapist and client refine the initial formulation as more information from the client is acquired.

Skills and strategies

Cognitive therapists employ an active-directive counselling style. An important skill is the ability to develop a good therapeutic relationship. Beck maintained from the early days of the development of cognitive behaviour therapy that the context of a sound therapeutic relationship was very necessary although not sufficient to bring about change (see Beck et al., 1979). Today there is increasing recognition in the light of research that the quality of this relationship is central (Wills and Sanders, 1997). The core conditions described by Rogers (1957) of empathy, unconditional positive regard and congruence have to be in place to facilitate the effective use of cognitive and behavioural techniques. The cognitive and behavioural techniques used need the context of a sound therapeutic alliance to be most effective.

Cognitive therapists need to be committed to the cognitive model and fully understand the rationale for this approach to therapy. The skill of being a good educator is essential to help clients understand the relationships between cognitions, emotions, physiology and behaviour. The ability to teach clients to monitor, reality test and modify their dysfunctional and distorted beliefs is crucial.

Therapists need to be able to work in a collaborative way with their clients, teaching clients to become their own therapists. Collaboration empowers clients by giving them a say in their own therapeutic process and it fosters self-efficacy.

Cognitive counselling or psychotherapy uses a variety of skills and strategies to bring about change. Techniques are chosen on the basis of the case formulation and in collaboration with the client.

Cognitive strategies are central to this approach and are used to help the client identify, examine, reality test and modify automatic thoughts, errors in information processing and schema. They include:

- Socratic questioning (i.e. a form of challenging dialogue using systematic questioning and inductive reasoning);
- cost-benefit analysis – looking at the advantages and disadvantages of holding a particular belief;
- alternative perspectives – for example viewing their problem from the perspective of a close relative;
- the use of automatic thought forms to help clients identify their automatic thoughts and understand how they influence their emotions and behaviour;
- reality testing – looking at evidence 'for' and 'against' the dysfunctional and distorted thoughts;
- cognitive rehearsal – practising coping with difficult situations either in role-play with the therapist, in imagination, or in real life.

Behavioural strategies are used to reality test clients' dysfunctional thoughts, and more specifically to reduce the physiological components of anxiety and increase the activity in people who are depressed. They include:

- graded exposure – getting clients to face step by step their fears and anxieties either in imagination or *in vivo*;
- monitoring activities – keeping a record of daily activities and rating them on a 10-point scale for mastery and pleasure;
- scheduling activities – to increase a client's activity levels, the client and counsellor schedule a number of activities into the day;
- behavioural experiments – these enable the client to test out their fears. For example, a man who has lift phobia and does not believe he can stand in a stationary lift for even five seconds can be asked to carry out this experiment and discover that, although he is uncomfortable in the lift, he can tolerate it;
- relaxation techniques to provide a coping strategy for reducing anxiety and to facilitate carrying out behavioural experiments.

Cognitive therapy advocates homework assignments to encourage clients to practise their newly learned skills and thus to enhance the therapeutic process.

Research evidence

Beck's cognitive therapy is one of the best researched approaches. Many well-controlled studies on the effectiveness of cognitive therapy have been conducted on a wide range of client problems. The general consensus is that this approach is effective in resolving problems.

The first important study was carried out by Beck and his associates (Rush et al., 1977) and demonstrated that cognitive therapy was more effective at reducing symptoms of depression than an antidepressant. As a result of this seminal study, cognitive therapy achieved academic recognition and became popular in the USA and in Europe. Roth and Fonagy (1996), in their systematic review of a large number of studies, concluded that there was good evidence of the effectiveness of CBT for a range of psychological problems. Since then a number of studies have demonstrated the efficacy of CBT for treating, for example, depression (Hollon et al., 2002; Teasdale et al., 2000), PTSD (Blanchard et al., 2003) and panic disorder (Barlow et al., 2000).

References

Barlow, D.H., Gorman, J.M., Shear, M.K. and Woods, S.W. (2000) Cognitive-behavioural therapy, imipramine or their combination for panic disorder. *Journal of the American Medical Association*, 283 (19): 2529.

Beck, A.T. (1963) Thinking and depression. I. Idiosyncratic content and cognitive distortions. *Archives of General Psychiatry*, 9: 324–333.

Beck, A.T. (1964) Thinking and depression. II. Theory and therapy. *Archives of General Psychiatry*, 10: 56–71.

Beck, A.T. (1976) *Cognitive Therapy and the Emotional Disorders*. New York: International Universities Press.

Beck, A.T., Rush, A.J., Shaw, B.F. and Emery, G. (1979) *Cognitive Therapy of Depression*. New York: Guilford Press.

Beck, J.S. (1995) *Cognitive Therapy: Basics and Beyond*. New York: Guilford.

Blanchard, E.B., Hickling, E.J., Devineni, T., Veazey, C.H., Galovski, T.E., Mundy, E., Malta, L.S. and Buckley, T.C. (2003) A controlled evaluation of cognitive behavioural therapy for posttraumatic stress in motor vehicle accident survivors. *Behaviour Research and Therapy*, 41 (1): 79.

Hollon, S.D., Thase, M.E. and Markowitz, J.C. (2002) Treatment and prevention of depression. *Psychological Science*, 3 (supplement 2): 39–77.

Kabat-Zinn, J. (1990) *Full Catastrophe Living: Using the Wisdom of Your Body and Mind to Face Stress, Pain and Illness.* New York: Dell Publishing.

Linehan, M.M. (1993) *Cognitive Behavior Therapy of Borderline Personality Disorder.* New York: Guilford Press.

Rogers, C.R. (1957) The necessary and sufficient conditions of therapeutic personality change. *Journal of Consulting and Clinical Psychology*, 21: 95–103.

Roth, A. and Fonagy, P. (1996) *What Works for Whom? A Critical Review of Psychotherapy Research.* London: Guilford.

Rush, A.J., Beck, A.T., Kovacs, M. and Hollon, S.D. (1977) Comparative efficacy of cognitive therapy and pharmacotherapy in the treatment of depressed outpatients. *Cognitive Therapy and Research*, 1 (1): 17–37.

Ryle, A. (1989) *Cognitive Analytic Therapy: Active Participation in Change. A New Integration in Brief Psychotherapy.* Chichester: John Willey.

Segal, Z.V., Williams, J.M.G. and Teasdale, J.D. (2002) *Mindfulness-based Cognitive Therapy for Depression.* London: Guilford Press.

Teasdale, J.D., Segal, Z.V., Williams, J.M.G., Ridgeway, V., Lau, M. and Soulsby, J. (2000) Reducing risk of recurrence of major depression using Mindfulness-based Cognitive Therapy. *Journal of Consulting and Clinical Psychology*, 68: 615.

Wills, F. and Sanders, D. (1997) *Cognitive Therapy: Transforming the Image.* London: Sage.

Recommended reading

Burns, D.D. (1990) *The Feeling Good Handbook.* London: Penguin.

Padesky, C.A. and Greenberger, D. (1995) *Clinician's Guide to Mind Over Mood.* London: Guilford Press.

Salkovskis, P.M. (ed.) (1996) *Frontiers of Cognitive Therapy.* London: Guilford.

Trower, P., Casey, A. and Dryden, W. (1998) *Cognitive-behavioural Counselling in Action.* London: Sage.

5.14 Personal Construct Counselling and Psychotherapy (George A. Kelly, 1905–1967)

◯◯◯

FAY FRANSELLA

Brief history

Personal construct counselling is based directly and totally on George Kelly's *The Psychology of Personal Constructs* set out in his two volumes published in 1955. His first degrees were in physics and mathematics, followed by postgraduate degrees in sociology, education and, eventually, psychology. He spent much of his academic life at Ohio State University and overlapped there with Carl Rogers for a short time. In his theory of personal constructs, George Kelly aimed to encompass the person's experiencing of the world in its entirety. Feeling involves thinking and behaving just as behaviour involves feelings and thoughts. The theory had a mixed reception on its publication as it was explicitly against the current climate in psychology of behaviourism on the one hand and psychoanalytic theories on the other. Its influence, both as a theory of personality and as an approach to counselling and psychotherapy, was felt first in Great Britain and spread into Europe before being taken up in any substantial way in its birthplace, the United States of America. (See Fransella, 1995 for more details of the man and his theory.)

A major reaction to the theory was an insistence that it did not espouse dualism. Critics insisted that the theory explained 'cognitions' very well but did not deal adequately with emotions. In spite of arguments to the contrary, in 1980 Walter Mischel called George Kelly the first cognitive psychologist. He said, 'There is reason to hope that the current moves toward a hyphenated cognitive-behavioral approach will help fill in the grand outlines that Kelly sketched years before anyone else even realized the need.' The argument about this issue continues today.

Of great influence has been George Kelly's philosophy of *constructive alternativisim*, which underpins the theory throughout. That philosophy is seen as one of the main precursors of the movement of *constructivism* that has swept through psychology as well as psychotherapy and counselling during the last few years. The philosophy sees reality as residing within the individual. While 'true' reality may indeed be 'out there', we, as individuals, are only able to place our own personal interpretations on that external reality.

Personal construct counselling and psychotherapy is practised around the world, but is not as popular as, for instance, person-centred counselling. The main reason, no doubt, is the fact that it is based on a very complex theory about how all individuals experience their worlds. Personal construct therapy is one application of that theory designed to help those who are experiencing problems in dealing with their world.

Basic assumptions

Constructive alternativism states that there are always alternative ways of looking at events. That means no one need be the victim of their past since that past is always capable of being seen in a different way – it can be *reconstrued*. However, we can trap ourselves by our past if we construe it as fixed.

The philosophy gives a positive and optimistic view of life since there is always the possibility of change – no matter how difficult that change may be. We have created the person we now are, and so can re-create ourselves.

Personal constructs are essentially discriminations. We see some events, or people, or behaviours as being alike and, thereby, different from other events. These dichotomous personal constructs are formed into a system and it is through that system of personal constructs that we peer at the world of events milling around us.

We place an interpretation on an event by applying certain of our repertoire of personal constructs to it and, thereby, predict an outcome. You see someone smiling at you across the street and predict, perhaps, that he is about to cross the road to say hello. You act accordingly.

Behaviour is the experiment we conduct to test out our current prediction of a situation. The man does cross the street and you put out your hand to shake his only to find he is smiling at someone behind you. In the language of personal construct theory, you have been invalidated.

The theory is couched in the language of science. Kelly suggested we might look at each person 'as if' we were all scientists. We have theories (personal construing), make predictions from those theories and then test them out by behaving.

The person is a form of motion. No sooner have we conducted one behavioural experiment than the answer leads us into another situation and another cycle of construing.

Feelings are experienced when we become aware that our current ways of construing events are not serving us well. We become aware that the current situation means we are going to have to change how we see our 'self' – we are threatened; or we become aware that we cannot make sense of what is happening and, until we do, we experience anxiety; or we become aware that we have behaved in a way which is 'not me' – and feel guilty.

Personal construct therapists know some of the ways of helping the client find alternative ways of construing events and life that will enable them to conduct more productive behavioural experiments. But the client is the expert and the client has the answers. However, those answers may well not be available to conscious awareness.

Construing takes place at different levels of cognitive awareness. The lowest level of cognitive awareness is what is termed *pre-verbal*. That is, discriminations that have been made before the acquisition of language.

An essential feature of personal construct theory is its reflexivity. It accounts for the construing of the counsellor and therapist as well as of the client.

Origin and maintenance of problems

There is no list for the personal construct therapist of ways in which problems start. The answer lies with the client who is presenting that problem.

A person decides they have a psychological problem when their present way of construing and predicting events is not working well. Predictions and behavioural experiments are being invalidated but the person is not able to modify those predictions and behaviours in the light of experience.

In all cases, the client has the answer to the question 'why do you go on behaving in this way when you would rather not?'

Change

Each person is a form of motion and therefore change is the norm. The person with a psychological problem is seen as being 'stuck'. The goal of therapy and counselling is to help the person 'get on the move again' (see Fransella and Dalton (2000) for more detail of the change process).

The therapist must establish a good relationship with the client. As part of this, he uses the 'credulous approach'. The therapist believes everything the client relates – even if it is known to be a lie. Credulous listening helps the therapist get a glimpse into the client's world. A therapeutic plan cannot be drawn up and certainly not put into action until the practitioner has some idea of what certain changes may mean to the client.

Somewhere in the client's construing system are the reasons why he or she cannot get on with the business of living. The therapist uses the theory of personal constructs to make a temporary *diagnosis* of why the client has the problem.

That theoretical diagnosis leads to the therapeutic plan of action. It may, for instance, focus on the *looseness* of the client's construing process. The client cannot make enough sense of events to conduct meaningful behavioural experiments. Or the client may be thought to be resisting any change because that change has some unacceptable implications. For instance, being *anxious all the time* may be seen as indicating that one is a *sensitive, thoughtful* and *caring* person whereas being *anxiety-free* means one is the opposite.

Personal construct counselling and psychotherapy is largely value-free. There is little in personal construct theory that dictates how a person *should* be.

The focus of the process of change is mostly in the here and now. It is how the client construes things now that is important. Sometimes, the client links the present with a past event. In that case, the counsellor explores, with the client, that past event. But there is nothing in the theory that makes it mandatory to explore the past with the client.

A personal construct psychologist can make a distinction between counselling and psychotherapy.

A personal construct counsellor will not usually expect to be dealing with construing that has developed before the acquisition of adequate language skills – that is, with pre-verbal construing. Nor will he or she expect to help the client change some core values relating to the self. For instance, someone who has stuttered all his life will probably change so much that he becomes a different person when he gives up stuttering. That is a long and hard process of change and will not normally be undertaken by a personal construct counsellor.

One of the roles of the therapist and counsellor is to act as validator of the client's construing. That does not mean that the personal construct therapist does not act as a human being. Far from it. But it does mean that the therapist or counsellor is constantly aware of the interpretations being placed on him or her by the client. For instance, interpretations of what the client is expressing are only made to the client if the therapist thinks that interpretation is useful in helping the client see an alternative way of looking at an event.

Skills and strategies

The therapist or counsellor needs to be able to suspend his or her own personal construct system of values. Without that ability, it is not possible to step into the client's shoes and look at the world through the client's eyes, because the therapist's personal values get in the way.

In the place of a personal system of constructs, the therapist peers through the system of professional constructs provided by personal construct theory. That means the therapist needs to be well-versed in the use of theoretical constructs.

Kelly (1955/1991) suggests the personal construct practitioner needs several other skills, including creativity and good verbal ability. The need for creativity stems from the fact that the theory is eclectic in terms of tools available to the counsellor. The aim is to help the client find alternative ways of dealing with personal events and the counsellor may use any means to attain that goal. Kelly put it like this:

> Creation is therefore an act of daring, an act of daring through which the creator abandons those literal defenses behind which he might hide if his act is questioned or its results proven invalid. The … [therapist] who dares not try anything he cannot verbally defend is likely to be sterile in a [counselling/psychotherapy] relationship.

Kelly described three specific tools that could aid the client's reconstruing:

- *Self-characterization* – stems from Kelly's first principle: 'If you want to know what is wrong with a person, ask him, he may tell you'. It consists of a statement written by the client, in the third person, describing herself in a sympathetic way. The client is free to say whatever he or she likes.
- *Fixed role therapy* – consists of the therapist writing a self-characterization of the client, usually with the help of colleagues. The self-characterization does not describe the client as he or she is now, but as someone slightly different. The client must agree that the portrait is understandable and acceptable. At that point the client is encouraged to become that new person for a week or more. That new role shows the client that making changes to oneself also produces changes in how others respond to us, how we feel and so forth. Most importantly, it shows we can re-create ourselves (see Epting et al., 2005).
- *Repertory grid technique* – is a method for showing mathematical relationships between personal constructs and the elements to which they may be applied. It was a way Kelly suggested psychologists could 'get beyond the words'. This technique has been widely used in counselling and psychotherapy but, as with all else, its use is by no means a requirement (see Fransella et al., 2004, for details on how to use this technique).

Research evidence

There has been a great deal of research into changes in construing resulting from therapeutic and counselling interventions. Most of that has used the repertory grid. Details of the evidence base of personal construct psychotherapy can be found in Winter (2003).

References

Epting, F., Germignani, M. and Cross, M.C. (2005) An audacious adventure: personal construct counselling and psychotherapy. In F. Fransella (ed.), *The Essential Practitioners' Handbook of Personal Construct Psychology*. Chichester: John Wiley & Sons.

Fransella, F. (1995) *George Kelly*. London: Sage.

Fransella, F. and Dalton, P. (2000) *Personal Construct Counselling in Action* (2nd edn). London: Sage.

Fransella, F., Bell, R. and Bannister, D. (2004) *A Manual for Repertory Grid Technique* (2nd edn). Chichester: John Wiley & Sons.

Kelly, G.A. (1955/1991) *The Psychology of Personal Constructs*, Vols I and II. New York: Norton (re-published by Routledge in 1991).

Winter, D. (2003) The evidence base for personal construct psychotherapy. In F. Fransella (ed.), *The Handbook of Personal Construct Psychology*. Chichester: John Wiley & Sons.

5.15 Rational Emotive Behaviour Therapy (Albert Ellis, 1913–)

WINDY DRYDEN

Brief history

Rational Emotive Behaviour Therapy (REBT) was founded in 1955 by Albert Ellis, an American clinical psychologist who had become increasingly disaffected with psychoanalysis in which he trained in the late 1940s. Originally, the approach was called Rational Therapy (RT) because Ellis wanted to emphasize its rational and cognitive features. In doing so, Ellis demonstrated the philosophical influences (largely Stoic) on his thinking. In 1961, he changed its name to Rational-Emotive Therapy to show critics that it did not neglect emotions, and, over 30 years later (in 1993), Ellis renamed the approach yet again, calling it Rational Emotive Behaviour Therapy to show critics that it did not neglect behaviour.

In 1962, Ellis published *Reason and Emotion in Psychotherapy*, a collection largely of previously published papers or previously delivered lectures, but which became a seminal work in the history of psychotherapy. Most of REBT's major, present-day features are described in this book: the pivotal role of cognition in psychological disturbance, the principle of psychological interactionism where cognition, emotion and behaviour are seen as interacting, not

separate, systems, the advantages of self-acceptance over self-esteem in helping clients with their disturbed views of their selves, and the importance of an active-directive therapeutic style, to name but a few.

REBT is practised all over the world and has many different therapeutic, occupational and educational applications. However, it tends to live in the shadow of Beck's cognitive therapy, an approach to cognitive-behaviour therapy which has attracted a greater number of practitioners and is more academically respectable.

Basic assumptions

Rationality – a concept that is normally applied to a person's beliefs. Rational beliefs, which are deemed to be at the core of psychological health, are flexible, consistent with reality, logical and self- and relationship-enhancing. Irrational beliefs, which are deemed to be at the core of psychological disturbance, are rigid or extreme, inconsistent with reality, illogical and self- and relationship-defeating.

There are four types of rational belief: non-dogmatic preferences ('I want to be approved of, but I don't have to be'); non-awfulizing beliefs ('It's bad to be disapproved of, but it isn't the end of the world'); high frustration tolerance beliefs ('It is difficult to face being disapproved of, but I can tolerate it'); and acceptance beliefs (e.g. self-acceptance: 'I can accept myself if I am disapproved of; other-acceptance: 'You are not horrible if you disapprove of me'; and life-acceptance: 'Even though this tragedy happened, life is not all bad and comprises good, bad and neutral events').

Similarly, there are four types of irrational belief: rigid demands ('I must be approved of'); awfulizing beliefs ('If I'm disapproved of, it's the end of the world'); low frustration tolerance beliefs ('I can't tolerate being disapproved of'); and depreciation beliefs (e.g. self-depreciation: 'I am worthless if I am disapproved of'; other-depreciation 'You are horrible if you disapprove of me'; and life-depreciation: 'Life is all bad because this tragedy happened').

REBT advocates a situational ABC model of psychological disturbance and health. A stands for activating event, which occurs within a situation and can be actual or inferred. A represents the aspect of the situation that the person focuses on and evaluates. B stands for belief (rational or irrational). C stands for the consequences of holding a belief about A and can be emotional, behavioural and cognitive. Thus, As do not cause Cs but contribute to them. Bs are seen as the prime but not the only determiners of Cs.

Holding a rational belief about an A leads to healthy emotions, functional behaviour and realistic subsequent thinking, whereas holding an irrational belief about the same A leads to unhealthy emotions, dysfunctional behaviour and unrealistic subsequent thinking.

REBT's view of human nature is realistic. Humans are seen as having the potential for both rational and irrational thinking. The ease with which we transform our strong desires into rigid demands suggests that the tendency towards irrational thinking is biologically based, but can be buffered or encouraged by environmental contexts.

Clients often have the unfortunate experience of inheriting tendencies towards disturbance and being exposed to their parents' disturbed behaviour.

REBT is optimistic and realistic here. It argues that if such clients work persistently and forcefully to counter their irrational beliefs and act in ways that are consistent with their rational beliefs, then they can help themselves significantly. However, REBT also acknowledges that most clients will not put in this degree of effort over a long period of time and will therefore fall far short of achieving their potential for psychological health.

Origin and maintenance of problems

People are not disturbed by events but by the rigid and extreme views that they take of them. This means that while negative events contribute to the development of disturbance, particularly when these events are highly aversive, disturbance occurs when people bring their tendencies to think irrationally to these events.

REBT does not have an elaborate view of the origin of disturbance. Having said this, it does acknowledge that it is very easy for humans when they are young to disturb themselves about highly aversive events. However, it argues that even under these conditions people react differently to the same event and thus we need to understand what a person brings to and takes from a negative activating event.

People learn their standards and goals from their culture, but disturbance occurs when they bring their irrational beliefs to circumstances where their standards are not met and their pursuit of their goals is blocked.

REBT has a more elaborate view of how disturbance is maintained. It argues that people perpetuate their disturbance for a number of reasons including the following:

- They lack the insight that their disturbance is underpinned by their irrational beliefs and think instead that it is caused by events.
- They think that once they understand that their problems are underpinned by irrational beliefs, this understanding alone will lead to change.
- They do not work persistently to change their irrational beliefs and to integrate the rational alternatives to these beliefs into their belief system.

- They continue to act in ways that are consistent with their irrational beliefs.
- They lack or are deficient in important social skills, communication skills, problem-solving skills and other life skills.
- They think that their disturbance has pay-offs that outweigh the advantages of the healthy alternatives to their disturbed feelings and/or behaviour.
- They live in environments which support the irrational beliefs that underpin their problems.

Change

REBT therapists consider that the core facilitative conditions of empathy, unconditional acceptance and genuineness are often desirable, but neither necessary nor sufficient for constructive therapeutic change.

For such change to take place, REBT therapists need to help their clients to do the following:

- realize that they largely create their own psychological problems and that while situations contribute to these problems, they are in general of lesser importance in the change process;
- fully recognize that they are able to address and overcome these problems;
- understand that their problems stem largely from irrational beliefs;
- detect their irrational beliefs and discriminate between them and their rational beliefs;
- question their irrational beliefs and their rational beliefs until they see clearly that their irrational beliefs are false, illogical and unconstructive while their rational beliefs are true, sensible and constructive;
- work towards the internalization of their new rational beliefs by using a variety of cognitive (including imaginal), emotive and behavioural change methods; refrain from acting in ways that are consistent with their old irrational beliefs;
- extend this process of challenging beliefs and using multimodal methods of change into other areas of their lives and to commit to doing so for as long as necessary.

Skills and strategies

REBT therapists see themselves as good psychological educators and therefore seek to teach their clients the ABC model of understanding and dealing with their psychological problems. They stress that there are alternative ways of addressing these problems and strive to elicit from their clients informed consent at the outset and throughout the counselling process. If they think that a client is better suited to a different approach to therapy they do not hesitate to effect a suitable referral.

REBT therapists frequently employ an active-directive counselling style and use both Socratic and didactic teaching methods. However, they vary their style from client to client. They begin by working with specific examples of identified client problems and help their clients to set healthy goals. They employ a sequence of steps in working on these examples which involves using the situationally based ABC framework, challenging beliefs and negotiating suitable homework assignments with their clients.

Helping clients to generalize their learning from situation to situation is explicitly built into the counselling process as is helping clients to identify, challenge and change core irrational beliefs which are seen as accounting for disturbance across a broad range of relevant situations.

A major therapeutic strategy involves helping clients to become their own therapists. In doing this, REBT therapists teach their clients how to use a particular skill such as challenging irrational beliefs, model the use of this skill, and sometimes give the clients written instructions on how to use the skill on their own. Constructive feedback is given to encourage the refinement of the skill. As clients learn how to use the skills of REBT for themselves, their therapists adopt a less active-directive, more prompting therapeutic style in order to encourage them to take increasing responsibility for their own therapeutic change.

REBT may be seen as an example of theoretically consistent eclecticism in that its practitioners draw upon procedures that originate from other counselling approaches, but do so for purposes that are consistent with REBT theory. REBT therapists are judiciously selective in their eclecticism and avoid the use of methods that are inefficient, or mystical, or of dubious validity.

REBT therapists have their preferred therapeutic goals for their clients, namely to help them to change their core irrational beliefs and to develop and internalize a set of core rational beliefs. However, they are ready to make compromises with their clients on these objectives when it becomes clear that their clients are unable or unwilling to change their core irrational beliefs. In such cases, REBT therapists help their clients by encouraging them to change their distorted inferences, to effect behavioural changes without necessarily changing their irrational beliefs or to remove themselves from negative activating events.

Research evidence

There is quite a lot of research indicating that psychological disturbance is correlated with irrational beliefs, but studies indicating that these beliefs are at the core of disturbance have yet to be carried out. Most scales which measure irrational and rational beliefs are deficient in one respect or another and there is a need to develop a scale with excellent psychometric properties.

Numerous studies on the effectiveness of REBT have been carried out and various meta-analyses of REBT outcome studies have been conducted which have come to different conclusions about the effectiveness of REBT. Well-controlled trials of REBT need to be done with clinical populations, employing well-trained REBT therapists who can be shown to adhere to a properly designed REBT adherence scale. Work is currently in progress to design such a scale.

Reference

Ellis, A. ([1962] 1994) *Reason and Emotion in Psychotherapy* (revised and updated edn). New York: Birch Lane Press.

Recommended Reading

Dryden, W. (ed.) (1995) *A Rational Emotive Behaviour Therapy Reader*. London: Sage.

Dryden, W. (2001) *Reason to Change: A Rational Emotive Behaviour Therapy (REBT) Workbook*. Hove: Brunner-Routledge.

Dryden, W. and Neenan, M. (2004) *Rational Emotive Behavioural Counselling in Action* (3rd edn). London: Sage.

Ellis, A. (2001) *Overcoming Destructive Beliefs, Feelings, and Behaviors*. Amherst, NY: Prometheus Books.

PART V
Theory and Approaches

HUMANISTIC-EXISTENTIAL APPROACHES

5.16   Existential Counselling and Therapy

EMMY VAN DEURZEN

Brief history

Existential counselling and therapy find their origin in the ancient practice of applied philosophy. Philosophy, or the love of wisdom, started out as an active search for the secret of a well-lived life. Hellenistic philosophers used the Socratic method of dialectical discussion to reveal and unravel the truth about personal and universal issues and dilemmas. This practice fell into desuetude but was revitalized at the beginning of the twentieth century when a number of psychiatrists began applying the thinking of existential philosophers such as Kierkegaard, Nietzsche and Heidegger to their clinical work (van Deurzen, 1997). Karl Jaspers, Ludwig Binswanger and Medard Boss were the first to formulate principles for existential psychotherapy (May et al., 1958). Their work, based mainly in Germany and Switzerland, was known as 'Daseinsanalysis' or existential analysis.

Authors such as Paul Tillich (1952) and Rollo May (1969) then spread the approach far more widely in the United States. Their influence on the human potential movement and on humanistic psychotherapy and counselling was extensive. There are obvious existential elements in approaches such as person-centred counselling and gestalt psychotherapy, while Irvin Yalom (1980), James Bugental (1981) and Alvin Mahrer (1996) have made direct contributions to the development of existential psychotherapy in North America.

In Europe existential psychotherapy was further developed on the continent by Victor Frankl's logotherapy ([1946], 1964). In the UK the work of R.D. Laing (1960) was much inspired by Jean-Paul Sartre's existentialist writing (Sartre [1943], 1956). It facilitated the flourishing of existential psychotherapy in the UK, which was firmly established from 1988 with the founding of the Society for Existential Analysis. A number of training courses at the Philadelphia Association, Regent's College, Surrey University and the New School of Psychotherapy and Counselling were developed. This generated some significant publications that made the existential approach more systematic and better known (see Cohn, 1997; van Deurzen, 1998, 2002).

Basic assumptions

The existential approach focuses on helping people in coming to terms with life in all its confusing complexity.

Many of the problems that clients struggle with are the natural consequence of the challenges and limitations of the human condition.

Life is tough and most people can do with a little help in learning to live. Sooner or later many of us falter in our ability to comprehend the demands made on us and we have trouble in coping with the predicaments we find ourselves in.

The objective is not to cure people of pathology, which is an unhelpful and misleading concept, but rather to assist them in coming to terms with the contradictions, dilemmas and paradoxes of their everyday existence.

Anxiety is a valuable instrument in helping us become more aware of reality, and should not be avoided. It needs to be embraced and understood if life is to be lived to the full.

People are never in isolation. They are always in a given world, with other people, and in a situation which influences their experience. Problems need to be seen in their cultural, social and political context.

There is a human tendency to hide away and deceive oneself about life and one's own position in it. The capacity for understanding self and others will increase as we face truth and aim for authenticity.

Self is a relative concept. It is only as I act in the world that I create a sense of self. It is only when my actions and qualities of being are named and described that my identity is established.

There is no such thing as a solid, immutable, self. We are in constant transformation.

There is no such thing as a place called the unconscious, nor is there such a thing as absolute truth. There are multiple interpretations of reality and many layered levels of understanding and consciousness. By reflection and understanding we can expand our grasp of what is, but never know it completely.

It is essential that people tune into their own yearnings and longings. In formulating new and valuable projects life becomes more meaningful as we rediscover new purpose and live in a more engaged manner.

Vitality is based on the acceptance of both positives and negatives. There can be no life without death and no health without illness. Learning to work with these tensions is the *sine qua non* of being real.

We live in time. Living requires us to recollect ourselves from the past and be present to ourselves now in order to project ourselves anew into the future. All these dimensions of time are equally important and in constant interaction with each other.

We live our lives on a number of dimensions. First, there is the concrete physical world where we interact with material objects. Second, there is the world with other people where we interact with those around us. Third, there is a dimension of self-representation where we constitute an inner world. Fourth, there is an abstract dimension of spirituality where we create meaning and make sense of things.

Origin and maintenance of problems

Life is intrinsically problematic. Every day we encounter problems of all sorts and of various levels of magnitude. We need to build confidence in our own ability to tackle and solve these problems and improve our competence in dealing with increasingly tougher situations. We can then find pleasure in the stimulation and vitality that come with such a resolute and courageous attitude to living.

As we sometimes find life rather too difficult we have a tendency to try and make things easier for ourselves by escaping from reality and living with illusions. One of the major ways in which we deceive ourselves is by imagining that we are condemned to be what we are, instead of embracing our freedom and the responsibility of making our own choices and changes in life. This bad faith leads to passivity, which perpetuates our difficulty in dealing with our problems.

Sometimes human beings feel so overwhelmed by the complexity of the problems with which they are faced that they withdraw from the world completely, in isolation or madness, losing their foothold on reality and their remaining strength and vitality in the process.

One of our constant causes for concern is the presence of others. We often tend to see our fellow human beings as potential threats and much of our experience confirms the untrustworthiness of the other. Our destructive interactions or our avoidance of interaction with others can thus become another self-fulfilling prophecy of doom.

As fragile human beings we often live with regret over what happened yesterday, in fear of what may be demanded of us tomorrow and in guilt over what we have not yet accomplished today. We are quite capable of emotionally paralysing ourselves in this manner.

Some people find themselves in situations that significantly restrict or constrict their outlook and their freedom of action. Genetic, developmental, accidental, class, cultural or gender factors can all generate what may seem like insurmountable obstacles. Everyone's life presents a number of difficulties that we have to learn to accommodate or overcome. Some people manage to overcome substantial initial disadvantages or adversity, whereas others squander their advantage or flounder in the face of minor contretemps.

Every problem has several solutions. Our attitude and frame of mind make all the difference to our ability to tackle difficulties. There is no point in blaming oneself, others or circumstances and remaining trapped in a particular position. Facing the situation and putting it in perspective may be hard to do, but it is always possible, given some time and with some assistance.

Being ready to face our problems leads to resolute living and to a willingness to meet whatever may come with steadfastness and in a spirit of adventure.

Change

Change takes place continuously and human beings have to make considerable efforts to try and keep their situations stable. We often attempt to avoid change, even when our situation is not particularly good. We frequently fear the inevitable process of transformation that everything in this world is subject to.

When clients come to psychotherapy or counselling they do so because they want to find the strength and confidence to allow a change for the better to happen in their lives. They need the therapist or counsellor to believe in them and help them to be steady when confronting their fears and doubts.

The objective of existential work is to enable clients to become more open to their own experience in all its paradoxical reality. They can be helped to be more tolerant of their own anxiety and to become more understanding of it by becoming more self-reflective. An awareness of what is the case will change what is the case and as clients tell their story and discuss it with their therapist they will gradually alter their interpretation of their story and thus of themselves.

To enable people to be aware of their strengths, talents and abilities is as important as to help them explore the darker side of their own experience, passion and yearning.

Crisis is seen as a moment of danger and opportunity when transformation happens rapidly while everything is temporarily thrown into a state of chaos. New paths can therefore be chosen and our interaction with the world can be reorganized in a new way. Counselling and therapy ensure that the crisis is a point of breakthrough rather than breakdown.

Even when the circumstances you find yourself in are dire or unfair, it is still possible to change your attitude towards them and find new ways of improving your fate.

Skills and strategies

The existential approach is in principle against techniques, as these might hamper human interaction at a deep, direct and real level. Therapeutic skill is used to help clients face vital issues and the therapeutic encounter consists of a deep and authentic human exchange.

Nevertheless, a number of conversational strategies can be recognized as belonging to the existential approach. These include the emphasis on working with paradox when clients are helped to recognize their conflicts and confront reality in all its contradictions and ambiguity.

An attitude of openness is encouraged and clients are not mollycoddled, though treated with respect, care and understanding. In this process there is a strategic emphasis on making clients aware of the strengths they are already displaying and could learn to master more effectively.

Clients are helped to make explicit their implicit assumptions, values and beliefs, until a clear worldview emerges. This may be explored for the contradictions or implications embedded in it.

The therapist keeps track of the client's state of mind. Moods and attitudes, feelings and deep emotion are followed to their source so that a deeply felt sense of what truly matters to the person emerges. The client is taught to continue doing this emotional tracking independently.

Purpose and ultimate concerns are worked with until people feel reactivated to live life to the full in an engaged and committed manner and without hiding away from difficulties and fears. In rediscovering what it is you want to live for you get a renewed taste for your own creativity and ability, finding a new authority and playfulness on the way.

The therapist allows himself or herself to identify with the client's issues in order to find a way into and through dilemmas in a personal and direct manner. At the same time distance from the client's predicament will be preserved through the philosophical attitude, which allows problems to be seen in the broader perspective of universal human struggles.

Ideological matters might be discussed and debated and political and cultural issues will be addressed. Clarifying and creating a meaningful world is one of the important objectives. By modelling a tough and caring approach to life and others, existential therapists inspire clients with a vital desire to live to the full with courage and self-determination. This resoluteness is always set against the recognition of human and personal limitations and is matched by a growing acceptance of the forces of life and death that we are all bound by.

Research evidence

There is very little direct outcome research in existential psychotherapy and counselling because of the opposition of existential therapists to the reductionistic technology of research. There is, however, a certain amount of qualitative research that investigates existential factors. There is also a lot of research that indirectly deals with existential concerns.

- Yalom (1970) in his work with groups found existential factors to be much more important to client change than he had originally thought. From then on existential psychotherapy became the focus in his subsequent work.
- Much of the research on the person-centred approach is relevant to existential therapy, especially where it demonstrates the importance of genuineness

or authenticity on the part of the therapist (Carkhuff and Truax, 1965).
- Bergin and Garfield (1994) recognized a number of existential factors as determining positive outcome in psychotherapy.
- Rennie's qualitative research shows the importance of a number of existential factors (Rennie, 1992).
- There is much research that shows the importance of meaning-creation to the successful processing of traumatic events (Clarke, 1989).
- Recent research in positive psychology demonstrates the importance of such existential factors as authenticity (Seligman, 2002) and meaning (Baumeister, 1991).

References

Baumeister, R.F. (1991) *Meanings of Life*. New York: Guilford Press.

Bergin, A. and Garfield, S. (eds) (1994) *Handbook of Psychotherapy and Behavior Change* (4th edn). New York: Wiley.

Binswanger, L. (1963) *Being-in-the-World* (trans. J. Needleman). New York: Basic Books.

Boss, M. (1957) *Psychoanalysis and Daseinsanalysis* (trans. J.B. Lefebre). New York: Basic Books.

Bugental, J.F.T. (1981) *The Search for Authenticity*. New York: Irvington.

Carkhuff, R. and Truax, C. (1965) Training in counseling and therapy: an evaluation of an integrated didactic and experiential approach. *Journal of Consulting Psychology*, 29: 333–336.

Clarke, K.M. (1989) Creation of meaning: an emotional processing task in psychotherapy. *Pychotherapy*, 26: 139–148.

Cohn, H. (1997) *Existential Thought and Therapeutic Practice*. London: Sage.

Deurzen, E. van (1997) *Everyday Mysteries: Existential Dimensions of Psychotherapy*. London: Routledge.

Deurzen, E. van (1998) *Paradox and Passion in Psychotherapy*. Chichester: Wiley.

Deurzen, E. van (2002) *Existential Counselling and Psychotherapy in Practice* (2nd edn). London: Sage.

Frankl, V.E. ([1946], 1964) *Man's Search for Meaning*. London: Hodder and Stoughton.

Heidegger, M. (1927) *Being and Time* (trans. J. Macquarrie and E.S. Robinson). London: Harper.

Kierkegaard, S. ([1844], 1980) *The Concept of Anxiety* (trans. R. Thomte). Princeton, NJ: Princeton University Press.

Laing, R.D. (1960) *The Divided Self.* London: Tavistock.

Mahrer, A.R. (1996) *The Complete Guide to Experiential Psychotherapy.* New York: Wiley.

May, R. (1969) *Love and Will.* New York: Norton.

May, R., Angel, E. and Ellenberger, H.F. (1958) *Existence.* New York: Basic Books.

Rennie, D.L. (1992) Qualitative analysis of the client's experience of psychotherapy: the unfolding of reflexivity. In S. Toukmanian and D.L. Rennie (eds), *Psychotherapy Process Research: Paradigmatic and Narrative Approaches.* Newbury Park, CA: Sage.

Sartre, J.-P. ([1943], 1956) *Being and Nothingness: An Essay on Phenomenological Ontology* (trans. H. Barnes). New York: Philosophical Library.

Seligman, M.E.P. (2002) *Authentic Happiness.* New York: The Free Press.

Tillich, P. (1952) *The Courage to Be.* New Haven, CT: Yale University Press.

Yalom, I.D. (1970) *The Theory and Practice of Group Psychotherapy.* New York: Basic Books.

Yalom, I.D. (1980) *Existential Psychotherapy.* New York: Basic Books.

5.17 Gestalt Therapy
(Frederick Perls, 1893–1970)

○○○

MICHAEL ELLIS AND JONATHAN SMITH

Brief history

Gestalt theory and practice was first developed by Frederick (Fritz) Perls and Laura Perls along with Paul Goodman and others in New York in the 1950s. *Gestalt Therapy: Excitement and Growth in the Human Personality* was published in 1951. This has been for many years the definitive text on gestalt theory. Prior to this, while in South Africa, Fritz Perls published *Ego, Hunger and Aggression* in which he laid the foundations for this approach to therapy.

Perls was born in Berlin and educated at the University of Freiburg and Frederick Wilhelm University in Berlin. He received his MD in 1921. Before this he had served as a Medical Officer in the German army. He then trained in psychoanalysis in Berlin, Frankfurt and Vienna. Thus Perls brought a strong foundation in psychoanalysis, particularly influenced by Wilhelm Reich and Karen Homey.

Laura Perls studied gestalt psychology with Kurt Goldstein (from which the approach takes its name), worked with Paul Tillich and was greatly influenced by Martin Buber. Paul Goodman, a philosopher, libertarian and anarchist, contributed the social and political dimension.

The word 'gestalt' does not have a direct translation into English; definitions include pattern, configuration, form and whole. The work of the gestalt psychologists in the early part of the twentieth century focused primarily on perception and learning. Wertheimer and Ehrenfelds proposed that we perceive our environment in terms of 'wholes'. As best as we are able, we make meaning, we create a form or gestalt from what we experience. The gestalt includes what is 'figure' for us in relation to what is in the background. Hence the importance in gestalt work of figure and ground. An additional contribution of the gestalt psychologists was the concept of 'closure'.

In its original sense it refers to the tendency of the perceptual system to 'close' or round off any incomplete shape or form.

Gestalt psychology

The work of the above psychologists and others, including Koffka and Kohler, was developed into the realms of personality by Kurt Goldstein and Kurt Lewin. The work of these men was key for the development of gestalt theory and practice, although Lewin's influence has only recently been acknowledged. Goldstein developed his 'organismic theory' from gestalt principles, and particularly the centrality of 'self-actualization' for the unfolding of the individual's potential. Lewin, associated with Wertheimer and Kohler, developed the concept of the individual as part of a dynamic field. He emphasized the importance of the person in relation to their environment and also the significance of the present, the 'facts' of the dynamic field.

Existentialism

Gestalt theory has been influenced by a number of existentialist thinkers such as Paul Tillich, Martin Buber and Jean-Paul Sartre. It is an existential phenomenological approach and what is explored is the individual's existence as experienced by them. There is considerable emphasis on the individual being responsible for their own existence; on the importance of the here and now (experience in the present) and the meeting of therapist and client as persons in the 'I–Thou' relationship as described by Martin Buber.

Eastern religion

The influence of eastern religions, particularly Taoism and Zen, are evident in the importance of awareness of the present moment as a goal and a method in gestalt work which may lead to a 'satori-like' insight, an 'Aha' which brings about a new gestalt, a reorganization of the person's experience. Also significant is the focus on 'organismic functioning' rather than over-emphasis on thinking; the

use of paradox and the ideas and practice of non-doing, of standing out of the way and allowing things to emerge. (Fritz Perls spent almost a year in Japan studying Zen.)

Drama and movement

Fritz Perls was very interested in acting and made use of Moreno's psychodrama techniques and Laura Perls studied dance for many years. This originally gave gestalt methodology a strong expressive/creative bias.

Basic assumptions

Holism – that nature is a coherent whole; different elements are in relation with each other in a continually changing process. Holistically we cannot understand ourselves by analysing aspects in isolation because 'the whole is greater than the sum of its parts'.

Growth – the process of organismic self-regulation occurs through contact with our environment, of which we are a part. In health we do this by a process of forming figures against a background based on our current most important need. At a given moment a need will emerge, become 'figural', be met and recede into the background as another need emerges from the 'ground'. For example, I become aware of a dry mouth, decide I need a drink, take action to get a drink and then focus on the paper I was about to read.

The Field – Field theory, originally formulated by Kurt Lewin, maintains that the person is never separated from their environment, both their internal physical and psychological environment and their external social and cultural context. The meaning we give to any figure, or stimulus, will then be dependent on its context or field.

Self-actualization – we have an innate tendency to realize our potential, to become who we can be. Perls (1969: 31) wrote: 'Every individual, every plant, every animal has only one inborn goal – to actualize itself as it is.'

Awareness – increasing awareness is at the core of gestalt practice: through the development of organismic experienced awareness (rather than just intellectual awareness) we are able to be responsible, proactive and allow the healthy flow of organismic self-regulation.

Contact and dialogue – contact refers to the way we meet, interact and exchange with the environment, including other people. Gestalt work always aims for lively contact which can be enhanced through the use of dialogue. Dialogue means meeting in the here and now and recognizing one another 'in our uniqueness, our fullness and our vulnerability' (Hycner and Jacobs, 1995: 9).

Healing – occurs through meeting another as a person. Each individual, acknowledged as separate, is capable of risking meeting the other in an I–Thou relationship as defined by Buber. He described two contrasting attitudes that an individual can take towards others: the I–It way of relating and the I–Thou way of relating. Both are needed for living. The I–It attitude is more present when there is a purpose in the meeting, when one or other or both have a goal of some sort. The I–Thou attitude is one of being as present as possible with another in a purpose-less way, with no goal in mind and with an appreciation of the uniqueness of the other as a person.

We are neither intrinsically good nor bad.

Origin and maintenance of problems

A healthy person in gestalt theory allows him or herself a fluent exchange and adjustment in relation with the environment (organismic self-regulation). This healthy process of forming figures against the background based on our needs is known as the gestalt formation and destruction cycle and is also called the contact/withdrawal cycle.

Problems are seen as disturbances of this natural healthy functioning. Significant early relationships are important in the initial disturbance of the contact/withdrawal cycle. These may develop as a creative way of surviving in the face of danger, lack of love, care and attention. However, they become embedded in the personality and in adulthood limit 'creative adjustment' with the current environment, so healthy fluid functioning becomes rigid, habitual and over-controlled.

Perls defined four 'neurotic mechanisms' or contact boundary disturbances which can restrict and limit individuals' healthy exchange with their environment, whether physical, emotional or intellectual. All these processes have a healthy, functional aspect; it is when they are habitual and chronic that healthy functioning is limited:

- *Introjection* – in which something is taken in whole, 'swallowed down' without assimilation or reflection. This may be an attitude, belief, idea or behaviour.
- *Projection* – in which traits, attitudes, behaviours, beliefs, etc., are attributed to others or to objects in the environment.
- *Retroflection* – this involves turning energy 'back in' against oneself which in healthy functioning would be allowed to go out to contact the environment. For example, somebody who has learnt that expressing their irritation or anger is risky may come to withhold aggressive energy, possibly causing headaches, muscle tension or other physiological distress, thus turning energy against oneself.
- *Confluence* – is a state of being in which the individual is unclear about boundaries, with others, with the environment. There is a merging of ideas, beliefs, feelings, etc., and no clear sense of separateness.

Since Perls, more recent theorists have described another 'neurotic mechanism':

- *Deflection* – in which the individual turns away from healthy contact with the environment and the contact is experienced as unclear, weak, vague (a weak gestalt). These are processes by which problems are maintained and result in 'unfinished business' (incomplete *gestalten*) which inhibits energy and healthy functioning. If extremely chronic this can result in severe disturbance in functioning for the individual.

Change

Therapeutic change occurs with the rediscovery of the gestalt process of organismic self-regulation. This involves close attention to *how* the client does what she or he does, how they function in the world and in the relationship with the therapist.

Awareness is the key in this work: to become more aware of the sorts of disturbances described in the previous section brings a recovery of contactfulness with aspects of self and others. The sort of awareness sought is not just intellectual but is holistic in that it is an experience involving intellect, emotions and physical sensations.

As part of the therapy the client works to complete 'unfinished business' through closure and resolution of issues from the past which still affect the client's current functioning.

Another aspect of change is that of exploring/experimenting with new sorts of behaviour as the energy bound up in old patterns is released. Such experimentation develops from an underlying attitude that the client may discover more of who they are.

Change in gestalt therapy comes from becoming more fully ourselves: 'Change occurs when one becomes what he is, not when he tries to become what he is not' (Beisser, 1970: 88). This can only happen through awareness, now, of what we are actually doing and how we are functioning.

With the full awareness described above there is a re-organizing of the client's experienced sense of themselves, an 'Aha' of change.

Skills and strategies

The gestalt therapist's approach is phenomenological; to facilitate clients deepening their awareness of themselves, and their relationship with others through attending, engaging with the clients, exploring their experience, describing what *is*.

The authenticity of the therapist, their genuineness, their wholeness and presence are central. The therapist engages and participates in the relationship and also observes. The therapist interacts with the client with an I–Thou attitude, a willingness to relate authentically and meet the client as a person. What sort of contact is made and how that is 'interrupted' is the focus of the work.

Therapists must therefore use their creativity, working from a clear understanding of gestalt theory: the centrality of gestalt formation and destruction, awareness of present experience and the theory of change. A range of interventions may be utilized which might include:

- *Focusing on body awareness* – e.g. encouraging the client to become more aware of felt sensations within the body.
- *Attention to language* – e.g. noticing *how* the client constructs sentences, one aspect being whether the client uses impersonal pronouns (it, they, one) to distance themselves from their experience.
- *Psychodramatic work* – e.g. 'empty chair' work in which a client explores their relationship with others, or aspects of themselves by imagining them to be present and engaging in dialogue with them in some way.
- *Directed awareness experiments* – e.g. a client who consistently speaks in a cognitive mode and may be encouraged to become more aware of their feelings as well as their thoughts.

Joyce and Sills (2001) discuss a variety of skills and strategies which can be used in gestalt counselling settings, although it should be remembered that the use of such interventions will arise out of the ongoing dialogue and exploration between client and therapist rather than being used merely as techniques. The aim is always to enhance the awareness of clients, to facilitate their recovery of their organismic self-regulation. Houston (2003) has also shown how the gestalt approach can be tailored for use in short-term, brief therapy settings.

Research

Research has only recent begun to play a significant role in the development of gestalt theory and practice and the recent move of UK Gestalt Institutes to integrate with universities and offer Masters-level qualifications will mean that this trend is likely to accelerate. Since Eleanor O'Leary's (1992) review of the research literature, a number of gestalt-related research papers have been published, and in the latest edition of *Bergin and Garfield's Handbook of Psychotherapy and Behavior Change* (Lambert, 2004), gestalt theory is identified as one of the three 'major subapproaches' to experiential/humanistic therapy, alongside person-centred and existential approaches (Elliott et al., 2004).

Many of the studies are concerned with the effectiveness of the two-chair technique. For example, Paivio et al. (2001) found that the degree of engagement in imaginal confrontations with abusive carers in empty-chair work predicted resolution of child abuse issues. Johnson and Smith (1997) compared systematic de-sensitization and gestalt empty-chair procedures with a no-therapy control group in the treatment of phobia sufferers, and found that, following treatment, both treatment groups were significantly less phobic than the no-therapy group.

References

Beisser, A.R. (1970) The paradoxical theory of change. In J. Fagan and I.L. Shepherd (eds), *Gestalt Therapy Now*. Harmondsworth: Penguin.

Elliot, R.L., Greenberg, L.S. and Lietaer, G. (2004) Research on experiential psychotherapies. In M.J. Lambert (ed.), *Bergin and Garfield's Handbook of Psychotherapy and Behavior Change* (5th edn). New York: John Wiley.

Houston, G. (2003) *Brief Gestalt Therapy*. London: Sage.

Hycner, R.A. and Jacobs, L. (1995) *The Healing Relationship in Gestalt Therapy*. Highland, NY: Gestalt Journal Press.

Johnson, W.R. and Smith, E.W.L. (1997) Gestalt empty-chair dialogue vs systematic desensitisation in the treatment of a phobia. *Gestalt Review*, 1: 150–162.

Joyce, P. and Sills, C. (2001) *Skills in Gestalt Counselling and Psychotherapy*. London: Sage.

Lambert, M.J. (ed.) (2004) *Bergin and Garfield's Handbook of Psychotherapy and Behavior Change* (5th edn). New York: John Wiley.

O'Leary, E. (1992) *Gestalt Therapy: Theory, Practice and Research*. London: Chapman and Hall.

Paivio, S.C., Hall, I.E., Holowaty, K.A.M., Jellis, J.B. and Tran, N. (2001) Imaginal confrontation for resolving child abuse issues. *Psychotherapy Research*, 11: 433–453.

Perls, F. (1947) *Ego, Hunger and Aggression: A Revision of Freud's Theory and Method*. London: Allen and Unwin.

Perls, F. (1969) *Gestalt Therapy* Verbatim. Moab, UT: Real People Press.

Perls, F., Hefferline, R. and Goodman, P. (1951) *Gestalt Therapy: Excitement and Growth in the Human Personality*. New York: Julian Press.

5.18   Narrative Approaches to Therapy   ○○○

JOHN McLEOD

Brief history

Narrative approaches to counselling and psychotherapy emerged in the 1980s. Within psychology as a whole, theorists such as Jerome Bruner, Theodore Sarbin and Donald Polkinghorne had argued that storytelling represented a fundamental human means of communication and sense making. These writers proposed that it was essential for psychologists to become more sensitive to the actual stories people told, and the way they told these stories. This 'narrative turn' within psychology, which reflected similar developments within philosophy and the social sciences in general, soon began to have an impact on psychotherapy and counselling.

One of the most significant contributions to the evolution of narrative therapy originally grew out of the work of Michael White and David Epston in the field of family therapy. Their book *Narrative Means to Therapeutic Ends* (1990) is essential reading for anyone interested in the role of narrative within therapy. An excellent introduction to their 'narrative therapy' model can be found in Morgan (2000). Another important strand of thinking about narrative dimensions of therapy has been the work of Lester Luborsky, Donald Spence and Roy Schafer, from a psychoanalytic perspective. During the 1990s there was a proliferation of narrative approaches (Angus and McLeod, 2004). In this respect, narrative ideas can be seen as exemplifying one aspect of the movement within therapy as a whole in the direction of integrationism and eclecticism.

Basic assumptions

Narrative-informed approaches to counselling and psychotherapy have tended to share a core set of assumptions about the role of narrative in human communication, identity and meaning making:

Stories are the basic way in which people make sense of their experience. Relating a story about an event conveys the intentionality and purpose of the teller and their understanding of relationships and the social world, expresses feelings, and communicates a moral evaluation of what has happened.

We tell our own personal tales, but do so by drawing on a cultural stock of narrative forms. We are born into the story of our family and community, and the story of who we are (e.g. our birth story, the story behind our name). As we grow up we adopt narrative templates provided by myths, films, novels and other cultural resources to give shape and meaning to our individual life-narrative.

People are social beings, and have a basic need to tell their story. Holding back on telling the story involves a process of physiological inhibition that can have negative effects on health. Telling one's story promotes a sense of knowing and being known, and leads to social inclusion.

Personal experience and reality are constructed through the process of telling stories. The stories that we tell are always co-constructed, and are told in the presence of a real or implied audience. There is a dialogic aspect to stories. Constructing a story is a situated performance, a version of events created at a particular time and place to have a specific effect. A story is something that is created *between* people rather than existing in one person's mind. The narrativization of experience is an open-ended process. There are always other stories that can be told about the same events or experiences.

The concept of *voice* refers to the way in which a story is told. The life-narrative represents a weaving together of multiple voices. For example, the story of someone's life, or episodes in that life, can be narrated through an official, psychiatric/medical voice, a personal and vulnerable voice, or the harsh critical voice of an angry parent. One of the tasks of therapy is to distentangle these voices. The concept of voice also conveys something of the embodied nature of storytelling, by drawing attention to the physical qualities of *how* the story is told, in terms of volume, tone, rhythm and the use of speech forms such as metaphor, repetition and contrast.

It is useful to distinguish between oral and literary (written) forms of narration. Writing down a story tends to produce a more logically structured version, which can function as a permanent record. People attribute authority and legitimacy to written stories. Oral versions of stories, by contrast, are generally more relational, improvised, emotionally involving and transient.

Origin and maintenance of problems

The experience of being *silenced* is emotionally painful and problematic for most people. Silencing can be a consequence of the social isolation that can result in many situations, such as bereavement, emigration/exile, illness and disability. Silencing can also be produced through purposeful oppression of persons, for example those who may have been sexually, physically or emotionally abused by family members or those who are members of political, ethnic, religious or sexual orientation minority categories.

A life story that is silenced or that is habitual minimizes the possibility of dialogical engagement with other persons. 'Problems' can be understood as being those areas of personal experience around which the person is not able, or willing, to engage in conversation.

The life-narrative templates available within a culture, community or family may be difficult or impossible to reconcile with the circumstances of actual lived experience. For example, the *dominant narratives* within a culture may prescribe gender, age or social class 'scripts' which deny many or most of the possibilities for creative human encounter.

The trajectory of some lives may contribute to the production of narratives which are *incomplete* or *incoherent*.

Some people can develop a style of telling personal stories that is almost wholly *problem saturated*. This tendency can be exacerbated by over-involvement with mental health ideologies.

Change

People find it helpful to have an opportunity to tell their story in a setting in which what they have to say is accepted and valued by others. The basic experience of another person becoming a witness to one's account of troubles is meaningful and worthwhile.

It can be useful to be given the opportunity to generate different versions of a story concerning life issues. Usually, the telling and re-telling of the story produces *solution-focused* narratives alongside the more habitual problem-saturated accounts of troubles which people bring into therapy.

The ritual of therapy makes it possible for the person to articulate their life narrative with support and without interruption or competition. This gives the person a chance to reflect upon their story, and to consider whether there are any parts of it that perhaps they might seek to articulate in different ways. Unfolding the story in its entirety is a means of retrieving and preserving the meaning of that life narrative, and in itself leads to a more meaningful life.

The notion of *externalizing* the story (a key technique within White and Epston's (1990) narrative therapy) conveys the idea that the person creates the stories he or she tells (and therefore can tell different stories). The person is not identified with their story but has a relationship with it.

Narrative therapy methods involve the construction of a more satisfying or coherent life narrative through a process of broadening the narrative horizon. The person may find that stories of current troubles may make sense when understood in the light of earlier 'chapters' in the life story.

People who are seeking to change aspects of their life story may engage in a search for examples of more convivial or suitable narrative forms they can live within. This search may involve exploring literary sources, meeting new people, or learning from fellow members of a therapy or self-help group.

The act of narrating a life in a changed way may necessitate disrupting or deconstructing habitual narratives. This process can be facilitated by the use of figurative and concrete language and different modes of telling (e.g. writing). Therapists encourage the telling of vivid, meaningful and emotionally resonant personal stories rather than bland, abstract reports.

Telling a different story about oneself can require recruiting new audiences, and challenging the ways in which pre-existing audiences and communities promote problem-saturated narratives.

Skills and strategies

The role of the counsellor or psychotherapist includes being both witness to, and co-editor of, the stories told by the person seeking help.

The skills of the narrative therapist are built on a sensitivity and awareness in relation to language use and narrative forms.

Narrative therapists seek to minimize the danger that the therapeutic experience will function as a means of reinforcing dominant cultural narratives. One of the ways in which they do this is by adopting a *not-knowing* stance, which involves honouring the teller as the expert on their own story. Users of therapy are seen as consultants to the therapeutic process, and are asked for advice on what is helpful. Therapists are also sensitive to the political and cultural meanings of the language they use and stories they tell and develop a critical approach to theory.

Many narrative-informed therapists use techniques based on writing, rather than relying solely on spoken dialogue (Bolton et al., 2004).

The goal of narrative therapy is to assist the person to enter a mutual conversation about whatever it is that is troubling them. The therapist must be willing actively to participate in this conversation.

Research evidence

The research literature on narrative approaches to therapy has focused mainly on the development of methods for exploring narrative processes (see Angus and McLeod, 2004); there is little evidence regarding the effectiveness of narrative therapy or narrative-informed practice.

Many narrative therapists are highly critical of existing research methods and instruments, for example those which rely on psychiatric diagnostic categories, on the grounds that they function to maintain the hegemony of a destructive dominant professional 'language of deficit'.

References

Angus, L.E. and McLeod, J. (eds) (2004) *Handbook of Narrative and Psychotherapy: Practice, Theory and Research*. Thousand Oaks, CA: Sage.

Bolton, G., Howlett, S., Lago, C. and Wright, J.K. (eds) (2004) *Writing Cures: An Introductory Handbook of Writing in Counselling and Psychotherapy*. London: Brunner-Routledge.

McLeod, J. (1997) *Narrative and Psychotherapy*. London: Sage.

Morgan, A. (2000) *What Is Narrative Therapy? An Easy-to-read Introduction*. Adelaide: Dulwich Centre Publication.

Schafer, R. (1992) *Retelling a Life: Narration and Dialogue in Psychoanalysis*. New York: Basic Books.

White, M. and Epston, D. (1990) *Narrative Means to Therapeutic Ends*. New York: Norton.

5.19 Person-centred Counselling and Psychotherapy
(Carl R. Rogers, 1902–1987)

○○○

TONY MERRY* AND KEITH TUDOR

Brief history

Person-centred (also widely known as client-centred) counselling and psychotherapy developed in the USA from the late 1930s on. For a short while the approach was known as non-directive therapy, a term that quickly fell out of use. A key date is December 1940, when the founder of this approach, Carl Rogers, spoke

---

* As this revised edition was being prepared, Tony Merry was taken seriously ill. Not wishing to disturb him, the editors asked me to step in and edit Tony's original chapter, which I have done, hopefully keeping the spirit of his clear thinking and accessible writing, while expanding the view of Rogers' therapeutic conditions and the chapter as a whole. Sadly, as the book was going to press, Tony died. This now stands as a co-authored publication, based on a dialogue with and development of his ideas, which, for my part, I dedicate with great affection to a valued colleague who devoted much of his professional life to presenting and elaborating the integrity of the person-centred approach to psychology. KT

at the University of Minnesota on 'some newer concepts of psychotherapy'. The approach was further expanded by Rogers and his colleagues at the University of Chicago and included the development of a theory of personality and behaviour, as well as a more detailed description of the characteristics of person-centred therapy.

Between 1953 and 1954 and based on his research, Rogers formulated his now famous hypothesis of certain necessary and sufficient conditions of therapeutic personality change (published in 1957 and 1959). These papers established Rogers and his colleagues as innovators in the field of counselling, and stimulated a great deal of debate and research, for a summary of which see Patterson (1984/2000) and Tudor and Merry (2002). Person-centred counselling or therapy – within this tradition the two activities are viewed as indistinguishable and, therefore, synonymous – became established as one of the most influential of the humanistic approaches. Mearns and Thorne (2000: 27), however, suggest that, in 'its forsaking of mystique and other "powerful" behaviours of therapists', person-centred therapy is as different from many humanistic therapies as it is from other traditions such as psychoanalysis. Currently, person-centred therapy is widely practised and studied in Europe, though its influence in the USA has diminished in recent years. In the later years of his life Rogers became interested in the wider application of the principles of person-centred psychology to education and learning; groups, group facilitation and conflict resolution; and politics. Person-centred therapy is now viewed as one application of what has become more broadly referred to as the 'person-centred *approach*', for a contemporary outline and development of which see Embleton Tudor et al. (2004).

Basic assumptions

The organism's tendency to actualize – the tendency towards the fulfilment of potential and wholeness – represents the sole motivational construct in person-centred psychology. The theory of actualization is a natural science theory, not a moral theory. While no specific moral values are implied by the theory, two values implicit in the person-centred approach to the person are fluidity (as distinct from fixity or rigidity) and creativity.

One function of the human organism's tendency to actualize is to differentiate a portion of an individual's experience into an awareness of self and the organization of a self-concept. The self-concept, or self-structure, is a fluid but consistent pattern of perceptions of the 'I' or 'me' in relation to the environment, personal values, goals and ideals.

Self-actualization, one aspect of the organism's tendency to actualize, appears after the development of the self-concept and acts to maintain that concept. Self-actualization does not always result in optimal functioning because each person, whether psychologically healthy or unhealthy, is self-actualizing to the extent that each has a self-structure to maintain and enhance. Thus, if an aspect of someone's self-concept is to be pleasing, then he may act socially to support that, at the expense of his organismic direction.

Awareness of self is termed self-experience. When any self-experience is evaluated by others as being more or less worthy of positive regard, a person's self-regard becomes vulnerable to these external judgements. When self-experiences become sought after or avoided because they are more or less deserving of self-regard, the individual is said to have acquired conditions of worth.

People have, within themselves, the resources needed for personal change. These resources can become available in a climate of facilitative psychological attitudes or conditions (described below). This climate can exist within a therapeutic setting or elsewhere, for example in a group, community, family or classroom.

The view of human nature is positive, optimistic and constructive. This, however, does not deny the capacity for destructive, anti-social and aggressive behaviour. Rather, it focuses on the potential for positive change to occur throughout life, and takes the view that environmental influences, particularly those concerning relationships with others, are critical factors in determining either positive or negative self-concepts, and hence healthy or unhealthy functioning.

People are regarded as potentially fully functioning, trustworthy, creative, social and congruent, or integrated in themselves and in relationships. In other words, given the right conditions, we are able to admit all experiencing into awareness without distortion or denial, which are the two defence mechanisms postulated in person-centred psychology.

Each individual client has the capacity to rediscover their organismic valuing process and direction in a relationship in which power and control are shared between therapist and client.

Origin and maintenance of problems

Disturbance exists whenever there is antagonism between a person's tendency to actualize in one direction and self-actualization which may lie in another direction. Incongruence exists to the extent that these two tendencies diverge.

At the beginning of life, a person is fully congruent, that is, able to allow all experiencing into awareness without distortion or denial. Later, the person encounters disapproval, rejection or other threats and becomes anxious in the face of the continuing need for positive regard from significant others. The formation of the person's self-concept becomes conditioned by these negative experiences, conditions of worth become internalized, and the person seeks protection from further negative experiences. The conditioned self-concept can become so reinforced that the person becomes completely alienated from any sense of themselves and their organismic direction. The dichotomy between the self-concept and experiencing leads to increasingly distorted perception. A condition of incongruence now exists, and the person's psychological functioning is disturbed.

Disturbance is maintained through the continuation of a high degree of reliance on the evaluations of others for a sense of self-worth or self-esteem.

Anxiety, threat and confusion are created whenever incongruence is experienced between the self-concept, with its internalized conditions of worth, and actual experience. Whenever such anxiety arises, or is threatened, the person will continue to default to defences of distortion or denial of experiencing. If experiences are extremely incongruent with the self-concept, a person's defence system may be unable to prevent such experiences from overwhelming the self-concept. Resulting behaviour may be destructive, disorganized and chaotic.

Change

Effective therapy occurs in a relationship in which the therapist holds certain attitudes or conditions and is successful in communicating those to the client over time. In addition, Rogers identified certain client conditions which, in our view, prefigures more recent concerns about the relational, dialogic and co-creative nature of therapy. Indeed, Rogers first referred to his work as 'relationship therapy'. Here, in summarizing the conditions, we distinguish between the therapist's conditions and the client's conditions (while retaining the original numbering).

The therapist's conditions (from Rogers, 1959: 213) are:

1. 'That two persons are in contact', a condition which requires both therapist and client to be actively present, both in a social sense of meeting and agreeing to work together (or not), and in a more psychological sense. Clearly some, more disturbed, clients are less contactful or contactable and, with advances in the theory and practice of 'pre-therapy' (Prouty, 1994), this condition is currently receiving more attention.

3. The therapist is congruent within the relationship, that is, is genuine or real, putting up no professional façade. This includes the therapist admitting into awareness all experience of the relationship so that such experiencing is available for direct communication to the client when appropriate. This condition is more about experiencing than self-disclosing. It is not necessary for the therapist directly to communicate any particular experience of the

relationship, except when the failure to do so impedes the practitioner's ability to experience unconditional positive regard and to understand the client empathically. Under such circumstances it may become necessary for the therapist to communicate their experiencing.

4. The therapist experiences unconditional positive regard for the client, that is, he or she maintains a positive, non-judgemental and accepting attitude.

5. The therapist experiences an empathic understanding of the internal, subjective frame of reference of the client.

There is a difference between Rogers' two formulations of these hypotheses about the extent to which the therapist should communicate these last two conditions.

The requirements on/of a client, which we may refer to as the 'client's conditions' (see Tudor, 2000), are:

1. 'That two persons are in contact' (as above).

2. That, by virtue of being vulnerable or anxious, the client is in some way incongruent or (as discussed above) experiencing a discrepancy between organismic and self-actualizing tendencies.

6. That he or she perceives the therapist's unconditional positive regard and empathic understanding 'at least to a minimal degree' (whether the therapist directly or explicitly communicates this or not). In one paper, Rogers (1958/1967) refers to this as the 'assumed condition', by which, in effect, all therapy is evaluated or assessed.

A major characteristic of person-centred counselling and psychotherapy is that it is in essence non-directive. In other words, the therapist has no specific goals for the client and does not suggest the client attend to any particular form of experiencing. The therapist refrains, for example, from interpreting clients' experience, but focuses on empathic, non-judgemental understanding and acceptance of it.

It is important to note that being in contact, congruence, unconditional positive regard and empathic understanding are not conceptualized in terms of skills, strategies or techniques. Rather, person-centred therapy is better thought of as a relationship in which

the client experiences another person (the therapist) as one who is acceptant of the client's subjective world, and who endeavours to understand the client's experiencing and meaning system. Therapeutic progress follows from the client experiencing being empathically understood without judgement.

A skilled therapist is one who can communicate his or her contactfulness, authenticity, positive regard and empathic understanding in ways that the client experiences as non-threatening. Experiencing these conditions without threat enables the client to become increasingly free of the need for denial or distortion.

Moments of therapeutic movement consist of experiences of self-acceptance and integration. Typically, such moments have the following characteristics: they are immediate and consist of total experiences, not thoughts or intellectual understandings (though these may follow or accompany the experience); they are new in that, while they may have been experienced before (at least, in part), they have never been experienced completely or with awareness combined with appropriate physiological reactions; they are self-accepting in that they are owned as a part of the self; and they are integrated into the self-structure without distortion.

Skills and strategies

The therapist's role is to maintain an attitude of unconditional positive regard and empathic understanding, coupled with being open to contact and personal congruence or integration. It is unhelpful to conceptualize person-centred therapy in terms of behavioural strategies since the therapist's only intention is to maintain a relationship with the client based on the conditions described above.

The skill most commonly associated with person-centred therapy is sometimes referred to as reflection of feelings. Though useful in that it describes some aspects of the therapist's behaviour in the relationship, it can be misleading in that it is only a partial description. The therapist concentrates on empathic understanding of the client's internal, subjective frame of reference. In communicating empathic understanding, the counsellor does not focus attention on feelings at the expense of other experiences that may be present within the client's frame of reference. These experiences may include, for example, thoughts, bodily sensations, fantasies and memories, etc.

Although opinions among person-centred therapists vary, many would agree that it is possible, even within the strictest theoretical confines of person-centred therapy, to utilize techniques associated with other forms of counselling and psychotherapy *providing* that such techniques, as Rogers (1957: 102) put it, 'serve as channels for fulfilling one of the conditions'. We may add that they are not imposed by the therapist, are requested by the client to further a particular purpose, and that the client retains control over the extent of their use. However, the use of such techniques by person-centred practitioners is minimal.

Research evidence

Rogers himself was one of the leading pioneers of research into counselling and psychotherapy (see Rogers and Dymond, 1954), conducting a major research study of psychotherapy with schizophrenic patients (Rogers et al., 1967). Partly because of its longevity, person-centred therapy itself has both been the subject of and generated more research than many other approaches. In the 1950s, using the Q-sort technique, Rogers and Dymond (1954) showed that person-centred therapy results in changes to the self-concept. The perceived self becomes closer to the ideal self, and the self as perceived becomes more comfortable and adjusted.

Research evidence that the therapeutic conditions are both necessary and sufficient is not unequivocal, though much of it suffers from inadequate methodology and the possibility of poorly reported and discussed results (for a useful summary of four decades of research see Bozarth, 1993). Most research strongly supports the hypothesis that the conditions are necessary for effective counselling, whether this is person-centred or not. This research forms the basis of the mainstream view in counselling and

psychotherapy that the therapeutic relationship is the key factor in successful outcome.

Finally, two relatively recent independent studies, based on randomized, controlled assessment (Friedli et al., 1997; Bower et al., 2000), have concluded that person-centred, non-directive psychotherapy/ counselling more than holds its own in comparison with other forms of therapy and helping.

References

Bozarth, J. (1993) Not necessarily necessary, but always sufficient. In D. Brazier (ed.), *Beyond Carl Rogers*. London: Constable. pp. 92–105.

Embleton Tudor, L., Keemar, K., Tudor, K., Valentine, J. and Worrall, M. (2004) *The Person-centred Approach: A Contemporary Introduction*. Basingstoke: Palgrave.

Friedli, K., King, M., Lloyd, M. and Horder, J. (1997) Randomised controlled assessment of non-directive psychotherapy versus routine general practitioner care. *Lancet*, 350: 1662–1665.

King, M. et al. (2000) Randomised controlled trial of non-directive counselling, cognitive-behaviour therapy and usual general practitioner care in the management of depression as well as mixed anxiety and depression in primary care. *Health Technology Assessment*, 4 (19).

Mearns, D. and Thorne, B. (2000) *Person-centred Therapy Today: New Frontiers in Theory and Practice*. London: Sage.

Patterson, C.H. (1984/2000) Empathy, warmth and genuineness in psychotherapy: a review of reviews. In C.H. Patterson, *Understanding Psychotherapy: Fifty Years of Client-centred Theory and Practice*. Llangarron: PCCS Books. pp. 161–173.

Prouty, G. (1994) *Theoretical Evolutions in Person-centred Experiential Therapy: Applications to Schizophrenic and Retarded Psychoses*. Westport, CT: Praeger.

Rogers, C.R. (1957) The necessary and sufficient conditions of therapeutic personality change. *Journal of Consulting Psychology*, 21: 95–103.

Rogers, C.R. (1958/1967) A process conception of psychotherapy. In C.R. Rogers, *On Becoming a Person*. London: Constable. pp. 125–159.

Rogers, C.R. (1959) A theory of therapy, personality and interpersonal relationships, as developed in the client-centred framework. In S. Koch (ed.), *Psychology: A Study of Science*, Vol. 3: *Formulation of the Person and the Social Context*. New York: McGraw-Hill. pp. 184–256.

Rogers, C.R. and Dymond, R.F. (eds) (1954) *Psychotherapy and Personality Change*. Chicago, IL: University of Chicago Press.

Rogers, C.R., Gendlin, E.T., Kiesler, D.J. and Traux, C.B. (eds) (1967) *The Therapeutic Relationship and Its Impact: A Study of Psychotherapy with Schizophrenics*. Madison, WI: University of Wisconsin Press.

Tudor, K. (2000) The case of the lost conditions. *Counselling*, 11 (1): 33–37.

Tudor, K. and Merry, T. (2002) *Dictionary of Person-centred Psychology*. London: Whurr.

5.20 Primal Therapy/Integration (Arthur Janov, 1924–)

○○○

COLIN FELTHAM

Brief history

This section focuses primarily on the primal therapy of Arthur Janov, but also refers to primal integration therapy, a variant of primal therapy, and tangentially to related therapies characterized by catharsis, emotional flooding, etc. Janov, an American clinical psychologist and psychiatric social worker practising psychoanalytically in Los Angeles, stumbled serendipitously upon a method of inducing dramatic, abreaction-like states in his clients in the 1960s. He developed these methods and an associated theory into a systematic psychotherapy for which he had applied for legal ownership. Primal therapy was popularized by Janov's publication in 1970 of *The Primal Scream: The Cure for Neurosis*, and updated in Janov (1991).

Although Janov regards his work as a unique and fortuitous development away from psychoanalytic/ insight methods, others have claimed that it belongs to a tradition stemming from the early Freud (experiments with hypnosis and catharsis), Wilhelm Reich (emphasis on the body, muscular defences, etc.), Otto Rank (emphasis on birth trauma), Fritz Perls

(emphasis on psychodramatic methods and confrontation) and object relations (emphasis on early child–caregiver bond, separation, 'murderous rage', etc.). Some early American practitioners broke away from Janov, establishing 'intensive feeling therapy'.

Rowan (1988) discusses the contributions of Swartley, Verny, Grof, Freundlich, Lake and others to the international primal movement. *Primal Integration (therapy)* stems from this separate tradition which accommodates notions of spirituality, joy and human potential (and, in some versions, claims of re-experiencing past lives) in a way that Janov's pain-centred, science-orientated theories do not (Brown and Mowbray, 1994). The methods of Frank Lake (founder of clinical theology) originally differed from Janov's, including the use of LSD and special breathing techniques. Various *rebirthing* therapies are associated with these developments, although Janov has always distanced himself from them (as well as from those listed later) and refers to these as 'mock primal therapy' which he considers ineffective or dangerous.

Primal therapy may be regarded as belonging to that family within the humanistic therapies which includes Reichian therapy, psychodrama (Moreno), gestalt (Perls), re-evaluation counselling (Jackins), focused-expressive psychotherapy (FEP, Daldrup et al.), implosive therapy (Stampfl), focusing (Gendlin), experiential psychotherapy (Mahrer) and others. Alice Miller's popular writings on child abuse and its long-term effects also endorsed (and later rejected) the related *Primärtherapie* of Swiss therapist Konrad Stettbacher. These all share a concentration on re-experiencing full-bodied feelings as central to understanding and resolving psychological problems and ventilation of feelings, or emotional flooding, as the key to healing.

Primal therapy is a non-mainstream therapy practised by Janov and his colleagues in only a few centres (principally Los Angeles). Primal *integration* is found more commonly in Britain, for example at the Open Centre in London. There is reason to believe, however, that in spite of its status as a relatively minority therapy, its ideas have influenced other approaches; for example, some person-centred practitioners acknowledge the occurrence of spontaneous birth primals occurring in the course of therapy.

Basic assumptions

Feelings and their authentic expression are the essence of healthy human functioning. Civilization has forced cultures and individuals to suppress their real feelings – and hence their real selves – usually from early infancy onwards.

Most people live in a state of *neurosis* which is a condition of psychobiological distress and under which all clinical psychopathology is subsumed (i.e. there is no true depression, obsessive-compulsive disorder, etc., but simply different expressions of the same underlying neurosis).

Human beings have a natural state of somatosensory-affective-cognitive equilibrium (the body, feelings and thoughts in harmony), which is 'knocked out of' them as children, but which can be restored via appropriate therapy so that they become their real, relaxed, organismic selves, and not individuals who are constantly 'coping', monitoring thoughts, rehearsing behaviours, and living in hope.

Feelings, *not* cognitions, are primary, and it is unfelt emotions that lead to irrational behaviour. The primal approach dictates that feelings cannot be bypassed therapeutically but must be fully experienced and integrated.

Primal therapy, in Janov's view, is essentially child-friendly and can be aligned with Leboyer's non-violent birth procedures and A.S. Neill's methods of free schooling.

All these are, however, against the grain of contemporary control-orientated ideologies in our 'postemotional society' (Meštrović, 1997). The vogue for 'emotional intelligence' bears little resemblance to the depth of feelings involved in primal therapy.

Origins and maintenance of problems

Human development may go awry from intrauterine existence onwards. Physical and emotional traumas experienced by pregnant women, the effects of smoking, drugs and alcohol, natural birth complications, and intrusive obstetric technology may all have profoundly negative results. Some practitioners even refer to conception and implantation trauma (Rowan, 1988: 28).

Early childhood experiences of emotional deprivation/neglect (minimal or absent warmth, inconsistent parenting, etc.), and emotional, physical and sexual abuse – quite common in various degrees across different cultures – add to any prior negative experiences an accumulation of painful experiences.

The growing child, instinctively aware of being powerless in a world dominated by unfeeling adults, is obliged to ward off assaults on his or her psychobiological integrity by using various defences (shutting off/ repression of real feelings, adoption of a false self/ front, outward compliance, psychosomatic illnesses, etc.) which may also lead to varieties of acting out in adult life (e.g. intellectualization, compulsive sex, addictions, self-harming, workaholism, mental illness, compulsive altruism, bullying).

The need to defend against overwhelming and cumulative (psychophysiological) *primal pain* leads to a state of *neurosis* characterized by detachment from real needs and feelings, and often by strenuous *denial* of feelings (particularly vulnerable, painful, even life-threatening feelings).

Denial and distance from feelings are compounded throughout an individual's life by (a) gradual enmeshment in avoidant or symbolic activities and relationships that render the expression of real, raw, 'uncivilized' and inconvenient feelings too risky, and (b) socio-cultural conditions generally, whereby emotional openness and unguardedness is rendered unsafe.

Janov (and others, including Alice Miller and Alvin Mahrer) opine that most if not all other psychotherapies ironically act as defences against feeling profound inner pain, by offering relatively non-threatening, intellectualized methods and explanations in emotionally uncongenial settings. The continuing dominance of the cognitive-behavioural therapies and the *Zeitgeist* of managed care have overshadowed the impact of most 1970s-inspired, feelings-orientated humanistic therapies.

Janov has argued for a neuroscientific correlate of psychological pain and neurotic defences. He developed from others' work a tripartite view of brain functions, beginning with the developmentally earliest – somatosensory (first line); affective (second line); and cognitive (third line) – and a gating process between these providing protection against overwhelming pain. Early, pre-verbal experiences (e.g. birth trauma) may be sealed off from awareness until triggered by a present-day trauma powerful enough to perforate cognitive defences; the person may become emotionally upset, but even more deeply may experience profound somatosensory discomfort, sometimes verging on psychosis (Janov and Holden, 1975).

Change

Most people cannot change spontaneously because primal pain is cumulative and the powerful defences keeping it at bay automatically become compounded and irreversible by will, insight or cognition.

Investment in neurotic lifestyles, relationships and ideologies makes serious personal change unlikely and extremely difficult unless one experiences a crisis which disables normal defensive coping strategies.

Unless one is fortunate enough to have escaped significant traumas, as described earlier, real – rather than symbolic, superficial – change is possible only via (usually long-term) primal therapy, effected by sometimes confrontational, defence-dismantling procedures and commitment to non-neurotic lifestyle choices.

In therapy, clients experience *primals* – deeply felt connections between current and past emotional wounds. Primals are, however, *not* in Janov's view synonymous with 'infantile regressions, play-acting, role-playing, hysteria, catharsis, or abreaction' (pseudo-primals); they are more than simply a form of tension release (as in 'scream therapy', meditation, sex or jogging). Nor are they simply retrospective constructs. Clients feel only as much pain, in primals, as they can tolerate at any one time.

Primals are often characterized by current painful stimuli leading to expressions of anger and frustration which in turn lead to felt recognition of emotional hurt, thence to deep crying and grieving for the lost self and/or for grief at one's own self-betrayal.

Therapeutic change, once under way, is an organismic process necessitating constant exposure to authentic feelings, and to re-experiencing whenever necessary the eruption of 'old hurts', their full impact and subsequent gradual integration, until the process becomes irreversible. Exposure to primal pain often causes clients to feel worse before they feel better.

Primal clients come to a point beyond which old unhealthy ways of behaving (maintaining a phoney persona, sustaining meaningless relationships, enduring uncomfortable, stressful jobs) become intolerable, and sometimes radical lifestyle (often 'downshifting') changes are chosen.

Skills and strategies

Therapy commences with a defence-dismantling contract which may or may not involve a period of voluntary isolation and deprivation (e.g. spending time alone, suspending obvious neurotic comforts such as nailbiting, drinking, masturbating, over-eating).

Therapists (who must have had substantial primal therapy themselves), adopt a caringly directive style, use active confrontation judiciously, identifying and disallowing clients' habitual defences, intellectualizing and acting out.

There is a focus on live, here-and-now, significant feelings which are viscerally linked to earlier childhood feelings and painful experiences.

Transference is eschewed and indeed the 'therapeutic relationship' is played down in favour of clients making direct identifications of emotionally significant others and gaining purchase on their own therapeutic process. However, therapists may sometimes touch or hug clients, for example, specifically to effect recall of past tactile/emotional deprivation or abuse.

Clients are directed in sessions to address significant others (e.g. parents, abusers) as 'You', to express real feelings fully (e.g. 'Please love me', 'Don't hurt me' or 'I hate you'), to repeat emotive phrases, speak more loudly, complete half-finished sentences, 'Say it the way you mean it', and so on.

Clients are encouraged to 'go with' (trust) gut feelings and bodily reactions, however apparently bizarre these may initially seem. This may involve shouting, screaming, punching cushions, deep crying, and convulsive body movements.

Appropriately sound-proofed, dimly lit, padded rooms, floor cushions, props, etc. and longer (up to two or three hours or occasionally longer 'marathon' sessions are employed) and sometimes more frequent sessions may be utilized to facilitate breakthrough, and full and safe exploration of feelings.

Groups are used for trying out therapeutically relevant risky behaviours, deepening feelings, debriefing following primals and for solidarity and support. In primal integration, groups are often the *primary* source of therapy.

Therapists encourage clients to link spontaneous insights (following completed primals) with the potential (if not imperative) for new, non-neurotic behaviours in everyday life. Exercise and nutrition may be discussed as components of healthy recovery. Feelings *in themselves* are not enough.

The need for authenticity/congruence in everyday situations and relationships is constantly reinforced, as is the need for on-going commitment to the sometimes frightening and daunting primal process across years. 'Homework' may include assertive confrontations, watching emotive films, visiting emotive places, etc.

Research

From the outset Janov initiated small-scale research using (a) self-report questionnaires and (b) measures of EEG activity, and vital signs (pulse, core body temperature, blood pressure), and claimed evidence of significantly reduced tension levels in those who had been in therapy for some time; as well as more satisfying lives, disappearance of symptoms and some unexpected results (such as body hair or breasts growing for the first time, supposedly signalling reversal of arrested development). Janov has also published photographs of clients showing old bruises re-appearing in therapy which are said to confirm objectively clients' subjective experiences of birth traumas. Janov (2000) continues to cite neurobiological research findings in support of his focus on prenatal and perinatal damage.

Janov has been criticized for not co-operating with independent appraisals of his work, his research being called 'largely uncontrolled, non-comparative, and short-term' (Prochaska and Norcross, 1994: 247). Videgard (1998) calculates a 40 per cent success rate for primal therapy, contradicting Janov's 98 per cent claim. Primal therapy and its variants tend to be non-mainstream and do not find their way into meta-analytic studies.

Alvin Mahrer, founder of experiential psychotherapy, argues like Rowan for the validity of subjective, experiential change to be recognized; and suggests that new qualitative research methods and intensive study of audio recordings are needed for investigating therapeutic process.

References

Brown, J. and Mowbray, R. (1994) Primal integration. In D. Jones (ed.), *Innovative Therapy: A Handbook*. Buckingham: Open University Press.

Janov, A. (1970) *The Primal Scream: The Cure for Neurosis.* New York: Putnam.

Janov, A. (1991) *The New Primal Scream: Primal Therapy 20 Years On.* Chicago: Enterprise.

Janov, A. (2000) *The Biology of Love.* New York: Prometheus.

Janov, A. and Holden, E.M. (1975) *Primal Man: The New Consciousness.* New York: Crowell.

Meštrović, S. (1997) *Postemotional Society.* London: Sage.

Prochaska, J.O. and Norcross, J.C. (1994) *Systems of Psychotherapy: A Transtheoretical Analysis* (3rd edn). Pacific Grove, CA: Brooks/Cole.

Rowan, J. (1988) Primal integration therapy. In J. Rowan and W. Dryden (eds), *Innovative Therapy in Britain.* Milton Keynes: Open University Press.

Videgard, T. (1998) *The Success and Failure of Primal Therapy.* New York: Prometheus.

5.21 Psychodrama
(Jacob Levy Moreno, 1889–1974)

○○○

PAUL WILKINS

Brief history

Psychodrama is an action method of psychotherapy originated by Jacob Levy Moreno. Moreno worked initially in Vienna and moved to the USA in 1925 where, at his centre in Beacon, New York State, he continued to practise and develop psychodrama until his death. In a way, the early history of psychodrama and the history of Moreno are inseparable. Although he had many students who themselves made significant contributions to the approach, he was a dominant and charismatic figure who many identified with psychodrama (and the related disciplines of sociodrama and sociometrics) *per se.* As a writer, Moreno was prolific. The classic texts of psychodrama are *Who Shall Survive* and *Psychodrama* (Volumes 1–3) (the two latter volumes written with Zerka Moreno), and it is in these that Moreno sets forth not only the principles of psychodrama psychotherapy but also his ambitions for his approach as a philosophical and political force. An account of

the colourful life and ideas of Moreno can be found in Hare and Hare (1996).

Many other practitioners and theorists have contributed to the development of psychodrama. One way in which this has been done is to incorporate the theories and practices of other modalities (e.g. object relations and systems theory) into the practice of psychodrama (see Wilkins, 1999: 3), but the application of psychodrama to a variety of client groups and various clinical settings is also continually being evaluated and new techniques or ways of thinking are being suggested. For example, Casson (2004) has recently demonstrated the usefulness of psychodrama in working with people who hear voices, and Bannister and Huntington (2002) describe working with children.

It was from the stronghold in Beacon, through the agency of students of Moreno, that psychodrama first spread across the world. Although there had been previous initiatives, Marcia Karp is credited with bringing psychodrama and psychodrama training to the UK. She established the first course and (with one exception) subsequent training courses have been started by its graduates. Currently, in the UK and Republic of Ireland, training courses in psychodrama are verified and monitored by the professional body, the British Psychodrama Association, and graduates are eligible for registration as psychodrama psychotherapists by the UKCP.

Basic assumptions

The theory of psychodrama is rich in original concepts – for some of which Moreno had to invent new words (see below) – but its fundamental assumption is that it is through enacting scenes from the past, present or future, real or imagined, that change, healing and growth may be facilitated. It is experiential, usually takes place in a group and centres on the whole person, not cognitive or emotional faculties alone. A psychodrama saying is that 'what the mind forgets the body often remembers' and, sometimes, the path to change is via this somatic memory. Underpinning the value of enaction is a set of ideas about intrapersonal and interpersonal relationships.

First, people are naturally creative and spontaneous and the free expression of these qualities is necessary for healthy living. These qualities are primary, primal and positive and in no way derivative. To be creative is to respond constructively to new situations and spontaneity, springing from it, is described as a new approach to an old situation or an appropriate response to a new one. Spontaneity and anxiety are opposites. The more anxious a person is, the less spontaneous and therefore the less likely they are to meet challenge and change in a healthy way. Life events may block creativity and psychodrama is a way of releasing these blocks.

Second, there are interpersonal processes which, while not confined to psychodramatic action, are essential to its success. These include *tele* and *encounter*. *Tele* may be understood as a form of mutual empathy or as including empathy and transference, that is a reciprocated 'insight into, appreciation of, and feeling for the actual make-up of another person' (Hare and Hare, 1996: 36). There is a core belief in psychodrama that the *protagonist* (the person whose psychodrama is being performed) will choose the most appropriate person for a role, however unlikely that choice may seem at first. It is the (often intuitive) mutual appreciation and understanding of tele which allows this. *Encounter* is the true meeting of individuals – the process of seeing another as they see themselves – and *always* takes place in the 'here-and-now' (a term which Moreno is credited as coining) even when apparently part of an enactment of the past. 'The objectives of encounter are increased self-acceptance, authenticity, openness to others, enhanced spontaneity and a realisation of innate creativity' (Wilkins, 1999: 66).

The concept of *role* is important in psychodrama. Perhaps confusingly, this term is used in two ways. Parts in a psychodramatic enaction may be referred to as 'roles' (and thus the person or thing playing the part is said to be 'in role'), but roles are also fundamental to psychodrama personality theory. In this case, role refers not only to a function (e.g. mother, wife, teacher, cook, nurse, all of which are *social roles*; sleeper, eater, which are *psychosomatic roles*), but also to something akin to subpersonality or configuration of self. Indeed, Moreno was one of the first psychotherapists to suggest that the 'self' was actually a multiple entity, in his case calling these personal aspects *psychodramatic roles*. It is from the various roles that the self emerges. Psychosomatic roles may be innate but social roles and psychodramatic roles are at least in part responses to the *social atom* of an individual.

A social atom is an individual's immediate social network – originally that into which the person was born and which continues to affect them throughout life, but also the 'significant others' surrounding an individual in the present. So, the primary social atom is formative and psychodramatic and social roles are relational.

Origin and maintenance of problems

The social atom is the basic determinant of mental (ill) health. To be spontaneous and creative, people need support from their social atoms. Individuals who endure, for example, abuse or neglect in their social atoms are likely to experience psychological disturbance. The separation from one or more components of the social atom (e.g. by bereavement) too may result in impairment. In the simplest analysis, the disturbance is the product of blocked or disrupted spontaneity. Without a natural flow of spontaneity, the individual will be unable to be creative. If people are insufficiently creative to respond to change, symptoms of anxiety and distress are likely and this in turn will be reflected in the disturbance of the individual's interpersonal relationships. Moreno does not appear to have offered a definitive statement as to what limits an individual's spontaneity. What can be garnered from his writing is that he believed humankind is particularly efficient at discouraging the development of spontaneity, that we tend to fear our own spontaneity (and that of others) and that we do not know how to use it. Nevertheless, some conclusions as to the contribution of disrupted spontaneity to psychological disturbance can be derived from Morenian concepts.

It is mutual, positive tele and the opportunity to experiment with a variety of roles which maintains spontaneity. Deprived of these, an individual suffers. For example, if, from an early age, a boy is surrounded by people (or even one significant person) with whom there is little or no mutual positive connection, then the likelihood is that he will feel unaccepted (and therefore unacceptable). This leads to feelings of alienation, perhaps resentment, and isolated and isolating behaviour. Once isolated, he will have little or no opportunity to practise a variety of roles (a necessary aspect of child development, see Hare and Hare, 1996: 39–40). It is the maintenance of a sense of isolation and alienation over time which leads to deeper psychological disturbance but other factors too are important. Disturbance is likely to be more severe if the social atom as a whole is experienced as rejection or one or more of the most significant individuals of which it is comprised (e.g. the primary care giver) is particularly unsympathetic. However, equally, there may be at least partial amelioration from elsewhere within the social atom. For example, a child with abusive or neglectful parents may find that an attentive, affectionate and accepting grandparent or sibling satisfies some of the need for positive tele.

Disturbance can also result from role conflict and role confusion. First, roles can be held too tightly, restricting the ability to adapt. For example, someone with a strongly defined 'masculine' role may experience stress if confronted with the requirement to act in a way he perceives to be 'girly'. Similarly, roles can become frozen in the past (perhaps because the opportunity to experiment with and develop roles was curtailed), often preserving behaviour acceptable in a child into adulthood, where it is inappropriate. Role confusion occurs when just what is expected of an individual is unclear. Perhaps an individual gets mixed messages about their roles in the social atom – for example, is a 16 year-old required to be an adult or a child? How can they be certain which way of being suits the current need? Whatever its cause and to whomsoever it happens, role confusion can cause anxiety and stress.

The prolongation of any of the above may lead to chronic psychological disturbance. Also, there is a cycle of distress. Loss of spontaneity results in being unable to respond to new situations or to re-address old one differently. This threat of change, for which there are no coping strategies, results in anxiety and anxiety leads to a loss of spontaneity, and so on. Behaviour becomes rigid, compulsive and habitual, and this may be seen as psychopathological. Similarly, if the primary social atom is faulty, then the individual is unlikely to build satisfactory interpersonal relationships and so exists as a part of a faulty social atom in the present, which means social relationships will be unsatisfactory, even harmful, and so on. Early confusion between fantasy roles and 'real' roles may become self-perpetuating, as would misplaced telic attraction (e.g. a preference for imagined people or objects over positive social relationships).

Change

In essence, change comes about through increased spontaneity/creativity. In psychodrama psychotherapy, the way of achieving this is through the skilled facilitation of an enaction by a *director* (the usual label for a psychodrama psychotherapist in action). This enaction usually takes place in a group setting (although one-to-one psychodrama is also effective). Group size may vary considerably but many psychodramatists would consider a group of around a dozen people most desirable. Psychodrama is available privately and through agencies of health and social care. Suitable clients range across the spectrum from the deeply disturbed to those who are seeking more effective functioning in their everyday lives.

With enhanced spontaneity, an individual is better equipped to play existing roles effectively and can more easily develop and employ new ones. Enaction can also promote insight and (when this insight is 'felt' as well as 'understood') this too may promote change. Insight may come about through the exploration or, for example:

- an individual's social atom in the past, present or even the future
- the roles an individual habitually occupies
- life events (as they are remembered or intuited).

Whatever its source, any insight gained through psychodramatic exploration is only useful if it can be integrated in the present. This too may be done through enaction. It is said that a psychodrama comprises at least three scenes. This is because it is supposed that the normal progression will be:

1. A scene which identifies or demonstrates the 'problem' in the present or near past. This leads to a heightened awareness of the issue in another time and place, usually the past.
2. One or more scenes in which the past incident is established and explored more fully.
3. A final scene in which the protagonist returns to the present with some new knowledge, increased awareness and, perhaps, resolution.

It is this pattern of present–past–present which gives rise to the notion of a necessity for three or more scenes.

One of the agencies for change, healing and resolution, perhaps leading to integration, is *surplus reality*, that is an imaginative strategy involving the enactment of something which did not happen, can never happen or will never happen. This is an opportunity to address 'unfinished business', for example, to say goodbye to a dead relative, or to replay a life event differently and so experience something which did not happen but which might be beneficial (e.g. good parenting from a tender, loving and respectful mother for a protagonist from an abusive background).

Skills and strategies

The function of a psychodrama psychotherapist is to encourage, manage and support enaction *and* to facilitate encounter (including group process) throughout the session (Wilkins, 1999: 66–68). Typically, a psychodrama session will have three stages. These are:

- warm-up
- enactment
- sharing.

Warm-up is about preparing, getting ready, toning up as individuals and as a group; enactment is the phase in which the protagonist, through action, tells a story, experiments, addresses an issue; and sharing is a coming together of the group in such a way as to give expression to common experiences and emotions.

There are five 'instruments' essential to the psychodramatic method. These are:

1. The *stage*, the designated space, formal or informal (Wilkins, 1999: 20–22), in which action will take place.
2. The *protagonist*, that is the person who is the subject of the psychodrama and its principal actor.
3. The *director*, who uses a set of professional skills to facilitate the enactment and to ensure the safety of the protagonist and the group.
4. The *auxiliaries*, who are the people who assist in the action by taking on roles.
5. The *audience*, who are the people witnessing the drama.

The protagonist may be identified as part of the warm-up, emerge from group process, be elected by the group or selected by the director, usually in response to the apparent *act hunger* (the conscious or unconscious need to give expression to emotional tension through enaction) of the individual. Auxiliaries are normally chosen by the protagonist and, as well as being important agents for change in the protagonist, may themselves have a therapeutic experience. The audience is those members of the group not directly involved in the action. For the protagonist, they serve a therapeutic function as witnesses.

In the facilitation of an enaction, psychodramatists have a variety of techniques at their disposal. These include:

- *Role reversal* – in the everyday language of the approach, this is 'the engine which drives psychodrama'. Role reversal is the process by which the protagonist temporarily becomes someone or something else in the psychodrama by adopting the position, characteristics and behaviour of the 'other'. The auxiliary performing that role temporarily holds the part of the protagonist. Role reversal has a number of functions. It is a way of instructing the auxiliary by demonstration, it conveys to the group the protagonist's perception of important people in the drama and it enables the protagonist to see the world form the perspective of the other person:

  > It is a strange fact but it often seems that the protagonist 'knows' more about the other when they become them, words are spoken, images come to mind, feelings are experienced of which, as themselves, the protagonist would seem to have no knowledge. Role reversal is a way of offering the protagonist a deeper understanding of the processes between themselves and other elements of their drama. (Wilkins, 1999: 34)

- *Doubling* – this is a term now used for two different techniques, permanent doubling and spontaneous doubling. A permanent double is a group member who stands with the protagonist throughout the drama, adopting their posture and mannerisms. The permanent double is principally a supporter and ally for the protagonist but (through empathy) may at times voice the thoughts and feelings that the protagonist cannot. Spontaneous doubling occurs when

a member of the audience has some sense of what isn't being said or what might be helpful and, with the agreement of both the protagonist and the director, offers this, speaking as the protagonist and while in contact with them. In both kinds of doubling, protagonist may accept the offered words and repeat them in their own way or, if they don't fit, reject them.

- *Mirroring* – this is a way of letting a protagonist view a scene from outside. The protagonist is replaced by an auxiliary and leaves the scene and watches as the action continues or is replayed. This has been likened to 'instant replay' and encourages a more objective awareness on the part of the protagonist.

Research evidence

Much of the research about the efficacy of group therapy is likely to hold true for psychodrama but, as with other approaches to psychotherapy, published results of systematic quantitative or qualitative investigations of psychodrama are scarce. Wilkins (1999: 124–126) summarizes some of what was then known from psychodrama research. Much of this research explores 'psychodrama in practice' rather than addressing theoretical concepts or the relative usefulness/efficacy of psychodrama with respect to other forms of treatment, psychological or medical. Studies of the client experience of psychodrama of one form or another or in one setting or another are increasingly common (see, for example, *British Journal of Psychodrama and Sociodrama*, *Journal of Group Psychotherapy* and *Psychodrama and Sociometry*), as are studies of the application of psychodrama to particular problems.

References

Bannister, A. and Huntington, A. (2002) *Communicating with Children and Adolescents: Action for Change*. London: Jessica Kingsley.

Casson, J.W. (2004) *Drama, Psychotherapy and Psychosis: Dramatherapy and Psychodrama with People who Hear Voices*. London: Brunner-Routledge.

Hare, A.P. and Hare, J.R. (1996) *J.L. Moreno*. London: Sage.

Wilkins, P. (1999) *Psychodrama*. London: Sage.

5.22 Psychosynthesis Therapy
(Roberto Assagioli, 1888–1974)

○○○

DIANA WHITMORE

Brief history

Roberto Assagioli was a student of Freud and a contemporary of Jung. He pioneered psychoanalysis in Italy and although deeply influenced by his studies with Freud and his exploration of the unconscious psyche, Assagioli quickly became dissatisfied and was inspired to delve into the further reaches of human nature. As early as 1910 he began to formulate a holistic theory of human development which he called Psychosynthesis. This includes the groundwork of Freud but also explores the higher aspects of being human – creativity, inspiration, spiritual understanding and higher values such as love, compassion, joy and wisdom. It also recognizes human beings' existential search for meaning and purpose in life – a search which Assagioli considered an urge as basic and natural as any biological drive.

In the late 1950s a radical shift occurred in the field of psychology, one which is still not fully integrated. It was the emergence of the third (humanistic) followed quickly by the fourth (transpersonal) forces of psychology. While Freud's theory of the unconscious psyche stressed the impact and consequences of childhood experience on adult behaviour, it tended to limit itself to pathology. Humanistic psychologists focused on what the human being is capable of becoming – they studied self-actualized people and psychological health. Psychosynthesis had held a similar perspective since 1910.

With the birth of transpersonal psychology, psychosynthesis gained further acceptance and recognition, and took psychology one developmental step further. It enlarged the vision of health to include the search for meaning and purpose and postulated in the human being, at core, a deeper spiritual identity which included the individual's experience and aspiration for transcendence as well as the healing potential of self-transcendence.

In over 70 years of research and verification, psychosynthesis has developed into a unified concept of human development and an organized system of therapeutic techniques which can be applied in the fields of therapy, medicine, education and personal development and training. It is concerned with the realization of individual potential, and, at the same time, in order to avoid unbalanced growth, with the harmonization of all elements of the personality.

Basic assumptions

Psychosynthesis ascribes a transpersonal context which illuminates and gives meaning to the client's particular circumstances. This context, which holds the 'ground' for all psychological processes, is *psychospiritual*.

The transpersonal realm includes experience of the Self, awareness of superconscious content, the evocation of potential and the emergence of meaning and purpose. These are considered to be essential components of psychological health and successful therapy.

The client is most essentially a Self, a Being who has a purpose in life and is on a path of unfoldment which includes challenges and obstacles of a psychological nature.

Pathological processes are viewed as being within this larger life journey, and are diagnosed as awakenings to be worked through, rather than symptoms to be cured. They also represent fundamental steps towards an emerging sense of identity.

The shadow, the lower unconscious (the darker side of human behaviour which contains unredeemed and repressed aspects) is integral to the human condition and is addressed in the therapeutic process. This includes the individual's potential capacity for both self-destructive and aggressive behaviour.

Psychosynthesis therapy values the development and integration of all psychological functions (thinking, feeling, sensation, imagination, intuition and desires).

The client's issues are not viewed as exclusively the result of childhood conditioning, but as containing a creative possibility which can provide opportunities for transformation and growth. Transpersonal work in therapy is not a substitute for psychological or psychodynamic work, but a vivifying and practical complement.

Psychosynthesis therapy works with the pivotal role of consciousness in determining the outcome of therapy, as both the instrument and the object of change and it acknowledges the potential for meaningful change to occur throughout a person's life.

The individual cannot be perceived in isolation, but within a wider context of culture and society, with an even wider context of the human being's global predicament. Social, cultural, historical and environmental influences are critical factors to be addressed in therapeutic work and are considered essential to the experience of well-being.

Psychosynthesis offers no predetermined therapeutic model of psychological health to be applied to all individuals. Each client is seen as a unique individual with his or her own set of needs and resources. The Self is abundant and complete and is the source of healing within the client.

Origin and maintenance of problems

Our early experiences exert a multi-dimensional, often indirect and pervasive influence on our adult behaviour and the degree to which we will experience psychological health and well-being. They may profoundly affect our capacity for love and intimacy; for assertion and self-affirmation; our perception of life and our deepest attitudes and values.

Few have had a childhood free from negative conditioning and the limitations of their primary caretakers and culture. There was a time when each of us 'ran towards life with open arms'; open and trusting, only to experience a sense of betrayal by the very adults we were so dependent upon and vulnerable to. Pain and psychological dysfunction may lie in the client's original relationships with primary caretakers who were not psychologically mature, who lacked positive models themselves, and who had fallen prey to unfulfilled needs and expectations and to conditional loving.

This conditional loving causes children to seek to mould themselves to become and to behave as they *imagine* necessary in order to be loved and indeed be lovable, often sacrificing their true individuality and natural qualities and gifts. The child truly is not seen, perceived, appreciated or welcomed in life as a unique soul with his or her own unique qualities and being. This *soul wound* leads to a deep implicit experience of having *betrayed* one's Self, one's own being. Where there is a loss of individuality, there is a loss of Self.

Further betrayals of Self, our conscious awareness that by conforming, adapting and settling for a minimized existence, we are not honouring our deepest experience of identity. This causes personal despair and meaninglessness which can only be redeemed through re-contact and re-connecting with our own depth of being.

The pain of the lack of a meaningful existence which is congruent with our deepest sense of identity and values, will be masked by many personal behaviours, both functional and dysfunctional. A lack of a sense of purpose in life will be covered by behaviours which seek to compensate for the lack of connection to Self and as such will be distorted and futile. Social norms and expectations, the superficiality of modern life, can further cloud our experience of a deeper value system which could provide a sense of purposeful life direction.

Change

Psychosynthesis therapists work with different levels of consciousness – both the depths and the heights – and with personality structures as well as facilitating the awakening of potential.

As there is no predetermined therapeutic model to be applied to all clients, psychosynthesis holds that clients have all the answers to their dilemmas and it seeks to empower clients and enable each to envisage his or her own psychospiritual health.

Psychosynthesis therapy holds the human relationship and interaction between client and therapist as central to the work, and as requiring an I–Thou relationship, one which recognizes the client as a spiritual Being. Within this context interruptions to I–Thou relating provide important therapeutic material to be addressed.

Psychological well-being is best facilitated by addressing the *past*, the *present* and the *future*.

The past

The past must be thoroughly addressed in terms of liberating the client from their childhood and historical conditioning which continue to inhibit self-acceptance and self-expression. Early learned behaviour patterns which are distorted and dysfunctional must become conscious in order for the client to be liberated from their destructive impact and to create consciously new and more congruent ways of being and doing – ways which contain more of the client's unique qualities and capacities.

The present

Congruence between an individual's inner experience of who they know themselves to be and their outer behaviour is sought by helping him or her to become conscious of behaviour patterns and ways of relating that are distorted and restrictive. In psychosynthesis therapy, the *presenting issue* is not taken simply at face value. The breadth and depth of its impact on the client's current life will be explored, including how the issue manifests in the client's everyday life, the situations which evoke the problem, the interpersonal relationships involved and the beliefs, attitudes and opinions that it stimulates. The therapist helps the client to reframe areas of pain and difficulty as progressive, and as indicators of a positive thrust towards integration.

The future

At their deepest level, problems and obstacles are inherently meaningful, evolutionary, coherent and potentially transformative. The client's presenting issues are not viewed as mere inadequacies, but as containing a creative possibility and an opportunity for growth. As a snake sheds its skin, the client can outgrow old behaviour patterns which are contained within a problem. He or she will experience pain and the need for change in precisely the areas where a larger or new identity is trying to emerge. The more counsellor and client consciously explore and co-operate with this, the greater progress is possible. On the other hand, if the client blindly repeats old patterns, much suffering will be generated through the perpetuation of old identities and the resistance to change.

The psychosynthesis therapist recognizes that it is no accident that certain issues have become foreground at certain moments in the client's life. Old psychological forms (the past) die in order for new ones (the future) to be born. Working with this *potential* in the process of change involves client and counsellor together working to recognize what potential is contained *within* the problem and to value this creative dissonance.

Skills and strategies

In psychosynthesis therapy, the therapeutic relationship is seen as the very heart of the therapeutic process. Without a bifocal vision – one which sees both the light and the shadow in the client – without a context that sees clients as *essentially more than* their pathology, the effectiveness of the work will be greatly reduced. Without authentic human relating, trust will not be established between the therapist and the client, and without this essential ingredient, little growth is possible. Moreover, a primary strategy is for the therapist to perceive the client as having a spiritual identity, as well as a personality which is struggling to address its problems.

The therapist's ultimate strategy is to facilitate the client's uncovering of a personal centre or identity which enables an expansion of awareness and the capacity to make choices. Psychosynthesis values *inner freedom* and the client gaining mastery over his or her state, through evocation and development of the will. The therapist's task is to support the client in enlarging possibilities and choices about their inner development and outer behaviour.

It is the responsibility of the psychosynthesis therapist to choose appropriate therapeutic techniques. The work may be on any level – physical, emotional, mental or imaginative. Although therapists are aware that clients are ultimately responsible, they will offer choices in the ways they might work. Active dialogue can be appropriate for understanding psychological problems, and awareness of harmful images and complexes may help to disintegrate them, but do not necessarily produce positive change. The cognitive aspect may need to be complemented with experiential techniques, designed to evoke deeper awareness, facilitate emotional experience and to support behavioural changes. The psychosynthesis approach is primarily pragmatic and existential. Although the overall goals and perspective are similar among practitioners, the methods they employ may vary considerably – from mental imagery to gestalt chair work, from free drawing to the training of the will, from journal keeping to physical expression.

Research evidence

Research in various fields, probably the best known being the work of Viktor Frankl, has shown that the sense of life having meaning enhances an individual's sense of well-being and psychological health. Furthermore, in over 70 years of practice of psychosynthesis the inclusion of the soul or spiritual identity of the individual has proved to enhance the effectiveness of therapeutic work. When treated as a spiritual crisis, addiction has often been addressed successfully by psychosynthesis.

Recommended Reading

Assagioli, R. (1965) *Psychosynthesis: A Manual of Principles and Techniques.* Wellingborough: Crucible, Aquarian Press.

Ferrucci, P. (1982) *What We May Be: The Vision and Techniques of Psychosynthesis.* Wellingborough: Crucible, Aquarian Press.

Ferrucci, P. (1990) *Inevitable Grace, Breakthroughs in the Lives of Great Men and Women: Guides to Your Self-realisation.* Wellingborough: Crucible, Aquarian Press.

Whitmore, D. (1991) *Psychosynthesis Counselling in Action.* London: Sage.

5.23 Transactional Analysis
(Eric Berne, 1910–1970)

○○○

KEITH TUDOR AND CHARLOTTE SILLS

Brief history

Transactional Analysis (TA) is a theory of personality, including theories of child development and psychopathology, all of which provide the basis for a theory of psychotherapy. It also provides a theory of communication which may be applied to individuals and systems such as groups and organizations.

Founded by Eric Berne, a Canadian psychiatrist who originally trained as a psychoanalyst, TA has theoretical roots in the psychoanalytic tradition, although it is also substantially influenced by the cognitive behavioural and humanistic/existential traditions. Berne was particularly influenced by Paul Federn who, from 1941, was his training analyst in New York. Federn's system of ego psychology was seminal in Berne's later development of the ego state theory of personality. In 1943 Berne joined the US Army Medical Corps where, as a psychiatrist, he conducted group psychotherapy and pursued his studies in the field of intuition, the results of which again may be seen in his later development of TA theory, especially the importance of checking intuitive judgements against objective observations. Having left the Army, Berne moved to California and in 1947 became an analysand of Eric Erikson, from whom he learned about sequential life stages and the importance of the social influences in psycho-social development. In the early 1950s Berne was beginning to take a more critical view of psychoanalysis and its conceptualization of the unconscious; his break with it came in 1956 with the rejection of his application for membership of the San Francisco Psychoanalytic Institute. Berne threw himself into activity – in his public psychiatric posts and, by now, in his private practice as well as his writing. By 1958, he had published articles which contained all the principal terms and concepts of TA. In 1956 he established a series of weekly meetings of mental health professionals interested in TA, under the name The San Francisco Social Psychiatry Seminar which, in 1960, became an incorporated educational body which, in turn, led to the foundation in 1964 of the International Transactional Analysis Association (ITAA). In 1961 Berne published *Transactional Analysis in Psychotherapy*, which drew together all his previous writings on TA and still presents a complete view of TA personality, psychotherapy and communication theory. The publication in 1964 of Berne's *Games People Play* marked a blossoming of interest in TA, especially in the USA, which was demonstrated by the passage into common usage of TA terms such as 'OK', 'games' and 'strokes' (a unit of recognition).

Since the 1960s TA has developed its theory, applications and organization. The ITAA and its sister organization EATA (the European Transactional Analysis Association) now comprise over 8,000 members in nearly 100 countries and provide a system of international accreditation of practitioners, supervisors and trainers. In Britain, TA has grown from initial seminar groups in the early 1960s, through the first national conference of the (British) Institute of Transactional Analysis in 1974 to a flourishing community comprising over 1,000 members with involvement in and recognition by the current national registering organizations of psychotherapy and counselling.

Basic assumptions

People are born with a basic drive for growth and health – in TA terms 'OKness'. Berne added the 'I'm

OK, You're OK' (or I+ U+) life position to the 'positions' or internal psychological conditions understood by Melanie Klein and object relations theory – the paranoid (I+ U-), depressive (I- U+) and schizoid (I- U-). Later, Berne also explored a third-handed position 'They're OK/They're not OK', thereby acknowledging the wider social context of such life positions.

Similarly, there is a creative force in nature which strives for growth and completion. Alongside Freud's instinctual drives – *thanatos* (death instinct) and *eros* (sexual instinct) – Berne proposed that there is a third drive – *physis* – which describes the creative life instinct. In his work and writing Berne also referred to *vis medicatrix naturae* or the curative power of nature.

A general goal in life for people is autonomy, which Berne defined as the release or recovery of our capacity for awareness, spontaneity and intimacy. In this sense, autonomy is not a selfish, individual goal; it is an outcome which requires others and, indeed, one which may be viewed as a social goal not only for individuals but also for groups, organizations, communities and societies.

Everyone has the capacity to think – and take responsibility for their actions.

People decide their own destiny and these decisions can be changed – this is the basis of redecision work in TA. (These decisions may be cognitive and conscious in the ordinary sense of the word, but they can also be unconscious, preverbal, bodily or visceral 'decisions'.)

Principles

TA is distinguished by its emphasis and reliance on the contractual method, by which all decisions about therapy (administrative, professional and psychological) are governed. A contract is a bilateral agreement or commitment between therapist and client to a well-defined course of action.

TA practitioners are committed to open communication in their transactions. Berne was one of the first psychiatrists (if not the first) to hold case conferences which were open to clients; he has been reported as saying 'Anything that can't be said in front of a patient isn't worth saying'.

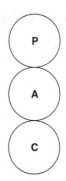

Figure 5.23.1 Structural diagram of a personality

Central theoretical concepts

Ego States

The personality may be categorized into three groups of 'ego states'. An ego state is 'the subjectively experienced reality of a person's mental and bodily ego with the original contents of the time period it represents' (Clarkson et al., 1996: 222). The three types of ego state are the Parent, Adult and Child, represented in Figure 5.23.1.

The Parent and Child ego states are archaic in that they represent past influences: 'the Parent ego state is a set of feelings, attitudes, and behavior patterns which resemble those of a parental figure .... The Child ego state is a set of feelings, attitudes and behavior patterns which are relics of the individual's own childhood' (Berne, 1961/1975: 75–77). By contrast, the Adult ego state is characterized by autonomous, here-and-now feelings, attitudes and behaviours. Ego states may be ascertained or diagnosed by four methods:

1. Behavioural – based on observable words, voice tones, gestures, expressions, etc.
2. Social – the reactions the subject elicits from other people.
3. Historical – the experience can be traced to a past which did actually occur.
4. Phenomenological – subjective self-experience (or examination of self-experience).

All four diagnoses are necessary for a sufficient identification of an ego state, and Berne emphasized the need for *both* observable and phenomenological verification of intuitive diagnosis.

Communication

All communication may be analysed in terms of transactions between ego states. This helps to understand how human beings engage with each other – both to achieve real contact and intimacy but also to repeat limited patterns of relating. In analysing such transactions, Berne (1966) identifies three 'rules' of communication.

Life Script

The origin of problems is understood in TA as the result of a person's *life script*. This has several elements, the definition of which is briefly elaborated:

- It is a *specific life plan*, laid out in the form of a drama with a beginning, middle and end.
- It is *decided in early childhood*, based on predispositions and needs balanced against the demands of the environment. Such decisions or survival conclusions are made on the basis of the infant's emotions and reality testing and his basic need to be in relationship. The script is understood to be the best decision or survival conclusion the infant can make at the time.
- It is *reinforced by parental influence*, that is through actual, specific, observable transactions with the parents or carers. Such script messages are both non-verbal and verbal.
- It *directs behaviour* in the most important aspects of a person's life in that the person's script culminates in a chosen (decided) alternative and, *out of awareness*, we choose behaviours which lead to the conclusion or 'script payoff'.

Psychological disturbance is understood in terms of *child development* (i.e. ego state development) and of *psychopathology* (i.e. in terms of the structure of the personality); for example the exclusion or contamination (unaware influence) of ego states; or symbiosis, that is when two (or more) individuals develop a co-dependent relationship based on script decisions.

Disturbance is maintained through the development of an interlocking system of beliefs about self, others and the world, and repressed authentic feelings; observable behaviours, internal experiences and fantasies; as well as reinforcing memories. This is known as a 'racket system' (Erskine and Zalcman, 1979) (after the notion of a protection racket). This system is closely linked to *games*, that is repeating patterns of interaction with others in which script beliefs are enacted relationally and lead to a reinforcement of the script pay-off.

Origin and maintenance of problems

In common with most psychological theories, TA acknowledges the influence of the past, especially childhood, on the present. In TA this repetition of past patterns is understood through the process of *script*. Script is a 'life plan' formed largely in the first few years of life, as a result of the interplay between the child's natural temperament and needs with her experiences in and of the world, including parental (and societal) influence. According to Berne, the infant is born with, in addition to physical needs, certain *psychobiological hungers*. The chief of these are hungers for *structure* and predictability, for novelty and *incident* and for relationship. Indeed, relationship is not simply a need but a given; from the first moments of life the infant is in relationship with another person. Her very identity is shaped by the interwoven experiences of self and other as well as by the 'messages' (*injunctions, program, counterscript*) and instructions she receives about how to be in the world.

As a result of her early experience, the child forms conclusions – some cognitive and conscious, many non-verbal, bodily-affective patterns of being – called *script decisions* about self, others and the world. This *frame of reference* acts as a template for future life, patterning relationships, aspirations and limitations.

As a result of this deeply held world view, the grown adult sees the world through a lens with which she filters or *redefines* her experience. As a result, her patterns of feeling and thinking are well repeated, which lead to patterns of behaviour (*psychological games*) that are likely to bring about repetitions of her early experiences. She does this partly because unconsciously it is familiar and predictable, and also because it provides a source of *strokes* (relating) and incident in a way that she expects and believes is essential to her survival. If the person's script is very rigid and impermeable, she will succeed in co-creating this vicious circle again and again. A less impermeable script system is open to updating and reshaping as the person engages in relationship with the here-and-now world.

Change

Change may broadly be seen as the manifestation of *physis* and the expression of autonomy. More specifically, Berne identified cure as a progressive process involving four stages:

1. Social control – the control of dysfunctional social behaviours.
2. Symptomatic relief – the personal relief of subjectively experienced symptoms.
3. Transference cure – when the client can stay out of their script, as long as the therapist is around either literally or 'in their head'.
4. Script cure – by which the person's own Adult ego state takes over the previous role of the therapist and the person makes autonomous decisions.

Skills and strategies

A central skill of the TA practitioner is detailed observation. In discussing the requirements of the group therapist, Berne (1966: 65) summarizes them as an ability to 'ideally use all five senses in making a diagnosis, assessing the situation, and planning the treatment: sight, hearing, smell, touch and taste' (although he acknowledges that the sense of taste is seldom used!). Berne pays particular and detailed attention to facial expressions and pasimology, the science of gestures. This is not to suggest that the therapist comments on all that they observe; it is to suggest that all this is available to their awareness. Observing in such detail has direct implications for

the training of therapists in general and of group therapists in particular.

TA originally took an operational, actionistic approach to change and 'treatment'. Based on the contractual method and their diagnosis of the client, TA practitioners negotiated, defined and generally followed a mutually agreed treatment plan. TA has developed a sophisticated treatment planning sequence comprising 12 stages (see Clarkson et al., 1996), including agreeing the contract, decontamination, building inner support, impasse resolution, therapy with the Parent ego state, integration, etc.

Berne (1966) identified eight 'therapeutic operations' which characterize TA therapy:

1. Interrogation or Enquiry – inviting the client to talk about himself.
2. Specification – categorizing and highlighting certain relevant information.
3. Confrontation – using previously specified material to point out inconsistencies; often this has the purpose and effect of disconcerting the client's Parent, Child, or contaminated Adult.
4. Explanation – explaining a situation with a view to strengthening the client's Adult.
5. Illustration – using an anecdote, simile or comparison to reinforce a confrontation or explanation.
6. Confirmation – using new confrontations to confirm the issues and patterns that emerge in the client's discourse.
7. Interpretation – offering ways of understanding a client's underlying motives, designed to stabilize the client's Adult control and 'deconfuse' his Child.
8. Crystallization – making summary statements to help the client make autonomous choices.

Since the early days, the original methodology has been developed in a number of ways. The early approaches (Classical, Cathexis and Redecision) relied on the 'concrete' analysis of script elements that were amenable to conscious cognitive awareness. Later developments have reflected changes in the wider field of psychotherapy. These include narrative or constructivist approaches that take account of new understandings in relation to memory and meaning making. They also include psychoanalytic TA (e.g. Moiso and Novellino, 2000) and relational TA where the relationship between therapist and client is the vehicle in which the client can express his or her, sometimes unconscious, self-experience and patterns of relating. Relational TA (Hargaden and Sills, 2002) and Co-creative TA (Summers and Tudor, 2000) also introduce the intersubjective into their understanding of the therapeutic endeavour, the former in examining the 'deconfusion' of the Child (elaborating Berne's operations into *empathic transactions*), and the latter in describing a present-centred theory of expanding Adult (see Tudor, 2003).

Research evidence

Berne (1966) argues that research and therapy must be clearly separated, to the extent that a research group should be designated as such and any therapeutic results regarded as secondary. He also discusses issues of motivation and possible psychological games involved in research, as well as the effect of the presence of the investigator. Nevertheless, Berne himself pre-figured the more recent concept of the reflective practitioner who is more aware of research. Berne's own writing, as well as that of other TA practitioners, reflects a broad concern in the TA community to observe the external manifestations of internal, phenomenological realities and to operationalize the conclusions.

It follows that most TA concepts are amenable to research – the life script through questionnaires, functional modes of ego states through the egogram, passivity and discounting through the discount matrix, the stroke economy through the stroking profile, etc. (for explanation of these and other TA concepts, see Stewart and Joines, 1987). Given that such therapeutic and treatment tools reflect and represent the technology of TA, it is surprising that comparatively little research has been conducted into the overall effectiveness of TA therapy and this is the subject of some discussion in the international TA community.

Nevertheless, in the last ten years research articles have appeared in the *Transactional Analysis Journal*

(the official journal of the international TA world) and the *EATA News* on, for example, self-esteem in a self-reparenting programme; the impact of TA in enhancing adjustment in college students; ego states; the effects of TA psychotherapy on self-esteem and quality of life; stress among high-school students, egograms; functional fluency (using the functional modes of ego states); and the use of TA in treatment centres for addiction.

References

Berne, E. (1961/1975) *Transactional Analysis in Psychotherapy*. London: Souvenir Press.

Berne, E. (1964) *Games People Play*. New York: Grove Press.

Berne, E. (1966) *Principles of Group Treatment*. New York: Grove Press.

Clarkson, P., Gilbert, M. and Tudor, K. (1996) Transactional analysis. In W. Dryden (ed.), *Handbook of Individual Therapy*. London: Sage. pp. 219–253.

Erskine, R.G. and Zalcman, M.J. (1979) The racket system. *Transactional Analysis Journal*, 9 (1): 51–9.

Hargaden, H. and Sills, C. (2002) *Transactional Analysis: A Relational Perspective*. London: Brunner-Routledge.

Moiso, C. and Novellino, M. (2000) An overview of the psychodynamic school of transactional analysis and its epistemological foundations. *Transactional Analysis Journal*, 30 (3): 182–191.

Stewart, I. and Joines, V. (1987) *TA Today*. Nottingham: Lifespace.

Summers, G. and Tudor, K. (2000) Cocreative transactional analysis. *Transactional Analysis Journal*, 30 (1): 23–40.

Tudor, K. (2003) The neopsyche: The integrating Adult ego state. In C. Sills and H. Hargaden (eds), *Ego States*. London: Worth Reading. pp. 201–231.

Recommended reading

Berne, E. (1972/1975) *What Do You Say After You Say Hello?* London: Corgi.

PART V
Theory and Approaches

ECLECTIC-INTEGRATIVE APPROACHES

5.24 Cognitive Analytic Therapy (Anthony Ryle, 1927–)

○○○

JAMES LOW

Brief history

Cognitive Analytic Therapy (widely known as CAT) was developed by Anthony Ryle in the 1980s while he was Consultant Psychotherapist at the United Medical and Dental Schools of Guy's and St Thomas's Hospitals in London. This approach developed out of various strands of Ryle's research interests and clinical experience: (a) Kelly's Personal Construct approach and in particular the Repertory Grid depiction of the predictability of interpersonal interaction; (b) Alexander's and French's focus on active intervention on specific psychodynamic issues; (c) the diagrammatic description of the psychological process developed by Mardi Horowitz in his ground-breaking attempt to map different 'states of mind' and the procedures effecting shifts between them; and (d) the identification of several types of commonly repeated interpersonal procedures which were then presented to patients for personal customization and rating of applicability. These and several other features (Ryle, 1990) have been incorporated into the CAT integration of cognitive-behavioural and object-relations thinking and practice.

The model is now widely practised in the UK and increasingly in Europe and Australia. A key principle in the development of this approach has been the wish to offer a time-limited and effective intervention which allows public sector health care services to offer at least minimum sufficient help to many people. New developments in the model are making it particularly useful for helping patients with borderline and other personality disorders (Ryle, 1997; Ryle and Kerr, 2002).

Basic assumptions

A collaborative approach grounded in a contractually defined working alliance helps to mobilize the patients' competencies and potential in the areas of thinking, feeling and acting.

Psychological problems are not entities but are manifestations of procedures, both intra-psychic and interpersonal. Procedures are patterns of relating which are regular in form, logical in each step (though the total sequence is often highly destructive of self and other), and usually invisible to the person until they are accurately described. These procedures can be identified and contextualized in terms of origins and ongoing maintenance. The CAT reformulation seeks to empower the patient to a re-vision of their identity, their resources, and their possibilities.

The therapist needs to be continuously watchful to avoid (a) confirming and colluding with the patient's procedures, and (b) enacting their own procedures.

By helping patients to define a clear focus for therapeutic work that can be discussed in terms of resolution, the therapist models for the patient how to identify and work on discrete problems. A brief therapy cannot deal with all the patient's problems but by supporting the development of skills in observation, analysis, reflection, prediction, impulse recognition and control, evaluation and self-feedback, the patient is educated and empowered to continue problem solving for themselves.

Human identity is generated through and maintained by dialogic interpersonal communication. Dialogic patterns are usually re-enacted out of awareness, often while each person is thinking of themselves as an autonomous agent. Conscious attention to the dialogic nature of identity brings a creative shift, a radical decentering of attention from the private individual to the shared matrix of emergent identities.

The patient's ability to revise their procedural patterns of thinking, feeling and acting is limited by fixed attributions of meaning. The therapist endeavours to engage the patient in the joint creation of conceptual tools which can then be internalized.

This helps to relativize the prior fixed attributions and empowers the patient to use new ways of behaving as a support for developing and maintaining new forms of meaning and value. This strengthens the ability to perceive options and to mobilize resources towards effective choice making.

Patients and therapists bring great stores of experience, lifeskills, and creative potential to the therapy. The clearly defined structure of the time-limited (usually 16 sessions) 'package' acts as a scaffolding around which the energy of the collaborative pair can be mobilized. The focus of the CAT is on removing the blocks that the therapist and patient identify as leading to suffering. This model encourages a pragmatic approach to removing these blocks and to identifying exits but has no overarching view of how the patient should live once these blocks are removed.

Origin and maintenance of problems

Problems arise from the development of fixed interpersonal positionings in response to the particularities of the early environment. These positionings are interactive and are known as reciprocal roles. Thus an infant growing up in a family where the imposition of parental control is a major feature of the interactive mood is likely to start processing a lot of what is going on, both interpersonally and intrapsychically, through the reciprocal roles of controlling–controlled. Both positions are available

to the person, though a common pattern would be to seek another to occupy the controlling position so that one can maintain the familiar controlled position oneself. The reciprocal role is also enacted on oneself by, for example, carrying on an internal critically controlling conversation so that one inducts oneself into the reciprocal position of hopelessly criticized and controlled. This internalization of early experience is the key contribution of object relations thinking to the model. Each individual's on-going behaviour of eliciting specific reciprocating roles from the other becomes a means of understanding both the power of the structure's self-maintenance and the clinical phenomena of transference and counter-transference. Positionings which were useful for survival in childhood frequently remain unrevised in adult life even when they are of little help in managing changed environments and new social roles.

Early experiences of invasion and abandonment give rise to patterns of conflict and deficit maintained through the reciprocal roles (R–R). When the child is responding to an environment whose overpowering intensity endures for a long period of time, the range of possible responses is experientially reduced. This leads to a felt enclosure within one R–R formation so that other options become invisible. Thus repeated abuse can result in a person feeling hurt, lost, anxious, mistrustful – and thereby unable to shift to a different mode of relating. In extreme cases the person can develop a limited repertoire of R–R, each of which operates as a quasi-autonomous self-state separated by dissociation leading to a very fragmented experience of being-in-the-world (Ryle, 1997).

The problematic R–Rs feed into a sense of core pain which is the chronically endured affect-ridden sense of badness, hopelessness, worthlessness, etc. Although the child was being subjected to unnecessary and/or unhelpful experiences where they would riot the causal agent, he or she will often ascribe a moral agency to their own position, feeling that it is their fault that they were hit, abused, abandoned, etc. This is often encouraged by the adult environments. Interpersonal procedures are largely responses to the environment, developed as attempts to manage the intolerability of the core pain.

The R–R structures are supported by procedures which arise from and return to them via the core pain creating a force of maintenance generated through an interplay of thinking, feeling and acting. This is described in the Procedural Sequence Object Relations Model (Ryle, 1990). This understanding is used to work with the patient towards a reformulation of their history and experience in order to help the patient avoid painful repetition. Procedures are organized in three categories though the same material can be arranged in any of these forms depending on the ease of comprehension by the patient. *Traps* are circular procedures arising from a core negative belief – no matter what is done to escape that belief it is always the final point of the procedure. *Dilemmas* are falsely dichotomous constructs of interpersonal behaviour which narrow the perceived choices to the stalemate of 'I'm damned if I do, I'm damned if I don't.' *Snags* arise where an implicit commitment or prohibition impedes an explicit goal which one mobilizes to satisfy. Thus I may long for intimacy and work hard to develop a relationship but just when security and depth of engagement become possible I sabotage or snag this effort due to the force of a parallel but consciously quite separate belief that intimacy will rob me of my sense of self and so I find a reason to withdraw.

Figure 5.24.1 shows how the causal patterns are embedded in the maintenance procedures. The terms used here are rather abstract; with an actual patient their own words would be used as much as possible to integrate the mobilizing energy of affect with the clarity of recognition promoting description. The procedure demonstrated in this example is a trap.

Change

The vehicle of change is the therapist's ability to establish and maintain a warm and empathic working alliance with the patient. The model supports the therapist's confidence that even the most disturbed and disadvantaged patient is able to achieve significant change for the better. It also supports the therapist in their focused attention on not confirming the patient's habitual R–R and procedures.

The collaborative style of the therapy provides the patient with ongoing feedback on how they continue or change their patterns of thinking, feeling and acting. The key stages of the therapy are description, recognition and revision.

Change occurs when the patient is able to step back from their familiar perceptions and observe new options which can be evaluated before a decision is made. This approach clearly demands that the patient is willing and able to engage in the tasks of stepping back, observing, reflecting, deciding, communicating, acting, reviewing. The therapist helps the patient do this by being fully present and useful on the creative edge of the patient's 'zone of proximal development'. This is the area for development created by the interface of the patient's potential and desire and the therapist's presence and ability to respond in the service of the other (Ryle, 1990).

The therapist helps patients to develop the new tools they need in order to think, feel and act differently. The poor parenting and environmental invasion and abandonment that are seen as strongly influencing the development of problems in adult life also cause gaps in knowledge as to how the world operates. The therapist through the reformulation letter highlights not only how the problems have occurred but what needs to be learned and explored in order for new and happier experiences to occur.

The therapist is not attempting to provide a regressive experience. The therapist is not the good mother providing a warm breast of generous and understanding nourishment. Rather, CAT is a 'post-rusk' therapy where patients are encouraged to work on their own tasks in and with the presence and help of the therapist. This style of 'doing with' as opposed to 'being with' or 'doing for' is vital in a brief therapy and works from the beginning to increase the patient's sense of self-esteem and self-efficacy. The therapist is active and interventionist – but this is directed towards the task jointly decided on as the focus of therapy. This active collaboration comes under attack when the patient or therapist loses focus and reverts to habitual patterns of expectation and response. This is why a clearly agreed jointly formulated description of the core positions (R–R)

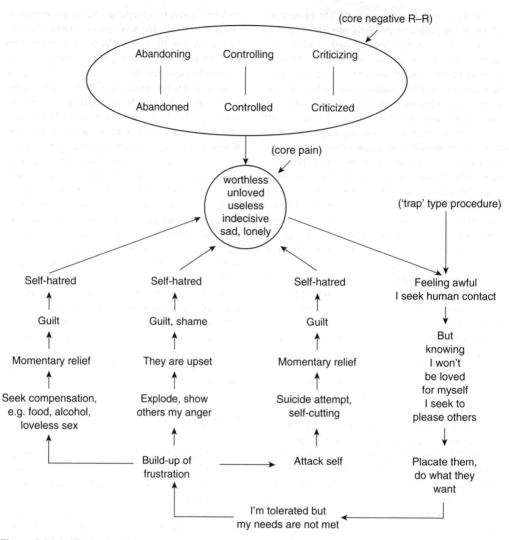

Figure 5.24.1 Example of sequential diagrammatic reformulation

and their supporting procedures is so vital to success in this form of therapy.

Skills and strategies

The therapist's key skills are empathic attunement, task focus, attention to the impact of their own and the patient's procedures on the task, and the ability to work effectively with the patient's zone of proximal development.

These skills are employed within the specific framework of a CAT as it progresses through the stages of description, recognition and revision.

Description is the early focus of the therapy during the reformulation phase (usually sessions one to four).

The therapist explores the patient's life history in relation to the problems that have brought them for treatment. The patient is encouraged to fill in the *psychotherapy file* (a self-selection list of common procedures), to write an account of their own life, and to keep a specially designed diary to identify the factors which intensify or alleviate the problems.

The therapist helps the patient to identify a clear focus for the therapy. Usually this is in the form of a deeper understanding of the presenting problem. For example, a person who presents with depression and social isolation may, through discussion of their desire and how it gets blocked, find the following to be a useful targeted problem to focus on: 'I don't know how to get close to others.' This formulation of the issue has the advantage of highlighting the learning aspect of the solution and opens the way for the therapeutic relationship to be a laboratory for experimentation and focused learning.

The therapist writes the patient a reformulation letter which shows the historical development of the problematic procedures. The patient is able to really check out whether the therapist has heard and understood them. They can correct details and this empowerment of their position is often a key factor in stabilizing the working alliance. Experiencing reformulation as an empowering joint activity is very important, for the retelling of the patient's life-story helps to loosen the attachment the patient often has to an absolute sense of how things were and especially to how bad they seem. This prose reformulation is then distilled into a sequential diagrammatic reformulation (SDR) – a diagram of the type illustrated in Figure 5.24.1.

Once the patient is clear about the description and can see how it pertains to past and present experience the next phase is *recognition*, in which the patient must struggle to use the description to make sense of what is going on. Often this starts with recognizing the pattern after the event has occurred but then, because the procedural description has already been checked against a wide range of experience, the patterns start to become clear as they are occurring and the observing self is strengthened. Building on this with discussion of events on the horizon, the patient starts to be able to predict how they might get hooked into a procedural response.

Once this perception is established the third stage of *revision* begins, whereby new options can be explored and so the closed circuit of the procedure is broken and fresh choices can be made.

With this basic CAT structure supported by the use of rating sheets for on-going joint evaluation of the therapy, and with patient and therapist exchanging review goodbye letters at the end of the 16 sessions, there is a great focus on conscious intentionality. This allows therapists to integrate into the treatment other skills that they may have, including dream analysis, use of creative arts, transpersonal exploration, and the use of gestalt contact to subvert the insistence of procedures. Thus the structure supports the therapist so that their own creativity and that of the patient can arise in the service of the contractually agreed task.

No matter what skills, strategies and techniques the therapist employs, the clarity of the agreed aim serves to support the collaborative nature of the work. CAT therapists try to be transparent in their practice and to be willing to discuss with the patient why they do the things they do. This modelling of self-reflective practice and accountability should help the patient to sustain the gains they make from therapy and continue to reflect on and be open to the richness of life's possibilities.

Research evidence

A research focus has been part of the development of CAT from the beginning (Ryle, 1990: ch. 14). Indeed, the structure of each therapy involves the joint development of a hypothesis which is then investigated. This encourages the development of an observing self in the patient which supports them in forming a research attitude towards themselves, leading to curiosity and a willingness to step back and evaluate how they are getting on.

Therapists also focus on single-case research as a major part of their training using tape analysis to gain a deeper and more precise sense of how their own procedures interact with those of the patients during the sessions. Investigation rather than belief forms the basis of CAT therapists' approach to their work.

Numerous descriptive studies have been published (Ryle, 1995: ch. 10), including the use of CAT with violent female offenders, cases of deliberate self-harm, and CAT groups. Reports on controlled trials have been published, including a comparison of outcomes of 12-session CAT and 12-session therapy according to Mann's model, and a study of the use of CAT to improve compliance in insulin-dependent diabetics. The results are very positive, particularly in showing an increase in patients' ability to control destructive impulses.

Major research projects are underway in Finland, Australia, Spain and the UK.

References

Ryle, A. (1990) *Cognitive-analytic Therapy: Active Participation in Change*. Chichester: Wiley.

Ryle, A. (ed.) (1995) *Cognitive-analytic Therapy: Developments in Theory and Practice*. Chichester: Wiley.

Ryle, A. (1997) *Cognitive-analytic Therapy and Borderline Personality Disorder: The Method and the Model.* Chichester: Wiley.

Ryle, A. and Kerr, I. (2002) *Introducing CAT Principles and Practice*. Chichester: Wiley.

5.25 Multimodal Therapy
(Arnold A. Lazarus, 1932–)

○○○

STEPHEN PALMER

Brief history

During the 1950s Arnold Lazarus undertook his formal clinical training in South Africa. The main focus of his training was underpinned by Rogerian, Freudian and Sullivanian theories and methods. He attended seminars by Joseph Wolpe about conditioning therapies and reciprocal inhibition and in London he learned about the Adlerian orientation. He believed that no one system of therapy could provide a complete understanding of either human development or condition. In 1958 he became the first psychologist to use the terms 'behavior therapist' and 'behavior therapy' in an academic article.

Lazarus conducted follow-up inquiries into clients who had received behaviour therapy and found that many had relapsed. However, when clients had used both behaviour and cognitive techniques more durable results were obtained. In the early 1970s he started advocating a broad but systematic range of cognitive-behavioural techniques and his follow-up inquiries indicated the importance of breadth if therapeutic gains were to be maintained. This led to the development of Multimodal Therapy which places emphasis on seven discrete but interactive dimensions or modalities which encompass all aspects of human personality.

Basic assumptions

Individuals are essentially biological organisms (neurophysiological/biochemical entities) who behave (act and react), emote (experience affective responses), sense (respond to olfactory, tactile, gustatory, visual and auditory stimuli), imagine (conjure up sights, sounds and other events in the mind's eye), think (hold beliefs, opinions, attitudes and values), and interact with one another (tolerate, enjoy or suffer in various interpersonal relationships). These dimensions of personality are usually known by the acronym, BASIC I.D. derived from the first letters of each modality, namely Behaviour, Affect, Sensations, Images, Cognitions, Interpersonal and Drugs/biology.

Modalities may interact with each other – for example, a negative image or cognition may trigger a negative emotion. Modalities may exist in a state of reciprocal transaction and flux, connected by complex chains of behaviour and other psycho-physiological processes.

The multimodal approach rests on the assumption that unless the seven modalities are assessed, therapy is likely to overlook significant concerns. Clients are usually troubled by a multitude of specific problems which should be dealt with by a similar multitude of specific interventions or techniques.

Individuals have different thresholds for stress tolerance, frustration, pain, external and internal stimuli in the form of sound, light, touch, smell and taste. Psychological interventions can be used to modify these thresholds but often the genetic predisposition has an overriding influence in the final analysis.

Individuals tend to prefer some of the BASIC I.D. modalities to others. They are referred to as 'cognitive reactors' or 'imagery reactors' or 'sensory reactors', depending upon which modality they favour.

Human personalities stem from interplay among social learning and conditioning, physical environment and genetic endowment. Therefore each client is unique and may need a personalized therapy.

Individuals usually benefit from a psycho-educational approach to help them deal with or manage their problems.

Although the therapist and client are equal in their humanity (the principle of parity), the therapist may be more skilled in certain areas in which the client has particular deficits. It is not automatically assumed that clients know how to deal with their problems or have requisite skills, and the therapist may need to model or teach the client various skills and strategies.

No one theory has all the answers when helping clients. Multimodal therapy is underpinned by a broad social and cognitive learning theory, while drawing on group and communications theory and general systems theory. However, multimodal therapists can choose not to apply these theories obsessively to each client.

Technically speaking, 'multimodal therapy' *per se* does not exist, as multimodal counsellors and psychotherapists, as technical eclectics, draw from as many other approaches or systems as necessary. To be accurate, there is a multimodal assessment format and a multimodal framework or orientation.

Origin and maintenance of problems

Human problems are multi-levelled and multi-layered. Few problems have a single cause or simple solution.

According to Lazarus, psychological disturbances are the product of one or more of the following: (a) conflicting or ambivalent feelings or reactions; (b) misinformation; (c) missing information which includes ignorance, *naïveté* and skills deficits; (d) maladaptive habits including conditioned emotional reactions; (e) issues pertaining to low self-esteem and lack of self-acceptance; (f) inflexible and rigid thinking styles and attitudes; (g) unhelpful core schemas; (h) tendency to cognitively or imaginally 'awfulize' events and situations; (i) unhelpful beliefs maintaining a low frustration tolerance (e.g. 'I can't stand it-itis'); (j) information-processing errors (cognitive distortions); (k) interpersonal inquietude such as misplaced affection, undue dependency or excessive antipathy; (l) biological dysfunctions.

Individuals avoid or defend against discomfort, pain, or negative emotions such as shame, guilt, depression and anxiety. This is known as 'defensive reactions' and should not be confused with psychodynamic concepts.

The principal learning factors which are responsible for behavioural problems and disorders are conditioned associations (operant and respondent);

modelling, identification, and other vicarious processes; idiosyncratic perceptions.

Non-conscious processes are often involved in learning. Stimuli that can influence feelings, conscious thoughts/images and behaviours may go unrecognized by the person concerned.

Interactions between two people or more involve communications and meta-communications (i.e. communication about their communication). Communication can disintegrate when individuals are unable to stand back from the transaction, thereby failing to examine the content and process of on-going relationships.

Individuals may have a genetic predisposition or vulnerability to certain disorders or distress.

Change

A good therapeutic relationship, a constructive working alliance and adequate rapport are usually necessary but often insufficient for effective therapy. The therapist–client relationship is considered as the soil that enables the strategies and techniques to take root. The experienced multimodal therapist hopes to offer a lot more by assessing and treating the client's BASIC I.D., endeavouring to 'leave no stone (or modality) unturned'.

Usually an active-directive approach to therapy is taken. However, this depends upon the issues being discussed and upon the client concerned.

The process of change commences with the counsellor explaining the client's problems in terms of the seven modalities, that is, the BASIC I.D., and then negotiating a counselling programme which uses specific techniques or interventions for each particular problem. This is usually undertaken in the first or second session and the completed Modality Profile is developed (see Table 5.25.1).

Multimodal therapists take Paul's (1967: 111) mandate very seriously: '*What* treatment, by *whom*, is most effective for *this* individual with *that* specific problem and under *which* set of circumstances?' In addition *relationships of choice* are also considered.

Positive, neutral or negative change in any one modality is likely to affect functioning in other modalities.

The approach is psycho-educational and the therapist ensures that the client understands why each technique or intervention is being used. Bibliotherapy is frequently used to help the client understand the methods applied and also to correct misinformation and supply missing information. A self-help coaching book provides details regarding the majority of multimodal techniques and how to develop a Modality Profile (Palmer et al., 2003).

The approach is technically eclectic as it uses techniques and methods taken from many different psychological theories and systems, without necessarily being concerned with the validity of their theoretical principles.

Multimodal therapists often see themselves in a coach/trainer–trainee or teacher–student relationship as opposed to a doctor–patient relationship, thereby encouraging self-change rather than dependency.

Flexible interpersonal styles of the therapist which match client needs can reduce drop-out rates and help the therapeutic relationship. This approach is known as being an 'authentic chameleon'. The term 'bespoke therapy' has been used to describe the custom-made emphasis of the approach.

Lazarus summed up briefly the main hypothesized ingredients of change when using the multimodal approach:

- Behaviour: positive reinforcement; negative reinforcement; punishment; counter-conditioning; extinction.
- Affect: admitting and accepting feelings; abreaction.
- Sensation: tension release; sensory pleasuring.
- Imagery: coping images; changes in self-image.
- Cognition: greater awareness; cognitive restructuring; modification of unhelpful core schema and information-processing errors.
- Interpersonal: non-judgemental acceptance; modelling; dispersing unhealthy collusions.
- Drugs/biology: better nutrition and exercise; substance abuse cessation; psycho tropic medication when indicated.

Skills and strategies

Therapist humility – Lazarus stresses that therapists should know their limitations and other therapists'

Table 5.25.1   John's full modality profile (or BASIC I.D. chart)

Modality	Problem	Proposed programme/treatment
Behaviour	Eats/walks fast, always in a rush, hostile, competitive: indicative of type A behaviour	Discuss advantages of slowing down: disadvantages of rushing and being hostile; teach relaxation exercise; dispute self-defeating beliefs
	Avoidance of giving presentations	Exposure programme; teach necessary skills; dispute self-defeating beliefs
	Accident proneness	Discuss advantages of slowing down
Affect	Anxious when giving presentations	Anxiety management
	Guilt when work targets not achieved	Dispute self-defeating thinking
	Frequent angry outbursts at work	Anger management; dispute irrational beliefs
Sensation	Tension in shoulders	Self-message; muscle relaxation exercise
	Palpitations	Anxiety management, e.g. breathing relaxation technique, dispute catastrophic thinking
	Frequent headaches	Relaxation exercise and bio-feedback
	Sleeping difficulties	Relaxation or self-hypnosis tape for bedtime use; behavioural retraining; possibly reduce caffeine intake
Imagery	Negative images of not performing well	Coping imagery focusing on giving adequate presentations
	Images of losing control	Coping imagery of dealing with difficult work situations and with presentations; 'step-up' imagery (Palmer and Dryden, 1995)
	Poor self-image	Positive imagery
Cognition	I must perform well otherwise it will be awful and I couldn't stand it	Dispute self-defeating and irrational beliefs; coping statements; cognitive restructuring; ABCDE paradigm (REBT) bibliotherapy; coping imagery (Palmer and Dryden, 1995)
	I must be in control	
	Significant others should recognize my work	
	If I fail then I am a total failure	
Interpersonal	Passive/aggressive in relationships	Assertiveness training
	Manipulative tendencies at work	Discuss pros and cons of behaviour
	Always puts self first	Discuss pros and cons of behaviour
	Few supportive friends	Friendship training (Palmer and Dryden, 1995)
Drugs/biology	Feeling inexplicably tired	Improve sleeping and reassess; refer to GP
	Taking aspirins for headaches	Refer to GP; relaxation exercises
	Consumes 10 cups of coffee a day	Discuss benefits of reducing caffeine intake
	Poor nutrition and little exercise	Nutrition and exercise programme

Source: Palmer, 1997: 159–160

strengths. The therapist tries to ascertain whether a judicious referral to another therapist may be necessary to ensure that the client's needs are met. In addition, a referral to other health practitioners such as medical doctors or psychiatrists may be necessary if the client presents problems of an organic or psychiatric nature.

Therapists take a flexible interpersonal approach with each client to maximize therapeutic outcome and reduce drop-out rates.

Techniques and interventions are applied systematically, based on client qualities, therapist qualities, therapist skills, therapeutic alliance and technique specificity. For example, research data will suggest various techniques that could be applied for a specific problem although the counsellor may only be proficient in using a number of them, while the client may only be able to tolerate one or two of the suggested interventions due to having a low tolerance to pain or frustration. Finally, a poor therapeutic alliance may thus increase the chances of attrition (dropping-out) occurring if a high-anxiety-provoking technique is applied.

A wide range of cognitive and behavioural techniques is used in multimodal therapy. In addition, techniques are taken from other therapies such as gestalt therapy (e.g. the empty chair). Table 5.25.2 (adapted from Palmer, 1996: 55–56) illustrates the main techniques used in therapy.

A 15-page Multimodal Life History Inventory (MLHI) (Lazarus and Lazarus, 1991) is often but not invariably used to elicit information about each of the client's modalities, general historical information, expectations about counselling and the counsellor. The client usually completes the MLHI at home between sessions one and two. If the client is not up to undertaking the task due to inadequate skills or severe depression, the therapist can use the MLHI questions as a guide in the session (Palmer and Dryden, 1995).

Second-order BASIC I.D. is a modality profile which focuses solely on the different aspects of a resistant problem. It is undertaken when the interventions or techniques applied to help a specific problem do not appear to have resolved it.

To obtain more clinical information and also general goals for therapy, a Structural Profile is drawn

(Lazarus, 1989). This can be derived from the MLHI or by asking clients to rate subjectively, on a scale of 1 to 7, how they perceive themselves in relation to the seven modalities. The counsellor can ask a number of different questions that focus on the seven modalities:

- Behaviour: How much of a 'doer' are you?
- Affect: How emotional are you?
- Sensation: How 'tuned in' are you to your bodily sensations?
- Imagery: How imaginative are you?
- Cognition: How much of a 'thinker' are you?
- Interpersonal: How much of a 'social being' are you?
- Drugs/biology: To what extent are you health conscious?

Then in the session the therapist can illustrate these scores graphically by representing them in the form of a bar chart on paper (see Figure 5.25.1). Then clients are asked in what way they would like to change their profiles during the course of therapy. Once again the client is asked to rate subjectively each modality on a score from 1 to 7 (see Figure 5.25.2).

Tracking is another procedure regularly used in multimodal therapy in which the 'firing order' of the different modalities is noted for a specific problem. Therapy interventions are linked to the sequence of the firing order of the modalities.

Multimodal therapists deliberately use a 'bridging' procedure to initially 'key into' a client's preferred modality, before gently exploring a modality (e.g. affect/emotion) that the client may be intentionally or unintentionally avoiding (Lazarus, 1997).

Research evidence

The majority of techniques used are taken from behaviour and cognitive therapy. These approaches, and more recently the techniques that are applied to specific problems and disorders, have been shown to be more effective than other forms of therapy.

Controlled outcome studies have supported the benefits of multimodal assessment and counselling programmes. In addition, Kwee's (1984) outcome study on 84 hospitalized clients suffering from

Table 5.25.2   Frequently used techniques in multimodal therapy and training

Modality	Techniques and interventions
Behaviour	Behaviour rehearsal
	Empty chair
	Exposure programme
	Fixed role therapy
	Modelling
	Paradoxical intention
	Psychodrama
	Reinforcement programmes
	Response prevention/cost
	Risk-taking exercises
	Self-monitoring and recording
	Stimulus control
	Shame-attacking
Affect	Anger expression/management
	Anxiety management
	Feeling-identification
Sensation	Bio-feedback
	Hypnosis
	Meditation
	Relaxation training
	Sensate Focus Training
	Threshold training
Imagery	Anti-future shock imagery
	Associated imagery
	Aversive imagery
	Coping imagery
	Implosion and imaginal exposure
	Positive imagery
	Rational-emotive imagery
	Time-projection imagery
Cognition	Bibliotherapy
	Challenging faulty inferences
	Cognitive rehearsal
	Coping statements
	Correcting misconceptions
	Disputing irrational beliefs
	Focusing
	Positive self-statements
	Problem-solving training
	Rational proselytizing
	Self-acceptance training
	Thought-stopping
Interpersonal	Assertion training
	Communication training
	Contracting
	Fixed role therapy
Interpersonal	Friendship/intimacy training
	Graded sexual approaches
	Paradoxical intentions
	Role-play
	Social skills training
Drugs/biology	Alcohol-reduction programme
	Lifestyle changes, e.g. exercise, nutrition, etc.
	Referral to physicians or other specialists
	Stop smoking programme
	Weight reduction and maintenance programme

Source: Adapted from Palmer, 1996: 55–56

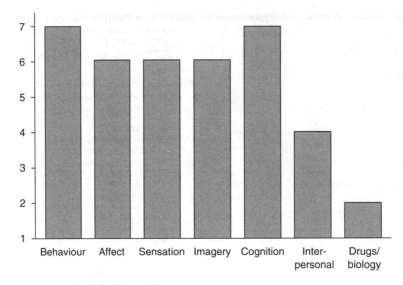

Figure 5.25.1   Natalies's structural profile

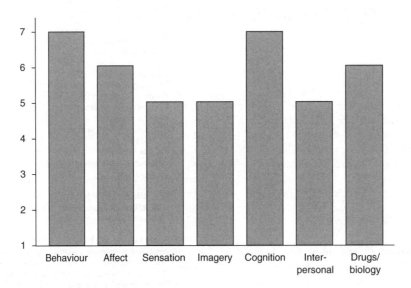

Figure 5.25.2   Natalie's desired structural profile

phobias or obsessive-compulsive disorders resulted in substantial recoveries and durable follow-ups.

References

Kwee, M.G.T. (1984) *Klinische Multimodale Gegragtstherapie.* Lisse: Swets and Zeitlinger.

Lazarus, A.A. (1989) *The Practice of Multimodal Therapy: Systematic, Comprehensive and Effective Psychotherapy.* Baltimore, MA: Johns Hopkins University Press.

Lazarus, A.A. (1997) *Brief but Comprehensive Psychotherapy: The Multimodal Way.* New York: Springer.

Lazarus, A.A. and Lazarus, C.N. (1991) *Multimodal Life History Inventory.* Champaign, IL: Research Press.

Palmer, S. (1996) The multimodal approach: theory, assessment, techniques and interventions. In S. Palmer and W. Dryden (eds), *Stress Management and Counselling: Theory, Practice, Research and Methodology.* London: Cassell.

Palmer, S. (1997) Modality assessment. In S. Palmer and G. McMahon (eds), *Client Assessment.* London: Sage.

Palmer, S. and Dryden, W. (1995) *Counselling for Stress Problems.* London: Sage.

Palmer, S., Cooper, C. and Thomas, K. (2003) *Creating a Balance: Managing Stress.* London: British Library.

Paul, G.L. (1967) Strategy of outcome research in psychotherapy. *Journal of Consulting Psychology,* 331: 109–118.

5.26 Neuro-linguistic Programming ◯◯◯
(Richard Bandler, 1950– and John Grinder, 1940–)

JO COOPER AND PETER SEAL

Neuro-linguistic Programming (NLP) is not, in itself, a 'therapy'. It can, however, be used therapeutically – and can be remarkably effective. NLP offers both a model and a modelling process. It can be used to model how other models (including therapeutic models) may work.

Brief history

Neuro-linguistic Programming was founded in the early 1970s by Richard Bandler, a mathematician and information scientist, and John Grinder, an assistant professor of linguistics at the University of California at Santa Cruz. They were interested in communication and influence and studied (modelled) people in many different fields. Their best-known subjects were three major therapists – the gestalt therapist Fritz Perls, the family therapist Virginia Satir and Milton H. Erickson, doctor and founder of the American Society of Clinical Hypnosis. Bandler and Grinder found that all three, despite their superficially different approaches, shared some common patterns in their use of language and behaviour to facilitate change.

In one of the earliest books, NLP was described as the study of the structure of subjective experience.

Bandler has described NLP as an attitude (of curiosity) and a methodology (of modelling), which leave behind a trail of techniques. The history of NLP has demonstrated the determination of Bandler, Grinder and their colleagues to model how human beings process their subjective experience and to develop ways in which apply the results of that modelling.

Bandler and Grinder's first books *Structure of Magic I* (1975) and *Structure of Magic II* (1976), were the result of their modelling of Fritz Perls, Virginia Satir and others and were primarily directed towards therapists. The first volume dealt with the way in which people use language to code, sequence and represent their experience. It presented the Meta Model, a language model for therapists (and other communicators). The second volume dealt with the intuitions and systematic behaviour of the therapists modelled, in relation to 'other ways a human being can both represent and communicate their world'.

Basic assumptions

NLP was not named until Bandler and Grinder had gone some way towards developing the methodology. Their first books had already been published and they were presenting increasingly popular seminars. The name that they chose can be thought of as descriptive:

Neuro refers to neuro-physiology, the functioning of the nervous system within the physiological structure of the human body, taken to be 'one system'.
Linguistic refers to the use of language to communicate.
Programming refers to the patterns and sequences evident in neurological processing, demonstrated in behaviour, which can be thought of as representing personal 'programmes'.

The domain of NLP is the functioning of the human system within its environment. At its simplest, NLP assumes that human beings use their senses (seeing, hearing, feeling, smelling and tasting) to perceive and process information from the 'outside world'.

As they continuously process their experience individuals develop their own unique models of the world which, in turn, inform their behaviour.

For practical purposes human modelling (the individual's creating and updating of their model of the world) can be thought of as the systemic inter-relationship of neuro-linguistic patterning and behaviour. All behaviour can be thought of as making sense within the individual's model of the world, however bizarre or extreme it may seem to others.

Indeed, Bandler and Grinder (1975) have said that identifying the assumptions in a client's modelling is the equivalent of understanding how the client's behaviour 'makes sense'. Similarly, there are basic assumptions to be appreciated in order for NLP to 'make sense' – these have become known as the *NLP presuppositions*.

The prime assumption of NLP is that *experience has structure* and all the presuppositions follow from this. Among these is the presupposition that *the map is not the territory* – the individual's model of the world is not the world itself. Many problems and misunderstandings occur when people confuse their model with the world, believing that their model is 'true' and that it is, or should be, shared by others. NLP presupposes that *each individual's model of the world is unique and is no more real or true than any other*.

NLP is a systemic model. It presupposes that *life and mind are systemic processes*, and that *whenever one element of a system changes the system itself changes*. Two other NLP presuppositions follow from this. The first is the idea that *the element of the system with the greatest flexibility of behaviour will be the most influential in the system*. The second, that *any change in one element of a system will, in some way, be detectable throughout the system*.

Cybernetic models were central in the development of NLP, including that the previously pervasive stimulus–response model could usefully be replaced by a model of behaviour as purposeful, incorporating the notion of feedback loops. This is encapsulated in the NLP presuppositions that *all behaviour has a positive intention* (in which positive refers to purposeful not to a value judgement) and that in communication *there is no failure, only feedback.*

These presuppositions generate the possibility of choice, in that a particular behaviour is chosen to accomplish a purpose. NLP presupposes that *individuals will make the best choice they can, given their model of the world and the resources they perceive available to them.* Implicitly, individuals may be limited as much by their models of the world and the choices they make, as by the world itself. Since 'internal' resources are a function of the development and sequencing of representational systems in internal processing, provided that they have the necessary neuro-physiology, *everyone either has, or has the potential to develop, all the resources they need.*

Origin and maintenance of problems

The domain of NLP is human subjective experience – how human beings model their experience. Bandler and Grinder proposed that three sets of 'filters' affect the way an individual models their experience. First, neurological constraints – the limits imposed by the human nervous system; second, social genetic factors which are shared by members of the same socio-linguistic community; and third, individual constraints. It is the individual constraints which provide the basis for the most far-reaching differences between individuals. It is the combination of these filters that ensures that the experience of each individual is unique and, therefore, that each individual creates their own unique model of the world. Bandler and Grinder said that 'these uncommon ways [in which] each of us represents the world will constitute a set of interests, habits, likes, dislikes and rules for behaviour which are distinctly our own' (1975: 12).

In NLP a 'problem' occurs when an individual is aware of a difference between their present state and desired state but perceives that they have little or no

choice. The objective of the NLP practitioner is to enable the client to enrich their model of the world so as to incorporate additional choices.

As NLP is a systemic rather than a linear causal model, practitioners do not attribute causes to problems, but explore how a problem is being maintained in the structure of the client's subjective experience. Their intention is to enable the client to restructure their experience in such a way as to enhance choice.

Change

Over the years NLP modelling has become more detailed and precise as finer distinctions have been made. In the early days, for example, it was recognized that human beings process their experience in sensory modalities. People see images in their mind's eye, hear internal sounds and voices (including their own voice) and have feelings that are internally generated, as well as taking in information from the 'outside world'.

The significance of changes in 'submodalities' was explored later. Submodalities are the finer distinctions within each representational system, including, for example, the colour, brightness, shape, location of an image; the tone, pitch, volume and tempo of a sound; and the location and intensity of a feeling.

In principle, deliberate and systematic NLP modelling can enable the practitioner to identify specific neuro-linguistic patterns and sequences so as to be able to make sense of, and recreate, aspects of the behaviour of their 'subject'. In the therapeutic context, this process is used to find out how the client is maintaining their 'problem' and to design suitable ways of facilitating change.

Bandler and Grinder (1975) claimed that all successful therapy, whatever its emphasis or form of treatment, characteristically involves a change in the client's representation/model of the world.

In the process of creating and maintaining their models of the world, individuals process vast amounts of sensory information. Some of this is in conscious awareness but most is processed unconsciously (in NLP 'unconscious' is used simply to refer to processing that is outside conscious attention).

Sensory experience is transformed by what Bandler and Grinder have referred to as the three universal modelling processes – deletion, generalization and distortion. Deletion occurs, in modelling, when information is left out, generalization when information is expanded so as to exclude counter-examples, and distortion with the assumption of causal connections and equivalencies. These are natural processes and can be both limiting and empowering.

In *Structure of Magic I* Bandler and Grinder showed how the universal modelling processes can be identified in an individual's language patterns. The words and phrases that people use can be regarded as 'surface structure', which is derived from 'deep structure' (full linguistic representation), which in turn is derived from the sensory representation of the individual's model of the world.

By observing the client's behaviour and listening to their language patterns, it is possible for an NLP practitioner to identify deletion, generalization and distortion in the client's modelling. By using language and behaviour in specific and precise ways, the NLP practitioner can help the client enrich their model and to expand its boundaries.

When an NLP practitioner and client work together it is always with the active, creative participation of the client. The practitioner uses sensory acuity, an understanding of modelling processes and behavioural flexibility to influence the system and to create a context in which the client is able to access new choices. Provided that the NLP practitioner has integrated the NLP presuppositions in their own behaviour, has the skills to model the client's processing and to detect the limits of the client's model, they can use whatever behaviour they choose to influence the system and create a context for change.

Skills and strategies

The skills needed by the NLP practitioner can be thought of from three perspectives – conceptual, analytical and behavioural. Conceptual skills include the understanding of, and ability to apply, NLP conceptual models. Analytical skills include the ability to analyse the system (including the practitioner's own and the client's behaviour) in terms of its component parts. Behavioural skills include the practitioner's ability to vary their own behaviour to influence the system and to facilitate the client's ability to change.

Perhaps the key conceptual model in NLP is the TOTE model, developed by Miller et al. (1960). The TOTE (Test–Operate–Test– Exit) model maintains that all behaviour is goal-oriented and feedback is provided by testing the goal against the evidence criteria for its achievement. The NLP practitioner makes use of the TOTE to model the client's behaviour and as a structure for their own participation in the system (Dilts, 1998; Dilts and DeLozier, 2000).

Other conceptual models include the NLP language models (the Meta and Milton models), representation systems (the way in which human beings process their experience in the different sensory systems), accessing cues (how individuals access information in their internal experience), anchors (the patterns of association between external cues and internal experience) and rapport (pacing and leading).

Analytical skills can be thought of as the ability to analyse the 'system', to chunk at different levels, to identify, for example, the TOTEs in the practitioner's and the client's behaviours, patterns and sequences of behaviour, language patterns and naturally occurring anchors.

Behavioural skills include the ability to use sensory acuity to be aware of what is happening in the system as it occurs. There is always external evidence of internal processing, including posture, gesture, breathing rate and location, eye movements, language patterns, voice tone, tempo and pitch and much more in every sensory system. The more highly developed the acuity of the practitioner, the better the feedback in the system and the more the practitioner will be able to vary their behaviour to influence the system. Behavioural skills include the ability to match the client's behaviour in a variety of ways and to lead the client to change their behaviour, to anchor specific states and to use language precisely to achieve specific outcomes.

In the early days of NLP, Bandler and Grinder summed up the necessary components of NLP as to gather information, evolve the system and solidify change. Over the years there has sometimes been a tendency for the methodology of modelling to be set aside and the application of recipe-like formats to be confused with NLP. This has tended to limit what is an exciting, inventive and creative process. NLP actually provides limitless opportunity for applying the attitude of curiosity and methodology of modelling to bring about change.

Research evidence

There have been many efforts to research NLP and related topics and many of them are listed in a database of NLP research, published on the internet, compiled and edited by PD Dr Daniele Kammer and associates at the University of Bielefeld.

NLP research can be thought of in two categories: first, research into the conceptual models formulated by Bandler and Grinder; and, second, research into the efficacy of the application of NLP 'techniques'.

The conceptual models present a difficulty for researchers in that Bandler and Grinder used the word *model* advisedly. They said in *Frogs into Princes*:

> We call ourselves *modelers*. ... We are not psychologists, and we're also not theologians or theoreticians. We have *no* idea about the 'real' nature of things, and we're not particularly interested in what's 'true'. The function of modelling is to arrive at descriptions which are *useful*. So, if we happen to mention something that you know from a scientific study, or from statistics, is inaccurate, realize that a different level of experience is being offered you here. We're not offering you something that's *true*, just things that are *useful*. (1979: 7)

Research into the application of NLP 'techniques' is equally fraught. Skilled NLP practitioners who have integrated NLP into their own models of the world are aware of sensory feedback within the system and vary their behaviour accordingly to achieve their outcomes. Their choice of behaviour is made in relation to the way in which the client is structuring their own experience, rather than the application of a standardized format.

Traditional research, however, has typically required the construction of a boundary around some particular aspect of behaviour in the belief that it is possible to measure the effectiveness of one element of behaviour in isolation. When NLP practitioners are working with their clients it is not their behaviour in isolation that is NLP; the NLP is in the intentional and purposeful application of the model.

References

Bandler, R. and Grinder, J. (1975) *Structure of Magic I*. Palo Alto, CA: Science and Behavior Books.

Bandler, R. and Grinder, J. (1979) *Frogs into Princes*. Moab, UT: Real People Press.

Dilts, R. (1998) *Modeling with NLP*. Capitola, CA: Meta Publications.

Dilts, R. and DeLozier, J. (2000) *Encyclopedia of Systemic NLP and NLP New Coding*. Santa Cruz, CA: NLP University Press.

Grinder, J. and Bandler, R. (1976) *Structure of Magic II*. Palo Alto, CA: Science and Behavior Books.

Miller, G.A., Galanter, E. and Pribram, K.H. (1960) *Plans and the Structure of Behavior*. New York: Holt, Rinehart & Winston.

The NLP Research Data Base, www.nlp.de/research/ is compiled and edited by PD Dr Daniele Kammer, Bielefeld, Germany, and published by Dr Franz-Josef Hücker, Berlin, Germany.

5.27 The Skilled Helper Model
(Gerard Egan, 1930–)

VAL WOSKET

Brief history

Since it first emerged on the counselling scene in the mid-1970s, the skilled helper model developed by Professor Gerard Egan of Loyola University, Chicago, has been continuously revised and expanded. The model has evolved from Egan's early writings on interpersonal skills in group and individual contexts and has moved through presenting a sequential process model of individual counselling to the development of change agent models and skills within the broader field of organizational change. In this section we will consider the model as it applies to one-to-one counselling.

An early and enduring influence on the skilled helper model is the work of Rogers and Carkhuff, which provides its person-centred values and principles. The model's cognitive-behavioural elements are closely informed by figures such as Bandura, Beck, Ellis, Seligman and Strong. While a three-stage map of the helping process (see below) has remained a constant during the various editions of the model, there have been a number of significant adjustments that take account of emerging research and developments in integrative practice. For instance, the third edition, published in 1986, evidenced a shift from problem management to opportunity development; and in 1990 the fourth edition carried an increased emphasis on challenge and action, as running through all stages of the counselling process. In 1994 the fifth edition engaged more forcefully with debates about eclecticism and integrationism. The fundamentally flexible, non-linear characteristics of the model and the importance of addressing shadow-side elements of the helping process were highlighted.

The model is now in its seventh edition (with an eighth edition in preparation) and in his latest revision, Egan (2002) has noticeably adopted a positive psychology approach to helping. Positive psychology is concerned with 'the enhancement of happiness and well-being, involving the scientific study of the role of personal strengths and positive social systems in the promotion of optimal well-being' (Carr, 2004: no pages). Positive psychology stands in opposition to the more traditional, remedial focus of clinical psychology. Rather than concentrating on psychological deficits, disability and dysfunction, the approach emphasizes instead clients' resourcefulness, resilience and capacity for constructive change. Egan's newest publication on the skilled helper model, designed to appeal particularly to para-professional helpers and called *Essentials of Skilled Helping* (2006), carries forward this emphasis on positive psychology. It also includes a companion brochure, *Skilled Helping Around the World*, which addresses the importance of developing cross-cultural sensitivity in applying the model.

Stated in simple terms the three stages of the skilled helper model are concerned with:

1 Problem definition.
2 Goal setting.
3 Action planning.

Egan has used different terminology in the various editions of *The Skilled Helper* to describe the three stages. In the current edition these are as follows:

Stage 1: 'What's going on?'
Stage 2: 'What solutions make sense to me?'
Stage 3: 'How do I get what I need or want?'

Underpinning the three stages of the model is an emphasis on action: 'How do I make it happen?'

It is sometimes debated whether the model, as currently practised, is integrative or eclectic, as such divisions are not always clear cut. The model can be thought of as integrative in that it provides an overarching framework for the helping process, yet it does not have an over-reliance on theory. It is derivative in that it draws on person-centred values and principles and cognitive-behavioural approaches. At the same time it has been described as atheoretical, meaning it moves beyond theory in searching for a framework or map which is built on pragmatism (what has been shown to work), rather than theoretical constructions.

The model is designed to provide a versatile and adaptable framework for developing a personal style of working that takes proper account of different client populations, issues and contexts. At its best, it is a shared map that helps clients participate more fully in the helping process. The stages and steps of the model become orientation devices that keep the helping process on course and prevent it deteriorating into a random set of events.

Basic assumptions

As noted above, Egan has explicitly adopted a positive psychology approach to helping in the current edition of *The Skilled Helper*. This involves seeing managing problems as more of a pro-active than a re-active process. As such, problem managements is considered to provide opportunities for clients to learn effective, life-enhancing skills.

Egan outlines the two principle goals of helping encompassed by the model as:

GOAL 1: Help clients manage their problems in living more effectively and develop unused resources and missed opportunities fully.
GOAL 2: Help clients become better at helping themselves in their everyday lives. (2002: 7–8)

In the service of these two goals for the helping process, counsellors need to be both skill learners and skill trainers.

The key values that underpin the culture of helping, as understood by Egan, are client empowerment and the Rogerian core qualities of respect, genuineness and empathy. These core values suffuse the communication skills that drive the model. While Rogers considered empathy to be a facilitative condition and one of the core qualities of the helping relationship, Egan views empathy both as 'a basic *value* that informs and drives *all* helping behavior' and as 'an *interpersonal communication skill*' (2002: 48, original emphasis). As a value, empathy places a requirement on the counsellor to understand clients as fully as possible in three particular ways:

1. Understanding the client from his or her point of view.
2. Understanding the client in and through the context (the social setting) of her or his life.
3. Understanding the dissonance wherever it appears to exist between the client's point of view and current reality.

Client empowerment is described as 'an outcome value' (Egan, 2002: 55) that is linked to the second goal of helping outlined above. It is recognized that counsellors are, by virtue of their role and status, in a more powerful position than those who seek their help. On the negative side, helpers can misuse their power wherever they encourage deference or dependency and when they oppress others. More positively, helpers can use the power inherent in their position within a social-influence process that can enable clients to become more effective at managing their own problems. A positive psychology approach encourages helpers not to see their clients as victims, even 'if victimising circumstances have diminished a client's degree of freedom', but instead to 'work with the freedom that is left' (Egan, 2002: 56). Egan therefore suggests that helpers who use the model think of themselves as consultants and facilitators who provide as much or as little assistance as the client needs in order to better manage the problem situations in their lives. Minimum intervention is considered to be the optimum way of working.

Origin and maintenance of problems

Egan's view of the person comprises a 'deficit' rather than a pathology model. The problems that clients bring to counselling arise, in most part, from their difficulties in harnessing energy and resources (both internal and external) to realize their best potential. Egan considers that unused human potential constitutes a more serious social problem than psychological or emotional disorders because it is more widespread.

He identifies the healthy and functional personality as someone who has the necessary knowledge, skills and resources to successfully complete developmental tasks and to handle upsets and crises when they occur. The individual's ability to accomplish life's challenges will be affected by external factors in the environment and may be reduced by these. Such limiting factors might include economic and social constraints, racism and oppression of minority populations and dysfunctional family environments.

Psychological disturbance is mainly attributed to:

- Being out of community – i.e. isolated or alienated from key social systems.
- The inability to successfully negotiate developmental tasks.
- Being out of touch with developmental resources (intrapersonal, interpersonal and environmental).

The helper is dealing with unique human beings at particular points in their lives. Pathologizing clients through general diagnostic labels is seen as unhelpful and perpetuates a remedial rather than a positive psychology approach to helping. Psychiatry and psychoanalysis have been too focused on the individual at the expense of the social and cultural context in which the individual exists. The horizons of the helper need to be expanded to include these systems and settings.

People become estranged from the capacity to realize their full potential through factors such as passivity, learned helplessness and their experience of undermining social systems and environmental conditions. Abnormal behaviour and emotional disturbance are seen as ineffective behaviour and its consequences, arising from lack of knowledge or skills. Skills and knowledge have to be acquired at each stage of development in order for the individual to accomplish increasingly complex tasks and fulfil new roles. Helpers need to be accomplished skill trainers or act as points of referral to external sources of information and skills that clients may need to make progress through developmental impasses. For instance, the counsellor might spend time helping the client to develop and practise the interpersonal skills of conflict management to help them move out of established patterns of deference to others.

Change

Changes in self-concept come about through empowerment as clients learn to be more effective at problem management and opportunity development. Therapy can help to overcome early developmental deficits by enabling the client to acquire skills in living, in particular interpersonal and problem-management skills.

Counselling is seen as a social influence process. People are capable of realizing their potential and rising above 'the psychopathology of the average' when given optimum amounts of supportive challenge within a solid therapeutic relationship. Helpers aim to be directive of the process but not the content of therapy. The client is considered to be the expert on him or herself and the counsellor acts as consultant to, and facilitator of, the client's process. The quality of the therapeutic relationship importantly mediates the effectiveness of the change process but is not an end in itself. Reluctance and resistance are seen as natural aspects of the change process.

The skilled helper model is one of a number of models that view the process of counselling as unfolding over definable stages. The emphasis on skills learning that is apparent in the skilled helper can suggest a disjointed and mechanistic approach. To guard against this, Egan is at pains to emphasize the need for helpers to mediate their use of skills through spontaneous engagement with the client.

Egan further asserts that it is a mistake to over-identify the helping process with the communication skills that are merely the tools that serve it. Communication skills do not, in themselves, constitute the problem-management process and 'being good at communication skills is not the same as being good at helping' (Egan, 2002: 135). Communication skills are principally helpful in establishing a good working relationship with the client. The working alliance provides a solid foundation for intentional counselling which Egan views, first and foremost, as a systematic process of 'social-emotional reeducation'.

Change comes about through action. However, action is not limited to behavioural change outside counselling sessions. Action can be understood both as internal (an inner shift or change in thinking or feeling) and external (observable action in behavioural terms) and as happening both within and outside sessions.

Skills and strategies

The first stage of the counselling process is about helping clients to construct a coherent personal narrative or story. Stories may consist of both problems and missed opportunities. The counsellor enables the client to tell their story through the active listening skills of attending (verbal and non-verbal), listening, reflecting back (content, thoughts and feelings), summarizing and clarifying. These communication skills help to convey the key quality of empathy, through which the counsellor demonstrates their understanding and acceptance of the client.

In order to elicit as clear a story as possible, the counsellor encourages the client to give concrete examples of behaviours, experiences and feelings. Empathic challenges are introduced to invite the client to begin to explore possible blindspots and to develop new perspectives on their situation. Through a balance of support and challenge, the counsellor helps the client search for leverage (something to work with that will make a lasting difference) using the skills of advanced empathy, immediacy, probing, questioning, summarizing and clarifying.

The second stage of the counselling process is about helping the client gain a clearer view of what they need and want. Where people have difficulty managing problems this is frequently down to a tendency to link problems to actions ('what do I *do* about this?') rather than link action to outcomes ('what do I need to do to get what I want?'). An axiom that Egan continuously emphasizes is that 'goals, not problems, should drive action' (2002: 248). Stage two of the process involves helpers assisting their clients, first, to see options for a better future and then to turn these into workable objectives that can drive action. The additional skills needed by the helper here are those related to goal setting, including future-oriented questioning, goal shaping and working with reluctance and resistance to generate hope and commitment.

The third stage of the helping process is concerned with enabling the client to identify and implement strategies for action that will result in positive and sustainable outcomes. Here the helper assists the client in achieving their identified goals using the skills of creative and divergent thinking, force-field analysis and sequential action planning.

Although this brief summary is presented in a linear fashion for ease of understanding, it is important to emphasize that in skilled hands the model is rarely applied in this fashion. The truly skilled helper learns to offer the stages of the model in a flexible and fluid manner where steps frequently overlap and merge into one another as counsellor and client move back and forth in the ebb and flow of the helping process.

Research evidence

As with any integrative model that is largely mediated by the way the individual therapist adapts and applies it, the skilled helper is not accessible to outcome research in the way that a more singular approach might, arguably, be seen to be. The model is not a set of treatment techniques that exists in any useful way independently of the practitioner who uses it. As such, the model is not accessible to empirical research in the way that a therapeutic approach with strictly definable techniques that can be replicated using a treatment manual might be. Rather, it is a framework that provides a 'geographical' map for the terrain of helping while also outlining the tasks of helping and how these tasks interrelate. Within this framework the helper utilizes their own unique blend of skills and awareness so that one counsellor's way of working with the model may be very different from another's.

This may in part account for the noticeable lack of formal studies into the model's effectiveness. A new book on the skilled helper model (Wosket, forthcoming) endeavours to include qualitative data on the client's experience of the model through a range of clinical case studies showing its application to different contexts and client populations. Further research into the model is needed to provide concrete evidence of its continued validity as the most widely used counselling model in the world (Egan, 2002).

While empirical studies into the effectiveness of the model may be lacking, the model itself is built on a firm foundation of research into the helping process. Egan is at pains to point out the bedrock of research upon which the various components of the model are founded. So, for instance, he draws extensively on research into cognitive dissonance theory, social learning, motivation and positive psychology to inform past and current versions of the model. That the skilled helper model continues to be highly

influential in the training and supervision of therapists in the UK and beyond (Connor, 1994; Page and Wosket, 2001) attests to its enduring popularity as a pragmatic and adaptable framework for students and established practitioners.

References

Carr, A. (2004) *Positive Psychology: The Science of Happiness and Human Strengths*. London: Brunner-Routledge.

Connor, M. (1994) *Training the Counsellor: An Integrative Model*. London: Routledge.

Egan, G. (2002) *The Skilled Helper: A Problem-management and Opportunity-development Approach to Helping* (7th edn). Pacific Grove, CA: Brooks/Cole.

Egan, G. (2006) *Essentials of Skilled Helping: Managing Problems, Developing Opportunities*. Pacific Grove, CA: Brooks/Cole.

Page, S. and Wosket, V. (2001) *Supervising the Counsellor: A Cyclical Model* (2nd edn). London: Brunner-Routledge.

Wosket, V. (2006) *Egan's Skilled Helper Model: Developments and Applications in Counselling*. London: Brunner-Routledge.

5.28   Solution-focused Therapy*

BILL O'CONNELL

Brief history

The key founders of Solution-focused Therapy (SFT) in the 1980s were the family therapists Steve de Shazer, Insoo Kim Berg and their colleagues at the Brief Family Therapy Center in Milwaukee, USA. Bill O'Hanlon, a therapist in Nebraska, also made a significant contribution. Other influential ancestors in the solution-focused family tree include George Kelly (founder of Personal Construct Theory);

* This approach should, properly speaking, be included in a separate 'constructivist' section and appears here as an editorial compromise to keep sections minimal.

John Weakland, Paul Watzlawick and Robert Fisch, who developed a problem-focused model at the Mental Research Institute (MRI) in Palo Alto, California, and Gregory Bateson and Milton Erickson whose ideas and clinical practice were seminal to the philosophy and application of SFT.

The approach has branched out from its origins in family therapy to applications in many other fields, such as mental health, psychology, group work, education, nursing, drug and alcohol work, counselling, social work and business.

In the early days of the model's evolution, the Milwaukee team of family therapists, headed by Steve de Shazer and Insoo Kim Berg, observed that their clients made significant changes following conversations about their preferred futures, even when there had been minimal attention to their problems or complaints. When clients described their solutions, these sometimes related directly to the problem, but often not. When clients articulated their solutions, they often saw the original problem in a different light. The more they focused upon their solutions, the less time and attention they paid to the 'problem'.

Following the clients' lead, the therapy team suspended judgement about the reported problems and focused upon the clients' non-problematic behaviour, competences and personal strengths. They discovered that by skilful prompting they could evoke solutions from clients. These standard interventions ('skeleton keys') could be used with all clients, irrespective of their presenting problems.

These interventions included:

- seeking exceptions to the problem – paying attention to what works when the problem is being managed better
- encouraging clients to 'do something different' – on the basis that many people become entrenched in their problems because they keep repeating the same failed solutions
- using the miracle question – to engage clients in imagining their preferred future without the problem dominating their lives
- scaling – to measure progress and build motivation
- taking small steps – to encourage clients to be realistic and not to be overwhelmed by the scale of change required

- giving feedback about the client's strengths, qualities and accomplishments based on the evidence of the session
- negotiating between-session tasks.

Basic assumptions

The solution-focused approach aims to help clients achieve their preferred outcomes by evoking and co-constructing solutions to their problems (O'Connell, 2001). Its primary emphasis is upon clients' resources, strengths and personal qualities. It makes a number of assumptions:

- Clients have ideas about their preferred futures.
- Clients are already carrying out constructive and helpful actions (otherwise things would be worse!).
- Clients have many resources and competences, many of which go unacknowledged by themselves and by others.
- It is usually more helpful to focus on the present and the future. The past can be useful as a source of evidence for prior successes and skills.
- It can be useful to find explanations for problems, but it is not essential, and in some cases this quest can delay constructive change.
- Constructing solutions is a separate process from problem exploration.
- The 'truth' of a client's life is negotiable within a social context. Fixed objective 'truths' are unattainable. There are many truths about the client's life.

Origin and maintenance of problems

Solution-focused therapists do not hold a theoretical position about the origin and maintenance of clients' problems. This is partly due to the fact that they do not see their primary function as helping clients to understand why they have their problems. It is also because they think that searching for the causes of problems assumes that such a quest is both desirable and useful – that there is an objective truth about the client out there to be uncovered.

Solution-focused therapists take the social constructionist view that 'reality' is socially negotiated by people through the use of language. The emphasis is therefore on the power of language to shape 'reality'. This epistemological stance explains why many solution-focused therapists feel uneasy about assessment processes controlled by professionals, who claim a privileged position in determining what constitutes a problem, and what 'treatment' is required. When professionals, from within their own power base define 'reality' by controlling the linguistic agenda, they can easily disempower clients and marginalize their voices.

Professional control of the 'problem agenda' is likely to increase client defensiveness. While acknowledging and validating client problems, it is often more productive to move away from problem talk and encourage the client to explore solutions. As therapist and client engage in talk about the client's preferred future, there is an accompanying sense of partnership – provided the therapist gets his or her timing right. Solution-focused therapists encourage clients to change their perceptual priorities from 'seeing' problems in all areas of their lives, to paying more attention to those things in their lives which are positive and are working for them.

Owing to the volume of information bombarding our senses and brains, we need to edit and select what we judge to be most appropriate at any given time. We can process information by either prioritizing the search for solutions or by turning on our problem filter. As a result, we tend to see what we are looking for!

Solution-focused clients are asked to pay attention to:

- their hopes for the immediate and their long-term future
- how they manage to make exceptions to the problem happen
- skills, qualities and strengths they show in one part of their lives that can be transferable
- the first steps they need to take.

The solution-focused understanding of the nature of problems is that they are an integral part of the human condition – they happen! They are 'normal'. In fact, overcoming adversity is what helps us to grow as human beings. Problems are not the problem! If

you haven't got a problem, you've missed the point! Sufferers with Obsessive Problem Disorder, a disease prevalent in professional circles, see problems in every aspect of their lives. Even when clients claim to have overcome their problems, it is interpreted as evidence that they are not aware of the deep and hidden nature of their problems!

Solution-focused therapists see clients as the experts in their lives. Their 'local' knowledge (i.e. what they know works in their particular context) is privileged above 'professional' knowledge. The professionals cannot possibly know what the 'right' solutions are for clients. Solutions need to fit clients, not the problem, and only the clients know what fits. The relationship in which the therapist 'joins with' the client is more important than any particular technique. Who you are with the client is more significant than what you do.

Change

Observation of clinical practice led solution-focused therapists to conclude that certain types of conversation are more likely than others to motivate and support clients towards change. These empowering interactions stress the competence, skills and qualities that clients can utilize to achieve their preferred futures. These conversations, characterized by optimism, hope and respect, create an awareness in clients that change is always happening and that they have the ability to determine, at least to some extent, the direction of change.

The solution-focused approach generates *descriptions* of clients' experiences, rather than attempt to diagnose and define conditions or disorders. It privileges language that conveys the ever-changing experience of the client. In this way it is easier to become aware of 'the difference that makes the difference'.

Skills and strategies

- *Pre-session change* – On initial contact with an agency or therapist, clients are asked to notice any changes that take place between then and the time when they come for their appointment. At the first session many clients report that they have managed to contain their problem, or indeed improve their situation. When this happens, therapy can 'hit the ground running'.

- *Problem-free talk* – In a sense, all solution-focused interventions encourage problem-free talk, but therapists also give clients the specific opportunity to talk about themselves and their interests, without reference to the problem. These conversations often yield information that is helpful to the therapist in knowing (a) how to work with the client, (b) which metaphors or examples will connect with the clients' world, and (c) clients' strengths, qualities and values pertinent to solution construction.

- *Listening for evidence of clients' strengths, qualities and skills* – While acknowledging clients' concerns and feelings, therapists also listen for evidence of the client's resources. An important element of the therapist's skill is in knowing the right time to help clients become more consciously aware of these strengths and skills. One way to describe the role of the therapist is that of bringing the client out of a state of perceived conscious incompetence to one of conscious competence.

- *Building on exceptions* – Instead of focusing upon the times when clients are experiencing their problems, therapists question them about times when they are managing the problem better. These exceptions (which are inevitable because people are constantly up and down) reveal evidence of clients' constructive strategies. By highlighting and exploring these times, clients can find ways in which they can extend these exceptions and thus reduce the problem areas in their lives.

- *The Miracle Question* – The Miracle Question is an intervention used by therapists to help clients bypass 'problem talk' and generate a description of life without the problem. Their answers identify goals and strategies they would like to use or have already begun to use. The question originated with de Shazer (1988) and his colleagues. Its standard form is:

> Imagine one night when you are asleep, a miracle happens and the problems we've been discussing disappear. As you were asleep, you did not know that a miracle had happened. When you wake up what will be the first signs for you that a miracle has happened?

Therapists question clients in some detail about what is happening that tells them that something has changed for the better. They explore the impact of the client's miracle on significant people and situations. As clients enter into their miracle their awareness of what they want to happen in their lives and 'what needs to happen for that to happen' becomes heightened.

- *Scaling* – Therapists use a scale of zero to ten to help clients measure progress, to set small identifiable goals, and to become aware of strategies they are already using. Ten represents 'the best it could be' and zero the worst. Therapists invite clients to explore the meaning of where they are on the scale and to consider whether they want to move up the scale and how they can do that. Scaling is a simple, practical technique which clients can take away and use between sessions.

- *Feedback* – The ending of a session is characterized by the therapists giving brief feedback to their clients. This consists of relevant compliments, summarizing client achievements and, where appropriate, negotiating a between-session task.

- *Tasks* – In negotiating tasks therapists follow principles such as:

(a) if it works for the client, encourage them to keep doing it
(b) if it doesn't work, invite them to stop doing it
(c) take small steps as small changes can lead to big changes
(d) give the client space to do something different from what was agreed.

Research evidence

Macdonald (2003) summarized studies of SFT in a wide range of client groups and settings, from offenders to patients with orthopaedic injuries. Most produced positive outcomes, although many did not meet the criteria for peer-review research. Only one randomized controlled trial has been published. This research took place in Sweden in a prison for recurrent offenders. Of the offenders who received five solution-focused treatment sessions, 60 per cent re-offended within 16 months, compared to a figure of 86 per cent in the control group. At the time of writing there are major SFT research projects, which are being co-ordinated by the European Brief Therapy Association, taking place across Europe.

References

De Shazer, S. (1988) *Clues: Investigating Solutions in Brief Therapy.* New York: W.W. Norton.

Macdonald, A. (2003) Research in solution focused brief therapy. In B. O'Connell and S. Palmer (eds),

The Handbook of Solution Focused Therapy. London: Sage.

O'Connell, B. (2001) *Solution Focused Stress Counselling.* London: Continuum/Sage.

5.29   The Transtheoretical Model
(James O. Prochaska, 1942– and Carlo C. DiClemente, 1942–)

PAUL JACKSON

Brief history

Prochaska and DiClemente considered that the initial impetus for the transtheoretical approach emerged from several different sources. Perhaps most significantly, in the USA from the mid-1970s to the early 1980s there was an increasing disquiet with the perceived rigidity and narrowness represented in many of the existing psychotherapeutic approaches. It appeared that each school of therapy tended to focus on its own, discrete mechanisms of change and sought to establish theories that solely supported these ideas, as opposed to exploring more generally the process of change as a whole. In 1977 Prochaska endeavoured to establish those change factors that are common to all forms of therapy, across all theoretical approaches. The culmination of this work in 1984 concluded that all theories of therapy share ten separate processes of change (see 'Processes of change' section on the next page). What at this time represented a framework or theoretical

construct was subsequently expanded, developed and researched to provide the empirical structure upon which Prochaska and DiClemente based their transtheoretical approach. This approach was welcomed into a climate already moving towards a more integrated and comprehensive method of psychotherapy, as it proposed a coherent account of how people change their behaviour. In particular, what is often referred to as the 'intuitive' appeal of this approach to therapists was, and generally still is, immediate.

Initially, the transtheoretical approach was embraced most readily in the field of addictions, where it remains very influential, not least because a new paradigm was sought in working with a client group that often presented as reluctant and unwilling to change. Additionally, addictive behaviours tend to be directly observable so any change is readily measurable, which in turn facilitates research and development. For some time, the approach became more commonly known as the 'model of change', as this seemed to capture both aim and content succinctly. More recently, however, it is referred to very specifically as the Transtheoretical Model (TTM) of intentional human behaviour change. While this refining of definition is subtle, it is also very significant, and represents an expansion of the model from a framework to aid exploration and understanding of behaviour change generally, to that of a 'template' to use in the development and delivery of specific interventions that increase the likelihood of a person progressing productively through the change process. The most obvious example of this is the integrated use of the TTM and motivational interviewing in the early stages of change, whereby these models are now considered clinically to be a 'natural fit'. Accordingly, the TTM has become influential far beyond its use in treating addictions, and is used to inform interventions and responses across a variety of generic health risk and protective behaviours such as mammography screening, dietary modification, exercise adoption and so on. However, within the context of more generic counselling and psychotherapy, the TTM remains less well accepted, in part because its overtly behavioural language can jar with milieus that conceptualize change more in terms of feeling-based, human experiences such as personal development, growth and potential.

Basic assumptions

The TTM recognizes, addresses and learns from the fact that many people make healthy, behavioural changes without ever seeking formal help.

The TTM is equally applicable to the many ways in which formal help is offered, from maximal to minimal interventions.

The TTM assists in the integration of the many and varied therapeutic approaches.

The TTM is applicable to the whole variety of presenting problems that people wish to change. It advances our understanding of how change is made, given such different presentations, and seeks to establish commonalities of change that may assist

in explaining success and failure in the person's attempt to address their difficulties.

The TTM encompasses the full course of change, from the point the person becomes aware of their difficulty to that robust resolution.

Origin and maintenance of problems

The TTM seeks to address the complexities of intentional behaviour change as a whole and as such is not concerned with the origin of the presenting problems in themselves. In this context, the emphasis is not on why and how a problem has developed but, rather, how best can change be understood and facilitated.

Change

The TTM seeks to integrate and apply therapeutically the *processes* of change, at certain *stages* of change, according to the identified problem *level*.

Processes of change

A process of change represents a form of overt or covert intervention that is either experienced or initiated by a person in addressing their thinking, feeling or behaviour in relation to their presenting problems. A common set of ten change processes are identified that span the diversity of problems experienced. Studies suggest that self-changers tend to use the full range of these change processes, whereas most systems of therapy are limited by adhering to the restrictions of their specific theoretical approach. The TTM requires that therapists be at least as creative as their clients. The processes of change fall into two groups: the experiential and behavioural. The experiential focus on those internal thought processes concerning the person's perception of their situation and are most relevant in the early stages of change. The behavioural are more concerned with the 'doing' of action and behaviour and are central to the later stages of change.

Experiential change processes

1. *Consciousness raising* – increasing information about oneself in relation to the problem.
2. *Dramatic relief* – experiencing and expressing the feelings surrounding the problem.
3. *Self re-evaluation* – reviewing thoughts and feelings about oneself in relation to the problem.
4. *Environmental re-evaluation* – considering if and how one's problems and subsequent behaviour affect others and the immediate environment.
5. *Social liberation* – recognition and creation of alternative possibilities in the social environment that may encourage behavioural change.

Behavioural change processes

1. *Stimulus control* – avoiding or resisting stimuli that promote problem behaviours.
2. *Counter conditioning* – introducing alternatives to the problem behaviours.
3. *Reinforcement management* – rewarding oneself or being rewarded by others for making change.
4. *Self-liberation* – belief in the ability to effect change and acting upon this with a commitment to alter behaviour.
5. *Helping relationships* – being open and trusting about problems with those who care, accept and support.

Stages of change

While there are various refinements to, and perceptions of, this model, presented most straightforwardly, making change involves moving through the stages of pre-contemplation, contemplation, preparation and action, to that of maintenance.

- *Pre-contemplation* – the person is not aware of, or does not acknowledge, their difficulties due to factors such as ambivalence, denial, rationalization and lack of knowledge. Commonly, any problems are most obvious to others who see, or are affected by, the person's difficulties.
- *Contemplation* – the person tentatively concedes something may be wrong, considers both what this might be and the possibility of change.
- *Preparation* – the person feels ready to change in the near future, and is on the verge of taking action.
- *Action* – the person overtly modifies their behaviour, implementing the planning of preparation.

- *Maintenance* – the person has implemented the change, consolidated and seeks to establish behaviours necessary to maintain this position.

In reality, of course, people tend not to change in such an ordered, linear fashion and this model is more realistically understood as a circular, revolving-door or spiralling out concept – in essence, a cycle of change. This, then, accommodates the reality of individuals often exiting by relapsing into old patterns of behaviour, re-entering the cycle and moving through the stages several times before establishing long-term maintenance which may, in turn, be exited from by moving into a life free from the identified difficulty. Alternatively, the person may remain fixed at a certain stage, or move backwards and forwards between stages, such as pre-contemplation and contemplation without really progressing beyond this. In its simplest form, this 'recycling' within the cycle of change can be represented diagrammatically, illustrating the dynamic movement therein (see Figure 5.29.1).

Levels of change

This dimension represents, in hierarchical order, the five discrete but interrelated levels of pyschological functioning at which interventions may be made. Although discrete, these levels are not in isolation and changes initiated at one level are likely to prompt change at another. The levels of change are:

1. Symptoms/situational – presenting difficulties.
2. Maladaptive cognitions – unhelpful thought patterns and beliefs.
3. Current interpersonal conflicts – difficulties within relationships.
4. Family/systemic conflicts – specific conflicts within the immediate system.
5. Intrapersonal conflicts – difficulties within the self.

Skills and strategies

The therapist's first task is to promote a healthy therapeutic relationship based on respect, trust and

Exit to termination/resolution

Maintenance

Action

Relapse
and
recycle

Preparation

Contemplation

Enter from pre-contemplation

Figure 5.29.1   The cycle of change

understanding which supports the client in making change.

The therapist is required to approach the task of change systematically, while integrating a broad range of skills and interventions relative to the specific needs of each client.

The therapist needs to assess whereabouts the client is in the cycle of change, and establish the level at which to incorporate the most appropriate intervention process. Working with the client non-prescriptively in matching intervention to stage will enhance the therapeutic alliance and further help facilitate change. The distinction needs to be made at this point between commitment to change and commitment to engage in a formal, helping relationship. A person can be committed to the former, but not the latter, and this discrepancy would need to be a vital consideration in establishing the appropriate degree of formal help offered.

Usually, but not exclusively, the presenting difficulty (level 1) is responded to with practical and behavioural strategies; maladaptive cognitions (level 2) with cognitive approaches; interpersonal and family conflicts (levels 3 and 4) with more systemic interventions; finally, intrapersonal difficulties (level 5) with in-depth counselling and

therapy. These levels are not static, and different levels can be worked with concurrently. For example, the presenting difficulties can be addressed while also exploring those systemic factors that may otherwise perpetuate the problem. It is important that the therapist remains aware of the level to which they tend to attribute problems in the client as this may be more an expression of the levels they feel competent to work in, rather than an accurate assessment of the situation. Change must remain client-centred, not therapist-centred.

By definition almost, those at the pre-contemplation stage are unlikely to seek help without some sort of external pressure. Strategies will primarily be aimed at increasing cognitive dissonance around the problem behaviour by enabling the client to articulate any previously unexpressed ambivalence. The aim is to engage the client's interest, build a relationship and promote helpful unease concerning the problematic behaviour to aid movement towards the contemplation stage.

Strategies appropriate to the contemplation and preparation stage include education, self-monitoring, questionnaires, identification of behaviour patterns and exploration of significant events. The aims are to raise consciousness, re-evaluate the problem behaviour, prepare and plan specific action and consider alternative ways of fulfilling needs. It is in these first three stages that the specific use of motivational interviewing skills and techniques are considered most productive in strengthening commitment to change.

Strategies for the action stage include cognitive-behavioural intervention at the symptom/problem level, learning new skills, controlling anxiety about the situation and finding support for the changed behaviour. The aims are to promote self-efficacy, self-esteem and develop alternative reward systems.

For the maintenance stage, appropriate strategies include further developing an alternative reward system, translating behavioural change into lifestyle change, counter-conditioning, stimulus control and addressing deeper intra- and interpersonal conflicts. The overall aim is to support the client in reinforcing their changed behaviour.

Useful responses to relapse revolve around helping the client view this as an opportunity for positive learning rather than failure, examining the preceding behaviour and events, continuing to stress those aspects developed in the maintenance stage, and reinforcing the advantages of their changed lifestyle. This helps preserve the client's belief that they do have a choice and can regain the necessary control in their lives if they so wish.

Research evidence

The TTM has been extensively researched, particularly within the field of addictions, using measures such as the 'Stages of change' and the 'Processes of change' questionnaires, comparing self-changers with those who receive formal help and over short- and long-term follow-up periods. The findings can be separated into those that concentrate on the TTM's proposed mode of action and those that examine client outcome with TTM-based interventions. With the first, it remains that research does not support unequivocally the view that change necessarily occurs through discrete stages or that matching particular processes to stages prompts movement to subsequent stages. In this context, it was suggested that the model be viewed not so much as an accurate description of how people change, but rather as a model of ideal theoretical change which, in turn, will continue to guide in devising useful modes of intervention. However, with the latter, literature supports the usefulness of treatments using various components of the TTM in a variety of behaviours. In addition, and this is more anecdotal than empirical at this stage, an increasing number of generic services are using the TTM to inform their treatment programmes. In the therapeutic setting, therefore, it perhaps remains the 'intuitive' appeal of the TTM for practitioners that facilitates its efficacy in clinical practice.

Recommended Reading

DiClemente, C.C. and Velasquez, M.M. (2002) Motivational interviewing and the stages of change. In W.R. Miller and S. Rollnick (eds), *Motivational Interviewing: Preparing People for Change*. New York: Guilford Press. pp. 201–216.

Hubble, M.A., Duncan, L.B. and Miller, S.D. (2000) *The Heart and Soul of Change*. Washington, DC: American Psychological Association.

Prochaska, J.O. and DiClemente, C.C. (1986) Toward a comprehensive model of change. In W.R. Miller and N. Heather (eds), *Treating Addictive Behaviors: Processes of Change*. New York: Plenum. pp. 3–27.

Prochaska, J.O. and DiClemente, C.C. (1992) The transtheoretical approach. In J.C. Norcross and M.R. Goldfried (eds), *Handbook of Psychotherapy Integration*. New York: Basic Books. pp. 300–334.

Prochaska, J.O., Norcross, J.C. and DiClemente, C.C. (1994) *Changing for Good*. New York: Avon Books.

Sutton, S. (1996) Can 'stages of change' provide guidance in the treatment of addictions? A critical examination of Prochaska and DiClemente's model. In G. Edwards and C. Dare (eds), *Psychotherapy, Psychological Treatments and the Addictions*. Cambridge: Cambridge University Press. pp. 189–205.

Velasquez, M.M., Maurer, G.G., Crouch, C. and DiClemente, C.C. (2001) *Group Treatment for Substance Abuse: A Stages of Change Therapy Manual*. New York: Guilford Press.

PART VI
Client Presenting Problems

6.1 Introduction

COLIN FELTHAM AND IAN HORTON

The following section examines a selection of some of the most common problems presented to counsellors and psychotherapists in and across different settings. To some extent this reflects what may be found in the *DSM IV TR* or elsewhere, although a notable difference perhaps is that some of these categories of problem are specific to situations, agencies, gender, the British experience, and so on. Obviously, it is not exhaustive, but hopefully it is representative. The selection is based mainly on the extensive practice experience of counsellors and psychotherapists. Writers come from a wide variety of clinical professions and their individual perspectives usefully reflect the catholicity of views in the therapy field. The term 'problems' has been chosen as common parlance, but of course different practitioners may prefer to think of psychodiagnostic categories, symptomatology, presenting problems, issues or concerns, goals, aspirations or simply different areas of clients' ongoing experience. A focus of this kind is likely to become more common with the increasing influence of the evidence-based

lobby. For ease of reference, an alphabetical ordering has been adopted here.

While each of these problem categories has been presented from a particular perspective, and with some emphasis on impressionistic and indicative themes, this part of the book is intended broadly to raise awareness of some of the following:

- description and recognition of a fairly distinct problem;
- nature of the problem – signs and symptoms, degrees of severity, accompanying psychological or physical problems;
- extent or prevalence of the problem, including, for example, social contexts, gender specificity, etc.;
- aetiology – single or multiple causes or associated exacerbating factors;
- contra-indications of therapy or treatment;
- therapeutic procedures – i.e. 'treatments of choice', including medication, etc.;
- clinical management, course, prognosis, time factors;
- relevant research findings, evidence and indications;
- (optional) recommended further reading.

6.2 Psychopharmacology ○○○

LINDA GASK

It's difficult to do justice to a complex subject in a small space, so this section will focus on the basics and what it is helpful for a counsellor or psychotherapist to know about the subject. The most up-to-date information on psychotropic drugs (drugs which act on the brain) can be found in the *British National Formulary* (online at www.bnf.org). Here you can find essential information on:

- effective dose range
- side effects
- drug interactions.

Specific drug groups and the generic (pharmacological) and trade (proprietary) names of drugs can be found in Tables 6.2.1–6.2.4. When a drug goes off patent (usually after ten years on the market) companies other than the original manufacturer can produce it under the generic name at low cost.

Withdrawal is much more difficult from drugs with a shorter 'half-life' (the half-life of a drug is the time taken for half of it to disappear from your system) and this includes Lorazepam and (in the antidepressants) notably Paroxetine (Seroxat).

There are three major groups of drugs that are used in mental health: the antidepressants (Table 6.2.1), the antipsychotic drugs also known as 'major' tranquillizers (Table 6.2.2) and the 'minor' tranquillizers (Table 6.2.3). The first major discoveries in these groups were all made in the 1950s. The next really important period came in the 1990s.

Antidepressants

Antidepressants may be helpful in combination with psychotherapy or counselling, particularly if the person is severely depressed, when they may be unable to formulate thoughts clearly and concentrate sufficiently to utilize talking treatments without additional medication.

All of the antidepressants work by raising the level in the brain of a substance called serotonin which is a neurotransmitter, a molecule that carries messages in the brain. In severe depression, there is evidence that the level of serotonin in the brain drops. Raising the level takes time, so antidepressants do not work immediately (usually 2–3 weeks). Some antidepressants (the tricyclics, and the newer combined-action drugs Venlafaxine and Mirtazepine) also have an impact on another neurotransmitter called noradrenaline.

In people who have bipolar disorder, antidepressants can trigger the onset of mania if used to treat depression without additional treatment with a 'mood stabilizer' (see Table 6.2.4) such as Lithium or Sodium valproate.

The first antidepressants commonly used were the tricyclics (see Table 6.2.1) but in the UK their use is being superseded by newer SSRIs (Selective Serotonin Reuptake Inhibitors) such as Fluoxetine (Prozac) and Sertraline (Lustral). The tricyclics (TCAs) are effective but cause numerous side effects and can be lethal in overdose (they cause heart arrythmias and a lethal dose may be small, less than ten tablets). Thus they have generally been prescribed in small doses, which can be a problem to people who have to pay for prescriptions. TCAs continue to be extensively used across the developing world because they work and they are very, very cheap.

Another older group of antidepressants, the Monoamine Oxidase Inhibitors (MAOIs) are rarely used now outside specialist centres because of the multiple interactions that they have with both other drugs and food (famously cheese).

Table 6.2.1   Antidepressants (commonly used types)

Group name	Generic name	Proprietary name
Tricyclic	Amitriptyline	*
	Clomipramine	Anafranil
	Dothiepin	Prothiaden
	Imipramine	Tofranil
	Lofepramine	Gamanil
SSRI	Citalopram	Cipramil
	Fluoxetine	Prozac
	Paroxetine	Seroxat
	Sertraline	Lustral
Others	Trazodone	Molipaxin
	Mirtazepine	Zispin
	Venlafaxine	Efexor
	Moclobemide	Manerix

*The tricyclics have been available for many years so it is unusual for anything other than generic versions to be prescribed. Fluoxetine is now also off patent so is available generically.

Table 6.2.2   Antipsychotic drugs (commonly used types)

Group name	Generic name	Proprietary name
Older drugs	Chlorpromazine	Largactil
	Flupenthixol	Depixol
	Haloperidol	Haldol, Serenace
	Sulpiride	Dolmatil
	Thioridazine	Melleril
	Trifluoperazine	Stelazine
Newer 'atypical' drugs	Olanzapine	Zyprexa
	Amisulpride	Solian
	Resperidone	Risperdal
	Clozapine	Clozaril*
Injectable (long-acting)	Flupenthixol decanoate	Depixol
	Fluphenazine decanoate	Modecate
	Haloperidol decanoate	Haldol

*People taking Clozapine require regular blood counts to monitor for serious blood side effects.

The SSRIs arrived in the 1990s and prescriptions have increased dramatically, particularly to younger people who have not previously had antidepressants. They also have side-effects but are generally easier to tolerate at effective doses than the older drugs. They may, however, cause significant irritability and agitation (which can rarely lead to suicide) and some have significant withdrawal reactions. This is not the same as addictiveness. Antidepressants are not addictive – people do not psychologically crave them or deal in

Table 6.2.3 Drugs used in anxiety and as sleeping tablets (commonly used types)

Group name	Generic name	Proprietary name
Benzodiazepines	Diazepam	Valium
	Chlordiazepoxide	Librium
	Lorazepam	Ativan
	Alprazolam	Xanax
Beta blockers	Propranolol	Inderal
Buspirone	Buspirone	Buspar
'Z' drugs	Zaleplon	Sonata
	Zopiclone	Zinovane

them on the black market. However, when they are stopped, there may be a multitude of unpleasant symptoms, including anxiety, aches and pains, headaches, flashing lights. Withdrawal should therefore always be a gradual process.

The final addition to the antidepressants have been the newer 'combined-action' drugs that work on both serotonin and noradrenaline, just like the TCAs did, but they are easier to take than the older drugs. These tend to be used when others (SSRIs) have failed. Venlafaxine (Efexor) also has a significant withdrawal syndrome.

Antipsychotic drugs

These drugs (see Table 6.2.2) are mostly used in psychotic illness, schizophrenia or mania, but also in smaller doses to control agitation in depression. Chlorpromazine (Largactil) is the best known, but much less used now. Thioridazine (Melleril) used to be widely used for agitation in depression but was found to be responsible for sudden death through its impact on the heart and is now less used. Many people with a diagnosis of schizophrenia receive injectable drugs which have a prolonged action.

In the late 1980s a drug that had been around for a long time, Clozapine (Clozaril) was discovered to have a significant impact on people with severe, previously drug-resistant illness. A political battle ensued to allow it to be made available, since it is

expensive. It can also cause serious blood problems and people receiving it require close monitoring. Newer 'atypical' antipsychotic drugs have appeared which do not have the side effects of the older drugs, and current prescribing guidance from the National Institute of Clinical Excellence (NICE) is that they should be available first-line. These drugs also have their own inherent problems, such as increasing weight, which has led to concern about the occurrence of diabetes in people on antipsychotic medication. Olanzepine can be effective in people with depression who have not otherwise responded to treatment. All the antipsychotic drugs may be used to treat agitation in severe depression but Thioridazine is now only licensed for use in schizophrenia.

Drugs used in anxiety

The most well-known members of this group (see Table 6.2.3) are the benzodiazepines ('benzos'), Diazepam (Valium) and Lorazepam (Ativan), which are prescribed much less than in the past for anxiety ('anxiolytics') because of their propensity to addiction, but are still going strong, particularly on the black market. New learning of the variety that is achieved in behavioural treatment for anxiety (particularly overcoming panic attacks) is difficult to achieve if the person is also taking anxiolytics, however there *may* be a place for very short-term treatment with

Table 6.2.4 Drugs used to stabilize mood

Group name	Generic name	Proprietary name
Lithium	Lithium	Camcolit, Priadel
Anticonvulsants	Sodium valproate	Epilim, Depakote*
	Carbamazepine	Tegretol

*Depakote is the version developed specifically for use in mental illness.

benzodiazepines in acute crises or to enable a person to initially engage with potentially traumatic therapy, and they are still used in short-term 'reducing regimes' (gradually decreasing dosage over several days) during withdrawal from alcohol.

Beta blockers can be helpful for people with primarily physical symptoms of anxiety. They help performance so are often used by people taking driving tests or professional musicians and are banned in competitive snooker (they cause unfair advantage in steadying the hand holding the cue).

Low doses of tricyclic antidepressants are also used for anxiety as they have the major advantage of being non-addictive. So too have low doses of antipsychotic drugs, which may be used in anxiety, however, these carry the risk of long-term side effects such as abnormal movements of the face and mouth (tardive dyskinesia) which can be seen in people who have been on the older antipsychotic drugs for some years and can be caused even by low doses.

Sleeping tablets

Benzodiazepines are still also used as 'hypnotics' (sleeping tablets). However, the newest group of hypnotics are the 'Z' drugs which are not licensed for long-term use and do cause dependence in a number of people (see Table 6.2.3).

Drugs used to stabilize mood

People who have a diagnosis of bipolar disorder, as well as those who have depression which does not respond to antidepressants alone, or which recurs, may be prescribed a mood stabilizer (see Table 6.2.4). Lithium is the best known of these, and has been found to promote recovery in depression when given along with an antidepressant ('augmentation'). The major problems with Lithium are that it is potentially lethal in overdose and blood levels have to be checked regularly (every three months) to ensure that the level falls within the safe and the therapeutic range. High levels of Lithium can cause severe tremor and confusion, but a mild tremor and thirst are common side-effects even at therapeutic doses. Lithium can also block the thyroid gland and cause hypothyroidism. The other mood stabilizers (apart from Lithium) are primarily used in epilepsy.

6.3 Conceptualizing Clients' Problems ○○○

COLIN FELTHAM

> As a practising clinician, the psychiatrist [or therapist] is concerned with individuals, each of whom is in his own fashion 'unique'. Yet if he is to function as a competent clinician, he requires certain general concepts and laws as a basis for his work.
>
> (Clare, 1980: 77)

Like many other aspects of therapeutic theory and practice, how we understand and conceptualize clients' distress, presenting problems and goals is a subject filled with interestingly conflicting views. Means of classifying different kinds of distress or problems in living, and associated terminology, have differed widely and changed significantly historically, culturally and according to the different clinical professions and their various theoretical orientations. Critics have also added to the debate by querying the very principle of classifying people in terms of 'psychopathology' – psychological disease or sickness. Counsellors and psychotherapists must balance allegiance to training-oriented theoretical loyalties against a wide range of factors idiosyncratic to each client. Arguably, the focus on 'clinical reasoning' shown by certain other helping professions (medicine, speech therapy, etc. – see Higgs and Jones, 2000) has not been well developed within our own profession due to training loyalties (Davies and Bhugra, 2004; Milner and O'Byrne, 2004), competing knowledge claims and an emphasis on the therapeutic relationship rather than on the actual, complex cluster of client characteristics calling for attention.

Historical views of psychopathology

Probably the first kinds of human 'psychological' problems were those related to fear of natural threats, including environmental hazards, fierce or abruptly changing weather conditions and hostile animals and humans, combined with an acute awareness of mortality. In addition, competition for resources and for sexual mates, along with anxious protection of the young, may all have begun to sow the seeds of later susceptibility to the counter-productively extended emotions of anxiety, hyper-vigilance, etc. (Stevens and Price, 2000). While names for these states would have taken a considerable time to develop, early cave paintings, charms and rituals testify to non-verbal attempts to ward off evil spirits. All long-established religions contain allegories or theories about the origins of suffering and propitiatory methods, and much 'psychopathology' was and is, in religious terms, understood as aspects of divine testing, as evil, karma, and so on.

Hippocrates in the fourth century BC devised a system of classification of illnesses into the humours of blood (sanguinity), phlegm (dullness), black bile (melancholy) and yellow bile (choler). Later Greeks applied more philosophical analyses, remedies and terminologies to problems of human distress. The Buddha had spoken in the sixth century BC of 'all worldlings as deranged' (Goleman, 2003: 341) and Buddhism developed the concept of *kleshas* (mental afflictions). The Middle Ages saw in Europe the gradual replacement of the idea of demonic possession (and the occasional admiration of those believed to be possessed as visionaries) with concepts of madness. Burton's *Anatomy of Melancholy*, published in 1621, interpreted depression and allied states as forms of divine retribution for sin. Concepts of lunacy, idiocy and insanity have waxed and waned, but by the end of the eighteenth century the Frenchman Pinel had arrived at a classification of mania, melancholia, dementia and idiotism. Westphal named agoraphobia in 1871. (Interestingly, it was named *Platzschwindel* (dizziness in public places) in 1870, but this coinage, although descriptively accurate, has not survived.) The 1880 United States census led to the seven categories of mania, melancholia, monomania, paresis, dementia, dipsomania and epilepsy. In 1898 the German Kraepelin coined the term 'dementia praecox', which was largely replaced by 1908 with Bleuler's term 'schizophrenia'.

This highly condensed selection is intended only to begin to suggest that religion, philosophy, medicine and other disciplines have variously staked their claims to understanding and naming human beings' multifaceted problems of distress and demoralization. But it also shows that interpretations and names change (Berrios and Porter, 1995). Even within the relatively short span of time from the late nineteenth century to the beginning of the twenty-first century, the following psychopathological labels have come and mostly gone: neurasthenia, hysteria, shell shock, nymphomania, inferiority complex, neurosis. In other words, diagnostic entities are to a considerable extent constructs of their own time and place. Hence, post-traumatic stress disorder (PTSD) came into being as an official (APA, 2000) clinical entity only in 1980, and the Vietnam war seems heavily implicated in its 'invention' (Young, 1997). Homosexuality was until 1972 (*DSM*) and 1992 (WHO, 1992) classified as a psychopathological condition, and alcoholism remains a disputed term. 'Road rage' has yet to become a recognized impulse-control disorder, nor has 'technophobia' yet become a recognized species of anxiety disorder.

Transcultural views of psychopathology

While all cultures recognize signs of 'something awry' with individuals' minds or souls and have their own terminology for varieties of distress, there is usually no exact correspondence between these and traditional western, scientific classifications. There is also considerable scope for misunderstanding the signs and symptoms presented to western therapists working in multicultural societies.

Social and medical anthropologists have charted some of what are often called *culture-bound syndromes*. Indeed, the *DSM-IV-TR* (APA, 2000) includes a specific outline section for culture-bound syndromes. As an illustration, an anthropological study of the Chewong (aboriginal Malaysians) found a very limited vocabulary for emotions, and showed that distress for the Chewong is conceptualized in *socially* oriented terms. Hence, transgression of rules and customs leads to shame: *tola* is an illness arising from disrespect; *maro* is a kind of dizziness associated with meanness.

Gopaul-McNicol and Brice-Baker (1998: 83) draw from several sources to demonstrate culture-bound syndromes. These include: *ataque de nervios* (Hispanic – 'an out-of-consciousness state resulting from traumatic events'); *falling-out* (African American – 'seizure-like symptoms resulting from traumatic events'); *Taijinkyofusho* (Asian – 'guilt about embarrassing others; timidity resulting from the feeling that one's appearance, odor, facial expressions are offensive to other people'); *Wacinko* (American Indian – 'anger, withdrawal, mutism, suicide resulting from reaction to disappointment and interpersonal problems'). Indigenous classifications may refer to supernatural causes and environmental factors. Hence, the Yoruba of Nigeria may speak of *Inarun* ('a condition which comes from God' – involving weakness, skin rashes, memory loss, irrational talking, etc.) and of *Ori ode* ('hunter's head' – involving the psychosomatic symptoms of a burning sensation, thumping in the head, visual problems, insomnia, etc.). A small-scale research survey of depressed Asian women in Britain includes discussion of what the women called 'thought sickness' (*soochne ke bimaari*), which was often comprised of a mixture of bereavement, isolation, poverty, racism and other contributing factors. As the publication reporting on this challengingly puts the diagnostic dilemma: 'Depression, or just life?' (CRE, 1993: 4).

Transculturally, reports of spirit possession and somatic symptoms are common, and easily misconstrued by western mental health professionals. The disproportionate number of black people in British psychiatric hospitals and prisons is often attributed to such misunderstandings. Almost by definition, the loss, dislocation, trauma and problems of adaptation and poverty, as suffered by many migrants and refugees in a new cultural environment, are too easily misunderstood (Van der Veer, 1998). A tortured refugee, for example, will find it hard to trust strangers (e.g. mental health professionals), may be legitimately suspicious, but this could easily be misconstrued as *paranoia*. It is also true to say that the number and kinds of psychopathologically oriented labels used for the distress or emotional difference experienced by or associated with women, is a cause for concern. Psychiatric abuses in the former Soviet Union, whereby political dissidents were often hospitalized for holding 'incorrect' views, should have alerted us to such dangers. More recently, the North American vogue for diagnosing *multiple personality disorder* (now *dissociated identity disorder*) has raised questions about different (and perhaps sometimes erroneous) diagnostic patterns in different countries. Practitioners claiming that their practices are 'colour blind' or neutral regarding race, culture and gender, should pause to consider the implications of the transcultural challenge. Additional helpful guidelines may be found in Eleftheriadou (1999), Paniagua (1998) and Ridley (1995).

Bio-medical views of psychopathology

Just as organized religion gradually displaced the dominance of magical practices, so science in the last three centuries has eroded the territory of religious practice. Physical and mental sickness (and their definitions) have been regarded as legitimate territory for scientific conceptualization, research and treatment. Many believe that our understanding – scientific or otherwise – of emotional or psychological problems or disorders is still at a fairly primitive, somewhat hit-or-miss stage. Clare (1980) argued that we might think in terms of four approaches to understanding mental distress: (i) organic (biological); (ii) psychotherapeutic (or psychological in the sense of having a focus on inner, subjective, mental and emotional life); (iii) sociotherapeutic (relating to social functioning and change); and (iv) behavioural

(psychology which concerns itself purely with symptoms and their removal). Ridley (1995) discusses alternative models of mental health in relation to multicultural awareness and the need to overcome unintentional racism in therapy by adopting models which are not inherently racist.

Psychiatrists are often attacked for their alleged adherence solely to the first of the above approaches, and have often been vilified for the practices of psychosurgery, electro-convulsive therapy (ECT), and use of psychotropic medications. While this is probably not a balanced portrayal, it is true to say that the medical and psychiatric professions are enormously powerful in leading research, influencing policies and dictating what is and is not psychopathology. Hence, a great deal of energy and public and private funds are dedicated to genetic, psycho-pharmacological and related research. The scientific model of mental distress, based on biology and behaviour ((i) and (iv) above) is clearly differently orientated from typical models of counselling and psychotherapy which are concerned with subjectivity and context. In other words, reflecting (ii) and (iii) above, psychological therapies (especially the psychodynamic and humanistic) tend to assess individuals more in terms of their holistic existence – inner (psychic) functioning; self-determination; (non-dualistic) body–mind system; psycho-social factors; spirituality; and potentiality as well as problem focus.

The western scientific tradition led inexorably, it seems, to the systematic categorization of forms of mental illness or disorder. The first edition of the *DSM*, now in its fourth edition, was published in 1952. Of very similar status and aims is the *International Classification of Diseases and Related Health Problems* (*ICD* – 10th edition), published by the World Health Organization (WHO, 1992). We now have a 2000 'Text revised' edition of *DSM* but, for simplicity's sake, the *DSM IV International Version with ICD – 10 Codes* is focused upon here. The *DSM IV* is an extremely influential text, indeed an institution, a necessity to most North American mental health professionals but also of considerable importance in Britain. Its aim is to offer comprehensive standardized categories for diagnosis that can be shared by all clinicians and agreed by third parties such as health agencies and funders. Acknowledging that *mental disorder* is an unsatisfactory term, the editors of the *DSM* nevertheless define it as

> a clinically significant behavioral or psychological syndrome or pattern that occurs in an individual and that is associated with present distress ... or disability ... or with a significantly increased risk of suffering death, pain, disability, or an important loss of freedom. (APA, 1995: xxi)

To qualify as a disorder, the client's condition must 'cause clinically significant distress or impairment in social, occupational, or other important areas of functioning' (1995: 7).

The *DSM* is a huge collaborative endeavour that attempts to set out some 340 mental disorders in the following groups:

- disorders usually first diagnosed in infancy, childhood or adolescence
- delirium, dementia, and amnestic and other cognitive disorders
- mental disorders due to a general medical condition not elsewhere classified
- substance-related disorders
- schizophrenia and other psychotic disorders
- mood disorders (mainly depressive and bipolar disorders)
- anxiety disorders (includes PTSD and phobias)
- somatoform disorders (e.g. hypochondriasis)
- factitious disorders (feigned illnesses, etc.)
- dissociative disorders
- sexual and gender identity disorders
- eating disorders
- sleep disorders
- impulse-control disorders not classified elsewhere (e.g. kleptomania)
- adjustment disorders (extreme negative reactions to stressors)
- personality disorders
- other conditions that may be a focus of clinical attention (e.g. sexual abuse, bereavement, phase of life problems).

The *DSM* gives criteria and guidelines as to severity and course of disorder: mild, moderate, severe, in partial remission, in full remission. Prior history, recurrence, principal diagnosis or 'reason for visit' are also key concepts. Concepts of prevalence, specific culture, gender and age features are given. It does not focus on treatment or therapy (see, however, Bellack and Hersen, 1990; Reid et al., 1997; Roth and Fonagy, 1996). The *DSM* commends multi-axial assessment, and the axes are: clinical disorders, and other conditions that may be a focus of clinical attention; personality disorders and mental retardation; general medical conditions; psycho-social and environmental problems; global assessment of functioning. The realities of 'diagnostic uncertainty' are acknowledged.

The *DSM*, it must be said, is regarded as a clinical bible by some, and as anathema by others (Kutchins and Kirk, 1997). It quite clearly suits the ethos of psychiatry and clinical psychology, particularly since many of the 'disorders' referred to are severe and more likely to come to the attention of statutory mental health professionals. However, in terms of discretionary clinical judgement, therapeutic tradition and ideology, client presentation and preferences, agency brief and so on, the *DSM* may be seen as at best one among many useful but fallible guides to understanding and assessment. What it does do, along with similar influential clinical traditions, is to call attention to problems that may be beyond the remit and power of counselling and psychotherapy to address successfully. In other words, it raises the question of limitations and contra-indications. Certain conditions such as very entrenched depression may benefit from medication as well as psychological therapy; some may benefit primarily from bio-medical treatment; and others will benefit primarily from psychological therapy or alternatives.

Lay or client views of psychopathology

For the most part ordinary people – non-professionals sometimes referred to as 'lay' – do not use the vocabulary of psychopathology (except where influenced by prevalent therapeutic discourse to present as 'depressed' or as having 'panic attacks', etc.). Rather, their first words and phrases to therapists may often include: 'I don't know where to begin'; 'I'm unhappy'; 'I can't cope'; 'I can't stop crying'; 'I think I'm cracking up/having a breakdown, going mad/losing my mind'; 'I can't face going to work'; 'I'm having trouble sleeping'; 'I can't seem to pull myself together'; 'I don't know what's wrong with me/what to do.'

Clients also quite often present using borrowed terminology – 'The doctor thinks it's a stress reaction'; 'I think perhaps I'm in shock'; 'Am I having a nervous breakdown?', etc. Such usage may be a combination of terms from the media and popular psychology, and is not necessarily helpful. Clients' own stories, faltering narratives in their own words, probably offer a better guide than pseudo-diagnostic language. When such terms *are* used, it is important to try and discover exactly how they are being used. 'I'm depressed' can mean 'I've been told I'm depressed' or 'I just can't cope with my job' or 'I'm really sad' or have many other nuances. Sometimes, as humanistic therapists have recognized, the core of a client's 'problem' – their deep inner pain, profound sorrow or self-loathing, for example – is best identified and most usefully conveyed experientially, by non-verbal and emotional expressions rather than by inexact, standardized pathological terms. Very often images and metaphors too are more effective personal labels than generalized medically oriented terms.

Critics' views of psychopathology

Broadly speaking, most practitioners of the humanistic and existential therapies are opposed to psychodiagnostic concepts, terms and procedures on the grounds of *inaccuracy, gratuitousness, stigmatization, disempowerment, abuse* and *'shrinkage'* (this last colloquialism referring to the tendency of psychiatric labels to shrink or reduce the totality of the human being to a spuriously named *part* of themselves, to dissect them psychologically and treat them accordingly). Many humanistic therapists are largely unconvinced by or uninterested in diagnostic assessment, and may commence therapy on the basis of non-judgemental acceptance and 'trial

therapy'. Usually emphasizing the importance of clients' self-determination and self-knowledge, as well as the trustworthiness of authenticity and emotional experience, some of these therapists have been known as 'anti-psychiatric', and many counsellors are opposed to the '(bio)-medical model' of diagnosis and treatment, with its perceived unwarranted use of medical or psychiatric nomenclature and uncritical use of psychotropic drugs. In spite of such critiques, somewhat paradoxically, some therapists have spoken of the 'trauma of eventlessness' (psychological damage done by an oppressively understimulating environment); 'hypophobia' (being less than appropriately anxious or fearful); and of 'the psychopathology of the average' (the tendency towards unhealthy conformity, the common failure in self-actualization).

Although psychodynamically affiliated therapists have closer links with the medical model, their assessments are often more influenced by clients' 'psychological-mindedness and quality of object relationships'. This is sometimes referred to as *dispositional assessment* rather than diagnostic. According to Roth and Fonagy, 'some orientations – particularly psychodynamic – consider that "suitability for therapy" is more important than formal diagnosis when considering which patients to accept into therapy' (1996: 29). However, the North American turn to empirically supported managed care, which influences even psychodynamic practitioners to adapt their therapy to brief treatments for diagnostic categories (Barber and Crits-Christoph, 1995), combined with increasing emphasis on evidence-based practice, may yet affect psychodynamic assessment and therapy in Britain (Fonagy, 2003).

Thomas Szasz is one of the most outspoken critics of psychopathology, arguing that 'mental illness' as such cannot exist because illness is physical, and furthermore that psychiatry and psychotherapy overreach themselves self-servingly when their ideologies colonize ordinary 'problems of living'. Szasz argues that psychiatry has taken over from religious domination and oppression; our version of the persecution of witches is the 'manufacture of madness', the unjustified labelling and involuntary incarceration or medicalization of people simply suffering, to different degrees, from a world that is often difficult to live in.

Experiments in which professionals have reported to psychiatric services with minimal or transient symptoms of mental illness (e.g. Rosenhan – see Clare, 1980) have resulted in detention on the basis, for example, of a single symptom (hearing voices) and subsequent difficulty in obtaining release. Concerns about the potential for misdiagnosis are very natural. It was at one time the habit of many psychiatrists to commit to hospital women who had had children outside marriage, and community care measures as late as the 1990s led to the 'decarceration' (release) of many such women, in some cases after 40 or more years in hospital, mainly on the basis of an implied pathological promiscuity.

Hare-Mustin and Maracek (1997) and Parker et al. (1995) point out that psychodiagnosis has always been abnormality oriented, and has frequently led to stereotyping 'mad people' as completely beyond the range of normal humanity and often beyond help. Alternatively, they have been regarded as objects of medical and psychiatric analysis, and have been benignly *pathologized* instead of being empathically understood or helped. Willingness to listen to their stories, to understand and value their differences (including 'delusions'), is recommended as a better way forward. As Parker et al. and other writers (e.g. Szasz, Cooper, Gergen,) have noted, the official language of madness, abnormality, psychopathology and clinical treatment tends subtly to spread so that ordinary people unwittingly think of themselves, when sad or demoralized, as depressed or stressed, or as in need of 'being in touch with my inner child' and so on.

Some clients no doubt seek the reassurance of official labels (and the associated understanding and 'cure' implied in them) and a small proportion are known to abuse such classificatory systems. 'Factitious PTSD' (fabricated PTSD symptoms), for example, can lead to financial compensation and the psycho-social rewards of adopting a 'sick role' (Young, 1997). In all such ways, therapeutic discourse may be consciously exploited, or unwittingly internalized and made to seem natural, but this cultural tendency is not necessarily in the true interests of individuals' welfare.

Informed and flexible assessment

Having weighed up some of the complex issues involved in the conceptualization of clients' problems, therapists obviously have to develop their own appropriate style of assessment. This will depend on the variables of training, profession, setting, on the abilities and preferences of therapist and client, and on the uniqueness of each therapeutic encounter. Certain facets of practical assessment have been referred to in section 3.5 on pages 109–117. Here, an informed and flexible model of assessment is briefly outlined.

A simple classical model of assessment is given by Lemma (1996: 46) which is reproduced in Figure 6.3.1.

Added to such a model are some proposed variations, complexities and problems for consideration.

Procedural variations

Depending on theoretical allegiance, the therapist may conduct a full formal assessment (using *DSM*-like criteria and possibly involving a good many questions), or may eschew assessment altogether, or devise an approach that is midway between these. A useful alternative to a full, formal, written assessment is an informal mutual assessment session or sessions. Therapists may rely more on clinical experience, impressions and intuition than on objective criteria. Alternatively, they may utilize multiple-item inventories that are not classification-centred but aim to gather comprehensive information, such as the Multimodal Life History Inventory (Palmer and McMahon, 1997: 188–196). They may engage in ongoing assessment, in which the client's active participation forms an integral part, possibly with regular reviews and evaluation mechanisms built in (1997: 168–186). Trial therapy – inviting the client to try or taste the therapy – is a typical variation that serves to test out the match between client problem and therapeutic offer.

Another variation is to place real emphasis on assessment of the client's strengths, resources and aspirations rather than on problems or psychopathology (Milner and O'Byrne, 2004). Many

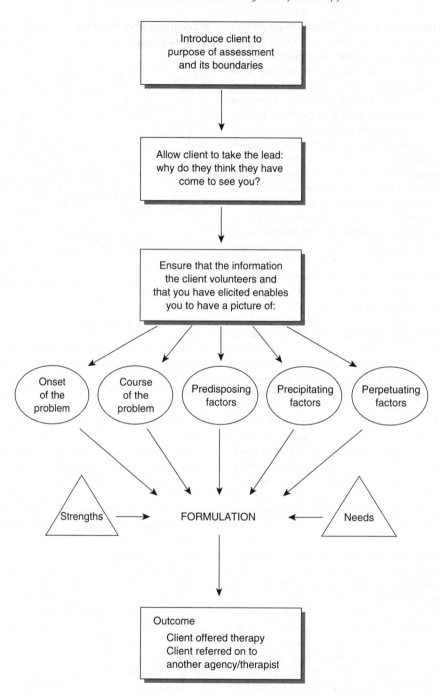

Figure 6.3.1 The content of assessment

Source: Lemma, 1996.

brief therapists, for instance, allow for the possibility that the client may need either *no therapy* or only *very brief therapy*, which is partly assessed by a question like, 'Why is this otherwise reasonably well-functioning person presenting for help only *now*?' Alternatively, problematic character traits and everyday problems of living, or hassles, may be construed by humanistic therapists as of equal (but no more) interest than clients' other experiences, stories and goals.

Assessment also includes, of course, the therapist's judgement as to their own competence to tackle the client's problem. This is often best decided in consultation with a supervisor. Where onward referral is decided upon, careful consideration obviously has to be given to the suitability of an alternative therapist or service (Leigh, 1998). The concept of *prescriptive matching* (optimum match of client and client problem with appropriate therapist, therapeutic approach, therapeutic modality, etc.), while attractive in some ways, is extremely difficult to accomplish in practice (Palmer and McMahon, 1997: 93–114).

Problems of assessment

There is an unhelpful tendency for some texts to disguise the fact that diagnosis and assessment are inexact procedures, involving as much art and educated guesswork as science (Mace, 1995). Although a warning is given in the *DSM IV* against 'excessively flexible and idiosyncratic' assessments (APA, 2000: xxiii), potential pitfalls lie in wait for *all* practitioners. The client may be opposed to diagnostic assessment (sometimes due to previous bad experiences) and/or the therapist, due to training orientation, ideology or temperament, may be opposed to formal assessment. An ideology of non-directiveness inevitably precludes assessment made from an 'external locus of evaluation'.

In some cases, the client *may* be 'resistant' and 'non-compliant' and/or the therapist may indulge in covert clinical conjectures. Varieties of collusion, impasse or mismatch can result from such unpredictable interplays of differences. Accordingly, assessment of likely therapeutic alliance (often based on the client's previous relational history) is always

a crucial procedure. The range of possible presenting problems, complicated by the need to judge severity, and to factor into the assessment equation a knowledge of therapeutic specificity, contra-indications, the therapist's own competence, etc., must lead to some inevitable degree of uncertainty. (Please also see section 3.5: Assessment and case formulation, pp. 109–117.)

In problem-specific agencies (e.g. alcohol treatment centres, rape crisis centres, HIV/AIDS counselling agencies) a tendency can exist to take the presenting problem for granted as the singular, real, significant problem. Often enough, however, a drinking problem, for example, can *mask* or *compound* other serious problems or conditions, such as depression, PTSD, childhood sexual abuse. Community-based services often attract clients whose problems are multiple, not only in psychological but also in psycho-social terms. Such agencies may have particular assessment challenges when access to their services is easy, yet therapy is necessarily time-limited, and alternative local mental health services may have long waiting lists. Sometimes clients are then seen and worked with as a compromise. A degree of compromise also exists where practitioners need to stretch their competence by taking on clients whose kind or severity of problem they have not worked with before, in order to gain clinical experience.

It is more than likely, in an era of increasing emphasis on evidence, that more stringent training and practice in assessment will be called for, as well as far better understanding of the clinical reasoning of practitioners which underpins assessment and early therapeutic decisions (Higgs and Jones, 2000).

References

APA (2000) *Diagnostic and Statistical Manual of Mental Disorders* (4th edn. text revised). Washington, DC: American Psychiatric Association.

Barber, J.P. and Crits-Christoph, P. (eds) (1995) *Dynamic Therapies for Psychiatric Disorders (Axis I)*. New York: Basic Books.

Bellack, A.S. and Hersen, M. (eds) (1990) *Handbook of Comparative Treatments for Adult Disorders*. New York: Wiley.

Berrios, G. and Porter, R. (eds) (1995) *A History of Clinical Psychiatry: The Origin and History of Psychiatric Disorders.* London: Athlone.

Clare, A. (1980) *Psychiatry in Dissent: Controversial Issues in Thought and Practice* (2nd edn). London: Tavistock.

CRE (1993) *The Sorrow in My Heart: Sixteen Asian Women Speak about Depression.* London: Commission for Racial Equality.

Davies, D. and Bhugra, D. (2004) *Models of Psychopathology.* Maidenhead: Open University Press.

Eleftheraidou, Z. (1999) Assessing the counselling needs of the ethnic minorities in Britain. In S. Palmer and P. Laungani (eds), *Counselling in a Multicultural Society.* London: Sage.

Fonagy, P. (2003) The research agenda: the vital need for empirical research in child psychotherapy. *Journal of Child Psychotherapy,* 29 (2): 129–136.

Goleman, D. (2003) *Destructive Emotions: And How We Can Overcome Them.* London: Bloomsbury.

Gopaul-McNicol, S. and Brice-Baker, J. (1998) *Cross-cultural Practice: Assessment, Treatment, and Training.* New York: Wiley.

Hare-Mustin, R. and Maracek, J. (1997) Abnormal and clinical psychology: the politics of madness. In D. Fox and I. Prilleltensky (eds), *Critical Psychology: An Introduction.* London: Sage.

Higgs, J. and Jones, M. (2000) *Clinical Reasoning in the Health Professions.* Edinburgh: Butterworth-Heinemann.

Kutchins, H. and Kirk, S.A. (1997) *Making Us Crazy: DSM – The Psychiatric Bible and the Creation of Mental Disorders.* London: Constable.

Leigh, A. (1998) *Referral and Termination Issues for Counsellors.* London: Sage.

Lemma, A. (1996) *Introduction to Psychopathology.* London: Sage.

Mace, C. (ed.) (1995) *The Art and Science of Assessment in Psychotherapy.* London: Routledge.

Milner, J. and O'Byrne, P. (2004) *Assessment in Counselling: Theory, Process and Decision-making.* Basingstoke: Palgrave.

Palmer, S. and McMahon, G. (eds) (1997) *Client Assessment.* London: Sage.

Paniagua, F.A. (1998) *Assessing and Treating Culturally Diverse Clients* (2nd edn). Thousand Oaks, CA: Sage.

Parker, I., Georgaca, E., Harper, D., McLaughlin, T. and Stowell-Smith, M. (1995) *Deconstructing Psychopathology.* London: Sage.

Reid, W.H., Balis, G.U. and Sutton, B.J. (1997) *The Treatment of Psychiatric Disorders: Third Edition Revised for DSM-IV.* Bristol, PA: Brunner-Mazel.

Ridley, C. (1995) *Overcoming Unintentional Racism in Counseling: A Practitioner's Guide to Intentional Intervention.* Thousand Oaks, CA: Sage.

Roth, A. and Fonagy, P. (1996) *What Works for Whom?: A Critical Review of Psychotherapy Research.* New York: Guilford Press.

Stevens, A. and Price, J. (2000) *Evolutionary Psychiatry: A New Beginning* (2nd edn). London: Routledge.

Van der Veer, G. (1998) *Counselling and Therapy with Refugees and Victims of Trauma* (2nd edn). Chichester: Wiley.

WHO (1992) *International Classification of Diseases and Related Health Problems* (10th edn). Geneva: World Health Organization.

Young, A. (1997) *The Harmony of Illusions: Inventing Post-traumatic Stress Disorder.* Princeton, NJ: Princeton University Press.

PART VI
Client Presenting Problems

SPECIFIC PROBLEMS

6.4 Alcohol Problems

ROSEMARY KENT

Defining alcohol problems

While the simplest definition is 'any problems resulting from drinking alcohol', there are a number of areas to explore when attempting to define, and assess, 'alcohol problems' or 'problem drinking':

- *Level of consumption* – refers to the quantity and patterns of a person's drinking, changes over time and how the pattern compares with others in his or her peer group. This is linked to:
- *Consequences of drinking* – which include (a) observable negative consequences (i.e. legal, social, family-related, and physical harm) and (b) subjective perceptions (i.e. relationship breakdown, lack of self-esteem, sense of shame and guilt, and other aspects of psychological distress). Many clients may not fully recognize the links between levels of consumption and consequential problems, tending instead to view problems as causing increased consumption. Alternatively, they may privately acknowledge the possibility of a link, but outwardly defend themselves by appearing not to. This in turn may by related to:
- *Degree of dependence* – which is best understood as the extent to which a person experiences discomfort in the absence of alcohol. The severely dependent drinker may try hard to ignore the links between the first two points above, through fear of having to give up alcohol, which has become a primary source of comfort. A key aspect of dependence is the physiological discomfort (withdrawal symptoms) which normally occurs when drinking ceases abruptly. Tolerance – the body's gradual adjustment to coping with increasing amounts of alcohol – also increases as dependence becomes more severe, and is an important element in assessment.

While some in the UK regard severity of alcohol problems as lying on a continuum, others maintain that there is a specific disease-like entity, which can be diagnosed as 'alcoholism'. Labels are often unhelpful and stigmatizing, but some people with high levels of consumption, severe dependence, and chronic resultant difficulties, may apply the term 'alcoholic' to themselves, and use it as a stepping-stone into treatment.

Who develops alcohol problems?

Attempts to predict who is more likely than another to develop an alcohol problem, and efforts to achieve some kind of epidemiology, have tended to rely on consumption levels and patterns as the key indicators for the likelihood of social, medical or psychological problems resulting.

The General Household Surveys of England and Wales have found that women's drinking has gradually been increasing since 1984, as have the drinking levels of men and women over 65. Nearly six and a half million drink at harmful levels (i.e. around 35 units a week for women and 50 units for men).

The availability of alcohol and peer pressure to drink heavily are major factors in certain groups, particularly young people (who are constantly being told of the dangers of illicit drugs and tend to see alcohol as fairly harmless). Those in high-stress, unsupervised jobs are also vulnerable and tend to show higher levels of consumption. Other social groupings may also experience social pressure to drink heavily, for example lesbians and gay men, and students. Alcohol serves as an effective self-medication (either as temporary or long-term relief) for many people. Thus, people experiencing chronic pain, those who are bereaved, and many who feel socially isolated because of disability or mental illness, may rely on alcohol. Finally, there are those who are vulnerable to alcohol-related problems at lower levels of consumption: elderly people, those who have certain physical impairments (such as liver damage), women in the early stages of pregnancy and those who have significantly low body weight.

Why do alcohol problems occur?

After decades of research in the fields of genetics, biochemistry, sociology, psychology and other disciplines, it has become acknowledged and accepted that there is no single cause for drinking behaviour which persists in the face of damaging consequences. Availability, familial and social factors and personal vulnerability (of a psychological and/or a biochemical nature) all play a part.

Psychological explanations

Social Learning Theory has in the last 30 years contributed much to our understanding of alcohol misuse, for example the role of cognitions, modelling and inappropriate self-regulation. The functional nature of alcohol drinking is emphasized: both the activity, and the sedating and disinhibiting effects of the drug. The United Kingdom has been at the forefront in promoting the idea of alcohol dependence as a learnt behaviour, rather than a disease.

Family history

A family history of alcohol misuse is common among those currently drinking to excess: similar drinking habits occur in up to 50 per cent of fathers and 20 per cent of mothers. Sociological and anthropological studies suggest that environmental factors are stronger than genetic ones in accounting for this, but there is some evidence that there may be a genetic susceptibility to developing alcohol dependence.

Psychodynamic theories

The attachment theories of Bowlby and others suggest that the drinker forms an exceptionally strong bond with alcohol, with symbolic significance, while classic psychoanalytic theory looks at deficits in early parenting as directly contributing to dependence on mood-altering substances, particularly the comfort of 'the bottle'.

The disease model

The idea espoused by Alcoholics Anonymous, many medical practitioners and perhaps the majority of the general public is that some people are 'born alcoholic', and once they start drinking they will never be able to drink in socially acceptable, harm-free ways. Some form of inherent chemical imbalance within the central nervous system is seen to be the cause, perhaps of genetic origin. Alcoholism is likened to an allergy in that alcohol is always dangerous for certain individuals, and is termed a chronic, progressive disease, with fatal consequences if left untreated. Treatment is synonymous with total abstinence from alcohol.

Public health explanations

This simply states that the more alcohol is available and affordable in any given society, the more health-related alcohol problems will occur. This model implies that by manipulating the availability and cost of alcohol, a society can affect the prevalence of alcohol-related problems.

Interventions and treatment settings

A key feature of helping people to change any behaviour about which they feel ambivalent (and thus people with alcohol problems) is that a high degree of trust and co-operation between practitioners and clients is required. Any intervention in someone's drinking behaviour cannot therefore be effective until and unless an appropriate therapeutic relationship has been established. This needs to be borne in mind, whether clients are coerced, or come willingly for help.

In addition, for most clients, enabling them to become alcohol-free (initially short-term, to enhance self-efficacy and to enable therapeutic work to begin) should be the focus of any helping intervention, before tackling with them the difficulties of sustaining sobriety and before any attempts are made to explore the origins of their alcohol dependence. Careful assessment will ensure client and practitioner agree on how long this should last. This will vary from a goal of lifelong sobriety for the severely dependent heavy drinker, through to a temporary period for the client with minimal dependence and problems. Agreement should also be reached at an early stage that clients will be alcohol-free when attending sessions with their counsellor (or other practitioner).

Problem drinkers are likely to be able to obtain help from:

- *Primary care practitioners* – such as general practitioners, social workers, health visitors, and probation officers, who should be able to recognize links between their clients' or patients' presenting problems and the drinking behaviour. Their role is primarily to engage with the drinker, make an initial assessment, provide basic information, and support, encourage and facilitate him or her to access the most appropriate type of help.
- *Specialist medical help* – will normally be needed for severely dependent drinkers when they stop drinking, and anyone who reports having previously had withdrawal symptoms (sweats, shakes, nausea, agitation, disrupted sleep patterns and occasionally hallucinations or paranoia) when they have stopped drinking abruptly in the past. Close monitoring, plus a reducing dose of Diazepam are normally recommended for a period of four to ten days.
- In addition to supervised detoxification (either at home or in hospital) many health settings and private facilities offer follow-on help, on an in-patient or out-patient basis. Day programmes, consisting of therapeutic groups, social skills sessions and – in some settings – guidance on following a Twelve-Step approach to recovery – are common. Medication, particularly anxiolytics, minor tranquillizers and antidepressants may be prescribed. Disulfiram

('Antabuse') may be prescribed for drinkers who find a chemical deterrent useful: the active ingredient of Disulfiram is potentiated when alcohol is swallowed, leading to unpleasant side-effects.
- *Specialist non-medical help* – covers such services as counselling, advice and 'drop in' centres, self-help groups, and residential rehabilitation projects.

Those facilities providing a non-residential service tend to have counselling as a core activity; groupwork, social activities, training for other professionals and public education may also be offered. However, with current social policy in the UK focusing on treatment services for users of illicit drugs, it may be easier to locate specialist help in facilities which provide 'addiction' or 'substance misuse' treatment.

As residential treatment and rehabilitation centres are more expensive than community-based facilities, public funding is becoming less readily available now for individuals needing such help. The theoretical approach of these centres is commonly the 'Minnesota Model' or a variation of this model, which broadly follows the Twelve-Step tradition of Alchoholics Anonymous. Most residential projects aim to be holistic in their approach, often emphasizing spiritual dimensions as well as social skills, education about alcohol and the development of psychological insight.

The best-known self-help group is Alcoholics Anonymous (AA). Many severely dependent drinkers find AA helpful, with its clear philosophy, ready availability and mutual support. 'Alanon' is a network of self-help groups for the partners and spouses of people with an alcohol problem, and can be a useful source of support for many people.

Current debates and recent research

Alcohol dependence and alcohol-related problems continue to generate many controversies and passionately held views about their nature and treatment. Some of these reach the public arena – such as the debates in the 1970s and 1980s about whether people diagnosed as alcoholics could ever return to harm-free drinking following treatment. 'Controlled drinking' as a goal is a tenable theoretical position for those who support the idea that because dysfunctional behaviour (i.e. excessive drinking) is learned, it can be un-learned. Individual problem drinkers vary in their willingness and ability to learn new, problem-free drinking habits, and teaching these skills is a complex and demanding process.

Many practitioners argue for a multifaceted approach, an example being the enthusiasm with which 'motivational interviewing' (Miller and Rollnick, 2002) has been embraced in the UK. This collection of principles and strategies – more recently elaborated into 'Motivational Enhancement Therapy' – is a combination of techniques drawn from person-centred and cognitive-behavioural therapy.

A major, multi-site trial in the USA in the late 1990s, entitled 'Project MATCH', endeavoured to establish whether a particular therapeutic approach would be more effective with one category of problem drinkers rather than another (Project MATCH Research Group, 1997). The therapies tested were: cognitive-behaviour therapy, Motivational Enhancement Therapy, and a Twelve-Step approach. There was no support for the idea that some types of client do better with one treatment approach, rather than another.

A transtheoretical model which, like motivational interviewing, has been welcomed but also hotly debated in the UK, is Prochaska and DiClemente's (1984) 'Stages of Change' model. This has been criticized on theoretical and empirical grounds, but pragmatists have argued that at the very least it alerts practitioners to the notion that decisions to change habitual behaviours are rarely either instantaneous or irreversible.

Fashion, politics and developments in other areas of the social and medical sciences will no doubt mean the continuation of many different models of research, theoretical debates and practice controversies, for there is still much we need to understand about alcohol problems. In particular, there is an urgent need for the general public, government policy and helping professionals to recognize the extent to which heavy drinking is causing increasing health, economic, psychological and social problems in this country, far outstripping those related to illicit drug use.

References

Miller, W. and Rollnick, S. (2002) *Motivational Interviewing*. (2nd edn). New York: Guilford Press.

Project MATCH Research Group (1997) Matching alcoholism treatments to client heterogeneity: Project MATCH. Post treatment drinking outcomes. *Journal of Studies of Alcohol*, January: 7–29.

Prochaska, J.O. and DiClemente, C.C. (1984) *The Transtheoretical Approach: Crossing Traditional Boundaries of Therapy*. New York: Dow-Jones Irwin.

Recommended reading

Reading, B. and Jacobs, M. (eds) (2003) *Addiction: Questions and Answers for Counsellors and Therapists*. London: Whurr.

Velleman, R. (1994) *Counselling for Alcohol Problems*. London: Sage.

6.5   Anger Control

EMMA WILLIAMS AND MICHAEL SCOTT

Anger is a common emotion experienced by us all. Indeed, if used constructively, it can be a positive and empowering emotion. Anger can be defined as an *emotional state* experienced as the impulse to behave in order to protect, defend or attack in response to a threat or a challenge. Of itself, anger is not classified as an emotional disorder (APA, 2000). It becomes problematic only when experienced with such a frequency or intensity that, for example, it frustrates the attainment of desired goals, interferes with the ability to connect with others or is detrimental to health. Problematic anger, associated with poor impulse control, is commonly evidenced in domestic violence and other forms of criminal behaviour.

Nature, signs and symptoms

Anger, like all other emotional states, is influenced by our cognitions (thoughts, images or values), our behaviours and our physiology.

Cognitions involved in an angry response commonly include thinking errors such as personalizing: 'He did that deliberately to upset me', and catastrophizing: 'I'll never get another job'. Common anger-inducing beliefs typically include, for example, that life should be fair or that one is entitled to take revenge for perceived injustice. Brondolo (1998) has suggested that anger arises when a person perceives that their core values have been violated.

The behavioural response to anger can include 'adaptive' responses such as problem solving, assertiveness, tactical withdrawal and 'maladaptive' responses such as social withdrawal, self-harm, verbal and physical aggression, the latter two being the target of most anger control therapies.

The physiological response is that triggered in the autonomic nervous system by adrenalin which produces symptoms such as increased heart rate, sweating and flushing, common to all emotions. It is the individual's labelling of these symptoms as 'anger' which differentiates it from other emotions.

Aggression, perhaps the most important sequela of anger, can be defined as any form of *behaviour* directed towards the goal of harming or injuring another living being or object.

Typical accompanying psychological, social and physical problems

People with anger control problems frequently experience associated problems with interpersonal relationships, low self-esteem and mental and physical health problems. The interrelationships of these problems are illustrated in Figure 6.5.1.

Treatments might focus on the various associated problems as well as on anger control *per se*, for example enhancement of self-esteem, ability to cope with stress, communication skills or examination of the person's goals and values.

Extent/epidemiology

Compared to emotional disorders such as anxiety and depression, the psychological research of the last 30 years has largely ignored anger as an emotional disorder, and few researchers have addressed anger as an important emotion in psychological disturbance. The extent of anger control problems is difficult to define as it is dependent on the levels of

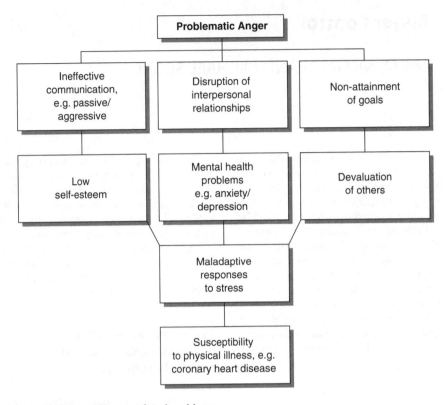

Figure 6.5.1 Anger and its associated problems

expressed anger and aggressiveness tolerated in our society. Aggressive behaviours in the form of arguments, indirect hostility, threats and displaced aggression are commonplace. However, the more severe consequences of loss of anger control are legally defined by criminal offences. Although not all acts of aggression are anger related, crime statistics can give an indication of the extent of the problem. The British Crime Survey estimated that there were 2,715,000 violent incidents experienced by adults in England and Wales in 2003. Over a million violent offences were recorded by the police. In over half of violent incidents the offender was known to the victim in some way (Smith and Allen, 2004).

With regard to domestic violence, it has been found that physical violence between spouses occurs in almost one-third of marriages in the USA (Straus et al.,

1980). Other statistics also illustrate the enormous extent of the problem of anger and aggressive behaviour. For example, typically, a woman is physically abused approximately 35 times before she reports to police. Seventy-five per cent of domestic violence is never reported to police, 27 per cent of abused women said their partner also physically assaulted their children and 3–5,000 children die each year in the USA from parental abuse (Pagelow, 1984).

There is a notable gender difference in anger expression, and hence in referrals to anger control therapy, with men being highly predominant. The expression of anger is strongly socially and culturally determined: women tending to suppress anger, become depressed or self-injure. Those women who do behave aggressively are more likely to be seen as suffering from mental disorder.

Aetiology

The major origin or causes of anger control problems for any individual are likely to be an interaction of both internal and external factors. Internal determinates are often rooted in childhood formative experiences. These commonly include a family history of violence or aggression, experience of bullying, experience of physical, sexual, emotional abuse or neglect. In addition, biological predisposition or vulnerability factors might also play an important role.

External or social factors also have a role in determining aggression, for example, frustration, provocation and peer influence. Environmental factors such as noise, overcrowding and poor living conditions, can also be influential determinants.

Treatments of choice

The aim of therapy for anger problems is the control of anger, not its suppression.

The treatment approach chosen will in part be dependent upon the theoretical background of the therapist. The development of treatments for anger control problems has generally followed the course of the development of psychological treatments for other emotional disorders: from the early instinct and evolutionary theories to motivational and drive theories, and more latterly to social learning and cognitive-behavioural theories.

The treatment implications stemming from psychological theories of anger and aggression are briefly summarized below:

- Instinct theory (e.g. Freud). The positive redirection of aggressive drives, for example, into combative sports, the displacement of aggressive urges and use of catharsis.
- Evolutionary theory (e.g. Lorenz). The prevention of accumulation of anger by engaging in lower-level non-injurious behaviour, the experience of emotions incompatible with aggression, for example, happiness.
- Motivational theory (e.g. Berkowitz). Modification of cues to aggression, cognitive restructuring, reduction of physiological arousal.

- Social learning theory (e.g. Bandura). Cognitive reappraisal, re-learning, examination of consequences of aggression.
- Feminist theories (e.g. Rohrbaugh). Challenging gender identity and sex-role stereotypes.
- Humanistic theories. Changing the subjective experience of anger, enhancing understanding, ownership, examining personal values.
- Stress-inoculation theories (e.g. Meichenbaum). Exposure to manageable levels of stress, cognitive preparation, skills acquisition, application training, self-instructional training.
- Cognitive-behavioural theories (e.g. Beck). Anticipation of triggers to aggression, reduction of physiological arousal, challenging thoughts, modifying beliefs, changing behaviours.
- Relapse prevention theories (e.g. Marlatt and Gordon). Increasing awareness, antecedents, behaviour and consequences of aggression, use of early warning signs, and high-risk situation management, behavioural rehearsal, relapse prevention planning.

The treatments of anger with the strongest research database are cognitive/relaxation approaches (Edmondson and Conger, 1996). These authors concluded, from their review of 18 studies, that it was difficult to recommend one treatment approach, be it relaxation training, cognitive restructuring or social skills training, above another because different anger treatments produce large effects for some aspects of anger and small effects for others. Thus treatment should be targeted to specific presenting problems, for example, focusing on the reduction of physiological arousal for clients who are habitually tense. Focusing on cognitive techniques such as distraction, self-calming statements, rationalizing and task-focusing would be appropriate for clients who tend to ruminate or present with significant cognitive distortions.

Brondolo (1998) has suggested that listening to clients' stories about anger-evoking situations gives a clue to their core values. The therapeutic task is to make the values explicit, identify their origins, and elaborate a viable expression of these values. Brondolo points out that values might compete, for example 'to achieve' and 'to care', and that the values may have to be expressed sequentially rather than simultaneously.

Table 6.5.1 Suggested components for the treatment of problematic anger

---

Phase 1   Engagement, motivation and preparation for change

- Educate about the cycle of anger, thoughts, feelings, beliefs and behaviour.
- Focus on acceptance of and responsibility for, anger control problem.
- Clarify expectations, help clients to set personal goals.
- Promote clients' motivation to change their behaviour, e.g. decision matrix, cost-benefit analysis.
- Encourage practice of self-monitoring techniques, e.g. personal anger diaries, anger charts, hassle logs.

Phase 2   Anger and aggression focused interventions

- Develop individual formulation of the factors underlying problematic anger for the client, e.g. beliefs, social, familial and environmental influences, common triggers, anger cycle and coping strategies.
- Develop coping strategies to deal with anticipated triggers, e.g. escape, de-escalation techniques and alternative responses.
- Help client to recognize and manage automatic thoughts and cognitive distortions by applying a range of cognitive strategies, e.g. thought stopping, self-talk, replacement thoughts, cognitive restructuring, reattribution, de-centring, reframing, de-catastrophizing.
- Identify, understand and challenge key beliefs that underly and maintain anger control problem.
- Increase clients' repertoire of responses to conflict situations, e.g. defusing, assertiveness, conflict resolution, problem solving, negotiation, compromise.
- Construct behavioural experiments to enable client to test their predictions and learn about their thoughts, behaviour and its consequences.
- Enhance clients' control of physiological responses, e.g. tension release techniques, relaxation and stress management.

Phase 3   Relapse prevention, maintaining gains

- Review clients' personal aims and set new ones.
- Develop a comprehensive relapse prevention plan, including high-risk situations, early warning signs and coping strategy enhancement.
- Focus on lifestyle change.
- Develop 'problem profiles'; what to change and how to do it.

Williams and Barlow (1998) have presented a comprehensive treatment programme for clients with anger problems. Their programmes include:

1. Motivational techniques, including an examination of the consequences of anger and aggressive behaviour for self and others.
2. An understanding of anger as an often self-defeating coping strategy by addressing clients' personal predisposing factors, triggers and anger aetiology.
3. The development of more adaptive coping strategies by modifying core beliefs and thinking errors that underlie the expression of anger.
4. The identification of early warning signs, high-risk situations, escalating and defusing behaviours,

lifestyle balance, and the detailing of Relapse-Prevention strategies such as self-statements, reducing physiological arousal, emergency tactics, challenging beliefs and increasing repertoire of responses.

Suggested components for the treatment of problematic anger are presented in Table 6.5.1.

What works for whom

No treatment intervention for anger will work unless the client is enabled to recognize it as a problem and indeed as *their* problem. Motivational work is often a prerequisite to successful engagement in anger control treatments. Clients who deny they have any problem with anger control, who have no motivation to change or have very significant impulse control problems might benefit from pre-treatment preparation, such as building a therapeutic relationship, enhancing self-esteem, competency and control recognition, personal anger awareness and basic anger and aggression monitoring. Recent publications have indicated treatment successes with clients previously thought to have intractable anger control problems, for example seriously assaultative violent populations (Novaco, 1997) and violent psychotic forensic patients (Becker et al., 1997). In some cases there might be physical reasons, such as head injury, that interfere with the person's ability to benefit from psychological treatment. The general rule in the treatment of any psychological condition is that alcohol and substance abuse have to be controlled before the underlying condition can be addressed, and this applies equally to the treatment of anger. Obviously, the more other conditions are associated with anger (e.g. personality problems, mental illness, impulse control problems), the more difficult it will be to effect successful treatment.

Anger control is often an important component of marital therapy focusing on moving the couple from an 'I win, you lose' to a 'both win' framework. However, with regard to domestic violence, caution should be exercised to ensure that issues such as perpetrator accountability and responsibility are successfully addressed before anger control strategies are employed as one part of a comprehensive treatment approach. Similarly, anger control training can be an important component of teaching parents child management strategies within the framework of understanding the parent–child relationship, and adult acceptance of responsibility for non-violence. Generating 'emergency tactics' and aggressive incident analysis can be particularly useful. The development of uncharacteristic irritability is one of the diagnostic features of post-traumatic stress disorder, and strategies for tackling this are outlined in Scott and Stradling (2001).

Clinical management and typical prognosis

From primary referral source (e.g. the General Practitioner) to attendance at therapy, the drop-out rate might be expected to be between 30 per cent and 60 per cent. Good professional liaison, explicit client suitability criteria and provision of information regarding the therapy can reduce inappropriate referrals and drop-out rates. Those clients who do engage in therapy, and who are motivated, can be expected to show lasting improvements in anger control.

Following therapy, clients might be offered:

- maintenance sessions to focus on their relapse prevention plans; formally examine incidents of loss of anger control and rehearse coping strategies;
- support or self-help group;
- supplementary sessions to focus on associated problems, such as low self-esteem, confidence building, assertiveness training and coping with stress.
- referral to other agencies or colleagues to explore specific problems identified in anger control therapy, for example, experience of childhood sexual or physical abuse.

Clients with anger control problems, more than any other emotional disorder, are at risk to others. The clinical management of anger should therefore focus not only on helping the client to maintain control over their anger, and potential aggressive behaviour, but also on assessment and management of their risk of violence and aggressive behaviour. Once assessed, the client's potential risk to others should be managed by isolating the critical factors identified and drawing up a treatment plan or supervision plan to attempt to reduce the risk. Good liaison and communication with other professionals involved with the client is essential. The limits of confidentiality should be made explicit to the client.

References

APA (2000) *Diagnostic and Statistical Manual of Mental Disorders* (4th edn text revision). Washington, DC: American Psychiatric Association.

Becker, M., Love, C.C. and Hunter, M.E. (1997) Intractability is relative: behaviour therapy in the elimination of violence in psychotic forensic patients. *Legal and Criminological Psychology*, 2 (1): 89–101.

Brondolo, E. (1998) Affirming core values: a cognitive approach for use in the treatment of anger and anxiety problems. *The Behaviour Therapist*, 21: 60–87.

Edmondson, C.B. and Conger, J.C. (1996) A review of treatment efficacy for individuals with anger problems: conceptual, assessment and methodological issues. *Clinical Psychology Review*, 16 (3): 251–275.

Novaco, R.W. (1997) Remediating anger and aggression with violent offenders. *Legal and Criminological Psychology*, 2 (1): 77–88.

Pagelow, M.D. (1984) *Family Violence*. New York: Praeger.

Scott, M.J. and Stradling, S.G. (2001) *Counselling for Posttraumatic Stress Disorder* (2nd edn). London: Sage.

Smith, C. and Allen, J. (2004) *Violent Crime in England and Wales*. Home Office online report 18/04. London: HMSO.

Straus, M.A., Gelles, R.J. and Steinmetz, S.K. (1980) *Behind Closed Doors: Violence in the American Family*. Garden City, NY: Doubleday/Anchor.

Williams, E.E. and Barlow, R.S. (1998) *Anger Control Training: A Practitioner's Guide*. Bicester: Speechmark.

Recommended reading

Beck, A.T. (1999) *Prisoners of Hate: The Cognitive Basis of Anger, Hostility and Violence*. London: Harper Collins.

Kassinove, H. (ed.) (1995) *Anger Disorders: Definition, Diagnosis and Treatment*. Washington, DC: Taylor and Francis.

Williams, E.E. and Barlow, R.S. (1998) *Anger Control Training. A Practitioner's Guide*. Bicester: Speechmark.

6.6   Anxiety and Panic

GILL DONOHOE AND TOM RICKETTS

Problematic anxiety is a common and pervasive difficulty which manifests in many ways. Phobic conditions, obsessive compulsive disorders, and the specific difficulties resulting from severe trauma are dealt with elsewhere. Here the focus will be on 'pure' anxiety difficulties as represented by the conditions labelled panic disorder and generalized anxiety disorder. Given the increasing effectiveness of cognitive behavioural approaches to these disorders, this is the perspective which will be taken throughout.

This section will first outline the features of panic disorder and generalized anxiety disorder. Models for understanding these difficulties will be introduced, and the treatment implications deriving from these models outlined. Finally, research into the area will be briefly reviewed, and areas of contention discussed.

Clinical features

Two different types of anxiety disorder can be distinguished. In the first, panic disorder, the main problem is recurrent panic attacks which occur unexpectedly at times when the individual does not anticipate anxiety. A panic attack is a discrete period of intense fear or discomfort that is accompanied by a range of somatic or cognitive symptoms (see Table 6.6.1). Panic attacks are often accompanied by a sense of imminent danger or impending doom and an urge to escape. They may be cued, that is triggered by specific situations, such as in phobic conditions or following trauma, or spontaneous. Unexpected or spontaneous panic attacks are important in the *diagnosis* of panic disorder, where at least

Table 6.6.1 Criteria for a panic attack

A discrete period of intense fear or discomfort, in which four (or more) of the following symptoms developed abruptly and reached a peak within 10 minutes:

1 palpitations, pounding heart, or accelerated heart rate
2 sweating
3 trembling or shaking
4 sensations of shortness of breath or smothering
5 feeling of choking
6 chest pain or discomfort
7 nausea or abdominal distress
8 feeling dizzy, unsteady, lightheaded, or faint
9 derealization, or depersonalization
10 fear of losing control or going crazy
11 fear of dying
12 paresthesias (pins and needles in extremities)
13 chills or hot flushes

two attacks need to have occurred spontaneously, that is, not in situations which commonly cause the individual anxiety. Panic disorder and agoraphobia commonly occur together, with the fear and avoidance of a wide range of situations common in agoraphobia often being linked to a fear of the recurrence of panic attacks. Other features of panic disorder are that sufferers experience either a persistent concern about having additional attacks, worry about the implications of the attack or its consequences, or a significant change in behaviour related to having had a panic attack.

Individuals may also experience panic attacks as a result of substance use, or as part of a medical condition such as hyperthyroidism. These possible explanations for symptoms should be explored in assessment.

In the second type of anxiety disorder, generalized anxiety disorder, the main defining feature is excessive anxiety and worry. To meet diagnostic criteria these must be experienced more days than not for at least six months, to be about a range of different events or activities, and cause significant interference with the individual's functioning. Table 6.6.2 shows other diagnostic features for generalized anxiety disorder.

Overall, the symptoms experienced in generalized anxiety disorder are less intense than in panic disorder,

onset is more gradual, and the central feature is the repeated experience of excessive worry.

Understanding panic disorder and generalized anxiety disorder

In the cognitive model of panic disorder, it is proposed that panic attacks result from the misinterpretation of certain bodily sensations, with the sensations being perceived as much more dangerous than they actually are. Examples would be an individual perceiving palpitations as evidence of an impending heart attack, or perceiving a shaky feeling as evidence of loss of control and insanity.

Figure 6.6.1 illustrates the model. Triggers can be either external (e.g. a department store for a client suffering from agoraphobia), or internal, (e.g. bodily sensations, thoughts or images). If the trigger is experienced as threatening, a mild state of apprehension occurs. This is accompanied by a range of bodily sensations, which are then interpreted as catastrophic. This interpretation becomes the next perceived threat, and the vicious circle continues, culminating in a panic attack.

Once panic attacks have become established, the individual develops further responses to panic

Table 6.6.2   Diagnostic features of generalized anxiety disorder

Excessive anxiety and worry, occurring more days than not for at least six months, about a number of events or activities (such as work or school performance). At least three out of the following symptoms:

1   restlessness or feeling keyed up or on edge
2   being easily fatigued
3   difficulty concentrating or mind going blank
4   irritability
5   muscle tension
6   sleep disturbance

The anxiety, worry or physical symptoms must lead to significant distress or impairment in important areas of functioning.

The focus of the anxiety or worry is not exclusively related to another psychiatric disorder.

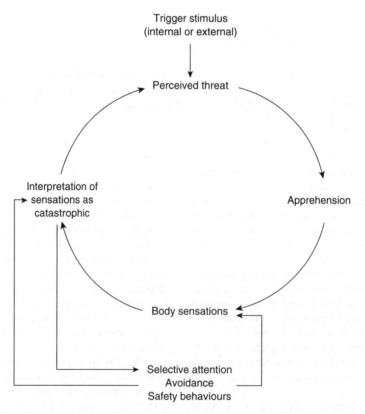

Figure 6.6.1   Cognitive model of panic disorder (adapted from Clark, 1986; Wells, 1997)

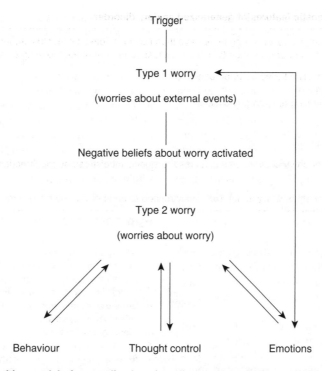

Figure 6.6.2 Cognitive model of generalized anxiety disorder (adapted from Wells, 1997)

which serve to maintain the problem, namely selective attention, safety behaviours and avoidances. Selective attention relates to the way in which clients are watching out for physical symptoms constantly, and therefore notice them more, activating the panic cycle. Safety behaviours develop to prevent the feared catastrophic consequence from occurring, and include such things as holding on to walls or sitting down to prevent collapse. These behaviours give the individual an alternative explanation for why the feared event did not occur, and prevent changes in thinking during panic attacks. An example would be the individual thinking that they did not collapse because they sat down. Avoidances develop which restrict the individual's contact with anxiety-inducing situations, thereby reducing opportunities for discovering that the feared consequences do not occur.

The cognitive model proposes that panic disorder develops as a result of the triggering of pre-existing learnt assumptions about physical symptoms such as 'bodily symptoms are always an indication of something being wrong'. These assumptions are viewed as being developed through a range of routes such as parental response to illness, perceived medical mismanagement and sudden deaths of significant others. Such assumptions are argued to be relatively stable (Beck, 1976), but to become more pertinent when triggered by events such as the individual experiencing illness themselves, or a first panic attack.

Models of generalized anxiety disorder (Wells, 1997) have focused on the central element of worry, with the development of a differentiation between two types of worry. Figure 6.6.2 outlines a model. Type 1 worries concern external daily events, such as the well-being of loved ones, and non-cognitive internal events such as concerns about physical symptoms. Type 2 worries concern themselves with the nature and occurrence of thoughts themselves, that is they are worries about worry. Examples would be 'My worrying will never stop', and 'I'll go crazy from worrying'. This cognitive model proposes that in generalized anxiety disorder there is a preponderance of type 2 worries, with associated inappropriate responses which maintain the problem. In addition, sufferers from generalized anxiety disorder may hold inappropriate positive beliefs about the benefits of worrying, such as 'Worrying helps me solve my problems'. This helps to explain the repeated use of type 1 worry as a voluntary strategy by some individuals.

In a similar way to panic disorder, cognitive models of generalized anxiety disorder propose that learnt assumptions regarding the need to control mental responses will be associated with the development of the disorder.

Responses which follow on from type 2 worry will include behaviours to avoid triggers to type 1 worries, efforts at thought control, such as distraction and positive thinking, and trying to control thoughts, and emotional responses such as anxiety, anger and frustration. All these (ineffective) strategies will lead to a confirmation of the uncontrollability of worry, and therefore a strengthening of beliefs underpinning type 2 worry.

These explanations of panic disorder and generalized anxiety disorder have led to the development of specific interventions, which will be outlined below.

Treatment

In both conditions cognitive-behavioural approaches deriving from the work of Beck (1976) have been shown to be effective. Treatment is based upon a detailed assessment and analysis of the presenting difficulty along with any other associated problems. This includes the client keeping a diary of their symptoms, and the taking of a history of the development of the problem. The assessment information is then discussed with the client within a cognitive-behavioural framework. This forms the first stage of therapy, the main purpose of which is to educate the client on the principles of the approach and the rationale for the treatment plan based upon their difficulties.

A considerable proportion of individuals with anxiety may be managed within primary care, adopting a self-help approach with more limited therapist involvement but still within the framework described in this section. Self-management approaches provide the client with access to guidance and information on panic and anxiety and how to apply therapeutic strategies. These methods are considered in further detail within the research section.

Approaches to panic disorder

- Education about anxiety – Given the importance of catastrophic misinterpretations of bodily symptoms in panic disorder, education regarding the features of normal anxiety is a first stage in treatment.
- Dealing with misinterpretations of physical symptoms – This part of the treatment focuses on enabling the client to identify thoughts associated with concerns about physical symptoms, and then to begin to develop alternative perspectives on those same symptoms. The previous educational intervention regarding the nature of anxiety and panic provides the client with a starting point for identifying an alternative perspective. Once an alternative perspective has been developed, current evidence for each of the two perspectives should be considered in detail, and a behavioural experiment agreed. Within this process the therapist is directive in engaging the client in consideration of their thoughts regarding symptoms, but the alternative views need to be elicited from the client, rather than presented by the therapist. An example would be the client who views palpitations as indicating the risk of an imminent heart attack coming to recognize that the symptom can be understood as being the result of the release of adrenalin into the bloodstream. The behavioural experiment could take the form of exercising when the person is anxious, thereby reducing the belief in the dangerousness of the symptom.
- Dealing with avoidance – Following a reduction in the degree of belief in the dangerousness of physical symptoms, the client should gradually resume all avoided behaviours, utilizing a graded exposure approach as described within the phobias section.

1. Place one hand on your stomach (little finger level with your waistband) and the other over your breast bone. See diagram opposite.
2. Notice which hand is moving as you breathe.
3. If it is the hand on your chest that is moving, then try and switch your breathing so the hand on your stomach is moving. Perhaps try to imagine that you have something tight around your chest so that you have to breathe from your stomach.
4. Breathe in and out gently through your nose. Feel the movement under the lower hand as your stomach expands. The upper hand should be still.
5. Breathe out for longer than you breathe in, at about 10 breaths a minute.
6. Once aware of how you are breathing, take the hands away from the rib cage. When you fill your lungs with air your stomach should push out too. If your breathing is too shallow your chest will move up and down. This should not be happening if you have mastered the technique.

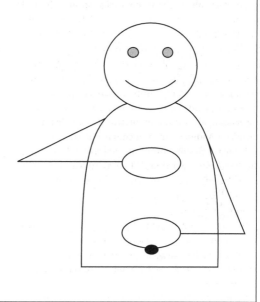

Figure 6.6.3   Breathing retraining instructions

- Reduction of safety behaviours – The use of safety behaviours by panic sufferers helps to explain how, despite the repeated failure of their feared consequence to occur during panic attacks, they continue to believe that it may, next time. Safety behaviours will therefore prevent the cognitive approach outlined earlier from being effective. As for avoidances, safety behaviours should be gradually reduced as the client becomes more confident in the alternative explanations for their symptoms.
- Relapse prevention – Consideration of the patterns of unhelpful behaviours which the client had engaged in, together with discussion and reconsideration of any longstanding assumptions regarding the dangerousness of physical symptoms, should occur towards the end of treatment, with a view to maintenance of change.
- Breathing retraining – Where hyperventilation is a feature of an individual's symptoms it may be helpful to teach the client a diaphragmatic breathing technique. Instructions on breathing retraining are

outlined in Figure 6.6.3. This is particularly helpful with clients who have beliefs regarding the uncontrollability of panic symptoms. Caution should be exercised to ensure that the technique is not overused, as it may become another safety behaviour.

Approaches to generalized anxiety disorder (GAD)

- Education – As with panic disorder, educating the client about the normal features of anxiety is a first component of treatment. Specifically, type 1 and type 2 worry should be differentiated, and type 1 worry normalized, as a universal mental phenomenon which the client has become over-concerned about.
- Modifying beliefs about worry – As with panic disorder, a process of identifying and then reconsidering

beliefs about the nature of symptoms, in this case worry, is central to treatment of generalized anxiety disorder. Other strategies seek to disconfirm beliefs, both positive and negative, about worry, specifically through behaviour change. Behavioural experiments which can be used include controlled worry periods, in which a 15-minute period each day is set aside to actively worry about issues. Throughout the rest of the day, when worry is identified, it is deferred until the planned worry period. This can be utilized to challenge perceptions of the uncontrollability of worry. Another means of doing so is an experiment where the client is encouraged to 'lose control' of worry, or actively exaggerate their worries, so that the individual's feared consequence of mental illness or complete loss of control is disconfirmed. Letting go of worries, or the purposeful abandonment of the use of worry as a positive strategy to deal with difficulties, can be used to disconfirm positive beliefs about the benefits of worry. Again, these changes should be framed as behavioural experiments to test out alternative perspectives regarding the individual's beliefs about worry.

- Abandoning thought control – In common with the strategies identified above to deal with safety behaviour in panic disorder, once the client has begun to be able to identify their misinterpretations about worry, all strategies that they are using to maintain control of their thoughts should be faded out, to remove an alternative explanation for why feared consequences do not occur.
- Relaxation training – Given the tension and restlessness evident in GAD, there is a place for the teaching of applied relaxation for some clients. Caution should be exercised that doing the relaxation 'right' does not become another source of worry for the client.
- Problem-solving training – Problem solving provides a structured method for identifying and dealing with problems or decision making. The client is provided with guidelines on the stages involved in the process and taught how to apply these to problems which may be contributing to anxiety and worries.

Research

Treatment outcome studies into the cognitive treatment of panic disorder have shown generally good results, despite some studies having relatively small sample sizes. Cognitive therapy has been shown to be more effective than supportive therapy (Beck et al., 1992), applied relaxation (Clark et al., 1994), and Imipramine (Clark et al., 1994). Cognitive therapy targeting catastrophic misinterpretations of physical symptoms, and excluding all exposure elements, has been found to be successful in reducing panic frequency. The addition of exposure-based approaches does appear to strengthen treatment effects, however. Where research has focused on panic disorder with agoraphobia, the superiority of cognitive therapy over exposure therapy alone is less clear cut, with Bouchard et al. (1996) finding no significant difference.

Research into the treatment of generalized anxiety disorder by cognitive therapy is more recent, but results are promising. Cognitive behaviour therapy has been found to be more effective than behaviour therapy alone (Butler et al., 1991), having good effects on thoughts, expectations and beliefs about worry in something less than half the clients. Borkovek and Costello (1993) have shown superior outcomes for cognitive therapy over applied relaxation.

For both panic disorder and generalized anxiety disorder, if medication is to be offered, an antidepressant from the selective serotonin reuptake inhibitor (SSRI) group has generally been shown to be most effective. The National Institute for Clinical Excellence (NICE, 2004) recommend that psychological therapy (cognitive-behavioural therapy), medication or some form of self-help should be made available to the client within the primary care setting. A combination of two of these, either staged or in conjunction, should be adopted before a referral is made to specialist mental health services (NICE, 2004).

The inclusion of self-help within the recommendations reflects increasing evidence on the value and range of methods which are more readily accessible to clients and less demanding on services. Self-management approaches can include the use of written materials (bibliotherapy), access to relevant charities and organizations, large group therapy and limited or remote (e.g. telephone) access to a therapist for advice. Computerized therapy programmes have also been developed and show considerable promise. However, further research is recommended before these are fully introduced into routine health service settings (Kaltenthaler et al., 2004).

Debates

Two main areas of continuing debate in the treatment of panic disorder and generalized anxiety disorder can be identified. These are the differential benefit of the cognitive approach over exposure alone, and the use of control rather than disconfirmatory strategies in treatment.

Cognitive therapy for both panic disorder and generalized anxiety disorder includes what are termed 'behavioural experiments'. There is a continuing debate as to whether the active elements in treatment are those claimed by the model, that is disconfirmation of beliefs, rather than the reduction in fear resulting from exposure. As with any therapy with a number of elements, the impact of any specific approach is difficult to distinguish. Evaluation of the effectiveness of individual elements of therapy, specifically through the comparison of cognitive and behavioural techniques, is required to clarify this issue. However, as behavioural aspects are central to cognitive therapy, such studies may be difficult to undertake. Research into panic disorder with agoraphobia indicates the clear effectiveness of exposure alone, which indicates the need for an individualized approach following assessment.

A second issue is that in both the treatment of panic disorder and generalized anxiety disorder there are competing treatment models which include control strategies for symptoms. In panic disorder, these take the form of the breathing retraining strategy (outlined earlier). In generalized anxiety disorder, the use of controlled worry can be understood as a control strategy. Use of control strategies does not readily fit with the cognitive model, where the focus is on the misinterpretation of normal phenomena. As such, the inclusion of these elements in therapy is the subject of debate.

References

Beck, A.T. (1976) *Cognitive Therapy and the Emotional Disorders.* New York: International Universities Press.

Beck, A.T., Sokol, L., Clark, D.A., Berchick, B. and Wright, F. (1992) Focused cognitive therapy for panic disorder: a crossover design and one-year follow-up. *American Journal of Psychiatry*, 147: 778–783.

Borkovec, T.D. and Costello, E. (1993) Efficacy of applied relaxation and cognitive-behavioral therapy in the treatment of generalized anxiety disorder. *Journal of Consulting and Clinical Psychology*, 61: 611–619.

Bouchard, S., Gauthier, J., Laberge, B., French, D., Pelletier, M.H. and Godbout, C. (1996) Exposure versus cognitive restructuring in the treatment of panic disorder with agoraphobia. *Behaviour Research and Therapy*, 34: 213–224.

Butler, G., Fennell, M., Robson, P. and Gelder, M. (1991) A comparison of behavior therapy and cognitive behavior therapy in the treatment of generalized anxiety disorder. *Journal of Consulting and Clinical Psychology*, 59: 167–175.

Clark, D.M. (1986) A cognitive approach to panic disorder. *Behaviour Research and Therapy*, 24: 461–470.

Clark, D.M., Salkovskis, P.M., Hackmann, A., Middleton, H., Anastasiades, P. and Gelder, M.G. (1994) A comparison of cognitive therapy, applied relaxation and imipramine in the treatment of panic disorder. *British Journal of Psychiatry*, 164: 759–769.

Kaltenthaler, E., Parry, G. and Beverley, C. (2004) Computerized cognitive behaviour therapy: a systematic review: *Behavioural and Cognitive Psychotherapy*, 32: 31–55.

NICE (2004) *Anxiety: Management of Anxiety Panic Disorder, with or without Agoraphobia, and Generalized Anxiety Disorder in Adults in Primary, Secondary and Community Care.* London: National Institute of Clinical Excellence.

Wells, A. (1997) *Cognitive Therapy of Anxiety Disorders.* Chichester: Wiley.

6.7 Bereavement

GABRIELLE SYME

During most people's lives at least one person close to them will die. In 2002, 530,967 people died in England and Wales; 515,388 from natural causes, 10,310 accidentally and 3,269 either through suicide or self-inflicted harm. Further details are given in Table 6.7.1. This makes it surprising that most people know so little about the normal grieving process until they or close friends are bereaved. A major reason may be denial of mortality. In ordinary speech, 'if I die' rather than 'when I die' is the more common expression.

Bereavement is the reaction to the loss of someone or something that really matters both personally and emotionally. Thus bereavement is part of a much broader phenomenon; the response of social animals to loss. While this section will centre on bereavement through death, it is important to realize that the emotional response to any other major loss and the appropriate therapeutic interventions will probably be similar. Examples of other major losses are: amputation, separation and divorce, emigration, moving house, burglary, miscarriage, infertility, imprisonment, a major life-threatening illness, disability, redundancy, retirement, rape, abortion, leaving home, and disfigurement.

Grief is the complex emotional response to bereavement. A number of people have sought theoretical explanations of grief, while others have attempted to produce a model of grief by describing and categorizing the responses to loss. The psychological process involved in recovery is known as mourning. It is this process that can be helped by people who will listen and understand in a sustained way. Obviously well-trained

Table 6.7.1   Deaths from natural causes – England and Wales, 2002

Age	Male	Female
All ages	243,240	274,148
<1	1,787	1,287
1–4	263	198
5–14	353	275
15–24	846	509
25–34	1,782	1,213
35–44	4,440	3,281
45–54	11,629	8,176
55–64	26,755	17,291
65–74	65,347	39,035
75–84	87,202	88,744
85+	52,746	114,139

Source: Figures supplied by the Office for National Statistics.

counsellors and therapists can do this, but often the bereaved have their own network of support who must not be sidelined if the bereaved are to remain part of their own social group. On occasions, the best intervention by the professionals is to support and possibly inform the concerned family and friends as they journey with someone who is grieving.

Theories of grief

The main theories of grief, all derived from western cultures, seek to explain the origin of grief. Although developed independently, none is self-sufficient. They need to be integrated to get the most complete understanding of the psychological process involved in grieving. Stress theory (Cannon, 1929) sees the response to bereavement as one example of the complex physiological and psychological responses of animals to danger. These responses were essential when early humans were hunter-gatherers living in a hostile world of unforeseen dangers and predators. To survive in a dangerous and terrifying situation the response was fright, then fight, and if the worst came to the worst, flight (Cannon's 'fright, fight and flight' response). Nowadays human beings still respond both physiologically (their metabolism responds so they can run away at high speed) and psychologically (they think more quickly and try to avoid the situation again by being hypersensitive to it) when fight and flight are not appropriate responses. This theory partly, but not totally, explains the occurrence of post-traumatic stress disorder (PTSD) after being involved in a life-threatening event, such as a major fire, the sinking of a ship, a car crash or a mass murder.

The stress theory was elaborated further by Caplan (1964) to take into account that almost any stressful event happens to not just one person but a group of people who can help each other live through dangerous situations. He also observed that people respond less severely if they have some preparatory knowledge of how to deal with a crisis and the effects of trauma, and that survivors are helped considerably by the support of others who have also been through the same or a similar traumatic event. Even adding crisis theory to stress theory, it is not sufficient to explain the response to loss in general.

A psychoanalyst, Lindemann (1944), after observing the reaction of survivors from a fire in a night-club in which almost 500 people died, noticed that some people had a delayed or distorted grief reaction. This led him to propose that in these situations grief was being repressed and this was causing the delayed response. Thus repression was added to the theories to explain grief, but of course repression was only being observed in a tiny minority of people. It is not a major component of the normal grief reaction.

Bowlby (1979) developed with his co-workers a theory to explain the immediate reaction to separation and loss. Their observation of infants separated from their mothers led them to propose that the formation of an attachment between these two in the first year of life was critical for survival. If a baby is separated from its mother, its first urge is to cry until she returns or, in other words, until she is found (see Section 5.11). This is the basis of the immediate reaction to separation and loss at any point in our lives. Extensive studies have shown four attachment patterns in infants; secure, and insecure with three sub-categories, which are avoidant, ambivalent and disorganized/disoriented. There are corresponding attachment patterns in adults; secure and insecure with three sub-categories, which are dismissing, preoccupied and unresolved/disorganized. The quality of attachment, whether it is secure or insecure, has a profound effect on the parenting styles of people in adulthood with attachment styles being transmitted from parent to child. Thus secure parents have secure infants, dismissing parents have avoidant infants and so on. The ability to manage loss is also influenced by attachment patterns. Those with an insecure attachment are much more likely to show prolonged and chronic grief when a relationship is lost. More recent research by psychoneurobiologists such as Eisenberg, Hobson, Schore and Trevarthen has produced neurological evidence for the crucial role of attachment behaviour and emotional communication in brain growth

Table 6.7.2 Phases of adult mourning and related feelings

Phases	Predominant feelings	Time from death
1 Numbness	Shock Disbelief	2 weeks to 1 month
2 Yearning	Reminiscence Searching Hallucination Anger Guilt	6 months
3 Disorganization and Despair	Anxiety Loneliness Ambivalence Fear Hopelessness Helplessness	1 year
4 Reorganization	Acceptance Relief	2 years or more

Source: Based on Parkes (1972)

of the orbitofrontal area of the brain and in emotional development. This is the socio-emotional part of the brain; the area responsible for empathy and attunement (Schore, 2001).

What attachment theory does not do is attempt to explain the recovery from bereavement (though not all people do so), and the way in which some people change, develop a new identity and in some instances noticeably mature as a result. This possible change is called the psycho-social transition by Parkes (1971) and is based on the work of Marris (1974). Bereavement, along with a number of other life events, challenges people's presumptions about their world. Many assumptions that had been made on the grounds of previous experience are no longer correct. For instance, the world is less predictable; some plans are no longer relevant; the person who has died is no longer a natural reference point. Part of the grief work is coming to terms with a different relationship with the deceased, the world and oneself. In many ways the work is learning about and coming to terms with a new 'I'.

Models of grief

Many people have described and systemized the reactions to bereavement. One of the first was Lindemann, who described five characteristics of the normal acute grief response:

1 somatic or bodily distress of some type;
2 preoccupation with the image of the dead person;
3 guilt relating to the deceased or circumstances of the death;
4 hostile reactions;
5 the inability to function as one had before.

Anyone who has worked with the bereaved would recognize these responses and that, alongside these, there are characteristic feelings, physical sensations, behaviours and ways of thinking.

A number of writers, the most notable being Bowlby and Parkes, separated all these responses into phases. Bowlby identified three phases when a child was separated from their parent or significant care-giver. These were angry pining, depression and despair followed by detachment if the parent did not return soon enough or at all. Parkes, on the basis of interviews with London widows, added an additional phase of numbness before the pining or yearning. These phases, and the associated feelings, are shown in Table 6.7.2. Though this pattern of response was constructed from interviews with women, it is essentially the same for men.

There has been a lot of unjust criticism of these phases on the grounds that they suggest that grieving is a linear process, something that Parkes never suggested. The process is very much one of two steps forward and one step back and the phases overlap. One moment it seems to the griever that life is improving and there are things to enjoy again – the acceptance phase – and then the next moment the mourner is plunged back into acute grief – the phase of despair and disorganization. Another criticism is that the phases also suggest a time scale. While for many the numbness lasts about two weeks, the acute yearning six months, and the whole process approximately two years, there are huge variations which, when they occur, should not be interpreted as abnormal. On the other hand, counsellors and therapists must be able to assess what parts of the grief have been experienced and whether they have been worked through, and also to recognize when the grieving is complicated and severely delayed. For this reason it is important that counsellors and therapists know what to expect but not to have rigid expectations of the process. The different phases and their suggested timings offer a checklist and no more.

It will be noted that Parkes' phases of grief focus exclusively on feelings. Stroebe and Schut (1995) studied grieving in a variety of cultures and realized that there are many differences. For instance, in some cultures, such as Muslim communities in Bali, grief is neither confronted nor expressed, with no serious psychological consequences. In others, such as Japan, a family shrine in memory of the dead ancestors is normal, yet in western communities it is viewed as a sign of unresolved grief. This led them to propose the Dual Process model of grief. They recognized that the two components of grief are loss-orientation (essentially the feeling part of the process observed by Parkes) and the restoration-orientation. This latter process is the necessary focus on new tasks and the development of new skills to be able to manage the momentous life changes that result from the death of a significant person. Recovery from bereavement involves both loss- and restoration-oriented activities.

A further development has been the recognition by the theoreticians of something that the bereaved always knew, that is that the deceased are never forgotten, the wound, albeit healed, is always present and that there are continuing bonds, both tangible and intangible, with the deceased. The tangible ones are keepsakes, such as letters, personal belongings and photographs of those who have died. Intangible ones are memories held in the heart. Klass et al. (1996) have written extensively on the necessity of continuing bonds and the inappropriateness of terms like 'letting go', which were commonly found in the bereavement literature.

Clinical management: normal grief reaction

The majority of the bereaved who seek help do so at least two months after the death. This may well be because immediately after the death family and friends rally round and are very supportive. The combination of their lack of awareness of how long the road of recovery is for the bereaved and having a less close relationship with the dead person means that after about two months all but the bereaved have returned 'to normal' and expect that of the bereaved as well. In reality, the bereaved are probably at their lowest ebb, perhaps thinking they are going mad, feeling acute fear and such loss of self-esteem that they do not believe anyone is interested in them. This latter feature may make it extremely difficult to ask for help.

For most bereaved what is needed is supportive counselling and an environment in which all the emotions associated with the death can be expressed. Many people need help in expressing anger and understanding guilt. Anger, because the person the griever is most likely to be angry with is the dead person, and frequently there is an almost superstitious belief that if 'ill is spoken of the dead' punishment is inevitable. Guilt, because it is rarely absent and is often expressed as 'if only …'. To an outside observer, this often seems misplaced when it is only too obvious just what the griever did for the dead person before the death. It is important to allow this guilt to be expressed and linked to reviewing the relationship with all its imperfections, and all the unkind things people say to one another in normal living. For some people, it takes a lot to be honest enough with themselves to admit there were occasions in the past when they had wished their partner or other close relatives and friends absent, if not dead.

Working with the bereaved is different from conventional therapy in that a lot more normalizing of the experience is necessary. This may be because so few people seem to know anything about bereavement unless it has happened to them. There are several powerful feelings and experiences that result in the bereaved fearing or even thinking they are going mad. The initial numbness, which is often both physical and emotional and gives a 'cotton-wool' feeling, seems to be an experience unique to loss. It is often a comfort to know that this is usual. The constant searching, which means going over and over in one's mind (or out loud) the details of the last days, hours or minutes before the death can be frightening, in particular because some of the images can be very disturbing. To know that this non-stop 'noise' in one's head is usual and not a sign of madness is comforting. Very often, once the terrible image has been shared, it fades. The third common experience which makes the bereaved, and frequently their family, query their sanity is the occurrence of hallucinations, which may be auditory, visual, sensual or olfactory. These are very vivid and can actually be comforting to the bereaved, but they are also disturbing because the person is dead. It is as if the brain has only partly accepted the death and at the same time expects the

person to be around. This is also seen in how many routine actions are done unnecessarily, such as laying the table for five people when there are now only four.

What the counsellor or therapist is doing is facilitating the grief work, which in uncomplicated grieving will often be a short piece of work in the range of two to ten sessions. The grief work (Worden, 1991) will be to help the client to:

- accept the reality of the death;
- experience the pain of grief;
- adjust to an environment in which the deceased is missing;
- relocate the deceased emotionally and move on with life.

Grief work involves both facilitating the expression of grief by focusing on feelings and emotions, and also focusing on the new skills, which are necessary distraction from the emotional side of grieving, that need to be acquired. In general, women choose to do the former and men the latter. However, Stroebe and Schut (1995) suggest that both areas need to be attended to and thus men need encouragement to talk about their feelings and women to be more practical.

The tendency for women to focus on their feelings and men to look practically to the future can cause enormous conflict in families. Frequently, a death means several people in a family are affected and they can become very angry with one another if they are grieving differently. Indeed, the person not showing much emotion is often accused of not caring, when that is far from the case. Such families may need a great deal of support. It is common for the death of a child in a family to cause such conflict that the couple often separate. Working through a bereavement will only strengthen a sound relationship.

When a death happens in a family, children need special help. They are often ignored because they move very rapidly through Bowlby's three stages and attach to another key adult. This misleads the adults into thinking the child is unaffected, but this is unlikely to be true. Depending on their age, they

Table 6.7.3   External circumstances affecting grief

Place of death	If person dies far away and particularly if dead body or grave not seen.
Coincidental deaths	Simultaneous and multiple deaths in family or community.
Successive deaths	If deaths or losses follow one after another in close succession, then the grief reaction and work over one may be incomplete before the next one and the whole process is interrupted.
Nature of the death	Where a death is sudden, untimely, violent or traumatic it is more difficult to grieve. Homicide and suicide are particularly difficult.
Social networks	Closely knit families and communities can be most helpful. The converse is also true. The attitude of a society to death and dying can help or hinder the grieving process.

Source: Lendrum and Syme (2004)

may not even understand what dying means and up to about the age of 5 expect the dead person to return. Between 8 and 10 years of age children develop an adult's concept of death. It is most important to understand that children up to at least the age of 10 are likely to think that they 'caused' the death, for instance linking a row with the death and believing that their anger has driven the person away. These irrational beliefs are found in adults too. Any belief of this sort must be explored and the child helped to understand that people do not die because the child has hated them.

Both children and adults need to be encouraged to value the importance of the continuing bonds found in memories, both tangible and intangible. The use of memory books or boxes for photographs, mementoes, significant letters and certificates can be very useful. Another helpful activity is writing a life history or creating a lifeline which helps to encapsulate significant events from the life of the deceased (Lendrum and Syme, 2004).

Another major strand of Stroebe's and Schut's work is to draw attention to cultural' differences in mourning and to warn against drawing wrong conclusions. For a Buddhist, it is usual to erect a shrine to a dead person while in some western cultures this is considered to be a sign of a chronic and complicated grief. Likewise, ritualized mourning is still normal in orthodox Judaism and at one time was usual

in Great Britain, but is now unusual and even considered morbid.

It is often assumed that people with a religious belief will be less upset by bereavement. For some, this will be true but it is unhelpful to make such assumptions. The feelings that even God has let them down and it is useless railing against a spiritual force, drives some people away from any religious beliefs. It is essential in bereavement work to have knowledge of the different religions and cultural groups in the UK as the rituals around death are very varied.

It is particularly important in bereavement work to hold the ending in mind in every session. Obviously, the ending of the therapy is in danger of being yet another loss. The reality of another loss must not be denied and it is very important that the ending in bereavement counselling is planned with the client. Indeed, a lot of clients find it useful to create their own ritual for the ending of therapy. If the client shows a marked reluctance to end, this would suggest that either the therapist has replaced the 'dead' person, always a danger as a therapist can seem much more understanding than any family or friends, or some part of the grief work has been omitted. A discussion with a supervisor about the ways to handle this is essential so that the problems can be confronted, understood and worked with.

Table 6.7.4   Internal factors affecting grief

Attachment history	If securely attached in childhood, can cope with anxiety in adulthood and will have a capacity to express emotion and grieve.
Loss and death history	If an earlier death or loss has been difficult to accept and grieve, then current grief will 'awaken' the earlier unresolved grief. The combination will then be harder to grieve.
Age and stage of griever	For children and young people and those in life transitions grief may be more challenging.
Intimacy level	The more intimate the relationship (e.g. spouse, lover, partner, child, parent, sibling), the more intense the grief.
Emotional complexity	The more straightforward the relationship, the less complicated the grief. If the relationship had many denied feelings or had unrecognized ambivalence, the grief will be more complex.
Social network	If the family and community is supportive and the griever has the capacity to use it, this will aid grieving. Similarly, if the attitudes of society are helpful.

Source: Lendrum and Syme (2004)

Chronic complicated grief

There are a number of factors that predict that the grieving could be greatly complicated and probably prolonged. These factors must be checked in the initial assessment. They are separated into two groups, the external circumstances surrounding the death and the internal factors linked with the life history and emotional development of the bereaved person. External circumstances that affect the grieving process are shown in Table 6.7.3. Internal factors affecting grief are shown in Table 6.7.4. The first three factors affect the person's capacity to grieve, the latter three will influence the reaction to the death because of the quality of the relationship which is lost.

It is not possible to predict exactly how the combination of these factors will affect the grieving process, but it is essential they are assessed. Their presence will help alert the therapist to the likelihood of a complex and/or a prolonged grieving process which may include severe, chronic depression and thus enable a decision to be made on what level of skill will be needed to work with someone and whether a psychiatric referral is necessary. If someone already has a psychiatric history, it would be unwise to work with them as bereavement can greatly exacerbate mental instability.

References

Bowlby, J. (1979) *The Making and Breaking of Affectional Bonds*. London: Tavistock.

Cannon, W.B. (1929) *Bodily Changes in Pain, Hunger, Fear and Rage*. London: Appleton.

Caplan, G. (1964) *Principles of Preventive Psychiatry*. New York: Basic Books.

Klass, D., Silverman, P.R. and Nickman, S. (eds) (1996) *Continuing Bonds: New Understandings of Grief*. London: Taylor & Francis.

Lendrum, S. and Syme, G. (2004) *Gift of Tears*. London: Routledge.

Lindemann, E. (1944) The symptomatology and management of acute grief. *American Journal of Psychiatry*, 101: 141.

Marris, P. (1974) *Loss and Change*. London: Routledge and Kegan Paul.

Parkes, C.M. (1971) Psychosocial transitions: a field for study. *Social Sciences and Medicine*, 5: 101.

Parkes, C.M. (1972) *Bereavement: Studies of Grief in Adult Life*. London: Tavistock.

Schore, A.N. (2001) Minds in the making: attachment, the self-organising brain, and developmentally-oriented psychoanalytic psychotherapy. *British Journal of Psychotherapy*, 17: 299–328.

Stroebe, M.S. and Schut, H.A.W. (1995) The dual process model of coping with loss. Paper presented at the International Work Group on Death, Dying and Bereavement, St Catherine's College, Oxford, 26–29 June.

Worden, W. (1991) *Grief Counselling and Grief Therapy*. London: Routledge.

6.8 Depression   ○○○

PAUL GILBERT

In 2004 the National Institute of Clinical Excellence (NICE) published its guidelines for the treatment of depression. This document discusses the nature of depression, its economic burden and treatment recommendations. It can be accessed at www.nice.org and is designed as a useful resource and guideline for identifying and treating depression. It is well known that depression creates a huge social burden for both sufferers and those who live with them.

Children growing up with a depressed parent can be affected in both their social and intellectual development. Rapid diagnosis and treatment is the key to helping depressed people. Although depression varies symptomatically (Beckham et al., 1995), psychologically (Arieti and Bemporad, 1980; Beck, 1983) and biologically (Thase and Howland, 1995) its core features are well recognized (see Table 6.8.1).

It has been estimated that about one in five people are at risk of suffering a depressive episode at some time in their lives (this figure varies according to social class and social circumstances) and women are over twice as likely to suffer an episode as men (Bebbington, 1998), largely for psycho-social reasons. Once depression has struck there is a high chance of relapse (over 50 per cent); early onset depression (on or before 20 years) being particularly vulnerable to relapse (Giles et al., 1989). There is also increased vulnerability in those from hostile and low-warmth families (Kessler and Magee, 1994). Although depression is a heterogeneous disorder (with some depressions, such as bipolar depression, have a high genetic loading) most depressions result from a variety of complex interacting factors – including biological vulnerability, early life history, current relationship problems, and life difficulties (Bifulco and Moran, 1988).

Beck et al. (1979) suggested that the internal experience of the depressed person revolves around a *negative cognitive triad* of feeling inferior and worthless (negative view of self), seeing the future as hopeless (negative view of the future), and the world as full of thwarting and frustrating obstacles

Table 6.8.1 The major domains of depression

Biological	Sleep disturbance, loss of appetite, loss of weight, fatigue, changes in circadian rhythms, hormones and brain chemicals (Healy and Williams, 1988; Thase and Howland, 1995).
Emotional	Low mood, anhedonia – cannot enjoy or find pleasure in things (Watson and Clark, 1988; Willner, 1993); feelings of emptiness, anger or resentment, anxiety, shame, guilt (Gilbert, 1992).
Motivation	Apathy, loss of energy and interest (Klinger, 1993): things seem pointless, hopeless (Abramson et al., 1989; Alloy et al., 1988).
Cognitive	Poor concentration and memory, commonly with worry about the changes (Miller, 1975; Watts, 1993).
Evaluations	Negative ideas about the self, the world and the future (Beck et al., 1979).
Behaviour	Lowered activity, social withdrawal, agitation or retardation. Problems in social relationships are common in depression, both as cause and consequence (Feldman and Gotlib, 1993; Segrin and Abramson, 1994).

Note: A key symptom in depression is anhedonia – the *loss* of pleasure and positive affect. However, negative emotions such as anger, shame, guilt and anxiety typically *increase* in depression.

(negative view of the world). This does, however, miss the anger that can sometimes lurk in depression. New work also suggests that feeling defeated and entrapped (the impossibility of escape from a difficult situation) is especially associated with depression (Gilbert, 1992, 2004; Gilbert and Allan, 1998) and more so than loss events (Brown et al., 1995). Depressed patients also have many interpersonal problems (Segrin and Abramson, 1994) and tend to behave submissively in conflicts (Allan and Gilbert, 1997).

Assessment

Counsellors are not expected to be able to make psychiatric diagnosis based on *ICD–10* or *DSM–IV*. More important is to understand specific problem areas. Asking questions about the symptoms in Table 6.8.1 will give you an assessment of the current mental state. This can be done by saying (for example), 'I would just like to ask you a few questions about how you're feeling and functioning at the moment', and then, 'How are you sleeping? What is your energy like?' etc. To explore emotions you might ask, 'Do you find yourself feeling very angry

inside and getting easily frustrated?' and for shame, 'Are there things in your life you would find very hard to talk about?' There are diagnostic criteria for depression but these don't do a good job in evaluating negative emotions such as anger, anxiety and shame and you will need to look at these especially. Depressed clients who are very shame-prone may not reveal the key things that are bothering them so you may need to be sensitive to what is hidden.

Some depressed people like to have a label for their difficulties and some do not. One can, however, talk in terms of exhaustion; of being exhausted in body and mind, and feeling that there is 'no more fight left in you'. This position can make it easier to negotiate for an anti-depressant if that is indicated by, for example, sleep disturbance, somatic symptoms, concentration problems and strong feelings that things can't improve. If you are unfamiliar with these decisions or with assessing *suicide risk* then you should contact someone who is and explain to your client why you may be referring them on for further assessment. You might, for example, talk of how states of mind lead us to think and feel things that we know we do not normally think and feel, and how depression is notorious for making the world seem dark, leading to a strong wish to escape it. It is important to assess suicide risk for all clients, especially depressed and hopeless ones. If you ask something like 'Do you have a strong wish to escape your present situation?' and get a strong affirmative, be especially wary. You might also say, 'We need to cover all the angles and I would like this other person [e.g. psychiatrist, CPN or psychologist] to have a talk with you and see if there is anything further they could offer.' Don't feel isolated with clients you are worried about, or get tied up in not being able to ask others for help.

Formulation

Formulations need to fit treatment. The formulation of a psychiatrist who is going to give medication will be different from that of a counsellor or therapist. Therapists need to formulate the problem of depression in terms of its psychological and/or social difficulties. Although the initial focus will be on the specific problem areas (for example, relationship problems), some insight into early life experiences is often helpful. Therefore, some time should be given within the first few sessions to find out what kind of relationship clients had with parents and significant others during their formative years. Attention should be given to the degree of warmth, control, neglect, aggression and shaming (such as criticizing, being disapproved of, and called names). Obviously any possible abusive experiences should also be considered (although these may not be revealed early in the therapy). Clients can be invited to reflect on how these early experiences may have shaped their inner world, and in particular their typical beliefs and feelings about themselves and others.

The next part of the formulation would focus on current beliefs about self and others. People who see themselves as inferior, worthless and inadequate will usually need to address these basic self-beliefs. In addition, of course, people who are very distrusting of others, and/or who have been abused in some way, may find it quite difficult to form an open and trusting relationship with the counsellor. It can sometimes be useful to reflect gently on that as a

potential area of difficulty, while acknowledging that it is in no way a criticism of the person.

It can be helpful to explore certain kinds of assumptions and attitudes about life in general (in cognitive therapy these are called attitudes). This may include beliefs such as 'I should never get angry with my children'; 'I should always be hard working'; 'I should never make mistakes'; 'I must be loved all the time', etc. These kinds of beliefs are going to lead to certain kinds of behaviours, and these behaviours may well be partly responsible for maintaining the depression (Segrin and Abramson, 1994). For example, people who believe they could not cope alone, may find themselves trapped if they get into unsatisfying and abusive relationships. Indeed, in recent research, feelings of defeat and entrapment proved to be extremely important to the experience of depression (Gilbert, 2004; Gilbert and Allan, 1998). If patients do feel trapped, it is useful to explore with them options for getting away, and also options for improving their current situation. Patients who feel very trapped may have trouble in focusing on the current environment and how to improve it, since their inner motive is so 'flight' orientated.

It is important to share your overview with clients, taking them through early life experiences, the way in which these may have shaped the way they see themselves and others, the way these in turn may have shaped how they think about the world and their role in it, and how this affects the way they behave in the world, particularly in relationship to interpersonal conflicts or seeking out various opportunities for relating (including employment).

It is important that the formulation is co-constructed and uses narrative to 'paint the story'. It should be agreed with the client because this provides the springboard to move on to therapeutic work. Out of the formulation comes an agreement of what would be helpful to change and work with. Sometimes this can be a focus on key beliefs or it may be a focus on key behaviours (such as difficulties in behaving assertively), or it may be offering an opportunity for clients to explore in their own way, in their own time, in a rather non-structured way.

Intervention

There are many types of intervention for depression. I prefer to approach depression via a biopsychosocial model (Gilbert, 1995). It is important that a full medical assessment is done to rule out physical disorders such as hypothyroidism, etc. Some people do benefit from anti-depressant drugs, whereas others do not. It is true, of course, that anti-depressant drugs do not help people re-train or understand the origins of the depression, or learn new coping skills – yet poor coping skills are a reason for relapse. Only psychological therapies and life experiences can help with new learning. On the social side it is important also to explore if the person has any major social difficulties requiring social work help, legal help, etc.

There is obviously a variety of psychological therapies that can be used for depression. These range from group therapy, family therapy and individual therapy, and follow different approaches such as behaviour therapy, cognitive therapy, interpersonal and psychodynamic. Therapists tend to mix and match these, sometimes in a rather arbitrary way. It is, therefore, useful to try to develop a focus with particular clients and to evaluate if certain types of therapy may be more appropriate for them than others. For example, under what conditions might you refer a patient for family therapy? If you choose to stay with individual therapy then there are often some very key themes to focus on. The negative cognitive triad in depression (Beck et al., 1979) is a very good place to start. In my own particular work, I tend to focus on current difficulties and coping, and then on negative views of the self, looking at the way in which individuals can feel internally very inferior, inadequate or worthless. Generally speaking, it is difficult to find people who are depressed who also feel confident and good about themselves. There are a number of specific ways in which one can intervene with patients' typical styles of thinking (Gilbert, 2000a). It can also be useful to be aware of a range of self-help books that people can use to find out more about depression and how they might help themselves (e.g. Gilbert, 2000b).

In general, therapists try to assist people to gain a different perspective on themselves and their current situations, so that they are not collapsed in a dark hole of pessimism and sense of worthlessness. This can be done by aiding individuals to look at the *alternatives* to their thoughts, to *test the evidence* for their thoughts and to try out new behaviours. Sometimes it is appropriate to help patients *break problems down* so that they can begin to tackle problems in a step-by-step fashion. Clients can be asked to focus on what they can do, rather than on what they can't do. Commonly, depressed patients have lost the capacity for a warm, caring and supportive inner approach to self. Therefore, assisting patients develop a compassionate, forgiving approach can be helpful and healing. Depressed patients often are very bullying of themselves (Gilbert, 2000, 2004).

Sometimes it is important to revisit past traumas and to enable patients to experience certain kinds of emotions while working through those traumas. If these traumas are related to abuse, and you feel unable to deal with them, then it is useful to steer the patient in the direction of therapists who do have experience of working with abuse. Try to be open on these issues rather than defensive.

Overview

Depression is obviously a complicated disorder, with many different causes, and presents in many different forms. When we come to treat depression we cannot afford to be 'a one-club golfer'. Sometimes we will need a mixture of treatments. And even when we focus on a psychological treatment, it is not always clear which psychological or social treatment would best suit that client (Roth and Fonagy, 1996). It is also the case that some individuals get on better with certain types of therapist, as opposed to certain types of approach. All of these enter into our reckoning of how best to help depressed people.

References

Abramson, L.Y., Metalsky, G.I. and Alloy, L.B. (1989) Hopelessness: a theory-based subtype of depression. *Psychological Review*, 96: 358–372.

Allan, S. and Gilbert, P. (1997) Submissive behaviour and psychopathology. *British Journal of Clinical Psychology*, 36: 467–488.

Alloy, L.B., Abramson, L.Y., Metalsky, G.I. and Hartledge, S. (1988) The hopelessness theory of depression: attributional aspects. *British Journal of Clinical Psychology*, 27: 5–12.

Arieti, S. and Bemporad, J. (1980) The psychological organization of depression. *American Journal of Psychiatry*, 137: 1360–1365.

Bebbington, P. (1998) Editorial: Sex and depression. *Psychological Medicine*, 28: 1–8.

Beck, A.T. (1983) Cognitive therapy of depression: new perspectives. In P.J. Clayton and J.E. Barrett (eds), *Treatment of Depression: Old Controversies and New Approaches*. New York: Raven Press.

Beck, A.T., Rush, A.J., Shaw, B.F. and Emery, G. (1979) *Cognitive Therapy of Depression*. New York: Wiley.

Beckham, E.E., Leber, W.R. and Youll, L.K. (1995) The diagnostic classification of depression. In E.E. Beckham and W.R. Leber (eds), *Handbook of Depression* (2nd edn). New York: Guilford Press. pp. 36–60.

Bifulco, A. and Moran, P. (1988) *Wednesday's Child: Research into Women's Experiences of Neglect and Abuse in Childhood, and Adult Depression*. London: Routledge.

Brown, G.W., Harris, T.O. and Hepworth, C. (1995) Loss, humiliation and entrapment among women developing depression: a patient and non-patient comparison. *Psychological Medicine*, 25: 7–21.

Feldman, L.A. and Gotlib, I.H. (1993) Social dysfunction. In C.G. Costello (ed.), *Symptoms of Depression*. New York: Wiley. pp. 65–112.

Gilbert, P. (1992) *Depression: The Evolution of Powerlessness*. Hove: Lawrence Erlbaum; New York: Guilford Press.

Gilbert, P. (1995) Biopsychosocial approaches and evolutionary theory as aids to integration in clinical psychology and psychotherapy. *Clinical Psychology and Psychotherapy*, 2: 135–156.

Gilbert, P. (2000a) *Counselling for Depression* (2nd edn). London: Sage.

Gilbert, P. (2000b) *Overcoming Depression: A Self-guide Using Cognitive Behavioural Techniques*. London: Robinsons; New York: Oxford University Press.

Gilbert, P. (2004) Depression: a biopsychosocial, integrative and evolutionary approach. In M. Power (ed.), *Mood Disorders: A Handbook of Science and Practice*. Chichester: Wiley. pp. 99–142.

Gilbert, P. and Allan, S. (1998) The role of defeat and entrapment (arrested flight) in depression: an exploration of an evolutionary view. *Psychological Medicine*, 28: 584–597.

Giles, D., Jarrett, R., Biggs, M., Guzick, D. and Rush, J. (1989) Clinical predictors of reoccurrance in depression. *American Journal of Psychiatry*, 146: 764–767.

Healy, D. and Williams, J.M.G. (1988) Dysrhythmia, dysphoria, and depression: the interaction of learned helplessness and circadian dysrhythmia in the pathogenesis of depression. *Psychological Bulletin*, 103: 163–178.

Kessler, R.C. and Magee, W.J. (1994) Childhood family violence and adult recurrent depression. *Journal of Health and Social Behaviour*, 35: 13–27.

Klinger, E. (1993) Loss of interest. In C.G. Costello (ed.), *Symptoms of Depression*. New York: Wiley. pp. 43–62.

Miller, W.R. (1975) Psychological deficit in depression. *Psychological Bulletin*, 82: 238–260.

Roth, A. and Fonagy, P. (1996) *What Works for Whom? A Critical Review of Psychotherapy Research*. New York: Guilford Press.

Segrin, C. and Abramson, L.Y. (1994) Negative reactions to depressive behaviours: a communication theories analysis. *Journal of Abnormal Psychology*, 103: 655–668.

Thase, M.E. and Howland, R.H. (1995) Biological processes in depression: an update and integration. In E.E. Beckham and W.R. Leber (eds), *Handbook of Depression* (2nd edn). New York: Guilford Press. pp. 213–279.

Watson, D. and Clark, L.A. (1988) Positive and negative affectivity and their relation to anxiety and depressive disorders. *Journal of Abnormal Psychology*, 97: 346–353.

Watts, F. (1993) Problems with memory and concentration. In C.G. Costello (ed.), *Symptoms of Depression*. New York: Wiley. pp. 113–114.

Willner, P. (1993) Anhedonia. In C.G. Costello (ed.), *Symptoms of Depression*. New York: Wiley. pp. 63–84.

6.9   Counselling Drug-related Problems

ANDREW GUPPY AND SALLY WOODS

Overview

This section provides an insight into the special challenges and opportunities within the field of drug misuse counselling. The next part outlines what we are referring to by the term 'drug-related problems', describing the types of substance and the expected range of problems. Following this, the types of intervention environment are then explored more deeply, focusing on the main approaches to counselling with some background to their underlying theory. Some practical considerations of counselling substance-related problems are then presented. The final part of this section looks at potential areas for development of this field and suggests ways of integrating drug counselling more closely into other fields.

Defining drugs, use and misuse

Initially, it is necessary to clarify what is meant by the concept of 'substance misuse'. According to the American Psychiatric Association (APA, 2000), misuse can include drug-related behaviour that may cause trouble in the short term through accidents, social or legal problems, though this behaviour need not have become a regular pattern. The APA definitions also include two more serious categories of 'substance abuse' (recurrent and continued misuse of a substance over the last 12 months) and 'substance dependence' (presence of tolerance, withdrawal and control loss features as well as those of abuse). It has to be noted that there remains some debate as to whether there can be non-problem use of illicit substances, given the above definitions. In other words, someone can very easily fulfil the label

of 'misuse' if they are prosecuted for unlawful use of a substance even if their pattern of use shows no other deleterious effects.

The range of illicit substances that are used and misused is quite wide and they vary in terms of their effects, legal status and population of users. Some of the main illicit drugs used in the UK are listed below, prevalence estimates are available from a number of sources (e.g. Ramsey et al., 2001).

Drugs with stimulating properties

Amphetamines – Short-term use results in feelings of energy and arousal. Long-term and/or heavy use may result in delusions, hallucinations and feelings of persecution. Around 5 per cent of 16–29 year-olds report annual use.

Ecstasy (MDMA) – Short-term use may be similar to LSD (calming, heightened senses) without hallucinations; larger doses may produce effects similar to amphetamines. Prevalence is assumed to be similar to amphetamines in younger groups.

Cocaine (including Crack) – Short-term use produces feelings of well-being and exhilaration. Long-term and/or heavy use may result in feelings of restlessness, sleeplessness and persecution. Around 5 per cent of 16–29 year-olds reported annual use.

Drugs with relaxing, depressing properties

Cannabis – Short-term relaxant that enhances perceptions and impairs psychomotor skills. Heavy use may result in perceptual distortions. There is an estimated prevalence of around 22 per cent of 16–29 year-olds in the UK.

Opiates (including heroin) – Short-term use produces feelings of contentment and warmth. Long-term and/or heavy use may result in dependence. Physical harm is usually related to needle use. **Morphine** and **codeine** are commonly prescribed; **heroin** is usually illicit; **methadone** is mainly prescribed as a heroin substitute, though it can be obtained illegally (usually through misuse of the prescription system). Annual heroin use was reported by around 1 per cent of 16–29 year-olds.

Minor Tranquillizers – Benzodiazepines are the most commonly prescribed (including Valium, Librium, Ativan). Short-term use depresses mental activity and alertness and can impair psychomotor skills. Withdrawal effects are common, as is psychological dependence. One in seven British adults are occasional users; one in 40 are long-term users.

Hallucinogenic drugs

Lysergic acid diethylamide (LSD) – Short-term effects include heightened visual and auditory sensations, and may include mystical, ecstatic or frightening experiences. True hallucinations are rare, and impairment of psychomotor and cognitive performance likely. Long-term effects relate to mental rather than physical well-being; prolonged serious disorders are rare as yet.

Psilicybin (magic mushrooms) – Short-term effects very much depend on the dose taken but can follow a similar pattern to LSD.

Counselling substance-related problems

Models of substance misuse and their implications for treatment

There are several different approaches in the drug and alcohol counselling field (e.g. see Miller and Hester, 1989: 3–14). One widely held view may be epitomized by Narcotics Anonymous (NA) and is designed to follow on from the approach pioneered by Alcoholics Anonymous (AA). This approach assumes that drug abuse is a pre-existing physical (biochemical) abnormality and it is almost as though some individuals have an incurable allergy to their substance of addiction (hence lifelong abstinence being the only answer). Another medically influenced approach views the important element as being the harm that is related to the drug misuse and seeks to minimize this by reducing risks, reducing intake (as opposed to cessation) and possibly changing to another substance with reduced harm implications. The third approach may be seen as viewing the drug misuse as principally a pattern of inappropriate coping and thus focuses on cognitive-behavioural elements to recognize and deal with situations likely to lead to drug use, to reduce unhelpful perceptions, to improve feelings of efficacy and to increase the range of coping behaviours that may be used as an alternative to drugs. Obviously, there are any number of other approaches that are available and successful, but the following are probably the most commonly encountered within the UK at present.

Narcotics Anonymous

Although this kind of 'intervention' may appear to be different from usual forms of 'counselling', Narcotics Anonymous quite clearly provide a well-known type of support for those with problems. The spread and level of activity of NA in the UK is considerably less than its sister organization AA. However, the broad philosophy of this approach can also be found in a number of residential and out-patient treatment facilities.

The principles of the NA (and AA) approach are covered in the 'Twelve Steps'. These steps principally involve six stages. First, there is an admission of powerlessness over substance use and that life has become 'unmanageable'. The second stage involves an acceptance of assistance from a 'higher power'. Stage three is about becoming aware of the 'nature of our wrongs', with the fourth stage working on removing 'defects of character' and 'shortcomings'. A penultimate stage is about promising to make amends to those who have been harmed and the final stage emphasizes the maintenance of progress through prayer, meditation and a commitment to helping others in similar need.

It has been noted that there are variations across AA (and perhaps more so, NA) groups in terms of the emphasis placed on the 'higher power principle' (some are more spiritual rather than religious); the principle that does not vary within the Twelve Steps approach concerns the goal behaviour of abstinence. This has some implications for those who are opiate abusers, where a common alternative involves methadone substitution (described below), which may be seen as incompatible with an abstinence approach by some.

Typical harm reduction approach

The essence of the harm reduction approach to substance misuse focuses on service provision on meeting and working with drug users on their terms. It is a feature of such an approach that at times these terms may be out of line with mainstream social, government or service provision policy. Critics of this approach have long argued that by being supportive, in reality giving drugs to drug users, the services may be encouraging these individuals to maintain their current patterns of use, with no compelling reason to stop (e.g. Edwards, 1969). Supporters of the harm reduction approach would argue that it is an attempt to bridge the gap between the expectations of drug users and service providers with realistic rather than moralistic methods of intervention.

Usually the first step in harm reduction involves the stabilization of the client's illicit use. This includes provision of sterile equipment and other harm reduction resources (e.g. condoms). The next step would normally involve reduction of use, sometimes paired with the provision of a 'script' to top up the reduced quantity of illicit drug. A number of drug dependency units (DDUs) adopt a policy of only providing scripts when the client is free from illicit drugs (usually monitored by urine screening).

Generally, counselling is offered throughout this process but is particularly encouraged during periods of change (reduction in script). Group counselling is generally available at most DDUs. However, the consistent uptake of counselling is generally felt to be low. Clients would normally keep close contact with a key worker whose remit includes social and welfare support as well as specific drug-related matters. To some extent, problem-oriented, directive counselling occurs with this key worker. In many environments this relationship may be maintained within a 'contract' situation where support from the key worker is dependent on the client complying with the 'script regime' (e.g. cessation of illicit use).

One of the primary benefits of this approach tends to be in the realistic perspective on relapse management. As the approach does not rely on abstinence as the only acceptable alternative to harmful use, the relapse event may be more accepted within the treatment regime and the re-establishment of the treatment process is much easier.

However, one possible drawback to the most commonly encountered harm reduction approach is the potential lack of detailed counselling support. To some extent, the process may focus on the management of the intake reduction and ignore underlying deficiencies in terms of self-perceptions and coping skills.

A typical psychological approach to substance misuse counselling

A number of community-based agencies focusing on alcohol and drug misuse can be seen as providing a mixture of intervention methods and a more traditional counselling approach. Thus one may see agencies providing certain features that are core to the harm reduction approach but also advocating a move towards abstinence while featuring a range of group and individual sessions focusing on elements central to cognitive-behavioural and rational emotive behavioural therapies.

The elements of harm reduction education and support in the provision of information and advice (as well as equipment in terms of syringes, etc.) would normally occur early on in the process. Later, the discussion of eventual outcome goals could be approached and specific input relating to unhelpful cognitions and behaviours would be the focus of later sessions. Particularly useful are the use of group sessions focusing on the uptake of alternative (to substance use) behaviours in order to positively replace the effects of drug taking.

Beyond the drug-specific information, the main difference in substance misuse counselling concerns the focus of activities (towards abstinence or 'controlled' use) rather than the actual activities themselves (e.g. role-playing within a general social skills development package). It is common for some time to be devoted to obvious substance-related issues such as 'saying no'. Additionally, a lot of effort is directed towards 'relapse prevention' within the substance misuse field (see later). Within this general package, material focusing on stress management and assertiveness training could be included, as would other exercises on self-awareness and the development of positive ways of spending leisure time (other than substance use).

Practical issues in drug counselling

One of the first lessons learned in substance misuse counselling concerns the difficulties of providing assistance to someone who is too intoxicated to talk coherently or to remember much of what was said. Although it is unlikely that much progress may be made, there is an opinion that intoxicated clients should not be refused contact with the counsellor (e.g. Lockley, 1995). This greatly depends on the situation. In our experience, there may be distinct problems with having intoxicated individuals participating in (or disrupting) group counselling sessions. However, as relapse is a commonly occurring feature of drug misuse, there is a danger that loss of contact and risk of harm may result if a regular client turns up intoxicated on an isolated occasion and is refused contact.

There are also some lessons to be learned in terms of structuring contact around known 'difficult times':

- Group sessions late on a Friday night may be useful for many early clients as it reduces the likelihood of weekend-long binges starting after work on Friday.

- Holding group sessions immediately before script handout when clients may be 'strung out' can lead to sessions being unhelpful with behaviour varying between aggressive and silent.
- Mixed-model group sessions may be more difficult to manage, although they can lead to useful discussion. The obvious clash comes between those on an abstinence route and those who are receiving scripts or who are trying to control their substance use.

Polysubstance abuse

In the field of drug misuse it is clear that while there may be a 'principal drug' that is misused, the client may well be using and misusing other substances. A very common pattern is the occasional or frequent heavy use of alcohol which can remain after use of the main problem drug has reduced (Gossop et al., 2001).

Dual-diagnosis patients

It is not uncommon to find additional psychiatric problems present in substance misusers. It is similarly likely that such underlying problems may be difficult to detect at the early points of contact when the client is still under the influence of drugs or alcohol. It is usually the case that such clients will benefit from psychiatric referral from the counsellor. Other underlying psychological problems may also come to light in the course of a programme of counselling sessions, which, depending on the environment, may also be appropriate to refer on. This very much depends on the expertise of the counsellor and the nature of the counselling environment (it may be inappropriate in some agencies focused on substance misuse). For a more detailed review of many of the significant issues related to this field, see Rassool (2002).

Relapse management

This has been one of the key features of substance misuse intervention (e.g. see Marlatt and Gordon, 1985). If substance use/misuse has become the most important and reliable method of coping behaviour within the individual over a period of years, it is quite likely that during or after assistance the client may 'return' to a pattern of substance use. The use of inverted commas around 'return' is important as the aim is for the individual to continue to progress so that they are not returning to substance use with the same set of cognitions or perspectives that they started with. Even in successful cases, relapse can occur, but the process is more likely to lead to eventual success if it is managed properly and the individual feels able to call on support as soon as possible. One of the criticisms of the NA/AA philosophy was that it made it difficult to maintain self-esteem following a relapse and that the distance in days from the last occasion of substance use seemed more important than how you may have developed along the way. However, this perspective is thankfully changing and one of the very useful elements of the group counselling environments found within NA/AA and elsewhere is the sharing of experience in relapse management, such as identifying high-risk situations or times and sharing ideas for alternative cognitions and behaviours.

Contracts and expectations

A number of substance misuse counselling agencies have developed an approach of agreeing a 'contract' with the client in terms of defining what sort of effort they are required to undertake and, in return, what sort of support may be expected from the agency. While it is felt important to discuss what both sides are expecting and willing to do, this may be developed over time and the use of a formal contract (especially early on) may be over the top.

It may be the case that the client is uncertain of what they actually want from the process and the focus of counselling may for some time be on developing the client's perspective on themselves and relevant others, their drug use and its advantages and disadvantages. As this develops, the process encourages users to develop perceptions of control over their patterns of use and works towards realistic decisions over where they are heading. To some extent, this approach does fit in with the notion of harm reduction in the sense that safer drug use (clean equipment

from needle exchanges; known content of drug from prescription; move towards non-injected substitute) may be preferred by the user as a treatment goal. There is, however, the alternative perspective that allowing the user to select the relatively easier option of harm reduction rather than abstinence as the treatment goal only delays the inevitable.

Outcome and maintenance

It is clear that success has been achieved by many different therapeutic approaches in the field of drug misuse. However, success needs to be carefully defined and must incorporate a number of dimensions rather than simply focusing on the volume or weight of the substance. Thus modern researchers advocate a range of outcome measures to include wider aspects of psychological and social functioning as well as the more usual substance- and symptom-oriented measures (Guppy and Marsden, 2002; Marsden et al., 1998; Moos et al., 1990).

Where outcome evidence has been examined in the field of substance misuse, there is support for all the interventions described above (e.g. Etheridge et al., 1999; Gossop et al., 2001; Maisto et al., 1994). Thus Twelve Step, harm reduction, REBT and CBT approaches have positive outcomes, though the prognosis tends to be less positive for those with heavier and longer patterns of misuse (Polich et al., 1981), perhaps particularly when misuse ranges over more than one substance. From experience, it seems that some individuals need to try a number of intervention approaches before they achieve much success. However, it remains unclear whether such success is necessarily dependent on a strength of that particular intervention or is a result of coincidental changes within the individual achieved largely outside the counselling process.

Future developments

It is easy to say, but one of the main difficulties in dealing with illicit drug misuse is the drug itself. For many years, the prescribing of drugs and substitute drugs has developed the possibility of moving the user away from the criminal sections of society and regaining some semblance of normal functioning. The continued development of this approach is viewed quite positively (see Gossop et al., 2001, for treatment outcome success). This is not to say that decriminalization should or should not be a future consideration, merely that we need to move away from a moral position that dictates that any illicit drug use is against the law and therefore must be clinically construed as misuse. While we have a society that regards non-problem use of alcohol as acceptable, there seems to be no strong psychological argument to support these double standards.

Of course the other main difficulty in dealing with illicit drug use is the person. Much of the policy and practice in relation to drug misuse has focused on the chemical rather than the person. Even the most common interventions struggle to acknowledge the subsidiary role that the substance takes in relation to the person choosing to take it. It may be viewed that all forms of addiction primarily relate to one small part of a wider model of mental health, that of inappropriate coping behaviour. Recent research and practice has begun to focus on other parts of the model in relation to how we appraise our interactions with the world, including expectations about our control over situations and outcomes and the efficacy of our coping. Thus it is considered that the long-term development in this field will be to bring it into the fold of other interventions in the promotion of psychological well-being to the mutual benefit of practitioners and clients all round.

References

APA (2000) *Diagnostic and Statistical Manual of Mental Disorders* (IVth edition, text revision). Washington, DC: American Psychiatric Association.

Edwards, G. (1969) The British approach to the treatment of heroin addiction. *The Lancet* (7598): 768–772.

Etheridge, R.M., Craddock, S.G., Hubbard, R.L. and Rounds-Bryant, J.L. (1999) The relationship of counseling and self-help participation to patient outcomes in DATOS. *Drug and Alcohol Dependence*, 57: 99–112.

Gossop, M., Marsden, J. and Stewart, D. (2001) *NTORS After Five Years: Changes in Substance Use, Health and Criminal Behaviour During the Five Years After Intake.* London: Department of Health.

Guppy, A. and Marsden, J. (2002) Alcohol and drug misuse and the organization. In M. Shabracq, J.A. Winnubst and C.L. Cooper (eds), *Handbook of Work and Health Psychology* (2nd edn). Chichester: Wiley.

Lockley, P. (1995) *Counselling Heroin and Other Drug Users.* London: Free Association Books.

Maisto, S.A., Galizio, M. and Connors, G.J. (1994) *Drug Use and Abuse* (2nd edn). Orlando, FL: Harcourt Press.

Marlatt, G.A. and Gordon, J.R. (eds) (1985) *Relapse Prevention.* New York: Guilford Press.

Marsden, J., Gossop, M., Stewart, D., Best, D., Farrell, M., Lehmann, P., Edwards, C. and Strang, J. (1998) The Maudsley Addiction Profile (MAP): a brief instrument for assessing treatment outcome. *Addiction*, 93 (12): 1857–1867.

Miller, W.R. and Hester, R.K. (1989) Treating alcohol problems: toward an informed eclecticism. In R.K. Hester and W.R. Miller (eds), *Handbook of Alcoholism Treatment Approaches.* New York: Pergamon Press.

Moos, R.H., Finney, J.W. and Cronkite, R.C. (1990) *Alcoholism Treatment: Context, Process and Outcome.* New York: Oxford University Press.

Polich, J.M., Armor, D.J. and Braiker, H.B. (1981) *The Course of Alcoholism: Four Years After Treatment.* New York: Wiley.

Ramsay, M., Baker, P., Goulden, C., Sharp, C. and Sondhi, A. (2001) *Drug Misuse Declared in 2000: Results from the British Crime Survey.* Home Office Research Study 224. London: HMSO.

Rassool, G.H. (2002) *Dual Diagnosis: Substance Misuse and Psychiatric Disorders.* London: Blackwell.

6.10   Eating Problems

SHEILA RITCHIE

In a women's eating problem group, members talked about diets they had tried, organizations such as Overeaters Anonymous and favourite binge foods. The therapist spoke about the fear of leaving food and diets outside and bringing hunger into the group. One group member responded: 'If I brought my hunger in here I wouldn't just gobble up everything in this room but would have to carry on down the corridor until there was nothing left of the centre.' This graphic example encapsulates a common fear women have of displaying emotional hunger – if they did, it would be destructive and out of control. The example demonstrates the concrete connection between emotional and physiological hunger.

This section will explore similarities and differences between eating problems, consider what they might be expressing psychologically, and look at practice issues for the counsellor or psychotherapist using the metaphors of food and body size in the work. Given the prevalence of women in this client group the client will be referred to as 'she'.

The link between eating and feelings

The terms eating problem or eating disorder are misnomers. Food and eating are not the core problem but represent an attempt at a solution, albeit a destructive one – an attempt to gain control over feelings which otherwise feel unmanageable. Eating problems are about a disorder of the self, a self which is unknown, hated or feared, and about a lack of capacity to think about emotional experience.

Food and love are so merged in many cultures that it is not surprising that food and the body are turned to in an attempt to deal with emotional problems.

Eating past the point of satisfying physiological hunger or going on a diet is perhaps something we can all relate to. Few women, and increasing numbers of men, have not at some time felt a sense of dissatisfaction with their bodies. When we talk about eating problems or eating disorders we are talking about a continuum with, at one extreme, an anorexic controlling her food intake to the extent of taking her life, an excruciatingly slow suicide attempt.

We are constantly faced with life and death issues in this field. The primitive nature of our need to eat to survive creates powerful feelings. They can make otherwise benign people feel and sometimes act in a punitive, controlling way towards clients. The work can stir feelings such as, 'I wouldn't mind a bit of anorexia.' We might wonder what is going on when we start to envy someone who is starving herself to death.

Particularly disturbing is the extent to which women will intensify their use of their eating problem to the point of requiring medical intervention, on an outpatient or inpatient basis; for example, in extreme cases of bulimia nervosa potassium levels drop because of the vomiting, causing an electrolyte imbalance and risk of cardiac arrest. When an anorexic gets below a certain body mass index (see p. 403) difficult decisions have to be taken as to whether naso-gastric feeding should be introduced to keep her alive.

Why predominantly women?

While eating problems are on the increase in both men and women, and while the gap is closing, there remains a wide gender imbalance. Estimates vary widely between 1:6 and 1:201. However, the Eating

Disorders Association in 2000 used the most commonly employed ratio of 1:10 male to female. This leaves us with the question of why it might be an issue which affects women more than men. We might look at the way women are socialized, starting with their early relationship with their mothers, and how they are subsequently influenced by the culture in which they live.

This mother–daughter relationship needs to be seen in its social context. Women tend to be encouraged to feed others and become preoccupied with food, and yet receive the social message to resist food and be thin, in perpetual pursuit of the 'ideal' female form. This has become thinner over time: the buxom female form of the post-war 1950s diminished to the anorexic, androgynous super-models of the twenty-first century. This societal overvaluing of thinness creates a disproportionate fear of fat. Even pre-school-age girls and boys are preoccupied with diets and the language of fat and thin, learning to control appetite rather than allow its satisfaction.

All women are affected in this culture. Women in different social groups are affected in different ways. A black woman might feel torn between cultures if she has been raised to believe that fat is beautiful and is then surrounded by images which tell her that thin is beautiful. Minority groups such as lesbians, disabled women and black and ethnic minority women might struggle with their own acceptability and identity in the absence of positive images of themselves reflected in society. An alternative view is, however, that these women are less likely than other women to be influenced by particular images of thinness and may feel more comfortable with their bodies. Anger and distress at being forced to ingest experiences of racism or homophobia can symbolically be enacted through food and the body in attempts to gain control over difficult feelings.

What is an eating problem expressing psychologically?

All eating problems have some common features. There is a relationship in each case between the language of food and the body and the language of feelings. In the absence of an emotional language to describe feelings the actions of the eating or food refusal and control of the body are used instead. An oversimplification of the world into the concrete-ness of 'fat' and 'thin' becomes an attempt to find some certainty in an uncertain world, both externally and internally. There is a preoccupation with food. Thinking about food may be used to structure time, to fill a sense of emptiness, loneliness or despair. A fear of fat and dissatisfaction with body size is often accompanied by a distortion in body image. Women with an eating problem have lost touch with using physiological hunger as a gauge for measuring what or when to eat. The parallels between physiological hunger and emotional hunger here are clear.

An eating problem is an attempt to work through earlier developmental issues, for example the need to define a separate sense of self in relation to others, to express autonomy, rebellion. If food has been used to sort out these issues in the past it is not surprising that it is used in order to resolve later conflicts – for example, around the dinner table a child requests a particular food but a parent makes her sit at the table and finish the food she is given until she is gagging. Her struggle to express her desires gets lost in a battle over food.

Each eating problem has its own distinctive features and expresses something different psychologi-cally. One of the problems with the categorizations of eating problems is that they prove inadequate to describe the complexity of the relationship with food and the body. Each woman's unique experience needs to be acknowledged and is crucial in under-standing her conflict. Her eating problem may change over time from anorexia to bulimia or compulsive eating at a different stage of her life.

Body mass index is a tool used in medical settings to ascertain the risk of someone being grossly over-weight or underweight. This index is calculated by dividing weight in kilos by height in metres squared. For example, if you are 1.63 m tall, multiply 1.63 by 1.63 to find the square of your height (2.66); then divide your weight in kilos, for example 64 kg by 2.66. The result is 24. In the case of anorexia nervosa concern begins to be expressed at a body mass index of 18 when periods stop, an index of 13 usually brings a hospital admission and at 11 the difficult decision of whether to introduce naso-gastric feeding is made. At the other extreme, a body mass index of 31–40 indicates that someone is seriously overweight and 41+ dangerously overweight.

Anorexia nervosa

Through anorexia a woman controls her food intake and attempts to create a closed self-sufficient system where she needs no input. Anorexia nervosa literally means nervous loss of appetite but is in fact more about a control of appetite. It is an attempt to transcend the needs of the body. An anorexic woman may indeed appear quite spiritual or asexual. Although she does not feel entitled to eat and satisfy her appetite, everyone else has the right to take in food and she may be interested in feeding others.

She will create a systematic regime of eating little and surviving on less and less. She may eat a bread roll and then run up and down stairs twenty times or go to the gym to burn off the calories in compulsive over-exercise. There are many physical problems associated with anorexia, the most extreme being starving to death. Howlett et al. (1995) estimate mortality rates in anorexic women to run at 13–20 per cent per annum. When the body's percentage of body fat drops below 15 per cent a woman ceases to menstruate. If we do not eat the body goes into survival mode and develops a soft downy hair termed 'lanugo'. An anorexic experiences all kinds of gut complaints, feels the cold due to poor circulation and has an increased risk of infertility and osteoporosis.

For the anorexic, eating is associated with showing need, expressing desire and being dependent and, therefore, constitutes failure. Allowing herself to be dependent is terrifying. The paradox around dependency for the anorexic woman is that while she wants to sustain the belief that she does not need to take in anything or depend on others, she might get to a point where she is hospitalized with 24-hour care and literally have someone feed her.

Bulimia nervosa

Bulimia nervosa is an encapsulated symptom with a ritualized element. It involves bingeing, purging, either by vomiting or misuse of laxatives (sometimes as many as 100 a day) and clearing up. Sometimes foods which we might otherwise consider inedible such as raw meat or frozen food are eaten as binge foods. A bulimic woman might perform this ritual once in a while when life becomes stressful, or, on the other hand, over 20 times a day. Unlike anorexia, which is very visible, bulimia is much more secret. Some bulimic women are the 'copers' in life, managing to hold down top jobs, often in the public eye, acting as if everything is fine, but might on the way home stop off at different shops (so that the amount of food bought is not conspicuous) get home and start her bingeing ritual in secret. Estimating the incidence of bulimia nervosa is difficult because of its very hidden nature.

Turnbull et al. (1996) focused their study on GP detection of bulimia and found that GPs identified 56.7 cases per 100,000 in the 20–39 age group and 41 per 100,000 in the 10–19 age group. These figures are clearly a conservative estimate, given that there are many women who would not disclose that they are bulimic to their GP. The study suggests a fivefold increase in the incidence of bulimia nervosa over a five-year period (1988–1993). Bulimia often results in a rotting of tooth enamel; digestive problems; risk of cardiac arrest due to a decrease in potassium levels which creates an electrolyte imbalance; and period problems.

Psychologically we might understand bulimia as being in touch with feelings and the need for relationships with others but to the degree that they are overwhelming and feel destructive. The bulimia is used to control these unmanageable feelings. Through the binge destructive feelings are allowed out through the action with the food. Once the food is inside it turns 'bad' and subsequent 'bad' feelings, such as shame at having let her feelings show, come to the fore. They then have to be got rid of down the toilet. She may start the binge with something colourful so that she knows that when she sees this colour in the vomit she will have totally evacuated the contents of her stomach. Once this is complete she can flush the toilet and go to bed exhausted, or tidy her hair, or put on make-up and go out and face the world again. She might feel some temporary relief but only until the next time. The bulimia has not met the underlying need to have her feelings understood and contained within a relationship.

Compulsive eating

For a woman with a compulsive eating problem, or binge eating disorder, the problem is that she feels too much. She will binge until she is unable to feel any more, the food serving as an anaesthetic, numbing the pain. She might binge on chocolate or a loaf of bread, not tasting the food. She is unable to wait and digest food. After a meal with the family she might continue bingeing in the kitchen, finishing off the leftovers. She is unable to distinguish one feeling from another. All feelings get merged in the body in a kind of blob and might be expressed as something like 'I feel fat.' Instead of experiencing her hunger and deciding what she might want to eat, she is terrified by the space, as if it were life-threatening. She has no capacity to hold on to the prospect that her hunger could be satisfied.

She looks in the mirror or gets on the scales to decide how she feels. She swings from putting on weight to losing it, using her body boundary to define who she is. She might talk of a size 12 woman inside her size 18 body. As a punishment for bingeing she might go through periods of dieting, holding on desperately to the belief that 'if only I were thin and back down to size 12, everything would be OK. I wouldn't feel sad, depressed or angry if I were thin.' Through dieting she might reach her 'ideal' weight but is unable to sustain it. She might feel threatened by the thinness, feeling vulnerable or more sexually attractive or insubstantial. She has not been able to 'get rid of' her anger or sadness.

Compulsive eating is the most widespread of all eating problems. Medical treatment is less common, although it is on the increase.

Preparing for the work

This work can stir powerful feelings about our own hunger, eating and the body. It is useful for therapists to think about their own attitudes to food and the body before starting work with clients. This will enhance our understanding of the client's issues and allow the therapists' own bodies and hunger to be accessed in the work. If we can do this we are less at risk of either over-identifying with the client's problem or feeling unable to identify due to our own unresolved difficulty with food and the body.

Ensuring that we get adequate 'feeding' for ourselves through supervision and other support is essential. We cannot 'feed' our clients if we feel starved.

Some psychiatric or medical liaison, with the client's permission, is important with people who are at the severe end of the continuum of eating problems. Medical professionals taking care of the more physical issues can be supportive. Even if the client protests about your contacting her GP or psychiatrist there is often some relief that you can demonstrate that you will intervene if necessary. She can feel held, which may be different to an earlier experience when problems went unnoticed. Some therapists set up a specific contract about weight loss if it goes below a certain weight.

When working with larger women, practical considerations such as providing a chair which will accommodate them are important to consider. During early stages of the work a bulimic client may need access to a toilet nearby so that she can vomit.

What to offer the client

Brief focal group therapy in mixed eating problem groups or specific groups, for example for compulsive eaters or for bulimic women, can be particularly helpful. Bulimic women are able to bring their more shameful feelings into a group where others do similar disgusting things with food. These feelings can be accessed and talked about more readily than in a more general group where there is a risk that the bulimia remains hidden for some time. Many women find group therapy less threatening than individual work.

Time-limited work is often more manageable for this client group than open-ended work which often confirms a sense of being out of control. Doing a piece of work which has a defined beginning and an end can help the client develop a sense of an internal boundary, that feelings can be expressed without going on forever.

A common response to anorexic people is to offer a lot of 'feeding'. They may, however, only be able to manage a little, especially at first. By contrast, a compulsive eater may feel that what is offered is not enough. In this case it may be important to stay with what you plan to offer and work with this feeling, without offering more.

For some women who are unable to make connections between their actions with food and their feeling world, a cognitive-behavioural approach might be more useful than psychodynamic work, especially in the initial stages.

Common themes arising in the work

Perhaps the first thing we have to remember in the consulting room is that the client's prime mode of emotional relating is through food and the body. Our aim as counsellors and therapists is to help our client put into words what she is struggling to express through the action of eating or food refusal and her relationship with her body. If she says 'I feel fat' we need to help her to decode this. What exactly is she feeling: angry, sad, vulnerable? A shift needs to take place from expressing her conflicts through her eating problem to expressing them in relationship with others.

However, we need to understand that she may not be able to give up the eating problem until something else begins to take its place. Therapeutic work might exacerbate the eating problem for a while. This can be disturbing for the therapist who might begin to feel that what is being offered is making the problem worse. In the initial stages, as feelings get stirred in the work, it is usual for the client to fall back on her established way of dealing with her feelings.

Entering the woman's world and language is useful as a point of engagement. Using metaphors of food and body size can be a helpful bridge. You might as the therapist see yourself as the feeder, or the food. The session might be a meal, or a binge,

the space in the room a body to be filled with food. How the space gets used is a key indicator of the woman's difficulties in relating. The punctuation of the beginning and end of the sessions can be difficult at first for the client to manage. Maintaining clear boundaries is important in this work to help the client develop a sense of her own.

A key theme in eating problems is a difficult relationship with the first feeder, usually mother. Even if problems are associated with father, such as abandonment or sexual abuse, there is often a precursor to this in the first relationship which might have been neglectful in an under-involved way or abusive or intrusive in an over-involved way. What the client does with food and her body is often a re-creation of the early failed relationship, externalized in a concrete way with food and the body, in an attempt to control or understand it. A binge might be an attempt magically to create the ideal mother who feeds on demand and never disappoints.

As the relationship with the therapist might be operating at an almost pre-verbal level, using the feelings engendered in us by the clients – that is our counter-transference feelings – is useful.

While sitting with an anorexic woman we might feel she is unable to use the time or that we don't know how we are going to get to the end of the hour. She may try to convince us that she is coming to therapy for others or to satisfy our need. Our stomach might rumble with ravenous hunger while she gives detailed accounts of her ability to survive on less and less. We may feel bored or disconnected as if there were no connection with her. We may be forced to watch the suffering of someone wasting away while she denies there is a problem. That may be the only way she can communicate to us how she has suffered in relationships.

With a bulimic woman we might feel we are having a good session, that the client is using the space well, then something suddenly changes, the client says she doesn't think counselling will help her and we end up feeling useless. It is as if the client has binged on us then vomited up the work we have done. We might feel controlled or wrong-footed, particularly at the beginning and the end of the session, as if the client is unable to recognize the boundary of where she begins and ends.

With a compulsive eater there may be little space or silence in the session as if a binge were filling the space to prevent any feelings from being felt. We might feel drowsy and lose our capacity to think as if we too had had a binge. We might feel the client is complying with the therapy, is very grateful for the work but then she forgets to pay, showing the split-off defiance which is unable to come into the session. Towards the end of a session the client may start talking incessantly or talk of what she is going to buy to eat on the way home. She is unable to imagine what it might be like to finish the 'meal', digest the food of the session in the week then come for a feed the following session. She has to carry on bingeing as if to allow hunger would threaten her very existence.

The relationship between eating problems and sexual abuse

There is much conflicting research about the link between eating problems and sexual abuse. In clinical practice, however, it is clear that the two often coincide. Eating problems and associated self-harm may follow from sexual abuse for many reasons: most families where sexual abuse happens are disorganized, so women may have literally had very poor experiences of being fed regularly; food or sweets given by the abuser as a 'reward' might be the chocolate which is turned into a binge food. The binge is an attempt to get rid of feelings about the abuse, but also a way of keeping alive the conflict in an attempt to deal with what feels unresolvable; starving or attacking the abused body can also be an attempt to make the abuse disappear. The client may be taking control of the body boundaries which weren't able to stop the abuse or it might feel preferable to her to identify with the abuser rather than the victim part of herself through a sadistic re-enactment of the hatred of the body.

Moving to a different phase of the work

The time it takes to address an eating problem in therapeutic work will depend on many factors: how long it has been used as a way of dealing with problems; the degree of insight and motivation to change; the severity of the underlying problems which the eating problem is covering up.

Women who present early for therapy often give up the eating problem within weeks or months. When the problem is more entrenched, longer-term work is necessary. If brief focal work has been successful there is an opportunity for women to shift into more on-going general work, the shift of identity having taken place from 'I'm a bulimic' to 'I need some help because of my difficulty with relationships.'

Therapists have to sit often with difficult feelings such as not believing they are good enough or that they are doing something damaging. These are important feelings to survive so that the client is able to accept the frustration that the therapist is not ideal without totally rubbishing her; an important outcome is to know that 'good' and 'bad' emotions can coexist.

Acknowledgement

I am grateful to the ideas of the Women's Therapy Centre, London, especially those of Susie Orbach and Marilyn Lawrence, and to my clients, who have taught me so much.

References

Howlettt, M., McClelland, B. and Crisp, A.H. (1995) The cost of the illness that defies. *Postgraduate Medical Journal*, 71: 36–39.

Turnbull, S., Ward, A., Treasure, J., Jick, H. and Derby, L. (1996) The demand for Eating Disorder Care: an epidemiological study using the General Practice Research Database. *British Journal of Psychiatry*, 169: 705–712.

Recommended reading

Bloom, C., Gitter, A., Gutwill, S., Kogel, L. and Zaphiropoulos, L. (1994) *Eating Problems: A Feminist Psychoanalytic Treatment Model*. New York: Basic Books.

Lawrence, M. (1995) *The Anorexic Experience*. London: The Women's Press.

Orbach, S. (1984) *Fat Is a Feminist Issue*. London: Arrow Books.

6.11   HIV/AIDS   ○○○

BERNARD RATIGAN

The constellation of diseases that are commonly understood as Acquired Immune Deficiency Syndrome (AIDS) is believed to result from the human immune system becoming infected with a virus. It is thought that the Human Immunodeficiency Virus (HIV) enters the body either 'horizontally' from another human being, usually through sexual contact or from blood products, or 'vertically' from a pregnant mother to foetus. After sero-conversion there is usually a period when the person is apparently symptom free. Not all people with the virus go on to develop symptoms. Without pharmacotherapy it is usual for the immune system to begin failing and, with the rise in viral load, infections weaken the person's organ systems, including the brain.

In the two decades since the identification of HIV there were slow but gradual developments of anti-viral medications which, if taken in the appropriate combination and frequency, appear to be making some inroads into the previously high levels of morbidity. There is still no effective vaccine but it is now clear that, where they are available, combinations of anti-virals are often effective in helping slow or even halt disease progression. It has not yet been established why some people infected with HIV make rapid progress to symptomatic status while others appear to be relatively well up to two decades after being infected.

Throughout the world it is estimated (2004) that there are about 40 million people infected with the virus; over 90 per cent live in Africa, Asia, Latin and South America. Globally, HIV is a disease that is transmitted mainly through heterosexual penetrative vaginal sexual intercourse. In North America and Europe it has been common for the virus to be transmitted by men who have penetrative anal sex with other men. To see HIV as affecting one category of person is both scientifically wrong and dangerous in public health terms. Nevertheless, HIV in the United Kingdom was initially linked with homosexuality and, to a lesser extent, with illegal injecting drug use, both of which are stigmatized and seen as morally transgressive activities. Because of this link with morality, HIV has never been just a physical condition but has always had a number of pyramidal psychological factors that impact on the person with the virus, their partners, relatives and friends as well as those who care for them. Although the prognosis is improving, the early view that HIV was a 'death sentence' still has considerable lay resonance, even though it is no longer accurate if patients have access to appropriate medications.

Therapists working with HIV-infected clients need a good working knowledge of both the basic clinical facts about the disease and new treatments. HIV is possibly the first disease where patients' knowledge bases can be as extensive as those attempting to treat them.

Psychological interventions in HIV

From the outset HIV has attracted the attention of psychological therapists; when HIV was first identified there was little else that could be offered to patients to help them cope with a strange and probably fatal illness. The strongly negative public and sometimes private reactions to those with HIV, because of the links with transgressive activities and stigmatized groups, led to the growth of HIV counselling as a way of supporting those infected. Mention should also be made of the range of voluntary support organizations and networks which have grown up along with the AIDS pandemic and which offer psychological as well as social and practical support.

Tracing the course of the illness of the person infected with HIV, we can see the opportunity for a number of psychological interventions. Before testing takes place it should be routine to offer all clients a counselling session to help prepare them for the results of the test, whatever the outcome. Taking the test and receiving the result are activities laden with potential for emotional disturbance, yet there is a tendency for the pre-test counselling session to be saturated with information giving. Fear of HIV and AIDS is sometimes a presenting problem for clients who are sero-negative and have no history of risk. Very occasionally, this is part of a psychotic illness, but is more often part of an obsessive-compulsive disorder, best treated by cognitive-behavioural therapy in the first instance.

Adjustment reactions to having an HIV diagnosis vary with a number of factors, one of which, previous history of emotional or psychological disturbance, is probably the most significant. Those with good social support systems probably do better than those without them. There is a problem with isolates, of which there can be many, in that they find it difficult to access sources of psychosocial support. One of the tasks of the psychological therapist can be in facilitating clients with HIV to explore problems in using such services. Among the isolates who can experience special difficulties are women who have been infected by their partners, prisoners and people living in one kind of exile or other from their domiciles.

What works for whom?

HIV counselling and psychotherapy reflect the spectrum of competing modalities currently found in the psychological therapies, though in the UK there has been a preponderance of humanistic, cognitive, systemic and existential models rather than those derived from psychoanalysis. The increasing involvement of specialist psychotherapists and clinical psychologists in hospital departments of infectious diseases and genito-urinary medicine have led to theoretical and clinical developments in cognitive, systemic and psychodynamic models. It is in the large voluntary sector that humanistic and eclectic models have found their strongest advocates. This sector is often permeated with a powerful ideology of self-help, voluntarism and suspicion of hierarchy, professionalism and the homophobia believed to subsist in psychoanalytically derived therapies. To date there has been little attempt to match psychological and psychotherapeutic interventions to the needs of clients in a systematic and evidence-based format. Most formal interventions are individual, although systemic, family and group therapy interventions have all been reported in the literature.

Counter-transference

In working therapeutically with clients with HIV the role of counter-transference cannot be too heavily emphasized. Because of the combination of internal intrapsychic forces and external socio-cultural stigma, the therapist has to keep a constant watch on their own emotional responses. Having often young, frightened clients undergoing a painful illness, sometimes deprived of family and other support because of secrets and disapproval, can evoke powerful responses in the clinician. One end of the spectrum is over-identification with its risks of a loss of therapeutic neutrality and possibly burnout. Another subtler and equally damaging risk is loss of emotional rapport because the client's material resonates, negatively or positively, with that of the clinician. Here the skilled clinician can give the superficial impression of staying engaged with the client while they have moved away, consciously or unconsciously, as a form of self-protection. There are many personal and existential issues in HIV which are bound to impact on any therapist as HIV links questions of sex and death. The skill is in being able to track these counter-transference events as they happen, second by second, in the clinical dialogue. To avoid burnout, specialist supervision is strongly advised.

Interventions: what to work on?

HIV counselling and psychotherapy can bring up important technical questions of where to pitch therapeutic interventions. Having a possibly life-threatening diagnosis and a prognosis of a reduced life expectancy gives opportunities for therapeutic work. The challenge for the psychotherapist is to assess, from what the client says and how they present, the appropriate and ethical level of any interpretations that should be offered (or not) and which focus is chosen to work on. From initial post-test denial or feelings of overwhelming chaos careful work with HIV clients can assist them in helping live more creatively with what faces them. A shortened life expectancy brings opportunities as well as threats. One danger is that people with HIV can get caught up in a culture of 'positivism' where hopeless, helpless and negative feelings are not deemed 'socially correct'. A safe therapeutic space can provide a facilitating environment in which the whole gamut of emotions, especially the social-culturally 'unacceptable', can be explored.

Testing HIV positive and living with HIV can threaten anyone's psychic equilibrium, melting the glue which holds us together psychologically. The therapist is faced with a number of technical questions about focus and pacing: the 'here and now' versus the historic, the surface versus the deeper, therapist-centred versus client-centred. Because of the manner of transmission of the virus many clients value the safety of the therapeutic space to think about difficult areas of their experience, such as guilt and shame. Even for gay men who are happy with their sexuality, having grown up surrounded by homophobic attitudes can leave deep narcissistic wounds. Family reactions to learning of an HIV diagnosis can open, or re-open, many painful areas of conflict. For those with the virus who are not happy with their sexuality, or for whom their homosexual activities are a secret in an otherwise heterosexually functioning life, therapists need to assess carefully what is usefully worked on. Therapeutic tact and confidentiality is at a premium in this work. Therapeutic relationships always risk attack from powerful unconscious forces in individuals, clinical and other teams, partnerships, families and the wider society.

Ethical questions in HIV work

Among the more problematic areas that can arise in HIV counselling and psychotherapy relate to sexual activities by infected clients which pose risks to others. For some, the struggle to keep practising 'safe(r) sex' for the rest of their lives becomes too much. Protected (vaginal, anal or oral) sex may come to be experienced as second rate. Others find the excitement of unprotected 'bareback' sex thrilling. A very few, at the disturbed end of the spectrum, may wish to infect others and actually do so. For the counsellor or psychotherapist there can be tricky technical and ethical questions that need addressing in supervision and consultation. Similarly, when groups of health care professionals become aware of some of the sexual activities of their patients, their capacity to keep thinking can be seriously under attack. There may be a pressure to break confidentiality as a knee-jerk action before adequate thought has been given. Sometimes professionals may not have confidence in the psychological therapeutic process to help patients understand and manage their risky behaviours. One of the major contributions that a counsellor or psychotherapist can make in this area is to act as consultant to colleagues who are struggling with the question of how to respond to patients who are putting themselves or others at risk.

Another area of ethical concern can arise where the immigration/nationality status of the patient is problematic. A number of refugees and asylum-seekers coming to the UK come from areas of the world with high incidences of HIV infection and are themselves infected. Counsellors and psychotherapists can find themselves supporting clients who are here illegally and have no official right to free NHS treatment. Sometimes clients are in danger of being deported to countries with very poor health care resources or where their being HIV positive puts them at risk, for example gay men with HIV may be at risk of deportation to countries where homosexuals are persecuted. Careful thought always needs to be given as to the most helpful, ethical and appropriate stance to take to therapists' involvement in extra-clinical proceedings like appeals against deportation.

Boundary modifications in HIV

From a psychodynamic perspective, where the stability of the therapeutic framework is so highly valued and the exchange is a purely verbal one, HIV can pose a number of problems. Clients can become too ill physically to attend sessions: should the therapist see them in their hospital rooms or even at home? What are clearly important here are the wishes of the client and the ability of the therapist to create as near an ideal setting as possible. Hospital wards can be very busy places and seeing clients in their own homes can require skilful management of the domestic environment to ensure privacy and confidentiality is maintained. The role of touch and physical contact in therapeutic work needs to be considered in supervision. In some areas, clinicians involved in HIV work will themselves be part of affected groups; an example of this is where gay clinicians working with gay clients live and socialize in gay communities. This can raise difficult ethical and technical questions, not just for psychodynamic therapists, that need airing for the safety of both clients and clinicians and for optimum effectiveness.

Issues in late-stage HIV psychological management

Working with people with HIV in the last stages of their lives can raise profound questions for the therapist. At all stages, but especially in the latter stages, it is important to consider if the person is suffering from clinical depression and needs appropriate treatment. Similarly, there needs to be an assessment of the person's mental state to establish whether or not they are cognitively impaired and suffering from dementia. Some clients want to discuss suicide and voluntary euthanasia. The therapeutic relationship, if well grounded and firm, is able to contain these important discussions. Many clients will want a say in their physical treatments and 'Living Wills' and other advance directives are common. Where so many people with HIV belong to marginalized and stigmatized groups matters such as next-of-kin, funeral arrangements and wills can be highly problematic and create psychological battlefields between the person with the illness, their partner(s) and their families.

Conclusion

This section has reviewed some of the issues in HIV counselling and psychotherapy, especially in the UK context. In a rapidly changing treatment environment, counsellors and psychotherapists are advised to access information sources such as the *National AIDS Manual, AIDS Care* and the medical pages of the HIV and gay community freesheets.

Acknowledgement

I would like to thank John Lippitt, GAI Project, The Health Shop, Nottingham City Primary Care NHS Trust for his comments on this section in draft.

Recommended reading

Barret, B., Anderson, J. and Barret, R (2001) *Ethics in HIV-related Psychotherapy: Clinical Decision-making in Complex Cases.* New York: American Psychological Association.

Merrick, M.V. and Catalan, J. (1999) *Mental Health Problems and HIV Infection: Psychological and Psychiatric Aspects.* London: UCL Press.

6.12 Infertility

CHRISTA DRENNAN

Although infertility is a medical condition – the inability of a woman to achieve pregnancy or carry a child to term, or a man to cause pregnancy – its emotional impact is often traumatic and far-reaching. Conceiving a baby is something that many of us take for granted, yet approximately 16 per cent of couples have problems conceiving and 4 per cent of couples remain childless involuntarily.

Clients with fertility issues request counselling for a number of reasons: for support and stress management while undergoing treatment or trying to conceive; to address other issues that have arisen or have been uncovered as a consequence of having problems conceiving; to facilitate decision making when facing treatment options; or to help them to come to terms with never having children. Many people believe that their psychological state has an impact on their ability to conceive, and may use counselling or therapy to address their problems.

The psychological impact of infertility

A grieving process

Most people assume they will have a choice about whether or not to have children. The loss or potential loss of one's ability to conceive require a reappraisal of the future, and time to grieve over what may never be. It is a grief process complicated by the absence of a body to mourn, and the ritual for saying goodbye. For some women, each menstrual cycle carries some hope, and can therefore produce fresh pain and despair. Carrying hope, however small, can inhibit the grieving process, making the short term a little more bearable, and putting off the acceptance of life without children.

Relationship difficulties

Although some couples find they grow closer as they face this problem together, many find that their relationship suffers from the increased pressure. Different ways of coping for each partner can mean that communication breaks down, leaving each person looking elsewhere for support.

Isolation

All societies are pro-natalist, encouraging the view that having children is a natural and fulfilling progression in adulthood. Infertility can mean that other members of the family have potential losses to deal with, such as never having grandchildren. The intimacy of the problem and feelings of failure can mean that clients tend to isolate themselves from family and friends, and in particular from those who are pregnant or have children.

Self-blame

Many clients feel guilt about past experiences such as terminations of pregnancy, and feel that they are somehow being punished. Those who have put off having children until later in life blame themselves for not having tried earlier. It is common for people to feel that they themselves are failures when they cannot conceive.

Psycho-sexual problems

The inability to conceive can have a detrimental effect on the libido of either or both partners. Sexual problems, such as sexual avoidance or arousal disorders, may develop as a side-effect or consequence of either the diagnosis of infertility, or as a result of the intrusive nature of many of the investigations and treatments that a couple or an individual undergoes.

Fertility treatment in the UK and its impact on the client

There is not always a clear dividing line between those who choose to have children and those who don't. Some may suspect infertility, but for a wide range of reasons choose not to expose themselves to investigation. Others opt for medical intervention and fertility treatment. Recent research has shown that women undergoing fertility treatment have significantly higher levels of anxiety, have lower self-esteem and are less hopeful than their male partners.

High hopes – low success rates

Clients presenting at their GPs with at least one year's history of failed conception are likely to be offered a referral to a fertility centre for further testing and, if appropriate, treatment. In many cases subfertility, and sometimes infertility, can be resolved by surgery or by drug treatment. Other kinds of infertility are essentially incurable, and in such cases treatments circumvent the infertility rather than cure it, allowing people who are technically infertile to have children. The best known method of achieving this is via *in vitro* fertilization (IVF) – the 'test tube' method. There are new developments occurring all the time and patients in the UK are now routinely offered procedures that were not available five years ago. For about one third of those who present for medical investigations, the cause of their infertility will remain unidentified. Success rates are relatively low. Less than one-quarter of those undergoing fertility treatment ever manage to conceive. Advances in reproductive technology have raised our expectations for a successful outcome, yet more often than not these expectations are not met by reality. The client has to try to balance being realistic and having hope.

Cost of treatment

In 2004 the National Institute for Clinical Excellence (NICE) issued national guidelines for the investigation and treatment of infertility. This is a positive step towards equality, although it will take several years for all the changes to be implemented and current idiosyncratic practice to be standardized. The issue of funding for treatment remains unclear. At present, waiting lists for funded treatment are long, and different organizations apply their own eligibility criteria. Many clients are therefore faced with a choice of either self-funding or forgoing treatment altogether. Most fertility treatment centres are private, and counselling may not be included in the cost of treatment.

Personal and physical intrusion

Investigations, treatments and monitoring procedures are personally and physically intrusive. Clients often feel that their privacy has been invaded, and may find routine visits to the clinic upsetting.

Powerlessness

Both men and women can feel vulnerable and out of control when undergoing fertility treatment. The client tends to take on the traditional role of patient, with all the powerlessness that tends to accompany it. Even when the fertility problem is the male partner's, treatment is focused on the female. During treatment the male is marginalized, and has only a supporting role, which some men find difficult. In cases where donor sperm is used the male partner may feel completely redundant.

Moral and ethical dilemmas with controversial issues

Fertility treatment is a controversial subject and is often in the media. New treatments create new moral dilemmas, and many people express concern about the techniques used, and interference with the natural 'miracle' of creating life. Clients not only have to deal with their own feelings and thoughts around these controversial issues, but also the opinions of those around them and those expressed by the media.

Personal feelings of failure

Some clients feel like failures when they have not conceived after fertility treatment. It can also seem to some as if the process has an inbuilt bias towards failure, that fertility treatment creates an emotional environment detrimental to conception. Some people find the whole process so stressful, and so intrusive, that they often wonder how they will ever conceive while under such strain.

Time factors

Fertility treatment is very time-consuming. There are often long breaks between appointments and treatment cycles, and during treatment cycles there are a lot of clinic appointments, and this can cause problems for those at work. Some women do not want to tell their employers that they are trying to get pregnant, fearing discrimination. Women can also feel pressure from their own 'biological clocks'.

Testing for transmissible diseases

Some fertility units test for transmissible infections such as HIV or hepatitis, and may not treat if clients test positive. Clients who test positive then have to cope with the double shock of discovering that they have a serious illness, and being refused treatment because of it.

When to say no

It can be very difficult for the individual to know when to give up trying to conceive. It may not be their choice – treatment centres may refuse treatment for various reasons, or financial factors may play a large part. Sometimes the emotional strain of going through another attempt is too much to bear. For others, the reality that they may never have children is much harder to accept, pushing them back on to the treatment path again, repeating an exhausting cycle of hope and despair.

Ambivalent feelings

Feelings of ambivalence when treatment does result in a pregnancy, particularly if it is a multiple pregnancy, are not uncommon. Many clients find these feelings hard to voice, as if somehow they are being ungrateful and hard to please.

Ways of working with infertility

No one counselling or other therapeutic approach has been identified as the most appropriate for working with infertility, but there are some key features: grief work, psycho-sexual counselling, couple counselling and stress management.

Techniques for relaxation and stress management, such as positive visualization and guided imagery can be effective for those clients who are coping with the stresses of testing and treatment. Some counsellors use art or drama therapy to facilitate emotional expression, and to help their clients deal with difficult and sometimes overwhelming feelings.

Many clients also feel that complementary therapies, such as aromatherapy, massage, acupuncture and hypnotherapy help to manage stress and to combat negative self-appraisal.

When to refer on

There are times when it would be more appropriate for a client to see a specialized fertility counsellor. Clients who wish to pursue treatment, or who are undergoing treatment, require a counsellor with a comprehensive knowledge of treatment options, their consequences and their implications. Fertility treatment centres are obliged to provide access to specialized counselling under the licensing laws of the clinics. Knowledge of the treatment process also assists the counsellor when facilitating the decision making that arises at each stage of treatment. Fertility counsellors are able to draw from the experiences of previous clients, which may help others to prepare for the treatment and its impact.

The treatment centre the client is attending will provide access to a specialized counsellor. The

British Infertility Counselling Association (BICA) also has a list of fertility counsellors, and ISSUE, the National Fertility Association, provides telephone counselling by professionally trained staff. It may also be appropriate to refer on if psycho-sexual issues are highlighted and need addressing by a specialist, and if couple counselling is appropriate and the counsellor cannot provide this.

The role of the fertility counsellor

The Human Fertilization and Embryology Authority (HFEA), the regulating body which licenses fertility treatment centres, identifies three different 'types' of counselling to be offered by the fertility counsellor: implications, support, and therapeutic. The code of practice states that each fertility centre *must* make implications counselling available, and *should* provide support and therapeutic counselling.

Implications counselling

Implications counselling aims to 'enable the person concerned to understand the implications of the proposed course of action for themselves, for their family, and for any children born as a result' (HFEA, 1995: 31). It combines the general issues relevant to infertility with the exploration of potential social and emotional issues. This is particularly important when a couple is considering treatment using donated eggs, sperm or embryos, and many treatment centres strongly advise couples to have counselling before deciding on this course of action.

Support counselling

At various stages throughout the whole process, from diagnosis to resolution, the client may benefit from support. This can be provided by friends, family or partner, but the process is long and many people lose their support as time goes on and people get on with their own lives. Support groups, both national and local, can also help reduce isolation and provide a much needed peer group.

Therapeutic counselling

Infertility may have the effect of unmasking other psychological problems. Any number of issues can be brought to the fore by the experience of infertility. In answer to the 'Why me?' question that plagues so many, past sexual behaviour, old losses and, frequently, previous terminations of pregnancy and miscarriages are linked by the client to their infertility. Depression, anxiety, low self-esteem, cultural issues, relationships, sexuality and many other issues may be brought to the counselling session (Naish, 1994), and the counsellor may decide to refer the client to other services outside the centre.

Assessment

Fertility counsellors are obliged to consider the 'welfare of the unborn child' (HFEA, 1995) as well as that of the infertile couple. In practice this means that some sort of assessment of suitability for treatment may take place. The fertility counsellor clearly separates counselling from any kind of assessment, and defines the boundaries of confidentiality by being explicit about any way in which the 'welfare of the unborn child' clause may impact upon the client–counsellor relationship.

Sometimes, a treatment centre asks the counsellor to be part of an assessment process. People who wish to donate eggs, sperm or embryos, or who wish to become surrogates, are generally screened for suitability. If the counsellor is participating in this process, the fact that an assessment is taking place is made explicit by the counsellor. The client's motives, expectations and understanding of the physical and emotional impact on themselves and their family, are all issues that may be discussed and evaluated.

The role of the genetic counsellor

Genetic counselling aims to support people diagnosed with genetic diseases. The process is focused on helping people to understand and come to terms with the diagnosis and its implications, and enabling them, where appropriate, to reach decisions about their future. People seeking genetic counselling may be newly diagnosed, planning a family, new parents, or family members concerned that they, too, may carry a disorder. Often difficult ethical issues are raised and need to be addressed in a sensitive and supportive environment. People with a genetic disease need to reach their own decisions about planning their family, based on their own unique medical and social circumstances. Although there are recurrent themes – guilt, grief, fear – each person bestows a very personal meaning to diagnosis, and weighs the risks in terms of their own personal values. Practical issues, such as what options there might be for prevention or testing, the risk of recurrence and the implications for other members of the family, require a specialist knowledge. Genetic counsellors are usually employed as part of a wider health care team, maintaining up-to-date, detailed knowledge of genetic diseases and their impact, enabling them to provide a family with an accurate vision of its future (Kidshealth, 2004; Wellcome, 2004).

References

HFEA (1995) *Code of Practice.* Human Fertilization and Embryology Authority, Paxton House, 30 Artillery Lane, London E1 7LS.

Kidshealth (2004) Section on genetic counselling. www.kidshealth.org (Accessed May 2004).

Naish, S. (1994) *Counselling People with Infertility Problems.* Rugby: British Association for Counselling.

Wellcome (2004) Section on genetic counselling. www. wellcome.ac.uk (Accessed May 2004).

6.13   Obsessive Compulsive Disorder

TOM RICKETTS AND GILL DONOHOE

Obsessive Compulsive Disorder (OCD) is a serious mental health problem whose defining features are the presence of obsessions and/or compulsions. These features are defined and described later. Until recently, the disorder was considered to be relatively uncommon, but this appears to have been due to the large extent of under-reporting by sufferers. Over 2 per cent of the population will experience OCD at some time (Roth and Fonagy, 2005), with an average age of onset in the mid-twenties. OCD commonly has a chronic course, with untreated individuals suffering difficulties for decades. Developments in understanding, and particularly behavioural and cognitive-behavioural treatment models, have improved the prognosis for sufferers. Therefore a priority is for the early identification of sufferers, and the offering of appropriate therapy.

This section will first outline the clinical features of OCD, exploring the range of common presentations. A behavioural model will then be introduced, and the link between this model and the approaches deriving from it outlined. Research supporting the utilization of exposure and response prevention will be briefly reviewed. Finally, developments and

Table 6.13.1   Examples of obsessional thoughts and linked behaviours

Content of obsessional thought	Nature of compulsive behaviour	Avoidances	Behavioural excesses
I may have come into contact with AIDS/other contamination.	Repeated handwashing. Showering for several hours at a time.	Avoids public toilets, touching 'dirty people'.	Scanning environment for needles/condoms. Wearing gloves.
Have I made a mistake which may harm others?	Repeated checking of items in home/at work, e.g. gas taps, switches, door locks.	Avoids switching on/off high-risk items.	Repeatedly requests reassurance from others. Engages others in checking.
Sexual, aggressive or blasphemous content.	Mental neutralizing by repeated praying and efforts to 'put a good thought' in place.	Avoids being alone with children.	Scanning environment for evidence of own evil.

debates in the area of therapy of OCD will be discussed.

Clinical features

Obsessions

Obsessions are defined in the *DSM IV* (APA, 2000) as recurrent, persistent and distressing ideas, thoughts, impulses or images. These are experienced (at least at some point during the disorder) as intrusive and senseless, and do not represent excessive worries about real-life problems. The person attempts to suppress or neutralize such thoughts or impulses with another thought or action. There is a clear recognition by the individual that the obsessions are a product of their own mind, and not imposed from without. Table 6.13.1 gives some examples of obsessions.

Compulsions

Compulsions are defined as repetitive and intentional behaviours or mental acts. These are performed in response to an obsessional thought, according to idiosyncratic rules that have to be applied rigidly, and which aim to reduce distress or prevent a dreadful event or situation. However, the behaviour

is not clearly linked to an outcome, or it is clearly excessive. The act is performed with a sense of subjective compulsion, with at least initially some sense of resistance. Table 6.13.1 gives some examples of compulsions and how they link to obsessional thoughts.

Insight

In OCD there is a recognition by the individual, at least at some point during the disorder, that their obsessions are senseless or excessive, and their actions excessive. At the point of assessment there may be wide variability in the degree to which the individual recognizes the inappropriateness of the extent of their behaviour.

While the different types of obsessive compulsive presentation can usefully be outlined (as in Table 6.13.1), there is much evidence of overlap between the different types, indicating common pathways to their development.

Biochemical aspects

In a review of biological models and treatment for OCD, Steketee (1993) highlights the strong evidence for a possible genetic predisposition for OCD, but with clear indication that environmental factors must also play a large part. Efforts to find biochemical markers for OCD have proved inconclusive.

Comorbidity

OCD often co-exists with other disorders, with over 50 per cent of OCD sufferers having a lifetime risk of specific phobia, and up to 25 per cent also meeting criteria for panic disorder. OCD is commonly complicated by depression, with studies identifying depression in 28–38 per cent of OCD sufferers. However, suicidal ideation or attempts among clients with OCD is reported to be rare. Despite claims in the past that OCD represented a pre-psychotic state, comorbidity with psychosis is rare, and the transformation of non-delusional symptoms during treatment into delusional ones is also uncommon (Steketee, 1993).

Understanding OCD

Behavioural models of OCD have been very helpful in enabling effective treatments to be developed. Figure 6.13.1 shows a behavioural model.

Within the model, intrusive thoughts are viewed as normal phenomena which, due to repeated association with fear-inducing stimuli, have become fear-inducing themselves. This fear is neutralized through the undertaking of voluntary behaviours (compulsions), either overt or covert, to prevent harm ensuing. For example, an obsessional thought regarding being responsible for harm coming to others through carelessness, may be followed by a checking behaviour. The undertaking of compulsive behaviours has a number of effects. First, it prevents the anxiety associated with the intrusive thought spontaneously reducing, a process termed extinction. Second, it increases the perceived importance of the intrusive thought. Because the thought is acted upon, the range of situations that will trigger it are increased, and it occurs more often. Third, as the compulsive behaviours are followed by a reduction in anxiety, they are more likely to occur again in similar situations. For example, an obsessional thought about having come into contact with AIDS may initially only occur where sexual activity by

others is suspected. Where the individual repeatedly responds to the thought by washing themselves thoroughly, an increasing range of situations come to be associated with the perceived contamination risk. Eventually, touching door handles, stains on clothes, or even being in the same room with others may be sufficient to trigger the obsessional thought, with the individual responding by repeated handwashing or other extensive decontamination activities.

In contrast, if the obsessional thought, discomfort and urge to engage in the compulsive behaviour are provoked but the individual refrains from carrying out the behaviour, the urge and discomfort will dissipate naturally, but more slowly than if the urges had been acted upon. With repeated induction there is a cumulative effect, with progressively less discomfort, less urge to engage in the compulsive behaviour, and progressively more rapid reduction in the urge to do so.

The process through which intrusive thoughts come to elicit anxiety and discomfort is the subject of some debate, with acquisition through a process of classical conditioning not finding general support (Jones and Menzies, 1997). However, the model of the maintenance of OCD has proved clinically fruitful, particularly in underpinning exposure and response prevention, which remains the treatment of choice, and is explained in the next section.

Therapy

Assessment

Assessment of OCD is similar to that for other disorders in that the aim is to obtain as full a picture as possible, utilizing a range of data collection techniques. Assessment is guided by the model, so that at the end of assessment a clear formulation of the development and maintenance of the disorder is possible, this being the basis of the individualized therapeutic plan. Data collection techniques include clinical interviews, self-monitoring of thoughts, emotions and behaviour, and, where possible, direct observation of the client undertaking their compulsive behaviours.

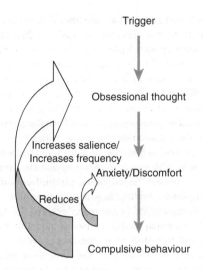

Trigger

Obsessional thought

Increases salience/
Increases frequency

Anxiety/Discomfort

Reduces

Compulsive behaviour

Figure 6.13.1 A behavioural model of OCD

Client education

Prior to undertaking exposure and response prevention the client is informed of the outcome of the assessment, as a means of making sense of symptoms that they may previously have found incomprehensible. They are also informed about the beneficial impact of experiencing obsessional thoughts in the absence of undertaking compulsive behaviours. This process should enable them to understand the rationale for the therapeutic plan, and enhance the collaborative relationship with the therapist. As they will be undertaking what may be frightening procedures it is important that they understand the purpose and process of therapy.

Exposure and response prevention

The key elements of exposure and response prevention are that the client is enabled to re-enter previously avoided situations while resisting the urge to undertake behaviours which would rapidly reduce subjective discomfort. This process is most effective when the exposure tasks are challenging but achievable, when the tasks are undertaken for an hour or

more, and on a daily basis if possible. Specifics are as follows:

- A list of trigger situations/tasks is developed with the client, and graded according to difficulty. Tasks to be undertaken with the therapist should be as difficult as the client is willing to undertake. Working with the therapist initially, the client is enabled to engage in contact with the previously avoided triggers, for instance holding an item considered contaminated, for a prolonged period, preferably over an hour. Where possible, the perceived extent of exposure should be maximized by such behaviours as touching other items, face, hair with hands considered contaminated. Throughout exposure, the urge to undertake the compulsive behaviour should be monitored, while the client is assisted not to undertake the behaviour. This subjective urge or discomfort should have reduced substantially (by at least 50 per cent) before the exposure session is terminated.
- A high frequency of exposure sessions is associated with more rapid processing of fear. In practice, the implications of this are that enabling clients to undertake self-managed exposure with response prevention between therapy sessions is essential. Encouraging the client to repeat what has been achieved within the therapy session is often sufficient, but clear written guidance is helpful.
- Therapist modelling of the desired behaviour prior to the client undertaking it increases client compliance and speeds up the process of exposure. Specific messages about the therapist not asking the client to do anything they would not do themselves should be given, with emphasis on a collaborative approach. Care should be taken to ensure that therapist involvement does not become a subtle form of reassurance for the client.

Medical treatment

Antidepressant medications have been utilized in the treatment of OCD. In a meta-analysis of drug studies, Ackerman and Greenland (2002) identify clear evidence for the effectiveness of clomipramine and other serotonergic compounds such as fluoxetine and fluvoxamine, with continuing evidence for the superiority of clomipramine. The combining of medication with exposure and response prevention appears to convey few additional benefits over exposure and response prevention alone, unless there is comorbidity between OCD and depression (Roth and Fonagy, 2005).

Research

In a meta-analysis of multiple randomized controlled trials, Abramowitz (1997) identified that exposure with response prevention was as effective as serotonergic medications. In a review of 20 studies, Steketee and Cleere (1990) identified that an average of 85.8 per cent of clients who accepted and complied with treatment were rated as improved or much improved (range 67–98 per cent). At follow-up, gains were well maintained, with 77.8 per cent of clients retaining this rating. They concluded that exposure and response prevention could be considered the treatment of choice for OCD.

Results from certain sub-groups of clients, however, are less impressive. First, there are problems with clients who do not undertake overt rituals. Second, there are those clients who regard their obsessions as rational, and therefore are likely to be highly resistant to the application of exposure strategies.

For the first sub-group, it has been proposed that the lack of overt rituals be understood as indicating the existence of covert compulsive behaviours, such as repeated praying, as in the third example in Table 6.13.1. One means by which clients can be exposed to their obsessional thoughts while being enabled to prevent covert compulsive behaviours is via the use of audiotaped exposure. The contents of the obsessional thought are recorded on a loop tape and listened to continuously until the urge to undertake a compulsive behaviour has reduced substantially, thereby preventing the behaviour from occurring. Evidence for the efficacy of this approach is still in the form of case studies.

For the second sub-group, cognitive procedures, aimed primarily at altering negative automatic thoughts, have been proposed. The focus is on thoughts evaluating the content of the obsessions, rather than the obsessions themselves, with the aim of reducing the belief in the accuracy of predicted outcomes, and thereby enabling the client to engage in exposure tasks. Studies investigating this approach indicate that cognitive therapy along these lines can be as effective as exposure and response prevention (Van Oppen et al., 1995).

Debates in the field

The major debates regarding psychological treatment for OCD currently centre on the extent to which cognitive-behavioural models and procedures will show additional benefits over the known efficacy of exposure and response prevention, and the development of self-management approaches.

Salkovskis (1985) and, more recently, Rachman (1997) have proposed cognitive-behavioural models regarding the nature of obsessions and compulsions. These models emphasize the importance of negative automatic thoughts appraising the existence and content of obsessional thoughts. Particular emphasis is given to beliefs regarding responsibility or blame for harm to self or others. The models have led to treatments focusing on enabling clients to alter perceived threat and responsibility beliefs. Although the models appear credible, treatment effects over and above those to be expected from the application of exposure and response prevention alone have not been shown at the time of writing (van Oppen et al., 1995).

Self-management approaches to anxiety disorders and their application to OCD have been the subject of debate. To date there is only limited evidence of the effectiveness of such approaches, but given the importance of widening access to known effective approaches, further work can be expected on both manual-aided and computer-delivered approaches (Greist et al., 2002).

References

Abramowitz, J.S. (1997) Effectiveness of psychological and pharmacological treatments for obsessive-compulsive disorder: a quantitative review. *Journal of Consulting and Clinical Psychology*, 65: 44–52.

Ackerman, D.L. and Greenland, S. (2002) Multivariate meta-analysis of controlled drug studies for obsessive-compulsive disorder. *Journal of Clinical Psychopharmacology*, 22: 309–317.

APA (2000) *Diagnostic and Statistical Manual of Mental Disorders* (4th edn, text revision). Washington, DC: American Psychiatric Association.

Greist, J.H., Marks, I.M., Baer, L. et al. (2002) Behaviour therapy for obsessive compulsive disorder guided by a computer or by a clinician compared with relaxation as a control. *Journal of Clinical Psychiatry*, 63: 138–145.

Jones, M.K. and Menzies, R.G. (1997) The relevance of associative learning pathways in the development of obsessive-compulsive washing. *Behaviour Research and Therapy*, 36: 273–283.

Rachman, S. (1997) A cognitive theory of obsessions. *Behaviour Research and Therapy*, 35: 793–802.

Roth, A. and Fonagy, P. (2005) *What Works for Whom? A Critical Review of Psychotherapy Research* (2nd edn). New York: Guilford Press.

Salkovskis, P.M. (1985) Obsessive-compulsive problems: a cognitive-behavioural analysis. *Behaviour Research and Therapy*, 25: 571–583.

Steketee, G.S. (1993) *Treatment of Obsessive Compulsive Disorder*. New York: Guilford Press.

Steketee, G. and Cleere, L. (1990) Obsessional-compulsive disorders. In A.S. Bellack et al. (eds), *International Handbook of Behavior Modification and Therapy*. New York: Plenum.

Van Oppen, P., de Haan, E., Van Balkom, A.J.L.M., Spinhoven, P., Hoogduin, K. and Van Dyck, R. (1995) Cognitive therapy and exposure in vivo in the treatment of obsessive compulsive disorder. *Behaviour Research and Therapy*, 33: 379–390.

6.14 Personality Disorders

LINDA GASK

Personality disorders are difficult to define and it is not easy to decide where normal personality changes into a personality problem and this then becomes serious enough to be labelled as a personality disorder. The World Health Organization defines personality disorders as:

> Deeply ingrained and enduring behaviour patterns manifesting themselves as inflexible responses to a broad range of personal and social situations. They represent either extreme or significant deviations from the way the average individual in a given culture perceives, thinks, feels and particularly relates to others. Such behaviour patterns tend to be stable and become multiple domains of behaviour and social functioning. They are frequently, but not always, associated with various degrees of subjective distress and problems in social functioning and social performance. (WHO, 1992)

Personality tends to be stable over time and disorders are usually recognizable in adolescence or early adult life and persist into middle age, when they generally seem to become less obvious – although this is not always the case, as people who work with the elderly will recognize. Psychiatrists have spent many years inventing (and failing to agree on) categorical labels for abnormal personalities but people

Table 6.14.1   A typology of personality disorders

Affective	Lifelong abnormality of mood which may be depressive, elated, changing from one to the other (cyclothymic).
Anti-social	Commonly called 'psychopaths' or 'sociopaths'. Anti-social behaviour with absence of conscience, inability to learn from mistakes, and a long history of disturbance and often violence problems with the law. Often described as superficially very charming and 'plausible'.
Avoidant	Also called anxious. Hypersensitive, timid, self-conscious.
Borderline	Instability of mood, interpersonal relationships and self-imaging.
Dependent	Inability to cope with normal demands. Submissive, helpless.
Depressive	Lifelong depressive temperament (can be confused with or co-exist with depressive illness).
Explosive	Uncontrollable outbursts of aggression, physical or verbal but not otherwise anti-social.
Histrionic	Sometimes called 'hysterical'. Demanding and attention seeking, emotionally shallow, dramatic, egocentric (often an abusive label applied without due grounds to difficult female patients by male doctors).
Narcissistic	Grandiose, self-important, hypersensitive to the evaluation of others.
Obsessional	Rigid, compulsive, inflexible and perfectionist. Also called 'anankastic'.
Paranoid	Sensitive, suspicious and may be jealous. Often litigious.
Passive/Aggressive	Passive resistance to demands for adequate social and occupational performance. Sulky, resentful, avoids obligations.
Schizoid	Withdrawn, introspective and detached. Indifference to social relationships. Restricted range of emotional experience and expression.
Schizotypal	Isolated, eccentric ideas.

rarely fit one exactly, and these labels should be used with some caution. A typology of the more commonly used terms can be found above (Table 6.14.1).

In practice most people, normal or abnormal, possess a number of different traits rather than easily fitting into one category, and there are probably many more varieties of abnormal personality than the classical 'types' described above. Some use the term 'character disorder' to describe a constellation of personality traits which may cause conscious distress to clients and those close to them but which does not warrant the frankly more pejorative term 'personality disorder'. The categorical approach has also been criticized by psychologists such as Hans Eysenck who described three dimensions (extroversion, neuroticism and psychoticism) which he in turn derived from the writings of Jung. A client can be plotted graphically on each of these dimensions. This approach may be more accurate but it can still be difficult to decide where the cut-off point lies between normal and pathological.

Risks

The diagnosis of personality disorder is highly stigmatizing and often leads to rejection from mainstream mental health services, when, with support and effective therapy, many people can make significant changes to the way that they cope with life stresses and relationships (NIMHE, 2003).

The presence of a personality disorder does not preclude the additional development of mental illness. Alternatively, some clients may demonstrate some of the features of a personality disorder when they have in fact developed a mental illness although no such signs were apparent before the onset of the illness. Here 'illness' is taken to mean onset of a range of symptoms such as thoughts, feelings and behaviours that have a clear and distinct point of onset and are severe enough to cause distress and interfere with everyday functioning. Clients with features of borderline personality disorder (see Table 6.14.2) may be particularly challenging and their problems

Table 6.14.2 Criteria for borderline personality disorder

Five or more of the following:

- Constantly attempts to avoid real or imagined abandonment.
- Unstable and intense relationships which tend to alternate between idealization and devaluation.
- Unstable self-image or sense of self.
- Impulsivity (spending, sex, substance abuse, reckless driving, binge-eating).
- Recurrent threats or episodes of deliberate self-harm.
- Instability of mood: rapidly changing in response to external events.
- Chronic feelings of emptiness.
- Intense anger and difficulty controlling anger.
- Brief psychotic episodes (losing touch with reality) when under stress.

Source: Adapted from *DSM IV* criteria (APA, 2000)

may not always become apparent until a therapeutic contract has commenced. More has been written about this disorder than about any other. Clients may superficially cope well in day-to-day life but later begin to disintegrate more overtly. Clients with personality disorders can generate strong and often negative emotions not just among those who are close to them and their therapists but also in other caring professionals who have been drawn into dealing with a crisis, and even members of the criminal justice system. Those involved in care may be implored to 'do something' when it is in fact not possible to save clients, who are unable to change, from themselves. It is crucially important for a therapist to utilize supervision fully in exploring the range of feelings, from a desire to rescue, to rage and even fear, which may be engendered within the counter-transference.

Epidemiology

Epidemiological studies vary considerably in their estimates of how common personality disorders are in the population. Before 1970 there were few reliable definitions that researchers could agree on but recent studies suggest that around 13 per cent of people drawn from a GP list, and predominantly in inner cities, will meet modern criteria. Among people who deliberately harm themselves, numbers may be as high as 50 per cent. Common categories to be found among such clients are 'borderline',

'anti-social' or 'explosive'. It is not surprising that estimates of the prison population suggest a high proportion (up to 75 per cent) of people with personality disorder, particularly those who are 'anti-social'.

Personality disorders are also common in clients who have received psychiatric out-patient treatment (often in combination with a diagnosis of mental illness or an alcohol or drug problem). The association between eating disorder and personality disorder is well recognized. In its severe form, bulimia may co-exist with anti-social, borderline, histrionic or narcissistic traits and such clients may not just binge and vomit, but deliberately harm themselves in other ways, including abuse of alcohol, drugs, taking overdoses and cutting. In contrast, anorexic clients may demonstrate more 'avoidant' features and be withdrawn. Depression and anxiety are common in people who have personality difficulties (indeed, the life problems that lead to depression may be caused by their problems in personal relationships). There is also a well-recognized link between the presence of personality disorder and alcohol and drug problems.

Aetiology

Information here is limited. The clearest evidence for genetic links seems to be for people with anti-social and schizotypal personality disorders, but personality traits are probably generally subject to hereditary influences. It may be that early experience in the family interacts with these inherited traits to exaggerate (or suppress) the development of more pronounced abnormal personality traits in adult life. Psychoanalysts have focused on early relationships with the mother, but rejection, violence and abuse by parents may all lead to personality difficulties (and also contribute to the development of mental illness) later. Personality change can come about after extremely stressful experiences and can also occur as a result of physical changes to the brain ('organic brain disease'), such as caused by a head injury, dementia, bleeding into the brain from an aneurysm (a weakness in the wall of a blood vessel) or brain tumour.

Treatments

Personality disorder used to be considered untreatable, at least by most mainstream psychiatrists. This is not always easy for the general public to understand as they see a person, who is suffering and/or causing suffering to others, as clearly 'crazy' and 'should be helped'. However, this person may either not be able to accept such help or have the capacity to change.

Psychotherapy

This is the treatment of choice and may take different forms. Psychotherapists and some counsellors have always been willing and interested to treat people with personality difficulties but often unwilling to take on for therapy those who are very disturbed. This has often been a source of conflict between professionals. Change is often very difficult to achieve, if at all, and may take many years.

A psychotherapist will first carry out an assessment to check out whether or she feels that the client is able to work within his or her chosen paradigm, be it psychoanalytic (individual or group), cognitive-behavioural (Beck et al., 1990; Linehan, 1993) or cognitive analytic (CAT; Ryle, 1997). Clients who are unable to work effectively within any of these models of therapy may benefit from a supportive relationship over a prolonged period of time with an interested and psychodynamically informed health professional with access to supervision. Many general psychiatrists, psychiatric nurses and even some general practitioners do this. Research evidence is limited but recent work suggests that CAT may be promising, even over a relatively brief period, and also with borderline clients (Ryle, 1997).

Medication

Some people with problems sufficient to render them psychiatric outpatients or inpatients are prescribed small doses of major tranquillizers. There is research evidence that this seems to be helpful. Antidepressants are often used to treat co-existent depressive illness but recently some research has suggested that they (particularly newer ones such as Prozac) may be effective in longer-lasting 'depressive' personality clients and if given over long periods and in people with borderline personality disorders. The benzodiazepines (such as Valium (diazepam) and Ativan (Lorazepam)) have been widely given in the past but almost certainly make matters worse, lessening ability to exercise self-control and encouraging dependence. Any type of medication brings with it the problem of risk of self-harm in overdose but the newer antidepressants and major tranquillizers are relatively safe. Some psychotherapists are unwilling to treat clients who are taking medication but in general any therapist who has extensive experience of working in this area will recognize that sometimes this simply cannot be avoided.

Outcome

Personality tends to be stable over time. There is evidence from research for an increased risk from homicide, accidents and the complications of substance misuse in anti-social personalities, and of violent death among those with criminal tendencies, but some do seem to stop indulging in criminal behaviour and apparently mature as they get older. Between 3 and 8 per cent of borderline clients will commit suicide. Some personality traits and associated character disorders (anti-social, borderline, explosive) seem to become less common with increasing age while others (obsessional) become more common.

Debates

The concept of personality disorder creates a conundrum for the clinician and does not sit easily within the medical model. Many psychiatrists consider that if a client does not have 'mental illness' *per se*, he or she does not warrant medical intervention. Nevertheless, people with the diagnosis of personality disorder both suffer and cause a good deal of pain and distress to others, not to say harm in the case of those who exhibit psychopathic traits. It is simpler to think of people as either 'mad' and 'ill' and, as such, worthy of care and 'bad' or 'personality disordered' and not worthy of care or mitigation under law – but the truth is probably much more complex than this. The debate about the 'treatability' of people with personality disorder has been further fuelled in England with the likely inclusion of a new diagnostic category – 'dangerous severe personality disorder' – within the revised mental health legislation.

Undoubtedly, many people with severe personality disorders may be difficult or impossible to treat, but there are many with less severe problems who do not deserve our rejection. Such people commonly present in primary care settings with 'stress', social problems or interpersonal conflicts represented by symptoms such as anxiety, depression or substance misuse. Beneath these presenting problems there frequently lie long-standing and deeply ingrained patterns of maladaptive thinking, feeling and behaviour. Understanding the way that these traits are likely to affect the therapeutic process, even if no major attempt is made within therapy to challenge underlying defences, is essential if any form of treatment, psychological or pharmacological, is likely to be successful.

References

APA (2000) *Diagnostic and Statistical Manual of Mental Disorders* (4th edn). Washington, DC: American Psychiatric Association.

Beck, A.T., Freeman, A. and Emery, G. (1990) *Cognitive Therapy of Personality Disorders.* New York: Guilford Press.

Linehan, M.M. (1993) *Cognitive-behavioural Treatment of Borderline Personality Disorder.* New York: Guilford Press.

NIMHE (National Institute of Mental Health for England) (2003) *Breaking the Cycle of Rejection: The Personality Disorder Capabilities Framework.* Leeds: Department of Health.

WHO (1992) *International Classification of Diseases and Related Health Problems* (10th edn). Geneva: World Health Organization.

Ryle, A. (1997) *Cognitive Analytic Therapy and Borderline Personality Disorder: The Model and the Method.* Chichester: John Wiley.

6.15 Phobias

GILL DONOHOE AND TOM RICKETTS

A phobia can be described as a marked and persistent fear that is excessive or unreasonable, cued by the presence or anticipation of a specific object or situation (APA, 2000). There is a strong desire to avoid the feared situation despite a recognition, when the phobic stimulus is not present, that the fear is irrational.

Table 6.15.1 Epidemiological data

Phobic disorder	Prevalence (lifetime risk)	Onset/course	Gender/distribution
Specific phobia	7.2–11.3 per cent	Childhood	Depends upon sub-type but generally higher proportion of women
Agoraphobia	1–2 per cent (panic with or without agoraphobia) of whom one-third to one-half with panic disorder also have agoraphobia (with higher rates in clinical samples)	Late adolescence to mid-thirties (agoraphobia usually within first year of panics)	Three times more frequent in women (panic without agoraphobia twice as frequent)
Social phobia	3–13 per cent	Mid to late teens	More frequent in women in epidemiological samples but equal in clinical samples

Source: APA (2000)

Phobic disorders can be broadly categorized into three main groups: specific phobias, agoraphobia and social phobia. Although in theory an individual can become phobic about any stimulus, and rare cases do exist, the list of five categories for specific phobias, as indicated later, addresses all types seen in clinical practice.

The aims of this section are to introduce readers to the various phobic disorders, focusing upon shared and specific clinical features and to provide a conceptual base for understanding phobias by outlining key theories. The main treatment approaches will be outlined with an emphasis on cognitive-behavioural methods, as indicated by research and current clinical practice. Recent advances and on-going debates in the field will conclude this section.

Description and clinical features

Phobic disorders all share the central feature of anxiety, which is experienced in anticipation of and/or upon confrontation with the feared situation or stimulus. Anxiety responses are intense and extreme and can present in the form of panic. Although symptoms are often negligible when the feared objects or situations are not encountered, some anxiety may occur at other times, for example in association with anticipation of confrontation. In addition, it is common for individuals with a phobic disorder to have at least one other anxiety disorder, with generalized anxiety being particularly common (Roth and Fonagy, 2005).

Individuals with phobic disorders may also experience panic attacks. These may only occur when faced with the phobic situation, and are referred to as situationally bound panic attacks. Panic attacks are more common in the case of agoraphobia, where they are often a central feature. Reference will therefore be made to panic attacks in this section although for a more comprehensive account readers should refer to the specific section on anxiety and panic.

In order to satisfy diagnostic criteria for a phobic disorder, the individual must experience difficulties carrying out daily activities impacting on the domestic, personal, occupational and relationship areas of their lives. If the person is able to avoid the feared stimulus, for example, in the case of snakes or plane travel, then treatment may not be warranted or sought.

Individuals with phobic conditions commonly suffer difficulties for many years, with little evidence of spontaneous remission. At the same time with current behavioural and cognitive-behavioural approaches, they are readily treated. Identification and the offer of intervention for sufferers is therefore a priority. Table 6.15.1 gives details of the prevalence, course and gender distributions of the different types of phobic disorder.

Specific phobias

Specific phobias have in the past been referred to as simple phobias as the fear is confined to one main stimulus. Specific phobias can be further categorized according to the following types:

- animal type, including mammals, insects and reptiles
- natural environment type, for example storms, water, heights
- blood/injection/injury type
- situational type, for example, airplanes, lifts
- other type, for example, illness, choking or vomiting (APA, 2000).

In the case of specific phobias, the extreme fear is experienced immediately upon contact with the feared stimulus and is usually proportionate to the proximity.

The symptoms of anxiety experienced upon anticipation or actual contact with the phobic stimulus include the usual range of autonomic symptoms. However, the pattern of arousal seems to differ in one particular type of specific phobia, namely, blood/injection/injury. These individual sufferers commonly experience a vasovagal response whereby the blood pressure may rise as usual initially, but then drops rapidly causing a fainting response. It has been suggested that approximately 75 per cent of individuals with blood/injection/injury phobias report a history of fainting in phobic conditions (APA, 2000).

Agoraphobia

Agoraphobia is a complex phobia as it involves a wide range of feared situations. Anxiety symptoms occur on entering a variety of public situations, for example, crowded places such as shops, queues, public transport; open spaces; confined places and any situations from which escape may be difficult or embarrassing and help unavailable. Distance from home or other places of safety and being alone are often key factors.

Agoraphobia appears to be closely linked to panic and this is reflected in diagnostic manuals (APA, 2000) which make the classification of 'panic disorder with or without agoraphobia'.

Panic attacks are characterized by the sudden onset of intense symptoms along with fears associated with the symptoms, for example, of dying or losing control. Symptoms include palpitations, sweating, trembling or shaking, shortness of breath or choking sensations, dizziness or feeling faint, numbness or tingling sensations, de-realization (feelings of unreality) or de-personalization (feeling detached from self). The experience of at least four of these symptoms is required to meet the diagnostic criteria (APA, 2000).

Social phobia

Social phobia is another more complex type of phobia although some individuals present with more specific social fears. Although triggered by social interaction, the nature of the fear is associated with prediction of less observable events, such as being rejected or viewed negatively by others. Specific fears may include public speaking or eating in public.

Understanding phobias

There has been, and remains, much debate about how and why phobias develop. Although one single theory does not appear to account for the acquisition and maintenance of all phobias, most of the progress in understanding has arisen from conditioning and learning theory accounts. Learning theories suggest that emotional responses such as fear can be learnt in a similar way to other aspects of human development.

The learning theory of phobias incorporates the principles of classical and operant conditioning. Pavlov and other Russian physiologists conducted animal experiments in the early to mid-part of the last century which demonstrated that dogs, for example, could be conditioned to salivate at the sound of a bell. Hence, it was shown that by repeatedly pairing food (an unconditioned stimulus) with the sound of a bell, this eventually became a conditioned stimulus resulting in salivation (conditioned response) even in the absence of food. Thus the principles are based upon the notion that previously neutral stimuli can develop stimulating properties and provoke new responses if repeatedly presented with another stimulus. In the case of phobias, the new or conditioned response is fear.

The second learning principle is based upon operant conditioning whereby learning is dependent upon the consequences following the behaviour. For example, if a behaviour is rewarded, then it is more likely to occur in the future. Similarly, a behaviour which is followed by the removal of something the individual finds unpleasant is also rewarded, and also more likely to occur again in future. These examples are termed positive and negative reinforcement respectively.

In applying these principles to the development and maintenance of phobias, they can be understood to be acquired through the process of classical conditioning and maintained by the effects of negative reinforcement, specifically the rapid reduction of anxiety which follows escape from or avoidance of the phobic situation.

To acquire a phobia through the above process, the individual must experience and associate traumatic or aversive stimuli with the phobic object until the latter develops these properties. While this is reportedly the case for many individuals suffering from phobias, there are cases where such conditioning events have not occurred. This has prompted the suggestion that phobic anxiety may also arise simply through the observation of fearful others, or through being told about potentially fear-invoking stimuli or circumstances. This 'three pathways to fear' model (Rachman, 1977) has found good empirical support, suggesting that the acquisition of phobic anxiety may come about through multiple routes.

Maintenance of phobias through negative reinforcement of escape and avoidance is best understood as preventing the spontaneous reduction of fear. In the absence of escape and avoidance, repeated contact with the phobic situation reduces the link between the situation and fear. After repeated contact, the previously fearful stimuli become neutral, no longer triggering an anxiety response.

Therapy

Research studies and reviews on the effectiveness of therapies for phobic disorders have found exposure therapy to be the primary treatment of choice with the incorporation of cognitive approaches and other strategies such as applied relaxation in some cases (see below). There seems to be no indication and little evidence for the use of non-directive counselling approaches or for the use of medication as the main approach (Roth and Fonagy, 2005).

Treatment is based upon a detailed assessment and analysis of the presenting difficulty along with any other associated problems. This includes a history of the development of the problem. The assessment information is then discussed with the client within a cognitive-behavioural framework. This forms the first stage of therapy, the main purpose of which is to educate the client on the principles of the approach and the rationale for the treatment plan based upon their difficulties.

Exposure therapy

Exposure therapy involves repeated, prolonged confrontation with the feared stimuli until the discomfort reduces and is no longer evoked by further contact. Exposure therapy should be *in vivo* (live) wherever possible and also should be graded, prolonged and repeated regularly (Marks, 1981). To achieve this, exposure tasks should be practised by the client as homework, either with or without the help of a partner or spouse.

The components of exposure can be summarized as follows:

1. *Education and instruction on the nature and principles of exposure therapy.* As homework practice is essential for successful therapy, the client's full understanding and active involvement is required. The therapist must enable the client to be their own therapist, giving them all the tools and knowledge available.
2. *Construction of a hierarchy for graded tasks.* This should be negotiated with the client based on agreed overall goals and assessment outcome. The hierarchy should represent the range of phobic and avoided situations in order of difficulty. Each situation can be rated according to the anxiety evoked or degree of avoidance (for example, on a 0–8 scale). Each step should be practical and realistic with equal spacing between steps where possible.
3. *Exposure tasks.* Exposure therapy may be therapist-assisted or self-directed. It can be conducted in a group or with a friend or spouse. If therapist-assisted exposure is the chosen method, it is important to consider the effects of the therapist's (or relevant others') presence and plan to phase this out. Ultimately, the client must be able to manage phobic situations alone and not have to depend on the presence of others.

   Whether alone or accompanied, within each session, the client monitors his/her level of anxiety and remains within the situation until this has reduced (at least 2 points on a 0–8 scale). The client is encouraged to focus upon the phobic object (e.g. spider) or the situation (e.g. supermarket) rather than distract themselves.

   The client may refer to other strategies if utilized, for example, applied relaxation or helpful self-talk (see below).
4. *Homework tasks.* If the exposure task has been conducted within a treatment session, whether accompanied or alone, this should be followed by further practice, which must be specified and agreed between client and therapist along with any relevant others. It is preferable that the task is based upon that which has already been completed so that the client can consolidate their learning.

Additional and alternative strategies

Although some form of exposure therapy should be the first treatment of choice in the majority of cases, some individuals and types of phobia may require additional strategies or a focus on cognitive approaches.

Applied tension

Individuals with blood/injury/illness phobias frequently experience fainting when presented with blood- or injury-associated stimuli due to the unique physiological response. Applied tension is a technique developed specifically for these individuals in order to control the fainting response and is therefore used in conjunction with exposure therapy. Individuals are taught to tense key muscle groups which in turn increases cerebral blood flow and helps to control fainting (see Ost and Sterner, 1987).

Applied relaxation

This is a form of relaxation therapy developed by Ost (1987) and seems to be the method which is the most effective and practical for phobic clients. The method can be taught to clients so that relaxation can be applied rapidly and in conjunction with exposure situations.

Cognitive therapy

Cognitive factors are clearly implicated in the maintenance of certain phobias and in the case of panic and social phobias, specific cognitive models have been developed (Clark and Fairburn, 1997). Whether cognitive approaches are superior or enhance traditional exposure therapy programmes for phobias has been the focus of research but so far real benefit has only been shown in the case of social phobia. Cognitive therapy has demonstrated significant benefits for depression (see Beck et al., 1979) and therefore should be considered if this is a major difficulty.

Cognitive strategies, as initially developed by Beck, focus upon identification and modification of faulty thinking styles by a variety of means, including verbal disputation and behavioural experimentation. For further reading, see Beck et al. (1979) and Wells (1997).

Skills training

Social skills and assertiveness training approaches may have an important role to play, particularly in the case of social phobia. Social skill deficits often accompany social phobic difficulties, therefore skill levels should be assessed and training approaches used if appropriate. Skills training may incorporate education, modelling, role play and rehearsal of specific skills, feedback and real-life practice.

Drug treatment

Antidepressant and anxiolytic drugs have been utilized although they have only demonstrated short-term benefits and have not been found to be superior to behavioural therapy programmes. Medication is certainly not indicated for specific phobias and most of the research has focused upon agoraphobia. This research has found that medication is not as effective as cognitive-behavioural approaches and relapse is more likely. There is some suggestion, however, that antidepressants may have some slight benefits when combined with psychological methods (Roth and Fonagy, 2005).

Advances and debates

The efficacy of exposure-based approaches is well established, but there is increasing recognition of the insufficiency of conditioning theories alone to explain fear processes (Clark and Fairburn, 1997; Rachman, 1977). Developments in cognitive psychology and cognitive therapy have led to models and interventions to help clients who have not benefited from purely exposure-based methods. In practice, the majority of clinicians now claim to be utilizing

cognitive-behavioural methods demonstrating how well these approaches have been integrated. However, research is still required to determine which aspects of therapy have what effect on which symptoms. For example, although we know that in the majority of cases exposure works, how does it work? Is it through the de-conditioning process or is it as a result of the client's reappraisal of the stimulus? Research has focused on the differences between specific approaches (e.g. cognitive versus exposure therapy) in order to determine which has more potency with which type of difficulty or symptom. As cognitive therapy would normally incorporate some aspect of fear confrontation, it has not always been easy to achieve. As suggested previously, for those with a diagnosis of social phobia or panic disorder, cognitive models have been developed and have received good research support. However, further research is required on the effectiveness of therapy, particularly in the case of social phobia.

The emphasis on tailoring treatment to individual clients has developed in conjunction with the need to investigate more efficient and client-led approaches. There has also been increasing concern about the availability of therapy for the large numbers of individuals with anxiety disorders. This has led to the incorporation of self-management approaches or interventions with limited therapist involvement. Such approaches should in theory be available to clients without being placed on lengthy waiting lists, although a proportion may still require more intensive therapy if identified at a later stage. Self-help approaches can include the use of written information and self-help packages (White, 1995), group approaches (e.g. Triumph over Phobia), advice clinics (Lovell et al., 2003) and increased use of technology resources such as telephones, computer therapy programmes and the internet. These developments are based upon the evidence that self-directed exposure therapy can be as effective as therapist-assisted programmes. Although self-help approaches have much to offer, further research is required before approaches such as computerized therapy programmes are fully integrated into services (see Kaltenhaler et al., 2004).

References

APA (2000) *Diagnostic and Statistical Manual of Mental Disorders* (4th edn, text revision). Washington, DC: American Psychiatric Association.

Beck, A.T., Rush, A.J., Shaw, B.F. and Emery, G. (1979) *Cognitive Therapy of Depression*. New York: Guilford Press.

Clark, D. and Fairburn, C.G. (1997) *Science and Practice of Cognitive Behaviour Therapy*. Oxford: Oxford University Press.

Kaltenthaler, E., Parry, G. and Beverly, C. (2004) Computerized cognitive behaviour therapy: a systematic review. *Behavioural and Cognitive Psychotherapy*, 32: 31–55.

Lovell, K., Richards, D. and Bower, P. (2003) Improving access to primary mental health care: uncontrolled evaluation of a pilot self-help clinic. *British Journal of General Practice*, February: 133–135.

Marks, I.M. (1981) *Cure and Care of Neurosis*. Chichester: John Wiley.

Ost, L.G. (1987) Applied relaxation: description of a coping technique and review of controlled studies. *Behaviour Research and Therapy*, 25: 397–410.

Ost, L.G. (1989) One session treatment for specific phobias. *Behaviour Research and Therapy*, 1: 1–7.

Ost, L.G. and Sterner, U. (1987) Applied tension: a specific behavioural method for treatment of blood phobia. *Behaviour Research and Therapy*, 25 (1): 25–29.

Rachman, S. (1977) The conditioning theory of fear acquisition: a critical examination. *Behaviour Research and Therapy*, 22: 109–117.

Roth, A. and Fonagy, P. (2005) *What Works for Whom? A Critical Review of Psychotherapy Research* (2nd edn). New York: Guilford Press.

Wells, A. (1997) *Cognitive Therapy of Anxiety Disorders: A Practice Manual and Conceptual Guide*. Chichester: John Wiley.

White, J. (1995) Stresspac: a controlled trial of a self-help package for the anxiety disorders. *Behavioural and Cognitive Psychotherapy*, 23: 89–107.

6.16   Post-traumatic Stress Disorder

PETER E. HODGKINSON

This section examines the effects of life traumas such as major disaster, road traffic accidents and violent assaults, and assesses the most promising kinds of psychological help. As up to 75 per cent of the population may experience an event which meets the criteria of being sufficiently traumatic to qualify for a diagnosis of Post-traumatic Stress Disorder (PTSD), trauma is clearly an experience that many therapists may encounter in their work.

The effects of trauma

The effects of experiencing major trauma can be summarized as follows:

- A proportion of trauma survivors, perhaps up to 25 per cent, may have no particular reaction, or may actually see benefit from their experience.
- Transient psychological symptoms, dissipating over six weeks, may be experienced by 25 per cent.

- More significant, persisting symptoms, needing professional assistance, will be suffered by 50 per cent, of whom half will go on to develop PTSD.
- Half of the cases of PTSD will remit within the first year, but half may become chronic, continuing over decades if not treated.
- Overall, up to one-third of survivors may develop chronic symptoms, including PTSD, anxiety and depression.

Post-traumatic stress disorder

The concept of PTSD was first described in 1980 in the third edition of the *Diagnostic and Statistical Manual of Mental Disorders* of the American Psychiatric Association (*DSM–III*), now in its fourth version (*DSM–IV–TR*; APA, 2000). However, the condition that this diagnosis attempts to describe has been recognized for literally thousands of years. PTSD has three main groups of symptoms: re-experience phenomena, avoidance or numbing reactions, and symptoms of increased arousal.

Qualifying criteria

First, the person must have 'experienced, witnessed, or [been] confronted with an event or events that involved actual or threatened death or serious injury, or a threat to the physical integrity of self or others' (APA, 2000). Second, the person's response must have 'involved intense fear, helplessness or horror' or, in the case of children, involved 'disorganized or agitated behaviour' (APA, 2000). If both of these criteria are met, then the person must have a requisite number of symptoms from the three areas of symptomatology.

Re-experience phenomena

These involve the traumatic event being persistently re-experienced in one (or more) of the following ways:

- recurrent and intrusive distressing recollections of the event, including images, thoughts, or perceptions;
- recurrent distressing dreams of the event;

- acting or feeling as if the traumatic event were recurring;
- intense psychological distress at exposure to internal or external cues that symbolize or resemble an aspect of the traumatic event;
- physical reactivity upon exposure to internal or external cues that symbolize or resemble an aspect of the traumatic event.

Avoidance or numbing phenomena

These include persistent avoidance of things associated with the trauma and numbing of general responsiveness, as indicated by three (or more) of the following:

- efforts to avoid thoughts, feelings, or conversations associated with the trauma;
- efforts to avoid activities, places or people that arouse recollections of the trauma;
- inability to recall an important aspect of the trauma;
- markedly diminished interest or participation in significant activities;
- feelings of detachment or estrangement from others;
- restricted range of affect (e.g. inability to have loving feelings);
- sense of foreshortened future (e.g. does not expect to have a career, marriage, children, or a long life).

Symptoms of increased arousal

These involve persistent symptoms including at least two of the following:

- difficulty in falling or staying asleep;
- irritability or outbursts of anger;
- difficulty in concentrating;
- hypervigilance;
- exaggerated startle response.

Duration and effect

Lastly, the duration of these symptoms must be more than one month, and the disturbance must cause 'clinically significant distress or impairment in social, occupational, or other important areas of functioning' (APA, 2000).

It is important to recognize that PTSD can co-exist with other conditions, such as generalized anxiety or depression. Similarly, many clients will not meet the full diagnostic criteria for PTSD, yet their lives will be significantly affected.

Psychobiology of PTSD

As might be predicted by stress research and indicated by the prominence of symptoms of increased arousal in the diagnosis of PTSD, trauma is a significant physiological event. In response to threat, adrenaline and noradrenaline are released and, together with sympathetic nervous system arousal, prepare the body for increased exertion (the 'fight or flight response'). Other hormones, including cortisol, support and modify this reaction.

Cortisol plays a crucial role in shutting down arousal after the threat is removed. Current research indicates that post-traumatic stress disorder differs from chronic stress or depression. In the latter, levels of cortisol increase but the responsiveness of cortisol receptors decreases, reducing negative feedback to the endocrine system, resulting in sufferers becoming less sensitive to further exposure to threat. With PTSD, cortisol levels decrease, the responsiveness of cortisol receptors increases, and there is stronger negative feedback to the endocrine system, resulting in PTSD sufferers becoming more sensitive to subsequent threat.

PTSD is therefore partly a state in which the body fails to suppress arousal. It is thought that arousal may be a key blocking process to a person's psychological processing of traumatic events. This has clear implications for the utility of stimulating arousal through emotion in therapy.

Influences on development of PTSD

There are three main influences on the development of post-traumatic reactions: dimensions of the person, the trauma and the recovery environment.

Dimensions of the person

These include previous mental health problems; prior victimization; previous adverse life events; and attitudes and beliefs which affect coping strategies. Once exposed to trauma, females more often develop PTSD and the risk for both sexes increases with middle age and beyond.

Dimensions of the trauma

These include duration of the event, whether the threats were single or multiple; whether experienced alone or with others; whether the trauma is likely to recur; or whether it also involved bereavement.

Dimensions of the recovery environment

These include isolation and levels of social support, coupled with perceptions of the helpfulness of such support; on-going stressors; cultural rituals for recovery; and community/society/media attitudes towards the event.

PTSD and trauma

The *DSM–IV–TR* PTSD criteria enable a therapist to gauge the range and severity of the response. They are not a comprehensive description of post-traumatic responses (survivor guilt is not mentioned, nor is substance abuse), and do not describe any underlying psychological process, understanding of which is important in the therapy of individuals with PTSD.

PTSD is not only a significant physiological event, it is a significant cognitive event. This is implicit in the first criteria of PTSD, where it refers to 'threat of death or serious injury', which reminds us that there is no objective scale of degree of trauma that we can measure events by. Threat is based on appraisal – the car crash from which we escaped unscathed may be rendered deeply traumatic by the process of 'what if?' thinking.

The experience of trauma may shatter the primitive, global, positive assumptions by which most individuals operate. Key assumptions which may be affected include those that:

- I am invulnerable.
- The world is safe, orderly, predictable.
- I am a good person.

In addition, there will exist a layer of attitudes towards expressing disturbed and disturbing feelings. Many of these attitudes are negative. Such feelings may be viewed as socially unacceptable, distressing to others, a sign of weakness, or a signal of madness or loss of control. If the world is now seen as chaotic and unpredictable, action to deal with negative feelings may be viewed as useless, and those to whom one might turn for help unworthy of trust.

What has been described as a 'traumatic memory network' may be formed, containing intrusive imagery which is, in turn, linked to arousal. These traumatic images are then subject to appraisal. It is here that 'what if?' thinking and the recognition (either in a more automatic or a more conscious way) that previous assumptions have been violated take place. For some, coping involves facing the intrusive imagery and rumination. Effective psychological processing will occur, for example 'what if?' thinking is put in a more rational perspective, avoidance and arousal decreases, and a new balance in the belief system is achieved.

However, it is as if there is a transitional point at which previous personality, including traditional ways of coping, assume prominence. For some, coping will involve avoidance of traumatic images or their triggers, and the associated arousal. While some successful avoidance is a part of coping, too much may lead to emotional numbing. At this point the survivor is trapped in a pit of rumination, worrying about what to do and reflecting on how they and life have changed. Not only may they be trapped in their particular 'fear structure', but a depressed mood may well be stimulated by the helplessness generated by this process of rumination.

Debriefing: early intervention

Studies of crisis intervention had predicted that if principles of early intervention were employed, people might return to normal functioning more quickly and might have a reduced likelihood of developing long-term problems. Thus, psychological debriefing as a tool of early post-trauma intervention gained considerable popularity.

After a decade of use, enthusiasm for psychological debriefing has become increasingly tempered. It will not prevent post-traumatic stress disorder (and given the complexity of PTSD it was unlikely that it would). However, many experienced trauma clinicians still use the processes of debriefing in their practice, holding that while it does not eradicate post-traumatic symptoms, it provides a heuristic method which enables people to build an account of their experience, highlighting predictable and manageable features and thereby moving them on to a more confident outlook. They employ it as a cognitive procedure focusing on thoughts rather than intentionally stimulating emotion, within a broader intervention.

Debriefing: purpose and structure

Debriefing is normally carried out (after a shared trauma) as a group procedure with perhaps 15 participants, or in a modified form with reduced benefit with individuals. It is best timed for 72 hours or so after the event, with a follow-up after three weeks, at which decisions concerning individual intervention may be made. Its objectives include:

- the ventilation of impressions and reactions;
- the promotion of cognitive organization, through clear understanding of both events and reactions;
- decrease in the sense of uniqueness or abnormality of reactions, achieving normalization through sharing;
- mobilization of resources within and outside the group, increasing group support, solidarity and cohesion;
- preparation for experiences, such as symptoms or reactions which may arise;
- identification of avenues of further assistance if required.

In practice, debriefing has four identifiable phases:

1   *Introduction.* This involves scene setting and the establishment of ground rules.
2   *Narrative.* The telling of individuals' stories enables group members to establish a coherent narrative of the event by a pooling of the facts, establishing the first stage of cognitive organization.
3   *Reactions.* A simple chronological structure allows the setting out of symptoms into a generally accepted pattern of developing reactions, both thoughts and emotions. These are set out in a step-wise fashion according to the following pattern:

    • reactions during the incident itself
    • reactions in the immediate aftermath
    • immediate reactions of family/significant others
    • reactions overnight
    • reactions the next and subsequent days (and so on).

    This promotes a decrease in the sense of uniqueness or abnormality of reactions and achieving normalization through sharing.
4   *Education.* The emerging picture of post-traumatic reactions can be reinforced with literature, with a summary bringing together the various elements of narrative and symptomatology so that participants have a model for their experience. This allows preparation for experiences such as symptoms or reactions which may arise later. The session concludes with forward planning. This allows mobilization of resources within and outside the group, increasing group support, solidarity and cohesion and will include identification of avenues of further assistance if required.

Debriefing: research and practice

Reviewing 11 reasonably well conducted studies (see Rose et al., 2003), it was noted that three had positive outcomes, six had neutral outcomes, and two studies of single early interventions reported negative outcomes. It was also noted that two of the studies that produced positive results were completed before psychological debriefing was formalized and used a more extended, less formal 'crisis intervention' format.

While it may be argued that debriefing was never conceived as a one-off procedure (involving both 'defusing' and follow-up), and that experienced trauma practitioners had never used it as an inflexible model, it is clear that early intervention must be conceived in a flexible way that is attuned to need rather than process.

Flexible early intervention

It has become popular to speak of 'psychological first aid' (see Freeman et al., 2001) that will enhance the normal adjustment process and provide a process of identifying those who need more focused psychological help. Three stages of intervention are identified:

1   *Initial stage.* It must be recognized that immediately after major trauma, the needs of survivors may be basic (following Maslow's 'hierarchy of needs'). Initial efforts must be directed towards providing practical help or support, comforting those involved and protecting them from further threat and distress. (This is essentially an expansion of the much misunderstood 'defusing' role set out in the debriefing model.)
2   *Middle stage.* Using a principle of 'not too much, not too soon', this will include:

    • Facilitating some telling of the trauma story. (By 'some' telling is meant identifying what the person wants to talk about rather than assuming that there is a need to tell, in detail, the whole account.)
    • Making a narrative. (By this is meant 'capturing the essence of the experience' rather than simply telling the story.)
    • Ventilating feelings as appropriate.

(The change of emphasis here from the debriefing process is to move away from prescriptive retelling and associated emotion to avoid the stimulation of excessive arousal. Any idea that catharsis is a desirable goal is hence mistaken, even though it was never seen as part of the debriefing process. However, it must be noted that advocates of the 'first aid' approach do not suggest debriefing should be abandoned, merely that it should be set within a process of practical assistance, be less formulaic/more tailored to the individual and that candidates should be more carefully selected, e.g. not mixing people with disparate experiences.)

- Linking people to systems of support. (People must be viewed and treated as resourceful and capable of adaptive recovery. Indeed, much recovery takes place without intervention. Their efforts to mobilize help within networks of friends, family and community must be supported.)
- Monitoring avoidance and beginning a sense of competence.

3 *Final stage.* The primary task of the final stage is to identify needs for future intervention, perhaps using brief screening procedures (see Brewin et al., 2003).

Therapeutic approaches with PTSD

Effective treatment of PTSD will comprise the summed effects of the following:

1 Non-specific effects:

- the survivor's decision to enter treatment, which is reflective of commitment;
- the quality of the therapeutic relationship, which is largely governed by the therapist having an appropriate attitude to the survivor's experiences, appearing trustworthy, and being competent and caring.

2 Appropriate skilled assessment to decide which treatments are appropriate.
3 Technique-specific effects:

- use of prolonged exposure;
- use of cognitive-behavioural techniques;
- use of techniques of stress inoculation training, including education;
- use of additional techniques such as medication or Eye Movement Desensitization and Reprocessing (EMDR).

The time-scale over which these may be effective, and the extent of effect will be governed by the skill and experience of the therapist, and the complexity and severity of the client's problems.

Prolonged exposure

This may involve properly selected clients retelling the account of the trauma over a number of sessions, exposing themselves to previously avoided aspects of the tale (imaginal flooding), over eight to ten sessions. Behavioural exposure to feared situations may also be used. Contra-indications include alcohol/drug misuse and depression. While exposure therapy is the first choice for clients with whom re-experiencing (or its avoidance) is a major issue, and may in itself lead to cognitive changes, these may not be therapeutically sufficient.

Cognitive therapy

Cognitive-behavioural therapy has been demonstrated (see Foa et al., 2000) to be clearly effective with PTSD, although not all clients who receive it benefit, and it is not clear what predicts success. As a technique, it involves discipline from both therapist and client.

During the account-giving stage, or in the re-living of exposure treatment, the therapist must attend closely to the client's statements, listening for areas of distorted thinking. The therapist may choose to focus further on the development of the client's narrative, reworking thoughts and reframing events and reactions, as a cognitive technique in its own right.

An early stage of cognitive treatment focuses on education, giving the client an understanding of the range of reactions and symptoms (a framework within which to place their own reactions) and providing a model for understanding post-traumatic reactions (within which the treatment method may be justified). This will also be a further adjunct to generating an alternative narrative.

Negative automatic thoughts and beliefs must be actively probed for, using the information the therapist has already gleaned as a starting point. These will then need to be monitored by the client.

Using techniques of Stress Inoculation Training, and guided by Socratic questioning, alternative self-statements and behaviours can be generated. These can be rehearsed in therapy before being tested out in practice.

Cognitive therapy may be carried out in group sessions, which makes it cost-effective. Eight hours of therapy (over four sessions) has been shown to be effective, but longer courses of treatment have generally been employed.

More specific techniques, such as EMDR (which involves the disruption of disturbing memories by rapid eye movements), may be used. While this has been demonstrated to have positive effect, it is not clear whether this is due to exposure, cognitive aspects, or some unknown ingredient. Psychodynamic therapy for PTSD remains unevaluated.

Drug treatment

Although the literature on drug treatment of PTSD is sparse, the following conclusions may be drawn:

- There is no case currently for using major tranquillizers or benzodiazepines and beta blockers in acute PTSD.
- There is clear evidence for the use of SSRIs (selective serotonin reuptake inhibitors) in treating all the symptom clusters of established PTSD.

Coda: counselling, therapy and post-traumatic stress

The past ten years have revealed the complexity of post-traumatic stress and PTSD as both a human experience and a disorder. Messianic fervour which developed among helping professionals to rush to assist survivors attracted public (and professional) opprobrium. Similar messianic fervour that attached itself to specific techniques, such as debriefing, was shown to be simplistic. However, the current shift in emphasis towards 'psychological first aid' will be very familiar to those who were involved in community disaster outreach in the UK in the late 1980s (Hodgkinson and Stewart, 1998).

What is clear is that adherence to any specific technique will not help survivors of trauma. Thus, for devotees of non-directive counselling, 'supportive counselling' has not been demonstrated to have any impact on intrusive or avoidant symptoms of PTSD. Just as PTSD is complex and is associated with comorbidity of anxiety and depression, so treatment of PTSD is complex and will rely on a cross-fertilization of techniques.

References

APA (2000) *Diagnostic and Statistical Manual of Mental Disorders* (4th edn, text revision). Washington, DC: American Psychiatric Association.

Brewin, C.R., Rose, S. and Andrews, B. (2003) Screening to identify individuals at risk after exposure to trauma. In R. Orner and U. Schnyder (eds), *Reconstructing Early Intervention After Trauma*. Oxford: Oxford University Press. pp. 130–142.

Foa, E.B., Keane, T.M. and Friedman, M.J. (2000) *Effective Treatments for PTSD*. New York: Guilford Press.

Freeman, C., Flitcroft, A. and Weeple, P. (2001) *Psychological First Aid: A Replacement for Psychological Debriefing*. Edinburgh: Lothian Primary Care NHS Trust.

Hodgkinson, P.E. and Stewart, M. (1998) *Coping with Catastrophe* (2nd edn). London: Routledge.

Rose, S., Bisson, J. and Wessely, S. (2003) A systematic review of single psychological interventions ('debriefing') following trauma. Updating the Cochrane Review and implications for good practice. In R. Orner and U. Schnyder (eds), *Reconstructing Early Intervention After Trauma*. Oxford: Oxford University Press. pp. 24–39.

6.17   Pregnancy, Miscarriage and Termination   ○○○

JOANNA BRIEN

Primarily, women present for counselling and psychotherapy with issues focused on interrupted pregnancies. In 2000, of approximately 800,000 conceptions in England and Wales, 77 per cent proceeded to live births, under 1 per cent were stillbirths and 22 per cent ended in abortion (ONS, 1990–2000). There are an estimated 400,000 miscarriages per year (Prettyman, 1995). This area, though so common, has been paid scant attention.

Pregnancy: emotional and psychological changes

The enormous physiological changes that occur as the body adapts to its pregnant state are accompanied by emotional and psychological changes which make thinking and acting more difficult (Brien and Fairbairn, 1996). Pregnancy is a major transitional event and is a potent symbol of regeneration and fertility, allowing women to be effortlessly creative or venerated as a mother. There are other desires that surround the wish to have a child or to be a parent, generated by the individual's own experience of being mothered.

Pregnant women are described as more emotional and aware of self, and demonstrate a more intuitive, pre-logical way of thinking (Condon, 1987) as well as an inability to concentrate (Jarrahi-Zadeh et al., 1969). The early narcissistic phase of pregnancy (when women intensively experience the pregnancy) is characterized by a tendency to depression and ambivalence which Dewl (1996) suggests leaves women feeling devalued and contemptuous if their pregnancy miscarries or is terminated.

Pregnancy is a temporary condition that involves some loss. Women and men can suffer the full impact of perinatal bereavement after a miscarriage or a termination for social or medical reasons. The unique aspect of grief connected with pregnancy is that there is no tangible person to mourn. It is dreams and fantasies that die with the lost pregnancy.

Optimal therapeutic approach

The most relevant approach, regardless of training, is one that lessens threat, allows the client to experience the counsellor or therapist as understanding and focuses on the client's needs. Some women may only want unbiased information and support.

The offer of counselling can imply that professional help is needed, or that abortion or miscarriage is necessarily traumatic. This is not inevitable – most women do not suffer psychological disturbance especially when a pregnancy is perceived as a physical mishap or illness (Moulder, 1995).

It is important for therapists and counsellors to have examined consciously their own religious or cultural views, any ambivalence to conception or unresolved feelings surrounding abortion and pregnancy losses. A non-directive approach is essential as even an implicit bias can be construed by the client as disapproval which can block the client working on their feelings. Regular supervision is required in order to understand these enmeshed feelings.

Interventions

Useful interventions are those that help facilitate decision making and mourning, while assessing potential risk. Time-limited counselling or therapy can provide gentle encouragement and empathic listening by using open-ended questions exploring the specific surrounding circumstances and meaning of the loss to the individual in their culture and context (Hertz, 1993). This may uncover extra vulnerability (abuse, addictions, depression, or family problems). Women can find that their pregnancy is a trigger for deeply embedded semi-conscious conflicts that they struggle to make sense of for the first time.

When there is significant illogical guilt and self-blame, clients may benefit from insight-orientated, interpretative, open-ended psychotherapy. These conflicts can be helped by therapy that enables the client to revive and mourn their losses. Therapists can find that buried feelings from a past negative experience of miscarriage or termination may surface years later. Unresolved grieving needs to be considered in assessments for non-specialized counselling, as women may refrain from mentioning abortion, miscarriage or perinatal loss. Psychological sequelae can be severe depression, persistent guilt, avoidance, nightmares, sexual and relationship problems. Some women make a poor adjustment after an abortion and may have similar symptoms to those associated with post-traumatic stress disorder.

It is good practice to offer to see partners after some individual time in consultation with the client. This is to avoid excluding significant others while ensuring that there is no coercion. All clients including those under 16 are entitled to confidential treatment. All women can receive counselling, contraceptives and in exceptional circumstances, abortion without parental consent. Victoria Gillick challenged the law relating to minors giving their consent to treatment. In 1985 the case went to appeal in the House of Lords. The Fraser ruling forms the basis of Department of Health guidelines that followed in 1986. This allows health professionals to treat young people without parental consent when they are satisfied that all the criteria laid down in this ruling have been met. In essence, a young person has to be mature enough to understand the risks and benefits of the proposed treatment; cannot be persuaded to inform a parent (or those with parental responsibility); is about to begin or continue having sexual intercourse with or without treatment; that their mental or physical health is likely to suffer and treatment is in their best interests

(Brien and Fairbairn, 1996). The recent Sexual Offences Act (2003) whose purpose is to enable the prosecution of abuse or exploitative sexual activity, in effect criminalizes sexual activity between under 18s and under 16s. However, those adolescents who have mutually agreed sexual activity and where there is no evidence of exploitation, are unlikely to be prosecuted under the Act. The Act has strengthened by statute the ability of anyone (this includes counsellors or therapists) to give confidential help if this prevents, protects or promotes an under 16's well-being and is not abusive.

Miscarriage

A miscarriage is a pregnancy that ends before the foetus is able to live independently at approximately 24 weeks. The depth of distress that clients experience is not related to the length of the pregnancy's gestation. The immediate reaction of shock may be accompanied by numbness that delays the impact of pain and loss. Fear and anxiety can overwhelm women unprepared for the time taken for the miscarriage to be completed or the pain and bleeding experienced.

Clients may show somatic distress. It is common for clients to experience yearning, irritability and depression. Some may endure intense jealousy at any reminders of others' motherhood. Women's angry feelings may be targeted at themselves, or displaced on to medical staff.

The medical profession and significant others may see miscarriage as a 'normal' event and, by focusing on the likelihood of having a baby eventually, try to minimize the distress caused. Friends may fear to intrude on grief and, feeling de-skilled, may distance themselves as a defence against the pain of their helplessness.

Women may want to understand the cause of their loss and the likelihood of further miscarriages. The aetiology of miscarriages is often speculative. Approximately half of all conceptions are naturally aborted and one in six known pregnancies end spontaneously. Seventy-five per cent of miscarriages occur within the first twelve weeks. Of these, 50 per cent are due to chance mutations at conception or in the early development of the foetus. Mid-trimester miscarriages account for 2 per cent of the total and can be caused by an incompetent cervix, uterine abnormalities, or pre-existing maternal disease. Those women with late miscarriages need adequate explanation of any findings after *post mortem* investigations. Written information is useful, as stress can make verbal information difficult to retain.

Clients may scrutinize every possible cause, deny reality or bargain (make secret resolutions) to regain a sense of control over an inexplicable event. Women can be secretly guilt-ridden, revealing nagging fears that their actions or omissions have caused a miscarriage, but can be helped by the knowledge that physical activities (including sex) are not responsible.

Women benefit from sensitive support when embarking on subsequent pregnancies. Investigations are not usually carried out until three miscarriages have occurred. This happens to 1 in 300 women and 68 per cent go on to have a successful pregnancy (Oakley, 1986). The standard advice, to wait three months before trying to conceive, can cause additional stress as each menstruation brings fresh grief at an opportunity lost.

Rituals are important in the healing process and these can alleviate grief. Individuals can be encouraged to mark and remember their baby and be offered appropriate memorial services. Women can present for help, only dimly aware that their feelings have been triggered by an anniversary.

The aim of counselling is to provide psychological space to acknowledge hidden loss, explore hopes, and rebuild shattered self-esteem while the natural healing process takes place.

Termination

Conceptions occur for a variety of reasons: reliable contraception can fail, be used inconsistently, or abandoned if the woman or couple has decided that there is little risk of pregnancy. Couples can instinctively avoid birth control as conjuring away their fecundity, causing sterility and killing spontaneity. Sexuality is not only a strong untamed instinct but can fulfil a tactile need for affection confirming that the individual is alive and separate. A completely effective contraceptive would remove all chance and burden us with the responsibility of making a choice.

Women are affected by ethical debates about abortion, as well as by the attitudes and actions of health professionals they meet. There is still a stigma attached to being unhappily pregnant and a taboo against abortion, as reflected in women's commonly expressed concerns about confidentiality. All the major world religions are pro-natalist and many prohibit abortion.

Counselling for abortion is not mandatory, aside from ascertaining whether two independent medical practitioners feel there are grounds under the 1967 Abortion Act. The availability of counselling, the qualifications and training of staff undertaking this role is often *ad hoc*. The Birth Control Trust has identified that '20% of women benefit from professional counselling in depth' (1994: 5.4). In 1981 Hare and Haywood found that although 48 per cent of pregnant women had made a clear decision about their pregnancy, 32 per cent were ambivalent and 20 per cent needed time to consider their decision.

Health professionals need to be aware that those women who are more likely to suffer psychologically and who benefit from counselling are: adolescents; those who have suffered a bereavement; women who have had difficult or traumatic gynaecological and obstetric histories (previous abortion for medical reasons, repeat abortions, ectopic pregnancy, stillbirth, miscarriage); and those who have had mental health problems, suffered abuse, or who show addictive or compulsive behaviours. Care needs to be taken with those who feel unwanted, are adopted, fostered or 'looked after' by social services; or those who are markedly calm or highly anxious.

Some women may block out both emotions and awareness of options in an urgent need for resolution, and to avoid responsibility. Other women can present as confused and be plagued by indecision, swinging from moment to moment from requesting abortion to deciding to continue with the pregnancy. Some clients will talk as if there is a right or wrong decision if only they could find it. There may be a seductive wish for a painless, magic solution. An effective strategy can be to help the client to concentrate on the positive outcomes of each alternative rather than viewing options negatively.

A woman's decision can pivot on complex socio-economic, ethical, cultural and religious considerations. The moral status and rights of the foetus, for many people, develop with the developing pregnancy and are balanced by the needs of the woman. Women can feel more anguish at terminating a late or twin pregnancy. The ability to make a decision is less important than accepting responsibility for their chosen path. Ultimately clients need to feel they have made their own decision, having examined all other options, including adoption.

Repeat abortion could indicate that the client is highly fertile or in an abusive situation where she has no control over her fertility. It is important to separate and validate each abortion experience. This care can help a client who has had repeat abortions to understand and avoid the compulsive and unconscious need to eliminate hidden difficult feelings along with the foetus.

Clients can ask for specific information – for example, whether a foetus feels pain *in utero*. Whatever the question or statement, the counsellor focuses on how this information will benefit the client. A client may need accurate, relevant information about continuing a pregnancy, or about termination methods and the immediate or future mental and physical risks.

Termination for medical reasons

There are around 2,000 abortions for medical reasons in England and Wales per year (ONS, 1990–2000). Section 1(1) d of the Abortion Act (as amended by the Human Fertilization and Embryology Act 1990) allows legal abortion if there is substantial risk that if the child were born it would suffer from such physical or mental abnormalities as to be seriously handicapped. Four per cent of births suffer some abnormality (De Crespigny and Dredge, 1991: 81–82).

Women can suffer grief reactions and serious psychological sequelae similar to those for miscarriage, with the additional stigma of requesting abortion. Medical staff tend to be more sympathetic to those seeking abortions for 'medical reasons', perhaps because the pregnancy is viewed as 'wanted' and the parent as 'blameless'. The voluntary organization, Support Around Termination for Abnormality provides excellent guidelines for health professionals

and support for women before and after termination (Brien and Fairbairn, 1996: 133). Their aim is for medical abortion to be treated as other perinatal bereavements, but there is little evidence that this happens. Once a decision has been reached, clients appreciate a quick referral with accurate, consistent information about the medical procedure.

In summary it is important for the therapist/ counsellor to help the client feel more supported and less isolated by listening to how the client feels and to what they believe is best for them.

References

Birth Control Trust (1994) *Model Specification for Abortion, 1994–5.* London: Birth Control Trust.

Brien, J. and Fairbairn, I. (1996) *Pregnancy and Abortion Counselling.* London: Routledge.

Condon, J.T. (1987) Altered cognitive functioning in pregnant women: a shift toward primary process thinking. *British Journal of Medical Psychology*, 60: 329–334.

De Crespigny, L. and Dredge, R. (1991) *Which Tests for My Unborn Baby?: A Guide to Prenatal Diagnosis.* Oxford: Oxford University Press.

Dewl, R. (1996) *Death and Bereavement: The Psychological, Religious and Cultural Interfaces.* London: Whurr.

Hare, M.J. and Haywood, J. (1981) Counselling for women seeking abortion. *Journal of Biological Science*, 13: 269–273.

Herz, M.D. (1993) Perinatal loss. In D.E. Stewart, N.C. Stotland and M.D. Herz (eds), *Psychological Aspects of Women's Health Care. The Interface between Psychiatry and Obstetrics and Gynaecology.* Washington, DC: American Psychiatric Press.

Jarrahi-Zadeh, A., Kane F.F.J., Van de Castle, R.L., Lachenbruch, P.A. and Ewing, J.A. (1969) Emotional and cognitive changes in pregnancy and early puerperium. *British Journal of Psychiatry*, 115: 797–805.

Moulder, C. (1995) *Miscarriage: A Woman's Experiences and Needs.* London: Pandora Press.

Oakley, A. (1986) Miscarriage and its implications. *Midwife, Health Visitor and Community Nurse*, April: 123–124, 126.

ONS (1990–2000) *Annual Publication Birth Statistics Conception Series, FMI number 30.* London: Office for National Statistics.

Prettyman, R.J. (1995) The psychological sequelae of miscarriage. *Journal of Maternal and Child Health*, 20 (6): 207–209.

6.18 Psychosomatic Problems ○○○

DIANA SANDERS

Between 30 to 80 per cent of people attending General Practitioners and medical outpatient clinics have symptoms which cannot be clearly medically diagnosed. The majority find these symptoms transient, are reassured that there is nothing seriously wrong, and one way or another find their own solutions. However, a proportion continue to believe that there is something seriously wrong, and remain worried and concerned. They may seek medical help numerous times, and have numerous tests and investigations, over perhaps many years. These people have traditionally been poorly managed by the medical profession, using up considerable resources in investigations and treatments that have not resolved the problems but have contributed to further distress and disability. They often invoke negative reactions, being described in the medical and psychiatric literature as the 'hard to help', 'difficult to manage', 'fat-file' and 'heart-sink' patients. Their distress may be dismissed as psychosomatic or as all in the mind, and therefore not real.

As counselling and psychotherapy services grow in primary care and medical settings, a number of these clients will be referred for psychological help for their difficulties. The route into counselling or therapy is often different from that of many other clients within a counsellor's caseload: they may be referred with some reluctance, with an element of last-resort desperation on the part of the medical profession, and perhaps with the message that the problems are all in the mind. This leads to issues in engaging and working with these clients, adapting the therapeutic relationship and style of therapy to integrate clients' medical views of their difficulties, and adaptations of therapeutic goals to their needs. This section aims to offer an overview of the definition of psychosomatic problems, the range of clients

within this category, a model of psychosomatic problems which conceptualizes the interaction between somatic, psychological, emotional and behavioural factors, and describes ways of working with these clients.

Defining psychosomatic problems

Counsellors may encounter clients with a number of problems when working in this area. These are briefly described below and include:

- psychosomatic problems
- medically unexplained or functional symptoms
- somatization
- hypochondriasis or health anxiety.

Psychosomatic problems can be defined as a broad range of somatic problems which cannot be accounted for by known organic disease, but where psychological problems in some way maintain the symptoms. They are also known as *medically unexplained symptoms* (Hotopf, 2004). The range of such symptoms and syndromes is shown in Table 6.18.1.

The list of such symptoms does not imply that they are solely caused by psychological factors, but that there is an interaction, particularly where psychological issues are maintaining the problems. Very common symptoms, which most of us may have experienced, include stress-induced headaches, aches and pains, rashes and tiredness, or when physical symptoms we are normally able to put up with become much more significant when we are feeling stressed or low. Psychosomatic symptoms may occur in association with physical illness: for example,

Table 6.18.1   Symptoms and syndromes which may be medically unexplained

Somatic symptoms	Syndromes
Breathlessness	Chronic pain syndromes
Diarrhoea	Dysmorphophobia
Dizziness	Factitious syndromes
Dysphagia	Hyperventilation syndrome
Dysphonia, aphonia	Irritable bowel syndrome
Fatigue	Post-traumatic syndromes
Incontinence and urgency	Premenstrual syndrome
Nausea	Somatization disorder
Pain (abdominal, chest, muscle and joint, low back, headache, facial, pelvic, neuropathic)	
Palpitations	
Pruritis	
Tinnitus	
Tremor	
Worry about benign tissue lumps and inconsistencies	

Source: Sanders (1996)

people with angina caused by diseased coronary arteries may also experience non-cardiac chest pains. Very occasionally, so-called medically unexplained or psychosomatic symptoms later turn out to have a measurable organic basis.

Regardless of the relation to organic factors, psychological factors play an important role both in the individual's distress and in the decision to seek help. Somatic symptoms characterize many psychological problems, particularly depression and anxiety. Around one-fifth of new consultations for physical symptoms in primary care are found to be due to primary, or co-existing, psychological problems, mainly anxiety and depression. An emotionally distressed individual is far more likely to consult a general practitioner with physical symptoms than to consult directly with emotional or social problems, and while the majority will, with appropriate questioning, reveal the true reasons for their distress, a number will not wish to make the links with psychological or social difficulties, and continue to seek help in the medical realm.

'Somatization' was originally defined as the hypothetical process whereby a deep-seated neurosis could cause a bodily disorder. The concept of somatization

arises from earlier ideas from Freud and Breuer, who developed concepts such as unconscious conflict, defences and resistance. Unexplained physical symptoms were considered to be outward signs of psychological disturbance, which became transduced into somatic forms, via hysteria and conversion. Patients' insistence that their symptoms were 'real' and organic was taken to represent their defence against the outpouring of intra-psychic conflict. The definition has moved on since then, losing some of its psychoanalytic overtones: somatization is generally defined as the process whereby people with psycho-social and emotional distress articulate their problems primarily through physical symptoms (Hotopf, 2004).

A common problem within the field of psychosomatic therapy is health anxiety or hypochondriasis, where clients are extremely anxious about the possibility of serious illness and disease, become convinced, often with little or no evidence, that they are ill, and may repeatedly seek medical reassurance which they then disbelieve (Salkovskis and Bass, 1996). Health anxiety may be a primary problem, or may accompany other psychosomatic problems as well as a range of physical difficulties. It is not always the case that clients with psychosomatic problems are also anxious: many are reassured that they are not suffering from serious disease, but remain understandably puzzled and disabled by their symptoms.

Conceptualizing psychosomatic problems

The literature on psychosomatic problems, somatization and health anxiety includes a number of ways of conceptualizing the problems, offering an understanding of the links between the somatic and psychological (Sanders, 1996; Sanders and Wills, 2003; Taylor and Asmundson, 2004). One model is influenced by cognitive therapy, which takes into account the interaction between physical symptoms, emotions, behaviour and interpretations of the symptoms, and considers the client's beliefs and assumptions which may underlie the problems. The model, which makes sense both for clients and counsellors, and can be adapted to working in different models of counselling or therapy, is summarized in Figure 6.18.1

The model suggests that *physical symptoms* arise from many sources, and include innocent physiological variations, symptoms arising from anxiety, depression or low mood, or symptoms of physical disease. Stress is an important mediator of physical changes: for example, stress leads to changes in the colon in individuals with irritable bowel syndrome; stress can lead to sleep disturbances, leading in turn to physical problems; and muscle tension is common in depression and anxiety, also associated with pain. We all vary in how much we notice such symptoms, and emotions can influence what sense we make of them. Regardless of the cause of the symptoms, the way the client *interprets* them is crucial. If they are interpreted as signs of physical damage or danger, or in terms of not being able to cope, the individual is likely to feel emotionally upset or anxious, which then leads to further physical symptoms. The way these are interpreted also determines how the individual copes with the symptoms, such as acting as though seriously ill, resting or taking medication. These ways of coping may in themselves

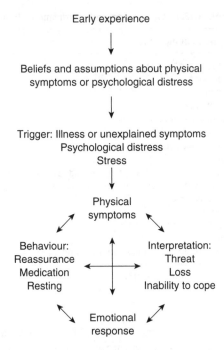

Figure 6.18.1   A model for psychosomatic problems (adapted from Salkovskis and Bass, 1996; Sanders, 1996)

exacerbate the symptoms, such as too much rest causing further fatigue or breathlessness. In addition, the individual may continually check the symptoms, as though a spotlight is on one particular part of the body, or may poke or rub lumps, which inadvertently makes the symptoms worse. Seeking medical reassurance and medical tests, while a natural and understandable response to health concerns, can in itself maintain the symptoms and the individual's distress. Repeated investigations themselves carry a risk of further physical damage; medical reassurance may be phrased in a way which is ambiguous ('There's nothing wrong now but come back if the problems don't get better and we'll send you for tests'; 'Your blood pressure is not bad for someone your age'), causing further anxiety; and to be told there is nothing wrong is incorrect because the individual is indeed experiencing difficulties (Salkovskis and Bass, 1996).

The client's background, beliefs and assumptions are all relevant to psychosomatic problems. A proportion will have experienced abuse during childhood, prevalent in, for example, clients with functional bowel problems (Toner et al., 2000). The development of 'somatization' may be a means of coping with background trauma. The kinds of assumptions and beliefs underlying a range of somatic problems can be divided into two main areas: first, those concerning the meaning of physical symptoms, which influence the extent to which the individual sees him- or herself as vulnerable to serious illness and its consequences; and second, beliefs concerning the meaning of psychological distress, which influence the way in which the person deals with difficulties and stresses (Sanders, 1996). Beliefs about the meaning of physical symptoms may include ideas such as 'My body should always function perfectly any symptoms must indicate something is seriously wrong'; 'If I have symptoms, the doctors should always be able to explain and treat these symptoms'; 'My health is the doctor's responsibility'. Personal and family history of illness and illness behaviours relates to the development of assumptions and beliefs, such as illness as a child, the way significant others responded to their own or children's body sensations or symptoms, and illness or death in the family. The second category of assumptions is of those concerning psychological distress. The notion that somatic symptoms represent a conversion of psychological distress into physical outlets has had a strong influence on the understanding of functional somatic symptoms. An extreme form of conversion, alexythymia, hypothesizes that the person is unable to express or verbalize distressing emotions, and so may convert them into somatic symptoms. Although it is sometimes the case that people with extreme somatization disorder appear free of affect, or blame their upset entirely on the physical symptoms and incompetence of the medical profession rather than on other difficulties in life, other 'somatizers' have much emotion associated with particular events or memories. Both the lack of emotion and failure of the individual to accept psychological factors in her or his distress may be more usefully conceptualized as a tendency to attend to somatic distress rather than to psychological events, which

are in turn related to underlying assumptions and beliefs about the relative importance or acceptability of physical symptoms as opposed to emotional ones. I have suggested elsewhere that four areas of assumptions may underlie psychosomatic problems (Sanders, 1996):

1   The individual is unable to find the words to express particular emotions; therefore the somatic component of psychological distress is attended to.
2   The belief that emotions are unacceptable or dangerous; therefore, feelings will be dismissed, and the somatic component of distress is attended to.
3   The belief that the individual is able to cope with all aspects of life, and to have difficulties is a sign of unacceptable weakness.
4   The individual believes that the only way to get one's needs met is through illness.

The evidence for these assumptions and beliefs is discussed in Sanders (1996). There is some research evidence supporting the notion that people with a tendency to express psychological distress in somatic ways feel that they have to be able to cope with all aspects of life, psychological problems such as anxiety or depression being regarded as evidence of weakness, failure or blameworthiness. Therefore, in response to life difficulties, the individual experiences physical symptoms, so preventing the loss of self-esteem associated with feeling bad (Toner et al., 2000).

Principles of counselling/ therapy for psychosomatic problems

Working with clients with psychosomatic problems involves careful adaptation of the counsellor's or therapist's usual model of working. A proportion of clients in this group may welcome the opportunity to talk through their problems, understanding the links with psychological difficulties and life events. However, some may be reluctant to come for counselling, not seeing it as relevant, and as implying that the symptoms are 'all in the mind'. An open invitation to talk about the problems may be threatening and difficult to the client, perhaps not seeing the point unless the counsellor can offer medical help. As a result, a more structured approach can be very helpful, working with the client to develop a model of the problems such as described in Figure 6.18.1, and negotiating specific goals for counselling. Some of the principles of counselling or therapy when working with this client group are outlined below.

The therapeutic relationship and engaging the client

Clients who are referred for psychological therapy for psychosomatic problems may well differ from those who are actively seeking help for other problems in that they may be less motivated to consider psychological factors, wanting to see their problems as purely physical. The client may not have requested counselling or therapy and may not see its relevance. Although some may acknowledge that they are psychologically distressed, they view this as a result of the physical symptoms and lack of appropriate medical help, and therefore may view counselling as secondary to the treatment of their main problems. One of the challenges for the practitioner is to engage the client actively in a way that does not threaten the individual's view of the self, takes account of their misgivings about counselling or therapy, and offers an understanding of the problems without either colluding with or rejecting the client's beliefs. It is probably the case that once the client is engaged in counselling, a substantial part of the therapeutic work has been done.

Listening to the symptoms and broadening the agenda

One way to begin to engage the client is to take a very full assessment of the physical symptoms and medical problems and gain an understanding of the client's medical treatment, and then broaden the agenda to look at psychological factors. Once the client has been given the opportunity to describe and discuss the somatic symptoms and medical treatment, it is useful to ask about their own explanation of the symptoms, such as abdominal pain caused by a food allergy or virus, or chest pain caused by spasm in the heart. Rather than attempting to challenge this assumption directly, or replace it with another, equally unhelpful explanation such as 'it's depression', it is more helpful to build on the client's view and work on the idea that precipitating factors, causing the symptoms in the first place, may differ from maintaining factors. Therefore, an illness or disease may have caused symptoms in the first place, but are no longer responsible for keeping it going. This leads to an introduction of the model of the problems shown in Figure 6.18.1, showing how cognitive, behavioural and emotional factors interact with physical symptoms, and so 'broadens the agenda' to a discussion of factors other than the symptoms. It also begins the process of developing a good collaborative therapeutic relationship.

Developing alternative hypotheses

Once the client's views about their symptoms have been discussed, it can be helpful to explore a number of hypotheses about what is causing the problems, other than physical illness. One hypothesis is that the client does indeed have a serious physical illness, and that the doctors so far have not been able to diagnose or treat it; the second hypothesis is that the individual is *concerned and anxious* about the possibility of illness, and that the anxiety is the central problem. The evidence for and against and the usefulness of each hypothesis is reviewed with the client. The therapist then proposes that they work together for a set time on the new hypothesis; after that time, if they have had a good try at a psychological approach and the problem has not improved, then it would be reasonable to review their original hypothesis. In this way, counsellor and client avoid 'getting into an argument' about the cause of the symptoms, the client's beliefs are respected, and the counsellor is able to offer a different perspective without asking the client to accept it immediately. Such an approach needs to be adapted to clients with psychosomatic symptoms who do not report being anxious, where it is helpful to stress that counselling aims to help the client cope better with the symptoms, and the uncertainty regarding diagnosis, rather than attempting to explain the symptoms.

Negotiating goals

It is vital when working with this client group to elicit and discuss their expectations about counselling or therapy and negotiate realistic goals. Clients frequently want the goal to be a complete cure and absence of symptoms. However, many trials of psychological approaches for psychosomatic problems indicate that, at the end of therapy, the physical symptoms may lessen or remain the same, but the client is less concerned or disabled. Therefore, it is important to negotiate realistic goals, such as coping better with the symptoms, reducing anxiety about the symptoms, decreasing the disability and limitation associated with symptoms, and reducing the level of consultations.

Offering alternative explanations for the symptoms

People with psychosomatic problems may report that they understand that the symptoms are not caused by serious disease; however, clients with health anxiety in particular are unlikely to accept that there is 'nothing wrong' in the absence of a convincing explanation for their distressing symptoms. There are a number of ways of demonstrating links between physical symptoms and psychological and other maintaining factors, such as keeping diaries of symptoms and stress, and demonstrating how stress or paying attention to symptoms can make them appear worse (Sanders and Wills, 2003). In addition, the client can be encouraged to experiment with discovering alternative explanations, using 'behavioural experiments' devised in cognitive therapy (Silver, Sanders et al., 2004; Silver, Surawy et al., 2004).

Dealing with maintaining factors

Psychosomatic symptoms can be exacerbated and maintained by a range of activities which the client uses to attempt to cope, such as seeking medical reassurance and further tests, illness behaviour, avoiding exercise, and checking or poking sore areas. It is important to identify what kind of unhelpful coping strategies the client may have evolved, and carefully negotiate with the client to

reduce or stop, and monitor how helpful this is. Again, behavioural experiments enable the client to discover the role of maintenance factors, and experiment with alternative ways of dealing with the symptoms (Silver, Sanders et al., 2004; Silver, Surawy et al., 2004). For example, the client can be encouraged to exercise gradually rather then rest, or to stop seeking reassurance or checking the internet, and monitor the impact on how he or she feels. Taking a systemic approach, looking at the role of the client's family and wider social context, is important: for example, while a client may be trying to get better, the spouse may be inadvertently reinforcing the sick role, or encouraging the individual to seek medical reassurance to allay his or her own fears.

Coping strategies

For some clients, learning appropriate ways of coping with symptoms may be helpful, such as breathing and relaxation exercises, learning to distract from symptoms rather than pay attention to them, and dealing with low mood, stress or anxiety. Mindfulness meditation has been shown to help clients with physical health problems as well as stress, anxiety and depression (see Kabat-Zinn, 2005; Segal et al., 2002), and may be a valuable adjunct to psychological therapies for clients with health anxiety and medically unexplained symptoms.

Working with other issues and difficulties

Once the client has accepted a psychological model for the symptoms, therapy moves on to focus on other difficulties. Life difficulties and stress may well be involved, and problem-solving therapy has been shown to be helpful for psychosomatic problems, enabling the client to look for solutions to the issues which may underlie and maintain the difficulties. Clients' assumptions and beliefs, as discussed above, can maintain the problems, requiring focus during counselling. A proportion of this client group will have experienced physical, emotional or sexual abuse in earlier years, and somatization may be one means the individual has developed to cope with such trauma. The counsellor, therefore, needs to proceed with care and caution, only gently exploring these areas as and when the client is ready. It is sometimes the case that it is preferable for the client to experience physical distress than to look at the pain from the past.

Effectiveness of counselling and psychological approaches for psychosomatic problems

There have been a number of trials of psychological therapies for a range of medically unexplained physical symptoms and health anxiety (reviewed by Hotopf, 2004; Sanders and Wills, 2003; Toner et al., 2000). Psychodynamic therapy, focusing on developing a therapeutic relationship in which the client can explore difficulties, using metaphor to make the link between somatic symptoms and emotions, and helping the client to address current life problems and cope with stress, has been shown to be an effective treatment for irritable bowel symptoms (Creed et al., 2003). Brief dynamic therapy, group psychotherapy and cognitive-behavioural therapy have been shown to be effective for a range of psychosomatic problems, chronic pain and health anxiety (Clark et al., 1998; Kroenke and Swindle, 2000; Lidbeck, 2003). One trial showed counselling and cognitive therapy to be equally effective in helping clients with chronic fatigue (Risdale et al., 2001) although others have shown cognitive therapy to be more effective (Deale et al., 2001). Overall, the research shows that counselling and psychological therapies are helpful to people with a range of psychosomatic problems. The active ingredients include offering the client a feasible alternative explanation for the maintenance of the symptoms, by making links between the symptoms and thoughts, emotions and behaviour; helping the client see how stress or emotional upset affect physical well-being; offering practical means of dealing with symptoms; modifying unhelpful thoughts and assumptions; and problem solving. The importance of engaging the client, and offering a therapeutic relationship in which to re-conceptualize the problem and look for solutions is stressed throughout even the most behavioural of therapies.

When counselling is not appropriate

It is also important to consider when psychological approaches, particularly brief therapy, might not be helpful. One danger in working with this client group is that the counsellor becomes yet another 'expert' who has not been able to help the client, thus compounding their distress and dissatisfaction with the helping professions. Counselling and psychological therapies are more likely to be helpful if the client accepts that psycho-social factors affect their somatic problems, such as the symptoms being aggravated by stress or emotion, thus lending more credibility to a psychological model; if the client reports being psychologically distressed; if the symptoms were preceded by identifiable life events; and if client and counsellor are able to negotiate mutually agreed goals and work collaboratively towards these goals. Factors which may indicate a poor response to psychological approaches include an attempt by the client to claim compensation for the symptoms, an inability on the part of the client to see any link with psychological difficulties or stresses, the presence of persistent dysfunctional beliefs about illness, and if the client does not experience psychological difficulties. In many cases it is helpful for the counsellor to work very closely with those involved in the client's medical treatment, and, for some long-term somatizing clients, a structured, long-term medical management is most appropriate. Counsellors and psychologists working in medical settings have a great deal to offer in helping medical professionals to manage such clients.

References

Clark, D.M., Hackmann, A., Wells, A., Fennell, M., Ludgate, J., Ahmad, S., Richards, C. and Gelder, M. (1998) Two psychological treatments for hypochondriasis. A randomised controlled trial. *British Journal of Psychiatry*, 173: 218–225.

Creed, F., Fernandes, L., Guthrie, E., Palmer, S., Ratcliffe, J., Read, N., Rigby, C., Thompson, D. and Tomenson, B. (2003) The cost-effectiveness of psychotherapy and

Paroxetine for severe irritable bowel syndrome. *Gastroenterology*, 124: 303–317.

Deale, A., Hussain, K., Chalder, T. and Wessely, S. (2001) Long term outcome of cognitive behaviour therapy versus relaxation for chronic fatigue syndrome: a five year follow up study. *American Journal of Psychiatry*, 158 (12): 2038–2042.

Hotopf, M. (2004) Preventing somatization. *Psychological Medicine*, 34: 195–198.

Kroenke, K. and Swindle, R. (2000) Cognitive behavioral therapy for somatization and symptom syndromes: a critical review of controlled clinical trials. *Psychotherapy and Psychosomatics*, 69 (4): 205–215.

Kabat-Zinn, J. (2005) *Coming to Our Senses: Healing Ourselves and the World through Mindfulness*. London: Piatkus.

Lidbeck, J. (2003) Group therapy for somatization disorders in primary care: maintenance of treatment goals of short cognitive-behavioural treatment one and a half year follow-up. *Acta Psychiatrica Scandinavica*, 107 (6): 449–456.

Risdale, L., Godfrey, E., Chalder, T., Seed, P., King, M., Wallace, P. and Wessely, S. (2001) Chronic fatigue in general practice: is counselling as good as cognitive behavioural therapy? A UK randomised trial. *British Journal of General Practice*, 51: 19–24.

Salkovskis, P.M. and Bass, C.M. (1996) Hypochondriasis. In D.M. Clark and C.G. Fairburn (eds), *Science and Practice of Cognitive Behaviour Therapy*. Oxford: Oxford University Press. pp. 313–339.

Sanders, D. (1996) *Counselling for Psychosomatic Problems*. London: Sage.

Sanders, D. and Wills, F. (2003) *Counselling for Anxiety Problems*. London: Sage.

Segal, Z.V., Williams, J.M.G. and Teasdale, J.D. (2002) *Mindfulness-based Cognitive Therapy for Depression*. New York: Guilford Press.

Silver, A., Sanders, D., Morrison, N. and Cowie, C. (2004) Health anxiety. In J. Bennett-Levy et al. (eds), *The Oxford Guide to Behavioural Experiments in Cognitive Therapy*. Oxford: Oxford University Press. pp. 87–105.

Silver, A., Surawy, C. and Sanders, D. (2004) Physical health. In J. Bennett-Levy et al. (eds), *The Oxford Guide to Behavioural Experiments in Cognitive Therapy*. Oxford: Oxford University Press. pp. 327–347.

Taylor, S. and Asmundson, G.J.G. (2004) *Treating Health Anxiety: A Cognitive-behavioural Approach*. New York: Guilford Press.

Toner, B.B., Segal, Z.V., Emmott, S.D. and Myran, D. (2000) *Cognitive-behavioral Treatment of Irritable Bowel Syndrome: The Brain–Gut Connection*. New York: Guilford Press.

6.19 Rape and Sexual Violence Towards Women

SHEILA RITCHIE

This section will discuss briefly some of the social and psychological issues that emerge when preparing to work with women who have been raped or sexually assaulted and will then address approaches to therapeutic practice.

How can we begin to comprehend the violation of one human being by another? When we hear of a natural disaster our compassion is stirred. We might breathe a sigh of relief that it is not happening to us or temporarily feel unsafe in a world where it feels that nature controls our fate. We might try to work out who is to blame but we can eventually absolve ourselves from any feelings of guilt. It is the ruthless aspect of nature that is to blame.

When it comes to a trauma inflicted by another human being we are forced to think about the unthinkable and thrown into a state of disbelief. We are faced with aspects of our own nature which we would prefer to disown: our own capacity to commit unspeakable acts and our vulnerability as humans. It makes us seek to blame; to make someone else responsible as we are somehow more implicated than in the case of an act of nature. This can feel unbearable and make us not want to know or believe what has happened.

The social context

This is indeed one of the main problems facing a woman who reports a rape – being believed and having the offence taken seriously enough to result in a conviction. Reported rape has trebled in the last decade and yet conviction rates have dropped from 24 per cent to 6 per cent (Fawcett Society, 2003). Many rapes go unrecorded. The Rape Crisis Federation report that only 12 per cent of victims who contact them go on to make any complaint at all. One finding of the British Crime Survey (Myhill and Allen, 2002) was that the police come to know of about 20 per cent of rapes.

A woman may have low expectations of being treated fairly, aware of the mythology about rape which continues to pervade many of the institutions she has to encounter, for example that 'real' rape happens down dark alleyways at night or that if you dress in a particular way or have a relationship with your rapist, then you must have 'asked for it' or 'led him on'. The British Crime Survey (Myhill and Allen, 2002) findings show that only 8 per cent of rapes were committed by strangers. Nearly half (45 per cent) of rapes reported to the survey were committed by perpetrators who were the woman's partner at the time of the incident.

Rape complainants often feel that they are the ones on trial and not the defendant as the trial tends to focus on the complainant's credibility. With the increased sophistication of DNA testing, rapists are more likely to plead that the woman gave her consent, rather than use the defence of denial. The Sexual Offences Act 2003 aims to clarify issues surrounding consent in rape and sexual assault cases and make it easier for juries to make fair and balanced decisions on the question of consent. The onus of proof still, however, rests with the woman and the vast majority of guilty verdicts often involve the defendant pleading guilty to a lesser charge.

While over the years there have been improvements in the response of police to women who have been raped, and services such as sexualt assault referral centres have been established, inconsistencies remain. One report found that where 'consent' is the issue, investigating officers did not send samples to the national DNA database for matching in over 80 per cent of cases. Since many rapists are serial offenders, this means that vital evidence is being thrown away (Fawcett Society, 2003).

The after-effects of rape

A woman's recovery from the trauma of rape will be aided or inhibited depending on how she has been believed and supported by professionals. She may experience a 'secondary victimization' through her contact with professionals and institutions.

The complicated effects of rape must be placed in the context of the woman's history. A woman's response to the trauma of such an attack depends on many factors: the degree of viciousness of the rape and the extent to which she experienced threat to her life; her sense of self and the quality of her network of relationships before the rape and people's response to her since; her own emotional development and past experience of trauma.

Some women who have been raped are able, after some limited help, to integrate the trauma, never to forget it, but to function again in everyday life. For others, their response is much more complex, as the rape as an adult often triggers some earlier trauma such as child sexual abuse, violence from a parent or lack of emotional containment.

As Garland (1991: 508) explains, 'the traumatic event … will link up quite specifically and in a peculiarly locked in and intractable way with whatever is already damaged or flawed from the survivor's own past.' There are three distinctive feeling states that commonly follow a trauma such as rape which Herman (1992) categorizes as hyperarousal, intrusion and constriction.

Hyperarousal is a state where it feels that something dangerous might happen at any moment. If someone bumps into you in the street or looks at you on the bus it is as if they are about to attack. This feeling state may indeed leave the woman even more vulnerable to further attack. It is almost as if there is an unconscious dialogue which allows perpetrators to pick out as victims women who feel more vulnerable and who are expecting attack.

Intrusion is when our usual mechanisms of self-protection simply do not work. When faced with fear our fight–flight responses usually come to the fore to help us. But when we cannot resist or escape, this state of helplessness causes internal mental protections to break down and our capacity to think is disturbed. The threat and terror is re-experienced as memories of the rape intrude. Years after the event a woman might be reliving the event as if it were continually recurring in the present. It is as if the trauma is running the mind, or, as Herman (1992: 37) puts it:

> The traumatic moment becomes encoded in an abnormal form of memory, which breaks spontaneously into consciousness, both as flashbacks during waking states and as traumatic nightmares during sleep. Small, seemingly insignificant reminders can also evoke these memories, which often return with all the vividness and emotional force of the original event.

Experiences of racism and homophobia compound this sense of fragmentation and hyperarousal where enforced projections on to social groups are a further intrusion leading to increased fragmentation and fear of attack. Where your experience leaves you with a greater sensitivity to being targeted for attack for some irrational reason such as skin colour or sexual orientation, you might already be in a state of hyperarousal and intrusion, leaving you more vulnerable to further attack.

Constriction is a state of passive numbness, a state of detached calm where the woman might feel as if she is not in her body – a dissociated state. Dissociation often happens as a way of protecting the self from something which is unbearable. It

protects the feelings about the trauma from breaking through but it can go too far, leading to a sense of complete disconnection from others and disintegration of the self. As Herman (1992: 42) describes:

> Events continue to register in awareness, but it is as though these events have been disconnected from their ordinary meanings ... the person may feel as though the event is not happening to her, as though she is observing from outside her body, or as though the whole experience is a bad dream from which she will shortly awaken.

A further response is what Freud called 'repetition compulsion', an unconscious process which serves to keep the conflict alive in order to control and understand it. Feelings emerging about the trauma may compel the woman to a form of re-enactment both consciously and unconsciously – for example the victim may go back to the scene of the event or go back to the perpetrator, risking a repeat attack.

Our bodies are our most sacred space. When a woman's body has been attacked it can become a site of shame; shame at not being able to stop the assault or protect herself from intrusion. This feeling can be compounded if at the point of trauma an identification with the perpetrator takes place. The woman feels that she is to blame, that she should be ashamed and needs to be punished – all feelings which may have been unconsciously projected by the perpetrator.

Often the trauma is somatized and attempts to block out painful memories might involve attacks on the body such as self-harm and eating problems, or drug and alcohol abuse. The body might be hidden away with fat or literally kept away out of sight indoors. It may be over-exposed or used in a sexual way as a metaphor for the conflict, for example by engaging in painful abusive sex. The perpetrator–victim relationship is played out through the body in an attempt to deal with what feels like an unresolvable problem. An identification with the perpetrator as a woman self-harms might make her feel temporarily in control of her more vulnerable part.

Some physical damage to the body may also have occurred which can leave the woman feeling contaminated. This might be actual, in that she may have contracted a sexually transmitted disease or have become pregnant. The damage may affect her ability to conceive and inhibit her sexual functioning. At an unconscious level she may also have experienced a psychic contamination, believing that she will never be able to have children or that the inside of her body is irreparably damaged, even if this may not actually be the case. The potentially long-lasting effect of the rape on the body is not to be underestimated.

Preparing for the work

Listening to and thinking about the material a woman brings, while at the same time being in tune with her feelings as well as our own, can feel quite overwhelming for much of the time. The work has a cumulative effect, having to bear witness to such atrocious events. What the client cannot bear to think about gets communicated to the therapist, who has to sit with unbearable feelings, often for some time. Therapists need their own space to think and talk so that a good supervisor is as important to the therapist as the therapist is to the client.

One of the first questions that needs to be asked is why we might want to do this kind of work. What are we trying to work out for ourselves? What is our motivation? What are our own attitudes to sexuality and, in particular, to rape?

Counsellors and psychotherapists often fear being flooded by the material; not being able to cope; feeling disgusted and appalled, voyeuristic or sexually aroused. The desire not to know or hear about rape is powerful, however willing we may feel ourselves to be. Female counsellors may feel more exposed and vulnerable to the risk of sexual violence. Hopelessness and uselessness are common feelings, as is rage at the perpetrators who are not convicted and the systems which do not bring justice. There is a risk either of an over-identification with the client or of becoming paralysed by guilt. While the feelings evoked in the work may be experienced by both male and female therapists, men may experience particular difficulties arising from their gender. They may become more concretely associated with the rapist or experience more confusion around sexual excitement in the work.

Women who have been through this trauma will have difficulty in trusting both male and female therapists although they may prefer, at least initially, to speak to a female therapist. Work with men at a later stage can help the woman restore faith in her relationships with men.

Being sensitive to how race issues might arise in the work is crucial – for example, a white woman therapist working with a black client whose rapist was white, or a black woman in a group where a white client's rapist was black will stir a particular dynamic. Primitive feeling states might trigger racist mythologies around race and sexual aggression or over-sexualization, historically often attributed by white people to black people.

A client may be living with the risk of repeated attack if the rapist is still at large. She may have practical problems such as housing, especially if she was raped in her own home. She may suffer from agoraphobia where she fears coming to the session. Offering her an appointment time when she does not have to travel in the dark and displaying some sensitivity about how she is treated on arrival at an unknown place can help support her with these difficulties.

What to offer the client

While some women seek help immediately, others present many years later when some event or memory such as a new sexual relationship triggers feelings about the rape. A common time to present is at anniversaries of the rape. The timing of therapeutic work in relation to the trauma is crucial. An instinct may be to offer therapy immediately, but in the initial stages, support and physical care may be more appropriate until the woman is in a state where she is able to begin to think about the experience.

For some women short-term individual work may be sufficient to work on the trauma so that some kind of normal life can continue. For others, particularly if they have been raped several times, or where there is psychic damage before the rape, more long-term work is needed.

Focal group psychotherapy for women who have been raped can be very helpful. Hearing other women's stories of feeling isolated, fearing for their lives, sharing the level of shame and anger experienced can aid recovery. The impact of the power relationship between client and counsellor, often experienced as unhelpful, can be diluted and feel less intimidating in a group. For women who have been raped by a gang or by more than one rapist there needs to be some consideration about the suitability of a group, or some careful preparation of the client about the issues that might emerge for her in a group.

The aim of therapy

For longer-term work our aim might be for the client to tell her story in a way which helps her to relive in the present the feelings attached to the event of the past. Through reconnecting with these feelings in the presence of a witness she can begin to integrate the experience and restore her capacity to manage her feelings and be more in touch with her resources to protect herself.

It often feels as if there is a tightrope to be walked in this work. The social reality of rape needs to be acknowledged. Women are not to blame for male sexual violence and are at risk of rape at any time of day, or of their lives, and in any place. Women often enter counselling or therapy with questions about whether they were to blame for the rape or whether they contributed in some way. A woman who has been repeatedly raped often asks why it is that some women never get raped while others are repeatedly attacked: a capacity to ask the question is a good sign.

Through the work in an environment where she is not being blamed or judged, a woman can begin to face the question. For some women it is clear that the rape is arbitrary and she could not have done anything more to protect herself. She is able to work through her feelings to free herself from a social prejudice which activates her self-blame. For others, usually where there is psychic damage prior to the rape, there may be more of a question about her own vulnerability and how she might have been better able to protect herself from the risk of attack – such as trusting her instincts that something was wrong at the time, which might have allowed her to seek help or better protect herself from the possibility of attack. Some women speak of an almost unconscious, unspoken agreement and expectation that the same thing will happen again. If she can acknowledge this without blaming herself she can leave the therapy feeling better able to protect herself in the future. There is a crucial difference here between taking responsibility and blaming herself for what has happened.

Women who have been raped have often lost touch with, or feel out of control of, their own aggression, frightened that they too would commit some atrocious act if it were expressed. Feeling rage at her rapist about what has happened to her is appropriate. In addition to this there comes a time later in the work where the client also has to own her own aggressive feelings. Learning to manage these can make her less vulnerable in the future to being the victim of others' violence.

The dynamics of rape may be present in the consulting room

By the time a woman comes for counselling or therapy her encounters with other professionals will influence how she sees the work and her expectations of the therapist.

The woman often brings with her a lack of faith in justice, a feeling that she has been blamed and not heard or believed. She might, then, feel on trial again or that she needs to defend herself. Unlike some shared traumas where survivors have gone through a similar experience, the experience of rape is one in which the victim is alone with the rapist (or gang of rapists) and feels utterly isolated. She may have tried in vain to call out for help when she was being raped, and then when she asks for help from professionals she can feel that no one comes to her aid. She often feels isolated, stigmatized or disconnected from her community. This is particularly accentuated with women who have been displaced from their own community or culture. A woman's ability to trust has been betrayed at a fundamental level.

Regardless of the therapist's orientation, the dynamics of the rape will be central to the therapist–client relationship. Issues such as abuse of power, one person controlling another, sexualization of contact, humiliation or force are always close to the surface in any exchange.

The trauma can be present in the consulting room in many ways, even when it is not being talked about. The intention behind what we offer as counsellors or psychotherapists may be experienced as the exact opposite by the client. We aim to provide a non-abusive relationship but the client's experience may be that all relationships are abusive. There is a certain inevitability that the therapist will at some stage be seen as, and will feel like, the abuser: not the 'therapist' but 'the rapist'.

The provision of a room with the door shut and with minimal disturbances means that as therapists we aim to provide a safe space. Our client, however, might feel trapped or imprisoned like she did during the rape, locked away with her rapist, experiencing the slightest noise from outside as an intrusion into the body. The counsellor's words, however benign, can feel as if they have the same power to intrude as the penis which violated. Dependency on a therapist is potentially life-threatening and needs to be resisted by the client at all costs, particularly in the early stages of a relationship as it becomes associated with the rape.

Our willingness to listen to excruciating stories may be experienced as voyeurism or judging and our response likened to that of other services such as police and courts.

The therapist might feel trapped or unable to move, desperate for the session to be over, or feel humiliated by the client as if being asked to experience what it felt like to be violated. Or she might be acutely aware of the immense power she has to control things. She might feel sexually aroused and feel like acting it out violently. These can be particularly disturbing feelings but need to be seen as important communications about what is problematic for the client. The difference between the therapist and the perpetrator is that the former makes herself available to receive these feelings, tolerates them and thinks about them without acting on them and then helps the client to manage them.

The therapist may be required to engage in substantial liaison and correspondence with other professionals with this client group. They may be required to give support for claims such as criminal injuries compensation or rehousing. The therapist needs to consider her own boundaries in terms of

how much help with practical or legal difficulties she might offer. In many instances it may be better to encourage the client to gain support for these difficulties outside the therapy relationship, such as through women's groups and advocacy projects. This leaves the therapy free for thinking about the client's inner world. Talk in the therapy about issues such as the need to find safe accommodation clearly has a real element which needs to be taken very seriously. It might also be an expression of a feeling of not having a safe place inside which is free from intrusion. Both aspects need working on.

While the work is tough there are great rewards in watching women develop psychologically: moving from a position of victim to survivor; experiencing relief at no longer feeling totally consumed by the experience and becoming able to get on with their lives; perhaps trusting enough to have a relationship again and not feeling so fearful of walking down the street.

Acknowledgement

I am deeply grateful to my clients, particularly those at the Women's Therapy Centre in London, who have taught me so much about this field.

References

Fawcett Society (2003) *Commission on Women and the Criminal Justice System.* Interim report on Victims and Witnesses. London: The Fawcett Society.

Garland, C. (1991) External disasters and the internal world: an approach to psychotherapeutic understanding of survivors. In J. Holmes (ed.), *Textbook of Psychotherapy in Psychiatric Practice.* Edinburgh: Churchill Livingstone Press.

Herman, J.L. (1992) *Trauma and Recovery – from Domestic Abuse to Political Terror.* London: HarperCollins.

Myhill, A. and Allen, J. (2002) *Rape and sexual assault of women: findings from the British Crime Survey.* London: Home Office Research, Development and Statistics Directorate.

6.20   Relationship Problems   ○○○

DEREK HILL*

The relationship problems discussed here are those which arise out of the central, intimate relationships between two adults. Marriages, cohabitations, heterosexual, gay and lesbian relationships and other 'non-traditional' and culturally different arrangements are encompassed. Relationship problems frequently involve issues such as medical and psychiatric conditions, sexual dysfunctions, (un)employment, financial problems, housing difficulties, criminal acts and civil disputes, and inequalities of opportunity. The assumption is made that clients are referred to specialized sources of assistance where such issues would otherwise impede the resolution of distressing interpersonal dynamics.

The nature of relationship problems

Couples – those engaged in intimate relationships – identify a very broad range of problems:

- communication difficulties
- conflicted needs, alienation
- affairs
- sexual problems
- conflicts as parents
- enforced gender role changes
- violence
- substance abuse
- jealousy/possessiveness.

Some seek help to sustain the continuing growth and change which offers enrichment of the partners' individual and shared lives. Many describe a 'stuckness' to do with an incapacity to talk about or resolve specific aspects of their relationship and the associated differences in attitudes, values and behaviours displayed by the partners. A variety of cyclic phenomena are experienced as blighting other relationships. Partners present their 'intolerable yet inescapable' situations within relationships. Some seek help to retain personal integrity while ending a relationship. Living longer challenges many of those in 'good' relationships as the partners' capacities and interests change progressively. Others' relationships are destabilized by the lack of the influence of a religious morality, or of a social environment that asserts norms of behaviour. Those entering a first or subsequent relationship may look for support as they work to define its scope and boundaries, and its expected rewards and responsibilities.

Couple relationships engage the partners at every level of their being. Disrupted couple relationships may therefore present as philosophical disputes, moral dilemmas, paradoxes, emotional hiatuses, physical illness, or life-threatening conflict. Potentially, they are among the most stressful of all adult experiences and can involve intense emotions, disturbed mental states, and a variety of somatic conditions. Specifically, clinical depression is a common consequence of relationship problems, and also a precipitating factor. Suicide and the murder of partner and/or children may also be linked with them.

Occurrence

UK government statistics show that an ever-growing proportion of marriages fail. There were 254,400 marriages in 2002 and in the same year 171,812 petitions for divorce were filed (ONS, 2003). Statistics relating to other forms of couple relationship are less reliable but suggest even higher

---

* Statistical information in this chapter has been updated by Cheryl Turner (formerly of Relate).

failure rates. The numbers of relationships which break down irretrievably give some indication of the prevalence of relationship problems in contemporary western society. They are probably the most common source of distress among normal, healthy adults. Relate, the largest couple counselling organization in the UK, saw over 140,000 clients in 2003 and provided about 255, 000 counselling sessions.

Origins

The roots of the problems faced by the partners in couple relationships lie in the essential qualities of those relationships. Attachment, dependency, intimacy, sexual engagement, exclusivity, parenting and asynchronous individual life stages each offer threats as well as benefits to the partners as the individuals strive to find a balance between personal needs and those of the relationship. The family, cultural and socio-economic contexts in which couple relationships are lived out can resource or deplete the partners' tolerances for anxiety and their capacities to solve problems. However, it is the nature of the partners' self-descriptions, and the pictures they carry within them of their preferred form of couple relationship which largely determine whether difficulties turn into problems. There have been many typographies of relationship problems but their primary characteristic is that each is a unique consequence of the constellations of issues contributed by the partners individually, by the dynamics they have established between themselves, and by the many external influences which shape their living environment. Thus, they may be recognized and owned by both partners, or only by one. Further, there is substantial evidence that profoundly dysfunctional aspects of couple relationships may not be recognized or owned by either partner. Although 'not a problem' for the couple, such features of relationships commonly underlie issues that do distress the partners.

Treatments of choice

The counselling of relationship problems encompasses so great a range of issues, and such a span of degrees of distress, that a number of specialized services have evolved. Individuals and couples refer themselves to pre-marital counselling, counselling for sexual problems, infertility counselling, bereavement counselling, divorce counselling and the counselling of those engaged in second and subsequent relationships.

Most who seek help in dealing with their relationships speak in terms of a combination of issues which are contributing to their problem. When those problems are being assessed, it is critically important to determine whether or not one or both of the partners are already using, or need, the services of other professions. The initial contact with a counsellor may serve the clients' best interests by affirming a continuing priority for use of other specialized services, or by assisting the clients to access them. There is evidence that drop-in and telephone relationship counselling services are frequently used by clients for those purposes. The relationship counsellor may occupy a role akin to that of a general practitioner and exercise similar skills in determining the limits within which counselling interventions are used, and the appropriateness and timing of assistance from other specialists.

Counselling may take the form of sessions with a relationship focus for one or both of the partners. The nature and duration of that counselling may be determined largely by the theoretical orientation and preferred strategies of the counsellor. However, substantial numbers of relationship counsellors have developed the ability to offer a variety of interventions and make use of the clients' perceptions, goals and preferences as well as their own assessments in setting up a contract for the kind of work to be undertaken. Broadly, the depth and duration of that counselling can be related to the degree to which problem resolution involves change in the inner worlds of the partners. Brief, dynamic work can catalyse radical internal change and may offer a couple a point of departure for further work on their own to consolidate new patterns of relating. Brief, focused work can resolve issues which might otherwise aggregate and threaten the survival of a relationship. More extended interventions are appropriate when dealing with the prospect, or implications, of major life experiences and events.

They also offer partners who are so disposed to work more reflectively and take the opportunity to explore, and assimilate into the relationship, childhood trauma or the roots of persistent and destructive patterns of interaction. It is instructive to note that Relate records case lengths ranging between one and more than 30 sessions, with a median number of five.

McCarthy et al. (1998) have reviewed the research into the effectiveness of a variety of theoretical approaches to, and modalities of, relationship counselling. There is no convincing evidence that any one theoretical approach is more generally effective than any other.

Research which establishes modalities and approaches of choice for a comprehensive range of relationship problems might be seen to be an urgent requirement as relationship counselling is used by more and more people. But the counsellor's task is to find interventions which address partners' problems, respect their values and life choices, and make best use of their individual and shared resources. That *unique* and complex undertaking is as much a matter of forging a therapeutic alliance as it is of applying researchers' findings.

Contra-indicators and risk factors

Effective counselling responses to clients' relationship problems are, of course, dependent upon the client's willing collaboration. There are a number of situations in which one or both partners are advised or instructed to seek counselling, for example, when the adults' custody of children is under threat. If that coercion results in sustained hostility towards counselling, its early termination is indicated. Where clients approach counselling with a view to securing material for use in court hearings, and are unwilling to relinquish that purpose, a referral to an appropriate source of expert assessment such as a clinical psychologist should be made and counselling should be terminated. Evidence of a partner's alcoholism, eating problems, clinical depression or psychotic states, suicidal ideation or obsessive gambling all call for the suspension of relationship counselling while other, specialized forms of assistance are used. That

is to say, where influences are at work which cannot be addressed effectively by relationship counselling, yet which are amenable to other forms of professional intervention, the latter should be accessed by the clients before a sustained counselling intervention is offered.

The risks associated with relationship counselling are primarily those of serious (physical) harm to one of the partners, or another. Domestic violence may be contained by negotiation of a zero-violence contract, but may necessitate a disclosure to the authorities or assistance for a victim who needs safe accommodation. Evidence, or the suspicion, of child sexual or physical abuse is generally regarded as the justification for a prompt disclosure to the authorities, in some cases *without* prior notification of the clients.

Affairs, separation and divorce, and 'tugs of love' create situations in which numbers of murders have been committed. While such situations are infrequent, relationship counsellors need to be open to the possibility that they may be in a position to prevent loss of life either through the use of their own skills, or by acknowledging the limitations of the service they are offering.

Prognosis and management

The diversity of relationship problems makes it impossible to offer an overall prognosis. Research shows that most of those who experience relationship counselling become less emotionally disturbed, understand themselves better and have improved self-regard, and many understand their partner and their relationship better. Numbers are helped to sustain and enrich their relationships. Others are assisted to end them with somewhat less acrimony. Some learn to manage shared parenting while relinquishing partnership. McCarthy et al. (1998) offer a research insight into outcomes, which may help to inform prognoses.

Using contact with one or both of the partners, the relationship counsellor helps couples find a balance between individual needs and those of their relationships. The issues faced are those of difference, affiliations, and respect for self and others. The challenges for partners and counsellor alike are those of one or other form of triangular relationship; collusions based on culture, gender, attitudes and unconscious agendas; and defences used to guard against intimacy, isolation, dependency, power differentials and conflict.

Within the bounds of a respect for the right of others to life and well-being, it is the task of the counsellor to help partners to sustain relationships which offer them a maximum of shared and individual fulfilment. Clinical management of that work may involve:

- negotiation of a contract for counselling, its boundaries, purposes, working methods and duration;
- renegotiation of the counselling contract to accommodate change in the needs of one or both partners;
- maintenance of the overall confidentiality and privacy of the content of counselling if under threat of use for other purposes;
- maintenance of a continuing working focus on the couple's relationship;
- use of work with partners' individual material for the purposes of the relationship;
- maintenance of an impartial engagement with each partner;
- avoidance of counter-productive dynamics within the counselling (see challenges listed earlier);
- balancing attention given to potentially intrusive third-party relationships (children, parents, other adults) with the needs of the couple relationship;
- clients' referral to, and (concurrent) engagement with, other specialized sources of assistance;
- the duty of confidentiality to individual partners and the holding of secrets;
- the safety of the partners, and of the counselling, where individuals are predisposed to violence;
- disclosure to the authorities of (risk of) serious harm to clients or others.

Current issues

The proposed Family Law Act 1996 had among its provisions access to relationship counselling for those contemplating divorce. The desire of government to 'save those marriages which are saveable' was creditable, as was the opportunity for more couples to benefit from counselling. However, there were risks that the authorities would determine the nature of the counselling provided. The association of relationship counselling with that legislation and the final stages of relationship breakdown might also have reinforced the current tendency to use it as a 'treatment of last resort'. Numerous studies provide evidence that relationship problems are much more effectively addressed earlier on.

The use of counselling provided through 'managed care' as a response to relationship problems is much more prevalent in the USA than it is currently in Britain. However, the growth of counselling delivered through primary health care practices, employee assistance programmes, and by charities with strictly limited financial resources and soaring costs, has put 'brief relationship counselling' on the agenda and has added to the attractions of those forms of counselling which adopt objectives allowing outcomes to be evaluated relatively easily. Those influences will have an important effect on the future of all forms of counselling. It will be important for those with a particular concern for relationship problems to give similar consideration to the impact of society on the nature of adult intimate relationships and family life. There is already ample evidence that couples exercise an ever greater freedom to make choices about lifestyle and patterns of relationships. The nature of relationship problems changes as those involved in them experiment with and change their assumptions and priorities. Formulaic interventions can fall far short of responding to their needs. It seems likely that new ways of offering insights into fundamental human capacities and needs will be called for if counselling's response to relationship problems is to be more than a superficial exercise in relieving distress.

References

McCarthy, P., Walker, J. and Kain, J. (1998) *Telling It As It Is: The Client Experience of Relate Counselling.* Newcastle: Newcastle Centre for Family Studies.

ONS (Office of National Statistics) (2003) *Popular Trends 117.* London: HMSO.

Recommended reading

Clark, D. and Haldane, D. (1990) *Wedlocked?* Cambridge: Polity Press.

Clulow, C. (ed.) (1993) *Rethinking Marriage: Public and Private Perspectives.* London: Karnac.

Clulow, C. and Mattinson, J. (1989) *Marriage Inside Out: Understanding Problems of Intimacy.* London: Penguin.

Dicks, H. (1967) *Marital Tensions.* London: Routledge and Kegan Paul.

Gottman, J. (1997) *Why Marriages Succeed or Fail and How You Can Make Yours Last.* London: Bloomsbury.

Hooper, D. and Dryden, W. (eds) (1991) *Couple Therapy: A Handbook.* Buckingham: Open University Press.

Karpel, M.A. (1994) *Evaluating Couples: A Handbook for Practitioners.* New York: W.W. Norton.

OPCS (Office of Population Censuses and Surveys) (1996) *General Household Survey 1994.* London: HMSO.

6.21 Schizophrenia   ○○○

RICHARD GATER AND ANN GLEDHILL

Schizophrenia is a complex disorder affecting all aspects of an individual's life. There are many approaches to the treatment of schizophrenia. These need to be brought together in an appropriate, effective and timely fashion to maximize the benefits to the individual. This section begins with a brief overview of schizophrenia and its causes. This is followed by the general principles of treatment, which is included in order to place therapy in the context of the overall management of schizophrenia. The main part on therapies describes the use of supportive counselling and specific therapies, along with the problems that can arise working with this client group.

What is schizophrenia?

Schizophrenia is a disease of the brain. In its most severe form it is a disabling and devastating illness for the individual, family and friends. This is not simply due to the direct effects of the illness itself, but also the lost opportunities, mythology, rejection and stigma that are associated with severe mental illness. Schizophrenia occurs in all races, and all

walks of life. Two surprising facts about schizophrenia are that it is a *common* disease affecting about 1 per cent of the population during the course of their lives, and that, although it cannot be cured, it is an eminently *treatable* disorder. Most people who have schizophrenia respond well to drug therapy and can lead productive and satisfying lives. Although schizophrenia has probably existed for thousands of years, it has only been conceptualized as a disease entity since the middle of the nineteenth century. In 1899, Kraepelin described the symptoms and course of 'dementia praecox', which corresponds closely with the current concept of schizophrenia. When, in 1908, Bleuler introduced the term schizophrenia, he acknowledged that this included a group of psychoses rather than a single disease entity. During the second half of the twentieth century, efforts have been made to develop a reliable and uniform approach to the diagnosis of schizophrenia. In the 1950s, Schneider identified the 'first rank' symptoms, which in the absence of organic disease signify schizophrenia. These have been refined into operational definitions in the two major international classifications of diseases: the World Health Organization's *International*

Classification of Diseases (ICD), and the American Psychiatric Association's *Diagnostic and Statistical Manuals* (DSM). These classifications provide a sound basis on which to make a reliable diagnosis, and for research and its findings to be applied consistently in clinical practice and service planning.

Schizophrenia affects equal numbers of men and women. The onset is typically slightly earlier in men (late teens or early twenties) than women (twenties or early thirties), though it can start at any age. The onset may be sudden, but sometimes occurs as subtle changes over a number of years (insidious onset).

An episode of acute schizophrenia is characterized by positive psychotic symptoms. These include impaired ability to think clearly and logically (thought disorder), which is expressed as disjointed speech that can be impossible to follow. False beliefs, often persecutory, are held with absolute conviction despite evidence to the contrary (delusions). There may be the belief that thoughts, feelings or actions are controlled by, or known to, others. False perceptions (hallucinations) most commonly take the form of voices heard only by the individual, which may threaten or comment on them. These symptoms are accompanied by impaired ability to distinguish that the psychotic experiences are not real, and impaired appreciation that the symptoms are due to illness and that treatment is needed (loss of insight). Positive symptoms are mediated through imbalance in the chemical transmitters in certain parts of the brain.

Positive symptoms occur during a relapse of schizophrenia, but they are often greatly reduced with effective treatment. Some people have just one episode of acute schizophrenia and make a full and complete recovery. Others suffer several episodes during their lives but are able to lead relatively normal lives between episodes. A third group, those with 'chronic schizophrenia', are liable to recurring episodes. They do not make a full recovery between episodes but have continuing positive and negative symptoms. Negative symptoms are deficits in normal behaviour, for example loss of drive, social withdrawal, and a lack of emotional expression.

Alongside the distinctive positive and negative symptoms of schizophrenia, people with schizophrenia also experience other symptoms of emotional distress such as depressed mood, anxiety and poor sleep.

Moral weakness or bad parenting does not cause schizophrenia. The concept of the schizophrenogenic family, for example, has been largely discredited. Schizophrenia does not have a simple single cause. In common with many physical diseases, it results from the interplay between genetic, environmental and psychological factors. Schizophrenia is more common in some families due to a genetic predisposition. Other biological factors affecting the foetus in the womb or perinatal complications also influence the development of schizophrenia. These factors produce vulnerability to schizophrenia, which may be subsequently triggered by stress, physical illness or some street drugs. The social environment has a profound effect on the course of schizophrenia. Stressful events, increased responsibilities, heavy criticism, hostility or over-involvement from someone in close contact, increase the likelihood of relapse. On the other hand, under-stimulation, isolation or even prolonged hospitalization can contribute to loss of social, occupational or daily living skills.

General principles of treatment for people with schizophrenia

Modern treatment of schizophrenia is many faceted, and usually involves different professional groups. The core mental health team of nurses, psychologists, psychiatrists, occupational therapists and social workers provides care along with the general practitioner and various organizations, according to the needs of each individual. Family members often provide daily care or support, and are the first to identify problems. Others may provide care or help in particular cases, including people with expertise in benefits, education, employment or housing, the police, probation, voluntary organizations, counselling or psychotherapy.

Co-ordination of such a diverse collection of people is complex. In different parts of the world, a variety of approaches has been used to bring care providers together to ensure that care is flexible and effective. In 1991 the Department of Health introduced the Care Programme Approach, in which a written care plan is agreed after careful assessment of the clinical and social needs. A 'key worker' ensures that the care plan meets the identified needs and that care is offered in a co-ordinated and appropriate way. The care needs and plan are regularly reviewed and revised at care plan review meetings. When counselling or psychotherapy is offered to someone receiving a complex package of care, it is important that the therapist liaises closely with other care providers to ensure that their work is supported, and the rest of the care team is aware of their input.

In 1999, the Department of Health further strengthened services for people with severe mental illnesses with the publication of the *National Service Framework for Mental Health* (Department of Health, 2000). This aimed to ensure appropriate, comprehensive and timely care by anticipating and planning for crises. The NICE guidelines on the core interventions in the treatment and management of schizophrenia in primary and secondary care (NICE, 2002) build upon this foundation, giving detailed guidance on services for people with schizophrenia from initiation of treatment in the first episode and treatment of an acute episode through to promotion of recovery. The guidelines highlight the importance of psychological interventions, particularly cognitive-behavioural therapy and family interventions to prevent relapse, reduce symptoms, enhance insight and promote adherance to medication.

Schizophrenia is a disorder in which the balance of neuro-chemical transmitters in the brain is disrupted. At the centre of treatment of schizophrenia is anti-psychotic medication to redress this imbalance. In most cases, positive symptoms respond to anti-psychotic medication, thus allowing the individual to function more effectively and appropriately, and to take advantage of other social and therapeutic activities. Anti-psychotic medicine does not cure schizophrenia, and for those at risk of further episodes continuing preventive use of anti-psychotic medication is required. Oral treatment is used in the short term, but this is often replaced by long-acting intra-muscular depot injection for maintenance treatment and prevention. In a depot preparation the anti-psychotic medicine is injected in an oily base, which delays absorption so that the anti-psychotic is slowly released over a period of weeks. Relapse is more likely if anti-psychotic medication is stopped or taken irregularly. Therefore, it is important that people with schizophrenia work with their care team to adhere to the care plan. Depot injections improve compliance, because they can be given every few weeks. Anti-psychotic drugs are not addictive, and at appropriate doses they do not turn people into 'zombies'. However, they may have troubling side-effects, such as sedation or muscular stiffness or trembling. Often these side-effects can be minimized by adjustment of the dosage, change of medication or use of another medicine to counteract the muscular side-effects, supervised by the doctor and psychiatric nurse.

Anti-psychotic drugs are the mainstay of treatment of positive symptoms, but there are often residual positive symptoms, or behavioural difficulties in communication, motivation, self-care and occupation that benefit from psychosocial treatments. Rehabilitation programmes focus on graded social and vocational training, to build skills and performance in daily living activities, problem solving, use of public amenities, communication and job training. In-patient treatment may be necessary in acute relapse if there are significant risks, and effective treatment cannot be provided in the community. Because the person with schizophrenia may not have insight, they may not recognize the importance of treatment. Therefore, many countries have legal provision for compulsory admission to hospital if the individual has a mental illness, is at risk to themselves or others, and does not agree to treatment. Recent service developments have attempted to improve care and reduce the rate and length of admission by providing access to acute day hospital as an alternative to admission, or intensive 24-hour support in the community targeted at those at greatest risk of admission (assertive community treatment). However, as yet, these are not widely available, and vary from place to place in what they provide and how effectively they achieve their objectives.

Therapies

Given the constraints imposed by the shortness of this chapter and the complexity of this client group, it is not our intention to suggest that readers will be able to go on to carry out therapy. Nevertheless, the chapter should provide an awareness of the therapeutic approaches available, and maximize use of existing skills. This understanding will be of benefit in helping readers to develop an important supportive relationship both with people with schizophrenia and with their carers.

One of the pervasive myths surrounding working with people with schizophrenia is that one should not challenge their delusions or encourage them to talk about their voices. In order to develop any supportive therapeutic relationship it is essential to acknowledge and not to deny the individual's experiences. This does not mean colluding with them. It is also important to remember that most people with schizophrenia hold perfectly rational conversations most of the time.

Supportive counselling

Various studies have used supportive counselling as a control condition and found that, although less effective in terms of symptom reduction/relapse than cognitive-behavioural therapy (CBT) approaches, it has benefits over routine care (Tarrier et al., 1998). Unfortunately, it appears that being offered empathic listening may not be a common experience for people with schizophrenia. Supportive counselling may play an important role in enhancing self-esteem and reducing distress.

In general, counselling skills are all applicable to working with people with schizophrenia and, in particular, for working with carers. People who go on to obtain specialist training to work therapeutically will find counselling skills an essential prerequisite. However, several additional factors should be emphasized and taken into consideration when engaging with someone with schizophrenia.

Additional counselling skills/factors when talking with someone with schizophrenia

Taking time to ensure that a good relationship has developed may take time and perseverance but is essential. Factors which may make this easier include being flexible with the location and duration of sessions to fit in with clients. When people have paranoid beliefs, developing a trusting relationship will take more time and persistence. Being open and not evading direct questions can help with engagement.

Often people with schizophrenia experience difficulties in concentration. This may be due to distracting voices, organic changes in the brain, depression, and/or medication. During a session it is important to obtain feedback regularly and to summarize frequently both in verbal and written forms. Avoid using abstract terms and strive to be clear and concrete in your communication. Reducing the length of a session or taking breaks can help with concentration.

When working with people who have delusions, remain open-minded: one person's delusion is another person's strong belief and reality. At times the other person's beliefs may appear so bizarre that you may be tempted to challenge them forcefully. Instead of helping, this causes the false beliefs to become more firmly entrenched as the challenge is met with resistance and the beliefs are defended, and thus strengthened. A golden rule here is 'Don't get into arguments. If stuck, agree to differ.'

Background to specific therapy approaches

Psychological approaches for working with schizophrenia have as their basis a stress vulnerability model: that is, that symptoms may have a biological origin but their occurrence and maintenance may be determined by psychological and environmental factors such as stress. Interventions to identify and change the occurrence or perception of these psychological factors may be of benefit.

Specifically, hallucinations can be viewed as mis-interpretations of one's own intrusive thoughts or of ambiguous external stimuli. Delusions are viewed as strongly held beliefs that are maintained by normal cognitive processes such as selective attention and the perceived consequences of giving up the belief. Therefore, in principle, cognitive therapy approaches should be effective. However, given the strength, duration and emotional attachment to these beliefs, and the impact of these beliefs on the person's functioning, intervention can be extremely difficult and should only occur collaboratively and with client consent. Further, the provision of specific therapeutic interventions will require specialist training and on-going supervision.

Interventions that have been shown to be effective are family interventions, residual symptom management or acute symptom management. The aims of these interventions include reduction in frequency or preoccupation with symptoms, reduction in the distress, disruption and stigma caused by symptoms, and increase in control and self-esteem.

Specific therapy approaches

A summary of these approaches is given, but for fuller descriptions please refer to the indicated references.

Family interventions

Psycho-educational approaches involve working with carers (Barrowclough and Tarrier, 1992). Clients living with relatives with high expressed emotion (EE, defined as over-involvement, critical comments and hostility) are more likely to relapse. Interventions aim to reduce EE via education, problem solving and stress management, and to enhance client functioning through goal setting. The provision of accurate information can be extremely useful in reducing stress within families/care settings. For example, a carer who assumes that someone with schizophrenia does not get up in the morning and does not wash because they are lazy, can be helped by knowing that this behaviour is a negative symptom of schizophrenia and that the sedative effect of the medication may make them more tired.

Living with a relative who has schizophrenia can be extremely stressful and it is not surprising that some relatives display high levels of expressed emotion. Furthermore the stress of caring can lead to psychological problems in carers. Counsellors working alongside other mental health professionals can play a key role in supporting carers in understanding, coming to terms with, and coping with caring for someone with schizophrenia. Such support may help to prevent anxiety and depression in carers and can serve to engage carers in the detection of early signs of relapse and in treatment compliance.

Residual symptom management

Coping strategy enhancement helps the individual identify and utilize existing strategies, develop new strategies and reduce the use of maladaptive strategies, such as drinking to cope with positive symptoms.

Psycho-education and normalization involve explaining and de-stigmatizing symptoms by relating symptoms to normal experiences, such as the occurrence of positive symptoms as a result of sleep deprivation (Kingdon and Turkington, 1994).

Belief modification involves sensitively questioning and evaluating the function and utility of delusional beliefs.

Focusing is an approach primarily for auditory hallucinations. It involves encouraging the person to focus on their symptom, its physical characteristics and associated beliefs (Haddock and Slade, 1996). Focusing aims to help the individual to reduce anxiety associated with hallucinations and to understand and address their occurrence, and factors maintaining them.

Relapse prevention involves helping the person to identify signs (emotional, behavioural, and physical) which commonly precede a relapse of symptoms (early signs), and to devise an action plan to deal with these. This may include stress reduction, respite or changes in medication. By helping the individual to identify these early on and act sooner, relapse can be prevented or severity reduced and the individual's sense of self-efficacy enhanced. Further advantages include reduced likelihood of stigmatizing behaviour or the need for crisis interventions.

Acute symptom management

Early intervention or acute management aim to reduce the duration of untreated illness and first psychotic episode. These involve the early detection of 'at risk' mental states, and interventions targeted during the early phase of psychosis (the 'critical period') (Drury et al., 1996; Lewis et al., 2002). New developments in this area include the identification of people who are at high risk of developing psychosis and interventions to prevent onset.

Combined CBT strategies

This is the most commonly used and advocated approach in clinical settings (Fowler et al., 1995). It involves combining the above specific approaches into an individually tailored package of care. This may include coping strategy enhancement, collaborative discussion of a new model, cognitive therapy strategies for delusional beliefs and beliefs about voices, cognitive therapy for delusional assumptions or social disability, and relapse management strategies. The use of cognitive behavioural therapy in addition to standard psychiatric care can reduce positive symptoms more effectively than standard psychiatric care alone.

Potential problems of working with clients with schizophrenia

Therapy with a client who has schizophrenia carries similar risks to therapy with other client groups, and caution should be taken to agree clear and realistic objectives, and to establish clear limits. A special risk in this client group is that therapy may potentially trigger or aggravate a relapse of psychosis. This can occur if positive symptoms are validated, forcefully challenged, or if the therapy proves to be so stressful that it results in a significant increase in the client's arousal. Close liaison with the mental health team may alert the therapist to the risk of relapse, and under some circumstances adjustment of medical treatment and close monitoring may be useful to give added protection against psychosis during a stressful phase of therapy. Likewise, therapists may be disappointed or disillusioned if their expectations are unrealistic or they enter a therapeutic relationship without supervision and find themselves out of their depth. An ambitious programme of psychotherapy without medication will not cure schizophrenia.

Close liaison with the mental health team is also crucial if the client reveals symptoms associated with risk to themselves or others. These include suicidal ideation, perceived threats, persecutory delusions that identify specific individuals, delusions of being controlled, statements of intentions to harm someone, command hallucinations and disorientation. Although the great majority of people with schizophrenia are not violent, three key features that should alert the therapist to the possibility of violence are a past history of violence, continuing substance abuse, and non-compliance with treatment. It is good practice for the mental health team to carry out a formal risk assessment, and they may be able to alert you to the level of risk and cues for violence. As a general principle, clients should be seen in a safe environment from which you can call for immediate assistance or make a judicious exit. If the client becomes agitated or threatening, try to maintain calm, and avoid confrontation or intrusion of their personal space. If violence does occur, training in breakaway techniques can give you the skills to remove yourself to safety. Most mental health professionals are encouraged to have regular training in breakaway techniques. After a violent incident ensure that you have opportunity for de-briefing and ventilation, and immediately inform the key worker and other relevant professionals of the incident.

New frontiers

Psychosocial interventions for psychosis are increasingly being shown to be an effective adjunct to drug therapy in reducing relapse rates, reducing positive symptoms and reducing distress. Interventions are now focusing on combinations of problems that were previously seen as difficult to treat. A motivational interviewing and CBT approach has been developed for people who have a dual diagnosis of schizophrenia with drug or alcohol problems. Other developments include looking at the relationship between psychosis and post-traumatic stress disorder (Morrison et al., 2003). New research is underway looking at the impact of treatment at an early stage, and at clients who also abuse drugs and alcohol. In contrast, less research has been focused on developing effective interventions for negative symptoms and social functioning.

References

Barrowclough, C. and Tarrier, N. (1992) *Families of Schizophrenic Patients: Cognitive Behavioural Intervention.* London: Chapman and Hall.

Department of Health (2000) *National Service Framework for Mental Health.* London: Department of Health.

Drury, V., Birchwood, M., Cochrane, R. and Macmillan, F. (1996) Cognitive therapy and recovery from acute psychosis, 1: Impact on psychotic symptoms. *British Journal of Psychiatry,* 169: 593–601.

Fowler, D., Garety, P. and Kuipers, L. (1995) *Cognitive Therapy for Psychosis.* Chichester: Wiley.

Haddock, G. and Slade, P. (eds) (1996) *Cognitive Behavioural Interventions with Psychotic Disorders.* London: Routledge.

Kingdon, D.G. and Turkington, D. (1994) *Cognitive-Behavioral Therapy of Schizophrenia.* Hove: Psychology Press.

Lewis, S., Tarrier, N. and Haddock G. (2002) Randomised controlled trial of cognitive-behavioural therapy in early schizophrenia: acute-phase outcomes. *British Journal of Psychiatry,* 181 (suppl.): s91–s97.

Morrison, A.P. (2002) *A Casebook of Cognitive Therapy for Psychosis.* London: Routledge.

NICE (2002) *Core Interventions in the Treatment and Management of Schizophrenia in Primary and Secondary Care.* NICE Guidelines. London: National Institute of Clinical Excellence.

Tarrier, N., Yusupoff, L., Kinney, C., McCarthy, E., Gledhill, A., Haddock, G. and Morris, J. (1998) Randomised controlled trial of intensive cognitive behaviour therapy for patients with chronic schizophrenia. *British Medical Journal,* 317: 303–307.

Recommended reading

Birchwood, M. and Tarrier, N. (1994) *Psychological Management of Schizophrenia.* Chichester: Wiley.

Chadwick, D. and Birchwood, M. (1994) The omnipotence of voices. A cognitive approach to auditory hallucinations. *British Journal of Psychiatry,* 164: 190–201.

Chadwick, P., Birchwood, M. and Trower, P. (1996) *Cognitive Therapy for Delusions, Voices and Paranoia.* Chichester: Wiley.

Mace, C. and Margison, F. (eds) (1997) *The Psychotherapy of Psychosis.* London: Royal College of Psychiatrists.

Nelson, H. (1997) *Cognitive Behaviour Therapy with Schizophrenia: A Practice Manual.* Cheltenham: Stanley Thornes.

6.22 Sexual Abuse in Childhood

MOIRA WALKER

What is sexual abuse?

Any discussion of sexual abuse has to acknowledge that many children who are sexually abused are also abused physically and emotionally and that many children who are not abused sexually are damaged by other forms of abuse. In working with adult survivors it is particularly important to be aware of this as some survivors feel their abusive experiences are somehow insignificant if they were not sexual in nature. Indeed, the NSPCC suggest that emotional abuse is the most hidden and underestimated form of child maltreatment (Cawson et al., 2000).

My definition of sexual abuse is based on recognizing the essential misuse of power and authority, combined with force or coercion, which leads to the exploitation of children in situations where adults, or children sufficiently older than the victim, have greater strength and power, seek sexual gratification through those who are developmentally immature and where, as a result, consent from the victim is a non-concept. What is central is the exploitation of the child, the denial of their rights and feelings, and the essential gratification of the abuser through the child, the child being regarded solely as an object for the perpetrator's use and to meet their needs.

Sexual abuse occurs in all communities, ethnic backgrounds, religions, cultures and social and economic classes, and is experienced by both males and females, although to date research suggests that the majority of victims are female and the majority of perpetrators male. Some abuse is particularly violent, long-lasting and frequent, while other abuse is a single incident. There is current and serious concern about the use of the internet for child pornography as a form of child sexual abuse that is particularly difficult to police but that horribly involves many children. It is now also increasingly recognized that adolescent abuse of younger children is a serious problem.

It is crucial to recognize the complexities of defining sexual abuse to avoid falling into over-simplified stereotyping that prevents survivors seeking help. For example, it appears frequently difficult for male survivors to present for counselling and therapy, and as female abuse has been underestimated and denied in the past, it can be similarly difficult for those abused by women to come forward. Much that was previously firmly believed to be true has been proved wrong in the light of new evidence, and child victims and adult survivors have suffered as a consequence. Working with survivors is working in a field where much remains unknown and where counsellors are often faced with believing the apparently unbelievable.

The extent of sexual abuse

Statistics for England up to 31 March 2000 show 30,300 children on the child protection register: of these, 5,600 were registered for sexual abuse. Although this had dropped to 2,800 by March 2002, it is unlikely to represent a significant decrease, rather a different method of collating statistics. Retrospective studies and clinical work with survivors suggest that official child protection figures are the tip of the iceberg, with many children suffering in isolation and in silence. An NSPCC study, published in 2000, on young people aged 18–24 showed that 1 per cent had suffered sexual abuse by a parent or carer and 3 per cent by another relative during their childhood, with 75 per cent of those reporting sexual acts against their wishes being female (Cawson et al., 2000).

Estimates of abuse do vary considerably. Some recent studies suggest that at least 25 per cent of males and 33 per cent of females experience sexual abuse before the age of 18. Others suggest figures of 8 per cent for males and 12 per cent for females. In the UK, the first set of figures would mean that over 20 per cent of the population (in excess of 10,400,000 people) are survivors of sexual abuse. Variations in the figures reflect the real difficulty in defining, researching and measuring sexual abuse. But even if the most conservative of estimates is taken, a very large number of the adult population are survivors of abuse.

A 1997 report (National Statistics, 1997) indicates that of men born in England and Wales in 1953, seven in 1,000 have a conviction for sexual offences against a child by the age of 40. Home Office figures show that in 1997 the police were notified of 1,269 offences of 'gross indecency with a child under 14 years' and that at least one-quarter of recorded rape victims are children. Other studies show that men convicted of sexual offences against a child claim five or more undetected sexual assaults for which they were never caught. Given that many perpetrators will not be honest about the extent of their offending, that many will not be caught and others will not be prosecuted, these figures also provide some idea of the potential extent of the problem.

An adult retrospective study demonstrated that 50 per cent of adults abused as children never reported the abuse and that in 67 per cent of cases the abuse started before the age of 11 years old. Another NSPCC study (Ghate and Daniels, 1997) took a national sample of 998 children aged 8–11 years and found that 15 per cent said they would not talk to someone if they had a problem. It may therefore be difficult to precisely state the size of the problem of sexual abuse but what is clear is that it is a major problem and one that remains frequently hidden from the view of a wider world, and maintained as a dreadful secret by both the child victim and the adult survivor.

The impact of sexual abuse on the child

The impact of abuse on the child is well documented and researched (Bray, 1997; Walker, 1992). The basic needs of children for love, security, care and nurture, safety, appropriate boundaries and respect for self and body are consistently undermined by sexual abuse. The abused child learns to confuse love and sex, and love and violence. Life is unpredictable and unsafe; personal boundaries are invaded physically, sexually and emotionally. What should be the safest place for the child – their home – is the most dangerous for many abused children, so nowhere is safe, and no time is safe and bribery serves to effectively silence and frighten the child into submission.

The existence of a safe attachment and a secure base is essential for satisfactory development: children learn who they are and what sort of person they are through their earliest relationships. Safe and secure attachment can be wrecked or damaged by abuse. Children abused by significant care givers are in an impossible position: the person they need and trust for protection is also the one the child needs protection from, and the impact on development is huge and negative.

Sexually abused children are frequently isolated, mistrustful and deeply confused. They live in a climate of fear, often experience considerable pain, and for children who are abused by one parent or carer, but are unable to tell the other, they effectively become a psychological orphan. Education frequently suffers and they can become labelled as attention-seeking, difficult, naughty or bad – all reinforcing their sense of unacceptability. Feelings of shame, guilt, dirtiness, badness and of being unlovable and unlikeable are often experienced and extend into adulthood.

The impact of childhood abuse on the adult

Sexual abuse in childhood frequently leaves the adult with a catalogue of losses to deal with that render assimilation into the wider world extremely problematic. The long-term effects of child sexual abuse have been well documented, and a meta-analysis carried out by Neumann and colleagues (1996) of 38 studies of the impact of child sexual abuse on later adult problems identified these as anxiety, depression, re-victimization, sexual problems, self-harm, suicidal tendencies, post-traumatic stress symptoms, dissociation, interpersonal problems, problems of self-esteem and substance abuse. In addition, other studies have shown a high proportion of survivors in the psychiatric population. Ainscough and Toon (1996) state that 50 per cent of women and 23 per cent of men receiving psychiatric help have been sexually abused.

This is not to say that all survivors of abuse will experience severe difficulties during adult life. Some clearly do not, raising the interesting question of what are the protecting factors. As a rule of thumb, it appears that the following are likely to intensify the negative long-term effects of abuse:

- the younger the child when abused
- the closer the relationship of the abuser to the child
- the significance of that person as an attachment figure
- abuse that is repeated over many years
- the involvement of others in the abuse (e.g. in an abuse ring)
- the absence of other supportive or loving figures.

If the abuser is a close care giver and the child is very young, the damage is likely to be considerable and long-lasting. But while it is recognized that the extent of the impact of abuse is related to its severity, duration and closeness of the victim to the abuser, the impact of single incidents should never be underestimated, particularly when the abuser is a trusted adult on whom the child depends. A girl of 13 who was sexually abused on one occasion only by her previously apparently trustworthy and loved and loving father felt this had destroyed her trust, wrecked her relationship with both parents, and had long-term and very serious consequences for her.

Therapeutic issues in counselling abuse survivors

These are many and complex. The provision of a safe, trustworthy and appropriately boundaried space is essential for the abuse survivor – remembering that abuse invades the boundaries of the self and damages the child's trust. Being believed and being heard are essential and central. Most children have been abused by a person whom society deems to be trustworthy (e.g. parents, step-parents, other family members and carers) and counsellors and psychotherapists arrive with the same label. Consequently, trust has to be worked at and earned and may be constantly tried and tested and re-tried by the client.

In early sessions the counsellor may or may not know if abuse is an issue, and even if the client's presentation indicates this, counsellors should never suggest abuse. Even when abuse is on the agenda, words should not be put into the client's mouth. Counsellors need to listen carefully, framing interventions in the client's own language and not pushing the client into revealing what they are not yet ready to reveal.

One of the central dilemmas in working with abuse survivors is that of remaining gently supportive while also being effectively containing. There is always a danger of the therapist being experienced as being ineffective or uncaring or uninterested (just as abuse survivors will have experienced in childhood), or being seen as abusive and invasive (as with their experience of the abuser). It is a delicate therapeutic balance.

While it is crucial to be empathic and connected to the client's experience, it is important to make contact without the client feeling the counsellor is somehow getting inside them, or has magical powers to 'know' about them. This resonates powerfully with the original experience of sexual abuse. Thus, enormous care has to be taken not to be invasive or inappropriate and, while helping the client to recognize a theme, not trapping them into uncomfortable exploration.

Being aware of the misuse of power in the adult's own childhood, and not misusing the power implicit in the counselling situation, is central. The client had no control over their abuse, but should control the pace and development of counselling sessions. It is also significant that women who have been abused in childhood are a particular target for the small but significant group of male therapists who have sexual relations with women clients.

Although gender issues in working with survivors are complex, if the counsellor is the same gender as their abuser, this may be an impossible scenario for the client. A choice of counsellor is important, although difficulties may still remain. For example, a woman abused by a man may see a woman counsellor as helpless and as impotent as she was.

Some survivors will decide while they are in counselling that they wish to take legal action against their abusers. Although counsellors can assist the client in exploring their reasons for doing so, help them to consider what they may hope to achieve, and support them during this process, it is crucial that clients who are seriously considering legal action seek legal advice. Counsellors need to take care to only work within their own area of expertise. They may be called to give evidence in such cases and therefore would need to take appropriate advice themselves.

Therapeutic approaches

Research on what works best is limited (Dale et al., 1998) but anecdotal evidence from survivors is strong. Although Dialectical Behaviour Therapy (DBT) seems to be having a promising effect in terms of reducing self-harm by abuse survivors, many survivors themselves are not positive about short-term approaches.

Generally speaking, there is not a good match between a survivor struggling to seek help for the first time and short-term or time-limited work, particularly where this is for only six to eight sessions. In short-term work the process does not easily go at the client's pace, since both clear focus and speed are of the essence. However, some survivors find a 'bite-sized chunk' approach helpful, whereby an agreed issue is worked with and further help given later. This can be combined with couple work and group work.

Some survivors prefer working in a group as the one-to-one relationship may replicate too closely the abusive situation and may not feel safe. Conversely, other survivors cannot initially manage group therapy, but may find this helpful later.

In counselling survivors counsellors can expect to encounter powerful feelings, both in themselves and from their clients. Distress, anger, horror and hopelessness are often evident and counsellors may feel de-skilled, inadequate and overwhelmed. In the light of such powerful emotions and disturbing material there is an obvious question of how much is enough: should the work be time-limited or open-ended?; should clients be seen weekly or more frequently?; and how should counsellors react if the client cannot manage between sessions and wants more time and contact?

These are all major questions and are addressed fully in the literature cited elsewhere in this section. As noted earlier, a key feature of abuse is the invasion of the child's boundaries of body, self and psyche, and it is vital that therapy and counselling in no way recreates this, and that secure boundaries are established and safely maintained. These may be challenged by the client, in the same way as theirs were by the abuser, but the counsellor's job is to hold, manage and contain boundaries. Different models have different views on frequency of sessions and ultimate length of the counselling, and, for instance, telephone contact between sessions. What is most important is that there is a model, that there is clarity for the client and if any change is made, this should be on the basis of carefully considered therapeutic need. It should never be a knee-jerk reaction – an inappropriate response to unprocessed, unconsidered and uncomfortable feelings in the counsellor. Therefore, for example, a desire to rescue, feelings of guilt and inadequacy,

and experiencing pressure from the client to give more should always be discussed with a supervisor. It is absolutely crucial that counsellors do not commit to more than they can safely and realistically give, and that changing the frame and the implications of this are explored before changes are made. To work safely with abuse survivors, counsellors must be able to contain and make therapeutic sense of very difficult feelings.

The approach should match the needs of that particular client, although sadly the opposite is often the experience of survivors (especially those who cannot afford to seek private help). They are offered what is available, not what they need. The voluntary sector, however, has some excellent services in some parts of the country, although others are sadly bereft of these. Many are run by survivors for survivors.

Some survivors have a strong need to work their way through the abuse, to describe it, to explore it, to have the counsellor act as witness to it, and attempt to make some sense of the awfulness. Others do not find this helpful, while yet others do not have a clear enough recall to enable them to do this. In that event, the therapeutic task is often helping someone to come to terms with, and move on from, uncertainty and not knowing.

A controversial field

Working with abuse has always involved controversies, reflecting both societal and individual denial and genuine difficulty in believing the horrors that can be perpetrated on children. These change over time but controversy is ever present. It has moved from whether sexual abuse is fantasy or real, to difficulty in acknowledging boys as victims and women as perpetrators, to having to face the widespread and often extreme abuse perpetrated by those in the care sector and in religious groups, to the question of recovered memory and the role of therapy within this, to the existence or not of satanic and ritual abuse.

Working in this field therefore requires a robustness and an ability to note the controversies, to consider them and act appropriately as a practitioner, but not to be stopped by them. If practitioners become frightened off in this way, then survivors of sexual abuse will become further alienated and isolated.

References

Ainscough, C. and Toon, K. (1996) *Breaking Free: Help for Survivors of Child Sexual Abuse.* London: Sheldon Press.

Bray, M. (1997) *Sexual Abuse: The Child's Voice. Poppies on the Rubbish Heap.* London: Jessica Kingsley.

Cawson, P., Wattam, C., Brooker, S. and Kelly, G. (2000) *Child Maltreatment in the UK: A Study of the Prevalence of Child Abuse and Neglect.* London: NSPCC Publications.

Dale, P., Allen, J. and Measor, L. (1998) Counselling adults who were abused as children: clients' perceptions of efficacy, client–counsellor communication, and dissatisfaction. *British Journal of Guidance and Counselling,* 26 (2): 141–157.

Ghate, D. and Daniels, A. (1997) *Talking About My Generation: A Survey of 8–15-year-olds Growing up in the 1990s.* London: NSPCC Publications.

National Statistic (1997) *Criminal Statistics in England and Wales 1997.* London: Home Office.

Neumann, D.A., Houskamp, B.M., Pollock, V.E. and Brier, J. (1996) The long-term sequalae of childhood abuse in women: a meta-analytic review. *Child Maltreatment,* 1: 6–16.

Walker, M. (1992) *Surviving Secrets: The Experience of Abuse for the Child, the Family and the Helper.* Buckingham: Open University Press.

Recommended reading

Cawson, P., Wattam, C., Brooker, S. and Kelly, G. (2000) *Child Maltreatment in the UK. A Study of the Prevalence of Child Abuse and Neglect.* London: NSPCC Publications.

Walker, M. (2003) *Abuse: Questions and Answers for Counsellors and Therapists.* London: Whurr.

6.23   Sexual Dysfunction

LLYNWEN WILSON

As attitudes to sexuality in our society are becoming more open and relaxed there is a greater expectation for satisfaction and fulfilment in sexual functioning and relating.

Every person has sexual feelings, attitudes and beliefs but each experience of sexuality is unique because it is processed through an intensely personal perspective. This perspective is developed from private and personal experience within a wider social and public context. It is impossible to understand human sexuality without recognizing its multidimensional nature. According to Freud sex is a basic and fundamental drive. However, like everything else about us which makes us unique, this drive varies in intensity. The whole subject of human sexuality has been studied, researched, debated, written about and commented on in the popular media and academically for the last few decades. It would be easy to imagine that we all know everything about sex and feel free to explore and express our sexuality, but the social and the personal are totally different experiences. It is much easier to talk about something outside of ourselves than to look at what is happening inside. Seeking help when difficulties arise can for some people feel quite overwhelming and it is therefore crucially important when working in the field of human sexuality to approach with the utmost sensitivity those who seek help.

Sexual and relationship therapists come from a multidisciplinary background and may include doctors, nurses, psychiatrists, psychologists, counsellors and psychotherapists. In order to become accredited as psycho-sexual counsellors or relationship and sexual therapists a two-year postgraduate training course followed by at least 100 post-qualifying hours must be completed. The British Association for Sexual and Relationship Therapy (BASRT) validates Diploma and MSc courses in psycho-sexual therapy and accredits those who fulfil the academic criteria and have shown their practice fully incorporates the ethical and professional standards set by them.

What is a sexual dysfunction?

There are many classifications which are derived from different perspectives, but perhaps to look at the most common problems which present to a sexual dysfunction clinic and the treatments available would give the reader a useful insight and understanding. Couples in relationship and sexual difficulty and individual men and women concerned with aspects of their sexuality are referred usually by their GP. Some people choose to see a therapist privately because of their discomfort with relating the problem to their doctor or because they do not want intimate details of their difficulties recorded in their medical notes.

A sexual dysfunction may have a physical or psychological orientation, it may be a primary problem or caused by external factors, but in order to understand fully what is happening a thorough assessment must be made. To make a formulation the therapist has to ask specific questions in order to clarify the diagnosis, and predisposing, precipitating and aetiological factors.

The following need to be ascertained:

- presenting problems – symptoms, duration, precipitants
- relationship history – duration, present state, past and recent stresses
- social and family histories

- psychological and psychiatric history
- physical and medical history to include medications, medical and surgical interventions
- reproductive histories to include *for women* – menstrual, gynaecological, obstetric history, contraceptive history; *for men* – urological and contraceptive history
- substance use – alcohol, nicotine and illicit drugs.

Diagnostic formulation

Female dysfunction:

- impaired sexual interest and/or arousal
- orgasmic dysfunction
- vaginismus – the involuntary contraction of the vaginal muscles which inhibits penetration
- dyspareunia – pain during sexual intercourse either at the entrance of the vagina or resulting from deep penetration
- phobias – a phobia can vary between total sexual avoidance due to a persistent and irrational fear to a specific phobia aversion such as that of touching a partner's penis or having contact with seminal fluid.

Male dysfunction:

- impaired sexual interest
- erectile dysfunction
- ejaculatory/orgasmic dysfunction (premature, retarded, retrograde)
- fetishes – the enhancement of sexual arousal and gratification when a non-living object is introduced into sexual activity. Many fetishes involve articles of clothing, footwear or textures such as fur, rubber, plastic and leather. A common fetish is that of men becoming more 'turned on' by their partner wearing stockings and suspenders. Fetishistic behaviour becomes problematic when the object becomes the essential feature for satisfactory sexual response.

Couple dysfunction:

- differences in interest
- communication difficulties
- relationship problems leading to sexual difficulties
- relationship problems secondary to sexual difficulties.

It is important to develop an initial diagnostic formulation before any treatment plans can be introduced. It must be borne in mind that all the above sexual dysfunctions could have a psychological, physical or a mixed cause for the difficulty.

Expectations are an important element in working with sexual dysfunction as many couples come into a relationship with preconceived ideas about what is normal and acceptable sexual practice. These ideas might have their basis in how a previous relationship worked, what they learned in their family situation, what popular magazines and books say is normal and so forth. These attitudes and expectations need to be tested.

Example

A middle-aged couple present with the problem of *impaired sexual interest*. In the assessment interview the information elicited is that they had both been married previously for a number of years and had lived alone for some time before they met and married. His sexual relationship had been non-existent for much of his married life while she had enjoyed a healthy and open sexual relationship up until the sudden early death of her husband. They were both in their *late fifties* when they presented and had been together for five years. Both had *traditional attitudes* to sexuality. The male makes the first move, sex should not be so important later in life and one should deal with problems on one's own in the privacy of home. It was therefore a difficult decision to ask for help but indicative of the depth of their misery. In therapy it became apparent that he felt the full responsibility for their difficulties as he was the one who avoided intimacy. His fear was of rejection and failure. On the occasions they had attempted intercourse his erections were unreliable and unspontaneous. She felt he was not attracted to her and became frustrated and depressed. They could not talk about the problem together because they felt it should not be a problem in as much as they were both older and sex was something younger people had a right to. They both *avoided situations* which they felt might develop into sexual confrontation and each on their own believed they were not interested any more.

The *expectations* they took into the marriage were different. He imagined she would avoid sex (as his wife had done up to the divorce) while she was expecting him to initiate sex frequently as had her husband. She felt quite guilty that she had a strong sexual drive and was afraid of what he might think of her and so said nothing. Things came to a head when the GP who was treating her migraines asked some insightful questions about her relationship and she broke down in the surgery.

The therapist was able to help them question their attitudes, look at their expectations, to educate them on aspects of sexuality and the effects of the ageing process and discover what they both wanted and how to attain their goal. The anxiety they both experienced about the lack of sexual intimacy and their inability to communicate with one another had exacerbated the problem. Just talking openly was a huge relief and by the time a sensate focus programme was introduced they were both highly motivated and worked well towards the goal they set.

Treatments

There are a number of treatment strategies which might be appropriate for different problems. If the problem in the male is physical there are a number of physical treatments available, but it is most important that a medical examination is undertaken first to ensure what the physical cause of the problem is. Physical treatments for men with impotence problems include vacuum devices, penile implants, injections of vaso-active agents, viagra and testosterone supplements. Before and during treatment good counselling should be available. For females there are not the same options for physical treatment. If a woman presents with vaginismus she is usually offered a desensitizing programme using vaginal trainers graded from very small and getting bigger as she becomes more confident. Again sensitive and supportive therapy must accompany the process.

Sexual/relationship therapists work in a number of ways. They may use a systems approach, cognitive or behaviour therapy or psychodynamic therapy and they also both educate and inform. The model around which these approaches are used is the sensate focus model based on the work of Masters and Johnson (1966). The model has three stages: (i) non-genital focus; (ii) genital sensate focus; and (iii) vaginal containment. These stages can vary in duration depending on the quality of the relationship and the commitment of both parties. The model acts also as a good diagnostic tool because problems that are encountered while couples do their homework assignments can be analysed in therapy. The first stage of the model provides couples with the opportunity for tactile intimacy without the need to achieve sexual goals. They are required to focus only on sensations experienced through body massage and caress and are forbidden to touch the genital or breast areas. This allows them both relaxation and discovery. When it is appropriate they move to the next stage which incorporates the sexual areas but not for sexual stimulation and so towards sexual stimulation before moving on to the third stage which is vaginal containment. Usually the male lies on his back with his erect penis held upright for his partner to lower herself on to with the help of KY jelly to aid penetration. No movement or thrusting is necessary initially but as the couple gain confidence they can become more active and eventually try other positions.

This model can be tailored for different problems associated with fear of pain, fear of failure, ejaculatory problems, and so forth. If the fears are with the woman then the process moves at her pace and within her control. There is usually a favourable outcome with this model when accompanied with sensitive therapeutic support.

People who are not in relationship and present with difficulties regarding their sexuality are offered a similar range of treatment options. There are specific behavioural programmes pertinent to the needs of men and women who want to deal with erectile and ejaculatory problems or vaginismus, fear of pain or low libido. Gender dysphoria, sexual orientation confusion, fetishes, phobias, aversions, and those practices which may constitute an offence would be better worked with cognitively or psychodynamically. Very specialized psychiatric assessment is necessary for those seeking sex reassignment surgery or advice.

The reasons why problems develop are sometimes quite complex and often have their roots in early childhood experience. For example there may have been a traumatic occurrence during the oedipal stage of development, childhood sexual abuse may have taken place or expression of sexuality forbidden within family norms. These feelings and experiences could have been internalized until such time as a present trigger (e.g. a new relationship) has brought the feeling up to consciousness without a cognitive understanding of why. Other reasons are more obvious and accessible, such as avoidance of sexual intimacy due to a fear of failing based on earlier failures and brought into the present relationship, or fear of pain because of traumatic childbirth.

Physical illness such as diabetes, multiple sclerosis, vascular problems and pelvic inflammation may be among the reasons brought to a sexual dysfunction clinic. These difficulties can be worked with if the couple or individual are open to exploring the possibilities of changing their goals and discovering new ways of expressing their sexuality. Whatever the causes of sexual difficulty, one of the main reasons why the problems feel untenable is lack of communication between the parties concerned or embarrassment at discussing an intimate part of life experience with a third party. This inevitably compounds and maintains difficulties. One of the most important elements of the therapeutic process is the facilitation of an environment which enables a client to feel free to express feelings openly. Once a problem is brought to the surface then there is something concrete to work on. Ageing, illness and physical disability may preclude full intercourse but by helping couples discuss their feelings new ways of sexual intimacy and fulfilment can be discovered.

A sexual dysfunction for one person may not be seen as a problem for another. The attitudes and expectations as to what is normal in our society have an important effect on how individuals perceive their sexuality and this can sometimes cause immense pain and suffering. There is a growing number of highly qualified therapists who are trained to help people discover and accept their own possibilities and limitations.

Reference

Masters, W.H. and Johnson, V.E. (1966) *Human Sexual Response*. Boston: Little Brown.

Recommended reading

Daines, B. and Perrett, A. (2000) *Psychodynamic Approaches to Sexual Problems*. Buckingham: Open University Press.

Hawton, K. (1985) *Sex Therapy – A Practical Guide*. Oxford: Oxford University Press.

Kleinplatz, P. (2001) *New Directions in Sex Therapy: Innovations and Alternatives*. Philadelphia, PA: Brunner-Routledge.

Leiblum, S. and Rosen, R. (2000) *Principles and Practice of Sex Therapy*. New York: Guilford Press.

6.24   Suicide and Deliberate Self-harm   ○○○

LINDA GASK

Terminology

Suicide requires little definition except to add that a coroner will only record a verdict of suicide where there is evidence of clear intent. Possible suicides are reported to the coroner and an inquest is held. In England and Wales there is a strict definition of suicide which requires proof of intention to die. When there is doubt over the victim's intent, a coroner is obliged to bring in an open verdict or a verdict of accidental death. A recent term incorporating coroner's suicide and open verdicts is consciously self-inflicted (CSI) death.

It is only in the last 40 years or so that it has been recognized that a person who 'attempts suicide' is not always intent on ending his or her life. The literature has come to recognize two distinct but overlapping groups and has struggled to find the best terminology. The term 'attempted suicide' has been superseded by 'parasuicide', 'self-poisoning' and more recently by '*deliberate self-harm*', which includes cutting, burning and other self-mutilatory acts.

Non-fatal deliberate self-harm (DSH) has been defined as:

> A deliberate non-fatal act, whether physical, drug overdose or poisoning, done in the knowledge that it was potentially harmful. And in the case of drug overdosage, that the amount taken was excessive. (Morgan, 1979)

'Attempting suicide' ceased to be a crime in 1961.

Suicide

The average annual suicide rate of England and Wales is 10.0 per 100,000 population, accounting for around 5,000 deaths per year (Appleby, 2001). In the last 20 years there has been a rise in the suicide rate in young males, and in those under the age of 35 suicide is now the commonest cause of death. The elderly are still at greatest risk but in this age group the rate is falling. In all groups men are at greater risk than women. Before the change to natural gas, carbon monoxide poisoning took place in the home but now car exhausts are increasingly employed. Men are more likely to use violent methods, such as hanging and shooting, while women tend to use either prescribed medication (the older antidepressants are particularly lethal) or over-the-counter medication such as paracetamol.

In the 1970s, a majority of the people who killed themselves had seen their GP within the previous month. This is still true for those over the age of 35 but not for the group in which the rate of increase is greatest, those under 35 years.

Based on 'psychological autopsy' research, in which all available information is collected after a person's suicide and key informants are interviewed, there is evidence that over 90 per cent of people who kill themselves are mentally ill. The vast majority are depressed, but others would meet diagnostic criteria for schizophrenia, alcohol dependence, drug problems and personality disorder. The following factors are known to be associated with suicide:

- male sex
- depression
- alcohol or drug-related problems
- separated, widowed or divorced
- social isolation
- recent discharge from psychiatric care
- serious physical illness
- impending or recent job loss
- current involvement with police
- prison
- certain occupations (e.g. farmer, doctor, dentist, lawyer).

Emile Durkheim, the sociologist, described the impact of 'anomie', a term used to denote the disintegration of normative codes and alienation that can occur in modern western society, particularly in the inner cities. However, the relationship between unemployment and suicide is far from clear. Certain occupational groups (dentists, certain groups of doctors such as anaesthetists) are at higher risk and there has been much concern over the increasing rate of suicide in farmers.

Non-fatal deliberate self-harm

The full extent of DSH is unknown. Many people who harm themselves do not see a doctor, and most that do are cared for entirely in primary care. There was a massive increase in the rate of DSH in the 1960s and 1970s. In contrast with suicide, women predominate, and DSH is the commonest reason for acute medical admission in women and the second in men. This may begin to explain some of the negative attitudes often encountered among doctors and nurses to people who harm themselves.

The factors known to be associated with DSH are:

- female sex
- divorced
- under 25 years old
- social class V (i.e. unskilled workers)
- unsuitable, overcrowded accommodation
- unemployment
- at present address for less than one year.

A minority of clients have mental illness (30 per cent are depressed) but eating disorders (bulimia nervosa) and personality disorders are associated with DSH (anti-social or borderline) and alcohol misuse is common. Within a few hours of harming themselves 50 per cent of men and 25 per cent of women take alcohol. Episodes of DSH may be best seen as a maladaptive form of communication with significant others in response to relationship problems and other life stresses.

Ethical and legal issues

When a client expresses suicidal ideas this can potentially raise a number of ethical and legal issues (see Daines et al., 1996). From a psychiatric point of view, suicide is seen as essentially preventable if the person is suffering from a treatable mental illness such that the suicidal ideation would no longer be expressed if the person received and responded to treatment adequately.

Bond (1993) usefully discusses striking the balance between the ethical responsibilities of respecting autonomy and confidentiality on the one hand, and protecting clients from self-destruction on the other. He concludes that:

> Best practice with regard to suicidal clients works in ways which respect the client's autonomy and right

Table 6.24.1 Risk assessment strategies

Ascertain
- **Is there evidence of mental illness?**
  Screen for depression, alcohol and drug problems, severe mental illness.

Explore
- **Hopelessness**
  'How do you see the future?' 'Do you still have hope that things will work out?'
- **Wishes to be dead**
  'Do you ever feel that life isn't worth going on with?'
  'How often does that go through your mind?'
  (**differentiate** *between passive thoughts of death 'I wouldn't mind if I was run over by a bus' and active thoughts of suicide 'I've been thinking about jumping in front of a car'*)
- **Ask about specific plans for suicide**
  'Do you think that you might do something to harm yourself ... or end it all?'
  'Have you made any specific plans? ... Tell me about them ...'
  'How close have you come to carrying it out?'

Take note of any measures taken to prevent detection.
- **Explore for factors likely to increase or decrease risk (Box 6.24.1)**
  'What stops you from carrying it out?'
  'What would need to happen to make you do it?'
- **Explore background: past suicidal episodes and difficulties in coping**
  'Have you ever felt like this before? ... What happened then?'

---

to choose until there are substantial grounds for doubting a client's capacity to take responsibility for himself; and there is a serous risk of suicide and there is the possibility of an alternative way of intervening. (1993: 122)

If there is, however, any suggestion that psychiatric intervention might avert suicide, such that, when treated, the client would feel differently about ending his life, the question of such an intervention must be debated with the client, if not by the therapist, then by his GP or mental health professional. Bond also argues for the importance of being able to carry out a thorough assessment in order both to inform decision making and to provide evidence that the duty of care has been honoured.

Assessment of people who may be at risk of harming themselves

Questionnaires are used by some clinicians as risk assessment tools but are really no substitute for being able to broach the topic sensitively face-to-face and

ask direct questions (Table 6.24.1). The phenomenon of apparent improvement in mood just prior to finally carrying out suicide has been observed and probably occurs as the person feels calmer for having disengaged from problems and made the decision to end his or her life.

Box 6.24.1 Factors to assess which may increase or decrease level of risk

Risk increased by:

- immediate plan to carry out suicide
- choice of violent method
- plans for death – e.g. Will changes, suicide notes
- recent escalation of:
  - suicidal behaviour
  - manipulative behaviour
  - help-seeking behaviour
- current symptoms of mental disorder
- recurrent drug/alcohol intoxication

- past high-risk attempt
- likelihood of further bad news 'last straw'
- a self-imposed deadline passes without the good news the suicidal person hoped for

Risk decreased by:

- a statement that suicide will not occur if a particular event occurs (lowers immediate risk only)
- looking forward to future events
- being afraid of
  - death
  - attempt not working and being left physically/mentally damaged
  - no effect on family/friends
  - no one to look after children/significant others
- no access to means of suicide

Working with suicidal clients is difficult and taxing on the therapist. Important general themes include the need for consistency and regularity, sharing an acknowledgement of pain and suffering, working with and challenging hopelessness and the issues that may be making it difficult to move forwards. When crises occur it may be necessary to switch modes of working and temporarily take control. Such events test the skills of both the therapist and supervisor. Future crises may be avoided by helping the client to recognize both the situations that are likely to cause problems and the emotional and behavioural 'warning signs' of impending crisis. Alternative ways of coping can then be reviewed. Some therapists do use formal 'contracts' and these are discussed in more detail by Sills (1997). There is no clear evidence that such contracts are effective, and they should be used with caution. As a rule, it is probably better to set limits by discussing at the beginning of therapy how the client can show commitment to the therapeutic process by not harming themselves, rather than contract to end therapy if the client takes an overdose. There is always the risk that a contract could be perceived as punitive and in practice be counter-productive.

Similar strategies may be used with those who deliberately self-harm and, indeed, the only therapeutic approach that has been demonstrated to be effective in this group is the problem-solving approach (Hawton and Catalan, 1987). Self-mutilation is difficult to treat but behavioural approaches have been used. Limit-setting techniques may be necessary when deliberate self-harm occurs in the therapy context with the borderline patient, and focusing on the act may, in some clients, actually make the situation worse. This often occurs when people with personality disorders are hospitalized.

Prognosis of non-fatal deliberate self-harm

The people who are more likely to repeat the behaviour tend to be those who have done it before, have a personality disorder, have been in psychiatric treatment, are unemployed, in social class V (i.e. unskilled workers), misuse alcohol and/or drugs, have a criminal record, a history of violence and are aged between 24 and 35 years, single, divorced or separated.

The risk of suicide after deliberate self-harm is 100 times that of the general population. Those who do kill themselves tend to be older, male, have a mental illness and poor physical health. They may have made repeated attempts and there is also an association with the long-term use of hypnotics (sleeping pills).

Debates

Assessment after deliberate self-harm must always take the form described above in order to clarify the intent at the time of the act in addition to the present risk. In the past this was generally always done by psychiatrists for those admitted to hospital, but there has been a trend for increasing involvement of nurses, social workers and junior doctors. This raises questions of whether a professional who has attempted such an assessment has had adequate training and supervision. Considerable concern has been expressed over the quality of assessment carried out by GPs, junior doctors and in Accident and Emergency departments, and there is a need for appropriate training for those working in the front line in both the general hospital and the community (for example, see www.storm.man.ac.uk[1]).

Linked to this is the debate about whether professionals can intervene to lower the suicide rate, which has been a key target in public health policy. Critics of this target point to the fall in the numbers of people who kill themselves having consulted a doctor within the previous month compared to 20 years ago. Suicide prevention strategies probably need to be focused on those at high risk, such as young men in the community, people recently discharged from psychiatric hospital and deliberate self-harmers. A number of public health measures, such as limiting access to over-the-counter paracetamol purchase and the introduction of catalytic converters on cars, may also help. Older antidepressants (tricyclics, particularly Prothiaden (Dothiepin)) are undoubtedly more lethal in overdose and are still widely prescribed, but it has yet to be proven that a change to newer, less harmful drugs would have an impact on the suicide rate, even though most clinicians now take this factor into account when considering what to prescribe.

Note

[1] STORM (Skills Training On Risk Management) is an evidence-based training package on risk assessment for health professionals developed by the University of Manchester.

References

Appleby, L. (2001) *Safety First: Five Year Report of the National Confidential Inquiry into Suicide and Homicide by People with Mental Illness.* London: Department of Health.

Bond, T. (1993) When to prevent a client from self-destruction. In W. Dryden (ed.), *Questions and Answers on Counselling in Action.* London: Sage. pp. 118–123.

Daines, B., Gask, L. and Usherwood, T. (1996) *Medical and Psychiatric Issues for Counsellors.* London: Sage.

Hawton, K. and Catalan, J. (1987) *Attempted Suicide: A Practical Guide to Its Nature and Management.* Oxford: Oxford University Press.

Morgan, H.G. (1979) *Death Wishes? The Understanding and Management of Deliberate Self-harm.* Chichester: Wiley.

Sills, C. (ed.) (1997) *Contracts in Counselling.* London: Sage.

Recommended reading

Duffy, D. and Ryan, T. (eds) (2004) *New Approaches to Preventing Suicide: A Manual for Practitioners.* London: Jessica Kingsley.

PART VI
Client Presenting Problems

SPECIAL ISSUES

6.25 Recovered Memories of Sexual Abuse: Theoretical and Practical Issues

SUSAN GOODRICH AND DEBRA BEKERIAN

In recent years, there have been many reports of adults claiming to recover memories of previously forgotten childhood sexual abuse (henceforth referred to as recovered memories). The most controversial cases are those where people have recovered memories subsequent to some kind of therapeutic intervention, and these memories have been used as evidence in criminal and civil prosecution. Initially, the arguments here were polarized. Some advocates suggested that such memories always represent historical truth (e.g. Bass and Davies, 1988) and that therapy facilitates recovery of true memories. On the other hand are those who challenged the notion that memories of childhood abuse could be forgotten and later remembered. Rather, it was argued, such memories were manufactured as a result of intense pressure placed on vulnerable clients by therapists (Loftus and Rosenwald, 1993).

Several recent papers have taken a more moderate stance, accepting that memories of childhood sexual abuse can be recovered following periods of amnesia for the abuse and that sometimes therapy can facilitate that recovery. At the same time, concern has been expressed about the possibility of false memories being induced, albeit unknowingly (Lindsay and Read, 1994).

The possibility that false memories could be created within therapeutic settings has received indirect support from years of memory research showing how susceptible our memories are to distortion and misinformation (see Ceci and Brook, 1993, for a historical review). Possibly the most widely cited findings in relation to recovered memories are those showing that people can be misled into generating detailed memories of childhood events that did not, in fact, occur (e.g. Hyman et al., 1995; see, however, Bekerian and Goodrich, 2000).

In response to this climate of uncertainty, papers have been written discussing findings from memory research and considering the implications of these for practitioners (BPS, 1995; Lindsay and Read, 1994; see also Walker, 1996). This section will continue on this line and consider more about the nature of our memories and the possible consequences of this for practitioners and their clients.

Our memories take many forms. We have stories about our lives that we relate verbally. We have memories for smells, and motor skills such as riding a bike. We also have 'memories' where the precipitating incident(s) themselves may not be consciously remembered, yet they influence our behaviour. For instance, few of us can remember and talk about early childhood experiences. Yet these first years are held to have a profound impact on later development with 'memories' being retained and expressed in 'non-verbal' forms, for example, somato-sensory sensations and feelings or body movements (e.g. Howe et al., 1994). As with early memories, it has been suggested that memories for trauma may sometimes be 'forgotten' and fail to reach conscious awareness. However, they too might be expressed through alternative pathways like dreams, body language, inexplicable fears, flashbacks, etc. (Erdelyi, 1990).

Given that so much of our behaviour is non-verbal, special therapeutic techniques have been developed. These might involve the client getting in touch with, and giving a voice to, body sensations. Clients might be encouraged to act out, and describe the previous context of symbolic behaviour, interpret dreams or be placed under susceptible states such as hypnosis. Techniques such as guided imagery and journalling are also used to facilitate recovery of memories.

The problem is that while therapeutic techniques that encourage the individual to interpret non-verbal behaviour, act out symbolic behaviour (e.g. engage in and enact fantasies), or place the individual under susceptible states (e.g. hypnosis) have been shown to facilitate remembering, they can also promote false 'recovery' (e.g. AMA Council on Scientific Affairs, 1985; Bonano, 1990). An additional, related, concern is that these 'memories'/body sensations are open to interpretation. Hence, a consistent choking sensation could be indicative of early sexual abuse. However, it might also result from forgotten childhood experience(s) that, although frightening, were not necessarily abusive in nature (Bekerian and Goodrich, 2000; Bekerian and O'Neill, 2000).

Taken together, the above findings suggest that in at least some cases, memories of previously forgotten childhood sexual abuse will be manifested initially in the form of non-verbal sensations or feelings. A person might come to therapy and work on these, possibly using techniques designed to explore such non-verbal memories. The problem arises if these non-verbal experiences are subsequently interpreted and placed within a context, say of sexual abuse. Similarly, dreams and fantasies can incorporate symbols that are grotesque and frightening in nature. However, although they clearly represent a person's 'inner world', there is a danger of putting too literal an interpretation on them. Many body states and ways of being may be culturally acquired and not necessarily gained through personal experience (Bekerian and Goodrich, 2000).

These ideas are supported by a study showing that when recovering memories for trauma (including child sexual abuse), subjects' memories were initially 'in the form of dissociated mental imprints of sensory and affective elements of the traumatic experience' (van der Kolk and Fisler, 1996: 505). Crucially, van der Kolk and Fisler suggest that the original sensory or affective experience is not subject to distortion. In contrast, they argue that the verbal description, being a constructed narrative,

is susceptible to misleading influences, and can, therefore, be a misrepresentation of what actually occurred.

Given the above, two conclusions seem warranted. First, where a client experiences non-verbal feelings, sensations or movements, practitioners need to stay with the facts, with what the client is experiencing without attempting to interpret, or place their experience within a context. Clients may know they have many of the hypothesized sequelae associated with sexual abuse and, in the absence of corroboration, they may never know the truth about what happened to them. It might be the case that both practitioners and their clients have to live with uncertainty. Second, practitioners should not encourage clients towards a course of action, such as litigation, if the primary evidence is recovered memories and these are uncorroborated. Encouraging litigation under such circumstances is not in the best interests of the client, the practitioner, or the legal system.

References

AMA Council on Scientific Affairs (1985) Scientific status of refreshing recollection by the use of hypnosis. *Journal of the American Medical Association*, 253: 1918–1923.

Bass, E. and Davis, L. (1988) *The Courage to Heal: A Guide for Women Survivors of Child Sexual Abuse*. New York: Harper and Row.

Bekerian, D.A. and Goodrich, S.J. (2000) Recovered memories of child sexual abuse. In G.E. Berrios and J.R. Hodges (eds), *Memory Disorders in Psychiatric Practice*. Cambridge: Cambridge University Press.

Bekerian, D.A. and O'Neill, M.H. (2000) Therapeutic techniques and memory. In G. Davies and T. Dalleish (eds), *Recovered Memories of Sexual Abuse: Seeking the Middle Ground*. Mahwah, NJ: Lawrence Erlbaum Associates.

Bonano, G. (1990) Remembering and psychotherapy. *Psychotherapy: Theory, Research, Practice, Training*, 27: 175–186.

BPS (January 1995) *Report on Recovered Memories*. Leicester: British Psychological Society.

Ceci, S.J. and Bruck, M. (1993) The suggestibility of the child witness: a historical review and synthesis. *Psychological Bulletin*, 113: 403–439.

Erdelyi, M.H. (1990) Repression, reconstruction and defense: history and integration of the psychoanalytic and experimental frameworks. In J.L. Singer (ed.), *Repression and Dissociation*. Chicago: Chicago University Press. pp. 1–32.

Howe, M.L., Courage, M.L. and Peterson, C. (1994) How can I remember when 'I' wasn't there: long-term retention of traumatic experiences and emergence of the cognitive self. *Consciousness and Cognition*, 3: 327–355.

Hyman, I.E., Husband, T.H. and Billings, F.J. (1995) False memories of childhood experiences. *Applied Cognitive Psychology*, 9: 181–197.

Lindsay, D.S. and Read, J.D. (1994) Psychotherapy and memories of childhood sexual abuse: a cognitive perspective. *Applied Cognitive Psychology*, 8: 281–338.

Loftus, E. and Rosenwald, L.A. (1993) Buried memories, shattered lives. *ABA Journal*, November: 70–73.

van der Kolk, B. and Fisler, R. (1995) Dissociation and the fragmentary nature of traumatic memories. *Journal of Traumatic Stress*, 8: 505–525.

Walker, M. (1996) Working with abuse survivors. In R. Bayne, I. Horton and J. Bimrose (eds), *New Directions in Counselling*. London: Routledge. pp. 124–138.

6.26 Mental Health Law   ○○○

LINDA GASK

Mental health law serves to formalize the removal of certain civil liberties from some people with serious mental health problems, and some form of legislation exists throughout the countries of the developed world. There has always been differing but similar legislation across the countries of the UK. However, with devolution, some greater differences have emerged. Commentators have questioned whether the law as it now stands strikes the correct balance between the civil rights of individual patients and the rights of society protection (Eastman, 1996). A new mental health act has been expected for some time in England and Wales and has been the subject of considerable debate (see below). New mental health legislation was passed in Scotland in 2003.

The Mental Health Act (1983)

The sections of the Mental Health Act which are most likely to be met in practice are:

- Emergency and short-term orders for assessment for up to 28 days (Sections 2 and 4). These apply to any mental disorder, which does not need to be specified.
- Longer-term orders for treatment (Section 3). These apply only to four specified types of disorder:

1. *Mental illness* – is not defined but the Act states that a person should not be treated as suffering from mental disorder 'by reason only of promiscuity, or other immoral conduct, sexual deviancy or dependence on alcohol or drugs'. This means that a person cannot be detained in hospital simply on grounds of addiction but only if there is associated mental illness (for example, if the person is a drinker but also depressed and suicidal or in 'delerium tremens' (or DTs) because of withdrawal from alcohol and clearly hallucinating).
2. *Severe mental impairment* – learning disability associated with abnormal aggressive or seriously irresponsible conduct.
3. *Mental impairment* – similar to above but of lesser degree.
4. *Psychopathic disorder* – with associated aggressive conduct. The place of 'psychopathic disorder' in the

Mental Health Act remains controversial and its use as a basis for 'sectioning' (a slang term in common usage which stands for detaining a person under the Act) depends on the notion of 'treatability' of the disorder. Mental health professionals are divided about whether it is possible to treat such severe personality disorders as witnessed by the debate over recent high-profile cases. Use of the Act in detaining people with psychopathic disorder is largely restricted to the courts when imposing hospital treatment orders (covered in other sections of the Act and used to enforce treatment on mentally disordered offenders).

An *approved social worker* (ASW) is one approved by the local authority as having special experience of mental illness. Approved social workers undergo special training.

An *approved doctor* is one who has been approved under Section 12 of the Act as having special experience of mental disorder and is usually a psychiatrist but can also be a GP who has had some experience in this field. Both now need to have attended brief training courses on the implementation of the law.

Section 2: admission for assessment

This lasts up to 28 days. Application can be made by an ASW or the nearest relative and requires two doctors, one of whom must be approved and the other of whom should preferably know the patient (usually the GP). It is used to detain someone who is either a risk to themselves or to other people and needs admission to hospital. The patient has the right to appeal. In practice it is almost always now a social worker rather than a relative who actually makes the application in consultation with the family.

Section 3: admission for treatment

This lasts up to six months in the first instance. Application can be made by an ASW or the nearest relative as before and requires the opinion of two doctors, as for Section 2. In addition, the nature of the disorder to be treated must be specified. It is used to detain someone who is either a risk to

themselves or to other people and needs admission to hospital for treatment to be carried out. The patient has the right to appeal.

Section 4: admission for assessment in case of emergency

This gives the police power to convey a person who appears to be in need of assessment to hospital. The use of this power is controversial and varies widely across the country. Common reasons for instituting it include assault, suicidal gestures, removing clothing in public places and 'bizarre' behaviour.

A person cannot be 'sectioned' in order to treat physical illness, although this has been the subject of recent controversial cases where unborn children are involved. Treatment can only be enforced for the mental disorder. So if a person who is hearing voices refuses to have surgery, treatment can be provided for the 'voices' under the Act, for example by use of medication, but the surgery itself cannot be enforced.

The 1995 Mental Health (Patients in the Community) Act

This Act was introduced because of the recognition that the 1983 Act is based on admission to hospital and does not allow for people who refuse to continue treatment once they are discharged from hospital. It is undoubtedly hurried through because of public (and media) concern about the risk posed by the mentally ill living in the community and the much-publicized 'failure of community care'. This Act introduced the Supervised Discharge Order, under which there is a community treatment agreement made with the patient before discharge. If the patient then defaults from treatment, he or she can be conveyed under the Act to a treatment facility but the Act does not provide any additional powers to enforce treatment or admission which must then be judged under the grounds set out in the 1983 Act. Critics have described the 1995 Act as 'fudged compromise that does not move the Mental Health Act towards greater congruence with community care' (Eastman, 1996: 208).

Legal aspects of deliberate self-harm and medical care

A doctor may only administer treatment when a patient gives consent. A competent adult can reject medical or surgical treatment, or investigations, even if this is life-threatening. So a competent adult who has taken an overdose and who refuses treatment, in the knowledge of the potentially fatal risks, cannot be legally treated even if he or she becomes unconscious. The issue of whether a person has the capacity to make such a decision thus becomes crucial, and the law concerning this will soon be clarified (see below).

Debates

The proposals outlined in the government White Paper for the reform of the Mental Health Act have united in opposition all mental health professionals, including psychiatrists, users of services and carers, against a move towards linking mental health law with public protection issues such as homicide rates. Their general concern has been that mental health legislation will move towards inappropriately applying medical care to people where it is not in their best interests. Particular concerns can be summarized thus:

- Proposals to widen the criteria for detention (with the added risk that people with a diagnosis of personality disorder might be detained even if there is no clear indication that being in hospital might be beneficial to them – which is not the case at present).

- Application can be made by any health care worker, not just an approved social worker.
- Psychiatrists can be prevented indefinitely from discharging a patient.
- The person in charge of a patient's treatment will not necessarily be a doctor. (Some psychologists have welcomed this opportunity.)
- Duration of compulsion in the community may be indefinite.

It remains to be seen what the outcome will be.

Legislation for 'incapacity' to make decisions about medical treatment will probably precede a new act, as it did in Scotland. The role of advance directives, allowing a competent person to give instructions about the type of treatment he or she wishes/does not wish to receive later is also likely to be further supported.

Reference

Eastman, N. (1996) The need to change mental health law. In T. Heller, J. Reynolds, R. Gomm, R. Muston and S. Pattison (eds), *Mental Health Matters: A Reader*. Basingstoke: Open University and Macmillan. pp. 205–211.

Recommended reading

Bluglass, R. (1993) *Guide to the Mental Health Act 1983*. Edinburgh: Churchill Livingston.
Jones, R. (1994) *Mental Health Act Manual*. London: Sweet & Maxwell.
Updates on the legal process in England and Wales: www.rcpsych.ac.uk/press/parliament
Scottish legislation: www.scotland-legislation.hmso.gov.uk/ legislation/scotland/acts2003/20030013.htm

PART VII
Specialisms and Modalities

7.1 Introduction

○○○

COLIN FELTHAM AND IAN HORTON

There are a number of therapeutic approaches that do not fall into the category of a distinct theoretical orientation, yet have significant identities or areas of application of their own. This part of the book brings together some of the most significant such specialisms and modalities. In principle it might be possible to organize these into subgroups but we have decided simply to present them in alphabetical order for ease of reference. Traditionally, couple, family, group and systems therapies are often presented as alternative arenas to individual therapy. Some writers have added to these the subjects of child psychotherapy and brief therapy (Bloch, 1990).

Therapy with older clients has often been neglected but is presented here. Therapies relating to clients with disabilities, multicultural therapy and feminist therapy have some affinity as areas of attention in terms of anti-oppressive and affirmative practice. Co-counselling or peer therapy appears here in order to challenge its neglect in many textbooks. A focus on the subject of therapy (and its special features) for therapists seeking their own therapy or personal growth, is also an often neglected 'specialism'.

Sometimes found grouped together as 'settings', the subjects of counselling/therapy in primary care, student counselling, and workplace counselling are presented here in order to identify and honour the particular challenges posed by their contexts. Similarly, career counselling is presented as an important specialism. Telephone counselling or therapy, again often neglected or subtly demeaned, has a special place here as a distinct and increasingly significant medium. The inclusion in this edition of electronically delivered therapies marks the growth – not without some resistance and problems to be overcome – of forms of therapy that are not face to face; for some, this may represent one of the greatest challenges to the tradition of the direct therapeutic relationship. Finally, since they are so commonly needed in our still fast-moving and arguably dehumanizing society, stress management and assertiveness training have been retained here.

Reference

Bloch, S. (ed.) (1990) *An Introduction to the Psychotherapies.* Oxford: Oxford Medical Publications.

7.2 Assertiveness

ROWAN BAYNE

Assertiveness theory and skills have several applications in therapy. Most obviously they are worth considering for any relationship or interpersonal difficulty of clients and as a strategy for coping with stress. They appear to be effective with a wide range of client groups (Rakos, 1991).

Although assertiveness training is often seen as a behavioural technique, it can equally well be seen as humanistic, as 'self-actualization' in action. Some books, trainers and counsellors focus on skills and techniques more than on self-awareness, some on self-awareness alone, and some (e.g. Albert and Emmons, 2001; Dickson, 1982) on both. A useful definition is 'being able to express and act on your own rights as a person while respecting the same rights in other people' (Nicolson et al., 2006). Assertiveness has been around for many years as a behavioural technique (Rakos, 1991), but at its heart is a basic existential question which is much older: how much do I do what *I* want to do (or concentrate on finding out what that is), and how much do I do what *others* want me to do?

Examples of the 'rights' in the definition offered above are 'expressing thoughts and feelings' and 'saying no without feeling guilty', and also respecting those rights in other people. Working through a list of assertive rights (there are typically about 12 of these) either in the abstract or when upset by something or someone, can be a salutary and clarifying experience. For example, someone might consider the suggested right 'To change my mind' for themselves first, and ask: 'Do I believe I have that right? What limits do I see for it as a right? When do I *behave* as if I have that right and when not?' Then the person might ask similar questions of their beliefs, feelings and behaviours about other people changing their minds. Here, the relationship

between assertiveness and the emphasis on irrational beliefs in cognitive therapy is very direct, but assertiveness is concerned with self-expression in all respects.

Perhaps the most useful levels of assertiveness theory are styles of behaviour and skills. Four styles of behaviour are usually distinguished: aggressive, which can be defined as blatantly ignoring other people's rights; manipulative – ignoring other people's rights in a more subtle way, e.g. through 'emotional blackmail'; passive – ignoring your own rights; and assertive. A crucial point here is that there is an assertive right *not* to be assertive. It is not that anyone actually is continually assertive – most people can and do behave in two or more of the four styles and indeed can readily demonstrate the ability to behave in all of them in assertiveness workshops and courses – but that a main principle of assertiveness is to increase options, not to impose a new orthodoxy.

Assertive skills usually include saying no, making requests, giving and receiving compliments, giving and receiving criticism and developing and maintaining self-esteem. The non-verbal element is central and again readily demonstrated by clients and in workshops. These are familiar, everyday concepts, both in broad terms and in the specifics of voice tone, posture, etc. In workshops and with clients, it is usually quite easy to agree on whether a particular way of saying no, for example, is assertive or not.

Assertiveness theory and skills can be applied with varying degrees of formality, ranging from a thorough, systematic analysis of situations and 'skills deficits' in a standard behavioural approach, to a discussion of possible ways of feeling and behaving differently in a more humanistic one. Rakos (1991) refers to the more formal approach as assertiveness *therapy* and the less formal as assertiveness *training*.

In either therapy or training, role-play with coaching can be helpful, and some consideration of likely costs and benefits is very desirable before trying out the new skill in a real situation.

'Coaching' may sound as if there is one right way to be assertive. On the contrary, good coaching values individuality, authenticity and spontaneity, not a mechanical, polished but lifeless performance. The cost-benefit analysis also points to a limitation of assertiveness: there is a risk of aiming too high, with subsequent frustration and sense of failure.

As an example of applying assertiveness theory in therapy, take a client who wants to ask someone for a date but is scared. At some point in helping your client explore and clarify this wish and fear, it may be helpful to try out various elements of an assertiveness framework. A particular 'right' or rights may be involved, most obviously 'I have the right to ask for what I want' and 'Others have the right to say "no" without feeling guilty.' (The rights can look trite but I think the reality behind them is quite different.) Then the assertive skills could be examined for their possible relevance. For example, applying the skills of making such a request would include the following steps:

1 Discussion of possible costs and benefits.
2 Assuming the benefits matter more, the person prepares what she or he wants to say. It helps considerably if the words feel comfortable, and if there is a key phrase.

Preparation can take into account the following guidelines:

- Be brief and fairly direct (see Dickson, 1982, for numerous excellent examples).
- Speak clearly and confidently, and watch out for inappropriate apologies.
- Try to assume that the answer might be Yes or No and not to sabotage the reply. Assume there's a good enough chance it will be yes (or that at least it's worth a try!).

Rehearsal and coaching might also take into account possible reactions to a range of replies, setting aside a time for constructive analysis of the outcome, and deciding when and where to make the request. Contingency plans appeal to some clients. Overall, the idea is to help clients use assertiveness theory and methods flexibly and creatively and in a way that suits them.

Another limitation of assertiveness theory and skills is that the social and multicultural context can be neglected. For example, suppose you work with a client who is being sexually harassed at work and who wants to be more assertive, for example to make a clear request to the person harassing him or her, such as: 'You say that touching me on the shoulder doesn't mean anything, but it matters to me. I would like you to stop doing it.' Your client can be very pleased with the results, which is fine as far as it goes. However, it leaves the norms of the organization intact. One response to this issue is to say that, after considering costs and benefits, your client may choose to take it further. Another response is that all techniques and theories have their own field of application and limits. Assertiveness operates at the individual level and other methods are more useful at the level of organizations or cultures. However, actually implementing other methods at these levels may call upon assertive skills.

'Bicultural competence' (Rakos, 1991) is another useful notion here. It underlines the principle that teaching assertiveness skills in a prescriptive way is too simple, and respects the fact that different cultures and groups have different norms. For example, looking someone straight in the eye is impolite or worse in some cultures, but part of being assertive in others. Bicultural competence treats assertiveness as a widening of the range of options: a person can practise saying no, for example, both while looking someone (perhaps their therapist) in the eye and while looking away.

Assertiveness can also be applied in therapy itself. It can play a crucial role in negotiating contracts and setting and maintaining boundaries, in the core qualities of acceptance (respect) and genuineness, and in the skill of immediacy. Immediacy is a pure application of assertiveness in its respect for and expression of both the therapist's and the client's views and feelings.

Dickson (1982) is still the last practical book on assertiveness in my view, for men too, and Rakos (1991) is the most recent detailed review of research.

References

Albert, R.E. and Emmons, M.L. (2001) *Your Perfect Right: A Guide to Assertive Behavior* (8th edn). Atascadero, CA: Impact.

Dickson, A. (1982) *A Woman in Your Own Right. Assertiveness and You.* London: Quartet Books.

Nicolson, P., Bayne, R. and Owen, J. (2006) *Applied Psychology for Social Workers* (3rd edn). London: Palgrave.

Rakos, R.F. (1991) *Assertive Behavior: Theory, Research and Training.* London: Routledge.

7.3   Brief/Time-limited Therapy   ○○○

COLIN FELTHAM

The title of brief/time-limited therapy is used generically to refer to the many varieties of brief psychotherapy and counselling, time-limited therapies, short-term therapies and the question of time-conscious design and delivery of therapeutic services.

History and contributing factors

Relatively little interest in brief and time-limited counselling or psychotherapy was apparent in Britain before the 1990s. Commentators usually trace the development of brief therapy from Freud's own early short-term cases through to the work of Alexander and French in the 1940s, combined with the US experience of administering help to war veterans, also in the 1940s, and an increasing interest in helping people suffering from crises, rather than the kind of 'neurotic populations' of Freud's time. The 1950s and 1960s witnessed the advent of new humanistic and cognitive-behavioural approaches, the rediscovery and modification of hypnotherapy, and the 1960s in the USA saw the introduction of

health legislation that encouraged exploration of short-term approaches. Pioneers in the USA included Mann, Sifneos, Budman and Gurman, Cummings, de Shazer and many others. In the UK, the work of Balint and Malan has been highly influential. The rise of time-limited cognitive analytic therapy (Ryle), and research into very brief interventions by Shapiro, Barkham and others in the 1990s, have attempted to answer some of the problems of waiting lists in the NHS.

As quite widespread public acceptance of and demand for therapeutic services took hold in Britain in the 1990s, witnessed for example in the spread of counselling in primary care and in employee assistance programmes, so a number of trends combined to focus on time-conscious, accountable and rationally delivered therapy. These were:

- the concerns of funders and service providers that thought be put into realistic and accountable provision of therapy and reduction of waiting lists;
- the influence of North American systems of managed care through public health services and in association with insurers and employers;
- research findings suggesting that actual take-up of therapy frequently averages at around six sessions,

based on consumers' apparent preferences, in a variety of settings;

- the rise of evidence-based cognitive-behavioural therapies, group therapies, counselling by telephone, therapeutic writing, email counselling and other new forms of focused therapeutic practices;
- increasing awareness of therapeutic failures, the question of therapeutic specificity, and consumers' demands for effective therapies;
- the changing pace of modern working life, uncertain economics, and a turn towards a harsher work ethic, which spawned respect for stress management and crisis intervention but perhaps little sympathy for extensive psychological explorations with vague or unknown outcomes.

Models of brief therapy

Brief therapies can be understood as falling roughly into three categories:

1 Any therapy that is intrinsically concerned with efficiency, pragmatism, parsimony, rapid symptom amelioration, circumscribed aims, etc. (e.g. behaviour therapy, cognitive therapy, multimodal therapy, rational emotive behaviour therapy (REBT), reality therapy, neuro-linguistic programming (NLP), etc.).
2 Therapies designed or intended to be brief but where brevity is not defined and therapy may in fact be open-ended or intermittent (e.g. short-term dynamic psychotherapy, solution-focused therapy, focused-expressive psychotherapy, depth-oriented brief therapy, etc.).
3 Therapies designed to be, and delivered as, time-limited, in other words holding to a *pre-designated* time limit (e.g. Mann's time-limited psychotherapy (12 sessions), cognitive analytic therapy (16 sessions), Macnab's contextual modular therapy (6 sessions), the '2+1 model', single-session therapy, etc.).

The late 1990s saw the gradual birth of time-conscious adaptations of traditional models, for example many varieties of short-term dynamic therapies, brief REBT, etc. Of those implementing time limits, many have settled on 6 as a workable minimum number of sessions, especially in primary care and EAPs. Anything from 1 to about 40 sessions

has been put forward as 'brief', obviously depending on previous traditions, but typically brief therapy is considered to be up to 12 sessions. (In medicine and, for example, in community psychiatric nursing, *minutes or half hours* spent with a client may be the norm for thinking temporally.) As well as time limits, the issues of optimal, conscious use and organization of valuable therapeutic time, and of the *meaning* of time in therapy, have been raised (Elton Wilson, 1996; Feltham, 1997). Approaches and practitioners most opposed to shortening and rationing are probably independent therapists, who may recognize that their livelihood would be compromised by too rapid a turnover, but also by those in the humanistic tradition who eschew psychodiagnostic thinking, defend clients' rights to define their own personal growth goals and to work at their own pace.

Key principles and interventions

Classical psychoanalysis by its own admission is based on respect for the unconscious and its timeless nature. The 'lengthening factors' inherent in this tradition are thought to include: searching for putative origins of symptoms; preoccupation with clients' early histories; perfectionism; dwelling on mainly in-session phenomena; infantilization and dependency; the apparent aimlessness of free association; transference neurosis; and recognition of the economic convenience of long-term paying clients (Budman and Gurman, 1988; Molnos, 1995). It is no surprise then that many of the key operating principles common to most brief therapies are reversals of these factors.

Assessment

Views differ on exactly which conditions do and do not benefit from brief therapy, but a degree of consensus suggests that the most suitable clients may have mild to moderate problems, crises, and well-defined symptoms; motivation, readiness, social support, a reasonable level of everyday functioning, ability to make a rapid, good enough therapeutic alliance. Clients with longstanding personality and/or multiple problems, those with histories of childhood sexual abuse, substance or alcohol misuse, and those who attend reluctantly, referred by third parties, may not be suitable. Assessment should include realistic estimates of the fit between time available and severity of distress (Burton, 1998), and contracts with clients must always be clear and honest about time limitations and what can be achieved.

Commitment to brief therapy

In common with open-ended therapies, brief therapy must be delivered by practitioners who believe in the possibility and usefulness of brief therapy. Covert therapist resistance, including doubts about the rationale for brief work, is likely to adversely permeate the therapeutic work. Concern for client preferences, rapid reduction of distress, elimination of waste, addressing waiting lists, realism about the costs of therapy to clients or funders, are all factors likely to be embraced by brief therapy enthusiasts. The therapist's commitment should also engender the sense of expectancy in the client that can be a vital ingredient in change.

Rapid therapeutic alliance

It has been inferred from research on attrition that failure to make strong working alliances within the first three sessions is one reliable predictor of clients dropping out of therapy. Therefore, in order to engage the client and initiate an immediate sense of hope, collaboration and necessary action, the therapist must actively mobilize the client by clear contracting, early identification of transference factors and possible relational obstacles. *Collaboration* is emphasized in cognitive therapy and cognitive analytic therapy especially and is identified by research as a key variable in the strength of the therapeutic alliance and successful outcomes in *all* therapy.

Focal and active concerns

In very brief work time is not available for extreme non-directiveness, lengthy exploratory or speculative discussion and free association. Instead, early identification of crisis, symptoms, key personal issues or needs is crucial. This may entail what has been referred to as 'skilful neglect' of certain underlying or dormant issues, and concentration on live problematic issues. Focal concerns may be obvious (e.g. a phobia) or may require work to identify (e.g. a recurring pattern of self-destructive behaviour). Initial contracting must be linked with realistic focal concerns.

Flexible, creative and informed skills

To some extent adherence to traditional theoretical models needs to be adapted or even sometimes abandoned, allowing for the primacy of each client's pressing needs. A certain pragmatism may be required to address psycho-social, decision-making needs, for example, and therapists may need to be prepared to teach relaxation or assertiveness skills, utilize and/or improvise simple cathartic or cognitive techniques, or be prepared – on the basis of research-awareness – to refer elsewhere for specialized therapy (e.g. eye movement desensitization and reprocessing (EMDR) may be indicated for PTSD). *Brief therapy particularly challenges therapists to fit the therapy to the client, not the client to the therapeutic tradition.*

Parsimony

This refers to the practice of making the least radical intervention necessary and the most obviously indicated. Many clients (up to 25 per cent) attend for, and/or find satisfactory resolution in, only one session, and up to 62 per cent may improve significantly by 13 sessions (see Feltham, 1997: 140). Consumer surveys have produced some evidence that many clients have far less extensive agendas for personal change than do their therapists. Also, advocates of intermittent (as opposed to 'all at once') therapy, argue that sporadic therapy may be more realistic and economic. Interventions may therefore include non-therapy (assuring the client that she needs no therapy at this time), referral elsewhere, very short sessions, supportive work, practical and decision-making guidance.

Challenge

Contrary to the above, some brief therapists argue for the validity and desirability of highly challenging short-term work (Ecker and Hulley, 1996; Molnos, 1995). Brief dynamic therapy as practised by Malan, Davanloo, Molnos and others may entail 'trial therapy' from the very outset, which judiciously confronts defences in order to test out tolerance for this kind of therapy. Transferential behaviour may be noted and addressed immediately, and therapy may have a purposefully anxiety-arousing character. Ecker and Hulley propose working authentically with deep emotions and the unconscious immediately, in their depth-oriented contructivist approach; cognitive analytic therapy may include challenging, transference-interpreting work; and Mahrer's experiential therapy works with deep feelings from the first session. In the cognitive-behavioural tradition, clients may be challenged to undertake homework and various self-challenging exercises.

Time itself as containing and challenging

Contrary to common belief among some therapists, many clients have reported feeling contained (made safe) by firm time limits, and being less likely to drop out. Therapists informed by existentialist and other views on death anxiety (e.g. Mann) consider that the finiteness and less-than-ideal frame of a small number of sessions fixed in advance, usefully arouses existential anxiety. Many brief therapists explicitly utilize notions of time as precious and therapy as a valuable chance for change, applying these factors as leverage. Available time is also often enhanced by encouraging the client to take seriously their own between-session change attempts and their post-therapy lives as full of further such opportunities.

Specific techniques

While many brief therapy techniques are simply sharpened or more rapidly applied techniques from traditional approaches, some are peculiar to or have evolved from within the brief therapy tradition. In the solution-focused therapy (often referred to simply as 'brief therapy') of de Shazer and others, so-called *miracle questions* may be used, requiring clients to imagine and describe in detail their circumstances if they were magically transformed overnight. Such catalytically designed challenges can unleash or restore clients' optimism and forgotten constructive abilities. Similarly, asking for *exceptions* to the presenting problem can be powerful (e.g. requiring the client to identify times when they are *not* depressed or anxious). *Paradoxical interventions* have been advocated (e.g. asking clients to escalate a problem; 'prescribing the symptom'). *Scaling questions* require clients to self-score their problems, degrees of severity, amount of change and prediction of what would be necessary to progress one point on their scale. Variations on *hypnotherapeutic techniques* have been utilized by Milton Erickson and are advocated by Budman and Gurman (1988). Dramatic phobia-eliminating techniques based on behavioural and NLP principles involving hypnotherapy and exposure have been reported as successful in single sessions (e.g. a longstanding bee phobia resolved in seven minutes). Implied in this is a possible eclectic imperative – that effective brief therapists may need to add to their technical repertoires or be willing to refer on. (Readers may refer back to Section 3.4 of this book, on specific strategies and techniques (pp. 87–109), for further details; and see also O'Connell, 1998). Wright (2003) shows the value of combining therapeutic writing with brief therapy.

Preparation for ending

It is responsible, ethical and effective practice to incorporate into brief therapy elements of the following: (a) realism about end results and willingness to discuss likely degrees of disappointment; (b) discouragement of dependency on the therapist and reinforcement of coping self-images; (c) preparation for possible relapse by, for example, devising and rehearsing coping strategies; (d) discussion of possible follow-up sessions or extendable contracts (Elton Wilson, 1996), or alternative forms of help (e.g. self-help groups, bibliotherapy, co-counselling, etc.); (e) evaluation of outcomes – verbally, by questionnaire or other evaluation instruments and 'goodbye letters'.

Therapists' professional development needs

Brief therapy is still a relatively new field and training is still under-developed, but see Feltham (1997: 131–139) for relevant issues. Views differ on whether beginners or experienced practitioners are most likely to find brief therapy difficult to learn (since it may demand a good deal of 'unlearning' of traditional attitudes), but there is an emerging consensus that some specific training or re-orientation *is* necessary. Problematic, too, is supervision for brief therapy, particularly for very short-term (e.g. six-session) therapy, the rapid client turnover associated with it, the contexts in which it is increasingly obligatory, and the current evidence suggesting that the cognitive-behavioural therapies are most likely to be effective in a short time (Mander, 1998; Roth and Fonagy, 1996).

Critiques and limitations

Short-term therapy is sometimes regarded as a faddish, merely politically and economically motivated development; as a second best or even damaging practice, cheating clients of what they *really* need; encouraging superficial, transient 'flight into health' and possible symptom substitution; as overly problem focused instead of growth promoting; inviting dubious compliance with therapists; and likely to result in a false economy (i.e. clients will return with the same or worse distress later).

Much research has indicated equivalent outcomes across short-term and long-term therapies, has validated claims of phobia cures, removal of post-traumatic stress symptoms, and of significant positive impact on some personality disorders. However, early enthusiasm has given way to some extent to acknowledgement of research findings that therapeutic gains do not necessarily hold up reliably over time, that clients do sometimes outwardly comply with brief therapy but inwardly suppress some of their significant concerns, and so on. Many therapists and counsellors in primary care express frustration at unhelpfully inflexible time limits and, in some cases, a limit of six sessions is extended to 8 or 12 in the interests of clients. The tendency for innovative approaches to be hailed as panaceas is strong, and brief therapy should be placed in perspective.

Conclusions

The time-conscious lobby has forced all therapists to reconsider implicit philosophies of time in the therapeutic context. It is not only about time rationing, but also about the optimal organization of therapeutic time as a scarce resource. Traditional 50-minute hours do not necessarily provide what is best for all clients – longer, intensive sessions, very brief but frequent sessions, intermittently distributed sessions might all be considered on their merits. Strictly time-limited therapy is not necessarily desirable or perhaps even ethically defensible for all clients, and judiciously extended temporal contracts are to be recommended. It is important to regard brief therapy as one therapeutic option among others, and to use assessment skilfully to this end (Burton, 1998; Shipton and Smith, 1998). Finally, better clinical guidelines *via-à-vis* temporal factors are awaited.

References

Budman, S.H. and Gurman, A.S. (1988) *Theory and Practice of Brief Therapy*. New York: Guilford.

Burton, M.V. (1998) *Psychotherapy, Counselling and Primary Health Care: Assessment for Brief or Longer-Term Treatment*. Chichester: Wiley.

Ecker, B. and Hulley, L. (1996) *Depth-oriented Brief Therapy*. San Francisco: Jossey-Bass.

Elton Wilson, J. (1996) *Time-conscious Psychological Therapy*. London: Routledge.

Feltham, C. (1997) *Time-limited Counselling*. London: Sage.

Mander, G. (1998) Supervising short-term psychodynamic work. *Counselling*, 9 (4): 301–305.

Molnos, A. (1995) *A Question of Time: Essentials of Brief Dynamic Psychotherapy*. London: Karnac.

O'Connell, B. (1998) *Solution-focused Therapy*. London: Sage.

Roth, A. and Fonagy, P. (1996) *What Works for Whom? A Critical Review of Psychotherapy Research*. New York: Guilford.

Shipton, G. and Smith, E. (1998) *Long-term Counselling*. London: Sage.

Wright, J. (2003) Five women talk about work-related brief therapy and therapeutic writing. *Counselling and Psychotherapeutic Research*, 3 (3): 204–209.

7.4 Career Counselling

JENNY BIMROSE

Work is an important component of personal identity for many adults. Indeed, one way of considering an occupational identity, to which we are adjusted and that is relatively stable over a period of time, is as a psychological 'home' (Brown, 2004). Viewed in this way, it is easy to understand the sense of loss and dislocation that people may feel when they are made redundant, with little prospect of regaining their former occupational identity, or face a transition (from education to employment, for example) when they have to develop a completely new identity. Indeed, given the centrality of work to modern life, it is not unreasonable to assume its importance as a presenting issue for counselling, generally. However, the specialism of career counselling has developed around this area.

Defining the term 'career counselling' is surprisingly difficult. Changes in the labour market (for example, globalization and the development of information technology) have challenged the relevance of the traditional, narrow view of career transition as a one-off event at an early stage of an individual's development, replacing it with a broader understanding of how transitions into education, training and employment are more complex, more prolonged and often span lifetimes. Recent definitions try to capture the implications of these changes. For example, a recent review by the Organization for Economic Co-operation and Development (OECD, 2004) notes how terms like 'information', 'advice' and 'guidance', 'vocational guidance', 'vocational counselling', 'career counselling' and 'career development' are used to refer to a range of activities, which they define as: 'services intended to assist people of any age and at any point throughout their lives to make educational, training and occupational choices to manage their careers' (2004: 19).

This section reviews career counselling in the United Kingdom, examines theoretical frameworks that underpin its practice together with some of their implications for practice, and reflects on the future of the profession.

Career counselling in the UK

Responsibility for career counselling in the UK has rested variously with the government departments for education and/or employment since the beginning of the twentieth century, when politicians and philanthropists became concerned about difficulties experienced by young people who were making the transition from compulsory education into employment (at this time, predominantly young men). In addition to changes of government departments taking overall responsibility for the service, operational control has also been shifted from central to local government and back again to central government (Peck, 2004). Perhaps the considerable changes imposed on career counselling are a consequence of the emphasis placed on its strategic importance, particularly over the past two to three decades. Government reports and papers published throughout the 1980s and early 1990s positioned it as crucial in the general drive to increase the country's economic competitiveness. This replaced an emphasis on career counselling as key in the personal and educational development of individuals. Most recently, career counselling has been 'refocused' on socially excluded young people and low-skilled adults by, first, the creation of the 'Connexions' service (bringing with it the new profession of 'personal adviser') which is mandated to reintegrate disadvantaged and disaffected young people into society and, second, the targeting of resources on adults with low-level qualifications. Despite differing ideological emphases of governments of the day regarding policy priorities for career counselling, its focus has consistently assumed that if individuals who are in transition from education, who are not in employment or who wish to change jobs are matched with the 'right' jobs, training or education courses as quickly and effectively as possible, then everyone gains.

Alongside changes to the policy priorities and delivery mechanisms for career counselling, government attention has been directed at training for career counselling practitioners with the dual aims of increasing the availability of suitably qualified staff and widening access to the profession. Most recently, the number of routes into the profession has been extended from a one-year postgraduate course to embrace National Vocational Qualifications and other specialist vocational training courses (Bimrose et al., 2003), with Foundation Degrees in prospect.

The arrival of the 'global economy', uncertainty about the existence of stable, bureaucratic careers, unemployment and the increased participation of women in the labour market have all contributed to the acceptance that most individuals require career counselling at some time in their lives and that some client groups (for example, women returning to the labour market after a break to have children, the long-term unemployed) have particular needs. However, sources of funding for services are diverse and sometime precarious, with the requirements of fund-holders interacting in a complex way with the theoretical frameworks that underpin practice. It is to these we now turn.

Theory underpinning practice

Like generic counselling, a wide range of theoretical frameworks or models exist on which career counsellors can base their practice. Three main categories can be identified. First, there are those providing structure for the interview; second, those which ensure that the focus of the interview relates specifically to career; and, third, those providing a broad understanding of vocational behaviour. Each of these categories will be briefly discussed.

First, interview models that provide structure for the interview – specifically, sequencing of phases in the interview. Various examples are available and a distinctive characteristic is that they can be used across a range of counselling situations, like marriage guidance and bereavement, as well as careers. Perhaps the best known is that developed by Gerard Egan (2001). Egan's practical, three-stage model emphasizes problem managing and action. It helps the client to explore the current situation, understand and identify change, identify strategies for achieving this change and then turn strategies into a plan. Alternative models include one developed by Ivey et al. (2002) for use with different cultural groups. They propose a five-stage model similar to Egan's, but place a different emphasis on some of the interview stages. For example, establishing rapport is identified as a discrete, initial stage, which is separate from the other four: gathering information about the client, establishing the desired goals, identifying ways of achieving these goals and finally implementing change.

Second, there are the frameworks which focus on career development. They complement those providing structure by placing a specific emphasis on career. Such frameworks can be used to guide the exploration, investigation or data-gathering stages of the career interview. Examples include Zunker's (1998: 484) model that identifies three types of client information that need to be explored in a career counselling interview. These are:

- information about the individual's current circumstances (e.g. work experience, medical, family and educational history, etc.);
- information about life roles and potential conflicts arising from various roles (e.g. work role and parental role);
- information which may impede progress (e.g. inaccurate perceptions of entry requirements for particular jobs).

Third, frameworks that provide a broad understanding of vocational behaviour. Theories of occupational choice provide competing explanations of the types of choice and decision process involved. The grand concepts, values and assumptions about human nature and behaviour contained in different theories exert a profound influence on the way in which a career counsellor approaches the interview. For example, whether she/he assumes the role of facilitator, expert or advocate and the types of skill used.

A range of academic disciplines has produced these theories, including those as disparate as geography, mathematics and anthropology. Psychology, arguably, has made most impact on the practice of career counselling, together with sociology. The key difference between approaches derived from these two academic disciplines relates to the question of choice. Psychological approaches generally assume a degree of individual choice and autonomy. In contrast, sociological approaches focus attention on structures that limit individual choice (for example, social class, gender, ethnicity, local and regional labour markets).

Psychological approaches to occupational choice include theories from various traditions. Differential (trait and factor) approaches emphasize the assessment of individual traits that are then matched to jobs. Developmental theories propose that vocational behaviour can be understood and predicted in terms of life stages. Behavioural theories (social learning) stress the importance of environmental influences and learned experiences of education and work. Psychoanalytic theories explain vocational behaviour as the result of the need of individuals to satisfy unconscious desires and impulses. Although humanistic psychology has not yet produced a theory of occupational choice, the person-centred approach to counselling has had a profound influence on career counselling, lending powerful insights about the core qualities required for effective counselling and the use of certain types of communication skills (for example, active listening).

Sociological approaches to occupational choice include the theory of occupational allocation that stresses the interaction of local labour market conditions with client characteristics such as gender and ethnic origin. One other example is community interaction theory that directs attention to the groups and agencies existing within local communities and the influence they exert on career development.

However, a consensus is emerging regarding the inadequacy of these established theories. Two distinct trends in theory development, which sometimes overlap, are emerging. One is towards developing theories that attempt to meet the needs of specific client groups, such as minority ethnic groups or girls and women. The second is towards those characterized by a post-modern approach, which marks a move away from 'logical positivism, objectivist science, and industrialism' towards 'a multiple perspective discourse' (Savickas, 1993: 205). Career theories are increasingly being developed which focus on meaning, invention and construction and are shifting away from objectifying clients by measurement to a preference for autobiography and meaning making.

Implications for practice

The implications for practice of selected psychological approaches are usefully summarized by Walsh (1990: 263). He examines the implications for various dimensions of the career interview, including the diagnosis phase, the process and the outcomes of the interview, techniques likely to be employed and the role of occupational information. Thus, a career counsellor adopting a differential approach would assess skills, abilities, motivation, progress and level of information processing. The goal would be to provide the client with information that would assist the rational decision-making process. Accurate information is stressed by this approach and techniques (for example, tests, interest inventories, and communication skills such as probing questions) that assist with accurate client assessment would be used. In contrast, a humanistic or person-centred approach would ensure that the client was in control of the interview content. The goal would be to promote self-discovery and skills used would include genuineness, empathy and unconditional positive regard. Little emphasis would be placed on occupational information during counselling.

These two examples illustrate some practical implications of psychological approaches to career counselling. Applying Walsh's analytical framework to sociological perspectives, the practitioner would be concerned to identify the social context of the client. Understanding the client's perception of the effect of certain factors (for example, ethnicity or gender) and ensuring they have access to relevant and accurate labour market information, together with the support necessary for interpreting this information, would be priorities. The counsellor's role may well extend beyond the interview to advocating on behalf of the client (for example, to an employer or course provider) or attempting to change systems (for example, recruitment and selection policies of employers).

Any one framework brings with it important implications for counselling. In reality, most career counsellors probably operate eclectically, or perhaps develop their own 'theory in action' that allows them to respond to and reconcile challenges and difficulties encountered. Research is needed which provides insights into the process of applying theory to practice and career counsellors need to be encouraged to contribute more to the development of the knowledge base which informs their practice.

Future practice

Matching approaches (from differential psychology) to career counselling have had (and probably still have) most influence on practice. Differential approaches undoubtedly offer many advantages, but also beg a number of important questions. For example, is it always the case that individuals are happiest (and therefore the most productive) in jobs that harness measurable abilities? Should career counselling concern itself with the social circumstances of the individual client? Should the career counsellor be regarded as the expert or facilitator? Should emotions be acknowledged, or priority given to rational decision making? Answers to these

and other questions will depend, in part at least, on what is regarded as the main purpose of career counselling.

Given the increasingly varied range of clients who seek career counselling, and the complexity and number of the activities implied by the term 'career counselling', it is unlikely that a single framework or theory can equip career counsellors to respond effectively to such varied and increasing demands. Rather, they need to be familiar with a relevant range of theories, able to select and apply theory appropriate to their clients' needs and be competent in the use of counselling skills and techniques.

Varied sources of funding bring an additional dimension to practice. Often fund-holders impose a view about the desirable outcomes of career counselling. These can sometimes be in conflict with the preferences and professional judgements of career counsellors, who must somehow resolve these conflicts in their practice.

Conclusion

Career counselling in the UK is a relatively new occupational area struggling to establish its identity as a profession. It has been manipulated by fund-holders to fit various political visions and delivery mechanisms have been subjected to fundamental change. Debates about definition continue and the profession is fragmented. Different occupational identities have formed around different professional contexts and their funding sources (for example, higher education, further education, schools, voluntary agencies, charitable organizations, workplaces and the private sector), with distinct training routes now aligned with different sectors. The fragmentation has consequences for issues like supervision and professional development which increasingly reflect the culture of the sector in which the service is based.

Career counselling has survived changes and risen to all the challenges imposed by different governments. It is time for career counsellors to develop a coherent professional identify and attract the recognition and achieve the status they have long deserved.

References

Bimrose, J., Mulvey, M.R. and La Gro, N. (2003) Careers guidance. In R. Bayne and I. Horton (eds), *Applied Psychology*. London: Sage. pp. 94–103.

Brown, A. (2004) Engineering identities. *Career Development International*, 9 (3): 245–273.

Egan, G. (2001) *The Skilled Helper: A Problem-management Approach to Helping* (7th edn). Belmont, CA: Wadsworth.

Ivey, A.E., Ivey, M.B. and Simek-Morgan, L. (2002) *Counseling and Psychotherapy: A Multicultural Perspective* (5th edn). Needham Heights, MA: Allyn & Bacon.

OECD (2004) *Career Guidance and Public Policy: Bridging the Gap*. Paris: Organization for Economic Co-operation and Development.

Peck, D. (2004) *Career Services: History, Policy and Practice in the UK*. London: Routledge Farmer.

Savickas, M.L. (1993) Career counselling in the post-modern era. *Journal of Cognitive Psychotherapy*, 7 (3): 205–215.

Walsh, W.B. (1990) A summary and integration of career counseling approaches. In W.B. Walsh and S.H. Osipow (eds), *Career Counseling: Contemporary Topics in Vocational Psychology*. Hillsdale, NJ: Lawrence Erlbaum Associates.

Zunker, V.G. (1998) *Career Counseling: Applied Concepts of Life Planning* (5th edn). Pacific Grove, CA: Brooks/Cole.

Recommended reading

Sharf, R.S. (2001) *Applying Career Development Theory to Counseling* (3rd edn). Pacific Grove, CA: Brooks/Cole.

7.5   Counselling Children

KATHRYN GELDARD AND DAVID GELDARD

Counselling children is different in a number of ways from counselling adolescents or adults. Whereas many adolescents and most adults seek counselling of their own volition, children are usually brought to see counsellors by their parents or significant other adults. The adults involved are likely to have agendas of their own. It is therefore imperative when counselling children that significant adults involved in the child's life are also involved in the therapeutic process in some way. The situation is also complicated because children live in families and their emotional and behavioural problems may relate to

the family system. Their problems certainly occur within the family system and will almost inevitably result in some consequences for the system. Therefore, when counselling children a counsellor will usually need to address not only the intrapersonal issues of the child in individual counselling, but also systemic issues involving the child's parents and/or family which may be causing and/or maintaining the child's problems or be a consequence of these problems.

Another important difference between counselling adults and counselling children is that adults are generally comfortable and able to explore and resolve their issues in a conversational relationship with a counsellor. Although some children may be able to do this, many are unable to share the things that trouble them with a counsellor who uses only conversational strategies. Consequently, most counsellors trained in counselling children will make use of media and activity to engage the child, to enable the child to talk about what is troubling them and to help the child find resolution of their issues.

Although many, if not most, of the children who are brought to counselling have underlying emotional problems, it is common for adults to bring children to counselling only after noticing behavioural problems. However, for successful therapeutic outcomes the counsellor needs to address both the emotional and the behavioural issues.

An additional difference between counselling adults and counselling children relates to confidentiality. With adults, confidentiality can be offered subject to the usual limitations imposed by ethical considerations, whereas with children the confidentiality issue is confounded by the rights of the parents to have information about their children. Clearly, if a child is to talk freely, he or she must have some confidence that the information they share will be treated respectfully and will not be disclosed to others without good reason.

Therapeutic approaches

There are several therapeutic approaches which can be used when counselling children, including:

- non-directive play therapy
- sand tray therapy
- Gestalt therapy
- time-limited play therapy
- cognitive-behavioural therapy
- family therapy.

Each of these approaches has some advantages and some limitations. The literature suggests that there is not one preferred way of working which is appropriate for all children. Some counsellors believe that they need to be flexible enough to select a method of working which is specifically suitable for a particular child and relevant for the child's issues. This idea was originally proposed by Millman and Schaefer (1977), who called it a 'prescriptive approach'. An alternative approach which is gaining acceptance is to use an integrative approach where ideas from a number of therapeutic approaches are integrated. Whatever approach is used, there are a number of goals which can usefully be achieved when counselling children. These include:

- To help the child gain mastery over issues and events.
- To enable the child to feel empowered.
- To help the child develop problem-solving and decision-making skills.
- To build the child's self-concept and self-esteem.
- To improve the child's communication skills.
- To help the child develop insight.

We will now discuss the range of individual approaches previously listed and will then explain how these can be combined in an integrative approach.

Non-directive play therapy

In this largely psychoanalytic approach the counsellor observes the child as the child plays without direction in an environment which contains suitable media. This material is likely to include typical children's toys, toy furniture, and materials such as clay, paint and crayons. The counsellor's observations might include observation of mood or affect, intellectual functioning, thinking processes, speech and language, motor skills, play, and the relationship with the counsellor. The presence of defence mechanisms such as suppression, avoidance, denial and indications of dissociation will be noted.

Various ways of working in non-directive play therapy were pioneered by Anna Freud, Melanie Klein, Donald Winnicott, and Virginia Axline (Cattanach, 1992). In non-directive play therapy the counsellor looks for unconscious motivation behind imaginative play, drawings and paintings. The counsellor then interprets the content of the child's play to the child. This psychoanalytic approach usually involves long-term work with the child and may be most suitable for young children with mental health disorders. Because it tends to require long-term work, this type of therapy may be unpopular in health services where financial resources are limited.

Sand tray therapy

This approach was pioneered by Margaret Lowenfeld in an attempt to find a way of helping children to communicate without the use of language (Schaefer and O'Connor, 1994). She used a variety of small objects as symbols in a sand tray to encourage non-verbal expression which was less influenced by rational thinking (Ryce-Menuhin, 1992). Many contemporary counsellors use sand tray work not only to observe non-verbal expression, but also as a tool to engage the child, and enable the child to talk openly and thus explore their issues. An advantage of using sand tray work is that it is suitable for children of all ages as it relies on symbolic rather than projective techniques. Sand tray work is very useful in helping a child to tell their story, explore issues, and express emotions. However, it may be less effective in promoting cognitive and behavioural change than other ways of working.

Gestalt therapy

Violet Oaklander (1988) has demonstrated a particular way of combining the use of Gestalt therapy principles and practice with the use of media when working with children. She works therapeutically with children by encouraging them to use fantasy and/or metaphor, and believes that usually the fantasy process will be the same as the life process in the child. She therefore works indirectly in bringing out what is hidden or avoided and relies on what is essentially a projective process. A limitation of Oaklander's approach is that it is an indirect projective technique. Although this works well for some children, others may have difficulty in making the connection between their fantasy and real life.

Other counsellors use a Gestalt therapy approach in a more direct way. While engaging the child in the use of media and/or activity they will use Gestalt techniques to help the child experience raised awareness while they are telling their story.

Time-limited play therapy

This approach uses ideas from brief therapy with a psychodynamic orientation (Sloves and Belinger-Peterlin, 1986). A brief assessment of the child's issues is made. The counsellor then selects a central theme and the therapeutic work is limited to this theme. The work with the child focuses on empowerment, adaptation and strengthening the ego. It focuses on the future rather than the past. Generally, individual work with the child is limited to 12 sessions. This form of therapy is both directive and interpretative. It is effective for some children and not useful for others (Schaefer and O'Connor, 1994). In particular, it has been found to be effective for children with recent post-traumatic stress disorder, adjustment disorders, and for children who have lost a parent due to a chronic medical condition (Christ et al., 1991).

Cognitive-behavioural therapy

An educational model, as described by Beck (1995), is used to describe the connection between thoughts, emotions and behaviours. The child's current thoughts, which are driving their emotions and behaviours, are explored. The counsellor's goal is to enable the child to replace unhelpful thoughts with more adaptive ones. When working with children using cognitive-behavioural therapy media and activity are useful. For example, worksheets, drawing and role-playing might be used in order to help the child explore their current thoughts and behaviours and practise new ways of thinking and behaving.

Cognitive-behavioural therapy tends to be popular with health services which have limited financial resources as the process is short-term, involving only a few counselling sessions. Cognitive-behavioural techniques are useful in enabling many children to gain a level of control over their emotions and behaviours. Limitations of this approach are that it does not directly target emotions or encourage emotional release. Also, the approach requires the child to have reasonably good language skills, and a level of cognitive development and emotional maturity. Without this, the child will not be able to makes sense of the educational model, and may not be able to interrupt emotional outbursts by making changes to their thinking. Consequently, it is not suitable for very young children.

Cognitive-behavioural therapy is often used in conjunction with behavioural psychotherapy where incentives are used to reinforce positive behaviour and there are consequences for undesirable behaviour. Behaviour therapy can be used with children of all ages.

Family therapy

This approach is discussed in section 7.10. Some counsellors believe that it is sufficient to explore and resolve a child's emotional and behavioural problems within the context of the family system. This can be a very effective way of working with some children. However, many children who come for counselling are troubled by emotional issues and/or thoughts which are of a highly personal nature and which they may not be able to talk about in the context of the family.

Eclectic and integrative counselling

The previous discussion has highlighted the advantages and limitations of a number of differing ways of working with children. Some counsellors like to use a particular therapeutic approach, but others prefer to work in an eclectic way. Some eclectic counsellors will choose to select and use the particular therapeutic approach which they think is most appropriate for helping a particular child with specific issues in the way that was described as prescriptive by Millman and Schaefer (1977). Other eclectic counsellors will select and make use of strategies from more than one therapeutic approach with the goal of meeting a child's specific needs. Both of these approaches can have positive outcomes.

However, although some eclectic counsellors have success in using the approaches described, it can be argued that there is a risk that the process of counselling might be compromised by the inappropriate selection and/or sequence of strategies used. An alternative is to use an integrative model where strategies from particular therapeutic approaches are deliberately used at particular points in the therapeutic process.

The SPICC model

An example of an integrative model is the 'Sequentially planned integrative counselling for children' model (the SPICC model), which we developed and use ourselves (Geldard and Geldard, 2002). This model divides the counselling process into a sequence of stages.

Wherever possible before using the SPICC model we try to engage the family in family therapy so that we can have a full understanding of the family dynamics and can see the child in the context of the family system. Sometimes after family therapy we will discover that the problem has been resolved and no further therapeutic work is required. At other times we will recognize that the child with the presenting problem, or another child in the family, may be experiencing emotional distress. We will then proceed to work individually with the child using the SPICC model.

The SPICC model involves the following sequence: joining with the child, enabling the child to tell their story, raising the child's awareness so that they get in touch with and express emotions, helping the child to cognitively restructure, helping the child to look at options and choices, and enabling the child to rehearse and experiment with new behaviours.

Sand tray work: In the initial stage the counsellor joins with and engages the child. To do this use will be made of media and/or activity. Typically, a counsellor might use symbols in the sand tray, or with older children who are cognitively able to use a projective technique, miniature animals can be used to represent family members. If working in the sand tray, the child can be encouraged to use objects as symbols to make a picture in the sand of their world as they perceive it, and/or their family. The activity component of the exercise enables the child to feel relaxed rather than pressured to talk. As the picture in the sand tray develops, the counsellor is able to explore its meaning for the child and help the child to talk openly about their life.

Use of Gestalt therapy: Once a trusting relationship has been established the counsellor can begin to use media and/or activity together with Gestalt therapy awareness-raising techniques to help the child connect with troubling emotions. The use of suitable media and/or activity maintains the child's interest, allows them to anchor their story, and ensures that the child has time to process thoughts in silence rather than to feel pressured to talk. As the child's awareness is raised the counsellor might encourage the release of troubling emotions. This might be done through the use of media such as clay or activity such as painting and drawing. The goal of therapy up to this point has been to facilitate a process which will allow the child to share their story, to get in touch with troubling issues and emotions, and to release those emotions in the safety of the therapeutic environment.

Use of cognitive-behavioural therapy and behaviour therapy: The next stage in the process is to target any unhelpful and/or maladaptive thoughts and behaviours. It is not sufficient just to help the child get in touch with and express emotions. Unhelpful thinking patterns need to be restructured using cognitive-behavioural therapy. The child is unlikely to change and emotional distress will probably reoccur if this stage in the process is overlooked. Similarly, the child needs to be encouraged to explore their options and choices regarding current and future behaviour. The new behaviour can then be reinforced using a behaviour therapy approach with the parents' co-operation.

Integration of individual and family work: During the individual counselling process with the child there may be times when it will be useful for the child to share information either with their parents or with the family. Certainly, towards the end of the therapeutic process it can be useful to re-engage the whole family in family therapy so that any changes can be reinforced and supported and remaining problems can be addressed.

Conclusion

Counselling children involves a range of specialist skills which can only be developed under the guidance of a counselling supervisor who is trained and experienced in working with children. Additionally, as with all counselling, ongoing supervision is necessary and essential to ensure good practice. Although there are several different approaches to counselling children it is generally advantageous for counsellors to combine the use of media and activity with suitable counselling skills to enable the child to feel at ease and to maximize positive outcomes of the counselling process.

References

Beck, A.T. (1995) *Cognitive Therapy: Basics and Beyond*. New York: Guilford Press.

Cattanach, A. (1992) *Play Therapy with Abused Children*. London: Jessica Kingsley.

Christ, G.H., Siegel, K., Mesagno, F. and Langosch, D. (1991) A preventative program for bereaved children: problems of implementation. *Journal of Orthopsychiatry*, 61: 168–178.

Geldard, K. and Geldard, D. (2002) *Counselling Children: A Practical Introduction*. London: Sage.

Millman, H. and Schaefer, C.E. (1977) *Therapies for Children*. San Francisco, CA: Jossey-Bass.

Oaklander, V. (1988) *Windows to Our Children*. New York: Center for Gestalt Development.

Ryce-Menuhin, J. (1992) *Jungian Sand Play: The Wonderful Therapy*. New York: Routledge, Chapman and Hall.

Schaefer, C.E. and O'Connor, K.J. (eds) (1994) *Handbook of Play Therapy*, Vol. 2: *Advances and Innovations*. New York: Wiley.

Sloves, R. and Belinger-Peterlin, K. (1986) The process of time-limited psychotherapy with latency-aged children. *Journal of the American Academy of Child Psychiatry*, 25: 847–851.

7.6 Co-counselling   ○○○

ROSE EVISON AND RICHARD HOROBIN

Co-counselling is a personal growth method involving participants working in reciprocal pairs, exchanging client and counsellor roles halfway through the session time. Theory and practice has evolved around the core experience that inbuilt body-mind processes of crying, shaking, *storming*, laughing and retching transform people's distressed rigid responses, called *patterns*, into flexible thinking and acting. A comprehensive theoretical underpinning, based on an integrative theory of emotions and supported by research, is available (Evison, 2001). [Note: co-counselling jargon is italicized]

Co-counselling is for anyone who is able to act as counsellor as well as work as client, and who is able to learn the techniques. Some heavily distressed people are excluded by these conditions, others are not. Co-counselling can cover therapeutic change from emotional first aid and problem solving, to dealing with strong or *chronic patterns* like *internalized oppression*. For ongoing growth using co-counselling, most people need to work within a supportive community of co-counsellors.

Key concepts

Emotions act as a motivating system, organizing our mind and body resources appropriately to meet task demands. Pleasurable emotions motivate us to look for meaningful elements in our environment, to solve problems and learn, and to care for each other and our children. They form our basic way of interacting with our physical and social environments – the learning mode.

Painful emotions motivate us to overcome physical and psychological threats to well-being, and organize body and mind resources for survival – they form our emergency response system. A threat's nature determines which muscles are activated, for fight or flight, to retch out poisons, to cry for help to replace loved ones, to repair threatened relationships. These preparations are associated with the inbuilt emotions – anger, fear, disgust, grief and shame. However, we do not experience these emotions when acting on them, all our attention being taken up by working to overcome the threat.

After successfully overcoming threats, we have no further need for our emergency response mode, so inbuilt emotional reset processes move us directly into positive feelings, with relaxed bodies and alert minds, adding the learning gained to our memories. This is termed a mastery reset to the learning mode.

When we fail to master a threat but survive, as happens frequently in childhood, our bodies remain aroused and our attention trapped by aspects of the threatening event. This results in locked-up resources, leaving us unavailable for new tasks. However, perceived absence of present threat, while mind and body resources are oriented to distressing situations, sets off failure reset processes – *discharge*. These are *storming* for anger, shaking for fear, crying for grief, laughing for shame, retching for poisonous ideas. The obvious physical aspects of the processes involve non-purposive actions that relax tense muscles, and the attention trapped by the threat is released by the physical relaxation.

However, socializing emotional expressiveness in childhood, by punishment, results in inhibition of these reset processes, producing *control patterns*. With release inhibited, we experience the pain of our aroused bodies. Seeking to minimize the pain results in those inadequate responses, occurring when the threat ceased, becoming conditioned to repetitions of the threat – *patterns*. When we meet reminders of such threats, these *patterns* are triggered and we act them out – *re-stimulation. Patterns* comprise rigidly connected thoughts, feelings, actions and body states, although not all these aspects may be noticed Everyone has *patterns,* which are readily recognized when people make lists of things they would like to change about themselves. *Patterns* vary in complexity, from nauseous responses to pain-associated smells, to the interlocking knots of low self-esteem. *Patterns* may be unique to individuals, or shared within a subculture.

To escape from *patterns* we must set up the conditions of failure reset: the absence of current threats plus re-experiencing the emotion that was not reset in the past. Given these conditions, termed a *balance of attention, discharge* occurs spontaneously; and a distress-triggered sequence ends in the positive feelings and relaxed alert mind and body of learning mode. The result is a disabling of *pattern* triggers, and spontaneous insights occur – *re-evaluation,* with new learning replacing distressed responses. Co-counselling techniques enable a *balance of attention* to be set up whatever emotional place the client is in.

Major techniques

Co-counselling uses three main strategies to obtain a *balance of attention,* which produces *discharge:*

- maximizing clients' awareness of freedom from current threat – *safety*;
- enabling clients to move from experiencing a *pattern* to re-experiencing the painful emotion that drives the pattern;
- enabling clients to gain attention outside strong or *chronic patterns* which are swamping them.

Maximizing clients' awareness of freedom from present threat is achieved by using an explicit session contract that minimizes threat-reminders from the counsellor. Counsellors avoid giving negative judgements, interpretations or advice, and aim to offer supportive attention at all times. Using these guidelines, along with the reciprocal roles, generates

safety for the client, providing high levels of non-judgemental warmth, empathy and genuineness.

Enabling clients to re-experience the painful emotion that drives a pattern is achieved by techniques which encourage reliving events in which distresses occurred, for example describing a specific event in the present tense while involving the body in relevant actions. Re-experiencing is enhanced by repeating and exaggerating *distress cues,* whether thoughts, feelings or bodily manifestations.

Enabling clients to gain attention outside the patterns swamping them is achieved using techniques in which clients put energy into words and actions which are the antitheses of the distress – ridiculous opposites or parodies. Useful phrases are those which trigger *discharge* on thinking or saying them quietly. For expanded accounts of co-counselling ideas and techniques see Evison and Horobin (1990, 1994).

Variations in UK co-counselling

Co-counselling grew from a counselling agency in Seattle, Personal Counselors. In the 1960s, the Re-evaluation Counseling Communities organization (RC) was set up, which spread beyond the USA, reaching the UK in 1971. Currently, RC exists in more than 40 countries. In the 1970s, Co-Counselling International (CCI) was set up by RC dissidents, and 'co-counselling' came into use as a generic name for the process. CCI has a presence in around 15 countries.

RC uses strong central control to maintain coherence in theory, practice and organizational form. Major developments have occurred, including working with oppressive distresses; sexism, racism, classism and adultism being tackled within RC and out in the world. An emphasis on skilled counselling encourages rapid client change, the potential downside being the unbalancing of the reciprocal relationship in favour of the counsellor role. The search for a good counsellor can replace individuals developing their own *inner-counsellor* skills. For an account of this variant by two of its experienced teachers, see Kauffman and New (2004).

CCI is a loose network without formal membership, providing an umbrella for a variety of ways of using reciprocal pairs for personal growth. CCI groups have diverged in theory, practice and organization both from RC and each other. Some common variants follow:

1   Some teachers have moved from the traditional co-counselling focus on *discharge* to include techniques from other therapies (e.g. from cognitive therapy, Gestalt and meditation). This is often diluting, or even contradictory, and encourages clients to search for the magic technique.
2   Some co-counselling organizations now promulgate clients' right to use any techniques from other therapies they find helpful. So co-counsellors from different groups can only work together if the counsellor role is downgraded.
3   An individualistic style has developed, using the premise that the client is in charge of their work all the time. This makes the client role the expert one, with counsellors not needing skills beyond that of providing supportive attention – co-clienting rather than co-counselling.
4   When the counsellor role is downgraded or deskilled, strong and *chronic patterns,* such as *internalized oppression,* cannot be worked with, resulting in oppressive practices within CCI not being tackled.
5   The original strategy of establishing a supportive group, where patterned behaviour is treated as material to be worked on, has changed. Many teachers and groups espouse a group dynamics model of group process, in which participants are asked to take individual responsibility for personally challenging destructive behaviour in others.

With these changes, the authors now use the term Cathartic Co-counselling to describe their own practice and teaching. They continue to use supportive group cultures, considering them optimal for learning and personal change, as supported by Evison's research review (2001). They emphasize the need for participants to develop skills in both client and counsellor roles, making change processes more efficient and enabling the tackling of *chronic patterns.*

Training and supervision issues

As a policy, RC remains outside the professional mental health field, regarding both professionals and institutions as oppressive, and runs its own training and supervision. Beginners' classes are conducted by teachers accredited by the central organization. For continuing membership, RC counsellors are required to take classes and attend workshops to develop their skills as counsellors and clients. Regional and national workshops are held. Teachers are expected to become skilled in the counsellor role and do demonstration counselling of class participants. Personal growth and supervision are combined in a system of teachers and leaders being regularly counselled by their organizational superiors, for instance during workshop demonstrations. Teachers are encouraged to work on what gets in the way of becoming better teachers. Teachers and members who contravene ground rules or deviate from accepted theory and practice are ejected from the organization. A journal devoted to teacher issues (*The RC Teacher*) is distributed to accredited teachers and is available to all those interested.

Within CCI, teachers are recognized as experts in passing on the skills, but training courses are *ad hoc,* often with the group the teacher belongs to having no say in the training content and processes. Rejection of hierarchy, authorities and directive counsellor roles largely results in the rejection of supervision as oppressive. Regional and national workshops offer possibilities for the exchange of skills and ideas, but these days are rarely used for advancing co-counselling skills. While there are skilled co-counselling teachers in CCI, there is no system for maintaining teacher quality or consistency. The consequences are loss of theoretical understandings, degrading of techniques, and increasing variations in theory and practice between groups.

Benefits of co-counselling for therapeutic practitioners

For therapeutic practitioners, using Cathartic Co-counselling provides ways to:

• participate in a support system independent of professional and job hierarchies, which can minimize the stresses inherent in the practitioner role and accelerate their own personal growth;

- experience being a client from the inside out, understand the difference made by a totally accepting relationship, and recognize the large overlaps in distresses between practitioners and their clients;
- experience enhanced learning of counsellor skills through participating as both client and counsellor in the reciprocal relationship, thereby developing their own *inner counsellor*;
- understand that a *balance of attention* is a core condition facilitating therapeutic change, and can be embodied in a variety of therapeutic methods. Learn to recognize the differences between emotional expressiveness and emotional acting out, and how to change acting out into emotional reset;
- understand that the conditions for *discharge* equate to those for in-built reset of basic painful emotions, and for the conditions for cathartic reset. Add methods of assisting emotional reset to their repertoire of therapeutic techniques.

Practitioners using co-counselling variants not based on techniques that facilitate *discharge*, and/or not developing counsellor skills for tackling chronic patterns, are unlikely to gain all the above benefits. However, the first two benefits remain,

and will be enhancing of practitioners' work with clients.

References

Evison, R. (2001) Helping individuals manage emotional responses. In R.L. Payne and C.L. Cooper (eds), *Emotions at Work: Theory, Research and Applications in Management*. Chichester: Wiley. pp. 241–268.

Evison, R. and Horobin, R.W. (1990) *How to Change Yourself and Your World: A Manual of Co-counselling Theory and Practice* (2nd edn). Pitlochry: Co-counselling Phoenix, Change Strategies.

Evison, R. and Horobin, R.W. (1994) *Co-counselling as Therapy* (2nd edn). Pitlochry: Co-counselling Phoenix, Change Strategies. (An expanded version of a chapter in J. Rowan and W. Dryden (eds) (1988) *Innovative Therapies in Britain*. Milton Keynes: Open University Press.)

Kauffman, K. and New, C. (2004) *Co-counselling: The Theory and Practice of Re-evaluation Counselling*. Hove: Brunner Routledge.

The RC Teacher: A Journal for People Interested in the Theory and Practice of Teaching Re-evaluation Co-counseling. Seattle, WA: Rational Island Press.

7.7 Couple Counselling   ◯◯◯

BARBARA MCKAY

What is a couple relationship?

A couple relationship could be described as two people striving to create sexual, physical, psychological and social intimacy with one another. Social,

cultural and religious influences may determine what measure of exclusivity is accorded within this relationship. The choices people make may be influenced by past relationships and attachment experiences, the desire for personal fulfilment as well as the desire to replicate previous relationships or create new and different future relationships. For homosexual and gay couple relationships, there may be additional factors to manage, such as prejudice and intolerance from some contexts within society. This may have to do with practices around power and the legacy of a historical perspective, pathologizing gay and lesbian relationships. In this section, I will focus on a heterosexual couple from two western cultures using a systemic social constructionist approach.

What couple relationships have in common is that they live their lives in stories, dialogues between two people and narratives within families. These stories begin before birth when a child's arrival becomes part of the family narrative. As we move through different phases of life we make and participate in multiple stories both in our family relationships and other contexts – schools, work and leisure.

Couples make and re-make the meanings they attach to events and ideas over the life of the relationship. These meanings include individual personal meanings and collective, couple meanings. Individual stories are of self-esteem, personal abilities and styles of communication. Couple stories are primarily relational, shifting the focus from the individual to the interpersonal. This is a move from an individualistic 'I' position to a collective, relational, 'We' position. In the 'We' position, individuals aspire to create 'fit' with one another by engaging in a series of dialogues. Some will be internal, measuring the developing relationships against a set of values or beliefs, some will be external, with significant others in the wider family and social system. In this way couples begin to create a set of feedback loops through which to understand and construct their relationship.

From these descriptions a picture is emerging of two individuals with their own sets of beliefs and behaviour, coming together to create a joint set of beliefs and behaviour that represent some kind of fit between them. This mutual relationship of giving and receiving also acts as feedback on the individual level, telling each partner about the kind of person they are as well as what kind of partner they are becoming. This joint relationship is then seen in the context of a wider family and social system, which both influences and can be influenced by the couple relationship.

What problems do couples bring to counselling?

Couples come into counselling for many reasons. They often bring a particular event, for example an affair, an argument or pattern of arguments or sexual problems. These are episodes of action and interaction that in some way challenge the stories about couple fit. Other concerns are less tangible: couples say they have grown apart, don't love one another any longer, have little in common. These couples might be talking about fundamental differences that have been part of the relationship for some time but have now become important. The meaning couples attach to these problems may influence the level of expressed emotion.

What approach might be useful?

If we take the position that couples live their lives in a series of connected stories, we might assume that each couple has within their repertoire the ability to recall and tell life-giving stories about their relationships as well as the stories of dissatisfaction and unhappiness they generally bring to counselling. With the couple, the counsellor has the task of creating a context where multiple versions of the stories can emerge. Each story style has a different effect on the couple relationship. The life-giving stories of love, success, mutuality and friendship create the 'we-ness', the shared beliefs and values that fit with the couple's view of how they should be. In these moments couples can draw upon collaborative stories of success from the past and present, and can envision these stories into the future.

The stories of dissatisfaction challenge the life-giving stories and the couple's resilience. This often has the effect of partners moving into an 'I' position and talking of blame in relation to the other. This shift can often be noticed in language, with couples

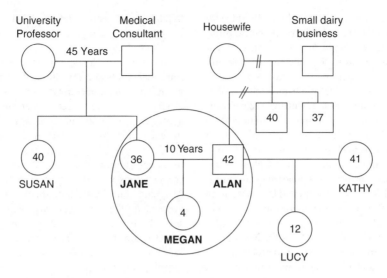

JANE	ALAN
• White American • Devout Christian • First marriage • Middle-class educated family • Parents married for 45 years	• White English • No religious conviction • Divorced 11 years • Middle-class rural community • Parents divorced after 11 years of marriage

Figure 7.7.1 Jane and Alan

using 'I' and 'you' much more than 'we'. Stories of blame are common in couple work and can be related to a specific event or can be more generalized across a range of events, situations and ideas.

The intention of the counsellor is to bring forth multiple versions of the various stories around an event or relationship in order to find some common ground through which to begin to develop new meanings and jointly create new possible future stories. This is based on the premise that language is not only descriptive of events but is constructive of them.

Working therapeutically, we take the position that it is unhelpful to hold on to notions of either individual or societal pathology, but rather construct meanings around behaviour within the relationships and circumstances in which they occur. These meanings and actions will be seen as stories located in a wider discourse, at the level of culture.

What should we do?

Alan and Jane, married for 10 years, came for couple counselling. Alan is 42, a self-employed accountant. Jane is 36, at home with the couple's daughter, Megan. Alan has a daughter from a previous marriage (Figure 7.7.1). The couple complained of frequent arguments that never seemed to resolve anything. Jane was thinking of leaving Alan, although this challenged her religious beliefs about marriage being sacred and permanent. Alan was worried that his second marriage was failing. Sexual issues were discussed but not considered to be the main focus for this couple at this time.

This kind of problem fits into the 'event' category and also what Gottman (2000) calls perpetual problems. These are described as repeating concerns that remain a feature throughout the relationship and despite frequent attempts to discuss and resolve them, little changes and they continue to cause dissatisfaction and unhappiness. Gottman (2000) calls this a 'gridlock position'. From a communication perspective, Oliver et al. (2003) might use the term 'strange loop'. Gridlock position and strange loop both describe those moments in a couple relationship when each partner is in a polarized and contradictory position to the other. This pattern of behaviour and its resultant communication becomes fixed and challenges the couple's version of how their relationship should be. This is further complicated by the unsaid but implicit message that 'if you were more like me' we would not have this problem.

Each episode or piece of interaction in the pattern will have an effect on and be affected by other interactions, which are in the context of culture, community, self and relationships. In order to make sense of these episodes, we, as counsellors, explore the way in which various stories are held together and kept in place. Cronen (1994) suggests that we hold stories of ourselves and our relationships which are strongly influenced by our past relationships and experiences, our gender, our communities, our religious beliefs and our culture. Because we can find ways of explaining our thinking and actions, we might imagine that nothing can change or that there is no other explanation or way of being and that we have no choices in certain situations. During these moments of the repetitive argument couples may be mostly occupied by stories of dissatisfaction and least available to their own life-giving stories of celebration and mutuality. Oliver et al. (2003) suggest that once a pattern is recognized the next step is to explore its uniqueness to the situation and the people involved, using this as a gateway to understanding and creating change.

Alan and Jane argued about small inconsequential things, which led to Jane shouting and Alan trying to get away. This made Jane even angrier as she believed that talk led to resolution. Alan believed that he needed space to reflect and take the heat out of the situation. The pattern they created did not fit for either of them.

One way of exploring this episode is to develop some ideas around the meaning of arguments. Each partner has the opportunity to witness the meaning given by the other, a process that encourages each to appreciate the 'I' position as well as the 'we' position in which they find themselves. Figures 7.7.2 and 7.7.3 and Table 7.7.1 show the multiple and complex meanings about arguments that emerged through conversations with Alan and Jane. It is clear that Alan and Jane have contradictory and polarized views about the meaning of arguments in relationships. Each is acting as if their own version is the only version, thus becoming stuck in one way of interacting and not able to see any other possible meanings or actions.

These different positions can be explored by tracking a piece of action from the initial point at which the pattern begins, which is often at a feeling level. This feeling or discomfort is connected with meanings, which are performed or shown in actions. This multilayered approach connects thinking, feeling and action in the present and takes the view that intervening at any one of these levels could subsequently influence the others. It also creates the opportunity for couples to become reflexive about their own processes and the significant influential forces emerging from previous experiences and relationships with the intention of creating changes that lead to different and preferred futures.

For Alan, the headline meaning of arguments was a signal for the end of the relationship. This led to Alan doing everything he could to avoid arguing to preserve the relationship. For Jane, the headline meaning was that arguments keep the relationship alive. This led to Jane pursuing arguments to cement their relationship. They felt they had no escape.

What next?

Exploring and understanding the pattern is only the first step. Counselling should make interventions at

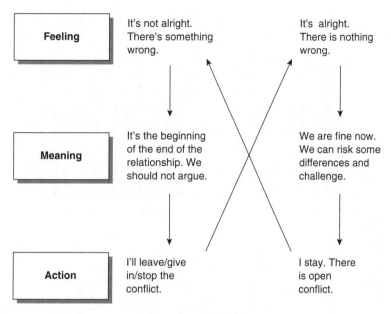

Figure 7.7.2   Arguments: Alan's position during an argument

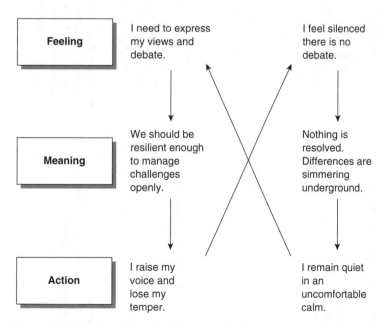

Figure 7.7.3   Arguments: Jane's position during an argument

Table 7.7.1 Mapping Alan and Jane's multiple stories of influence on the meaning of arguing

	Alan	Jane
Cultural (religious, community, gender)	• *Religious* – no religious influence mentioned. • *Community* – small rural English village, avoid scandal, don't wash dirty linen in public. • *Gender* – as a middle-aged man, anything for a quiet life. Arguments and fighting belong in the past.	• *Religious* – marriage should be for life. • *Community* – part of an American educational community where debate is regarded positively. • *Gender* – as a woman at home I sometimes need to shout to get my voice heard. Accustomed to woman using shouting over men to express opinions.
Relational (family beliefs, past experiences – how the individual stories collide relationally)	• *Family* – parents argued and this signalled the breakdown of the marriage. It was best to keep out of the way until things calmed down. • *Experience* – had one failed marriage. Need this to succeed so try to avoid arguments. Arguments cause problems.	• *Family* – parents were part of the educational context and regularly argued about social and political issues. This was fun. • *Experience* – this is my only long-term relationship. I thought we would be like my parents. Sparky relationships mean good relationships.
Identity (life script – the effect of family and community on 'I' position)	• *Good husband* – I should not shout at my wife (argue). This demonstrates my commitment to the relationship. • *Good father* – I should keep the place calm for the children.	• *Good wife* – I should have opinions and stay interesting. • *Good mother* – encourages independent thinking and ability to challenge men – especially for daughter.

Table 7.7.2 Circular questions used with Jane and Alan

Questions	Intention
Can you think of a time when you have seen the signs of an argument but have managed to do something different?	Challenge the fixed story that occupies the couple. Embed the idea of 'non-problem' times as an alternative story.
At what point in the arguments do you think you have an opportunity to take a different course, but have not managed to do so yet?	All communication is invitational, if the action is changed; this creates a different invitation to the partner and can build up a new repertoire of skills for both.
When you managed to do something different, what did Jane/Alan say/do?	Move between 'I' and 'we' positions.
If we imagine that these arguments are a style of communication that does not suit you, what would be your preferred styles?	Creating the opportunity for new visions of the relationship with them and preferred ways of being.
What connections do you make with other relationships or situations when you think about these arguments?	Widens the context to explore how current arguments may have a resonance and meaning located in other contexts that are exerting a strong influence.
In arguments with colleagues and friends, what resources do you call upon to create a resolution?	Moves relationships and demonstrable abilities in one context that might be transferable to this context. Begins to develop the life-giving stories.
If you were to argue less, what would you like to do more of in your couple relationships?	Invites the couple to think about the life-giving stories that can overshadow the problem stories and be the basis of new ways of interacting and relating.

the level of pattern both in terms of meaning and action. By bringing forth existing descriptions and inviting people to develop different relationships with these stories, opportunities emerge consciously to create a new pattern.

Ziegler and Hiller (2001) talk of helping a couple to develop 'good stories'. These, they say, are borne out of a shared vision of their future together and reinvigorate the couple relationship. Language should encourage strength-based dialogue rather than deficit talk, which often perpetuates problems and blame. Gottman (2000) suggests that the resolution of the repetitive, perpetual problems is not always necessary. What is important is the positive affect between the couple during discussions about the conflict.

How does this look in practice?

The exploration, development and sharing of meanings attached to each episode of arguing is an intervention in its own right, using a series of questions that are intended to help participants to see their own contribution to the pattern and also, in the context of new information, develop new meanings and practices for the future. The most useful types of question in this context are circular and reflexive questions. (See Tomm (1987, 1988) for a full description.) In short, circular questions are intended to be exploratory and seek to look for moments that challenge the dominant story, scanning for difference (Table 7.7.2).

Table 7.7.3 Reflexive questions used with Jane and Alan

Questions	Intention
Now that Alan has described arguments to mean the beginning of the end of your relationship, what impact do you imagine this will have on the next argument that emerges?	Alan and Jane now have an opportunity of being curious about the different meanings attached to arguments.
Having heard Jane describe the fun of arguments in her family while growing up, what new ideas do you have about your arguments?	The next argument does not need to follow the pattern.
If your parents could see the way you are facing different dilemmas in your couple relationship, what do you think they would say? Which aspects of the way you are managing would they be most proud of?	The intention is to continue to get the couple to see their relationship in the context of others. These types of question often bring forth appreciative comments and have the embedded suggestion that this couple are resilient and resourceful.

Table 7.7.2 shows some examples of questions intended to challenge the fixed stories about arguing by developing alternative explanations that emerge through the therapeutic conversation. The counsellor needs to maintain continued curiosity in order to be part of the emerging making and re-making of stories. The questions try to stay in a relational frame, while enquiring about the positions of the individuals and their contribution to the pattern.

Reflexive questions (Tomm, 1987, 1988) are intended to be facilitative and point to new ways of understanding and acting in the present and future. They encourage partners to see things from a point of view other than their own (Table 7.7.3).

The examples in Table 7.7.3 demonstrate the collaborative nature of couple work and the co-construction of possible solutions.

Conclusion

This section has attempted to show the complexity of couple work and offer some interventions that might be useful in this context. Underlying this is the belief that each couple's construction of their relationship is unique. As counsellors and therapists,

we need to maintain continued curiosity in order to bring forth multiple perspectives and stories about these couple relationships, with the intention of creating the possibility for new and preferred ways of being to emerge.

References

Cronen, V.E. (1994) Co-ordinated management of meaning: practical theory for the complexities and contradictions of everyday life. In J. Siegfried (ed.), *The Status in Common Sense Psychology*. Norwood, NJ: Ablex Publications.

Gottman, J.M. (2000) Marital therapy: a research-based approach. Clinical workshop video. Seattle, WA: The Gottman Institute.

Oliver, C., Herasymowych, M. and Senko, H. (2003) *Complexity, Relationships and Strange Loops: Reflexive Practice Guide*. Calgary: MHA Institute Inc.

Tomm, K. (1987) Interventive interviewing: Part II. Reflexive questioning as a means to self-healing. *Family Process*, 26: 167–183.

Tomm, K. (1988) Interventive interviewing: Part III. Intending to ask lineal, circular, strategic or reflexive questions. *Family Process*, 27: 1–15.

Ziegler, P. and Hiller, T. (2001) *Recreating Partnership: A Solution-oriented: Collaborative Approach to Couples Therapy*. New York: W.W. Norton & Co.

7.8 Disabled People

○○○

FRANCES BLACKWELL

Within the disability movement terminology has been debated over the years: in the 1980s some disabled people preferred to be known as *people with disabilities*, considering that this emphasized that they were people *first*. The term disabled people is now generally accepted and disability defined as:

> something imposed on top of our impairments, by the way we are unnecessarily isolated and excluded from full participation in society. Disabled people are therefore an oppressed group in society …. it is a consequence of our isolation and segregation in every area of life, such as education, work, mobility, housing, etc. (UPIAS, 1976: 3–4)

Professionals within the disability field tend to refer to blind and deaf people as having visual or hearing impairments. However, clients will soon say how they wish to be described and this may reflect their sense of identity, or lack of it.

There are many disabled people who write books and articles on disability. Barnes and Mercer (1996), for example, have edited an excellent book on disability and illness. However, few disabled counsellors or therapists have written anything for publication. I believe this is due to lack of energy or waiting, like myself, for more time to write. It is usually non-disabled counsellors who write about disability. Such literature abounds and is usually impairment-focused and concerned with theories of adjustment to new impairments. Lenny (1993: 233) writes 'As disabled people have begun the process of collective empowerment, they have articulated a need for counselling', and goes on to discuss the paradox between this and the rejection of general views and professional assumptions that it is impairments that are the problems for individuals.

Some clients express frustrations about their negative experiences of counselling and therapy. Their comments range from 'She wanted to know what separation and loss I had experienced', or 'He just wanted me to accept what has happened to me', to 'All he wanted to do was to ask me questions about my impairment; he did not want to hear about *me*.'

Counselling from a social model perspective means that ideas shift from focusing on impairments to providing the opportunity for clients to explore their vulnerabilities and potential for change within a social context, as well as within a humanistic or psychodynamic frame of reference.

There are many non-disabled counsellors seeing disabled clients but very few disabled counsellors. This is due to comparatively few disabled people being trained as counsellors (Blackwell, 1998); partly to lack of qualifications and to full access to education; and partly to some negative attitudes from training institutes. These attitudes rest on the general societal view that disabled people should not be encouraged to work in the area of counselling. The feelings are that it will 'put off' clients.

Some disability associations or coalitions may have a counselling project attached, or may be able to access the services of a local disabled counsellor. There is one disability counselling service within a health trust in East London which serves the local disabled population. It is the only one of its kind known to the writer which is funded totally by the area health authority.

Some disabled people would say that non-disabled counsellors should not see disabled people, but this is unhelpful; we need to encourage those who wish to work with disabled clients by sharing knowledge and experience. However, there is one key issue about *experience*. Non-disabled counsellors can never really know what it is like to be disabled. They will never experience negative attitudes or lack of access, segregated education and so on.

A few disabled counsellors are concerned as to whether they need to tell their clients about their impairments. This is not necessary, at least initially. Clients may ask, but this is usually not because they want to know, but because they are afraid the counsellor cannot contain their pain or fears. It is best to always deflect the question back, and then see what comes of this.

Non-disabled clients seeing disabled counsellors, it is argued from a psychodynamic perspective, will want to look after their counsellor, thus confusing transferential feelings; so they may be concerned for the counsellor because of the counsellor's disability, rather than staying within the working alliance. Disabled counsellors need to be aware of this.

In work with those who have always had impairments one of the issues often presented in counselling may be the client's experience of being in a 'special' school; some disabled children are educated in mainstream schools but most are still sent away to boarding schools, often as young as 3 or 4 years old. This can cause social dislocation and sometimes dysfunctional family life.

Counsellors may find that young disabled clients have experienced the death of friends; sometimes children have not been told their school friends have died. They have found this out later, resulting in a sense of loss which they quickly forget and push down into their unconscious. Disabled children may not have lost just one friend, but several while they are young. This 'multiple loss' is now better understood within communities where HIV and AIDS have been experienced.

Some practical issues

- *Assistance for the client* – a client may bring a personal assistant (carer), or a facilitator to aid communication, such as a British Sign Language interpreter for a deaf client.
- *Direct payments* – this is when disabled people themselves employ and manage their own personal assistants through payments from local social service departments; this can become a major issue brought to counselling/therapy.
- *Home visits or telephone counselling* – a counsellor might consider this if clients with mobility problems cannot come to the counsellor.
- *The venue* – clearly this needs to be accessible; however it is often a non-disabled person who makes the judgement about accessibility, but the best way is to invite a disabled person in to see if it is suitable for them.
- *Money* – many disabled people are on low incomes. Fees therefore may need to be negotiated.

Providing assistance to clients (for example, giving a drink, guiding a blind person, moving a client in their wheelchair, etc.) needs to be done in a professional and matter of fact way. On occasion, counsellors can become deeply moved and touch a client as an act of humanity when they hear, for example, that the client is dying, or someone close to them has died. Some counsellors may touch more than others, but it is always necessary to question whether this is appropriate.

Supervision

For non-disabled counsellors it is a good idea to get some supervision from a disabled supervisor, even if, because of distance, it is by telephone. It can be limited to only a few sessions, but enough to get adequate knowledge. It might help to go on a disability equality training day or to find some disabled people who can give support and assistance. Coping with fears about disabled clients' impairments can be quite upsetting or indeed shocking, especially when they are the result of a particularly violent or traumatic incident. Counsellors need to think about how they can cope with this, addressing it with supervisors, not with clients.

Some counsellors may feel tempted to infantilize disabled clients. Moreover, many disabled clients have experienced boundaries being broken, as counsellors have overstepped the line between warmth and actually abusing them with sexual or physical advances. It is a painful process, unpacking the lack of trust and disillusionment. For some clients who are desperately seeking respect and attention, the crossing of boundaries can be devastating. It happens when well-meaning counsellors believe that 'this' client is different; each client is unique but this does not mean that counsellors can breach their codes of ethics. It is important to keep this issue of boundaries in mind when bringing disabled clients to supervision.

Assessment

Disabled clients are assessed as any other client. The theoretical backgrounds may be different but counsellors usually seek similar information: name, address, telephone, GP. Counsellors need to know about family and friends, and social networks (and whether they only see professionals or have friends as well). Some disabled people have few friends because much of their time, particularly after acquiring an impairment, is taken up with medical appointments; disabled people then find they lose their friends and will often consider professionals as their main source of emotional support.

Counselling disabled people

Most disabled people who come to counselling or psychotherapy will have recently acquired an impairment. Counsellors will see fewer clients who have always been disabled – partly because they have seen so many professionals during their lives and partly because few seem to want counselling.

Why are some clients always late for a session by anything from a few minutes to half an hour? There could be a number of practical reasons such as a taxi not coming or trains being delayed, but counsellors need to realize that it may be because the content of the session and its length become too much to bear. In time clients learn to keep to a regular time once they understand the therapeutic reason.

Such examples illustrate how counsellors and therapists can wrongly assume a cause that has in fact nothing to do with the client's impairment but with their psychological needs, as with anyone else. The impairment is a separate issue and not necessarily the main one. Newly disabled clients may have difficulties in learning to live with their new impairment(s), but they have come to counselling for assistance in looking at their inner world. Counsellors may come from all sorts of training backgrounds, but can use that training to work with disabled people as they would work with any other client group.

An interesting issue which can be highlighted here is the dichotomy between working to bring into awareness the splitting within a client's psyche, and the need to reconcile the split off parts with the client's often obvious and visible impairment which cannot be healed. (*Splitting* is used here in the psychoanalytic sense of a defence mechanism whereby the individual denies some difficult aspect of self or environment. Rycroft (1968: 156–157) gives some useful definitions.)

What is the rewarding aspect of counselling disabled people? Principally it is to see the possibilities of their overcoming trauma from accidents, illnesses and physical impairments, and positively taking control of their lives. Professionals often want patients to accept, come to terms with, or cope with their impairments: counsellors need to seek to encourage disabled clients to *learn to live* with their impairment; such a phrase has a different emphasis and outcome, since it allows the disabled client to have a 'bad' day and not feel a failure. 'Acceptance' or 'coming to terms with' are phrases which put quite a strain on the individual as they struggle day by day with their new impairments. Being disabled takes up energy in constant forward planning. It is the understanding here of the social context: it is not just impairment that a client is coping with, but living within such a disabling environment which demands so much of a client's time and attention. Many clients express sentiments such as 'If I had not had my disability I would never have decided to …'. The counsellor may thus have the opportunity to witness this transition from helplessness to positive action in a client's life.

If the client has always had an impairment, they may never mention it. If someone comes with a marital problem and the counsellor feels it is due to their impairment, should it be mentioned? Why not? If the client denies their impairment it may be best to initially wait and listen, as with any client on any issue. However, counsellors and therapists need to work from their own theoretical approach and the more disabled people they see the more confident they will become.

Conclusion

The most important consideration for therapists providing counselling for disabled clients is to use the same training skills and techniques that they use for non-disabled clients, but in addition to understand the impact of the disabling factors of the social context on the lives of disabled clients. Some clients may never mention their impairments, while those with newly acquired impairments may need a place to explore how they are going to learn to live with their impairments. The counsellor's responsibility is to provide a safe and supportive environment for the client and irrespective of theoretical orientation, counsellors need to pay particular attention to the often very real social pressures on disabled clients, such as changed attitudes of family and friends, the specific needs of housing, or stays in hospital, and so on.

Finally, it is important to emphasize the enormous value of having supervision from a disabled supervisor, remembering that initially the impact of disability can be difficult for the counsellor or psychotherapist to deal with. It is easy for professionals who are disabled to forget that those who are non-disabled can be shocked or afraid when they first meet a disabled client. As experience grows, this will become less and less.

References

Barnes, C. and Mercer, G. (eds) (1996) *Exploring the Divide: Illness and Disability*. Leeds: Disability Press.

Blackwell, F. (1998) Access and attitude. *Counselling News*, May.

Lenny, J. (1993) Do disabled people need counselling? In J. Swain, V. Finkelstein, S. French and M. Oliver (eds), *Disabling Barriers, Enabling Environment*. London: Sage.

Rycroft, C. (1968) *Dictionary of Psychoanalysis*. Harmondsworth: Penguin.

UPIAS (1976) *Fundamental Principles of Disability*. London: Union of the Physically Impaired Against Segregation.

7.9   Electronically Delivered Therapies   ○○○

KATE ANTHONY

Since 1995, there has been a growing body of individual practitioners, organizations and dedicated service providers who have turned to new methods of communication to deliver counselling and psychotherapy. Despite the initial reservation, some would say resistance, of the profession to accepting this seemingly controversial method of service provision, there has been an increasing body of evidence that using text to conduct a therapeutic relationship is not only possible but in many cases more desirable from the client and practitioner point of view.

Almost ten years on from the first appearance of commercial websites that offered email and Internet Relay Chat (IRC) for therapeutic communication, many publications have provided a wealth of information and literature around the topic. Perhaps the most comprehensive of these, for further textbook reading, are Hsiung (2002), Goss and Anthony (2003), and Kraus et al. (2004), and an invaluable online resource is the work of John Suler (2004). Also available as a source of information for potential clients of online therapy is Stofle (2001).

As well as the work of international experts in the field, publishing literature and collaborating on research projects, the area of electronically delivered therapy (and in particular the ethical and legal side of it) has been addressed by mental health organizations worldwide. Professional bodies such as the British Association for Counselling and Psychotherapy (Anthony and Jamieson, 2005; Goss et al., 2001), the National Board of Certified Counselors (2001), and the American Counseling Association (1999) have addressed and published guidelines for their members who wish to offer an online presence. In addition, a dedicated body for online practitioners, the International Society for Mental Health Online, was formed in 1997 'to promote the understanding, use and development of online communication, information and technology for the international mental health community'.

This section describes the most essential elements that practitioners need to be aware of before considering an online presence, from a theoretical stance. It will concentrate on the use of text, via email, IRC (chatrooms), forums (also known as Bulletin or Message Boards) and mobile phone texting (SMS), for conducting an individual client–practitioner therapeutic relationship. However, the reader needs to be aware that many of these elements of working in cyberspace can be extended to online group work, supervision, training and research. It is not

possible to cover some of the developing uses of technology in counselling and psychotherapy, such as videoconferencing, stand-alone software, virtual reality and Avatar therapy, and so the reader is referred to Goss and Anthony (2003) for in-depth discussion, analysis and case studies of these facets of electronically delivered therapies.

Types of electronically delivered therapy

Using block-text email (asynchronous) for therapy

This is most people's perception of using email for therapeutic use – the exchanging back and forth of emails between two people within a contract, which is (usually) short-term, (usually) weekly, and which (hopefully) utilizes encryption software for privacy and confidentiality.

Using narrative dynamic email (asynchronous) for therapy

More popular in the USA, this type of email is where the practitioner inserts his/her responses *within* the client's email using different fonts and/or colours, and the client reciprocates in the same way, usually for a small number of exchanges before the dynamic text becomes two unwieldy and a new narrative is required. Again, it is (usually) short-term, (usually) weekly, and (hopefully) utilizes encryption software for privacy and confidentiality.

Using Internet Relay Chat (synchronous) for therapy

This method involves a dialogue between client and practitioner in real time, using an internet chatroom or Instant Messaging software (AIM, ICQ, etc.). The contracted sessions are usually weekly, and often incorporate a weekly exchange of asynchronous email (this is a useful function to allow the client to expand upon actual descriptive situations that would otherwise take up valuable time within the IRC sessions). They are also (hopefully) password protected.

Using forums (asynchronous) for therapy

More secure than any other form of electronically delivered therapy within this context, forums are held on the internet itself behind a password protected access system so that client and therapist visit a website to view and post responses to each other.

Using mobile phone texting (asynchronous) for therapy

An extremely recent method for therapeutic use, mobile phone texting (SMS or Short Message Service) is usually reserved for making and cancelling face-to-face appointments. Its use has, however, been documented as a facility for clients to end face-to-face relationships (Walker, 2004) and as follow-up for patients who have been treated for drug and alcohol addiction. The use of texting within therapy is anticipated to become more common in the near future.

The essential concepts of online textual therapy

The first aspect of working with text that may seem obvious but bears clarifying is that it is a distance method of communication. There are obvious benefits to those who cannot access therapy, for example, because of disability or geographical reasons, but apart from practical reasons it is important to understand the disinhibition effect (Suler, 2001) that makes for a more open and honest relationship. The ability for the client to reveal much more when working at a certain perceived distance (the one with which they feel comfortable) is significant. It also means that the level of disclosure occurs at a much faster pace than it usually does in a face-to-face

relationship or even within other methods of distance therapy, such as the telephone. This intensity of disinhibition is peculiar to using typed text over the internet for communication, and should not be underestimated, particularly when taking care of the self and the client. Many clients find that a one-off outpouring of emotion and narrative, due to disinhibition that affords a cathartic experience, means that they feel better and can disappear into cyberspace – a particularly distressing experience for the practitioner (also known as a black hole experience). For the most part, though, the disinhibition effect is a positive empowering experience, and one that is important to clients who cannot reveal sensitive information due to shame, embarrassment or being unable to 'look someone in the eye' while doing so.

The distance of the client also means that self-revelation of practitioner material, where appropriate within the work, can be a useful tool to facilitate a second aspect of working online – the concept of presence, described by Lombard and Ditton (1997) as 'the perceptual illusion of non-mediation'. This is described in my original research as occurring when 'the media used (in this case the computer and keyboard) is unimportant and you are interacting with another person in a separate space' (Anthony, 2000: 626). In this way, the media used to conduct a therapeutic relationship is secondary to the therapeutic relationship actually taking place as a mutual journey towards the client's recovery. Despite the lack of any body language, so often cited as the reason that online work via text can never be 'real' therapy, the practitioner is able to enter the client's mental constructs of their world through their text, respond in a similar manner, and so develop a rapport that transcends the hardware used to support the communication as *well* as the 'white noise' that a physical presence can induce.

The white noise of the physical presence, which can introduce bias and judgement into a face-to-face therapeutic relationship, is bypassed when working online. Rather than seeing this as a negative part of the method, many online practitioners believe that it is not only positive, but also essential to the development of the therapeutic relationship to encourage a fantasy of the other person via a visual, auditory and kinaesthetic representation system. In this way, the client can build an overall sense of their counsellor or psychotherapist and develop that fantasy to fit their perception of the person they are most able to work with. It can be argued that the person behind each other's defences is found and the therapeutic relationship becomes stronger much more quickly.

This construction of the fantasy is extremely important when practitioners are developing or planning the way any online work can fit into their current practice. Taking an existing face-to-face or telephone relationship online permanently is usually very successful, because the familiarity of the therapist is there but the disinhibition effect allows a deeper level of communication to be achieved. Using online communication during a break in the therapy, for example, when the client is travelling or has a temporary illness preventing the previous method of work, *can* work, but more often means that the relationship will be more strained when it resumes in its traditional format as the openness that was there at a distance is removed. But perhaps the most dangerous form of service provision is the one where online counsellors assume that introducing a physical presence into the process, by making the relationship face-to-face, is desirable. This is rarely the case as the fantasy of the ideal therapist is shattered when the real therapist is made evident, and the relationship rarely recovers.

Finally, we must consider how all this building of the therapeutic relationship can occur without the gestures, vocal interventions and eye contact that make up the traditional face-to-face relationship. The quality of the practitioner's written communication and their ability to convey the nuances of body language that facilitate the client's growth (empathic facial gestures, for example) is paramount when working online. However, it should be noted that respect for the client means that their ability to communicate in this way need not be expert (although the practitioner's work is made much easier if it is). The use of text to replicate body language takes many forms online, as does the use of netiquette (a combination of 'net' and 'etiquette'), but both aspects are integral to the success of the

communication and therefore the client's recovery. Both these aspects are also sometimes considered facile within the conventional profession, and yet their contributions to the online therapeutic relationship being established, developed and maintained are vital. While in no way exhaustive, the following should give the reader some insight into what is possible within the remit of using typed text:

- There are different ways of communicating in an appropriate manner, depending on the context of that communication. Danet (2001) identified two types of textual communication – business and personal. However, in Goss and Anthony (2003) I explain how a third definition is necessary because the 'therapeutic textual communication' is at once both a business transaction (contracted between therapist and client) and a personal communication (because of the nature of the content). It is essential to be trained in developing the ability to construct therapeutic textual communication on courses such as that offered at OnlineCounsellors.co.uk.
- One rule of netiquette that it is essential to be aware of, is that the use of CAPITALIZATION for an entire sentence or block of text is considered to be shouting and is usually disrespectful and rude.
- There are many ways of emphasizing certain words where necessary, such as *italicizing*, **bold**, underlining, _underscoring_, and *asterisks*. The latter two are necessary because of discrepancies of coding between email softwares. A use of colour can also show real care if used well.
- Overuse of exclamation marks generally makes the text difficult to read and is considered poor form.
- There are thousands of emoticons (emotional icons) that are used to convey facial expressions. Some are supplied in email and IRC packages and some have to be created and read by holding the head to the left (this does not apply in Asian countries – a cultural issue practitioners need to be aware of). Some of the more frequently used in online therapeutic work are:

☺ or :o) or :)	Smiles (smileys)
☹ or :o(or >:o{	Frowns
;) or ;o)	Winks (winkies)

this, in particular, is essential to indicate irony or a non-serious statement.
- Abbreviations and acronyms are also widely used. Some of the more frequently used in online therapeutic work are:

LOL	Laugh Out Loud
BTW	By The Way
PFT, k?	Pause For Thought, OK?

this is particularly useful for the client to use silence within a synchronous session.

- Emotional bracketing is also used to clarify emotion. As well as being able to hug your client by using parentheses, as in ((((Kate)))), some other uses are:

  <<crying>>
  [[sigh]]

- The use of automatic signature files, greetings and sign-offs also need careful consideration and use of personal style *within the appropriate context of the communication*.

Conclusion

As well as the above facets of using typed text for therapeutic communication, there are, of course, a wealth of both practical and ethical considerations that need to be taken into account when setting up an online presence to work with clients. In-depth analysis of these facets is available in Anthony (2004) and Goss and Anthony (2004), but some of the more obvious considerations are:

- confidentiality and data protection
- limitations of the method
- contracting and informed consent
- encryption
- fee structure
- assessment skills, suitability of client and referring on
- verification of parties (identity management)
- practitioner competence (both within IT and online work)
- boundaries
- licensing, regulation and quality control
- virus, worm and Trojan management
- crisis intervention and the suicidal client
- cultural differences
- technical breakdown

The world of technological development is one that moves and develops extremely quickly, and it is well known that the counselling and psychotherapy profession in particular has been playing catch-up with the arrival of technology for therapeutic use over the last ten years. What is certain, however, is that the profession has had to come to terms with the idea that sometimes the client is in a situation that means that they not only *cannot* sit with us face to face, but also that *they don't want to.* It is these clients that practitioners can now stop excluding from our services, ensuring that the world of counselling and psychotherapy becomes more accessible to our potential clients worldwide.

References

American Counseling Association (1999) *Ethical Standards for Internet Online Counselling.* Available at: www.counselling.org/resources/internet.html (accessed 12 June 2004).

Anthony, K. (2000) Counselling in cyberspace. *Counselling Journal,* 11 (10): 625–627.

Anthony, K. (2004) Therapy online: the therapeutic relationship in typed text. In G. Bolton, S. Howlett, C. Lago and J. Wright (eds), *Writing Cures.* Hove: Brunner-Routledge. pp. 133–141.

Anthony, K. and Jamieson, A. (2005) *Guidelines for Online Counselling and Psychotherapy* (2nd edn). Rugby: British Association for Counselling and Psychotherapy.

Danet, B. (2001) *Cyberplay.* Oxford: Berg.

Goss, S. and Anthony, K. (2003) *Technology in Counselling and Psychotherapy: A Practitioner's Guide.* Basingstoke: Palgrave.

Goss, S. and Anthony, K. (2004) Ethical and practical dimensions of online writing cures. In G. Howlett, C. Lago and J. Wright (eds), *Writing Cures.* Hove: Brunner-Routledge. pp. 170–178.

Goss, S., Anthony, K., Palmer, S. and Jamieson, A. (2001) *Guidelines for Online Counselling and Psychotherapy.* Rugby: British Association for Counselling and Psychotherapy.

Hsiung, R. (ed.) (2002) *e-Therapy.* New York: Norton.

Kraus, R., Zack, J. and Stricker, G. (eds) (2004) *Online Counseling.* San Diego, CA: Elsevier.

Lombard, M. and Ditton, T. (1997) At the heart of it all: the concept of presence. *Journal of Computer Mediated Communication,* 3 (2). Available at: www.ascusc.org/jcmc/vol3/issue2/lombard.html (accessed 11 August 2000).

National Board of Certified Counsellors (2001) *The Practice of Internet Counseling*. Available at: www.nbcc.org/ethics/webethics.htm (accessed 13 February 2004).

Stofle, G. (2001) *Choosing an Online Therapist*. Harrisburg, PA: White Hat Communications.

Suler, J. (2001) *The Online Disinhibition Effect*. Available at: www.rider.edu/users/suler/psycyber/disinhibit.html (accessed 29 August 2001).

Suler, J. (2004) *The Psychology of Cyberspace*. Available at: www.rider.edu/~suler/psycyber/psycyber.html (accessed 22 June 2004).

Walker, S. (2004) Counsellors Who Text. *BACP Counselling and Psychotherapy Journal*, 15 (3) (April).

7.10   Family and Systemic Therapy   ○○○

EDDY STREET

Area of concern

The challenge for us as human beings is to understand our place and role within the systems that we inhabit, that is the family, groups, the culture and the general environment in which we live. To do this we need to explore the beliefs, meanings and behaviour that we construct to explain our world of intimate relationships. This specialism deals with human beings in their interaction and in their relationships. It is an area that deals with human systems and the most significant of human systems – the family. The family can be defined in any way given the culture and the way the individuals consider that they are connected. Most of the work that is undertaken in this area covers typical family themes, such as bringing up and dealing with children, coping with relationship stress and dealing with the elderly. This is placed within the context of the difficulties that emerge in various forms of adversity and ill health. Given the nature of systems and individuals placed within it, some systemic therapists and counsellors organize their practice by seeing individuals, some have a speciality which deals with

work and staff groups, while the majority see families and couples.

History

Until about the 1950s the individual was the locus of attempts to understand and help people. Relationships were considered but only in terms of their past impact, via internal inquiry (psychoanalysis). The development of family therapy follows the consideration of relationships in another way and a number of influences led to this development. There were British psychodynamic individual practitioners who began to see the importance of interviewing clients conjointly rather than separately and US research projects that were looking at the family influences in schizophrenia, these being theoretically linked to the work of Gregory Bateson.

The original conception of the family system had an emphasis on patterns and process as observed from the outside; symptoms were seen as a function of these dynamics. The aim of therapy was to alter the patterns that are maintained in the problems. Minuchin's 'Structural' family therapy was an example of this approach as was the 'Brief Therapy' model outlined in different ways by Haley and Watzlawick. The metaphor from this phase of development was of the family as a cybernetic system with built-in processes of adapting to change such that there always could be equilibrium.

In line with postmodern movements in the social sciences, therapeutic models have developed away from a mechanistic understanding of systems. Patterns of communication are still important, but the emphasis is now towards an exploration of how these are shaped by meanings, beliefs, explanations and stories held by family members. The Milan School and the work of Lynn Hoffman characterize the beginning of this development. Problems are seen to arise from ways of viewing or punctuating events. Therapy is seen as involving the joint construction of meanings. In this conversational process of therapy new meanings are generated around and about the problem that then dissolves and disappears as a new context is constructed.

Because of its history, systemic thinking originally stood in opposition to those theories that considered individual processes. As a result, in the first decades of its development a dichotomy was created between the self and the system and between individual and family therapy. However, theoretical developments have led to a re-evaluation of the 'self' and relationships and there is now a process of integration as the earlier dichotomies collapse. Similarly, ideas that originated historically are now being innovatively integrated into current practice.

In the early professional development of this speciality in the USA there was an organizational amalgamation of those focused on the 'family' and those with a focus on the 'marriage'. Hence they became included under the same professional umbrella. In the UK, however, the history of service developments led to a professional separation between those who were interested in family and systemic practice and those with a focus that derived from

marital therapy, although organizationally this is now lessening.

Theory and key concepts

Human system and communications

A system is composed of interrelated parts, all of which combine to influence its overall and total functioning. It functions by means of connections between the parts; these connections can then be patterned. The connections are variously termed 'communications', 'interactions', 'transactions', 'beliefs', or 'ideas'; collectively these can be termed information. The system is described by what happens between parts, not by what happens in the parts themselves. The system utilizes the information that passes between constituent parts and a change of information at any point will result in a change elsewhere in the system. A simple example would be noting a change in the way a mother and father interact, this then having an impact on how one of them deals with their child whose behaviour then alters, the child's changed behaviour then having an effect on how the parents interact. This is known as circular causality or circularity. Human action and activity is therefore embedded within the connections, the interactions between people. To be involved in a communicating system is at the core of human identity as identity evolves socially.

The focus of interest is on the pattern of connection between one individual and another, with individuals' characteristics being seen as the behaviour illustrating the connection rather than being something located within the individual. Indeed, it may be more accurate to describe individuals as displaying certain behaviour rather than describing them as being particular types of people. Therefore, to say that a particular type of person is aggressive does not capture the sense of all the interactions around that person at any particular time. It is more accurate to report that from a particular point of view, when certain interactions occur, the person can be described as displaying aggressive type behaviour.

Development and change

Development means that there is a natural process of change within the family. In the developmental framework, families move through a cycle of forming relationships, dealing with their fertility, rearing children, watching children leave home, caring for elderly relatives, retiring and preparing for dying. Different generations are at different points of this cycle at different times in a way that intertwines with the development of individuals of different ages.

Change occurs naturally through development. There is change where individuals alter their own behaviour to accommodate their developing mastery of their situation, such as when a child learns a new skill. This involves *first-order change* – a person doing something differently which becomes a new base line. The next type of change is known as *second-order change* which refers to changes in the system's functioning rather than a simple change in one component. Second-order changes refer to the family system's adaptation to individual changes. Any first-order change requires a second-order change to deal with the effects of the difference that the members of the system notice. The consequence is an alteration of meaning and hence behaviour within the system, and thus new behavioural sequences are generated. For example, as a child becomes more mobile parents have to be watchful in different ways and they need to negotiate new parenting tasks to deal with a toddler (rather than an infant). Obviously one change feeds into the next in a circular fashion.

As the family moves forward through time its members have to deal with pressures that come from the predictable course of development (*developmental stresses*) together with the unpredictable stresses of chronic illness, untimely death, accident, divorce and re-marriage. There are also historical demands that include patterns of relating and functioning transmitted in the family down the generations that are referred to as *trans-generational stresses*. The developmental model provides a framework for considering the predictable elements of family life, although idiosyncratic histories and sudden events will produce the specific development tasks for each family. Stress in family development is at its highest level as the family moves from one phase of life to another, when significant second-order changes are necessary. This period of movement is known as a *transition* and includes events such as children leaving home, and retirement. New meanings and new structures are needed in order to adapt successfully to the changes that occur.

Therapeutic notions

Clearly, this particular view of human phenomena marks out family therapy from other approaches. Family therapists see themselves as, first, allowing the family to appreciate their own interactions and therefore consider what changes, particularly of the second-order nature, they need to make. The family therapist considers interventions that create information for the system such that there is a change. Family therapists differ in the way they categorize information and the emphases they place on particular information themes and processes. Some consider processes in terms of a behavioural event, others a feeling event and others a meaning event.

Within systemic models different thematic elements are emphasized and interactionally these are seen to occur over different time periods. Themes about who is a member or not (boundary/inclusion themes) are more obvious in shorter time-frames. Issues about power and discipline (control themes) occur over longer periods whereas even longer sequences of interaction are found to repeat from one generation to the next and are typically linked to issues of emotional involvement (intimacy themes). Hence different forms of family therapy focus on different time-frames within the developmental framework.

Assessments of applicability to particular clients

Family therapists have embarked on a variety of research studies to examine the process and outcome of its activity, the general conclusions being that the interactive therapies have produced beneficial outcomes in about two-thirds of cases, their effects being superior to no treatment. Research has also demonstrated that there is a greater chance of positive outcome with relationship difficulties when both partners are involved in therapy conjointly than when only an individual is seen. It has also been found that positive results from all types of interactive and systemically based therapies typically occur in treatments of short duration, that is less than 20 sessions. Generally speaking, therefore, in psychotherapeutic terms family therapy can be categorized as at the brief end of the temporal continuum.

Much research effort has been directed to estimating the effectiveness of various interactive therapies with specific disorders and problems. In keeping with other psychotherapies the more structured approaches have demonstrated effectiveness with a variety of problems, including anxiety disorders, juvenile delinquency, conduct disorders and marital discord. Those approaches known as the psychoeducational have been shown to make a considerable impact on how families deal with severe mental illness and in reducing the relapse rate of these disorders. Effectiveness has also been demonstrated when family therapy is used as part of a multimodal treatment programme, helping families deal with chronic illnesses, substance misuse, eating disorders, domestic violence and overcoming the effects of abuse.

Key procedures

To help the family in the discovery of new information relevant to their particular problem the therapist simply asks questions. The questions she asks are about how individuals think, feel and behave and how groups of individuals interact. The therapist asks questions of the system so that the information produced will reveal the way the family is interconnected and the means by which it operates as a system in its own circular fashion, including beliefs about itself. As this information is generated, the family is then provided with an opportunity of becoming aware of its manner of interaction and relating.

Regardless of the focus of particular schools of therapy, it is clear that the therapist needs to be able to demonstrate empathy, warmth and genuineness, though these may be labelled differently by different schools. Within the interactive framework these are best accomplished through the practical skills of active listening and reflection of interactions. Reflection of interaction or interactive empathy is important as it permits the therapist and family to move between individual frames of reference and the interactions those perspectives give rise to. Reflection processes are linked to questioning of the system as this allows the therapist not only to convey empathy for the family's interaction, but also to step back and observe where the family is taking her interactively. The skill therefore refers not just to mirroring back, but also to the process of thinking about and introducing a wider meaning about the observed and reported interaction. Each individual therefore hears an empathic feedback of his or her own statements, feedback on the family's interactions and wider reflections provided by the therapist's questioning. For her part, the therapist feeds back what she sees and hears as well as offering her own perspective, informed as it is by the family's thoughts, feelings and behaviours.

Active listening

Therapist asks question of client A.
A answers.
Therapist reflects feelings from A and asks B about A's answer.
Therapist reflects feelings from B and asks A about B's answer etc.

Interactive empathy

The reflection of interaction sequence has the therapist commenting on the nature of the interaction process that is implied by a statement or commenting on interactive sequences as they occur.

Therapist asks question of client A.
A answers, reporting on interaction with B.
Therapist reflects interactions including A's reply and asks question of B about these interactions.
B answers reporting on interaction with A.

Therapist reflects interactions from B's reply and reflects interactive links from both A and B. The questions continue.

Training and supervision issues

Family therapy has been the therapeutic approach that has taken the privacy of the counselling room into a more public domain. Techniques then developed such as observation through one-way screens, in which the observer provides information for the therapist to incorporate into her work, and this has moved on to the reflecting teams approach, in which the family listens to the team's discussions about family members. Such an attitude to therapy has fostered particular types of training and supervisory needs. Training at the highest level of family therapy has to occur where there is supervised observed practice and, for the beginner and experienced therapist alike, observation of on-going work leads to enhancement of therapeutic skills and outcomes.

As the principal practice context of family therapy is within a multidisciplinary service, training is required to address a variety of issues in broad systemic terms. With an increasing understanding of the developing self of the therapist, training needs to bring to awareness possible prejudices and biases with regard to race, culture, gender, age, etc. The question as to what constitutes personal and professional growth for a family therapist continues, with an important training issue being whether or not family therapists in training should have some sessions with their partners or families. Interestingly, evidence suggests that a considerable majority of family therapists have undertaken personal individual therapy for their own benefit. Practitioners are now required to have a knowledge of research processes in order to informatively rest on, develop and expand the considerable evidence base that now informs practice. The family therapy field is finding more in common with some schools of psychotherapy, such as the person-centred and psychoanalytic approaches and training needs to reflect this more.

Recommended reading

Carr, A. (2000) *Family Therapy: Concepts, Process and Practice*. Chichester: Wiley.

Dallos, R. and Draper, R. (2000) *An Introduction to Family Therapy*. Buckingham: Open University Press.

Rivett, M. and Street, E. (2003) *Family Therapy in Focus*. London: Sage.

Street, E. (1994) *Counselling for Family Problems*. London: Sage.

7.11   Feminist Psychotherapy

IRENE BRUNA SEU

What is feminist psychotherapy?

Feminist psychotherapy (therapy henceforth) has existed since the early 1970s, following the attempts of the women's movement to eliminate the social and cultural barriers that prevent women's full and equal participation in our society. However, despite its 20-year history, feminist therapy is difficult to define. Some have attributed this to the absence of a specific founding person, theoretical position or a set of techniques. Furthermore, that feminist therapy integrates complex bodies of knowledge about social structures and diverse therapy techniques has also prevented it from becoming monolithic and unified. It is therefore more appropriate to think about the subject as a pluralistic, fluid and negotiated set of techniques, albeit all centred round some fundamental shared principles.

One of the fundamental principles underpinning feminist therapy is that many of women's problems are related to the injustice and inequality of patriarchal society. More radical feminist therapists claim that in fact women's psychological suffering is the direct result of the contradiction in their experience between the stated ideology of equalitarianism in our society and the social reality of the patriarchal system (see Section 2.2 on gender (pp. 24–28), and Cammaert and Larsen, 1988: 12).

Generally speaking, the term 'feminist therapy' is used mostly in reference to the Humanistic Empowerment model of therapy in the USA. More recently, following the establishment of the Women's Therapy Centre in London, the term has also been used to refer to the work, particularly with eating disorders, initiated by the feminist object relations therapists, Luise Eichenbaum and Susie Orbach. There is also an increasing (albeit financially struggling) number of women's therapy centres in the UK, providing services to women by women.

Then and now

We can trace the origin of feminist therapy to the 'consciousness-raising' groups in the early years of the feminist movement. These groups started from the rejection of traditional studies of women's lives and problems as steeped in androcentric assumptions and reflected in the male-dominated structure of knowledge. As an alternative to the 'written' word and tradition, women turned to the direct exploration of their feelings as the only reliable source of information of what was going on. In these groups women were encouraged to go beyond their individual experience to examine with other women the

mechanisms of silencing and denial, and explore possibilities of action and liberation. In summary, consciousness-raising groups were based on the principle that personal problems can only be understood as political problems, hence 'the personal is political'.

However, by the mid-1970s it became clear that women joined consciousness-raising groups more in search of support and need of personal growth than for political aims. It also became clear that women found the sharing of feelings and experience in the groups very 'therapeutic' in themselves. It was at the point at which women psychotherapists realized the potential of utilizing their therapeutic skills for political aims that the possibility of feminist therapy emerged (Enns, 2004).

The alternative approach to counselling and psychotherapy proposed by feminists focused on two main issues. First, there was a strong dissatisfaction with traditional theories of female and male development, behaviour and sex-role stereotypes. Feminists argued instead that if there were differences between the sexes, they reflected inequalities in social status and interpersonal power between women and men. Second, feminists challenged the sexist biases of current theories on personality and psychopathology. Overall feminists rejected traditional psychological theories because they found them androcentric, gendercentric, heterosexist, intrapsychic and deterministic.

However, the relationship between psychotherapy and feminism hasn't always been straightforward. Many feminists believed that psychology had nothing to offer women and argued that in fact the 'therapeutic' relationship would reinforce old power relationships and further disempower women. This critique has been applied particularly to psychodynamic therapy, which is often criticized for being based on patriarchal theories and techniques. On the other hand, other feminists valued psychology and psychotherapy as extremely effective instruments of change for women. Most of them, however, did agree on the necessity for some changes in the therapy technique, for example, the necessity for the therapist to be a woman, for a heightened attention to power dynamics between client and therapist, and so on.

In the last 20 years feminist psychotherapy has undergone many changes and has diversified into overlapping but quite distinct approaches, varying from radical and extreme positions to what might appear to be more a statement of intention or of political identification than anything specific in the theory or technique. Currently, the *sine qua non* of feminist therapy could be defined in terms of a commitment to interrogate from a feminist angle one's theoretical orientation and therapy technique and to be continually aware of how gender, race, class, economic status and sexual orientation influence women's and men's lives. This commitment is coupled with an attempt to empower the client and to pay attention to power dynamics in the therapy situation. However, research (Marecek and Kravetz, 1998) seems to suggest a disconcerting lack of clarity about these issues and how to go about addressing them. Often therapists would describe their feminist stance in terms of process rather than goals and outcome, thus describing feminist therapy as containing more warmth and allowing more 'crossing of boundaries' than in traditional therapy. It is not surprising therefore that now, more than ever, what is feminist therapy appears to be an open question.

It has been suggested that feminist therapy needs to enter into a further stage of development, one that involves naming biases within the profession and adopting a reflexively deconstructive stance in clinical practice. The challenge comes from post-modern feminism, which questions the most taken-for-granted beliefs about power, knowledge and the self as well as the eurocentric and heterosexual biases which have come to dominate, and thus represent 'feminism' as singular. Because post-modern feminists believe that knowledge can never be neutral, they warn feminist researchers and practitioners against theories that ignore issues of difference by generalizing what it means to be a woman. It has also been argued that issues of race, class, ethnicity, age and sexual orientations should be as important as gender for feminists.

Theory and practice

All feminist therapists have a commitment to the belief that:

- external realities of women's lives influence women's problems (i.e. that the personal is political);
- women's problems and symptoms can be understood as methods of coping and surviving rather than as signs of dysfunction.

However, feminist therapists differ quite a lot in their approaches. Due to these differences, they have been grouped into (Enns, 2004):

- *Non-sexist/humanistic therapists* emphasize personal choice and growth issues. They do not focus explicitly on gender issues or external factors.
- *Liberal/gender role feminist therapists* encourage the client to consider how socialization has influenced their choices and to change traditional gender role definitions if alterations are consistent with her personal goal. Their focus is on individual development rather than social change. The major goal in this group is to re-socialize the client and to facilitate her personal growth.
- *Radical feminist therapists* believe that in order for women's psychological health and status to improve, society must be changed at its roots. They explicitly communicate their belief about the importance of equality in human relationships and encourage the client to become aware of the common issues that influence women. The major goal in radical feminist therapy is to equalize women's and men's power in all of society's institutions.

Bearing these differences in mind, these are the fundamental tenets, goals and techniques of feminist therapy.

The personal is political

This principle is based on the assumption that women's problems are either entirely or to a great extent the result of inequality in our patriarchal society. There are some important consequences to this. First, this implies a reframing of what, in traditional psychology, would be seen as *pathology* into creative solutions or coping tools for socially determined problems. Thus, contrary to traditional psychology, which tends to decontextualize and view women's problems as 'intrapsychic' processes, feminist therapists encourage their clients to distinguish between internal/psychological and external/social aspects of the issues they are dealing with and to find appropriate strategies for both. In this way the client is not blamed but recognized and validated in her struggle, and is thus empowered to find social and personal solutions to her problems.

The therapist–client relationship is not value-free

Feminist therapists believe that it is impossible for the therapist to practise value-free therapy. Research has suggested that even when one's values remain unstated, the therapist's techniques, roles, non-verbal behaviour and attitudes are likely to reveal important aspects of the therapist's views (Enns, 1998: 13). Nevertheless, therapists vary in their approach to self-disclosure: some consider it essential to clarify their beliefs to their clients; others feel more cautious and would not even define themselves as feminist to their clients. Overall there seems to be general agreement that, regardless of the implicit or explicit nature of each therapist's statement, it is impossible not to communicate one's values and that careful attention should be paid to how they affect one's client.

Respect for the client should be paramount

Two areas are considered particularly important: the empowerment of the client and the questioning of the therapist's power. As far as the first issue is concerned, feminist therapists believe that the client is the main expert and should be treated as such. Thus what in traditional therapy would be viewed as symptoms, should instead be validated as creative attempts at coping and surviving. In this way the client's self-reliance is enhanced and strengthened.

The therapist's power presents much more complex dilemmas because, although an attempt at sharing power with the client is recommended, it is also recognized that some power imbalances are impossible or inappropriate to erase. Humanistic principles like genuineness, confrontation and empathy have been advocated as ways of making the relationship more equal. Again, as has been discussed above, there seems to be a confusion between process

and goals. Furthermore, it remains questionable whether the presence of the above qualities in a therapeutic relationship actually changes the power dynamic or just makes it more hidden.

Self-disclosure, as a way to make the client feel that the therapist is also subjected to sexist behaviour and negative experiences, is perhaps the most controversial technique and has been the target of fierce criticism as unethical practice. Some feminist therapists have also been concerned that an extreme attempt to deny or eliminate the power differential might also restrict the full benefits of the therapist bringing into the relationship skills and professional expertise which cannot be shared. Generally speaking, it is still being debated whether it is actually beneficial to deny or attempt to eliminate power imbalance in the therapy situation, or whether it should be openly acknowledged and used as a creative opportunity for the exploration of strategies for dealing with similar situations elsewhere as well as in the therapy.

Women in therapy are clients and not patients

Feminist therapists feel that to position women as 'patients' is pathologizing and disempowering. Thus feminist therapists promote their clients' rights as consumers. This involves the use of clear, jargon-free language and the establishment of a clear contract at the beginning of therapy which is regularly reviewed together. The therapist should also provide clear information regarding her training and theoretical orientation. A safe atmosphere should be fostered to allow the client to feel entitled to ask questions about the direction of the therapy and about the therapist's interventions.

Liberation of the client rather than her adjustment should be the ultimate goal of feminist therapy

From the beginning, feminists criticized traditional psychology for functioning as a subtle but powerful instrument of oppression by manipulating women into blaming themselves for their suffering and finally making them adjust to their oppression. Instead, feminist therapists have as their main aim to enhance awareness of their clients' oppression and help them find psychological as well as practical means of liberating themselves. The client is thus encouraged, for example, to become financially independent and to become less gender-bound in her relationships. Some feminist therapists also feel it is their duty to provide the client with information and encouragement to join political groups and participate in action which will contribute to her and other women's liberation.

Empowerment and self-nurturance

Expressions of anger and needs are identified by feminists as particularly difficult for women because they bring up shame and self-hatred and clash with traditional stereotypes of women as passive and self-less. Feminist therapists aim to help women to feel comfortable with their anger, which is viewed as a self-empowering feeling, and to find more effective ways of expressing it. In this way women's sense of competence and self-esteem are enhanced. Feminists are also aware of how rarely women feel entitled and comfortable with their 'neediness' and tend to focus their energies into looking after others' needs instead. Feminist therapy aims to redress this imbalance,

helping women not to feel selfish when nurturing themselves, and to redefine the boundaries between themselves and others.

In recent years the development in feminist therapies is primarily of an applied nature. Particularly worthy of notice is the rich body of work exploring gender and cultural issues in family dynamics and mental health (Ballou and Brown, 2002; Zimmerman, 2001).

References

Ballou, M.B. and Brown, L.S. (eds) (2002) *Rethinking Mental Health and Disorder: Feminist Perspectives.* New York: Guilford Press.

Cammaert, L.P. and Larsen, C.C. (1988) Feminist frameworks of psychotherapy. In M.A. Ditton-Douglas and L.E. Walker (eds), *Feminist Psychotherapies: Integration of Psychotherapeutic and Feminist Systems.* Norwood, NJ: Ablex.

Enns, C.Z. (2004) *Feminist Theories and Feminist Psychotherapies: Origins, Themes, and Variations* (2nd edn). New York: Haworth Press.

Marecek, J. and Kravetz, D. (1998) Power and agency in feminist therapy. In I.B. Seu and M.C. Heenan (eds), *Feminism and Psychotherapy: Reflections on Contemporary Theories and Practices.* London: Sage.

Zimmerman, S.T. (ed.) (2001) *Integrating Gender and Culture in Family Therapy Training.* New York: Haworth Press.

7.12 Lesbian and Gay Affirmative Therapy

GRAZ KOWSZUN

Anti-oppressive practice

Since the first edition of this *Handbook*, lesbians, gay men and bisexuals (LGBs) have lobbied hard

for our rights and needs, and much has changed politically in Britain. At last we have achieved an equal age of consent, the recognition in law of the crime of male rape and of homophobic assault as a hate crime. As I write, Victorian anti-gay sex offences of gross indecency and buggery have finally been repealed.

Even while Wloszczyna (2003) can claim, 'it's in to be out these days', an LGB life can still be fraught. Philip Reilly, Counselling Co-ordinator of the Metro lesbian, gay and bisexual Centre in Greenwich, London, points out: 'Your attitude can make it easier for you, if you are middle-aged, out a long time, have a strong personal presence. But for many a client the world looks very different' (personal communication, 2004).

We live in a heterocentric (Herek, 1996) society, based on the assumption that everyone is heterosexual, and other sexualities are systematically discounted, marginalized, ridiculed and punished. For example, consider the vilification in the gutter press of the *Coronation Street* kiss or how the young people most likely to be bullied are those thought to be gay. LGBs have to make difficult choices around coming out and may face prejudice, rejection, discrimination, physical violence and harassment regardless. These painful processes are just as likely to occur within the biological family as in wider society and the lack of support, guidance and role modelling can augment internalized homophobia as well as stress and despair.

> Every person is like all persons, like some persons, and like no other persons. ... To gain a full understanding of individuals, it is necessary to explore the unique and simultaneous influences of cultural specificity, individual uniqueness and human universality. (Kluckhohn and Murray, 1953: 335)

Recognizing how clients of diverse sexualities will be no different from any other clients, utterly unique *and* will also share some group characteristics, such as living in a heterocentric culture, is the basis of a lesbian and gay affirmative perspective. This requires four elements: a *considered open attitude; self-awareness* (particularly relating to attraction and sexuality); *good theory*; and appropriate resources for *professional development*.

The therapist's attitude: openness and acceptance

Strong experiences form us. Coming to terms with and developing a minority sexual identity, against which there is much prejudice and discounting, is therefore likely to be a formative experience. A therapist who is comfortably LGB-oriented can create a sense of common ground which aids rapport, although there will also be limits to the commonalities. Heterosexual therapists with a commitment to practising in a non-oppressive way (BACP, 2002) can develop their empathy and acceptance, a process which makes it possible for clients and counsellors of various sexualities to work at relational depth.

When we listen to a client, we may be listening predominantly with interest, empathy and acceptance. Often, there will come a point when we are *affected* by the communication process to the extent that we become reactive or emotionally stirred, or blocked. Communication then becomes distorted and is more likely to be unhelpful. With an LGB client, we may be inhibited in trying to avoid saying the wrong thing. Alternatively, we may avoid topics that a LGB client wants to explore by inadvertently inhibiting, discouraging or diverting them.

Psychological treatment of LGBs has been traditionally pathologizing and damaging. As recently as 2000, Biaggio et al. found that clinical psychologists rated otherwise identically presenting clients as more impaired if they were described as LGB. Most therapists remain untrained and uninformed about LGB issues. Many espouse accepting beliefs, but still use pathologizing theoretical models and show subtle bias.

Warner (1998) offers a useful distinction between therapists whose style is likely or not to encounter client resistance. Therapists who draw on their training and experience in order to diagnose, construct treatment plans, interpret clients' defences or who use tactics of which the client may remain unaware (such as paradoxical interventions or conditioning procedures) fall in the former camp. Those who endeavour to remain within the client's frame of reference throughout, or who offer occasional suggestions of questions or strategies but readily drop these should the client demur, are unlikely to encounter resistance, for they are not opposing the client in any significant way. In psychodynamic therapy, resistance is conceptualized as a defence against unconscious material. Deference to the authority of the therapist is often viewed as healthy; its absence pathological. This position is questionable, however, particularly when working with minority groups. Walker (1992) takes a diametrically opposing view of resistance, when she asks 'what is the secret of joy?' The answer she proclaims is *resistance*, perhaps agreeing with Walt Whitman: 're-examine all you have been told … dismiss whatever insults your own soul' (1855, Preface to *Leaves of Grass*).

It could be argued that the risks of oppressive practice involved in adopting an attitude that is likely to evoke resistance in a LGB client may be unacceptably high, given the likelihood that the client's sense of identity and experience will have often been overridden. Therapists who focus on close-tracking their client's frame of reference and who are willing to question themselves non-defensively if the client's material evokes reactions are more likely to meet the LGB client's needs.

Self-awareness

One does not become enlightened by imagining figures of light, but by making the darkness conscious. The latter procedure, however, is disagreeable and therefore not popular. (Jung, 1945: 335)

The reader may wish to take some time out from reading to answer the questions below, or at least to notice how they rationalize choosing not to do so:

- Do you remember being a baby, a toddler or a small child? What were the first feelings of desire you recall? In what context and when did you learn, however vaguely, about sex?
- What were the earliest messages you remember about boys/girls/love/power and gender/families, etc.?
- Where did you first hear about gays and lesbians, and what were the words used?

- Who did you find attractive at primary school? At secondary school?
- What was your first sexual experience?
- If you were to live in a predominantly gay/lesbian area, what might you like and dislike about this? Explore your response further.
- Let yourself free-write for five minutes about being marooned for several months on a desert island with someone of your own sex, who was openly lesbian/gay. Take time to process your free-writing.
- How do you define your sexual orientation? Imagine a continuum from 'exclusively homosexual', through 'evenly bisexual' to 'exclusively heterosexual'.
- Where would you put yourself along this continuum in terms of your feelings and fantasies *this year*? And your sexual behaviour?
- Expand the time-frame to cover your whole life. Has your position on the continuum changed? Is there a difference between attractions and behaviour? Why?

The professional who says he or she has no homosexual feelings [is] about as well off as the psychotherapist who says he or she never dreams. It indicates you are out of touch with your inner emotions and would do well to consider another profession. (Clark, 1987: 233)

Good theory: generic and applied

Much of what has been written about *sexual diversity* is pathologizing, and a therapist aiming to be gay affirmative should read some of the more recent literature (Davies and Neal, 2000; Johnson and O'Connor, 2002; Ritter and Terndrup, 2002; Shelley, 1998; *Lesbian & Gay Psychology Review*; *Journal of British Psychological Society*), which challenges heterosexist notions of health and perversity.

A helpful attitude to theory in this context is to view it as short-hand for experience and consider whether the experiences informing the theory's creation and the client's life situation can usefully be compared. Does the theory take social context into account and include ways of conceptualizing social privilege and exclusion and its impacts? Does it recognize, for instance, the impact of class differences or urban versus rural lifestyles on the behaviours and self-perceptions of clients? Mark, for example, moved from a small town in the county of his birth, where he was regularly 'queer bashed', to a cosmopolitan inner city, where he was safer in his anonymity, but still occasionally harassed. His therapist's diagnosis of a paranoid personality style failed to take this into account.

Experience is subjective and strongly influenced by beliefs. Thus if the client is living in a society which finds him disgusting, immature or even exotic because of the object of his desire, his sense of belonging and self-esteem will be affected. If a client regularly finds her living situation is assumed to be quite different from what it is, her willingness to be open and approachable may suffer and she may collude in her marginalization.

If the theory informing a therapist's practice has a developmental aspect, is it normative or does it incorporate a plurality of definitions of family, health and developmental paths? What is its value in application? How usefully does it consider some of the concerns more or less specific to or differently experienced by LGBs? Does it, for instance, shed light on the coming out process? Does it explore lifespan development in a way that is pertinent to diverse lifestyles? To give some examples, relationships with previous partners and children were shattered when Joanna came out at the age of 51. Self-defining family and support networks provided some protection against the stigma of ageing for Barrie, but he considered the loss of his muscle tone and youthful good looks devastating to his life on the 'scene'. Ali found that considering having children with her partner Trish was a fraught complex issue; while a lack of family responsibilities contributed to Mellie continuing to drink like a young adult right into her middle age and thereby developing substance abuse problems.

Professional development

Therapists wishing to work anti-oppressively need to consider their training and supervision needs in this area. They may benefit most perhaps, through a safe space to explore assumptions or reactions to lesbian clients. Alternatively, formative input, such as knowledge of relevant resources (books, videos, workshops or models to inform your practice) may be required. Perhaps support of a restorative nature, such as encouragement to visit gay venues or a place to offload any sense of inadequacy, would currently be very useful? Therapists may find it important to consider how resourced and how lesbian and gay affirmative their regular supervisor is and perhaps to discuss whether they may need additional consultative support and/or training.

Endnote: A sample of guidelines for good practice in lesbian and gay affirmative therapy for consideration

Various authors have attempted to distil good practice into the form of guidelines (American Psychological Association, 2000; Clark, 1987; Garnets et al., 1991) and the list below is no more exhaustive or conclusive than its predecessors:

- Therapists should not assume their clients are heterosexual by default. Enquiring about a client's sexual orientation, living situation or whether they currently have a primary sexual partnership demonstrates more sensitivity and is more likely to generate the information desired.
- Sexual orientation may or may not be relevant to the client's concerns, either centrally, or as background.
- Sexual orientation is not reducible to sexual activity, nor should any particular lifestyle be presupposed.
- Lesbian, gay and bisexual clients may or may not be married. Similarly, they may or may not have children.
- Furthermore, lesbian, gay and bisexual clients may or may not be 'out' to families, friends, at work, in church, etc. This could be problematic, or it may be a well-considered, wise choice in their circumstances.
- Legal families or live-in relationships may not be the client's chief source of support. Many lesbian, gay and bisexual clients have developed extensive and varied networks for different forms of practical and emotional support.
- The attitude of lesbian, gay and bisexual clients to their orientation may be glad, mad, sad or a myriad other possibilities. While the likelihood is high that they have suffered from homophobia and heterosexism, and may have internalized it to some extent, this may be more or less conscious.

- Lesbian, gay and bisexual clients do not form a homogeneous group. Self-definitions vary. Clients may refer to themselves as lesbian, gay or bisexual. Alternately they may use queer, dyke or homosexual. Sometimes it is respectful to ask how the client wants to be considered.
- Therapists should not assume sexual orientation is fixed for life any more readily than they assume it may be changing.
- Clients may or may not be willing to educate the therapist in their lifestyle and lesbian, gay and bisexual issues. It is respectful at least to enquire, and for therapists to make sure they have alternative sources of information and support.

References

American Psychological Association (2000) Guidelines for psychotherapy with lesbian, gay, and bisexual clients. *American Psychologist*, 55: 1440–1451.

BACP (2002) *Ethical Framework for Good Practice in Counselling and Psychotherapy*. Rugby: British Association for Counselling and Psychotherapy.

Biaggio, M., Roades, L.A., Staffelbach, D., Cardinali, J. and Duffy, R. (2000) Clinical evaluation: impact of sexual orientation, gender, and gender role. *Journal of Applied Social Psychology*, 30: 1657–1669.

Clark, D. (1987) *The New Loving Someone Gay*. Berkeley, CA: Celestial Arts.

Davies, D. and Neal, C. (eds) (2000) *Issues in Therapy with Gay, Lesbian, Bisexual and Transgender Clients*. Buckingham: Open University Press.

Garnets, L., Hancock, K.A., Cochran, S.D., Goodchilds, J. and Peplau, L.A. (1991) Issues in psychotherapy with lesbians and gay men: a survey of psychologists. *American Psychologist*, 46 (9): 964–972.

Herek, G.M. (1996) Heterosexism and homophobia. In R.P. Cabaj and T.S. Stein (eds), *Textbook of Homosexuality and Mental Health*. Washington, DC: American Psychiatric Press. pp. 101–113.

Johnson, S.M. and O'Connor, E. (2002) *The Gay Baby Boom: The Psychology of Gay Parenthood*. New York: New York University Press.

Jung, C.G. (1945) *The Philosophical Tree*. In *The Collected Works of C.G. Jung (1953–1978)*. Vol. 13. *Alchemical Studies*. London: Routledge and Kegan Paul.

Kluckhohn, C. and Murray, H.A. (1953) Personality formation: the determinants. In C. Kluckhohn, H.A. Murray and D.M. Schneider (eds), *Personality in Nature, Society and Culture*. New York: Random House.

Ritter, K.Y. and Terndrup, A.I. (2002) *Handbook of Affirmative Psychotherapy with Lesbians and Gay Men*. New York: Guilford Press.

Shelley, C. (ed.) (1998) *New Perspectives on Psychotherapy and Homosexuality*. London: Free Association Books.

Walker, A. (1992) *Possessing the Secret of Joy*. London: The Women's Press Bookclub.

Warner, M. (1998) *Person-centred Psychotherapy: One Nation, Many Tribes*. Chicago: Chicago Counselling and Psychotherapy Center.

Wloszczyna, S. (2003) It's 'in' to be 'out' these days: TV, films, and stage now feature gays in unprecedented ways. *USA Today*, 2 June, pp. D1–D2.

7.13   Groups and Group Counselling/Therapy   ◯◯◯

KEITH TUDOR

Most people live and work in groups. Even people who live and work alone have some relation to groups by virtue of being a part of a family (however defined), a community and society. While for most therapists individual therapy is the therapy of choice or, more accurately, the assumed preferential modality of therapy, it is arguable that, due to the social nature of the human condition, group therapy is the therapy of choice (and that practitioners rather need to make the case for choosing to work with people on an individual basis). In this section on groups, I briefly consider the history of therapeutic groups, outline four key theoretical concepts, discuss their applicability and some procedures and strategies that group leaders/facilitators may adopt, and conclude with reference to some training and supervision issues.

Context

It seems that the first recorded reference to the use of therapeutic groups was in 1905 when Joseph Pratt, an internist in Boston, organized classes or groups of consumptive patients. In establishing a preventive programme of 'home sanatorium treatment', Pratt was initially only concerned to monitor patients' progress and to educate them about their diet and environment. He came to realize, however, the importance of the mutual support created by patients having 'a common bond in a common disease', and he later became more interested in the psychological aspects of the groups and the interactions between group members. At around the same time, in Vienna, Jacob Moreno was working with school children acting out plays, initially written for them, about various social and behavioural issues. Soon the children were presenting their own plays and Moreno was applying this impromptu role-playing or psychodrama to working with adults. Later, during the Second World War, Moreno and his colleagues developed sociodrama, in which the audience became the community, acting out and dealing with issues such as those of racial conflict.

Historically, perhaps the most influential development for our present understanding of therapeutic group practice was that the phenomenon of 'the group' began to be viewed from within the conceptual framework of psychoanalysis. In 1921 Freud published a short book on *Group Psychology and the Analysis of the Ego* (Freud, 1985) in which he drew heavily on the work of the French psychologist, Le Bon. Freud's views on group psychology have led to a number of distinct traditions of group therapy

within psychoanalysis (for a summary, see Tudor, 1999). One of these developed a group-dynamics approach to group psychotherapy, which emphasized the importance of viewing the group itself as a coherent entity and is associated with the work of Wilfred Bion, Siegmund Foulkes and the Tavistock Clinic in London. This focus on the dynamics of the group led these and other practitioners to develop theoretical concepts relevant to the group-as-a-whole as distinct from applying concepts to the group borrowed from individual psychoanalysis.

Another important influence on group therapy includes Kurt Lewin's field theory, whereby psychological relationships were viewed in terms of their surrounding field. From the 1960s, a variety of practitioners and theoreticians in the humanistic/existential tradition experimented with more experiential approaches to groups, in which the participants' experiencing of each other was the focus of the group. These practitioners included Will Schutz, the 'father' of encounter groups, Eric Berne (1966) and Carl Rogers (1973).

Over the last 30 years the different traditions of groupwork, group analysis, group psychotherapy and group counselling have all developed, been applied to more and a greater variety of settings, and have become integrated into a variety of fields of application. In psychotherapy and counselling a number of authors from different traditions or theoretical orientations have contributed to both specialists and wider understandings of group theory and practice, for example psychodynamic (Whitaker, 1985), cognitive-behavioural (Alladin, 1988), psychodrama (Davies, 1988), Gestalt (Feder and Ronall, 1994), and person-centred (Lago and Macmillan, 1999) approaches. As well as therapists, social and health care workers, psychologists, management and organizational consultants are leading/facilitating groups. Support groups and focus groups, as well as a plethora of social groupings (parents' meetings, choirs, parties), are not only part of our consciousness but also of our daily experience of social life. As our knowledge about and experience of groups has expanded, so has the confidence of people to establish and run their own groups, and 'self-help groups' abound. One search identified over 800 such groups in the UK alone – from 'Abducted Children' to people with 'XXY syndrome' – many with their own local branches. In the last ten years or so the internet has provided an electronic web through which many people can access and identify with others as a group or virtual group, a phenomenon which also includes self-helps groups. In an interesting study, King and Moreggi (1998) discuss the pros and cons of internet therapy and self-help groups.

Theory

Four key theoretical concepts of groups are briefly summarized.

Group development

This refers to the concept that, as an entity in itself, the group *as a group* has a life of its own which may be viewed in developmental terms. Thus, most theoretical psychological approaches, from Freudian to Rogerian, have, implicitly or explicitly, a conceptualization of group development. Perhaps the most famous of a number of meta-models of group development is Tuckman's stages of forming, storming, norming and performing. In his original article, Tuckman (1965) acknowledged a pre-forming stage and he later added an adjourning stage, thus making a six-stage model (Tuckman and Jenson, 1977). Although the very concept of developmental stages in groups is a debatable one, many group therapists find it useful in describing and sometimes predicting patterns of group behaviour. It is worth noting that Tuckman's sequence was based on a review of a number of *task* groups.

The image of groups

While group development is predominantly based on some objective view of the task and/or lifetime of a group, this refers to the subjective image (or *imago*) of groups everyone carries around with them: the 'mental image of the dynamic relationships between the people in the group, including the therapist; idiosyncratic for each individual patient' (Berne, 1966: 364). Berne identifies four phases in the

development of the individual's group imago (for a summary, including additions which parallel Tuckman's stages, see Tudor, 1999).

Therapeutic factors

In 1970 Yalom published his seminal work on *The Theory and Practice of Group Psychotherapy*, now in its fifth edition (Yalom, 2005), based on his research into the curative or therapeutic factors of groups. These factors refer to the elements of group therapy which contribute to improvement in the client and are a function and result of the actions of the group therapist, the other group members, and the client her/himself, although it is recognized that aspects of life outside the group may be experienced as therapeutic or healing. Yalom's factors are: the instillation and maintenance of hope; universality (the notion that we are not alone); imparting of information; altruism (helping others); the corrective recapitulation of the primary family group; the development of socializing techniques; imitative behaviour; interpersonal learning; group cohesiveness; catharsis; and existential factors.

The role of the leader

Much has been written about the role of group 'leader' (described variously as analyst, conductor, facilitator, therapist), both from the point of view of addressing the practical issues in establishing, maintaining and ending a group, and in working *in*, *through* and/or *with* the group. Depending on the group therapist's theoretical orientation and experience, and on the purpose of the group, different leaders will take different attitudes and make different interventions in, through or with the group. The advantages and disadvantages of co-leadership also need to be addressed by the potential group therapist/s.

Assessment

There are two key issues in assessing clients for group therapy: assessment and selection.

Assessment refers to the areas of concern and/or interest which both clients (potential group members) and the group therapist/s address in deciding whether to work together in a group setting. In addition to their usual means of (individual client) assessment, the group therapist needs to consider issues such as:

- whether group or individual therapy is the modality of choice for the client (or whether the therapist is prepared to offer or accept the combination of group and individual therapy);
- whether the client is looking for group therapy or some other kind of social group experience;
- whether the client is looking for a mixed therapy group or one which is homogeneous in its composition (e.g. a single-gender group).

The logic of taking a group relations perspective challenges the group therapist at least to consider conducting her/his assessment *in groups*, whether in assessment groups or in the context of an ongoing, 'open' group.

Selection refers to the practice whereby therapists select clients, usually through some form of assessment, for a specific therapy group. Reflecting on the literature, Yalom (2005) states that patients who are brain-damaged, paranoid, hypochondriac, addicted, acutely psychotic or sociopathic (anti-social) are poor candidates for a long-term, interactional outpatient therapy group. On the other hand, Berne took an unusual stance in favour of non-selection, arguing that heterogeneous groups are more representative of society and that selection is usually based on personal prejudices and untenable rationalizations: 'the real issue … is not the one commonly debated "What are the criteria for the selection of patients?", but the underlying, usually unstated assumption "Criteria for selection are good"' (Berne, 1966: 5). This is of particular relevance in promoting a heterogeneous, inter-cultural approach to groups and inter-group relations (see Tudor, 1999).

Key procedures and strategies

All therapeutic procedures and strategies depend on a combination of the therapist's theoretical orientation and experience; the client, their issues and experience; the contract or agreement as to the purpose of therapy for the particular client/s; and the context

and modality of the therapy. Nevertheless, there are a number of procedures and strategies which the group therapist needs to consider:

- *In preparing for the group* – having a coherent concept and theory of groups (see above) and a view about the therapeutic value and factors of the proposed group; defining the group in terms of its purpose, type, constituency, size, regularity and lifetime, duration, setting and fees; being clear about assessment and (if at all) selection, recording, research and evaluation; and arranging appropriate support and supervision.
- *In establishing the group* – deciding the group rules and negotiating group contracts, for example about confidentiality and social contact between members; and deciding about the style of leadership, including the group therapist's roles, tasks and attitude to power.
- *In 'leading' the group* – deciding on appropriate levels of interventiveness (from facilitative to executive) and how to respond to absence, collusion, conflict, hostility, norms, requests, scapegoating and silence, etc., in the group.
- *In closing or ending the group* – being able to manage endings and deciding when to end.

Training and supervision issues

Although the majority of training courses in counselling and psychotherapy are generic, the predominant emphasis in training therapists is on individual, adult clients. There is no requirement on generic courses to have either a theoretical or practical component on groups, although some writers on groups favour a required element in the training of *all* therapists to have some experience of running – and, indeed, in being in – groups.

The components of a good education/training in group therapy are:

1. The formal taught course, including observation of experienced group therapists.
2. Personal therapy or personal development – both personal group experience and individual therapy.
3. Supervised group practice (for further discussion of these components, see Tudor, 1999; Yalom, 1995).

Courses in group therapy (group analysis, group counselling, etc.) divide into those specialist courses which lead to registration with the UKCP and other independent courses in group therapy. A counsellor's groupwork practice still does not count towards individual accreditation as a counsellor with the BACP.

Despite the increase in interest, publications, courses and qualifications in supervision of therapy, there is surprisingly little on the supervision of groupwork. Exceptions to this are Sharpe (1995) and Proctor (2000). There are a number of relevant issues:

- The setting of supervision is important: clearly, there are advantages to the supervision of groups itself taking place in groups as this creates a forum for reflection (e.g. on parallel processes) and for creative options in supervision (e.g. role play).
- The supervision group provides a source of process itself: whether it is a group of trainees or qualified practitioners or a peer group, how the group is established, its composition, size, etc. all provide points for discussion about groups.
- The requirements of the supervisor are high: they should themselves be an experienced group therapist and supervisor and, preferably, a trained group supervisor.

References

Alladin, W. (1988) Cognitive-behavioural group therapy. In M. Aveline and W. Dryden (eds), *Group Therapy in Britain*. Milton Keynes: Open University Press. pp. 115–139.

Berne, E. (1966) *Principles of Group Treatment*. New York: Grove Press.

Davies, M. (1988) Psychodrama group therapy. In M. Aveline and W. Dryden (eds), *Group Therapy in Britain*. Milton Keynes: Open University Press. pp. 88–114.

Feder, B. and Ronall, R. (eds) (1994) *Beyond the Hot Seat: Gestalt Approaches to Group*. Highland, NY: The Gestalt Journal Press.

Freud, S. (1985) Group psychology and the analysis of the ego. In A. Dickson (ed.), *Civilization, Society and Groups* (trans. J. Strachey). London: Academic Press. pp. 77–109.

King, S.A. and Moreggi, D. (1998) Internet therapy and self help groups – the pros and cons. In J. Gackenbach (ed.), *Psychology and the Internet: Intrapersonal, Interpersonal and Transpersonal Implications*. San Diego, CA: Academic Press. pp. 77–109.

Lago, C. and Macmillan, M. (eds) (1999) *Experience in Relatedness: Group Work and the Person-centred Approach*. Llangarron: PCCS Books.

Proctor, B. (2000) *Group Supervision: A Guide to Creative Practice*. London: Sage.

Rogers, C.R. (1973) *On Encounter Groups*. Harmondsworth: Penguin. (Original work published 1970.)

Sharpe, M. (ed.) (1995) *The Third Eye: Supervision of Analytic Groups*. London: Routledge.

Tuckman, B.W. (1965) Developmental sequence in small groups. *Psychological Bulletin*, 63: 384–399.

Tuckman, B.W. and Jenson, K. (1977) Stages of small-group development revisited. *Group and Organization Studies*, 2 (4): 419–427.

Tudor, K. (1999) *Group Counselling*. London: Sage.

Whitaker, D.S. (1985) *Using Groups to Help People*. London: Routledge.

Yalom, I. and Leszcz, M. (2005) *The Theory and Practice of Group Psychotherapy* (5th edn). New York: Basic Books.

7.14 Managing Stress

ROWAN BAYNE

A useful working definition of 'stress' is 'the experience of unpleasant over or under stimulation, as defined by the individual in question, that actually or potentially leads to ill health' (Bond, 1986). This definition recognizes the fact that different people find radically different things stressful and it has a flavour of feeling strained to the extent of feeling overwhelmed, as in everything being 'too much to bear' (too much stimulation) or 'going out of my mind with boredom' (too little). The definition also includes a statement about the effects of stress on health, a controversial field discussed well by Sapolsky (1998) and Jones and Bright (2001). Stress is probably a minor factor in ill health compared to diet, smoking, poverty, genetic factors, etc., but still worth attention.

Bond's definition of stress, like most definitions, emphasizes the role of individuals rather than their organizations, social contexts or cultures. If the organization, for example, is too cold, too demanding or too hostile, then the organization itself is arguably the main source of stress and interventions for managing stress will be most effective at that level. For example, the organization could reduce its demands on employees and increase their sense of control (rather than just providing stress-management workshops or an EAP). However, it is probable that each of us as an individual contributes significantly to our stress and that working on ourselves is therefore vital. (The tension between the political and the personal is a familiar one in counselling and psychotherapy, and is discussed elsewhere in this book.)

The symptoms or signs of stress are often also possible symptoms of illness. Feeling 'tired all the time', aches, irritability, sleeping difficulties, lack of concentration and 'negative' mood are among the most common. One symptom, unfortunately, is ignoring such symptoms. Ideally, each person will notice *early* symptoms of stress and take action to reduce or remove them. The advantages of early action are obvious: less energy wasted and less damage done. Working out the cause(s) or stressors may also be more feasible.

This ideal way of coping with stress is fine when people are rational. However, there can of course be deeper, motivational problems. Why does X who knows all the arguments continue to overwork and ignore her feelings of futility and emptiness? Why does Y, who knows all the arguments and wants to eat more healthily and exercise, do quite well for a few days and then, as he sees it, fail again? The crucial points here are the wish to change (or not)

and the obstacles if we do wish to change. We have the right to, for example, work much longer hours than most people, smoke, and not exercise, though some of the writing on stress assumes otherwise and has a moralizing, patronizing tone. Conversely, when someone does want to exercise more, say, and gets frustrated and demoralized with their attempts, therapists can draw on theories of change and motivation to try to help.

There is a lot of research on the main causes of stress in different occupations, on ways of thinking about and measuring coping with stress, and on the effectiveness of different strategies (Jones and Bright, 2001). Much of this, like the work on stress and illness, is still at a fairly early stage – theory and conjecture rather than based on good evidence. Thus, faced with a particular client, we are not yet justified in saying, 'This technique has been shown to be the most likely to be effective with this kind of problem and for the kind of person you are.' Rather, it is a matter of discussing options and the obstacles to achieving them, and then individual experimentation and follow-up.

However, there are some fairly clear guidelines and some useful pieces of evidence. The rest of this section will touch on ideas and findings about (a) sources of stress for therapists and (b) several strategies for coping with or managing stress: relaxation, exercise, and social support. Other strategies, such as supervision, assertiveness and of course counselling itself, are reviewed elsewhere in this book.

Several sources of stress for therapists are discussed by Brady et al. (1995). Perhaps the most obvious are clients who are suicidal, hostile, etc., as well as clients who end therapy abruptly or who do not turn up. Each therapist is likely to be affected more by some of these ways that clients behave than others. Brady et al. also discuss emotional depletion, physical isolation, psychic isolation, therapeutic relationships, working conditions and personal disruptions. This is a bleak list and may raise the question 'Why become a therapist?' However, there are strategies for trying to cope with each of these sources of stress and Brady et al. recognize that therapy is also nourishing, enriching and a privilege.

A further, underlying cause of stress, is when therapists conceal from themselves one or more of their motives for being a therapist. The idea here is not so much that the motives themselves are a problem but how concealed they are and what their impact is. Motives include trying to help, trying to avoid loneliness, seeking praise, fear of intimacy, seeking power and playing various unhelpful roles such as those of victim, persecutor and rescuer. Skilful use of supervision, and reflection during and after therapy, are probably the most effective safeguards.

As for strategies, it is usually not known why a strategy works. For example, shopping is a distraction, physical exercise, and (for some people) a treat, so it may be any, some or all of these elements which matters. Similarly, 'sense of control' is inevitably an aspect of implementing any strategy successfully, and it may be that it is more important than the particular strategy.

The therapist may also be concerned with helping clients to manage stress by modifying coping techniques to suit themselves. No strategy, however strong the research evidence for it or one's own experience with it, is right for everyone. In practice it is easy to lapse, if only occasionally. Psychological type theory (discussed in Section 5.3, see pp. 231–234) is a useful antidote here, but even people who know and apply the theory expertly find themselves making the 'how to be more like me' error. Moreover, the theory suggests different styles or tones for people of different psychological types, for example, being more playful and very flexible with some clients; more organized and systematic with others; more scientific, creative and logical with others. In addition, perhaps the best overall strategy is one of trying something to see what happens, though a clear purpose rather than a haphazard, 'butterfly' eclecticism, and some persistence, are also desirable.

The strategy of physical relaxation illustrates some of the points above well. Generally it has a positive and cumulative effect, but for some clients, at least at a particular time in their lives, it may actually add to stress. For example, someone may try too hard to relax or may be afraid of losing control of certain images or emotions. Relaxation can also be boring and therefore stressful. The client and therapist

can then try either shaping the strategy accordingly, or another strategy, or a combination, for example several very brief sessions rather than the recommended two ten-minute sessions per day, meditation or visualization as possible ways of relaxing mentally, and so on (see Rosenthal, 1993 for an open-minded and empirical discussion of the use and effectiveness of guided imagery, pets, etc.).

Exercise is another strategy which the research suggests is generally among the most effective. The current view is that a relatively moderate level of physical activity – rather than 'exercise' – is enough to make a difference to physical health and to an ability to cope with stress. The moderate level is 30 minutes slightly out of breath (rather than sweaty and panting) accomplished most days. This is fundamentally different from an external standard such as so many miles per day, or vigorous exercise for 20 minutes in blocks three times a week. However, assuming the therapist or client wishes to experiment with physical activity, it may still need to be approached gradually – by, for example, sometimes using the stairs rather than a lift, or walking a bit more briskly.

Social support is one of the most used strategies and, as with relaxation and exercise, there is quite good evidence for its effectiveness (Jones and Bright, 2001). However, it is a more complicated and intangible strategy, with presumably much in common with counselling and therapy. Moreover, a person's friends and relatives (the usual sources of social support) may also be major sources of stress. When social support is effective it seems to be through giving or confirming a sense of belonging and identity, at one level, and being more directly supportive through giving information, listening and so on, at another level (see Bond, 1986 for discussion of giving and receiving support).

Finally, it is worth mentioning some more mundane factors. Sleeping badly, eating certain foods (especially, unfortunately, chocolate and other sources of sugar), and going without food for long periods, can all be causes as well as symptoms of stress. It may be worth considering these factors the next time you or a client are trying to understand and cope with stress.

References

Bond, M. (1986) *Stress and Self-awareness: A Guide for Nurses*. London: Heinemann.

Brady, J.L., Healy, F.C., Norcross, J.C. and Guy, J.D. (1995) Stress in counsellors: an integrative research review. In W. Dryden (ed.), *The Stresses of Counselling in Action*. London: Sage.

Jones, F. and Bright, J. (2001) *Stress: Myth, Theory and Research*. Harlow: Prentice-Hall.

Rosenthal, T. (1993) To soothe the savage breast. *Behaviour Research and Therapy*, 31 (5): 439–462.

Sapolsky, R. (1998) *Why Zebras Don't Get Ulcers. An Updated Guide to Stress, Stress-related Diseases and Coping*. Basingstoke: Macmillan.

7.15   Counselling Older Adults   ○○○

ELEANOR O'LEARY AND NICOLA BARRY

'I realize that I am not a write-off: there are still things I can do'. (Group member, Cork, 1998)

The term 'older adult' is generally based on a chronological definition of old age and is associated with an individual over 65 years of age. In 1996, the first author pointed out that this demarcation occurred for economic reasons in Germany at the end of the last century and that psychological, biological, social and spiritual definitions can also be used. Using a chronological definition, it becomes apparent that, in this century, a large increase in the number of older people has occurred. Figures for the over-65s ranged from one in 20 at the turn of the century to one in seven in 1996, while, by the year 2020, it is expected to be one in five (Walker and Maltby, 1997). Similar trends for those over 75 have been noted by Walker and Maltby. In 1996, one in 15 persons fell in this category while the anticipated figure for the year 2020 is one in ten.

Growing numbers of older people imply a need for increased attention from counselling and therapy professionals. Conwell et al.'s study (2002) indicated that the rate of suicide among older adults warrants significant concern and highlights the need for intervention to address the prevalence of mood disorders in this age group. The most frequently encountered difficulty relates to loss in all its manifestations – loss of loved ones through death, of a specific family role, of physical agility, of work identity and of economic independence. Other issues include loneliness, depression, physical illness, psychosexual difficulties, anticipation of death, insomnia and cognitive decline. The main therapeutic approaches that are used with older adults may be considered under the following headings: cognitive-behavioural, family, humanistic and group reminiscence. Each of these will be briefly outlined and the most pertinent research findings discussed. A new development, gestalt reminiscence therapy, will be considered in greater detail.

Counselling approaches and research

Cognitive-behavioural approaches involve detailed problem description, the application of specific therapeutic techniques and the formulation of concrete goals. They are guided by the assumption that clients can replace maladaptive patterns of behaving and thinking with more constructive forms.

Depression has been the major focus of therapeutic research investigations with older adults. Campbell's (1992) study involving 103 community-based older adults found that interventions based on the reinforcement of positive thought patterns were effective in the reduction of depression. More recently, a study of cognitive therapy by Floyd et al. (2004) indicated that both bibliotherapy and individual psychotherapy might be useful treatments to address depression in older adults. Both behaviour and cognitive-behaviour therapy have had a positive impact in treating insomnia (Engle-Friedman et al., 1992; Morin et al., 1993). While a one-year follow-up study of older adults by Rickard et al. (1994) provided further evidence for the efficacy of relaxation training in reducing subjective anxiety.

Humanistic approaches are guided by a number of underlying assumptions, including an anti-reductionist stance and the rejection of a narrow definition of human nature. Individuals are perceived as being in a continuous process of development and are viewed in the context of autonomy. Understanding the perspective of each person is central. Age does not place any limits on the potential for becoming increasingly self-actualized. Rather than being conceptualized as a period of stagnation and deterioration, the latter part of the life cycle is seen as a dynamic time in which ongoing emotional growth can occur.

Only three group humanistic studies (Johnson and Wilborn, 1991; Lieberman and Gourash, 1979); O'Leary et al., 2003) have employed a control group and the first two of these had methodological problems. Control group members in the Lieberman and Gourash study had higher pre-test scores on the dependent variables than the treatment group. In the case of Johnson and Wilborn's study, no information was available on the training and experience of the facilitator. In general, research investigations using humanistic counselling approaches with older adults are in an exploratory phase. As a result of these explorations, hypotheses are emerging, conceptualizations are being altered and theory is being developed. A study by O'Leary et al. (2003) was confirmatory in nature. In a randomized control investigation of 43 older adults over 65 years of age, it was found that participants in a gestalt therapy group had less anger control and more overall expression of anger than control group members. Thus it may be that loss of rigidity in the control of their anger allowed older adults to express it. At the conclusion of the group, the participants were significantly more agreeable and less hostile as well as more clear-headed and less confused. Younger members of the group were significantly more composed and less anxious than younger control group members. Qualitative results further supported the findings in relation to anxiety, clear-headedness and agreeableness and indicated substantial learning by the participants.

The application of family therapy to the older adult population has received little attention. The emphasis in this approach is on improved family functioning. The design of appropriate programmes for carers has been conducted by Myers (1989) and Sheehan and Nutall (1988). The lack of controlled outcome studies in the area is lamentable since it may be particularly relevant to clients whose presenting problems originate within their families.

Group reminiscence therapy has been the most frequently used psychodynamic approach with older adults. Members recount stories of their past to other participants, thus allowing them to share in their experiences. Reciprocal listening enables older adults to develop a new awareness of themselves and of each other while the act of story-telling adds a psychosocial dimension to the work.

Research on group reminiscence therapy has been conducted by a number of authors. Some of the reported investigations used controlled designs involving the random assignment of participants to a reminiscence-type group, to another intervention or a control group. Support for the effectiveness of group reminiscence in anxiety reduction and the use of life review to increase life satisfaction was provided by Haight (1988) and Rattenbury and Stones (1989). Haight reported increases in psychological well-being (O'Leary, 1996). According to Berghorn and Schafer (1987) group reminiscence was most suitable for nursing home residents who had difficulty in adapting and whose values were in conflict with those of others in their environment.

In research by Sherman (1987), community-based participants in both reminiscence and experiential groups experienced positive changes in life satisfaction and self-concept. Furthermore, Sherman stated that reminiscence groups were effective in developing friendships, in encouraging the establishment of ongoing peer support groups and creativity and in providing enjoyment for older adults. Haight and Dias (1992) discovered that reminiscence was the modality of choice in groupwork, while in a review of nine studies, half of which reported statistically significant reductions in depression scores, Hsieh and Wang (2003) concluded that it was a useful treatment intervention. One of the few longitudinal studies in the field which investigated 176 older adults over 18 months was that of Stones et al. (1995) who found that, when a reminiscence intervention was used, earlier measures of happiness predicted lower mortality.

A development in the field of working with older adults is that of gestalt reminiscence therapy (O'Leary and Barry, 1998). Within this group approach, individuals are involved in focusing on the emotional, social and spiritual dimensions of their lives. Older adults explore their inner psychological lives through centring on current experiencing. Facilitators also attend to their internal world to ensure that ageist attitudes are not hindering the process.

Within gestalt reminiscence therapy, the emphasis is on enabling clients to live a fuller and more satisfying life. Problems are viewed within this context. The approach integrates gestalt and reminiscence therapies by including story-telling, unfinished business, the present, the expression and location of emotion, the acknowledgement of contextual dimensions, the enhancement of contact, the sharing of spiritual values and attention to both interpersonal and group processes. Stories are not only recalled but feelings associated with them in the present are explored and participants facilitated in accepting responsibility for these experiences. Participants are encouraged to use the personal pronoun 'I' to increase their sense of responsibility as evidenced by the following excerpt:

CLIENT: Yes, because … I mean to say … when … you've had a very long life, what can you do about it?

FACILITATOR: Mmmm … Can you say: I've had a very long …

Gestalt reminiscence therapy assists individuals to think about bereavement and death. The death of a group member is viewed as both a time of sadness for other participants and an opportunity to explore feelings around their own deaths. Sharing the spiritual aspects of their lives can provide support and comfort in exploring their own future deaths.

The group context creates a supportive environment in which former achievements are celebrated and both past and present difficulties are understood by others and worked through with the assistance of the facilitator. The participants become aware of their personal and group identity. This was illustrated in one group of older adults when members of the group questioned what name they should give themselves.

Within nursing homes, the group can provide an important ancillary social support function during a period of life when immediate family contact is often lessened. This involves an expansion of personal boundaries to encompass a view of oneself as connected to other members through both emotional and social ties. In this manner, helplessness and dependency, which can be increased through institutionalization, can be partly counteracted.

Within gestalt reminiscence therapy, special attention is given to counsellor attitudes and client beliefs that may hinder progress. Counselling can be enhanced or hindered by the attitudes of either the client or the counsellor and the nature of their interpersonal relationship. Counsellors may fear ageing, hold the belief that problems are due to either organic brain disease or general deterioration associated with old age, or experience an inability to deal with death and bereavement. Client beliefs may be based on a cohort perception that only mentally ill people attend counselling, cultural views that consider the appropriate support for problem resolution to be the family or a higher power, and the image of the counsellor as the carer, the expert or the ideal. The interpersonal relationship can be hindered by the ageist attitudes on the present of either party. These attitudes and beliefs should be explored in counsellor or therapy training courses to ensure that misconceptions regarding old age are corrected and healthy attitudes developed.

To date, three qualitative studies relating to gestalt reminiscence therapy groups with older adults have been reported in the literature. In the first study, O'Leary and Nieuwstraten (1999) found that the initial expression of unfinished business by older adults can be in non-personal language. The therapists assisted participants in personalizing their issues, expressing accompanying feelings and completing the experience. Group members identified with the shared stories and gave different perspectives to the identified problem. In the second study, which focused on the exploration of memories, O'Leary and Nieuwstraten (2001a) found that the memories shared by older adults in a gestalt reminiscence therapy group were related to objects, locations and people, past achievements, historical occasions and personal events as well as to sensitive issues. Interpersonal bonding occurred through links between the reminiscing of participants. Through the recall of past achievements, self-esteem was enhanced and older adults empowered through viewing themselves as personal experts on the times in which they lived. Memories also helped to identify unfinished business. In the third study, which considered psychological issues relating to death and dying, O'Leary and Nieuwstraten (2001b) found support for the stages of denial, depression and acceptance outlined by Kubler-Ross (1969). Emerging psychological issues included the fear of being forgotten, depression and the coping mechanism of deflection. The resources of song, prayer and humour enabled participants to speak about death.

Conclusion

In addition to researching the effectiveness of therapeutic intervention, professionals should also be willing to explore values and attitudes which may hinder their work with older clients. An awareness of the potential impact of ageist attitudes, such as the perception that later life is synonymous with decay and decline, is central to good practice.

With its emphasis on development and psychological growth, gestalt reminiscence therapy is particularly suited for enhancing the potential of older clients and enabling them to be self-determining. The wealth of experience, wisdom and skills acquired during a lifetime can be explored to improve quality of life. This valuable resource can be used to contribute to the betterment of society as is indicated by the exploratory studies conducted to date.

References

Berghorn, F.J. and Schafer, D.E. (1987) *The Urban Elderly*. Montclair, NJ: Universe Books.

Campbell, D.T. (1992) Treating depression in well older adults: use of diaries in cognitive therapy. *Issues in Mental Health Nursing*, 13: 19–29.

Conwell, Y., Duberstein, P.R. and Caine, E.D. (2002) Risk factors for suicide in later life. *Biological Psychiatry*, 52 (3): 193–204.

Engle-Friedman, M., Bootzin, R.R., Hazel, L. and Tsao, C. (1992) An evaluation of behavioural treatments for insomnia in older adults. *Journal of Clinical Psychology*, 48: 77–90.

Floyd, M., Scogin, F., McKendree-Smith, N.L., Floyd, D.L. and Rokke, P.D. (2004) Cognitive therapy for depression: a comparison of individual psychotherapy and bibliotherapy for depressed older adults. *Behaviour Modification*, 28 (2): 297–318.

Haight, B.K. (1988) The therapeutic role of a structured life review process in homebound elderly subjects. *Journal of Gerontology*, 43: 40–44.

Haight, B.K. and Dias, J.K. (1992) Examining key variables in selected reminiscing modalities. *International Psychogeriatrics*, 4 (Suppl. 2): 279–290.

Hsieh, H. and Wang, J. (2003) Effect of reminiscence therapy on depression in older adults: a systematic review. *International Journal of Nursing Studies*, 40 (4): 335–345.

Johnson, W.Y. and Wilborn, B. (1991) Group counselling as an intervention in anger expression and depression in older adults. *Journal of Nursing Specialists in Group Work*, 16, 133–142.

Kubler-Ross, E. (1969) *On Death and Dying*. London: Tavistock.

Lieberman, M.A. and Gourash, N. (1979) Evaluating the effects of change groups on the elderly. *International Journal of Group Psychotherapy*, 29: 283–304.

Morin, C.M., Kotwatch, R.A., Barry, T. and Walton, E. (1993) Cognitive behaviour therapy for late life. *Journal of Consulting and Clinical Psychology*, 61: 137–146.

Myers, J.E. (1989) *Fusing Gerontological Counseling into Counsellor Preparation: Curricular Guide*. Alexandria, VA: American Association for Counseling and Development.

O'Leary, E. (1996) *Counselling Older Adults: Perspectives, Approaches and Research.* London: Chapman and Hall.

O'Leary, E. and Barry, N. (1998) Reminiscence therapy with older adults. *Journal of Social Work Practice,* 12 (2): 159–165.

O'Leary, E. and Nieuwstraten, I. (1999) Unfinished business in gestalt reminiscence therapy. A discourse analytic study. *Counselling Psychology Quarterly,* 12 (4): 395–412.

O'Leary, E. and Nieuwstraten, I. (2001a) The exploration of memories in gestalt reminiscence therapy. *Counselling Psychology Quarterly,* 14 (2): 165–180.

O'Leary, E. and Nieuwstraten, I. (2001b) Emerging psychological issues in talking about death and dying. *International Journal for the Advancement of Counselling,* 23: 179–199.

O'Leary, E., Sheedy, G., O'Sullivan, K. and Thoresen, C. (2003) Cork Older Adult Intervention Project: outcomes of a gestalt therapy group with older adults, *Counselling Psychology Quarterly,* 16 (2): 131–143.

Rattenbury, C. and Stones, M.J. (1989) A controlled evaluation of reminiscence and current topics discussion groups in a nursing home context. *Gerontologist,* 29: 768–771.

Rickard, H., Scogin, F. and Keith, S. (1994) A one-year follow-up of relaxation training for elders with subjective anxiety. *Gerontologist,* 34 (1): 121–122.

Sheehan, N.W. and Nutall, P. (1988) Conflict, emotion and personal strain among family caregivers. *Family Relations,* 37: 92–98.

Sherman, E. (1987) Reminiscence groups for community elderly. *Gerontologist,* 27 (5): 569–572.

Stones, M.J., Rattenbury, C. and Kozma, A. (1995) Group reminiscence: evaluating short- and long-term effects. In B.K. Haight and J.D. Webster (eds), *Art and Science of Reminiscing: Theory, Research, Methods and Applications.* Washington, DC: Taylor & Francis

Walker, A. and Maltby, T. (1997) *Ageing Europe.* Buckingham: Open University Press.

7.16   Personal Growth

PAUL WILKINS

For some clients, the objective of working with a therapist is personal growth. That is, they are not in crisis, nor are they wishing to focus on a particular problem or issue (although addressing chronic behaviour patterns, psychosomatic symptoms, etc., may be part of their agenda). Such clients see themselves as functioning adequately in the world but are looking for ways of improving this functioning. In the parlance of the early twenty-first century, they may even be seeking enhanced emotional intelligence/emotional literacy or 'life coaching'. Trainee therapists, for whom personal therapy is a course requirement, may also present in this way.

For them, the element of 'compulsion' may also be an issue.

There is a possibility that some aspects of personal growth may best be facilitated working with a therapist whose philosophy is not necessarily compatible with that of the client. For example, a person who functions best on a feeling or intuitive level may have something to gain by working with a practitioner of a cognitive-behavioural approach. Similarly, a person whose forte is logic and rationality may benefit from working with, for example, a psychosynthesist who would also value emotional and spiritual dimensions of the self.

This way of working may provide a stimulating challenge but caution is required. If the challenge of a different way of viewing people and the world is too great, it may be impossible to bridge and little profit will result. There must be at least a genuine willingness to try something different and an element of curiosity on the part of the client, and perhaps the therapist will also need to be flexible.

There is an assumption that the techniques and processes of therapy may serve the purpose of personal growth. Rowan clearly makes this assumption when he writes:

> Personal growth is what happens when a healthy person with no obvious problems decides on a process of self-exploration for self-understanding, simply in order to be more able. ... In personal growth all the methods of psychotherapy and counselling can be used, and they have exactly the same effect. In other words, problems are uncovered and dealt with, barriers taken down, blocks removed, insights obtained, and so forth. (1983: 9–10)

Theoretically, there is no agreement between different modalities as to just what constitutes growth and what is its basis. Rowan's words reflect the idea of growth as an innate process of *self-actualization* on which humanistic approaches are often assumed to be predicated. For a person-centred practitioner, 'growth' is a biological metaphor implying direction and the *actualizing tendency* (something quite different from self-actualization) impels movement towards the fulfillment of potential, not to an ideal state (see Wilkins, 2003: 51–54). Psychodynamic and cognitive-behavioural therapists will have their own understandings of personal growth, but perhaps there can be broad agreement that it is about functioning more effectively in the world and/or an enhanced ability to freely choose a way of being. Goals of personal growth may include:

1 Increased self-acceptance.
2 An increased reliance on one's self as the primary evaluator of experience.
3 A better understanding of intrapersonal and interpersonal emotional process (and possibly intuitive and imaginative processes).
4 Enhanced spontaneity and creativity, that is the ability to adapt and respond more readily to change.
5 An ability for 'self-in-relationship' that is to be intimate, to have a sense of social order and social belonging and an understanding of interpersonal dynamics.
6 The capacity to enter into the emotional worlds of others while maintaining a sense of self.

The extent to which the term 'personal growth' has meaning or is of relevance seems to depend on the context. It is widely used in discussions of therapist training and continuing development (although this is questioned by Irving and Williams, 1999), but less commonly when referring to work with clients. It seems like that, as practitioners, we 'know' the difference between therapy and personal growth, but I suspect that this difference varies between individual therapists and between orientations. Although it hasn't been so hotly debated, the issue is similar to the difference between counselling and psychotherapy. It appears to me that some therapists define these as the same, some define them as different, and to argue against the other perspective results in a circular and sterile debate. So, it is for individual therapists to make up their mind what is personal development and whether they are prepared to work with people for whom this is an aim. Contingent upon this, they might like to think about how, if at all, their practice with such people should be different from people who seek 'therapy'. Is the way of working to be the same? Do they have the same responsibility towards someone who experiences themselves as 'well' as towards someone who is experiencing emotional or psychological distress? If they operate formal assessment procedures and offer formal contracts can this be the same process or must it be modified? Is the same level of personal disclosure appropriate or could/should it be different?

A personal example may help to clarify this. I do not distinguish between psychotherapy, counselling and personal growth. My role is to form a relationship in which the person in the client role *may* change and grow (to tend towards a process of functioning more fully – see Wilkins, 2003: 52). It does not much matter to me what this process is called. It is my clients who dictate the content, direction and pace of our interactions and whether there is an acute or chronic need, a niggling feeling that all is not well, a perceived deep disturbance or a quest for improved functioning. What I do and how I think and feel are much the same. This is philosophically, theoretically and practically consistent with my espoused core model. For others it will be different.

What is important about facilitating the personal growth of another is that therapists are very clear what expectations they have of themselves in that role. Supervision is an appropriate place to raise and develop this.

It is likely that any therapist being approached by an informed potential client seeking personal growth is being asked to use the same range of techniques as they would expect to use with any other. It is certainly reasonable to proceed on this assumption. This belief is based solely in my own subjective experience and that of other practitioners that clients are instinctively quite good at selecting an approach that meets their growth needs. Someone who experiences themselves as having needs relating to their early development may seek out a psychodynamic practitioner or perhaps a primal integrationist; someone for whom oppressive power is an issue may be attracted to person-centred; if a spiritual dimension is important, a Jungian therapist therapy or psychosynthesis guide might be appropriate; and those for whom logic and rationality are important might well be inclined towards the cognitive-behavioural approaches. Of course, even if this is true, it does not release the practitioner from the obligation to ensure that the potential client *is* informed of the approach and techniques they may encounter.

All of this may go some way to helping individual practitioners decide how to proceed when they are faced with a client who wants (or is required to have) personal therapy but has no particular agenda. The decisions will be based largely in the personal philosophy and mode of practice of the therapist. A suitable focus may be on life events or one or more of the aims of the personal growth listed above or something else mutually agreed, but perhaps this still leaves the exact nature of the sessions unclear. Just what is the therapist to do with a client who is in effect saying, 'Now I'm here, I don't know what to do' or (worse still) 'I'm only here because I have to be'?

There is a whole range of techniques which are designed to facilitate self-exploration and self-expression and many of them can be used in a way appropriate to a majority of therapeutic orientations. There may be some value in looking back as a way of understanding the present. This may indicate some kind of life-history work. The person in the client role may be asked to review significant life events from (or even before) birth to the present, perhaps even to project into the future. This can be as words spoken or written, 'actual' or fictionalized (offering clients the opportunity to express their lives in heroic, fairy tale or mythological form), or in the form of drawing, perhaps as a map, perhaps a figurative or even an abstract picture. How this is processed will depend upon the desires of the client and the orientation of the therapist. Some clients find the expression in itself of value, others wish to reflect openly upon their story, some invite the intervention of the therapist. Similarly, a person-centred therapist may focus on the process of producing the picture or story, a psychodynamic therapist may offer insight into the meaning of its symbols and metaphors, and so on.

An alternative to looking back is to concentrate on the mood or experience of the moment and to invite clients to express this in any chosen safe way (literal, creative, expressive). Or perhaps the focus can be upon the relationship between client and practitioner. Just what is happening within each of us and between us in this place at this time? The possibilities are limited only by the imagination of the client–therapist dyad. What is important is to recognize that personal growth work and/or the agenda-less client may involve moving away from a conventional 'curative' focus to one in which aims of expression, creativity, or enhanced spontaneity take precedence. How this is then dealt with will depend upon the need of the client and the orientation of the therapist.

There may be a temptation to think of clients seeking personal growth as in some sense 'easier' to work with than those perceiving themselves (or being perceived) as in distress or acute or chronic need. However, this might be a mistake and it would certainly be an unwise assumption. First, there is the possibility that the quest for growth is, knowingly or unknowingly, a 'presentation problem' masking some other need. Second, it is undoubtedly not true that people who function well in the world are necessarily 'problem free'. It is in personal growth work (as group participants or therapists) that practitioners can witness some of the most painful and distressing stories and encounter the most seemingly intractable issues of their therapeutic careers. In many ways, this could demand more of the practitioner and (in the process) be more debilitating of the client than any other kind of work. Of course, not everybody wishing to address their personal growth has such stories to tell, but nevertheless good supervision and support are at least as necessary as for psychotherapy and counselling, even if these are considered to be different.

Arguably, there is no need for any particular additional training for therapists working in the area of personal growth but it may be necessary to make a perceptual shift. Although the majority of therapists see themselves as operating in a way different from the 'medical model' of diagnosis/treatment/cure, there is nevertheless implicit in much of counselling and psychotherapy the notion that there is something 'wrong' with the person in the client role (perhaps whether they know it or not) and that it is the job of the practitioner to facilitate change, healing or cure. Personal growth work may involve letting go of this notion and accepting that some clients really do not seek to address past trauma, irrational thought patterns or conditions of worth, for example, but simply wish to be better at something (or several things). An appropriate analogy

is with physical development. There is a level of physical fitness which we accept as healthy, free of impairment but which we know can be enhanced in any of several ways, perhaps in terms of strength or speed, perhaps in terms of endurance or suppleness. This can be just as true of mental, emotional or spiritual abilities and this enhancement may be the objective of personal growth. Brown and Mowbray (2002: 130–142) explore these issues, writing about 'visionary deep personal growth':

> Rather than work of a psychological nature being the 'privilege' of a minority regarded as 'disordered' or in need of 'help', the benefits for society of 'average maturing adults' engaging in deep work to expand awareness and to 'know themselves' better are potentially huge. (2002: 141)

To all this should be added a warning. As well as being accepting of a client's agenda for growth and working with it, the practitioner must also be watchful for any emerging issue which *does* indicate a need for a remedial, therapeutic, healing approach and be able to respond appropriately. It would be just as mistaken to ignore what appeared to be a need for therapy when the expressed agenda is personal growth, as it is to assume that the 'real' need is therapy.

References

Brown, J. and Mowbray, R. (2002) Visionary deep personal growth. In C. Feltham, (ed.), *What's the Good of Counselling and Psychotherapy? The Benefits Explained.* London: Sage.

Irving, J.A. and Williams, D.I. (1999) Personal growth and personal development: concepts clarified. *British Journal of Guidance and Counselling*, 27 (4): 517–526.

Rowan, J. (1983) *The Reality Game: A Guide to Humanistic Counselling and Therapy.* London: Routledge.

Wilkins, P. (2003) *Person-centred Therapy in Focus.* London: Sage.

7.17   Counselling in Primary Care   ○○○

JOHN EATOCK

The main features of this setting

Any counsellor intending to work in primary care needs to think carefully about their own personality, for example 'Am I a team player or do I prefer to work alone?' To work in the NHS is to work within a very large and complex system. The NHS is also a rapidly changing and developing organization that follows an agenda that is very sensitive to government demands and those of the general public. If a counsellor's personality is not able to cope with constant change, as the NHS constantly seeks to reform and improve, then this is not the place in which to seek employment.

Mental health is just one of the three target areas of concern for the new NHS and the majority of mental health issues are now dealt with in primary care. There appear to be five significant factors that will impinge upon any counsellor working in this setting. They are:

- public protection and the resulting concern for patient safety;
- the quality of services and the relatively recent requirements of Clinical Governance;
- the emphasis on collaborative working;
- the need for evidence-based and therefore cost-effective practice; and
- the place of patient involvement and their feedback on NHS services.

If counsellors are not prepared to realize the need for, and accept the possibility of, statutory regulation of the profession in the near future as one of the means towards the protection of the general public, then they will find themselves out of step with the

general view within the NHS for all health care professionals to be formally regulated.

Similarly, counsellors working in primary care need to be sufficiently appraised of the Clinical Governance requirements of the NHS and of NHS and local Trust protocols on many matters which will impinge upon their professional practice. Issues such as record keeping, waiting times, confidentiality, and so on will all become the necessary concern of a counsellor working in primary care. Although counselling usually takes place on a one-to-one basis in primary care, there is no professional isolation; collaborative working is the order of the day for primary care counsellors. Close collaboration with referring GPs, practice nurses or other colleagues working in the talking therapies and other health care professions is commonplace and encouraged in primary care. Therefore, if someone is intending to work in primary care, then they need to consider if they are able to be part of the primary care health care team rather than an independent practitioner. Confidentiality can be an issue for those counsellors newly arrived in the NHS, where information sharing and collective confidentiality is normal practice and included in local and national protocols.

In addition there is a need to take into account the increasing emphasis on evidence-based practice. The *National Health Service Framework for Mental Health* (1999) emphasizes the need to employ techniques and practices for which there is some evidence. The *National Service Framework* sets standards: 'each standard is based on the evidence and knowledge-base available'. This 'evidence' usually means that provided by Clinical Guidelines currently being produced with alacrity by the National Institute for Health and Clinical Excellence (NICE).

Counselling and psychotherapy do not sit easily with the hierarchy of evidence espoused by NICE and, although this is being challenged, there is some pressure to use cognitive-behavioural therapy (CBT) and other theoretical models that are easily measured using randomized control trials (RCTs). A counsellor who is not adaptable or amenable to some evaluation of outcomes of their work will find primary care counselling a difficult area in which to work. In addition, a primary care counsellor needs to be aware that patient/client feedback will be taken into account, whether is it formally assessed by the Healthcare Commission or locally by their employing Trust.

Main features of the clients/patients encountered in primary care

The types of client that counsellors work with in primary care are those generally described as suffering distress in the 'mild to moderate range' of psychological mental health. The competence of the counsellor concerned, their training, and their place in the primary care mental health team will, of course, determine the types of client with whom they work. Increasingly, the GP is the first person that patients in any sort of distress will see. The GP will usually refer the patient to the counsellor. Primary care is becoming ever more concerned with 'well-being' and not only physical or diagnosable conditions. This being the case, counsellors in this setting may well find themselves working with a range of problems, including:

- various crises, especially those of limited severity or duration
- adjustment disorders (e.g. coming to terms with a medical condition)
- behavioural problems, including anger management
- relationship difficulties
- anxiety and/or depression
- grief and loss reactions
- the need to adjust to a diagnosis of major illness
- a somatic fixation
- those who need help with the management of chronic pain.

Depending on their training, a counsellor in primary care may also be able to help with psychosexual problems, substance misuse problems or eating disorders. There is a richness and diversity of clients who can provide very satisfying work for the competent practitioner in primary care.

The very nature of primary care counselling is that it is part of a team approach to patient-centred care. Ideally, a patient will be seen quickly and for a relatively short period of time by the practice counsellor. There is evidence that on average, where the counsellor is given autonomy, the number of sessions (i.e. 50-minute hours) is 5.9 per patient (Mellor-Clark et al., 2000). The six-session model of counselling has for various reasons, many of which are historical and economical, become the expected duration of counselling in primary care. It is important to bear in mind that the evidence concerning the length of primary care counselling is based upon the notion of the counsellor having some autonomy. This means a counsellor may see a patient for only one session or for many more and yet the evidence is that the average number of sessions is around six. It is not surprising that many counsellors working in primary care are trained or become adept at offering briefer time-limited therapy.

Another feature of the setting that concerns patients/clients is the mode of referral. The suggestion that counselling may be helpful invariably comes from one of the primary care team. There are few opportunities in primary care where self-referral is encouraged or permitted. Once it has been suggested to a patient that counselling may be helpful, it is becoming common for patients to be offered an opportunity to 'opt in' to counselling via a letter from the counsellor to the patient. This is particularly the case where a patient has been on a waiting list for some time. This encourages the notion of autonomy in the patient and takes away the feeling that they have been 'sent' by a member of the primary care team. Various referral guidelines have been produced for counselling services and psychological therapies. Some of these protocols are based upon local practice and familiarity with the competencies of local counsellors and others are based upon the increasing number of guidelines previously mentioned. Chief among these is the *Treatment Choice in Psychological Therapies and Counselling: Evidence-based Practice Guideline* (Parry, 2001) produced by the Department of Health.

Specific postgraduate training for counsellors working in primary care

Those counsellors intending to work in primary care, and also within the NHS, might reasonably consider what additional training is appropriate and helpful following their initial training. There is a growing consensus among professional counselling organizations that further specialized training is highly desirable for primary care counsellors. It may be that it will be provided as CPD (continual professional development) by their employing Trust or obtainable via professional organizations or educational institutions. The specific areas that have been found to be helpful and relevant are:

- an understanding of NHS structure and policy
- Clinical Governance
- NHS multidisciplinary working and collaborative care
- knowledge of mental health referral pathways and procedures
- assessment, including risk assessment and risk management
- time-limited/brief therapy
- psychotropic medication and the effects of other medication on health and well-being
- chronic illness and its impact on mental health
- focused, evidence-based practice
- audit, evaluation and research.

There will, of course, be some counsellors who have completed a training placement in primary care during their initial training and others become trainee counsellors in this arena post-qualification. In either case, the professional associations recommend this additional training and offer guidance concerning such placements.

From the list of areas it is apparent that there are recurring themes for counsellors working in primary care: collaborative working within a large organization, the need to work competently and within an evidence base and also to produce evidence and to audit their work.

Professional support for counsellors working in primary care

It is imperative that counsellors working in primary care maintain their membership of professional organizations. Generally speaking, the professional counselling organizations set standards of training, offer advice, and attempt to ensure that counsellors, in this setting as in any other, work ethically (Sharman and Seber, 2004). It certainly is the case with primary care counselling. Most NHS advertisements for counsellors to work in primary care specify that a counsellor is BACP accredited, or the equivalent. Within BACP there is a specialist advisor for health care counselling and psychotherapy, and also a team of advisors who are part of their specialist division, known as the Faculty of Healthcare Counselling and Psychotherapy (FHCP). FHCP is the largest and oldest membership organization for counsellors working in the NHS, and especially primary care. There is also the Association of Counsellors and Psychotherapists in Primary Care (ACPC), which is part of the United Kingdom Council for Psychotherapy. There are slightly differing standards for members but both provide invaluable support for counsellors and link them to the wider professional world of counselling and psychotherapy.

Ongoing professional support will obviously be that of counselling supervision. The supervision of primary care counsellors can be a contentious issue as counsellors are more accustomed to professional supervision that is not managerial, or of the case study type, than their other colleagues in the NHS. Where psychological therapy teams are established, this may well be provided 'in house' and counsellors often have to strive to establish their need for counselling supervision provided by a qualified colleague. In other instances, external counselling supervision may well be funded. Issues such as the need for counselling supervisors to thoroughly understand their supervisee's organizational context should be addressed. Trusts also have to take into account the need for confidentiality to be kept within various protocols that apply to the NHS when engaging external counselling supervisors.

Other NHS issues

Being one of the most recent additions to the range of professions working within the NHS, primary care counsellors have for some years been working hard, both individually and via their professional organizations, to establish themselves as a natural and essential part of service provision within primary care. Since December 2004, under the NHS Agenda for Change agreement, National Job Profiles for counsellors working in the NHS have been established. Counsellors will generally find themselves being paid in Bands 5, 6 and 7. In the near future it is hoped that a National Job Profile will be established for NHS Counsellors who manage or head services at Band 8. It is important for NHS counsellors to understand their relationship with graduate mental health workers, link workers, community mental health teams, and other primary care mental health workers. As well as being employed by NHS Trusts, some counsellors in primary care may well be employed as a result of funding from the new GP contract. An example of this may be through the new National Enhanced Depression Service in which some GPs are involved, especially those who are 'GPs with Special Interest' (GPSIs) in mental health. From all of this it will be apparent that a familiarity with, and an interest in, the ever-changing face of the NHS and primary care services is an asset to the primary care counsellor.

The future of primary care counselling

The increasing pressure to deal with the majority of mental health patients within primary care and to de-stigmatize psychological distress, means that in one form or another counselling in primary care is here to stay. Counsellors working in primary care can feel threatened and unsure of themselves in the face of many colleagues who may appear to do some or a part of their job. Nevertheless, there is a growing sense that if counsellors working in primary care can confidently establish their unique identity while remaining adaptable, confident and informed, and engaged with their context, they are well on their way to becoming part of the normal provision available to patients within primary care.

References

Department of Health (1999) *National Service Framework for Mental Health.* London: DoH.

Mellor-Clark, J., Sims-Ellis, R. and Burton, M. (2000) *National Survey of Counsellors in Primary Care: Evidence for Growing Professionalisation?* Occasional Paper 79, April 2000. London: The Royal College of General Practitioners.

Sharman, K. and Seber, P. (2004) *Guidance for Best Practice: The Employment of Counsellors and Psychotherapists in the NHS.* Rugby: British Association for Counselling and Psychotherapy/Faculty of Healthcare Counsellors and Psychotherapists.

Parry, G. (2001) *Treatment Choice in Psychological Therapies and Counselling: Evidence-based Practice Guidelines.* London: Department of Health.

7.18   Student Counselling   ○○○

ELSA BELL

The term 'student counselling' is used here to mean the formal, and clearly contracted, activity undertaken by those who hold the title 'student counsellor'. Its therapeutic focus makes it distinct from situations in which others, within educational settings, use what can be broadly termed *counselling skills* as an adjunct to their primary role, for example as tutors and careers advisors. It follows, then, that those who take up this formal activity need to be appropriately trained and experienced practitioners.

Context

Post-compulsory education went through a process of radical change in the 1990s. At one time it was easy to define the client population. Full-time students in colleges of further education were predominantly young people in the 16–18 age group who had opted for this route as an alternative to academic study at school or because it offered a more vocational focus. Additionally, there was usually a large cohort of part-time, late adolescent and adult students who attended college on day release from work in order to gain necessary qualifications or for specific skills training. In the main they knew why they were there and (allowing for the vagaries of adolescent development) were reasonably well motivated. Higher education at polytechnics, universities and a small number of colleges of higher education was available to about 5 per cent of the population. Students were normally 18–21 years of age and had achieved the necessary academic qualifications for the highly selective entry process. There was a small number of mature undergraduate students and limited places for post-graduate studies for those who expected to follow an academic career.

While the types of student profiled above are still entering both further and higher education, access has been widened to many who would never have imagined that they were capable of, or would be accepted into, studies beyond school level. All institutions are now challenged to meet the needs of those who have come from less traditional routes. Colleges of further education typically now include disaffected young people who would rather be at work, adults who feel that they have failed within the education system so far, other adults who feel compelled to retrain after the hurt and disappointment of redundancy, and an increasing number who have been recommended to take up study as part of the 'care in the community' approach to mental health care. These students enter alongside new types of students who have less troubled histories – women taking up educational opportunities after bringing up children; adults gaining accreditation for the previously unrecognized skills they have learned at work; people for whom English is a second language using the college as the first step on a ladder of opportunity. In higher education the scene has changed just as dramatically. Polytechnics are now universities: of the 36 per cent (England)–40 per cent (Scotland) of the population who now enter universities (with the present government committed to raising this to 50 per cent) as many as 40 per cent in some universities are over age 25 when they begin their undergraduate studies and some inner-city universities can proudly state that 45 per cent of their students come from minority ethnic groups. There has been a 58 per cent growth in non-European Union students since 1997, with a predicted further increase, particularly in taught postgraduate courses. Those who join these courses add to the richness of the university community but, equally, students who come to the UK for one or two years can bring with them all the attending issues of transition and culture change.

This constantly changing scene has challenged not just academics but all, including counsellors, who work within these institutions, to review their methods and the quality of their relationships with students. While most of the changes have been welcomed by those who support the widening of access to education, the parallel changes in funding systems and the overt ethos of a more 'product-oriented' system have been less welcome for those who believe that education should allow time for personal reflection and development. Thus academics and counsellors can find themselves questioning how far they can work with integrity in organizations where there seems less time to 'be' and to 'discover' and where there is more emphasis on the need to perform and produce (Smith, 1996). Nevertheless, and undoubtedly because further and higher education, of itself, represents the possibility of change for individuals, education has always been, and continues to be, an exciting place for counsellors who can be flexible within the boundaries of their theoretical and ethical frameworks.

History and development of student counselling

In common with counselling in most institutional settings, there is no single moment in time when the practice of student counselling can be said to have begun. Nor did it begin with one individual. Rather there were a number of influences that came together to produce the establishment of the Association for Student Counselling (ASC) in 1970. There appear to be three main routes of influence (Bell, 1996):

- Those who came from psychoanalytic or analytic psychotherapy backgrounds, such as Mary Swainson, who began the formal counselling work at the then University College at Leicester in 1948 that was to become the highly regarded service at the University of Leicester.

- The North American influence through the work of Carl Rogers and the development of personal guidance and counselling in American universities which, for example, saw the establishment of a service at Keele University. In 1973 the service was already publishing a history of its development (Newsome et al., 1973) and describing the importance of a single unit to deal with educational, vocational, social, personal and emotional problems.

- Specific individuals within the UK university health services, such as Nick Malleson, who, between 1949 and 1976, wrote and spoke on the impact of emotions on students' capacity to study, and lobbied to set up professional counselling services within universities. He was also the driving force behind the establishment of the Association for Student Counselling.

The Association for Student Counselling (ASC) set about developing professional standards and, in 1979, the membership agreed an accreditation procedure which defined appropriate training, experience and supervision and also insisted on renewal on a regular basis. This procedure was used as the basis for the development of the BAC (now the BACP) accreditation scheme in 1983. Although by then a Division of the BAC, the ASC elected to run its own accreditation scheme in parallel until 1997. Since the merger of the two schemes, ASC, now called the Association for University and College Counselling (AUCC), has been developing with the BACP additional criteria that will identify the particular skills required to work in student counselling. The ASC was also the first Division within the BAC to develop a scheme for recognizing training courses, and the AUCC, at its annual general meeting in 1999, agreed a procedure for accrediting services. This scheme, again, formed the basis of a BACP scheme and in 2004 the AUCC agreed to end its own scheme and be part of the wider BACP procedure. These initiatives demonstrate the impetus to ensure the development of student counselling as a professional activity and indicate the influence that AUCC has on the development of counselling as a whole.

Recognition of the professional nature of the role is mirrored in employment and salary structures. Partly because of the length of time student counselling has been established but, more particularly, because of the influence of the ASC/AUCC, student counsellors enjoy conditions of service that are less frequently found in other settings. Most are on permanent contracts on academic, or scales related to academic, rates of pay. In 2002/03 the AUCC noted that counsellors in further or higher education colleges were most commonly paid between £20,000 and £24,000, with Senior Counsellors rising to £34,000. In universities the most common rate of pay was £20–29,000 for counsellors while Heads of Services tended to be in the £30–34,000 range, with a small but increasing number earning over £35,000. The permanency of the contracts, including sickness and holiday entitlement, gives a measure of emotional security to counsellors and contributes to their capacity to cope with their constantly changing clientele. In addition, recognition within contracts of the need for professional development has been of benefit to counselling as a whole. Student counsellors have had time and the resources to contribute to the national debate on counselling standards by, for example, taking up places on committees or publishing in established journals. However, the changing financial situation in educational establishments has begun to make an impact. In 1994, the annual general meeting of the ASC was informed of the difficulty in finding a Chair for the Association. The amount of time required to carry out the duties meant that potential candidates felt that they could not guarantee the support of their institutions. Since then the membership has agreed to a less demanding time commitment from its Chair, but has also had to agree to recompense services from which Chairs come. These difficulties, in a division of BAC that has had a high profile and is financially sound, have major implications for those who wish to see counselling continuing to develop as a professional activity in the twenty-first century.

A framework for practice

During the 1960s and early 1970s a number of counselling services were established, particularly in the new polytechnics, where there was a commitment to student support through the development of departments of student services. In parallel, the National Union of Students (NUS), at its 1974 conference, passed a motion calling for the appointment of trained professional counsellors. Thorne (1985) records an extract from the resolution and comments on the shrewdness of the proposal:

> Conference urges that counselling services should be set up in each institution on the following basis:
>
> 1 Staff working in these services should be fully trained.
> 2 The service should be seen as an integral part of the educational programme complementary to teaching.
> 3 Services should not merely tackle individual problems as they arise but should look constructively at ways in which they can (a) adapt institutions, (b) improve learning situations, (c) help individuals to take proper advantage of the opportunities available to them, so that the typical manifestations of student problems do not appear.

The NUS was echoing the basis on which the ASC was defining the function of student counselling – that it should deal professionally with the range of problems presented by individual students in counselling sessions and additionally, and importantly, it should work preventatively and developmentally within the institution. National data collected annually by the AUCC show that these three elements of the role are still in evidence today.

More recently, policies and guidelines have emerged from influential bodies within education and health that have underlined the importance of student counselling services. Universities UK (2000, 2002), a grouping of Heads of higher education institutions, has produced guidelines for developing policies and procedures on student mental health and reducing the risk of suicide. The Association of Managers of Student Services in Higher Education (AMOSSHE, 2001) published a good practice guide on duty of care and responsibility in responding to student mental health issues. The Royal College of Psychiatrists (2003) produced its own report on the mental health of students in higher education. All of these documents stressed the importance of the developmental and preventative roles of counselling services as well as identifying them as the prime source of support for individual students.

Work with individual students

Student counsellors encounter people within a wide range of ages and backgrounds. The range and depth of the problems presented are equally extensive. This means that counsellors need to be confident and experienced enough within their chosen theoretical framework so that they can respond flexibly to individual need. In one session they may be dealing with a circumscribed problem that requires a decision to be taken. In the next the student may be presenting with a complicated family or psychological history where the source and influence of the present distress may be deeply masked, and which calls for intricate and sensitive work over a protracted period.

The two most frequently cited theoretical models used within student counselling are psychodynamic (based on Freud, Klein and Winnicott) and person-centred (based on Rogers). Although few student counsellors have been formally trained in cognitive-behavioural therapy, the influence of this theory has gained ground and in recent years some services have made specialist appointments in CBT. Underpinning any theoretical framework is the need to listen to, and work with, the student's subjective experience of being a student. What do academic terms, with their alternating beginnings and endings (Heyno, 1999), or examinations (Coren, 1997) with their overtones of competition, rivalry and judgement, mean for this particular student? Whatever the student brings to counselling, the very process of being in an educational institution will be present and significant. That process, the interplay of the objective and subjective experience of being a student, is the vital key in every piece of counselling work.

Work in student counselling is characteristically brief. This is not simply because demand is high, but because it is in tune with students' developmental needs. All students, of whatever age, use the educational process to engage with issues of independence and personal autonomy. Counsellors respect this desire for change and harness it as a therapeutic tool. They know also that only in exceptional cases

is it productive to encourage a long-term and dependent relationship in the counselling room. However, in these few cases it may be essential. Thus student counsellors must be proficient in the theory and practice of both brief and long-term therapies.

The generally brief nature of work with students should not be taken to mean that it is necessarily simple. Although some students require only a few sessions, there are many more within the 4–12 sessions group who bring serious problems that can tax even the most experienced counsellor. Issues of abuse, depression, delayed mourning, relationship breakdown, sexual identity and extreme anxiety are part and parcel of the work of a student counsellor. In addition, the degree of severity in the presentation calls for sound assessment skills. The AUCC's data define the levels of severity according to nationally agreed criteria (on a scale of 1–7 with 7 being the most severe). The 2002/03 annual survey recorded:

> The most common severity ratings for clients in each type of institution were 3 and 4. These points denote a considerable degree of distress impacting on one or several areas of functioning. A significant minority of clients were also rated 5 (distress affecting all areas of functioning with limited ability to cope). Interestingly, a greater proportion of clients were recorded at the higher ratings such as 5, 6 and 7 within universities than in either FE or HE colleges. This again points towards a growing demand for counselling support by students experiencing severe mental health difficulties within these contexts. (AUCC, 2004: 23)

The AUCC data, now collected over ten years, supports the warning signs identified in its earlier report, *Degree of Disturbance: The New Agenda* (1999), and it was this publication that prompted the Royal College of Psychiatrists to form its own working party (referred to earlier) on student mental health. Its report notes:

> The increasing number of students presenting with mental health problems reflects the rapidly increasing access of young people to higher education and the associated growth in student numbers. It also reflects the growing rates of

mental health problems in young people generally. Given the trends in the general population, it is hardly surprising that rates of psychological disturbance and psychiatric illness among students are rising. The effects are profound. They are felt by the students themselves, both subjectively and through the negative impact on their education, but also by those around them, including peers and family, and by the educational institutions that the students attend. (Royal College of Psychiatrists, 2003: 10)

A further challenge has been produced by the Special Educational Needs and Disability Act (2001). The incorporation of those with severe and enduring mental health problems into the Act means that educational institutions must not discriminate against students with mental health problems and must make reasonable adjustments to ensure that such students are given every possible chance to complete their studies. It will be interesting to note, from future AUCC data collection, how this change in policy is reflected in the degree of severity reported by counselling services.

University counselling services are now seen to be the primary mental health care option for many students (Royal College of Psychiatrists, 2003: 8) and this can been seen as equally true in further education. It is, therefore, axiomatic to say that this level of severity requires student counsellors to have the experience and skill to identify those at risk of psychological breakdown, and to be familiar and in regular contact with local medical and psychiatric services. For those counselling services where there are no links with distinct student health provision, this can be problematic. It is particularly so in further education where students often live at home but are drawn from a wide geographical area, thus making it extremely difficult for counsellors to build the kind of relationship with medical practitioners that will facilitate speedy and appropriate treatment.

Preventative work

There are many examples of this throughout the country. These activities are designed to prepare students for the task of being a student and to address problems before they arise. They include:

- instructions on study skills
- groups on anxiety management
- pre-examination groups
- discussion groups for those who have newly arrived in order to help them settle in
- courses in basic helping skills for students so that they can listen constructively to peers who are troubled and, equally importantly, learn when and how to refer to professional help.

Developmental work

This is more difficult to define but is based on the premise that counsellors bring a unique view of the educational process and are able to contribute to the culture and development of an organization. If institutions will allow, counsellors can indicate ways in which the organization might make the experience of being a student more productive, and ways in which it might already be causing stress and lack of productivity. In order to do this, counsellors need an understanding of organizational dynamics and the subtle skills that allow them to express their views in a way that is intelligible and acceptable to the institution. Counselling services are often viewed with great ambivalence by the rest of the institution. They can be seen as the focus of a hope that everyone can be helped and supported but they can also represent the part that the institution would prefer to ignore – the fact that all is not well and there are problems to be faced. The impetus is then to marginalize the service so that problems can remain hidden and silent (Noonan, 1983). Conversely, counsellors who do not engage with the institution develop only a partial view. They see only troubled people and therefore a troubled organization. By working collaboratively on institutional tasks, counsellors and academics gain a more realistic view of each other and the work they are both engaged in on behalf of students. Equally importantly, knowledge of the strengths, weaknesses and stresses of the institution are essential for successful work with individual students. Without it, only part of the student will be understood.

Challenges

Confidentiality

Educational institutions have sophisticated systems so that information can be shared about students' progress. A counselling service, with its commitment to confidentiality, may be seen as a direct and unhelpful challenge to the institution's aims. While the ethical basis of counselling must be preserved, student counsellors have to find ways of working with others who are equally concerned with the welfare and development of students. It can be argued that the therapeutic space for students is not contained, simply, within the counselling room, that there are many opportunities for change within the whole experience of being a student (Bell, 1999) and that when students give counsellors and academics permission to liaise with each other, the therapeutic work can be enriched (May, 1999). However, this liaison is always a matter for careful consideration and is one of the most complicated aspects of a student counsellor's role.

A variety of skills

As well as the necessary training to provide good quality counselling to individuals and, increasingly, in groups, student counsellors need to be competent in the following areas (Butcher et al., 1998):

- general management
- information management
- information giving
- facilitating self-help groups
- advising (counsellors do sometimes have to give advice, although they often insist on defining themselves as someone who never does!)
- liaison with, and giving feedback to, providers
- teaching and training
- advocacy
- supporting other key pastoral workers in the institution.

Since these skills are very rarely taught on established training courses, counsellors have to learn them 'on the job'. This is possible in a large counselling team where there are more experienced counsellors. Where counsellors practise on their own, it is possible but it adds considerably to the stress of the job.

Evaluation

Educational establishments now have to behave like businesses. The books must balance and counselling services have to be seen to be productive. The challenge for counsellors is to join with others in the institution who understand that academic productivity is achieved through the subtle interaction of skilled teaching with social, emotional, psychological and environmental factors. However, to do this, counsellors have to learn the language that will convince and produce evaluations of their work that show them to be in line with the aims of the institution. Rickinson and Rutherford (1995), in recording their research on increasing undergraduate retention rates at the University of Birmingham, have given an outstanding example of how this can be achieved without compromising the values that underpin counselling work.

Conclusion

Student counselling is one of the best-established branches of counselling. It has defined clearly what it considers to be within its domain and has, through the ASC/AUCC, achieved considerable success in achieving the aim of encouraging institutions to employ well-trained and professional staff. However, changes in the context, and the increasing pressure on organizations to cut costs, mean that there are many – and some would even say, exciting – challenges to be faced.

References

AMOSSHE (2001) *Good Practice Guide: Responding to Student Mental Health Issues. Duty of Care Responsibilities for Student Services in Higher Education.* Winchester: Association of Mangers of Student Services in Higher Education.

AUCC (Association for University and College Counselling) (1999) *Degrees of Disturbance: The New Agenda.* Rugby: British Association for Counselling and Psychotherapy.

AUCC (2004) *Annual Survey of Counselling in Further and Higher Education, 2002/03.* Rugby: British Association for Counselling and Psychotherapy.

Bell, E. (1996) *Counselling in Further and Higher Education.* Buckingham: Open University Press.

Bell, E. (1999) The role of education in the role of counselling in further education. In J. Lees and A. Vaspe (eds), *Clinical Counselling in Further and Higher Education.* London: Routledge.

Butcher, V., Bell, E., Hurst, A. and Mortensen, R. (1998) *New Skills for New Futures: Higher Education Guidance and Counselling Services in the UK.* Cambridge: Careers Research and Advisory Centre.

Coren, A. (1997) *A Psychodynamic Approach to Education.* London: Sheldon Press.

Heyno, A. (1999) Cycles in the mind: clinical technique and the educational cycle. In J. Lees and A. Vaspe (eds), *Clinical Counselling in Further and Higher Education.* London: Routledge.

May, R. (1999) Doing clinical work in a college or university: how does the context matter? In J. Lees and A. Vaspe (eds), *Clinical Counselling in Further and Higher Education.* London: Routledge.

Newsome, A., Thorne, B. and Wyld, K. (1973) *Student Counselling in Practice.* London: University of London Press.

Noonan, E. (1983) *Counselling Young People.* London: Methuen.

Rickinson, B. and Rutherford, D. (1995) Increasing undergraduate student retention rates. *British Journal of Guidance and Counselling,* 23 (2): 161–172.

Royal College of Psychiatrists (2003) *The Mental Health of Student in Higher Education: Council Report CR112.* London: Royal College of Psychiatrists.

Smith, E. (ed.) (1996) *Integrity and Change: Mental Health in the Market Place.* London: Routledge.

Thorne, B. (1985) Guidance and counselling in further and higher education. *British Journal of Guidance and Counselling,* 3 (1): 22–34.

Universities UK (2000) *Guidelines on Student Mental Health Policies and Procedures for Higher Education.* London: Universities UK.

Universities UK (2002) *Reducing the Risk of Student Suicide: Issues and Response for Higher Education Institutions.* London: Universities UK.

7.19   Telephone Counselling   ○○○

MAXINE ROSENFIELD

History

The use of the telephone for counselling, as distinct from befriending or the incidental use of counselling skills, was almost unheard of until the late 1990s in the UK, which is surprising since more than 90 per cent of the UK population in 1990 had access to a telephone in their place of residence.

A few counsellors had used the telephone for the occasional session when a client was unable to attend a face-to-face session, but conducting all counselling sessions by telephone, with no face-to-face contact at all, was seen by many counsellors as impossible and not an appropriate medium for the counselling process. Fortunately those counsellors who were willing to explore new concepts and broaden their horizons persevered and telephone counselling became an accepted mode of counselling. The 'old school' objections to telephone counselling, relating to the imagined impossibility of successful counselling when there is a lack of the visible perspective, have been challenged further with the rapid development of counselling by email. There is also the option to work by textphone with hearing-impaired clients, which is confidential as long as both parties have access to a private textphone.

For 20 years there has been an increasing acceptance of the use of telephone helplines for talking about feelings, finding information and seeking advice. The proliferation of helplines in the UK, which between them respond to millions of calls each year, has helped to encourage people to seek more in-depth, ongoing support by telephone. There are helplines for almost any social, health or welfare related situation or condition: asthma, cancer, drug misuse; for carers, for children, for lesbians and gay men, for older people and for anyone in a crisis, seeking help, information or wanting to be listened to then and there.

The demand for in-depth work by telephone has come from the public seeking more than any helpline can offer, as well as from counsellors seeking to explore the medium. The telephone offers a versatile counselling medium because, in addition to individual telephone counselling sessions, some counsellors run closed counselling groups by teleconference.

Working as a counsellor by telephone is significantly different from face-to-face work, as this section will highlight. It will also consider the standards and ethical considerations that should be taken into account to ensure that clients receive the best possible service from their counsellors and that the counsellors develop high quality practice.

Theory of telephone counselling

The key concept of telephone counselling is that appropriately trained counsellors use the telephone to conduct entire therapeutic relationships with clients.

Telephone counselling can have many advantages over face-to-face counselling. The lack of the impact of any visual impressions and assumptions or prejudices that occur when client and counsellor see each other in a formal counselling room, at home or in an office, make both parties focus on each other's voice tones and words. The anonymity of the medium is liberating for many clients (and counsellors!). The intensity of the interaction, because there is less opportunity for distractions during the session, since both parties are focused on words and voice tone alone, further enhances the development of the relationship. This usually enables a deeper therapeutic relationship to become established sooner than occurs in much face-to-face work. The entire process of counselling is generally 'accelerated' so that fewer sessions are indicated for the client to gain insight, understanding and/or empowerment.

Telephone counselling is an excellent example of an integrative approach to counselling. It can utilize aspects of psychodynamic orientations, person-centred approaches, brief therapeutic interventions and other humanistic methods of working. Cognitive-behavioural techniques may be used alongside interpretive psychotherapeutic disciplines. There is no doubt that transference and counter-transference occur, triggered by language, subject matter and, perhaps most important of all, by voice tones, pitch and accents. Goal setting and action planning may be as much a part of some sessions as is exploring the emotional aspects of the client's situation. Much effective work by telephone can focus on helping the client to draw on their own strengths-based orientation or on Rogers' 'self-healing potential'.

The telephone is excellent for crisis intervention and short-term work because of its immediacy and the fact that the clients only need say what they want to say, retaining some degree of anonymity or privacy if they wish. Indeed, one of the key reasons why people say they phone telephone helplines is because they are in crisis and want to talk anonymously and confidentially.

When someone contracts for telephone counselling sessions, some of their anonymity and confidentiality goes. As with helpline work, a point of crisis may be the trigger for the person to seek counselling but, unlike calling a helpline, the client is not totally anonymous. The client has to agree a contract for the work (see later) and therefore provide some personal details which they might not reveal if they are calling a helpline for a one-off call. The counselling relationship will last more than one session but may be relatively brief in comparison with face-to-face work, for example, often a block of six sessions is all that is used with a client who has a specific issue to discuss and explore.

Telephone counselling is an excellent way of equalizing the power relationship between the counsellor and the client. Both parties have to work with the unknown in ways that face-to-face counselling does not present. This is no bad thing for broadening the horizons of any counsellor. Further, it could be argued that the ultimate power lies with the client, who can choose to hang up at any time.

Accessibility of telephone counselling

Many people can have relatively easy access to a telephone, but for a one-hour counselling session finding a place that is private, quiet and uninterrupted is more difficult. Call boxes are not ideal if they are in public places, so there is a very practical deterrent for some people from using telephone counselling. Similarly, mobile phones are not always ideal as they may be neither as confidential nor as reliable in sound quality as regular phone lines.

On the other hand, if one has access to a phone and a quiet room, telephone counselling makes it unnecessary for the client to have to travel to see a counsellor and means that the session can take place even if the client or counsellor are not in the same location for each session. This makes it a very accessible medium for people who travel in their working lives, for example. It also makes counselling more accessible for someone who has limited mobility or limited time.

Illness does not always prevent telephone counselling sessions from taking place, whereas face-to-face sessions might be cancelled. People who are terminally ill or limited in their ability to go out of doors can still receive counselling. Carers who might wish to go out but cannot find respite cover or cannot guarantee to be able to find cover regularly at a specific time for an appointment can benefit from telephone counselling.

The cost of a regular phone call is generally less than the cost in time and travel to go to a counsellor, making telephone work more financially accessible

in many cases (see also contracting, below). Clients can choose to work by telephone with counsellors who are not geographically accessible to them. This enables people to find a specific counsellor for a specific purpose if they wish. Some people even work together when one party is outside their own country.

From the counsellor's perspective, the telephone can be liberating, enabling them to operate from any environment that is quiet and where they are uninterrupted. It may also mean that the counsellor can work with a wider variety of clients at a greater range of times.

For telephone group work, the teleconference can bring together people from all over the UK and include people from overseas, as long as each can be in a quiet, private place. This can lead to groups being created for people who are linked through rarer situations, specific illnesses, age or any other common theme.

Contracting and ethics

Some of the issues to be considered for contracting have already been addressed, such as location and time.

A contract must be agreed at an assessment session which should be free of charge except for perhaps the cost of the phone call and can last for up to an hour. The contract should include:

- terms of reference for both parties, outlining the goals or aims of the sessions;
- the length of each session, which should be fixed at no longer than an hour and no less than 45 minutes;
- the time interval between sessions, ideally a week;
- the number of sessions before a review – a block of six with a review during the fifth is suggested. Further blocks of four to six sessions can be agreed as desired;
- the location, to ensure privacy and no interruptions;
- who calls whom and therefore pays for the cost of the call;
- what is considered a late start or no-show and what happens in these instances;
- what type of notes, tapes or other means of recording the sessions would be acceptable – if tape recording is to happen, both parties must give overt consent;

- what the client might do to 'leave the room' to adjust themselves psychologically after the session;
- methods of payment – how much, when and how it will be received;
- what the terms are for the cancellation of a session;
- whether or not photographs will be exchanged to provide a visual image (some counsellors prefer not to do this and to work with the impact of the lack of any visual clues if it is appropriate);
- what would constitute a breach of confidentiality and why;
- how confidentiality relates to technological issues for both parties (see technology, below);
- what happens if the client calls between sessions.

Ethical issues include the counsellor explicitly adhering to existing codes of conduct such as those published by BACP. There is also an ethical consideration regarding payment. It is possible for a counsellor to purchase a premium rate tariff telephone line. In this case, the client calling the counsellor pays more than the cost of a regular phone call and the 'profit' could constitute all or part of the counsellor's fee. If this is to be the case, the counsellor must inform the client or the potential client of the likely cost per session in advance. Ethically, it is considered inappropriate for the counsellor to use this premium rate telephone line for the assessment session. In addition, such a tariff does not permit any discretionary rate for clients.

Mixing face-to-face sessions and telephone sessions is not acceptable for telephone counselling. This is because the mixing of the media will affect the transference issues/power relationship/dynamics of the situation, with visual assumptions or judgements or prejudices changing the dynamic of the phone relationship thereafter. When a counselling relationship is being established, this could have quite an impact on the trust and the development of the partnership. It might be agreed at contracting that photos could be exchanged, with an awareness that this can bring a chain of judgements into being which could affect the development of the relationship. This could, of course, be addressed during subsequent sessions.

Confidentiality comes into both contracting and ethics. If the client calls the counsellor who operates anything other than a freephone service,

the counsellor's phone number will be itemized on the client's telephone bill. This might not always be desirable for the client and the counsellor cannot prevent this from happening unless the service is provided as a freephone service. Further, if anyone in the client's house dials 1471 they can find out the last number the client called. If they have the service '1471 Extra', the last 5 numbers dialled will be revealed. So if this presents a problem for a client they need to remember that after finishing the call they have to dial at least one and possibly five other numbers to prevent anyone else knowing that they have called the counsellor.

Telephone technology and the confidentiality of the relationship

Confidentiality is one key factor of which both parties need to be aware with regards to technology. For the client, this includes the itemized telephone bill mentioned above.

If the counsellor is calling the client and the counsellor's number is not permanently barred, they may wish to use the 141 one-off block (number withhold) code. This may not be a concern in the usual course of events, but perhaps the counsellor is calling at a time when the client would not expect the call and therefore the counsellor wishes to preserve the confidentiality of the relationship from anyone else who might answer the phone. The block will enable the counsellor's number to be anonymous.

There are other technological developments and services available, such as anonymous call reject (ACR), where if either party has their number permanently barred and the other has ACR, the call will not get through in the first place. Other technology options, such as call waiting, should not be used by the counsellor at all, since the tone that comes on the line if another call is trying to get through can be distracting. The implications of these and other technological developments should be fully explored by any counsellor seeking to work by telephone as they may affect the ability of either party to make safe and confidential contact.

Training and supervision

One assumption throughout this section is that the counsellor should hold at least a full Diploma or Degree in counselling and have experience of face-to-face counselling practice before they commence telephone work. Currently there is no specific, accredited training in the UK solely for telephone counselling although there is plenty of training for helpline counselling skills. One 'B' unit of a National Vocational Qualification within the advice, guidance, counselling and psychotherapy units is concerned with telephone skills, aimed at helplines. The Telephone Helplines Association also offers a range of training courses, again suitable for helpline work, rather than in-depth telephone counselling work.

Group facilitation requires additional skills for telephone groups and, again, there is no specific training qualification applicable to this at present.

It is not enough to assume that a good face-to-face counsellor will have, or be able to develop, the necessary skills for telephone counselling and there is a worrying trend in trained counsellors or therapists developing a telephone practice without ever receiving qualitative feedback about their voice, style and manner – things that should been assessed during a telephone training course.

A skills checklist for the trained counsellor/therapist starting telephone work

- How do you sound?
- Is your accent pronounced or could it be off-putting to the client group you seek to attract?
- Are you able to work with silence on the phone? Be aware that a silence of a few seconds on the phone often seems like many minutes and the usual counselling/therapeutic interpretations of silence and methods of responding to silence need to be adapted for successful work on the phone.
- Are you confident and skilled at handling distress by phone?

Supervision by telephone

This is growing as counsellors seek out supervisors for specific reasons. The issues relating to skills transfer and voice tones are the same as for the client–counsellor relationship, and not all supervisors can or should adapt to the phone. At the very least, a supervisor might ask a fellow supervisor to do an objective assessment for voice tone, manner and style before offering themselves in this medium.

Counsellor accreditation

It is possible to include some telephone counselling work as part of the individual counsellor accreditation process of the BACP. However, there are no specific criteria that acknowledge the specialism of the medium and case work will be presented in the same way as for face-to-face work, which seems to me to negate the impact of the specialism.

Cultural issues

Helpline statistics have shown that among some minority communities there is less use of the phone for support. While there is no reason to doubt this, it is essential not to make any assumptions, and so discussion of the ethnic origin and cultural identity of both client and counsellor should preferably form part of the assessment session.

Prejudice and/or assumptions can form a large part of telephone work based on voice alone and the counsellor should always discuss their frame of reference with a new client to reduce or, ideally, prevent this.

One example of what happens when this does not take place is linked to accents or dialects. An accent or dialect often sounds more pronounced on the phone than it would do if the people were face to face. If, for example, English is the counsellor's first language and the client has it as a second language, or vice versa, this could inhibit someone from attempting to explore the medium.

Conclusion

The telephone is an excellent medium for enabling the client to feel free to talk about anything. It is also an excellent way of broadening the counsellor's horizons. It is one of very few counselling techniques that enable an equalizing of power in the client counsellor relationship. Further, it constantly reminds the counsellor of the skills of listening and really hearing.

Further reading

Rosenfield, M. (1997) *Counselling by Telephone*. London: Sage.
Telephone Helplines Association (1999) *Guidelines for Good Practice* (3rd edn). London: THA.

7.20 Transcultural Therapy ○○○

CAROL MOHAMED

Counselling and psychotherapy aim to offer a safe relationship within which clients can explore personal difficulties and, through the development of a deeper understanding of themselves, move towards change. The therapeutic process is therefore primarily dependent on the quality of the relationship between the therapist and their client. The amelioration of pain and healing is achieved through this dynamic, creative alliance. An important starting point in this relationship is trust, a necessary part of any therapeutic alliance and, with this, the validation and integration of all aspects of a client's experience into the therapeutic work. This is particularly important where there is a culturally or racially differing pairing between the therapist and client.

Psychotherapy and counselling have avoided or made limited attempts at conceptualizing issues relating to racism and its impact. Approaches that focus on racism and cultural issues arose as a reaction to the failure of mainstream therapy to take account of experiences of racism, discrimination and prejudice, and the ways in which cultural and racial differences are addressed in a therapeutic relationship. Inter-, trans- or multi-cultural approaches have been embraced as therapeutic techniques that take account of the internal and external realities of the patient. They also advocate that therapists should have an awareness of their own prejudices and ways of stereotyping in order to be able to identify the way that racist metaphors appear within the therapeutic encounter.

I will explore some of the elements of this therapeutic application and attempt to investigate the significance of the effects that emerge as a product of racism. I will be using the term 'black' to include all who have a shared experience of denigration, genocide, hatred and slavery as a response to their skin tone.

I am also interested in the way that 'blackness' can be used as a container in a therapeutic situation and will examine some of the ways that intra-psychic conflicts can appear in the therapeutic situation and used, through interpretation, to uncover and expand an understanding of a patient's psychic structure and conflicts.

History and context

Black people in Britain have historically faced many social disadvantages, such as poverty, inadequate housing, unemployment and poor educational opportunities. This may be compounded by the experience of sexism, homophobia and other prejudices. Additional factors, such as migration and dislocation from the country of birth, can contribute further to the social difficulties experienced by black people in this society. The contemporary perception of Britain as a multi-ethnic society has fostered the view that *ethnic* or *immigrant* means *black*. When the experience of racism is added to the difficulties experienced by black people, it is hardly surprising that these stresses can have an impact on an individual's sense of well-being. Data about the mental health experiences of people from black and minority ethnic groups compared with native-born white people show worrying tendencies. The mental health organization Mind have produced a factsheet 'Race, culture and mental health' (Hatloy, 2002) which states that: 'This fact sheet explores statistical information relating to the disporportionately excessive numbers of Black people and Irish being diagnosed with mental health problems and entering psychiatric hospitals, both as formal and informal patients' (2002: 9). In addition, the report provides other statistics which raise questions about the basis of diagnoses and the extent to which racism and prejudice underpin this practice.

- Black people are more than twice as likely to be hospitalized for mental distress than their white counterparts.
- Recent research suggests that although more black Caribbean people are treated for psychosis, it is unlikely to indicate a greater predisposition to this illness but is more indicative of misinterpretation, by professionals, of the way that symptoms are expressed.
- African Caribbean men are 4.3 times more likely to receive a diagnosis of schizophrenia at their first admission and women 3.9 times more likely than their white counterparts.
- Although there is no evidence indicating that African Caribbean people are more likely to be aggressive than whites, psychiatric staff are more likely to perceive them as potentially dangerous to others (data from Hatley, 2002).

One of the consequences of racism is that black people become identified not as individuals, but by the perception of their skin colour and what it symbolizes. This means having to embody the negative projections that this society places on to blackness.

Therapeutic approaches

Kareem describes an intercultural therapeutic approach as:

> A form of dynamic psychotherapy that takes into account the whole being of the patient – not only the individual concepts and constructs as presented to the therapist, but also the patient's communal life experience in the world, both past and present. The very fact of being from another culture involves both conscious and unconscious assumptions, both in the patient and the therapist. I believe that for the successful outcome of therapy it is essential to address these conscious and unconscious assumptions from the beginning. (1992: 5)

I think that multicultural therapy approaches are based on a western structure but have as their fundamental underpinning an understanding and consideration of the internal and external experiences of being assigned as 'other' and then denigrated. This framework offers an arena, within a therapeutic situation, where these matters can be tackled. I would argue, however, that a weakness of this model is that it has limited itself thus far to gaining an insight into the impact on the 'object' of racism, black people, but stops short of expanding the thinking to encompass an understanding of the psychopathology of the subject of racism, white people.

It is important to remember that people are not static, but are able to change and adapt to their internal and external situations. The position of black women, in particular, shows how important it is to be able to address change in order to accommodate different circumstances. Black women have had to be adaptable to find a way through a history of subjugation during slavery, and, in the contemporary situation, to cope with the dual discrimination of racism and sexism, while maintaining an image of independence and strength. In doing so, they have been able to encompass an identity that has integrated the strengths and skills developed as a result of a history of adversity.

In order to avoid dealing with material that may be perceived by white therapists as frightening or too challenging, there may be a tendency to want to match culturally different clients with therapists of a similar background, rather than developing the skills required. The idea that black or Asian clients can *only* be seen by black or Asian therapists may be an opportunity to collude and avoid confronting the key issues. This therapeutic approach acknowledges difference and considers the way that external experiences are internalized, as well as transforming relationships with others. One of the main aims of therapy is to offer a relationship, within a structured environment, in which the therapist enables the patient to develop a better and deeper understanding of themselves and, in this way, achieve change. This is dependent on the therapist possessing an understanding of the psychology, pathology and social experiences of individuals as well as of themselves. I would therefore argue that therapists need to possess a deep level of self-awareness that enables them to recognize all the assumptions that they bring to the therapeutic encounter. The process of self-awareness involves not only intra-psychic factors, but also facing the oppression, discrimination, stereotyping and racism within this society. Lago and Thompson (1996: 48) argue that therapists need to have a 'structural awareness of society and a personal awareness of where they stand in relation to these issues'. Failure to do so, they suggest, may result in judgments being made on the basis of the individual's own prejudices. This is true for both the client and therapist. They state that:

> At worst, the white therapist might respond in all sorts of ways to the visibility of difference, the black skin, failing completely to recognise the inner 'being' of the client that may be profoundly rooted in the same culture as the therapist. Only difference will be seen, the similarity of culture perhaps goes unrecognised. (1996: 32)

Society's norms inevitably affect the way that individuals see themselves, particularly when these perceptions are embedded within language itself, and are used quite unconsciously and uncritically. In this society, black often represents bad and inferior, and white good and superior. A transcultural therapy approach takes account of a client's internal and external experiences. Kareem (1992: 14) suggests that 'the very fact of being from another culture involves both conscious and unconscious assumptions, both in the patient and the therapist'. In order to take account of a client's total experiences, these assumptions must be addressed at the beginning of therapy. The way that these issues are addressed is the essence of a transcultural approach.

The therapist and the therapeutic relationship

A transcultural approach requires therapists to be conscious of their own race-related attitudes and prejudices, and to be aware of the way that these may impact on their behaviour towards culturally and racially different clients. As the establishment of a working relationship is at the core of any therapy, it is important for therapists to understand what they are bringing from their own culture and history to this encounter. A therapist who is unaware of their own prejudices and stereotypes will form an opinion of a culturally or racially different client based on their own perceptions rather than on who the client actually is. Becoming conscious of parts of oneself that are unpleasant or uncomfortable is a difficult challenge for any therapist, but a client cannot be helped to think about their experiences of racism if the 'therapist is unable to think about it themselves. It may be experienced by the client as something that cannot be discussed and that is too contentious.

The relationship between the therapist and client may be more complex when the former is black. They will have experience of racism and oppression as well as having had to live within two cultures. In the therapeutic setting, they will be perceived as being in a position of power, but will probably become the object of a white client's racist projections. For a black therapist, their colour is likely to be a conscious or unconscious feature of the relationship, both with a black and white client. As a part of the therapeutic process, the black counsellor will be presented with the stereotypes and prejudices of society. These have to be worked through in the relationship by interpreting and enabling the client to understand what their prejudices mean to them. It is very difficult work for black therapists, who need to have an understanding of their own experiences of racism in order to be able to work with the negative projections of white clients. It is important, while examining the process of racism within the relationship, for a black therapist to be aware of the feelings that the client evokes in them. Failure to do so can lead, as Thomas (1992) suggests, to a distancing from a client who is experienced as racist and demeaning.

Transcultural therapeutic skills and knowledge

Through examining the meaning of a transcultural approach, it appears that therapists need to develop their knowledge and skills in specific areas, in order to offer a process that takes account of the client's total experience. Two areas of particular significance in transcultural therapy practice are language and the process of communication, and the dynamics of power in the therapeutic relationship.

Communication is the main tool of any psychotherapeutic relationship. The therapist's role is to make sense of what is expressed by the client, verbally and non-verbally, consciously and unconsciously. In a transcultural situation there is a great deal of potential for misunderstanding and miscommunication in a number of ways.

Language

Clients may find themselves trying to express thoughts and feelings in a language that is not their mother tongue. It is difficult enough to find the words to express emotions without the added burden of having to find the words in another language. How sensitive are therapists to the difficulties that clients of other races or cultures may be experiencing when trying to find the words to express themselves? One could argue that the process of psychotherapy and

counselling is so unlike the way that we communicate ordinarily that it is like speaking another language. In trying to achieve this using another language, it is hardly surprising that there is the potential for misunderstanding, and for the process to become counter-therapeutic. The use of interpreters is an important way of ensuring that a therapy is made accessible, as well as facilitating an understanding between the client and therapist. There are, however, potential difficulties that arise from the use of the interpreter as an intermediary. Meanings can change within a translation, as they are dependent on the interpreter's understanding and accurate conveyance of what is being communicated. For example, a client who says that they are feeling 'sick and tired' might be expressing a feeling of exasperation. Without an understanding of what the client is attempting to communicate, the interpreter might represent this as the client feeling ill.

Body language

The potential for misunderstanding is also possible when interpreting body language. Therapists can misread physical actions if they are not culturally aware. As with words, non-verbal cues can have different meanings or a different significance within different cultures. For example, in the Caribbean, direct eye contact while conversing might be considered rude or insulting. In Britain, however, not having eye contact could be interpreted as shyness, slyness, or even disrespect. Similarly, the tone and volume of the voice, or physical proximity, are other potential areas for misunderstanding.

Emotions

The manner in which emotions are expressed can be very different across cultures, and is a third area for potential misunderstanding by therapists. For example, consider the manner in which grief is expressed. In Britain, it is usually very private and rather hidden. In many other cultures (e.g. in the Caribbean and in Asia) death and grief are more open, public affairs. A lack of understanding can result in a mis-diagnosis or misrepresentation of an individual's state of mind. It was interesting to observe the media reaction to the public show of grief following the death of Diana, Princess of Wales in 1997. It caused much consternation because people were reacting in a manner that was outside the cultural norm. It was described by some as a sort of madness that threatened to upset and unbalance the status quo. The conclusion that difference necessarily means dysfunction is the perception that people of different cultures face every day. It may be difficult to hold on to one's identity when it is experienced as a threat to the majority culture.

The achievement of good communication is an important way of facilitating a therapeutic relationship. Poor communication can result in a lack of understanding and a difficulty in achieving trust in the relationship. Therapists therefore need to be conscious of the way that they use language themselves, and of the way that they interpret what others communicate.

There is an inevitable power inequality in any therapeutic relationship, because the therapist maintains a professional persona, revealing little about themselves, while the clients, who are typically in need, reveal a lot of detail about themselves. This dynamic is compounded when the therapist is white and the client is black, because it reflects the common power imbalance in this society. Therapists therefore need to consider what this means in the context of the relationship. It is important that a white therapist is aware of how this is perceived by the client, and is cautious not to replicate the societal imbalance within the relationship. If a therapist has been able to acknowledge and differentiate their own issues concerning power and oppression from those of the client, an opportunity for open dialogue is created.

Non-western healing models

Cultural norms have a profound impact on the way that individuals seek help, and on what is viewed as problematic. There is a danger in assuming that a western model of healing is necessarily what will be most helpful to culturally different clients. For example, in the West Indies, problems are more likely to be dealt with within the extended family, or by consulting a church minister or spiritualist, who

is a part of the community, rather than seeking help from a stranger.

Summary of transcultural skills and knowledge

To summarize, the specific skills and knowledge that transcultural counsellors need to possess include:

- an awareness of what assumptions they bring to the therapeutic situation – this should include cognizance of their prejudices, attitudes, stereotypes and racism;
- an awareness of their own cultural history, and knowledge of other cultures;
- knowledge of the histories of oppression and racism that form the context for their work with clients from other cultures;
- the ability to operate between diverse cultures;
- an openness to challenge and to review their own ideas and attitudes to issues of race and culture;
- a commitment to proactive anti-discriminatory practice.

Sue et al. (1995: 624–644) identify specific skills and knowledge that contribute to the achievement by counsellors of transcultural competence. These include:

- a sense of comfort with differences that exist between themselves and clients in terms of race, ethnicity, culture and beliefs;
- an understanding of the way that race, culture and ethnicity may affect personality formation, vocational choices and psychological disorders, help-seeking behaviour, and the appropriateness or inappropriateness of therapeutic approaches;
- an awareness of their negative emotional reactions towards other groups that may prove detrimental to their clients in counselling. Counsellors should be willing to contrast their own beliefs and attitudes with those of their culturally different clients;
- recognition of the limits of their competencies and skills;
- willingness to seek consultations with traditional healers or religious and spiritual leaders and practitioners in the treatment of culturally different clients where appropriate.

Supervision and training

Supervision and training provide important opportunities for therapists to explore issues concerning their transcultural work. Training courses for supervisors are now addressing transcultural issues as a theme worthy of consideration. It is therefore the responsibility of supervisors and consultants to consider these issues in respect of their own practice and their personal attitudes.

The therapeutic situation

Transcultural therapists need to listen and learn from their client, without making assumptions, and without being afraid to ask questions if they need to clarify meaning. As d'Ardenne and Mahtani suggest:

> clients from other cultures have already had to overcome many barriers in everyday life, and may find the counselling environment a further struggle. Transcultural counsellors understand this, and try to meet their clients more than half way. (1989: 5)

Clients will arrive with preconceptions and attitudes about the therapist and the therapeutic process. Clients from other cultures will also bring skills that they have had to acquire to enable them to function within different cultures. These include linguistic, interpersonal and social skills, and the ability to translate these functions in order to operate within different cultures. Furnham and Bochner (1986) suggest that these skills enable culturally different people to contend with an alien culture while holding on to their own cultural identity. This is an important issue for both therapists and clients, regardless of their colour.

It may be a very complex task for a therapist to offer insight or an understanding of the issues that a client is bringing if it is outside their cultural context. For example, with a client who is bringing issues about her relationship with her family, the therapist may not be able to understand the client's dilemma of both wanting to separate from the family and also feeling a bond and loyalty that makes this impossible. They also need to be aware of their own feelings about the issue. A client born in this society and raised within a different culture (e.g. British-born Asians and African Caribbeans) may feel caught between cultures, and experience conflicts. Therapists who do not have any insight into the cultural background of their clients may view cultural differences as a deviation from the 'norm' and as the client's failure, rather than as a reflection of who they are. A therapeutic framework that takes account of the internal and external world of a client is a good basis for working through cultural issues as well as the impact of racism on black and white people. Holding both of these perspectives is what will ensure that the individual's total experience and uniqueness is seen and acknowledged. A focus on racism alone casts individuals into homogeneous groups and loses sight of individuality. Agoro says:

> While an anti-racist perspective provides an analysis of the way racism impacts on the lives of black and white people, this in no way diminishes the reality that black people in Britain come from diverse cultural communities and religious backgrounds, and within black communities there is a complexity of individual experiences which are mediated by a multitude of factors such as age, class, gender, sexuality etc. (2003: 29)

Working transculturally requires an approach that increases the accessibility of counselling and psychotherapy to clients. The assessment should therefore take account of differences, and offer an approach that does not leave clients alienated by the 'rules' and culture of counselling and psychotherapy, which may occur if they have not been fully explained. An example is the importance of a time boundary around the beginning and ending of sessions. It is important to enable clients, who are largely unfamiliar with the tenets of therapy and counselling, to find a way into it that enables them to work comfortably and usefully within it. This may mean demystifying the process by explaining, for example, the meaning of boundaries, the style of therapy being offered, (e.g. non-disclosure by the therapist), and why the therapist may sit quietly at the beginning of a session, rather than setting the agenda.

The aim of the assessment is to determine the type of help that may be suitable for a client, or what other options may be available. It is possible that clients from other cultures do not meet the criteria prescribed by a therapist who has not taken account of cultural differences. A client who does not communicate in a manner that meets the expectations of the therapist may not be considered suitable as a counselling client. An example is where English is the second language, and the expression of feelings through language, particularly to a stranger, is not the custom for a client. It is therefore important that a flexible approach to the initial assessment is adopted, and that it is not structured in a way that is predominantly excluding rather than including. If therapists have a set of rigid and culturally specific criteria, they will inevitably eliminate all of those who do not fit or meet the cultural expectations. In describing different approaches to assessment, d'Ardenne and Mahtani (1989) conclude that assessments must recognize the problem and construct ways of resolving it in a manner that is reasonable to both the client and the therapist. In making therapy and counselling accessible to culturally different individuals, it is important to offer a demonstrable understanding of their life experiences, and a therapeutic relationship in which the reality of racism can be acknowledged and explored from the beginning.

It is important to explore certain features of the therapeutic relationship with the client at an early stage, to ensure that they are made explicit and can be talked about openly, such as a cultural or gender difference. Certain theoretical approaches advocate waiting for the client to raise issues, but it may be the responsibility of the therapist to identify and, in so doing, give the client permission to talk about differences between them, and to acknowledge the existence of a power imbalance in the therapeutic relationship. Therapists who are able to work through these issues for themselves will be able to work more creatively with culturally and racially different clients.

Thomas (1992) suggests that white clients bring assumptions about the superiority of whiteness and the inferiority of blackness to the therapeutic situation, and these may be hidden in symbols. The task for a black therapist is to contain the client's negative feelings and transform them into an understanding of themselves. Cultural and racial differences are fertile areas for the eradication of bad or unwanted feelings. A black therapist may, for example, be viewed by a white client as useless or second-rate, a view that is often expressed (or thought) within this society. The therapist may represent for the client unbearable feelings that the client has about her or himself, and will therefore need to be able to process what is being communicated in order to offer a useful interpretation of this to the client. It is a huge task, for a black therapist, to work with overt racism and prejudice. Where there is a black therapist and black client, there will be some shared understanding and experience of the issues, which provides a starting point of explicit understanding. The impact of these experiences will vary depending on social and psychological factors. The therapist may, however, have to face being seen as second best.

Clinical manifestations of racism and transference and counter-transference issues

The impact of racial differences in the transference mirrors what happens externally. Blackness inevitably acts as a potent trigger and container for the projections of unwanted feelings from the patient, but possibly also the therapist. If psychoanalysis does not engage with this issue directly, why assume that therapists and analysts have enough personal awareness not to use blackness as a container themselves, or that it is not embedded in the countertransference?

Black and white people are perceived differently, not just in terms of their skin tone. A white person will not immediately be predominantly defined by their colour or race, but by who they are or what they do. Black people, however, are immediately identified by their race, and all the accompanying stereotypes associated with 'blackness'. Who they are becomes a secondary factor. This is an important issue in a therapeutic situation because a white therapist may unconsciously see a black patient rather than the person they are. If therapists have not examined the way that they stereotype and make judgements, they may deny what they have projected into blackness. Most white people can choose how they are seen and, as such, individually identify themselves. For black people, the way that they are perceived and treated will usually be on the basis of stereotypes and projections. This means that they are already defined, which limits the ability to present oneself as an individual, with all of the complexity and contradictions that accompany this. A therapist cannot simply remove all the baggage of a history of oppression and degradation that a black person is forced to carry, based on a desire to see everyone as the same. Webb Johnson and Nadirshaw argue that:

> One of the prevailing assumptions about the 'Asian Community' ... is that it represents an homogeneous group of people who share a common culture and heritage. Since there are as many diversities as similarities between people of South Asian origin in terms of culture, language, religion and historical legacy, the existence of a monolithic 'Asian culture' becomes an untenable concept. (2002: 121)

These are the very issues that have to be openly confronted and accepted as an important aspect of a black person's experiences. It is comparable to issues of gender. A therapist who tries to view a patient as if their gender is irrelevant will deny major aspects of that person's internal and external experiences.

In my experience of working psychoanalytically with black and Asian women, I have found that in addition to other ordeals that bring them to therapy, the experiences of racism and depression are often cited as presenting problems. Black women have had to find a way of contending within a society in which sexism, racism and homophobia are deeply embedded. The image of beauty in this society is Euro-centric and white, which means that many black and Asian women do not fit the concepts of what is acceptable and desirable, and are, by implication, viewed with disdain. Many black women present a strong, self-reliant image, an understandable way of coping in an openly hostile society. A therapist who has not engaged in an understanding

of racism may not see this. They may not see the cost of having to present an external image that prevents the recognition of vulnerability and needs.

Evans-Holmes (1992) expresses a view of race within the transference as useful and facilitative. I will explore this view of the potential value of the manifestation of racism within the therapeutic encounter. Although potentially wounding for a black therapist, I believe that the presence of an easily identifiable container condenses and acts as a catalyst for the arousal and uncovering of unbearable aspects of the psyche which are made available for splitting and projection.

Evans-Holmes strongly argues for an elucidation and interpretation of racist material with patients because it inevitably conceals underlying conflicts. Racism within the transference could arguably be viewed as a manifestation of aggression – the death instinct. The elaboration of racism as a defence, through interpretation, enables a further exploration of the underlying conflicts. I am suggesting that blackness can be used in the transference in many ways, for example, a countertransference feeling of being a useless therapist related to a patient's envy of the therapist's capacities, and the projection of her own feelings of inferiority. I think that the technique in working with racism is similar to working with dreams, because racism often appears in material as a metaphor. This means working with symbolic representations, and the technique of uncovering the manifest content of the material through associations to get at the underlying meanings. Evans-Holmes, a black analyst, presents an interesting example of this in her work with a white patient. The patient was describing a conversation with his elder brother, who had been complaining about the proposed Martin Luther King national holiday:

> Mr D: I got very tense when he talked endlessly about gains and how we didn't need another national holiday. I got more and more upset and confused as I thought about death and sex. I thought again about how I used to shoot (the patient stuttered) racoons as a teenager. (Mr D switched suddenly to talking about what his brother had been telling him about his sexual exploits.) (1992: 6)

Associations to this uncovered a link between the dark and racoons. He eventually said, 'Black men are called "coons". They get shot down' (1992: 6). (Note the earlier reference to Martin Luther King). Evans-Holmes suggests that this racist metaphor was strongly related to ambivalent feelings that the client had towards his father. The therapist's blackness was used as a container, enabling his underlying murderous feelings towards his father to be projected on to blackness.

Discussion

I have attempted to demonstrate that racism operates at a deep psychological level and is a way of defending against deep-seated anxieties. These anxieties find a container that acts as the peg on which to hang the hat. Blackness is made into a suitable container because of the mythology or archetypal symbolism associated with it. The skin is a psychologically binding mechanism. In combination, blackness and the skin offer a powerful and easily identifiable container for anxieties and conflicts. I believe that the most basic and fundamental aspects of the psyche come into play within racism, and that its structure acts as a gladiatorial arena for our most basic fears and anxieties. Racism is rooted in a fantasy or false creation rather than objective truth and reality. Truth is disregarded as irrelevant because of internal psychological needs that have precedence over any regard for reality and objectivity. These psychological needs become sanctioned by cultural, economic, social and political factors. These external factors, coupled with individual needs, ensure that the objects of racism meet the stereotype that is imposed on them and is an important element of this dynamic. I believe that these fantasies emanate from unconscious wishes and desires, and attach to racist structures, which then act as a container within which they can be acted out, and anxieties relieved. Kovel (1970) argues that these fantasies are not unique to racism but are parts of the psychic struggles that we all face. He states that:

> racism is a specific historical situation in which some elemental aspects of human experience are turned toward the classification (and oppression) of people with different ethnic traits. Race fantasies are applied only at second hand to races; they are actually generated in the universal human setting of childhood, and used by culture to handle its historical problems. (1970: 47)

Conclusion

The therapeutic process is dependant on the therapist's ability to make a connection with a client that will form the basis of a trusting, working alliance. Therapists who do not have experience of forming relationships with culturally or racially different clients outside a therapeutic situation may form views based on a limited encounter and understanding of black people. White therapists who have no experience of communicating and sharing ideas with black people, and in operating outside their own cultural boundaries, will be limited in their ability to achieve a real dialogue, and form a trusting relationship with black clients. Under these circumstances it is important for therapists to develop an awareness of their own assumptions and to develop skills and knowledge that will enable them to work transculturally. Lago and Moodley argue that:

> If counsellors and therapists have also undergone self-exploration of their own 'race-thinking' and have a sophisticated awareness of their own cultural roots they will be in a better position to consider aspects of dissonance in their views of the client (countertransference, projections, stereotypical reactions, etc.). (2002: 45)

If white therapists only make relationships with black people in a professional setting, they maintain a position of power that is likely to adversely affect their ability to achieve an alliance based on trust. Therapists are taught to concern themselves with the inner realities of their clients without really understanding the way that social experiences have had an impact on their clients' lives. This means that they are relatively unprepared to help clients who bring real experiences of racism and oppression. Therapists therefore need to be careful not to deny or minimize experiences that their clients may bring simply because they are outside their own. Black clients have talked of feeling 'pathologized', as if their experiences of racism are their problem, and therefore not real. Agoro (2003: 29) says: 'Within anti-racism there needs to be an implicit recognition of the diversity and richness of black cultures, along with an explicit value base in the structural analysis of inequalities and an, unequivocal and proactive commitment to pathologizing and eradicating racism'. A lack of awareness can lead to a mirroring, in the therapy, of the inequalities and oppression within society. A black client will have had experiences of powerlessness and disregard. This can easily be replicated if the therapist is not genuinely accepting of, or accessible to, their client.

References

Agoro, O. (2003) Anti-racist counselling practice. In C. Lago and B. Smith (eds), *Anti-discriminatory Counselling Practice*. London: Sage.

d'Ardene, P. and Mahtani, A. (1989) *Transcultural Counselling in Action*. London: Sage.

Evans-Holmes, D. (1992) Race and transference in psycho-analysis and psychotherapy. *International Journal of Psychoanalysis*, 73: 1–11.

Furnham, A. and Bochner, S. (1986) *Culture Shock: Psychological Reactions to Unfamiliar Environments*. London: Methuen.

Hatloy, I. (2002) Race, culture and mental health. *Mind Factsheet*. London: Mind.

Kareem, J. (1992) The Nafsiyat Intercultural Therapy Centre: Ideas and experiences in intercultural therapy. In J. Kareem and R. Littlewood (eds), *Intercultural Therapy: Themes, Interpretations and Practice*. Oxford: Blackwell Scientific Publications.

Kovel, J. (1970) *White Racism: A Psychohistory*. New York: Pantheon and London: Free Association Books.

Lago, C. and Moodley, R. (2002) Multicultural issues in eclectic and integrative counselling and psychotherapy in perspective. In S. Palmer (ed.), *Multicultural Counselling: A Reader*. London: Sage.

Lago, C. and Thompson, J. (1996) *Race, Culture and Counselling*. Buckingham: Open University Press.

Sue, D.W., Arrendondo, P. and McDavis, R.J. (1995) Appendix III. In J.G. Ponterotto, J.M. Casas, L.A. Suzuki and C.M. Alexander (eds), *Handbook of Multicultural Counseling*. Thousand Oaks, CA: Sage. pp. 624–644.

Thomas, L. (1992) Racism and psychotherapy: working with racism in the consulting room – an analytic view. In J. Kareem and R. Littlewood (eds), *Intercultural Therapy: Themes, Interpretations and Practice*. Oxford: Blackwell Scientific Publications. pp. 133–145.

Webb Johnson, A. and Nadirshaw, Z. (2002) Transcultural counselling: an Asian perspective. In S. Palmer (ed.), *Multicultural Counselling: A Reader*. London: Sage.

7.21   Workplace Counselling   ○○○

ADRIAN D. COLES

Brief history and development of workplace counselling

The history of workplace counselling has not been extensively recorded. Most counselling texts mention the transition of welfare into counselling, and examples of how organizations and companies develop counselling for their employees can be found in Coles (2003). Usually, counselling 'evolves' in a company, sometimes introduced by an individual who has benefited from personal counselling and decided counselling would help others in the company as well. Sometimes counselling is directly introduced into an organization because of a specific event, for example, traumas that encouraged British Airways to establish Crewcare, or the Bradford fire in 1984 that enabled police authorities to offer counselling to their employees, such as the Northamptonshire Police Authority. Organizations seek counselling in much the same way as an individual does – something happens, something becomes unbearable, or preparation for a big event pushes the organization to seek other resources, resources they may not have.

Today, counselling is a regular feature of many diverse workplaces and often a service that most human resources/personnel departments are familiar with and have access to, or they will know how to access psychological help for employees. Workplace counselling is usually accessible to employees through employee counselling services or employee assistance programmes (EAPs). Many counsellors in the UK use workplace counselling as a regular source of income and often counsellors will be contracted to an EAP to provide short-term work.

There are various reports and research documents (McLeod, 2001) that claim to identify the incentives for providing counselling services to employees. Some employers seek counselling services to counteract legal action, and although these motives may not be ideal conditions for establishing a service, they are common features and need to be recognized by the counsellors involved. In 2002, the Court of Appeal made some important judgments on work-related stress cases and this may have an influence on the provision of counselling services as an employer can use a counselling service as part of their defence in court against stress claims. The Health and Safety Executive (HSE) in 2003 served an Improvement Notice against a hospital because of work-related stress suffered by employees. Kinder (2003) outlines some of the issues brought forward by the Court of Appeal decisions and the HSE, and their possible impact on contemporary workplace counselling services.

Other influences on the evolution of counselling in industrial, commercial and service sector settings include the actions and interests of certain key figures in the counselling world. In North America, individuals who developed early self-help programmes for employees with alcohol problems helped to establish EAPs. Gerard Egan (2002) provided a simple counselling model that was easily applicable in many different helping scenarios (the Three Stage Model). In the UK, individuals such as Michael Reddy developed a small company (now ICAS [Independent Counselling and Advisory Services]) and Michael Carroll (1996) wrote the first main 'text' for workplace counselling; both were instrumental in the development of workplace counselling. Currently, the EAP market is almost reaching saturation point, with some commercial EAPs engaged in a fierce price war.

Professional representation for counsellors and EAP workers continues to be developed by the Employee Assistance Professional Association (EAPA), the British Association for Counselling and Psychotherapy (BACP), the Association of Workplace Counselling (ACW) and Counsellors in Local Authorities (CILA). With more people spending more of their lives in their working environments, some employers have had to adapt to provide what employees need in order to keep them at work. Counselling can keep an employee functioning, on task and as part of the workforce. It can also enable employees to leave abusive working environments, or challenge the hostile and sometimes 'alien' experiences of being an employee.

Key characteristics

Counselling in a workplace is a different experience for counsellors and clients. It has important differences from counselling in private practice, health care settings or educational institutions. The organization/employer that pays the counsellor, either directly or indirectly, is always present in the session, consciously or unconsciously. This can take many forms, from the number of sessions contracted per employee, to specific confidentiality boundaries that are established between counsellor and client and employer. Clients in this setting are 'employee-clients'. The employer is providing the service for them. The counselling service may be part of a 'benefits package', an occupational health department, a human resources section or a one-off service brought in to help with specific events such as trauma or redundancy. Although many employee counselling services are open to self-referral, the employers' motivations for providing the service need to be explored and understood by a counsellor entering into a contract with an organization, as these background motives can contaminate a counsellor–client relationship.

There are several common models for contracting counsellors to provide workplace services: internal, external and mixed. Examples of internal services include the employee counselling service at Birmingham City Council or Hampshire County Council. Here the counsellors are paid employees of the council and employees refer themselves for short-term counselling. The counsellors are line-managed and some provide other function, such as training on stress, bullying, counselling skills, etc.

External services are provided for a variety of private and public sector services by an EAP provider. The counselling is delivered by sub-contracted independent counsellors and case-managed by the EAP for the company-clients that purchase the EAP's services.

An example of a mixed model can be found at Northamptonshire County Council where a network is case-managed by council employees and provided by a group of independent counsellors contracted to the County Council.

These models are successful for different reasons but are primarily designed to fit the organizations that need them. Usually, counsellors in any of these models will work to ethical guidelines and codes of good practice developed by the EAPA and/or the BACP and ACW.

Competencies of workplace counsellors

As well as any general or theory-specific counselling training, anyone entering the ethically fraught and complex world of workplace counselling needs to have a firm understanding of the following issues:

- the dominance of short-term work
- how confidentiality of the counselling relationship will be maintained
- whether the counselling role will remain a purely counselling role or will be expected to expand to encompass other roles and functions – dual and multiple relationships
- how the organization will measure the effectiveness of counselling – evaluation.

Short-term counselling

Most counselling in this setting is short term. Usually, companies will have a set number of sessions per employee, per annum. The average is usually around five 50-minute sessions per employee. Often finance determines the number of sessions, although in some organizations, the status of the employee may be a factor. For example, a senior employee may be entitled to more sessions than other employees (this can provide fascinating insight into a company and its hierarchy).

Confidentiality

A counsellor may find that the ethics of confidentiality, which are an essential part of their daily practice, may not be understood or acknowledged by a company contracting for their services. There may be fundamental divergences between counsellor and company around the need for confidentiality, the 'exceptions to the rule' and cultural expectations about secrecy, knowledge and power in a company. To ignore the dynamics of confidentiality, and of secrecy in a company, is unwise. Client consent is needed to breach confidentiality in some circumstances but rigid adherence by a counsellor to private practice principles of confidentiality may be inappropriate in this setting.

Egan's advice is useful. He usually starts a conversation with an employee by saying: 'Both of us are paid by this organization, and you might benefit from our discussion' (Coles, 2003: 58). He suggests that confidentiality is a concept that comes from contemporary concern for the individual rather than for the group. However, a confidentiality neurosis can be found in many organizations. Understanding an employee's anxiety about 'not letting others know' or 'I don't want to be seen using the counselling service' tells the counsellor much about the individual and culture of the organization. The counsellor needs to establish at the beginning of the work with an organization, or when taking on a contract with an EAP, what the expectations about 'feedback' into the company will be, what they are prepared to deliver and what use is made of information provided. A counsellor may be asked to provide the company with useful statistics and information about general themes, trends and problems in a workforce without compromising individual identity.

Dual relationships

Many counsellors are asked to deliver non-clinical functions and tasks inside companies. Often these roles will include training, team development and team building, stress audits, mentoring and conflict resolution. Sometimes referred to as 'multi-tasking' (Gabriel, 2002: 5), the workplace counsellor needs to be aware of the compromises and difficulties that can arise. Occasionally, a counsellor may be asked to provide counselling to a close colleague or line manager, and the counsellor needs to be clear, sensitive and firm in the face of such demands. Individual client–counsellor relationships may be damaged when a client sees a counsellor perform in a different environment, displaying other skills or being involved with other employees. Of course, the counsellor needs to be firm with their boundaries, but sometimes he or she will need to be part of the work community and this can be a struggle. Other employees in a company may have an interest in the counselling that an employee is receiving. For example, the human resources department may want to know how many sessions an employee has had and to report this back to line management, even though the counselling service is described as confidential. Or an employee may be *sent* to counselling as part of a disciplinary procedure. These interests and problems are common to many workplace counsellors and require sensitive understanding and clarity.

The Tavistock Consultancy Service (TCS) is a successful example of in-depth and structured applications of psychological theory and practice to organizational issues and, as such, represents some of the most profound benefits that companies can take from counsellors and therapists in these settings. Counsellors in the workplace can be rich and productive resources and can extend their value beyond the counselling room.

Evaluation

Measuring the psychological benefits to employees of workplace counselling is as difficult today as it was for Freud when he started developing his approach. There are some more sophisticated tools for evaluation now, and the era of evidence-based practice has made measurement part of modern therapeutic practice. Carroll (1996) described the need for counselling evaluation and Mellor-Clark et al. (1999) have been instrumental in the development of the CORE (Clinical Outcome in Routine Evaluation) system (CORE System Group, 1998). However, whatever tool is used to evaluate a counselling process, the counsellor's main concerns need to be who is using it and what for? As an EAP contractor, a counsellor will usually be evaluated on a routine basis with feedback forms completed by the client and returned directly to the EAP or organization.

Other important issues for a counsellor to explore further include close attention to the physical setting of the counselling/consultation room, case management, the acclimatization process, the management of counsellors and the absence of fees in the employee–counsellor relationship (Coles, 2003).

Conflicting values

Conflicting roles, functions and needs in a company can reveal a variety of opposing values, concerning confidentiality, integrity and efficiency, for example. The variety of boundaries, dual relationships and multiple roles in an organization can be a source of difficulties and ethical dilemmas for many counsellors. However, there are other problems that counsellors experience working in organizations, such as trying to apply psychological theory and practice in environments that function on principles directly opposed to the growth and development of individuals and groups. Marx (1844) described the alienation of labour in his economic texts and Freud ([1927] 2001) explored the function of work as a means of repressing and controlling instincts which can lead to profound dissatisfaction and uninterest in work, for many people 'are not spontaneously fond of work' ([1927] 2001: 186). A recent exploration of these themes can be found in Bunting (2004).

Workplace counsellors may need to reconcile (with their supervisors and peers) how they work ethically in unethical settings and how they reconcile their own internal conflicting values to turn up for work and help employees survive or leave organizations.

Trends

Counsellors and employers will decide the future of workplace counselling. The main developments will include:

- small businesses using counsellors
- the expansion of telephone counselling
- the customization of workplace counselling/ EAP services
- the development of 'behavioural risk' services for employers
- coaching and brokerage of EAP/counselling services
- joint-working and possibly amalgamation of work-place counsellor professional bodies and accreditation.

I offer this challenge to counsellors. Many of the workplace counsellors that I know and have met offer excellent therapeutic short-term interventions to thousands of employees every working day of the week, around the world. When I have asked them about their theoretical influences and training backgrounds, I am offered the whole spectrum of coun-selling, psychological and psychotherapeutic trainings that workplace counsellors have com-pleted. However, most of them operate in more or less the same fashion. What does this mean? Some areas of development for workplace counselling may include answers to the following questions:

- Is theory irrelevant to this setting? Does the setting take precedence over the theory?
- Is short-term work an entity in itself regardless of setting/training?

- Is any short-term training good enough for workplace counsellors?
- Can long-term therapy find a place in the workplace setting or are the only constraints financial? (I have met some therapists who use long-term contracts with employees, so maybe short-term is not the only fix?)
- The introduction of more theory into the setting may test our theories and further develop and expand them to include thinking more globally about what work means for practitioners and for employees. Would it be wrong to consider not just a 'workplace counselling' component on a Masters degree course, but a 'psychodynamic workplace counselling course', a 'person-centred workplace counselling module' or a CBT employee counselling programme'? What do the different counselling schools have to offer when exploring the workplaces that most of us spend most of our lives in?
- What are the career prospects for some counsellors in this setting and what training is available for them if they want to manage a counselling service?

Other future features for counselling in this setting include competition. Counsellors and com-mercial EAP providers may price themselves out of employee markets. Employers may lose interest and see counselling as a fashionable employee benefit, and litigation may make it more difficult to employ and use counsellors in a workplace setting. The watering down of counselling services into 'jack-of-all-trades' personnel professionals may aid the demise of counselling in this setting. However, therapy survives. Psychoanalysis has withstood a hundred years of criticism, exploration and develop-ment and still inspires and stimulates deeper interest in the human psyche. There are pitfalls and changes to come for workplace counsellors, but also many challenges for counsellor writers and practitioners to consider as we struggle, survive and develop in the time-consuming, alienating but necessary, endlessly fascinating world we know as 'work'.

References

Bunting, M. (2004) *Willing Slaves: How the Overwork Culture Is Ruling Our Lives.* London: HarperCollins.
Carroll, M. (1996) *Workplace Counselling.* London: Sage.

Coles, A. (2003) *Counselling in the Workplace*. Maidenhead: Open University Press.

CORE System Group (1998) *CORE System (Information Management) Handbook*. Leeds: CORE System Group (www.coreims.co.uk).

Egan, G. (2002) *The Skilled Helper* (7th edn). Pacific Grove, CA: Wadsworth.

Freud, S. ([1927] 2001) *The Future of an Illusion*. Standard edition, Vol. 21. London: Vintage.

Gabriel, L. (2002) Working in a multi-task job. *Counselling and Psychotherapy Journal*, 13 (4): 5.

Kinder, A. (2003) Stress in court: the consequences for employment tribunals. *Counselling at Work*, (Winter): 43. Rugby: BACP.

McLeod, J. (2001) *Counselling in the Workplace: The Facts*. Rugby: British Association for Counselling and Psychotherapy.

Marx, K. (1844) Estranged labour. *Karl Marx and Frederick Engels Collected Works*, Vol. 3. London: Lawrence and Wishart.

Mellor-Clark, J., Barkham, M., Connell, J. and Evans, C. (1999) Practice-based evidence and the need for a standardised evaluation system: informing the design of the CORE Systems. *European Journal of Psychotherapy, Counselling and Health*, 2: 357–374.

Postscript: Summary and Future Forecasting

COLIN FELTHAM AND IAN HORTON

We have, we believe, roughly the following scenario. Counselling and psychotherapy have gained in acceptance by the general public, in spite of initial cultural resistances and undermining by critics (see, for example, Furedi, 2004). In 2004, the Future Foundation found somewhat surprisingly – in a telephone survey of 1,008 people – that an estimated 21 per cent of people in the UK had now had counselling or psychotherapy. Previous estimates had been around 5 per cent at most. The BACP (2004) summarized this and similar trends towards greater acceptance:

- 83 per cent of British adults have had or would consider having counselling or psychotherapy.
- 72 per cent believed that people would be happier if they talked more about their problems to a counsellor or psychotherapist.
- Over 90 per cent consistently agreed that anyone can suffer from depression.
- 63 per cent agreed that they know someone who could benefit from counselling and psychotherapy.
- 45 per cent of employees expressed a desire for the opportunity to avail themselves of a confidential counselling service provided by their employer.

Counselling continues to expand – in particular in primary care – and to some extent this fortunate expansion also makes what some see as unfortunate medical and bureaucratic inroads on the largely humanistic culture of counselling. Psychotherapy continues to maintain a separate identity and to flourish and be modified in somewhat different ways but is also inevitably affected by wider trends. In 2004, a sharp tension appeared between the British Psychoanalytical Society and the newly formed College of Psychoanalysts, with serious questions raised about the rights to ownership and training

in psychoanalysis. Simultaneous expansions and adaptations of mental health nursing, psychiatry, psychoanalysis, clinical psychology and counselling psychology are accompanied by some inevitable misunderstandings and tensions between all these professions. The British Association for Counselling became the British Association for Counselling and Psychotherapy in 2000 and hence lent weight to greater rapprochement, but in most respects the mental health professions have not chosen to move forward on the agenda of professional convergence since the challenge issued by James and Palmer (1996).

The professionalization agenda came to an impasse in recent years over various matters: disputed distinctions between counselling and psychotherapy, frictions and altercations between professional bodies, disagreement over the best way forward *vis-à-vis* voluntary or statutory regulation, and so on. At the time of writing, definitive legislation is mooted to be in place by 2008 at the earliest. Norms are already in place with bodies like the BACP, in terms of training, accreditation and supervision, but the title of counsellor and psychotherapist will probably also be clarified and protected in the near future. This may offer protection to a majority of practitioners and clients but some therapists remain altogether opposed to professionalization, which they see as an unwise and fundamentally ethos-changing shift in values (House, 2003). Exactly where dissenters will take their objections, and even more importantly their practices, remains to be seen, but the mainstream battle over professionalization appears to be over. Counselling and psychotherapy are joining the established professions, just one of the signs of which is the increasing domination and influence of higher education institutions as providers of training and qualification.

One of the most significant planks of professionalization is evidence-based practice (EBP). Counselling and psychotherapy have followed medicine and other health care professions in engaging in and promoting research to establish the effectiveness and efficacy of the psychological therapies (Rowland and Goss, 2002). This is sure to yield short- to medium-term gains for this profession – in public relations, parity with other health care professions, enhanced employment opportunities, clinical guidelines, and clearer information available to clients – but it also contains dangers. While EBP adherents reassure us that therapeutic creativity and individuality will not be stifled, the tendencies for available evidence to favour short-term and cognitive-behavioural therapies is clear. In the long term, EBP holds many dangers and threats that require critical analysis (Feltham, 2004). It is important that some maintain a critical opposition to this trend, whether at the level of promoting alternative research methods or as an eloquent defence of the values of humanistic therapy.

Debates continue among therapists as to the needs for, and benefits of, empirical research, supervision, personal therapy and continuing professional development (Feltham, 1999). It is often taken for granted that continuous refinements in ethical underpinnings, complaints procedures, public relations and other endeavours bolster the value and effectiveness of therapy. A former emphasis on 'good enough', humanly fallible practice subtly concedes to the government-driven ethos of continuous improvement, value for money, efficient use of time, professional and clinical excellence. Counselling and psychotherapy – and their valuing of genuineness, difference and holistic aspirations – do not necessarily dovetail seamlessly with government socio-economic, health and educational policies, nor indeed with the pressures of increasingly globalized capitalism.

Integration of models of therapy has partly continued but has also partly been resisted. Hence, more and more practitioners identify themselves as integrative (and the brave as 'eclectic'). To some extent this tendency has been fostered by the day-to-day pressures and prompts of working in primary care settings and by short-term contracts with

clients: practitioners have, in the best interests of clients, frequently looked for and forged the most practical therapeutic packages. But in parallel with this, many 'new' models of therapy, including new brief models, have arisen. Expediency, market forces and innovation combine to produce a continuing abundance of new models in a manner that works against integrative convergence. Solution-focused therapy has now become well established as one of the most widely practised models of therapy, due not only to its brevity but also to its hopeful, anti-pathologizing, forward-looking ethos and interventions. Beginning to make an impression on the UK scene from the USA are models like interpersonal psychotherapy, dialectical behaviour therapy (DBT) and mindfulness-based cognitive therapy (MBCT), with the promise of addressing the needs of many 'difficult' clients in particular (often, those diagnosed with borderline personality disorder). Interestingly, DBT and MBCT both incorporate meditational features, a development that could signal a hitherto unlikely resonance between cognitive-behavioural, humanistic and transpersonal models.

It remains the case that the UK is primarily a recipient of American models rather than an exporter. It is also to the credit of the BACP that many countries still developing a counselling profession turn to the BACP frameworks and norms for guidance. It is of some concern that despite continuing calls for models and interventions that are non-American and non-Eurocentric, no truly multicultural model – or even modest experiments in culturally specific therapies or interventions – has emerged. There is little available formally to underpin Islamic values for Muslim clients, for example. Client-centred 'non-directiveness' remains the dominant value base and therapeutic style in much counselling despite voiced dissatisfaction from some quarters. There is continuing emphasis on verbal exchange in therapy instead of more creative and diverse forms of delivery and exploration, and the health, spiritual and socio-economic-related needs of specific client groups have not been focused upon as concertedly as they might have been. (For an excellent discussion of the poorly explicated topic of human needs, see Doyal and Gough, 1991.) While a certain amount of UK literature has brought a welcome focus on some of the above areas, typical training curricula do not appear to have altered substantially. Tensions do, however, exist between aspirations to respond creatively to such needs, and the real limitations of funding, time and suitable personnel.

While therapists develop research (mainly small-scale empirical studies) into the subtleties of the client–therapist relationship and the multifaceted micro-processes of therapeutic practice, developments in science slowly impinge on our field. In evolutionary psychology, neuroscience, genetics and psychopharmacology, significant advances are being made. All such endeavours hold potential for helping to explain parts of the aetiology of human distress and dysfunction, and all might potentially offer suggestive remedies of their own and/or challenges to the conversational norms of counselling and psychotherapy. Equally, it remains possible that some of their findings will confirm therapists' longstanding practice knowledge of the importance of early childhood experiences, the quality of parent–child interaction, emotional needs, and the potency of certain corrective emotional experiences in therapy. Difficult though it may be, it seems crucial that therapists are aware of scientific developments that could sometimes threaten and sometimes support their work.

As therapists we tend to react to present human need rather than to anticipate or forecast future scenarios. Arguably, however, we might be drawing on the values of therapy and the insights gained from practice, training and supervision, in order to visualize and attempt to address future social needs, trends and problems. It is predicted that we will have an increasingly ageing population, probably with extended employment, growing pensions problems and health care demands accompanying longevity. Alongside this, it is predicted that a population of fewer young people will have to support older citizens economically, and that immigration may have to be boosted to make good the shortage in the workforce. Varieties of conflict between young and old and different ethnic groups have been predicted. As we know, marriage and similar, if informal, partnerships have been enduring for less time than traditionally and typical family size has fallen and its constitution has changed. Pressures and expectations have increased on students at all levels, with mental health problems escalating accordingly. Work stress has remained a fairly high-profile issue for much of the 1990s and 2000s. Depression increases across populations and, while therapy has gained in acceptance, powerful pharmacological companies gain much more from such trends in problematic mental health (Ritzer, 2004). Concern has been expressed about the continuing rise in prescribed drugs for young people.

This general scenario, if accurate, challenges us in two main ways. First, it behoves us to consider how theory and practice may have to adjust to meet new and greater demands. A greater number of older clients may well seek help, for example, with attitudes and dilemmas that differ from those associated with traditional prospects for retirement and later life aspirations. Better and more accessible knowledge of our genetic profiles will generate a need for more specifically informed genetic counselling. An increasingly multicultural society will demand changing content in counselling and psychotherapy training. Increasing knowledge of the benefits of psychopharmacology, of neuroscientific understanding and the interplay between different available and documented therapies will probably require of counsellors and psychotherapists more stringent updating and/or choice of specialized further training modules. As yet, counsellors and psychotherapists have not had to 'think epidemiologically' (and strategically) in the way that many psychiatrists and clinical psychologists have begun to (Abernathy and Power, 2002).

Second, and much more difficult for therapists to respond to, perhaps, is the problem of how human suffering and psychological need should be conceived. A gradual shift from traditional aetiological models focusing primarily on individual psychology, parent–child interactions, personal traumas and so on is an almost inevitable prospect. Demographic changes, cultural and religious pluralism, geopolitical uncertainties, environmental degradation, terrorist threats and pervasive (if low level in many societies) death anxiety may come to be seen to drive compromised mental health as much as, if not more than, traditional analyses of clinical, psychic or cognitive dysfunctional tendencies. In other words, 'social contexts' will have to feature more prominently in our thinking, theorizing and training. We may also be forced rather uncomfortably to concede that therapy is not quite the panacea we have perceived it as being and does not hold quite the position of eminence in addressing personal insecurities that we may hope. In the UK population of about 60 million, even if there are, as estimated, 250,000 therapists, and even if all therapy had a great deal of reliable and durable success, exponential happiness expansion is still an unlikely scenario. In a world population of 6.5 billion, many of whom do not have even basic needs met and suffer from untreated diseases, shortened life expectancy, war and terror, and associated traumatic effects, there is far greater cause for caution (Ritzer, 2004; Williams, 2004). Therapy quite naturally addresses the near at hand, and seems likely to experience high demand and professional success in the short to medium term. But alongside this, long-term forecasting suggests that responses to human problems may need to emerge that are more socially potent than one-to-one therapeutic work.

Accepting that therapy is a meaningful but relatively modest part of the answer to our human problems is an arguably necessary step in the maturity of therapy, whether regarded as a profession or vocation. Balancing hope and enthusiasm for the growth of professional norms against vigilance and sensitivity to emergent social and global trends may be said to parallel the task faced by the individual therapist in believing in her or his work while remaining profoundly receptive to the client's subtly changing material, insights and experiences.

References

Abernathy, J. and Power, M. (2002) The epidemiology of mental distress. In C. Feltham (ed.), *What's the Good of Counselling and Psychotherapy? The Benefits Explained.* London: Sage.

BACP (2004) Press release, October. Rugby: British Association for Counselling and Psychotherapy.

Doyal, L. and Gough, I. (1991) *A Theory of Human Needs.* Basingstoke: Macmillan.

Feltham, C. (ed.) (1999) *Controversies in Psychotherapy and Counselling.* London: Sage.

Feltham, C. (2004) Evidence-based psychotherapy and counseling in the UK: critique and alternatives. *Journal of Contemporary Psychotherapy,* 35 (1): 131–143.

Furedi, F. (2004) *Therapy Culture: Cultivating Vulnerability in an Uncertain Age.* London: Routledge.

Future Foundation (2004) *The Age of Therapy: Exploring Attitudes Towards and Acceptance of Counselling and Psychotherapy in Modern Britain.* London: Future Foundation and British Association for Counselling and Psychotherapy.

House, R. (2003) *Therapy Beyond Modernity: Deconstructing and Transcending Profession-centred Therapy.* London: Karnac.

James, I. and Palmer, S. (eds) (1996) *Professional Therapeutic Titles: Myths and Realities.* Leicester: British Psychological Society.

Ritzer, G. (ed.) (2004) *Handbook of Social Problems: A Comparative International Perspective.* Thousand Oaks, CA: Sage.

Rowland, N. and Goss, S. (eds) (2002) *Evidence-based Counselling and Psychological Therapies: Research and Applications.* London: Routledge.

Williams, J. (2004) *50 Facts That Should Change the World.* Duxford: Icon.

Index

Oedipus complex, 251
O'Hanlon, Bill, 338
OKness, 310–11
older people, services for, 35–6, 186, 487, 542–6
O'Leary, E., 543, 545
Oliver, M., 28, 30
online therapy, 519–22
operant conditioning, 88, 263, 426
Orbach, Susie, 528
organismic theory, 286
Ost, L.G., 427
otherness, 52–3, 56–8, 566
outcome studies, 211, 326–9

Paivio, S.C., 289
Palmer, I., 131
Palmer, S., 110, 112
Palmer Barnes, F., 194
panic attacks, 374–81, 424–5, 428
paraphrasing, 80–1
Parker, I., 359
Parkes, C.M., 384–5
Parkinson, F., 147–8
Parry, G., 5, 209
Parsons, Frank, 4
past-present connections, 101–2
patient profiling, 206
patriarchy, 528–9
Patterson, C.J., 228–9
Paul, G.L., 324
Pavlov, Ivan, 263, 426
peer counselling, 14, 164, 487
peer group supervision, 167
peer review, 162
performance indicators, 221
Perls, Fritz, 285–7, 297, 329–30
Perls, Laura, 285–6
person-centred psychotherapy, 66–7, 109, 139–40,
    143–5, 147, 162, 197, 284, 292–7, 335, 497, 557
personal construct theory and therapy,
    102, 271–5, 317
personal development/growth, 158–9, 162–3,
    170, 546–9
personality change, 13, 66, 75
personality disorders, 319, 419–23, 475, 483, 494
    definition and typology of, 419–20
perspectival change, 101
phantasies, 254–5
phobias, treatment of, 265–6, 270, 326–9, 423–9
    see also agoraphobia
physis drive, 311

Piaget, J., 228
Pipes, R.B., 185
play therapy, 500–1
Ponterotto, J.G., 23–4
positive asset search, 103
positive psychology, 230–1, 334–5, 338
postmodernism, 529
post-traumatic stress disorder (PTSD), 4, 149,
    191, 266, 355, 359, 383, 429–35, 437, 462, 465,
    492, 494
Poznanski, J.J., 234–5
practice-based evidence, 208
Pratt, Joseph, 536
predisposing and *precipitating* factors, 269
pregnancy, 436–8, 449–50
Prevention of Professional Abuse Network, 199
primal therapy, 297–301
primary health care, counselling and
    psychotherapy in, 17–18, 167–8, 440–1, 456,
    490–1, 550–3, 579
private practice of counselling and psychotherapy,
    18, 35–6, 39, 126–7, 173–6, 190
problem-free talk, 341
problem-management model, 145–6
problem-solving therapies, 12, 36, 39, 182–3, 445, 475
Prochaska, J.O., 300, 342, 368
professional organisations, 159–60, 172, 179,
    196–200, 552
professionalism and professionalization, 157, 200, 580
    see also continuing professional development
progress monitoring, 123–4
projection, 287
projective identification, 255
psyche, the, 248, 252, 517
psychiatry, 357–9
psychoanalysis and psychoanalytic theory, 3–5,
    32–3, 37, 54–7, 65–6, 139, 148, 158, 162, 173,
    185, 203, 227, 250–8, 266–7, 275, 310, 491,
    497, 523, 536, 580
psychodrama, 301–5
psychodynamic theory and therapy, 65–6, 109,
    114–15, 139, 143, 146–7, 162, 228, 253–7,
    256–7, 358, 366, 446, 516, 528, 532, 557
psycho-educational work, 11, 324, 461, 526
Psychologists Protection Society, 174–5
psychology, 227–8
    see also analytical psychology; contextual
        psychology; developmental psychology;
        evolutionary psychology; positive
        psychology; social psychology; transpersonal
        psychology